Core MCSE: Windows 2000 Edition

ISBN 0-13-083458-0

90000

9 780130 834584

PRENTICE HALL PTR MICROSOFT® TECHNOLOGIES SERIES

.NET FRAMEWORK

- The Microsoft .NET Platform and Technologies
  Simmons, Rofail

NETWORKING

- An Administrator's Guide to Windows 2000 TCP/IP
  Networks
  Wilson
- IP Solutions for Windows 2000
  Ammann
- Microsoft Technology: Networking, Concepts, Tools
  Woodard, Gattuccio, Brain
- NT Network Programming Toolkit
  Murphy
- Building COM Applications with Internet Explorer
  Loveman
- Understanding DCOM
  Rubin, Brain
- Web Database Development for Windows Platforms
  Gutierrez

PROGRAMMING

- Pocket PC, Handheld PC Developer's Guide
  Nick Grattan
- Office XP Development with VBA
  Aitken
- Windows 2000 Kernel Debugging
  McDowell
- Windows Script Host
  Aitken
- The Windows 2000 Device Driver Book, Second Edition
  Baker, Lozano
- Win32 System Services: The Heart of Windows 98
  and Windows 2000, Third Edition
  Brain, Reeves
- Programming the WIN32 API and UNIX System Services
  Merusi
- Windows CE 3.0: Application Programming
  Grattan, Brain
- The Visual Basic Style Guide
  Patrick
- Windows Shell Programming
  Seely
- Windows Installer Complete
  Easter
- Windows 2000 Web Applications Developer's Guide
  Yager

- Developing Windows Solutions with Office 2000
  Components and VBA
  Aitken
- Multithreaded Programming with Win32
  Pham, Garg
- Developing Professional Applications
  for Windows 98 and NT Using MFC, Third Edition
  Brain, Lovette
- Introduction to Windows 98 Programming
  Murray, Pappas
- The COM and COM+ Programming Primer
  Gordon
- Understanding and Programming COM+:
  A Practical Guide to Windows 2000 DNA
  Oberg
- Distributed COM Application Development Using
  Visual C++ 6.0
  Maloney
- The Essence of COM, Third Edition
  Platt
- COM-CORBA Interoperability
  Geraghty, Joyce, Moriarty, Noone
- MFC Programming in C++ with the Standard Template
  Libraries
  Murray, Pappas
- Introduction to MFC Programming with Visual C++
  Jones
- Visual C++ Templates
  Murray, Pappas
- Visual Basic Object and Component Handbook
  Vogel
- Visual Basic 6: Error Coding and Layering
  Gill
- ADO Programming in Visual Basic 6
  Holzner
- Visual Basic 6: Design, Specification, and Objects
  Hollis
- ASP/MTS/ADSI Web Security
  Harrison

BACKOFFICE

- Microsoft Exchange 2000: Programming Collaborative
  Web Applications
  Ammann
- Microsoft SQL Server 2000 Optimization Guide
  Fields

- BizTalk: Implementing Business-To-Business E-Commerce
  Kobielus

- Designing Enterprise Solutions with Microsoft Technologies
  Kemp, Kemp, Goncalves

- Microsoft Site Server 3.0 Commerce Edition
  Libertone, Scoppa

- Building Microsoft SQL Server 7 Web Sites
  Byrne

- Optimizing SQL Server 7
  Schneider, Goncalves

ADMINISTRATION

- Samba Essentials for Windows Administrators
  Wilson

- Tuning and Sizing Windows 2000 for Maximum Performance
  Aubley

- Windows 2000 Cluster Server Guidebook
  Libertone

- Windows 2000 Hardware and Disk Management
  Simmons

- Windows 2000 Server: Management and Control, Third Edition
  Spencer, Goncalves

- Creating Active Directory Infrastructures
  Simmons

- Windows 2000 Registry
  Sanna

- Configuring Windows 2000 Server
  Simmons

- Supporting Windows NT and 2000 Workstation and Server
  Mohr

- Zero Administration Kit for Windows
  McInerney

- Windows NT 4.0 Server Security Guide
  Goncalves

- Windows NT Security
  McInerney

CERTIFICATION

- Core MCSE: Windows 2000 Edition
  Dell

- Core MCSE: Designing a Windows 2000 Directory Services Infrastructure
  Simmons

- MCSE: Implementing and Supporting Windows 98
  Dell

- Core MCSE
  Dell

- Core MCSE: Networking Essentials
  Keogh

- MCSE: Administering Microsoft SQL Server 7
  Byrne

- MCSE: Implementing and Supporting Microsoft Exchange Server 5.5
  Goncalves

- MCSE: Internetworking with Microsoft TCP/IP
  Ryvkin, Houde, Hoffman

- MCSE: Implementing and Supporting Microsoft Proxy Server 2.0
  Ryvkin, Hoffman

- MCSE: Implementing and Supporting Microsoft SNA Server 4.0
  Mariscal

- MCSE: Implementing and Supporting Microsoft Internet Information Server 4
  Dell

- MCSE: Implementing and Supporting Web Sites Using Microsoft Site Server 3
  Goncalves

- MCSE: Microsoft System Management Server 2
  Jewett

- MCSE: Implementing and Supporting Internet Explorer 5
  Dell

- Core MCSD: Designing and Implementing Desktop Applications with Microsoft Visual Basic 6
  Holzner

- MCSD: Planning and Implementing SQL Server 7
  Vacca

- MCSD: Designing and Implementing Web Sites with Microsoft FrontPage 98
  Karlins

MICROSOFT TECHNOLOGIES SERIES

TOM DELL

Core MCSE: Windows 2000 Edition

Prentice Hall PTR, Upper Saddle River, NJ 07458
www.phptr.com

Library of Congress Cataloging-in-Publication Data

Dell, Tom
    Core MCSE: Windows 2000 edition / Thomas Dell.
       p. cm.
    Includes bibliographical references and index.
    ISBN 0-13-083458-0
     1. Electronic data processing personnel--Certification. 2. Microsoft software--Examinations--Study guides. 3. Microsoft Windows (Computer file) I. Title.

    QA76.3 .D452 2001
    005.4'4769--dc21

                                    2001051342

Editorial/Production Supervision: Jan H. Schwartz
Acquisitions Editor: Jill Harry
Editorial Assistant: Justin Somma
Marketing Manager: Dan DePasquale
Development Editor: Jim Markham
Manufacturing Manager: Alexis R. Heydt-Long
Buyer: Maura Zaldivar
Cover Design Direction: Jerry Votta
Cover Design: Talar Boorujy
Art Director: Gail Cocker-Bogusz
Series Interior Design: Meg VanArsdale
Composition: Laura Bonnemaison

Pearson Education LTD.
Pearson Education Australia PTY, Limited
Pearson Education Singapore, Pte. Ltd.
Pearson Education North Asia Ltd.
Pearson Education Canada, Ltd.
Pearson Educación de Mexico, S.A. de C.V.
Pearson Education—Japan
Pearson Education Malaysia, Pte. Ltd.
Pearson Education, Upper Saddle River, New Jersey

*This book is dedicated to the memory of
all those who lost their lives in the attack on America,
September 11, 2001.*

CONTENTS

About the Author   *xvii*

Acknowledgments   *xix*

MCSE Exam 70-210 Requirements Matrix   *xxi*

MCSE Exam 70-215 Requirements Matrix   *xxxi*

MCSE Exam 70-216 Requirements Matrix   *xxxvii*

MCSE Exam 70-217 Requirements Matrix   *xlv*

Introduction   *li*

PART ONE

Windows 2000 Professional   *1*

1

Installing Windows 2000 Professional   *3*

Installation Planning *5*

Attended Installations *14*

Unattended Installations *21*

Upgrading *39*

Deploying Service Packs *42*

Troubleshooting Installations *44*

2

Administering Windows 2000 Professional Resources   *55*

File and Folder Access *56*

Shared Folder Access *71*

Working with Print Devices *90*

Working with File Systems *101*

3

Managing Windows 2000 Professional Devices   *111*

Working with Disk Drives *113*
Working with Display Devices *145*
Working with Mobile Computer Hardware *150*
Working with I/O Devices *155*
Updating Drivers *167*
Working with Multiple Processing Units *169*
Working with Network Adapters *170*

4

Optimizing Windows 2000 Professional Devices   *181*

Working with Driver Signing *182*
Using Task Scheduler *186*
Offline File Synchronization *191*
Optimizing the Desktop *198*
Managing Hardware Profiles *227*
Recovering System State and User Data *231*

5

Configuring Windows 2000 Professional Environments   *255*

Working with User Profiles *256*
Supporting Multiple Languages and Locations *268*
Working with Windows Installer Packages *275*
Working with Desktop Settings *281*
Working with Fax Support *287*
Working with Accessibility Services *289*

6

Networking Windows 2000 Professional   *301*

Working with TCP/IP *302*
Working with Dial-Up Networking *324*
Connecting to Shared Resources *338*

7

Securing Windows 2000 Professional   *351*

Encrypting Hard Disk Data *352*

Implementing Local Security Policy *361*

Implementing User Account Security *364*

Authenticating Local Users *388*

Implementing Security Configurations *393*

PART TWO

Windows 2000 Server   *407*

8

Installing Windows 2000 Server   *409*

Installation Planning *410*

Attended Installations *417*

Unattended Installations *426*

Upgrading *433*

Deploying Service Packs *438*

Troubleshooting Installations *440*

9

Administering Windows 2000 Server Resource Access   *449*

Network Services Interoperability *450*

Working with Printer Access *468*

Working with File and Folder Access *481*

Working with Web Site Access *503*

10

Managing Windows 2000 Server Devices   *517*

Configuring Hardware Devices *518*

Configuring Driver Signing *522*

Updating Device Drivers *524*

Troubleshooting Hardware Problems *528*

11

Optimizing Windows 2000 Server 535

Managing System Resources *536*
Managing Processes *546*
Optimizing Disk Performance *550*
Optimizing System State and User Data *554*
Recovering System State and User Data *561*

12

Administering Windows 2000 Server Storage 575

Working with Disks and Volumes *576*
Configuring Data Compression *591*
Working with Disk Quotas *593*
Recovering from Disk Failures *597*

13

Networking Windows 2000 Server 603

Working with Shared Access *604*
Working with Network Protocols *632*
Working with Network Services *649*
Working with Remote Access Services *651*
Working with Virtual Private Networks *662*
Working with Terminal Services *665*
Working with Network Adapters *669*

14

Securing Windows 2000 Server 677

Encrypting Hard Disk Data *678*
Working with Windows 2000 Policies *682*
Working with Auditing *690*
Working with Local Accounts *693*
Working with Account Policy *698*
Using the Security Configuration Toolset *702*

PART THREE

Windows 2000 Networking   *709*

15

Administering Domain Name Services   *713*
Working with DNS *714*

16

Administering Dynamic Host Configuration Protocol   *745*
Working with DHCP *746*

17

Administering Remote Access   *761*
Working with Remote Access *762*
Configuring Remote Access Security *780*

18

Administering Network Protocols   *789*
Working with Network Protocols *790*
Working with Network Protocol Security *810*
Working with Network Traffic *812*
Working with IPSec *820*

19

Administering Windows Internet Naming Service   *837*
Configuring NetBIOS Name Resolution *838*
Working with WINS *843*
Configuring WINS Replication *850*

20

Administering IP Routing   *857*
> Working with IP Routing *858*
> Working with NAT *872*

21

Administering Certificate Authorities   *883*
> Working with Certificate Authorities *884*

PART FOUR

Active Directory   *895*

22

Installing Active Directory   *897*
> Installing Active Directory *898*

23

Administering Active Directory and DNS   *919*
> Administering DNS for Active Directory *920*

24

Managing Change Configuration   *925*
> Working with Group Policy *926*
> Managing Change Configuration *933*

25

Optimizing Active Directory   *947*

> Managing Objects *948*
> Optimizing Performance and Replication *954*
> Backup and Restoration *960*

26

Securing Active Directory   *967*

> Working with Security Policy *968*

Appendix: Chapter Review Answers   *973*

Index   *997*

Tom Dell

This book was re-written by author, trainer, and IT consultant Tom Dell. His other recent books include the following:

- *MCSE: Implementing and Supporting Microsoft Internet Explorer 5*, ISBN: 0-13-014268-9.
- *MCSE: Implementing and Supporting Windows 98*, ISBN: 0-13-032250-4.
- *MCSE: Implementing and Supporting Microsoft Internet Information Server 4*, ISBN: 0-13-011392-1.
- *IIS Interactive Training Course* (CD-ROM), with Marine Leroux, ISBN: 0-13-017619-2.
- *The Complete IIS Training Course* (CD-ROM and paperback), with Marine Leroux, ISBN: 0-13-026308-7.
- *Core MCSE* (Windows NT 4.0 Server, Workstation, Windows 98), with Dan Goldberg, ISBN: 0-13-082861-0.
- *Core MCSE Interactive Training Course* (CD-ROM), with Marine Leroux, ISBN: 0-13-087416-7.
- *The Complete Core MCSE Training Course* (CD-ROM and paperback), with Marine Leroux, ISBN: 0-13-085256-2.
- *AppleShare IP*, ISBN 0-12-208866-2.

Dell's email address is trdell@scionnet.com.

Acknowledgments

The author would like to acknowledge the contributions of all the people at Prentice Hall who made the production and distribution of this book possible. In particular, thanks go to Acquisitions Editor Jill Harry and Development Editor Jim Markham, who guided this title through the editorial process, and Laura Bonnemaison, who composed its pages.

#	MCSE Requirements for Exam 70-210: Installing, Configuring, and Administering Microsoft Windows 2000 Professional	Prentice Hall Chapter/ Syllabus No.	Related Question(s)
1	Installing Windows 2000 Professional: Perform an attended installation of Windows 2000 Professional.	1.1	1-7
2	Installing Windows 2000 Professional: Perform an unattended installation of Windows 2000 Professional.	1.2	8
3	Installing Windows 2000 Professional: Perform an unattended installation of Windows 2000 Professional. Install Windows 2000 Professional by using Windows 2000 Server Remote Installation Services (RIS).	1.2	9, 10
4	Installing Windows 2000 Professional: Perform an unattended installation of Windows 2000 Professional. Install Windows 2000 Professional by using the System Preparation Tool.	1.2	11, 12
5	Installing Windows 2000 Professional: Perform an unattended installation of Windows 2000 Professional. Create unattended answer files by using Setup Manager to automate the installation of Windows 2000 Professional.	1.2	13, 14
6	Installing Windows 2000 Professional: Upgrade from a previous version of Windows to Windows 2000 Professional.	1.3	15
7	Installing Windows 2000 Professional: Upgrade from a previous version of Windows to Windows 2000 Professional. Apply update packs to installed software applications.	1.3	16, 17
8	Installing Windows 2000 Professional: Upgrade from a previous version of Windows to Windows 2000 Professional. Prepare a computer to meet upgrade requirements.	1.3	18, 19

#	MCSE Requirements for Exam 70-210: Installing, Configuring, and Administering Microsoft Windows 2000 Professional	Prentice Hall Chapter/ Syllabus No.	Related Question(s)
9	Installing Windows 2000 Professional: Deploy service packs.	1.4	20, 21
10	Installing Windows 2000 Professional: Troubleshoot failed installations.	1.5	22, 23
11	Implementing and Conducting Administration of Resources: Monitor, manage, and troubleshoot access to files and folders.	2.1	1
12	Implementing and Conducting Administration of Resources: Monitor, manage, and troubleshoot access to files and folders. Configure, manage, and troubleshoot file compression.	2.1	2, 3
13	Implementing and Conducting Administration of Resources: Monitor, manage, and troubleshoot access to files and folders. Control access to files and folders by using permissions.	2.1	4, 5
14	Implementing and Conducting Administration of Resources: Monitor, manage, and troubleshoot access to files and folders. Optimize access to files and folders.	2.1	6, 7
15	Implementing and Conducting Administration of Resources: Manage and troubleshoot access to shared folders.	2.2	8
16	Implementing and Conducting Administration of Resources: Manage and troubleshoot access to shared folders. Create and remove shared folders.	2.2	9, 10
17	Implementing and Conducting Administration of Resources: Manage and troubleshoot access to shared folders. Control access to shared folders by using permissions.	2.2	11, 12
18	Implementing and Conducting Administration of Resources: Manage and troubleshoot access to shared folders. Manage and troubleshoot Web server resources.	2.2	13, 14
19	Implementing and Conducting Administration of Resources: Connect to local and network print devices.	2.3	15
20	Implementing and Conducting Administration of Resources: Connect to local and network print devices. Manage printers and print jobs.	2.3	16, 17
21	Implementing and Conducting Administration of Resources: Connect to local and network print devices. Control access to printers by using permissions.	2.3	18, 19
22	Implementing and Conducting Administration of Resources: Connect to local and network print devices. Connect to an Internet printer.	2.3	20, 21

#	MCSE Requirements for Exam 70-210: Installing, Configuring, and Administering Microsoft Windows 2000 Professional	Prentice Hall Chapter/ Syllabus No.	Related Question(s)
23	Implementing and Conducting Administration of Resources: Connect to local and network print devices. Connect to a local print device.	2.3	22, 23
24	Implementing and Conducting Administration of Resources: Configure and manage file systems.	2.4	24
25	Implementing and Conducting Administration of Resources: Configure and manage file systems. Convert from one file system to another file system.	2.4	25, 26
26	Implementing and Conducting Administration of Resources: Configure and manage file systems. Configure file systems by using NTFS, FAT32, or FAT.	2.4	27, 28
27	Implementing, Managing, and Troubleshooting Hardware Devices and Drivers: Implement, manage, and troubleshoot disk devices.	3.1	1
28	Implementing, Managing, and Troubleshooting Hardware Devices and Drivers: Implement, manage, and troubleshoot disk devices. Install, configure, and manage DVD and CD-ROM devices.	3.1	2, 3
29	Implementing, Managing, and Troubleshooting Hardware Devices and Drivers: Implement, manage, and troubleshoot disk devices. Monitor and configure disks.	3.1	4, 5
30	Implementing, Managing, and Troubleshooting Hardware Devices and Drivers: Implement, manage, and troubleshoot disk devices. Monitor, configure, and troubleshoot volumes.	3.1	6, 7
31	Implementing, Managing, and Troubleshooting Hardware Devices and Drivers: Implement, manage, and troubleshoot disk devices. Monitor and configure removable media, such as tape devices.	3.1	8, 9
32	Implementing, Managing, and Troubleshooting Hardware Devices and Drivers: Implement, manage, and troubleshoot display devices.	3.2	10
33	Implementing, Managing, and Troubleshooting Hardware Devices and Drivers: Implement, manage, and troubleshoot display devices. Configure multiple-display support.	3.2	11, 12

#	MCSE Requirements for Exam 70-210: Installing, Configuring, and Administering Microsoft Windows 2000 Professional	Prentice Hall Chapter/ Syllabus No.	Related Question(s)
34	Implementing, Managing, and Troubleshooting Hardware Devices and Drivers: Implement, manage, and troubleshoot display devices. Install, configure, and troubleshoot a video adapter.	3.2	13, 14
35	Implementing, Managing, and Troubleshooting Hardware Devices and Drivers: Implement, manage, and troubleshoot mobile computer hardware.	3.3	15
36	Implementing, Managing, and Troubleshooting Hardware Devices and Drivers: Implement, manage, and troubleshoot mobile computer hardware. Configure Advanced Power Management (APM).	3.3	16, 17
37	Implementing, Managing, and Troubleshooting Hardware Devices and Drivers: Implement, manage, and troubleshoot mobile computer hardware. Configure and manage card services.	3.3	18, 19
38	Implementing, Managing, and Troubleshooting Hardware Devices and Drivers: Implement, manage, and troubleshoot input and output (I/O) devices.	3.4	20
39	Implementing, Managing, and Troubleshooting Hardware Devices and Drivers: Implement, manage, and troubleshoot input and output (I/O) devices. Monitor, configure, and troubleshoot I/O devices, such as printers, scanners, multimedia devices, mouse, keyboard, and smart card reader.	3.4	21, 22
40	Implementing, Managing, and Troubleshooting Hardware Devices and Drivers: Implement, manage, and troubleshoot input and output (I/O) devices. Monitor, configure, and troubleshoot multimedia hardware, such as cameras.	3.4	23, 24
41	Implementing, Managing, and Troubleshooting Hardware Devices and Drivers: Implement, manage, and troubleshoot input and output (I/O) devices. Install, configure, and manage modems.	3.4	25, 26

#	MCSE Requirements for Exam 70-210: Installing, Configuring, and Administering Microsoft Windows 2000 Professional	Prentice Hall Chapter/ Syllabus No.	Related Question(s)
42	Implementing, Managing, and Troubleshooting Hardware Devices and Drivers: Implement, manage, and troubleshoot input and output (I/O) devices. Install, configure, and manage Infrared Data Association (IrDA) devices.	3.4	27, 28
43	Implementing, Managing, and Troubleshooting Hardware Devices and Drivers: Implement, manage, and troubleshoot input and output (I/O) devices. Install, configure, and manage wireless devices.	3.4	29, 30
44	Implementing, Managing, and Troubleshooting Hardware Devices and Drivers: Implement, manage, and troubleshoot input and output (I/O) devices. Install, configure, and manage USB devices.	3.4	31, 32
45	Implementing, Managing, and Troubleshooting Hardware Devices and Drivers: Update drivers.	3.5	33,34
46	Implementing, Managing, and Troubleshooting Hardware Devices and Drivers: Monitor and configure multiple processing units.	3.6	35, 36
47	Implementing, Managing, and Troubleshooting Hardware Devices and Drivers: Install, configure, and troubleshoot network adapters.	3.7	37, 38
48	Monitoring and Optimizing System Performance and Reliability: Manage and troubleshoot driver signing.	4.1	1, 2
49	Monitoring and Optimizing System Performance and Reliability: Configure, manage, and troubleshoot the Task Scheduler.	4.2	3, 4
50	Monitoring and Optimizing System Performance and Reliability: Manage and troubleshoot the use and synchronization of offline files.	4.3	5, 6
51	Monitoring and Optimizing System Performance and Reliability: Optimize and troubleshoot performance of the Windows 2000 Professional desktop.	4.4	7

#	MCSE Requirements for Exam 70-210: Installing, Configuring, and Administering Microsoft Windows 2000 Professional	Prentice Hall Chapter/ Syllabus No.	Related Question(s)
52	Monitoring and Optimizing System Performance and Reliability: Optimize and troubleshoot performance of the Windows 2000 Professional desktop. Optimize and troubleshoot memory performance.	4.4	8, 9
53	Monitoring and Optimizing System Performance and Reliability: Optimize and troubleshoot performance of the Windows 2000 Professional desktop. Optimize and troubleshoot processor utilization.	4.4	10, 11
54	Monitoring and Optimizing System Performance and Reliability: Optimize and troubleshoot performance of the Windows 2000 Professional desktop. Optimize and troubleshoot disk performance.	4.4	12, 13
55	Monitoring and Optimizing System Performance and Reliability: Optimize and troubleshoot performance of the Windows 2000 Professional desktop. Optimize and troubleshoot network performance.	4.4	14, 15
56	Monitoring and Optimizing System Performance and Reliability: Optimize and troubleshoot performance of the Windows 2000 Professional desktop. Optimize and troubleshoot application performance.	4.4	16, 17
57	Monitoring and Optimizing System Performance and Reliability: Manage hardware profiles.	4.5	18, 19
58	Monitoring and Optimizing System Performance and Reliability: Recover system state data and user data.	4.6	20
59	Monitoring and Optimizing System Performance and Reliability: Recover system state data and user data. Recover system state data and user data by using Windows Backup.	4.6	21, 22
60	Monitoring and Optimizing System Performance and Reliability: Recover system state data and user data. Troubleshoot system restoration by using Safe Mode.	4.6	23, 24

#	MCSE Requirements for Exam 70-210: Installing, Configuring, and Administering Microsoft Windows 2000 Professional	Prentice Hall Chapter/ Syllabus No.	Related Question(s)
61	Monitoring and Optimizing System Performance and Reliability: Recover system state data and user data. Recover system state data and user data by using the Recovery Console.	4.6	25, 26
62	Configuring and Troubleshooting the Desktop Environment: Configure and manage user profiles.	5.1	1, 2
63	Configuring and Troubleshooting the Desktop Environment: Configure support for multiple languages or multiple locations.	5.2	3
64	Configuring and Troubleshooting the Desktop Environment: Configure support for multiple languages or multiple locations. Enable multiple-language support.	5.2	4, 5
65	Configuring and Troubleshooting the Desktop Environment: Configure support for multiple languages or multiple locations. Configure multiple-language support for users.	5.2	6, 7
66	Configuring and Troubleshooting the Desktop Environment: Configure support for multiple languages or multiple locations. Configure local settings.	5.2	8, 9
67	Configuring and Troubleshooting the Desktop Environment: Configure support for multiple languages or multiple locations. Configure Windows 2000 Professional for multiple locations.	5.2	10, 11
68	Configuring and Troubleshooting the Desktop Environment: Manage applications by using Windows Installer packages.	5.3	12, 13
69	Configuring and Troubleshooting the Desktop Environment: Configure and troubleshoot desktop settings.	5.4	14, 15
70	Configuring and Troubleshooting the Desktop Environment: Configure and troubleshoot fax support.	5.5	16, 17
71	Configuring and Troubleshooting the Desktop Environment: Configure and troubleshoot accessibility services.	5.6	18, 19
72	Implementing, Managing, and Troubleshooting Network Protocols and Services: Configure and troubleshoot the TCP/IP protocol.	6.1	1, 2

#	MCSE Requirements for Exam 70-210: Installing, Configuring, and Administering Microsoft Windows 2000 Professional	Prentice Hall Chapter/ Syllabus No.	Related Question(s)
73	Implementing, Managing, and Troubleshooting Network Protocols and Services: Connect to computers by using dialup networking.	6.2	3
74	Implementing, Managing, and Troubleshooting Network Protocols and Services: Connect to computers by using dialup networking. Connect to computers by using a virtual private network (VPN) connection.	6.2	4, 5
75	Implementing, Managing, and Troubleshooting Network Protocols and Services: Connect to computers by using dialup networking. Create a dialup connection to connect to a remote access server.	6.2	6, 7
76	Implementing, Managing, and Troubleshooting Network Protocols and Services: Connect to computers by using dialup networking. Connect to the Internet by using dialup networking.	6.2	8, 9
77	Implementing, Managing, and Troubleshooting Network Protocols and Services: Connect to computers by using dialup networking. Configure and troubleshoot Internet Connection Sharing.	6.2	10, 11
78	Implementing, Managing, and Troubleshooting Network Protocols and Services: Connect to shared resources on a Microsoft network.	2.1 2.2 2.3 6.3	12, 13
79	Implementing, Monitoring, and Troubleshooting Security: Encrypt data on a hard disk by using Encrypting File System (EFS).	2.4 7.1	1, 2
80	Implementing, Monitoring, and Troubleshooting Security: Implement, configure, manage, and troubleshoot local security policy.	7.2	3, 4
81	Implementing, Monitoring, and Troubleshooting Security: Implement, configure, manage, and troubleshoot local user accounts.	2.1 5.2 7.3	5
82	Implementing, Monitoring, and Troubleshooting Security: Implement, configure, manage, and troubleshoot local user accounts. Implement, configure, manage, and troubleshoot auditing.	7.3	6, 7

#	MCSE Requirements for Exam 70-210: Installing, Configuring, and Administering Microsoft Windows 2000 Professional	Prentice Hall Chapter/ Syllabus No.	Related Question(s)
83	Implementing, Monitoring, and Troubleshooting Security: Implement, configure, manage, and troubleshoot local user accounts. Implement, configure, manage, and troubleshoot account settings.	7.3	8, 9
84	Implementing, Monitoring, and Troubleshooting Security: Implement, configure, manage, and troubleshoot local user accounts. Implement, configure, manage, and troubleshoot account policy.	7.3	10, 11
85	Implementing, Monitoring, and Troubleshooting Security: Implement, configure, manage, and troubleshoot local user accounts. Create and manage local users and groups.	7.3	12, 13
85	Implementing, Monitoring, and Troubleshooting Security: Implement, configure, manage, and troubleshoot local user accounts. Implement, configure, manage, and troubleshoot user rights.	7.3	14, 15
87	Implementing, Monitoring, and Troubleshooting Security: Implement, configure, manage, and troubleshoot local user authentication.	7.4	16
88	Implementing, Monitoring, and Troubleshooting Security: Implement, configure, manage, and troubleshoot local user authentication. Configure and troubleshoot local user accounts.	7.4	17, 18
89	Implementing, Monitoring, and Troubleshooting Security: Implement, configure, manage, and troubleshoot local user authentication. Configure and troubleshoot domain user accounts.	7.4	19, 20
90	Implementing, Monitoring, and Troubleshooting Security: Implement, configure, manage, and troubleshoot a security configuration.	7.5	21, 22

#	MCSE Requirements for Exam 70-210: Installing, Configuring, and Administering Microsoft Windows 2000 Server	Prentice Hall Chapter/ Syllabus No.	Related Question(s)
1	Installing Windows 2000 Server: Perform an attended installation of Windows 2000 Server.	1.1 8.1	1, 2
2	Installing Windows 2000 Server: Perform an unattended installation of Windows 2000 Server.	1.2 8.2	3
3	Installing Windows 2000 Server: Perform an unattended installation of Windows 2000 Server. Create unattended answer files by using Setup Manager to automate the installation of Windows 2000 Server.	1.2 8.2	4, 5
4	Installing Windows 2000 Server: Perform an unattended installation of Windows 2000 Server. Create and configure automated methods for installation of Windows 2000.	1.2 8.2	6, 7
5	Installing Windows 2000 Server: Upgrade a server from Microsoft Windows NT 4.0.	1.2 8.3	8, 9
6	Installing Windows 2000 Server: Deploy service packs.	1.4 8.4	10, 11
7	Installing Windows 2000 Server: Troubleshoot failed installations.	1.5 8.5	12, 13
8	Installing, Configuring, and Troubleshooting Access to Resources: Install and configure network services for interoperability.	9.1	1, 2
9	Installing, Configuring, and Troubleshooting Access to Resources: Monitor, configure, troubleshoot, and control access to printers.	2.3 9.2	3, 4
10	Installing, Configuring, and Troubleshooting Access to Resources: Monitor, configure, troubleshoot, and control access to files, folders, and shared folders.	2.1 9.3	5

#	MCSE Requirements for Exam 70-210: Installing, Configuring, and Administering Microsoft Windows 2000 Server	Prentice Hall Chapter/ Syllabus No.	Related Question(s)
11	Installing, Configuring, and Troubleshooting Access to Resources: Monitor, configure, troubleshoot, and control access to files, folders, and shared folders. Configure, manage, and troubleshoot a standalone Distributed File System (DFS).	9.3	6, 7
12	Installing, Configuring, and Troubleshooting Access to Resources: Monitor, configure, troubleshoot, and control access to files, folders, and shared folders. Configure, manage, and troubleshoot a domain-based Distributed File System (DFS).	9.3	8, 9
13	Installing, Configuring, and Troubleshooting Access to Resources: Monitor, configure, troubleshoot, and control access to files, folders, and shared folders. Monitor, configure, troubleshoot, and control local security on files and folders.	2.1 9.3	10, 11
14	Installing, Configuring, and Troubleshooting Access to Resources: Monitor, configure, troubleshoot, and control access to files, folders, and shared folders. Monitor, configure, troubleshoot, and control access to files and folders in a shared folder.	2.1, 2.2 9.3	12, 13
15	Installing, Configuring, and Troubleshooting Access to Resources: Monitor, configure, troubleshoot, and control access to files, folders, and shared folders. Monitor, configure, troubleshoot, and control access to files and folders via Web services.	2.2 9.3	14, 15
16	Installing, Configuring, and Troubleshooting Access to Resources: Monitor, configure, troubleshoot, and control access to Web sites.	9.4	16, 17
17	Configuring and Troubleshooting Hardware Devices and Drivers: Configure hardware devices.	3.1, 3.2, 3.3, 3.4, 3.6, 3.7 10.1	1, 2
18	Configuring and Troubleshooting Hardware Devices and Drivers: Configure driver signing options.	4.1 10.2	3, 4

#	MCSE Requirements for Exam 70-210: Installing, Configuring, and Administering Microsoft Windows 2000 Server	Prentice Hall Chapter/ Syllabus No.	Related Question(s)
19	Configuring and Troubleshooting Hardware Devices and Drivers: Update device drivers.	3.5 10.3	5, 6
20	Configuring and Troubleshooting Hardware Devices and Drivers: Troubleshoot problems with hardware.	3.1, 3.2, 3.3, 3.4, 3.6, 3.7 10.4	7, 8
21	Managing, Monitoring, and Optimizing System Performance, Reliability, and Availability: Monitor and optimize usage of system resources.	11.1	1, 2
22	Managing, Monitoring, and Optimizing System Performance, Reliability, and Availability: Manage processes.	4.4 11.2	3
23	Managing, Monitoring, and Optimizing System Performance, Reliability, and Availability: Manage processes. Set priorities and start and stop processes.	4.4 11.2	4, 5
24	Managing, Monitoring, and Optimizing System Performance, Reliability, and Availability: Optimize disk performance.	4.4 11.3	6, 7
25	Managing, Monitoring, and Optimizing System Performance, Reliability, and Availability: Manage and optimize availability of System State data and user data.	4.6 11.4	8, 9
26	Managing, Monitoring, and Optimizing System Performance, Reliability, and Availability: Recover System State data and user data.	4.6 11.5	10
27	Managing, Monitoring, and Optimizing System Performance, Reliability, and Availability: Recover System State data and user data. Recover System State data by using Windows Backup.	4.6 11.5	11, 12
28	Managing, Monitoring, and Optimizing System Performance, Reliability, and Availability: Recover System State data and user data. Troubleshoot system restoration by starting in safe mode.	4.6 11.5	13, 14
29	Managing, Monitoring, and Optimizing System Performance, Reliability, and Availability: Recover System State data and user data. Recover System State data by using the Recovery Console.	4.6 11.5	15, 16

#	MCSE Requirements for Exam 70-210: Installing, Configuring, and Administering Microsoft Windows 2000 Server	Prentice Hall Chapter/ Syllabus No.	Related Question(s)
30	Managing, Configuring, and Troubleshooting Storage Use: Monitor, configure, and troubleshoot disks and volumes.	3.1 12.1	1, 2
31	Managing, Configuring, and Troubleshooting Storage Use: Configure data compression.	2.1 12.2	3, 4
32	Managing, Configuring, and Troubleshooting Storage Use: Monitor and configure disk quotas.	3.1 12.3	5, 6
33	Managing, Configuring, and Troubleshooting Storage Use: Recover from disk failures.	4.6 12.4	7, 8
34	Configuring and Troubleshooting Windows 2000 Network Connections: Install, configure, and troubleshoot shared access.	2.1, 2.2, 2.3 6.1 13.1	1, 2
35	Configuring and Troubleshooting Windows 2000 Network Connections: Install, configure, and troubleshoot network protocols.	6.1 13.2	3, 4
36	Configuring and Troubleshooting Windows 2000 Network Connections: Install and configure network services.	13.3	5, 6
37	Configuring and Troubleshooting Windows 2000 Network Connections: Configure, monitor, and troubleshoot remote access.	6.2 13.4	7, 8
38	Configuring and Troubleshooting Windows 2000 Network Connections: Configure, monitor, and troubleshoot remote access. Configure inbound connections.	6.2 13.4	9
39	Configuring and Troubleshooting Windows 2000 Network Connections: Configure, monitor, and troubleshoot remote access. Create a remote access policy.	6.2 13.4	10, 11
40	Configuring and Troubleshooting Windows 2000 Network Connections: Configure, monitor, and troubleshoot remote access. Configure a remote access profile.	13.4	12, 13
41	Configuring and Troubleshooting Windows 2000 Network Connections: Install, configure, and troubleshoot a virtual private network (VPN).	6.2 13.5	14

#	MCSE Requirements for Exam 70-210: Installing, Configuring, and Administering Microsoft Windows 2000 Server	Prentice Hall Chapter/ Syllabus No.	Related Question(s)
42	Configuring and Troubleshooting Windows 2000 Network Connections: Install, configure, monitor, and troubleshoot Terminal Services. Remotely administer servers by using Terminal Services.	13.6	15, 16
43	Configuring and Troubleshooting Windows 2000 Network Connections: Install, configure, monitor, and troubleshoot Terminal Services. Configure Terminal Services for application sharing.	13.6	17, 18
44	Configuring and Troubleshooting Windows 2000 Network Connections: Install, configure, monitor, and troubleshoot Terminal Services. Configure applications for use with Terminal Services.	13.6	19, 20
45	Configuring and Troubleshooting Windows 2000 Network Connections: Install, configure, and troubleshoot network adapters and drivers.	3.7 13.7	21, 22
46	Implementing, Monitoring, and Troubleshooting Security: Encrypt data on a hard disk by using Encrypting File System (EFS).	7.1 14.1	1, 2
47	Implementing, Monitoring, and Troubleshooting Security: Implement, configure, manage, and troubleshoot policies in a Windows 2000 environment.	7.2 14.2	3
48	Implementing, Monitoring, and Troubleshooting Security: Implement, configure, manage, and troubleshoot policies in a Windows 2000 environment. Implement, configure, manage, and troubleshoot Local Policy in a Windows 2000 environment.	7.2 14.2	4, 5
49	Implementing, Monitoring, and Troubleshooting Security: Implement, configure, manage, and troubleshoot policies in a Windows 2000 environment. Implement, configure, manage, and troubleshoot System Policy in a Windows 2000 environment.	7.2 14.2	6, 7
50	Implementing, Monitoring, and Troubleshooting Security: Implement, configure, manage, and troubleshoot auditing.	7.3 14.3	8, 9

#	MCSE Requirements for Exam 70-210: Installing, Configuring, and Administering Microsoft Windows 2000 Server	Prentice Hall Chapter/ Syllabus No.	Related Question(s)
51	Implementing, Monitoring, and Troubleshooting Security: Implement, configure, manage, and troubleshoot local accounts.	7.3 14.4	10, 11
52	Implementing, Monitoring, and Troubleshooting Security: Implement, configure, manage, and troubleshoot Account Policy.	7.3 14.5	12, 13
53	Implementing, Monitoring, and Troubleshooting Security: Implement, configure, manage, and troubleshoot security by using the Security Configuration Tool Set.	7.5 14.6	14, 15

MCSE Exam 70-216 Requirements Matrix

#	MCSE Requirements for Exam 70-216: Implementing and Administering a Microsoft Windows 2000 Network Infrastructure	Prentice Hall Chapter/ Syllabus No.	Related Question(s)
1	Installing, Configuring, Managing, Monitoring, and Troubleshooting DNS in a Windows 2000 Network Infrastructure: Install, configure, and troubleshoot DNS.	15.1	1
2	Installing, Configuring, Managing, Monitoring, and Troubleshooting DNS in a Windows 2000 Network Infrastructure: Install, configure, and troubleshoot DNS. Install the DNS Server service.	15.1	2, 3
3	Installing, Configuring, Managing, Monitoring, and Troubleshooting DNS in a Windows 2000 Network Infrastructure: Install, configure, and troubleshoot DNS. Configure a root name server.	15.1	4, 5
4	Installing, Configuring, Managing, Monitoring, and Troubleshooting DNS in a Windows 2000 Network Infrastructure: Install, configure, and troubleshoot DNS. Configure zones.	15.1	6, 7
5	Installing, Configuring, Managing, Monitoring, and Troubleshooting DNS in a Windows 2000 Network Infrastructure: Install, configure, and troubleshoot DNS. Configure a caching-only server.	15.1	8, 9
6	Installing, Configuring, Managing, Monitoring, and Troubleshooting DNS in a Windows 2000 Network Infrastructure: Install, configure, and troubleshoot DNS. Configure a DNS client.	15.1	10, 11

#	MCSE Requirements for Exam 70-216: Implementing and Administering a Microsoft Windows 2000 Network Infrastructure	Prentice Hall Chapter/ Syllabus No.	Related Question(s)
7	Installing, Configuring, Managing, Monitoring, and Troubleshooting DNS in a Windows 2000 Network Infrastructure: Install, configure, and troubleshoot DNS. Configure zones for dynamic updates.	15.1	12, 13
8	Installing, Configuring, Managing, Monitoring, and Troubleshooting DNS in a Windows 2000 Network Infrastructure: Install, configure, and troubleshoot DNS. Test the DNS Server service.	15.1	14, 15
9	Installing, Configuring, Managing, Monitoring, and Troubleshooting DNS in a Windows 2000 Network Infrastructure: Install, configure, and troubleshoot DNS. Implement a delegated zone for DNS.	15.1	16, 17
10	Installing, Configuring, Managing, Monitoring, and Troubleshooting DNS in a Windows 2000 Network Infrastructure: Install, configure, and troubleshoot DNS. Manually create DNS resource records.	15.1	18, 19
11	Installing, Configuring, Managing, Monitoring, and Troubleshooting DNS in a Windows 2000 Network Infrastructure: Manage and monitor DNS.	15.1	20, 21
12	Installing, Configuring, Managing, Monitoring, and Troubleshooting DHCP in a Windows 2000 Network Infrastructure: Install, configure, and troubleshoot DHCP.	16.1	1
13	Installing, Configuring, Managing, Monitoring, and Troubleshooting DHCP in a Windows 2000 Network Infrastructure: Install, configure, and troubleshoot DHCP. Install the DHCP Server service.	16.1	2, 3
14	Installing, Configuring, Managing, Monitoring, and Troubleshooting DHCP in a Windows 2000 Network Infrastructure: Install, configure, and troubleshoot DHCP. Create and manage DHCP scopes, superscopes, and multicast scopes.	16.1	4, 5

#	MCSE Requirements for Exam 70-216: Implementing and Administering a Microsoft Windows 2000 Network Infrastructure	Prentice Hall Chapter/ Syllabus No.	Related Question(s)
15	Installing, Configuring, Managing, Monitoring, and Troubleshooting DHCP in a Windows 2000 Network Infrastructure: Install, configure, and troubleshoot DHCP. Configure DHCP for DNS integration.	16.1	6, 7
16	Installing, Configuring, Managing, Monitoring, and Troubleshooting DHCP in a Windows 2000 Network Infrastructure: Install, configure, and troubleshoot DHCP. Authorize a DHCP server in Active Directory.	16.1	8, 9
17	Installing, Configuring, Managing, Monitoring, and Troubleshooting DHCP in a Windows 2000 Network Infrastructure: Manage and monitor DHCP.	16.1	10, 11
18	Configuring, Managing, Monitoring, and Troubleshooting Remote Access in a Windows 2000 Network Infrastructure: Configure and troubleshoot remote access.	17.1	1
19	Configuring, Managing, Monitoring, and Troubleshooting Remote Access in a Windows 2000 Network Infrastructure: Configure and troubleshoot remote access. Configure inbound connections.	17.1	2, 3
20	Configuring, Managing, Monitoring, and Troubleshooting Remote Access in a Windows 2000 Network Infrastructure: Configure and troubleshoot remote access. Create a remote access policy.	17.1	4, 5
21	Configuring, Managing, Monitoring, and Troubleshooting Remote Access in a Windows 2000 Network Infrastructure: Configure and troubleshoot remote access. Configure a remote access profile.	17.1	6, 7
22	Configuring, Managing, Monitoring, and Troubleshooting Remote Access in a Windows 2000 Network Infrastructure: Configure and troubleshoot remote access. Configure a virtual private network (VPN).	17.1	8, 9
23	Configuring, Managing, Monitoring, and Troubleshooting Remote Access in a Windows 2000 Network Infrastructure: Configure and troubleshoot remote access. Configure multilink connections.	17.1	10, 11

#	MCSE Requirements for Exam 70-216: Implementing and Administering a Microsoft Windows 2000 Network Infrastructure	Prentice Hall Chapter/ Syllabus No.	Related Question(s)
24	Configuring, Managing, Monitoring, and Troubleshooting Remote Access in a Windows 2000 Network Infrastructure: Configure and troubleshoot remote access. Configure Routing and Remote Access for DHCP Integration.	17.1	12, 13
25	Configuring, Managing, Monitoring, and Troubleshooting Remote Access in a Windows 2000 Network Infrastructure: Manage and monitor remote access.	17.1	14, 15
26	Configuring, Managing, Monitoring, and Troubleshooting Remote Access in a Windows 2000 Network Infrastructure: Configure remote access security.	17.2	16
27	Configuring, Managing, Monitoring, and Troubleshooting Remote Access in a Windows 2000 Network Infrastructure: Configure remote access security. Configure authentication protocols.	17.2	17, 18
28	Configuring, Managing, Monitoring, and Troubleshooting Remote Access in a Windows 2000 Network Infrastructure: Configure remote access security. Configure encryption protocols.	17.2	19, 20
29	Configuring, Managing, Monitoring, and Troubleshooting Remote Access in a Windows 2000 Network Infrastructure: Configure remote access security. Create a remote access policy.	17.2	21, 22
30	Installing, Configuring, Managing, Monitoring, and Troubleshooting Network Protocols in a Windows 2000 Network Infrastructure: Install, configure, and troubleshoot network protocols.	18.1	1
31	Installing, Configuring, Managing, Monitoring, and Troubleshooting Network Protocols in a Windows 2000 Network Infrastructure: Install, configure, and troubleshoot network protocols. Install and configure TCP/IP.	18.1	2, 3
32	Installing, Configuring, Managing, Monitoring, and Troubleshooting Network Protocols in a Windows 2000 Network Infrastructure: Install, configure, and troubleshoot network protocols. Install the NWLink protocol.	18.1	4, 5

#	MCSE Requirements for Exam 70-216: Implementing and Administering a Microsoft Windows 2000 Network Infrastructure	Prentice Hall Chapter/ Syllabus No.	Related Question(s)
33	Installing, Configuring, Managing, Monitoring, and Troubleshooting Network Protocols in a Windows 2000 Network Infrastructure: Install, configure, and troubleshoot network protocols. Configure network bindings.	18.1	6, 7
34	Installing, Configuring, Managing, Monitoring, and Troubleshooting Network Protocols in a Windows 2000 Network Infrastructure: Configure TCP/IP packet filters.	18.2	8, 9
35	Installing, Configuring, Managing, Monitoring, and Troubleshooting Network Protocols in a Windows 2000 Network Infrastructure: Configure and troubleshoot network protocol security.	18.2	10, 11
36	Installing, Configuring, Managing, Monitoring, and Troubleshooting Network Protocols in a Windows 2000 Network Infrastructure: Manage and monitor network traffic.	18.3	12, 13
37	Installing, Configuring, Managing, Monitoring, and Troubleshooting Network Protocols in a Windows 2000 Network Infrastructure: Configure and troubleshoot IPSec.	18.4	14
38	Installing, Configuring, Managing, Monitoring, and Troubleshooting Network Protocols in a Windows 2000 Network Infrastructure: Configure and troubleshoot IPSec. Enable IPSec.	18.4	15, 16
39	Installing, Configuring, Managing, Monitoring, and Troubleshooting Network Protocols in a Windows 2000 Network Infrastructure: Configure and troubleshoot IPSec. Configure IPSec for transport mode.	18.4	17, 18
40	Installing, Configuring, Managing, Monitoring, and Troubleshooting Network Protocols in a Windows 2000 Network Infrastructure: Configure and troubleshoot IPSec. Configure IPSec for tunnel mode.	18.4	19, 20

#	MCSE Requirements for Exam 70-216: Implementing and Administering a Microsoft Windows 2000 Network Infrastructure	Prentice Hall Chapter/ Syllabus No.	Related Question(s)
41	Installing, Configuring, Managing, Monitoring, and Troubleshooting Network Protocols in a Windows 2000 Network Infrastructure: Configure and troubleshoot IPSec. Customize IPSec policies and rules.	18.4	21, 22
42	Installing, Configuring, Managing, Monitoring, and Troubleshooting Network Protocols in a Windows 2000 Network Infrastructure: Configure and troubleshoot IPSec. Manage and monitor IPSec.	18.4	23, 24
43	Installing, Configuring, Managing, Monitoring, and Troubleshooting WINS in a Windows 2000 Network Infrastructure: Install, configure, and troubleshoot WINS.	19.2	3, 4
44	Installing, Configuring, Managing, Monitoring, and Troubleshooting WINS in a Windows 2000 Network Infrastructure: Configure WINS replication.	19.3	7,8
45	Installing, Configuring, Managing, Monitoring, and Troubleshooting WINS in a Windows 2000 Network Infrastructure: Configure NetBIOS name resolution.	19.1	1, 2
46	Installing, Configuring, Managing, Monitoring, and Troubleshooting WINS in a Windows 2000 Network Infrastructure: Manage and monitor WINS.	19.2	5, 6
47	Installing, Configuring, Managing, Monitoring, and Troubleshooting IP Routing in a Windows 2000 Network Infrastructure: Install, configure, and troubleshoot IP routing protocols.	20.1	1
48	Installing, Configuring, Managing, Monitoring, and Troubleshooting IP Routing in a Windows 2000 Network Infrastructure: Install, configure, and troubleshoot IP routing protocols. Update a Windows 2000-based routing table by means of static routes.	20.1	2, 3

#	MCSE Requirements for Exam 70-216: Implementing and Administering a Microsoft Windows 2000 Network Infrastructure	Prentice Hall Chapter/ Syllabus No.	Related Question(s)
49	Installing, Configuring, Managing, Monitoring, and Troubleshooting IP Routing in a Windows 2000 Network Infrastructure: Install, configure, and troubleshoot IP routing protocols. Implement Demand-Dial Routing.	20.1	4, 5
50	Installing, Configuring, Managing, Monitoring, and Troubleshooting IP Routing in a Windows 2000 Network Infrastructure: Manage and monitor IP routing.	20.1	6
51	Installing, Configuring, Managing, Monitoring, and Troubleshooting IP Routing in a Windows 2000 Network Infrastructure: Manage and monitor IP routing. Manage and monitor border routing.	20.1	7, 8
52	Installing, Configuring, Managing, Monitoring, and Troubleshooting IP Routing in a Windows 2000 Network Infrastructure: Manage and monitor IP routing. Manage and monitor internal routing.	20.1	9, 10
53	Installing, Configuring, Managing, Monitoring, and Troubleshooting IP Routing in a Windows 2000 Network Infrastructure: Manage and monitor IP routing. Manage and monitor IP routing protocols.	20.1	11, 12
54	Installing, Configuring, and Troubleshooting Network Address Translation (NAT): Install Internet Connection Sharing.	20.2	13, 14
55	Installing, Configuring, and Troubleshooting Network Address Translation (NAT): Install NAT.	20.2	15, 16
56	Installing, Configuring, and Troubleshooting Network Address Translation (NAT): Configure NAT properties.	20.2	17, 18
57	Installing, Configuring, and Troubleshooting Network Address Translation (NAT): Configure NAT interfaces.	20.2	19, 20
58	Installing, Configuring, Managing, Monitoring, and Troubleshooting Certificate Services: Install and configure Certificate Authority (CA).	21.1	1, 2

#	MCSE Requirements for Exam 70-216: Implementing and Administering a Microsoft Windows 2000 Network Infrastructure	Prentice Hall Chapter/ Syllabus No.	Related Question(s)
59	Installing, Configuring, Managing, Monitoring, and Troubleshooting Certificate Services: Issue and revoke certificates.	21.1	3, 4
60	Installing, Configuring, Managing, Monitoring, and Troubleshooting Certificate Services: Remove the Encrypting File System (EFS) recovery keys.	21.1	5, 6

#	MCSE Requirements for Exam 70-217: Implementing and Administering a Microsoft Windows 2000 Directory Services Infrastructure	Prentice Hall Chapter/ Syllabus No.	Related Question(s)
1	Installing and Configuring Active Directory: Install forests, trees, and domains.	22.1	1
2	Installing and Configuring Active Directory: Install forests, trees, and domains. Automate domain controller installation.	22.1	2
3	Installing and Configuring Active Directory: Create sites, subnets, site links, and connection objects.	22.1	3, 4
4	Installing and Configuring Active Directory: Configure server objects. Considerations include site membership and global catalog designation.	22.1	5, 6
5	Installing and Configuring Active Directory: Transfer operations master roles.	22.1	7, 8
6	Installing and Configuring Active Directory: Verify and troubleshoot Active Directory installation.	22.1	9
7	Installing and Configuring Active Directory: Implement an organizational unit (OU) structure.	22.1	10
8	Installing, Configuring, Managing, Monitoring, and Troubleshooting DNS for Active Directory: Install and configure DNS for Active Directory.	23.1	1
9	Installing, Configuring, Managing, Monitoring, and Troubleshooting DNS for Active Directory: Install and configure DNS for Active Directory. Integrate Active Directory DNS zones with existing DNS infrastructure.	23.1	2
10	Installing, Configuring, Managing, Monitoring, and Troubleshooting DNS for Active Directory: Install and configure DNS for Active Directory. Configure zones for dynamic updates and secure dynamic updates.	23.1	3

#	MCSE Requirements for Exam 70-217: Implementing and Administering a Microsoft Windows 2000 Directory Services Infrastructure	Prentice Hall Chapter/ Syllabus No.	Related Question(s)
11	Installing, Configuring, Managing, Monitoring, and Troubleshooting DNS for Active Directory: Install and configure DNS for Active Directory. Create and configure DNS records.	23.1	4
12	Installing, Configuring, Managing, Monitoring, and Troubleshooting DNS for Active Directory: Manage, monitor, and troubleshoot DNS.	23.1	5
13	Configuring, Managing, Monitoring, Optimizing, and Troubleshooting Change and Configuration Management: Implement and troubleshoot Group Policy.	24.1	1
14	Configuring, Managing, Monitoring, Optimizing, and Troubleshooting Change and Configuration Management: Implement and troubleshoot Group Policy. Create and modify a Group Policy object (GPO).	24.1	2
15	Configuring, Managing, Monitoring, Optimizing, and Troubleshooting Change and Configuration Management: Implement and troubleshoot Group Policy. Link to an existing GPO.	24.1	3
16	Configuring, Managing, Monitoring, Optimizing, and Troubleshooting Change and Configuration Management: Implement and troubleshoot Group Policy. Delegate administrative control of Group Policy.	24.1	4
17	Configuring, Managing, Monitoring, Optimizing, and Troubleshooting Change and Configuration Management: Implement and troubleshoot Group Policy. Configure Group Policy options.	24.1	5
18	Configuring, Managing, Monitoring, Optimizing, and Troubleshooting Change and Configuration Management: Implement and troubleshoot Group Policy. Filter Group Policy settings by using security groups.	24.1	6
19	Configuring, Managing, Monitoring, Optimizing, and Troubleshooting Change and Configuration Management: Implement and troubleshoot Group Policy. Modify Group Policy prioritization.	24.1	7
20	Configuring, Managing, Monitoring, Optimizing, and Troubleshooting Change and Configuration Management: Manage and troubleshoot user environments by using Group Policy.	24.1	8

#	MCSE Requirements for Exam 70-217: Implementing and Administering a Microsoft Windows 2000 Directory Services Infrastructure	Prentice Hall Chapter/ Syllabus No.	Related Question(s)
21	Configuring, Managing, Monitoring, Optimizing, and Troubleshooting Change and Configuration Management: Install, configure, manage, and troubleshoot software by using Group Policy.	24.2	9
22	Configuring, Managing, Monitoring, Optimizing, and Troubleshooting Change and Configuration Management: Manage network configuration by using Group Policy.	24.2	10
23	Configuring, Managing, Monitoring, Optimizing, and Troubleshooting Change and Configuration Management: Configure Active Directory to support Remote Installation Services (RIS).	24.2	11
24	Configuring, Managing, Monitoring, Optimizing, and Troubleshooting Change and Configuration Management: Configure Active Directory to support Remote Installation Services (RIS). Configure RIS options to support remote installations.	24.2	12
25	Configuring, Managing, Monitoring, Optimizing, and Troubleshooting Change and Configuration Management: Configure Active Directory to support Remote Installation Services (RIS). Configure RIS security.	24.2	13
26	Managing, Monitoring, and Optimizing the Components of Active Directory: Manage Active Directory objects.	25.1	1
27	Managing, Monitoring, and Optimizing the Components of Active Directory: Manage Active Directory objects. Move Active Directory objects.	25.1	2
28	Managing, Monitoring, and Optimizing the Components of Active Directory: Manage Active Directory objects. Publish resources in Active Directory.	25.1	3
29	Managing, Monitoring, and Optimizing the Components of Active Directory: Manage Active Directory objects. Locate objects in Active Directory.	25.1	4
30	Managing, Monitoring, and Optimizing the Components of Active Directory: Manage Active Directory objects. Create and manage objects manually or by using scripting.	25.1	5

#	MCSE Requirements for Exam 70-217: Implementing and Administering a Microsoft Windows 2000 Directory Services Infrastructure	Prentice Hall Chapter/ Syllabus No.	Related Question(s)
31	Managing, Monitoring, and Optimizing the Components of Active Directory: Manage Active Directory objects. Control access to Active Directory objects.	25.1	6
32	Managing, Monitoring, and Optimizing the Components of Active Directory: Manage Active Directory objects. Delegate administrative control of objects in Active Directory.	25.1	7
33	Managing, Monitoring, and Optimizing the Components of Active Directory: Monitor, optimize, and troubleshoot Active Directory performance and replication.	25.2	8
34	Managing, Monitoring, and Optimizing the Components of Active Directory: Back up and restore Active Directory.	25.3	9
35	Managing, Monitoring, and Optimizing the Components of Active Directory: Back up and restore Active Directory. Perform an authoritative and a nonauthoritative restore of Active Directory.	25.3	10
36	Managing, Monitoring, and Optimizing the Components of Active Directory: Back up and restore Active Directory. Recover from a system failure.	25.3	11
37	Managing, Monitoring, and Optimizing the Components of Active Directory: Back up and restore Active Directory. Seize operations master roles.	25.3	12
38	Configuring, Managing, Monitoring, and Troubleshooting Security in a Directory Services Infrastructure: Apply security policies by using Group Policy.	26.1	1
39	Configuring, Managing, Monitoring, and Troubleshooting Security in a Directory Services Infrastructure: Create, analyze, and modify security configurations by using the Security Configuration and Analysis snap-in and the Security Templates snap-in.	26.1	2
40	Configuring, Managing, Monitoring, and Troubleshooting Security in a Directory Services Infrastructure: Implement an audit policy.	26.1	3

#	MCSE Requirements for Exam 70-217: Implementing and Administering a Microsoft Windows 2000 Directory Services Infrastructure	Prentice Hall Chapter/ Syllabus No.	Related Question(s)
41	Configuring, Managing, Monitoring, and Troubleshooting Security in a Directory Services Infrastructure: Monitor and analyze security events.	26.1	4

Introduction

This book is designed primarily to support computing professionals preparing for the Microsoft Certified Systems Engineer (MCSE) core exams. This book prepares a candidate for four core requirement exams: Exam 70-210, *Installing, Configuring, and Administering Microsoft Windows 2000 Professional*; Exam 70-215, *Installing, Configuring, and Administering Microsoft Windows 2000 Server*; Exam 70-216, *Implementing and Administering a Microsoft Windows 2000 Network Infrastructure*; and Exam 70-217, *Implementing and Administering a Microsoft Windows 2000 Directory Services Infrastructure*.

This book will also benefit any computing professional who manages Windows-based computing environments, particularly in the enterprise. It is designed to be both a training guide and reference resource.

Who This Book Is For

This book is designed to provide concise and comprehensive information for computer professionals who manage computers running under the Microsoft Windows 2000 operating systems. Readers of this book should have a working knowledge of a Microsoft Windows operating system, such as Windows 98 or Me, Windows NT 4.0, or Windows 2000. This book will give the reader the knowledge needed to pass the core exam requirements of the MCSE program.

What You'll Need

Through the use of numerous illustrations and an interactive CD-ROM-based training supplement, we have endeavored to make this book as self-contained as possible. Nevertheless, we acknowledge that there is no substitute for hands-on experience. To practice the concepts explained in this book, you will need at least a Pentium or compatible processor-based computer with 32 MBs of RAM (64 MBs recommended), 650 MBs of free hard disk space, a network adapter card, a mouse (or other pointing device), a VGA monitor, a CD-ROM drive, and a printer. Optional equipment includes a modem and network adapter, a 1.44 MB 3.5-inch floppy disk drive, and a tape drive. Software requirements include Microsoft Windows 2000 Professional or Windows 2000 Server.

How This Book Is Organized

This book is divided into four parts, each containing material related to the following core MCSE and MCSE + Internet exams.

- Part 1: Exam 70-210, *Installing, Configuring, and Administering Microsoft Windows 2000 Professional*
- Part 2: Exam 70-215, *Installing, Configuring, and Administering Microsoft Windows 2000 Server*
- Part 3: Exam 70-216, *Implementing and Administering a Microsoft Windows 2000 Network Infrastructure*
- Part 4: Exam 70-217, *Implementing and Administering a Microsoft Windows 2000 Directory Services Infrastructure.*

Each part is further divided into multiple chapters, each corresponding to a basic exam objective. These include such issues as planning, installation and configuration, resource management, monitoring and optimization, and troubleshooting. Each chapter is further divided into subsections that correspond to specific MCSE exam contents, and is concluded with a list of related study questions. Some additional non-MCSE specific material is also provided to enhance readers' knowledge in certain areas.

Conventions Used in This Book

This book uses different features to help highlight key information.

Chapter Syllabus

The primary focus of this series is to address those topics that are to be tested in each exam. Therefore, each chapter opens with a syllabus that lists the topics to be covered. Each topic directly corresponds to the Level 1 headings in the chapter. So if there are six Level 1 headings in a chapter, there will be six topics listed under the Chapter Syllabus. If a syllabus topic and Level 1 heading are MCSE-specific, they will be accompanied by an MCSE icon (see the following icon description). However, there may be instances when the topics are not exam-specific. In these cases, the chapter syllabus highlights and corresponding Level 1 headings appear without the MCSE icon.

Icons

Icons represent called-out material that is of significance and that you should be alerted to. Icons include:

 This icon is used to identify MCSE-specific Chapter Syllabus topics and appropriate MCSE sections in each chapter.

 Use this icon to call out information that deserves special attention; one that the reader may otherwise run a highlight marker through.

 This icon is used to flag particularly useful information that will save the reader time, highlight a valuable technique, or offer specific advice.

 This icon flags information that may cause unexpected results or serious frustration.

Chapter Review Questions

Each chapter ends with a series of review questions. These questions are a combination of multiple choice, true/false, and open-ended designed to simulate a part of an actual exam and to reinforce what you have just learned.

The number of questions vary depending on the length and subject matter of individual chapters.

All of these questions are taken directly from the material covered in the chapter, and the author's answers can be found in the Appendix.

Although this book covers all of the material required by the MCSE exam, the author has reordered some material to make it as clear and concise as possible, as well as avoid repetition. While it is impossible to avoid some repetition in topics that are common to all four sections, the author has done his best to present previously described topics in new ways. While this repetition might elicit of feeling of déjà vu at times, it is useful in ensuring that important concepts will be remembered.

About the Web Site

This book is accompanied by a companion Web site on which readers can find additional exam preparation aids and updates to the enclosed material. It is located at *www.phptr.com/dellwin2000*.

Windows 2000 Professional

I**n** this book we cover material from MCSE exam 70-210, *Installing, Configuring, and Administering Microsoft Windows 2000 Professional.* This gives you the knowledge necessary to install, configure, and manage networked Windows 2000 Professional workstations. This section's topics include the following:

- **Installing:** Performing attended or unattended installations and upgrades, deploying service packs, and troubleshooting failed installations.

- **Administering:** Working with file and folder access, connecting to print devices, and configuring file systems.

- **Devices:** Working with such devices as hard disks, displays, mice, keyboards, and modems.

- **Optimizing:** Employing driver signing, Task Scheduler, and file synchronization, optimizing desktop features, managing hardware profiles, and recovering systems and data.

♦ **In This Part**

♦ **CHAPTER** 1: Installing Windows 2000 Professional

♦ **CHAPTER** 2: Administering Windows 2000 Professional Resources

♦ **CHAPTER** 3: Managing Windows 2000 Professional Devices

♦ **CHAPTER** 4: Optimizing Windows 2000 Professional

♦ **CHAPTER** 5: Configuring Windows 2000 Professional Environments

♦ **CHAPTER** 6: Networking Windows 2000 Professional

♦ **CHAPTER** 7: Securing Windows 2000 Professional

- **Configuring:** Working with user profiles, multiple languages and locations, installer packages, desktop settings, fax support, and special accessibility.
- **Networking:** Working with TCP/IP, Dial-Up Networking, and shared resources.
- **Securing:** Encrypting hard disk data, working with local group policy, managing user accounts, and configuring security.

Installing Windows 2000 Professional

▲ Chapter Syllabus

Installation Planning

MCSE 1.1 Attended Installations

MCSE 1.2 Unattended Installations

MCSE 1.3 Upgrading

MCSE 1.4 Deploying Service Packs

MCSE 1.5 Troubleshooting Installations

In this chapter, we examine the installation topics covered in the *Installing Windows 2000 Professional* section of Microsoft's *Installing, Configuring, and Administering Microsoft Windows 2000 Professional* exam (70-210).

The following material is designed to make you comfortable with installing the operating system on a single computer, multiple computers, and computers that are running under older versions of Windows.

In all cases, the installation is smoothest if you perform the following tasks ahead of time:

- Ensure that your hardware and software is compatible and meets or exceeds Microsoft's minimum system requirements. You might need to obtain new device drivers and/or software updates for some of your system's components.
- Determine whether you will be upgrading an existing operating system or starting afresh.

- Consider how you will partition the computer's hard disk, and which file system format(s) it will use.
- If you are upgrading, be sure to back up your important files in the event that something unexpected causes problems with the hard drive.
- Record network information, such as necessary protocols, network addressing information, dialup access numbers, domain names, and server addresses. If the computer targeted for the installation will participate in a Microsoft Networking domain, also make sure that either a computer account has been created for it, or that you have the administrative permissions to do so.

In addition to the material presented in this book, you should read the file READ1ST.TXT from the installation CD-ROM. It contains the latest information available at the time of the installation disk's pressing, including important preinstallation notes. To locate it, click on the Browse This CD link in the Windows 2000 Professional installation CD-ROM Autorun screen that appears when you insert the disk, as shown in Figure 1.1.

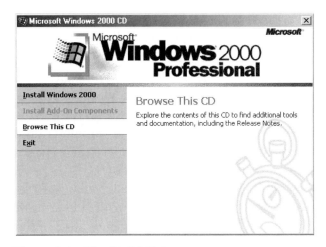

Figure 1.1   *The CD-ROM Autorun screen.*

You are presented with various files and folders, including the READ1ST.TXT text file, as shown in Figure 1.2.

Other important resources that come with your installation CD-ROM include the following:

- The README.TXT file, which covers post-installation and compatibility details.

- A set of text files, found in the SETUPTXT folder, that describe the installation of Windows 2000 Professional on a single computer.
- The Hardware Compatibility List (HCL) file (HCL.TXT), found in the SUPPORT folder, which lists the systems and components that are known to be compatible with Windows 2000 Professional. The most up-to-date version of the HCL can be found at the Microsoft Web site (*www.microsoft.com/hcl/*).
- In addition to the HCL, refer to the Windows 2000 Product Compatibility Web site at (*www.microsoft.com/windows2000/compatible*) for information on software compatibility.

One additional resource, particularly useful for IT professionals working with a large number of Windows 2000 desktops and configurations, is Microsoft's Windows 2000 Professional Resource Kit.

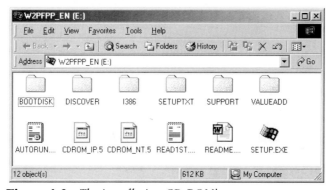

Figure 1.2   *The installation CD-ROM's contents.*

Installation Planning

In this section, we prepare you for the process of installing Windows 2000 Professional on a single or multiple computers.

Verifying System Requirements

To run Windows 2000 Professional, your computer must have at least the following components:

- A 133 MHz Pentium microprocessor (or equivalent). This includes the Pentium II, III, or 4 as well as the AMD K-6, K-6 II or III, and K-7 Athlon.

- Windows 2000 Professional provides up to two-way SMP (Symmetric Multi-Processing) support.
- 32 MBs of RAM is the minimum supported, although Microsoft recommends a minimum of 64 MBs. Windows 2000 Professional will support maximum of 4 GBs of RAM.
- 650 MBs of free hard disk space is the minimum required for a local installation. You will need a bit more if you install via a network. Microsoft recommends a minimum of 2 GBs.
- A VGA or better monitor.
- A Keyboard.
- A mouse.
- A CD-ROM or DVD drive. If your CD-ROM drive is not bootable so that you can start the Setup program from the installation CD-ROM, you will also need a 3.5-inch High-Density floppy disk drive from which to launch boot disks.
- A Windows 2000 Professional-compatible network adapter, if you are installing from a network share.

Considering Installation Methods

Once you have determined that your system meets the requirements, you must decide whether to install Windows 2000 Professional as a new operating system, such as on a new system, or as an upgrade to an existing system, such as Windows NT 4.0. Windows 2000 Professional can also be installed in a dual-boot capacity with such operating systems as Windows Millennium Edition (Me), MS-DOS, Novell NetWare, or UNIX/Linux.

PLANNING FOR UPGRADES

You may choose to upgrade if the target computer is running one of the following operating systems:

- Windows 98
- Windows 95
- Windows NT 4.0
- Windows NT 3.51

Upgrading overwrites your existing system but keeps most of your setting preferences and applications.

If the computer is running Windows NT 3.1 or 3.5, you must upgrade to Windows 3.51 or 4.0 and then upgrade again to Windows 2000 Professional.

If the computer is running Windows 3.1 or Windows for Workgroups 3.11, you are out of luck. These operating systems are too old, so plan for a clean install.

If the computer is running Windows Me, you are also out of luck. The operating system is too new! Since Windows 2000 Professional was released before Windows Me, no upgrade path was prepared. The newer system includes core changes, such as a Registry split and removal of real mode support, that make it unsuited to upgrade.

PLANNING FOR CLEAN INSTALLS

If the target computer has no operating system, or one that Windows 2000 cannot replace, you must perform a *clean install*. This will require you to manually configure all of the operating system's preference settings and reinstall your applications. It will also permit you to install Windows 2000 alongside other operating systems in a multi-boot capacity.

If you are preparing the computer for multi-boot, the file system becomes especially important.

Considering Formats and File Systems

One major distinction between Windows 2000 and other versions of Windows are the file systems they support. Among the factors that must be considered in choosing a file system is the size of the destination disk drive, the operating systems with which the drive will be used, and the level of file security that is desired.

In selecting a file system, you should initially plan for the physical and logical structure that is appropriate for your desktop's disk drive. On new disk drives—or existing disks on which you wish to irrevocably delete all existing data—this involves *formatting*. During this process you are given the opportunity to create *partitions*.

PLANNING FOR PARTITIONS

A hard disk can be formatted as a single drive with its own drive letter designation (e.g., "C"). This is commonly the case with smaller disk drives, often less than 1 GB. Alternately, a hard disk can be subdivided into multiple partitions. Although each partition resides on the same physical hard disk, each has its own drive letter designation and can be addressed by the operating system as if it were a separate drive. This method is commonly used with larger disk drives because it is easier to navigate a smaller directory structure.

It is also a common practice to create different partitions for multiple operating systems, thereby keeping their associated software separated.

Partitions result from the logical organization of a single physical disk. Creating a subdivision from the free space on a hard disk is the process of *partitioning*. When setting up a new hard disk on a Windows computer, one must define two types of partitions.

PRIMARY PARTITION • A primary partition can support a bootable operating system. Each disk drive can contain as many as four primary partitions. A primary partition cannot be further partitioned.

EXTENDED PARTITION • An extended partition will not support a bootable operating system. On single disk drive systems, then, an extended partition is used in addition to one or more primary partitions. An extended partition can, however, be subdivided into multiple logical partitions, each with its own letter designation (e.g., "D," "E," "F," and so on). Only one extended partition can reside on a disk drive.

There can be no more than four partitions on a disk drive in total, so if an extended partition is established, only three primary partitions can be used (as illustrated in Figure 1.3).

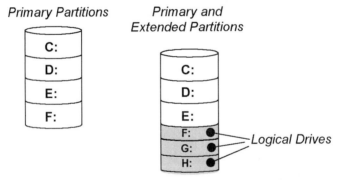

Figure 1.3   *A disk can be divided into as many as four primary partitions.*

ACTIVE PARTITION • On an Intel-based computer, it is necessary to mark one primary partition as active. This is the partition from which the computer will boot on startup.

Computers with disk drives containing multiple operating systems are typically formatted with a primary partition for each operating system. Computers with disk drives containing a single operating system are commonly formatted with either a single primary partition, or one primary partition and one extended partition.

On a new computer, the Windows Setup program creates an active partition when it installs the operating system. If an active partition already exists on a destination computer, it will be used.

SYSTEM VS. BOOT PARTITION • Under Windows NT and 2000, the system partition contains the files necessary to boot the operating system. By definition, this will also be the active partition. This need not be the partition in which the operating system is installed.

The boot partition contains the Windows NT/2000 operating system. It does not actually contain the boot files, however, which can lead to some confusion. A computer is booted using the system partition, not the boot partition. The boot partition simply contains the WINNT folder, as illustrated in Figure 1.4.

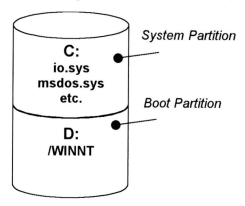

Figure 1.4 *The boot partition contains the system files (e.g., the WINNT folder).*

Partitions can be created on new hard drives, or drives on which you do not mind deleting the contents, using the **MS-DOS FDISK** utility. One common procedure is to copy this program onto a floppy disk formatted as a system disk, boot from the floppy disk, and run **FDISK** to reconfigure the hard drive. This limits you to 2 GB partitions, however (4 GBs in newer versions with "large disk support"). Alternately, you can use a third-party utility, such as Partition Magic, which is especially helpful when the drive will be shared with non-Microsoft operating systems such as UNIX or Novell NetWare. The easiest method, however, is to leave the work up to the Windows Setup program, as described further on.

PLANNING FOR FILE SYSTEMS

Your computer's hard disk must be formatted to support the file system that will organize and manage its data. Windows 2000 Professional supports three main file systems: File Allocation Table (FAT), FAT32, and New Technology File System (NTFS).

A fourth file system, Compact Disk File System (CDFS), is supported for use with CD-ROM drives. It cannot be used to format a hard disk partition.

FAT • The FAT file system, also known as FAT16 in contrast to its 32-bit off-spring FAT32, was introduced with MS-DOS. The 16-bit FAT is supported by Windows 3.x, 95, 98, Me, NT, and 2000, as well as IBM's OS/2. Because it is the most universally supported file system, FAT is still commonly used despite its age and inherent limitations.

At its most basic level, the File Allocation Table is like the directory in an apartment building. When you wish to visit people in an apartment complex, you usually locate their names in a directory and call up the appropriate unit numbers. Likewise, when you call on the computer to access a file, that file's location is first looked up in the FAT. Needless to say, this methodology is faster than walking through an apartment complex knocking on doors, or scouring the entire contents of a hard disk.

FAT works most efficiently with small partitions (400 MBs or less). It is the file system that must be used with multi-boot computers that host multiple operating systems that do not recognize FAT32 or NTFS (if one is to access that partition from all of them).

There are advantages and disadvantages to using FAT over newer file formats:

- FAT32 is only recognized by Windows 98, Me, and 2000, while FAT is supported by all Windows versions and MS-DOS.
- NTFS has higher system disk space overhead (as much as 10 MBs as opposed to FAT's 1 MB). As a result, you cannot create a NTFS boot disk on a traditional floppy disk (e.g., 1.44 MB).
- FAT32 and NTFS take less time to find and open files on partitions greater than 200 MBs.
- FAT cannot support file, directory, and partition sizes in excess of 4 GBs. (2 GBs on early versions.)

- NTFS offers a higher level of security.
- FAT can become corrupted with cross-linked files or orphan clusters in the event of a power loss.

FAT32 • Although the difference is seldom noted, when talking about FAT16 we are really talking about VFAT. The original FAT was available in MS-DOS through version 6.22, but was superseded with VFAT by the introduction of Windows 95. Among the limitations of the original FAT were file names of only eight characters plus a three character extension (the 8.3 convention), no more than 512 files in a root directory, no more than 65,535 files in a non-root directory, and a partition size of 2 GBs. VFAT is also limited to 512 files in a root directory, but it supports file names of up to 255 characters, unlimited files in a non-root directory, and a partition size of 4 GBs.

With the introduction of Windows 98 (actually Windows 95 Release B) came FAT32. This file system has the following advantages over FAT:

- FAT32 uses a smaller cluster size, resulting in an average of about 30 percent more disk space, according to Microsoft. For example, FAT uses a 32 kB cluster on drives of 2 GBs or greater. This means that if you were to store a 36 kB file on such a drive, two 32 kB clusters would be needed, wasting 28 kBs of disk space. FAT32 would use eight 4 kB clusters in the same situation, wasting no space. A comparison of FAT vs. FAT32 cluster sizes is provided in Table 1.1.

Table 1.1 *FAT Cluster Sizes*

Partition size	FAT32 cluster size	FAT16 cluster size
32 MBs	–	2 kBs
128 MBs	–	2 kBs
256 MBs	–	4 kBs
512 MBs	4 kBs	8 kBs
1 GBs	4 kBs	16 kBs
2 GBs	4 kBs	32 kBs
3–7 GBs	4 kBs	–
8–16 GBs	8 kBs	–
16–32 GBs	16 kBs	–
33 GBs or Greater	32 kBs	–

- FAT32 is optimized for disk access, allowing programs to open up to 36 percent more quickly, according to Microsoft.
- FAT32 can support partitions of up to 2 TBs (although you can only create FAT32 partitions of 32 GBs under Windows 2000 because of performance limitations).
- FAT32 can relocate the root directory and use backup copies of the file system, reducing the risk of crashes.

Although FAT32 is superior to FAT in many respects, it is not always the better choice when upgrading from a previous version of Windows to Windows 2000.

For example, FAT32 does not allow you to dual-boot with many previous versions of Windows (Windows 95 [Version 4.00.950], Windows NT 3.x and 4.0, or Windows 3.x). However, if computers running these operating systems access the Windows 2000 computer remotely over the network, they can still gain access to the FAT32 hard drive via file sharing mechanisms.

Although most programs are not affected by a conversion from FAT to FAT32, some disk utilities that depend on FAT do not work with FAT32 drives.

Most disk compression software is not compatible with FAT32. If your FAT drive is compressed, you will probably not be able to convert it. If you convert a removable disk and use it with other operating systems that are not compatible with FAT32, you will not be able to access the disk while you are running the other operating system.

If your computer has a hibernate feature, the conversion might turn this feature off. Your computer's manual should provide details on this feature.

FAT32 is a much more efficient file system than is FAT16 if it supports a large number of small files. However, if it supports a smaller number of larger files, its efficiency is reduced and it may be less efficient than FAT.

Neither FAT nor FAT32 provide file-level security like NTFS. If you require this type of security, you may wish to make a move to NTFS rather than FAT32.

Table 1.2 provides a comparison of some of the FAT file systems' other characteristics.

NTFS • Unlike FAT, NTFS can take advantage of all of Windows 2000's capabilities. Unfortunately, only the Windows NT or 2000 operating system can access an NTFS drive, so if you plan to run multiple operating systems on the same computer, its usefulness is limited.

If you plan to run Windows 2000 alone on the disk drive, you will almost certainly want to choose the NTFS format for its increased performance alone. As previously mentioned, FAT is best suited to disk drives in the 200-400 MB range. Beyond that size, NTFS is faster. In addition, FAT cannot handle disk drives larger than 4 GBs, while NTFS is good for up to 16 EB (exabytes) — that is one billion gigabytes.

Even if performance is not a prime consideration, you should choose NTFS because of its inherent safety. For example, NTFS is capable of *sector sparing* on Small Computer Serial Interface (SCSI) drives. Should a hard disk sector fail on an NTFS-formatted SCSI drive partition, NTFS will attempt to write the data from RAM to a good sector and then automatically map out the bad sector so that it will not be used again.

If that is still not enough reason for you, consider the fact that NTFS also supports far greater security. For example, an NTFS-formatted disk drive supports both directory level and file level permissions. The Windows 2000 version, NTFS5, also supports file encryption. Table 1.2 provides a brief summary of some of the file systems' various characteristics.

Table 1.2 *Comparison of FAT and NTFS File Systems*

Characteristic	FAT16 (VFAT)	FAT32	NTFS
Max. partition size	4 GBs	2 TBs	16 Ebytes
Max. file name length	255	255	255
Can use 8.3 convention	Yes	Yes	Yes
Case sensitive	No	No	No
Case preserving	Yes	Yes	Yes
Local security controls	No	No	Yes
Transaction log	No	No	Yes
Sector sparing	No	No	Yes
Disk space overhead	1 MB	1 MB	2-10 MBs
Accessible to MS-DOS	Yes	No	No
Accessible to Windows 3.x/95	Yes	No	No
Accessible to Windows 98/Me	Yes	Yes	No
Accessible to Windows NT/2000	Yes	Yes	Yes
Accessible to OS/2	Yes	No	No
Can be converted	To FAT 32 or NTFS	To NTFS	No
Best efficiency	200–400 MBs	400 MBs +	400 MBs +
Fragmentation level	High	High	Low
File compression	With utilities	With utilities	Built-in

To summarize, give preference to FAT if you must multiple-boot or have a small disk drive with a small number of large files. Give preference to FAT32 if you must dual-boot with Windows 98 or Me. Give preference to NTFS wherever possible.

Also be aware that traditional FAT compression utilities, including Microsoft's DriveSpace and DoubleSpace, cannot be used with NTFS. Windows 2000 has its own built-in compression capabilities, however.

Considering Licensing

Assuming your computer will be deployed in a network environment, you should consider the issue of licensing. Windows 2000 Professional computers require two licenses, one for the operating system, and one that permits it to access a Windows 2000 Server. The latter Client Access License (CAL) comes in the following forms:

- Per Seat. This license is for the client computer itself, which may then connect to as many servers as needed.
- Per Server. This license is for the server computer, which may then accommodate as many simultaneous client connections as it has CALs for.

CALs are not required for HyperText Transfer Protocol (HTTP), File Transfer Protocol (FTP), or Telnet connections. So, for example, connections to Microsoft's Internet Information Server (IIS) are exempt. Additional licenses are required for Microsoft BackOffice products.

MCSE 1.1   Attended Installations

In this section, we run through the process of installing Windows 2000 Professional manually on a single computer. Microsoft breaks this down into the following steps:

- Running the Setup program.
- Running the Setup Wizard.
- Installing Windows networking components.
- Completing the Setup program.

Running the Setup Program

If the target computer has a newly formatted hard disk or is running an operating system that will not recognize the installation CD-ROM, you will need to boot from either the CD-ROM drive or from a floppy disk drive using the Windows 2000 Professional Setup startup disks.

You can create installation floppy disks from the installation CD-ROM. Simply load the CD-ROM on a computer that is capable of reading it, open the Command Prompt program, and switch to the CD's BOOTDISK directory (see Figure 1.2). Next, insert a blank 1.44 MB floppy disk in the disk drive and type the command: MAKEBOOT A: (where A: is the floppy disk drive). Follow the directions to create four setup disks.

If the target computer is running an operating system that will recognize the CD-ROM, such as Windows NT 4.0 or Me, you can simply insert it and click the Install Windows 2000 link in the Autorun screen (see Figure 1.2) to launch the Setup Wizard, as shown in Figure 1.5.

Figure 1.5 *Choosing an upgrade or clean installation.*

You are given a chance to choose between an upgrade and a clean installation. If you choose the former, you can boot from either your old operating system or Windows 2000 after the installation.

Next, you are prompted to read and approve the Microsoft licensing agreement and supply the Product Key code, as shown in Figure 1.6.

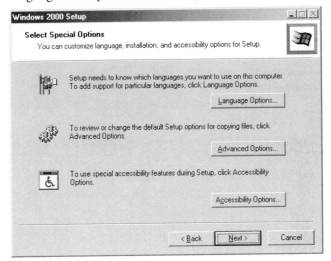

Figure 1.6   *Entering the Product Key.*

Next, you are given the chance to select special options such as those for languages and special accessibility, as shown in Figure 1.7.

Figure 1.7   *Choosing among special options.*

Of particular interest here is the Advanced Options button that opens the dialog box shown in Figure 1.8.

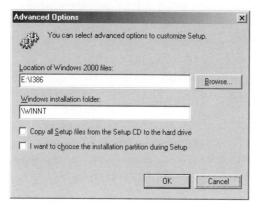

Figure 1.8 *Specifying setup file options.*

In the Advanced Options dialog box you can specify the source of setup files, such as the \I386 directory on the CD-ROM or a network share, and the name of the destination system folder (\WINNT by default). You may also enable options that will copy all of the setup files to the hard drive, making the subsequent use of the CD drive or network connection unnecessary, and to permit you to choose the installation partition in later steps.

Finally, the Setup Wizard copies setup files to the hard disk and reboots the computer, as shown in Figure 1.9.

Figure 1.9 *Rebooting the computer during setup.*

The computer restarts with a minimal version of Windows 2000 loaded into memory. This launches the text-based Setup program, which begins by prompting you to agree with Microsoft's licensing requirements.

When the program continues, you are asked to choose a partition for the installation of Windows 2000 Professional. The Setup program lets you select an existing partition, create a new partition from unused disk space, or delete an existing partition so that you may reconfigure the drive. As powerful as this feature is, it is best to create only the partition on which you plan to install Windows 2000 Professional at this point. Once the operating system is in place, you can use its Disk Management tool to make further modifications.

When performing a new installation, the Setup Program picks the active disk partition by default, although you can alter its choice by selecting Advanced Options.

Once you have created the installation partition, you are asked to choose a file system with which to format it. As previously described, your best choice is NTFS unless you are planning to run Windows 2000 Professional in a multi-boot capacity. If you are unsure, choose FAT. It is the most compatible file system, and you can always convert it to NTFS later.

Next, the Setup Program formats the hard drive according to your choices, copies its installation files to the disk (C:\WINNT is the default system directory), and saves its configuration information. It then restarts and launches the Setup Wizard.

Running the Setup Wizard

The Graphical User Interface (GUI)-based Setup Wizard asks you for the following information about the computer and its environment:

- **Regional Settings.** Windows 2000 can be configured for multiple languages and regional preferences. Choose a language, locale, and keyboard layout here.
- **Name and Organization.** Identify the person who owns the copy of Windows 2000 Professional that you are installing, and the organization that person is associated with (optional).
- **Your Product Key.** Type in the 25-character product key that came with this copy of Windows 2000 Professional, usually on a sticker attached to the CD-ROM's case.
- **Computer Name.** Here you must choose a name that is between one and 15 characters in length and is unique from any other computer, domain, or workgroup name on the network. Windows 2000 makes up a name by default.

- **Password for the Administrator Account.** The password you choose for the automatically created Administrator account grants you the administrative privileges necessary to fully configure and manage the computer. Do not forget it.
- **Modem Dialing Information.** Assuming the Setup Wizard has not already been clued in by the previously established regional settings, select the computer's geographic location here. You can establish the local area code, identify either pulse or tone dialing, and add any code needed for outside access (e.g., "9"). These options only arise if there is a modem installed in your computer.
- **Date and Time Settings.** Here you can establish the time, date, and resident time zone, if they have not already been read from the computer's BIOS. You can also choose automatic updates for daylight savings time.

Installing Windows Networking Components

The Setup program now moves on to installing networking components, beginning by detecting and configuring the computer's network adapter cards. It then copies networking software to the hard drive, and prompts you to choose between typical or custom settings for its default protocols and services:

- **Client for Microsoft Networks.** This component permits your computer to access Microsoft Networking-based resources, such as shared printers and file servers.
- **File and Printer Sharing for Microsoft Networks.** This component lets you make your computer a server, sharing folders and printers on the network for others to access.
- **TCP/IP.** The Transmission Control Protocol/Internet Protocol (TCP/IP) is required if the computer is to access the Internet, and is commonly needed for many private Local Area Network (LAN) and Wide Area Network (WAN) implementations as well.

Windows 2000 Professional ships with several other protocols and services, which are described further on.

WORKGROUP VS. DOMAIN

Along with the installation of Client for Microsoft Networks comes an important decision and the next question posed by the Setup Wizard: Does the computer participate in a domain?

Under Microsoft networking, Windows computers can reside on the network in either workgroups or domains. Like a group of people in an office that communicate for the purpose of collaboration, a Windows *workgroup* is a group of networked computers that share information and resources to perform common tasks. Each computer in the workgroup keeps track of accounts (e.g., names, passwords, and permissions) for all users that might need to use it locally. This works well enough in small network environments, but it can result in a great deal of administrative overhead when the workgroup becomes large.

Windows 95, 98, Me, NT, and 2000 computers can form workgroups. A Windows NT or 2000 Server computer can participate in a workgroup if it has been configured as a standalone, or *member*, server. Computers running the now discontinued Windows for Workgroups can also participate in workgroups (as the name implies).

Conceptually, a *domain* is much the same as a workgroup except that user accounts are kept in a central database instead of on each individual workstation. This database resides on a Windows NT or 2000 Server computer configured as a domain controller. Administrative overhead is greatly reduced under this model because users log on using one central account to access resources anywhere in the domain, rather than having a separate account for each of those resources.

The workgroup method lends itself best to the peer-to-peer networking model, wherein all computers may act as both servers and clients to each other. The domain method lends itself best to the *client-server* networking model, wherein one or more computers are dedicated to network services and other computers act solely as clients to them. It is possible to create a client-server workgroup, however, by dedicating one or more workstations as servers or by deploying one or more Windows 2000 Server computers in a standalone server capacity.

Perhaps the biggest difference between workgroups and domains is the way in which they implement security. Security under the workgroup model is applied to whatever a given computer is sharing on the network, and is referred to as share-level security. Under this system, resource passwords are used rather than user account authentication.

Security under the domain model involves the authentication of user accounts with a centralized server. The resources a given user may access is determined by the access permissions granted to that user throughout the network, or more commonly, to the permissions granted to the groups to which the user belongs. This model is referred to as *user-level security*.

For a Windows 2000 computer to join a domain, an administrator must have created a computer account for it on a domain controller ahead of time. Alternately, a computer account can be created from the target computer during the installation process if you have domain administrator privileges. The Setup Wizard prompts you for the administrator-level name and password needed to add your computer to a domain.

No such authentication is needed to make your computer part of a workgroup. You need only add the name of an existing workgroup to join it, or a new name to create a workgroup. The Setup Wizard then installs the selected networking components and moves on to its final stage.

Completing the Setup Program

In its final stage, the Setup Wizard installs Start menu items, registers the components, applies the settings that you selected, saves your configuration settings to the hard drive, deletes unnecessary installation files, and restarts the computer.

Study Break

Install Windows 2000 Professional Manually

Practice what you have learned by compiling the information you will need prior to installing Windows 2000, then by following the description provided in this section to install the operating system as a clean install.

If you are unable to install Windows 2000 as a clean install because you must upgrade a previous operating system, skip ahead and read Section 1.3, *Upgrading*, before proceeding.

MCSE 1.2 Unattended Installations

The attended installation of Windows 2000 Professional on a few desktops is fairly straight forward, as you have seen in the previous section. If you need to install the operating system on many computers or in multiple locations, however, it can become prohibitively time consuming. To address this, you must be able to install Windows 2000 Professional without physically being in front of each target computer. Microsoft makes this possible through the use of several unattended installation strategies.

The first methodology that can be applied to unattended installations is disk duplication, also know as *disk cloning* or *disk imaging*. At its simplest, disk duplication involves performing a clean install of Windows 2000 Professional on a master computer, then creating a disk image of the hard drive that can be redistributed to other similar machines. Microsoft provides two tools for this purpose. The System Preparation tool is used to create images that can be distributed by third party applications. The Remote Installation Preparation Wizard creates images that can be distributed from a Windows 2000 Server. The caveat is that you may only perform clean installs.

The second methodology that can be applied to unattended installations is scripting. Here you create an *unattended answer file* to automatically provide answers to the questions that you would ordinarily be prompted for if you were sitting in front of the computer while running Setup from a remote server. This method can be used for both clean installs and upgrades. Microsoft provides the Setup Manager to help you create answer files, although they can also be created with any text editor using the proper syntax.

Using Remote Installation Services

Remote Installation Services (RIS) is an optional component of Windows 2000 Server that lets you install Windows 2000 Professional remotely on multiple computers of the same or differing configurations. Under RIS, you create a disk image of a properly configured Windows 2000 Professional workstation using any disk duplication tool, preferably the companion Remote Installation Preparation Wizard. This image is then distributed to additional workstations from the RIS server. The Remote Installation Preparation Wizard strips hardware-specific settings and the security identifier (SID) from the master image, making its duplicates usable by any workstation.

In action, the RIS installation process works as follows:

1. A target client computer starts up from its Preboot eXEcution (PXE)-based BIOS or the boot ROM on its network adapter — if so enabled — or from a Remote Boot Disk that can be prepared on the RIS server using the Remote Boot Floppy Generator tool.

2. The client computer uses the Boot Protocol (BootP) to locate a Dynamic Host Configuration Protocol (DHCP) server and obtain an IP address. The DHCP server provides the client with an IP address, and Boot Information Negotiation Layer (BINL) extensions redirect the client to the RIS server.

3. The RIS server downloads the Client Installation Wizard (CIW) to the computer, which opens with a log-in screen.

4. When the user logs in, RIS uses the Domain Name System (DNS) to locate the Active Directory server.
5. Active Directory determines which options the CIW may display to the user, as well as which images the user is allowed to choose from. Active Directory then downloads the initial installation files to the client using the Trivial File Transfer Protocol (TFTP).
6. The user chooses the appropriate image, launching the setup.

It is a good solution, but one that requires careful planning since the client computer's boot mechanism, RIS, DHCP, DNS, and Active Directory must all work in harmony. Before you can use RIS, your network must have a Windows 2000-based Active Directory domain controller and a DNS server that is integrated with the domain (e.g., that supports RFC 2052 SRV records and RFC 2136 dynamic updates). Additional limitations of RIS are as follow:

- RIS can only be used to duplicate the Windows 2000 Professional operating system.
- Only a single partition, such as the C: drive, can be duplicated.
- The Remote Boot Disk only contains drivers for 25 Peripheral Connection Interface (PCI)-based network adapters. Laptops with PC Card adapters, for example, are therefore out of luck.

SETTING UP RIS

To set up RIS, you must perform the following steps:

1. Designate a Windows 2000 Server that is a member of a Windows 2000 domain to be a RIS server. The shared volume on which images are stored must be formatted as NTFS. The volume must have between 800 MBs and 1 GB of free space for an initial image, and it cannot contain the Windows 2000 Server system files.
2. Authorize the server as a DHCP server with Active Directory (even though it really is not). This is done using the DHCP Manager snap-in to the Microsoft Management Console (MMC).
3. Install RIS and reboot the server.
4. Run the RIS Setup Wizard (RISETUP.EXE) to prepare the share drive and install the initial image. If you have multiple images, there will be a great deal of file duplication that would consume server disk space. To lessen this impact, Microsoft creates a Single-Instance-Store (SIS) volume in which duplicate files are not saved.
5. Add new images as needed using the Remote Installation Preparation Wizard (RIPrep.exe). To use the Remote Installation Preparation Wizard, first install Windows 2000 Professional on a master computer

remotely from the RIS server. Next, install the appropriate applications (as determined by your organization's policies). Finally, run the Remote Installation Preparation Wizard on the master computer to create a disk image that will be uploaded to the RIS server. On the down side, you can only duplicate a single partition. On the up side, identical machine configurations are not required so long as they share the same Hardware Abstraction Layer (HAL). When differences occur between the master and target computers, Plug and Play support is employed.

6. Restrict user access to various images as necessary by applying group policy through the Active Directory Users and Computers MMC snap-in. This ensures that users will only apply the appropriate images to their workstations. If you only authorize a given user to download one image, the user will only be shown that image, which can then be installed automatically.

On the client side, users may be presented with some combination of the following four options after the Client Installation Wizard launches (depending on how you configured Active Directory):

- **Automatic Setup.** The default, this option only requires that the user select the appropriate image. The image is then installed using all of its preconfigured settings.
- **Custom Setup.** This option lets the user name the computer and select the Active Directory location in which its computer account will be created. Most of the installation's parameters can be specified manually using this option.
- **Restart a Previous Setup Attempt.** In the event of a connection failure, this option picks up where the previous setup left off without prompting the user for previously entered information.
- **Maintenance and Troubleshooting.** This option permits a third-party tool to be run prior to the installation.

Once users choose an option here, they are prompted to select the appropriate image, then setup begins (assuming that you authorized them to see more than one image).

A complete description of RIS setup and usage can be found in Chapter 24, *Managing Change Configuration*.

Using the System Preparation Tool

The System Preparation tool can be applied to computers with identical hardware and software configurations only. This makes it limited if you have computers from many different manufacturers or with many differing software environments, since a disk image must be created to support each machine. If you have large numbers of computers from the same manufacturer with standardized software configurations, however, it is a practical, simple to use tool.

As with the Remote Installation Preparation Wizard, you must configure a master computer from which to create a disk image using the System Preparation tool. The image can then be burned on to CD-ROMs or shared from a server. Third-party utilities, such as Symantec's Norton Ghost or PowerQuest's DriveImage, must then be used to replicate the image to target computers.

You must have a volume licensing agreement for Windows 2000 Professional before employing the System Preparation tool.

Technically, the target computers need to be "compatible" rather than "identical." In other words, they must have a similar HAL. Hard drives and their controllers, however, must be identical. For example, you cannot create a master on a SCSI-based hard disk and apply it to an IDE-based device. Also, the target computer's hard disk must be at least as large as that of the master computer's. Plug and Play devices, such as video cards and network adapters, may differ.

The System Preparation tool (Sysprep.exe, Setupcl.exe) can be extracted to your hard drive or a floppy disk from the following path on the Windows 2000 Professional installation CD-ROM:

```
D:/SUPPORT/TOOLS/Deploy.cab
```

The System Preparation tool can be executed from the Run dialog box using a command in the following format:

```
Sysprep.exe [sysprep.inf] [-quiet] [-nosidgen] [-reboot]
```

Table 1.3 describes its optional switch settings.

Table 1.3 *SYSPREP.EXE Switches*

Command	Purpose
-quiet	Suppresses the display of prompts.
-nosidgen	Suppresses the generation of a SID, allowing the user to customize the computer account settings. Use this option when you do not want to clone the master computer's settings.
-pnp	Forces the use of Plug and Play detection.
-reboot	Forces the restart of the master computer after image creation.

When creating an image, you must log on to the master computer with an Administrator account.

Another component of the System Preparation tool, the Mini-Setup Wizard, is used to regenerate the SIDs on target computers and to permit user customization of the following parameters:

- End-user license agreement.
- Product key.
- User name, company name, and Administrator password.
- Network configuration.
- Domain or workgroup selection.
- Date and time zone.

Alternately, you can automate the selection of these parameters by creating a "sysprep.inf" answer file. (We describe the creation of answer files in the next topic.) Any answer not provided by sysprep.inf will be presented to the user.

Using Unattended Answer Files

Scripted installations can be performed in a couple of ways. The first involves the use of command line switches associated with the Setup program (WINNT.EXE) that determine how setup will handle the preinstallation phases. The second involves Unattended Answer Files (UAFs), which supply the answers to questions that arise during the latter GUI-based installation phases. Associated with UAFs are companion Uniqueness Database Files (UDFs), the Setup Manager Wizard, and the System Difference (SYSDIFF.EXE) application.

WORKING WITH WINNT32.EXE

You can automate the setup process somewhat by running the WINNT32.EXE program from the command prompt or Run dialog box. Table 1.4 describes several switches that can be used with either clean installations or when upgrading from Windows NT or 9x.

Table 1.4 *WINNT32.EXE Switches*

Command	Purpose
/copydir: *folder_name*	Creates a subfolder within the folder in which Windows 2000 files are installed that is not deleted after Setup completes. Use additional /r switches to install additional folders. This is handy for copying down third-party drivers for later installation.
/copysource: *folder_name*	Similar to the previous option, creates a subfolder within the folder in which Windows 2000 files are installed that is deleted after Setup completes.
/cmd: *command*	Executes a command just prior to Setup's final phase.
/cmdcons	Installs the files needed to restart the system in command-line mode for the purpose of repair after a failed installation. It adds a Recovery Console item to the BOOT.INI file.
/syspart: *hard_drive*	Prepares a hard disk to be transferred to another computer by installing setup files and marking the partition as active. With it, you can put the installation files on a hard disk, remove the disk from the machine, install it in another machine, and complete the installation there. Use in conjunction with the /tempdrive switch.
/tempdrive: *hard_drive*	Specifies the drive to which Windows 2000 temporary files will be installed during setup.
/makelocalsource	Copies Windows 2000 source files to the target drive during setup, making it unnecessary to depend on a CD-ROM drive or network connection thereafter.

Table 1.4 *WINNT32.EXE Switches (continued)*

/noreboot	Prevents reboot after installation so that another command can be executed. You must then restart manually, after which time Setup will resume.
/checkupgradeonly	Checks the computer for incompatibilities that might interfere with a successful upgrade. This option will not actually launch the Setup program.
/unattend	Upgrades a previous version of Windows using unattended Setup mode that requires no user intervention. Settings are taken from the previous installation.
/unattend[#]:*unattended_answer_file*	As described further on in this section, Setup can use an UAF to provide specific information about setup options that would otherwise be asked of the user. In addition, a number can be specified for a time delay before reboot using this switch.
/udf:*id*[,*udf_file*]	Permits the application of an automatically generated computer name from a UDF, as described further on in this section.

There are actually two versions of the **Setup** program. **WINNT32.EXE**, described in Table 1.x, can be used to launch clean installs or upgrades to Windows 95, 98, or NT 4.0. **WINNT.EXE**, which has similar but has slightly different options, can be used to launch clean installs on computers running **MS-DOS** or Windows 3.x.

WORKING WITH UAFS AND UDFS

UAFs essentially replace an administrator so that a human does not have to sit at a computer and reply to every setup prompt that comes along. It is likely that a group of computers on a network will be operated by people with user-level rights and permissions. Equally likely, these computers will all be configured in much the same way. Thus, one UAF can often be applied to a series of computers.

Unfortunately, the only-one-text-file option also limits all the computers to a single computer name, domain membership, and other applicable network information such as IP address. In order to automate these variables as well, a different UAF could be created for each computer. But then, this option increases both the time required for installation and the probability of human error during the process, not to mention defeating the purpose of creating the text files in the first place.

Optionally, the installation process can be programmed to stop and wait for user input at those points at which unique setup parameters are required. Of course, this method defeats the purpose of an automatic setup, too. To complete the solution, you must call upon a UDF that can fill in unique information for individual computers, such as the computer name.

CREATING UAFS • The UAF is a text file that answers the Setup application's prompts (see Figure 1.10). Combined with the files described in the following paragraphs, the UAF allows for both automation and flexibility.

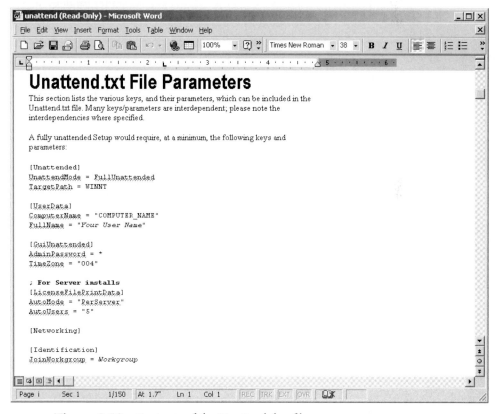

Figure 1.10 *Contents of the Unattend.doc file.*

The Windows 2000 Professional installation CD-ROM contains a sample UAF in the "unattend.doc" document. You can use the example as a template for your own UAF. Alternately, you can build an UAF from scratch by using the graphical Windows 2000 Setup Manager Wizard.

Both are located on the Windows 2000 Professional installation CD-ROM in the Support/Tools/Deploy.cab file.

CREATING UDFS • The best way to personalize an UAF during installation is with an UDF. An UDF is a text file that allows you to provide unique and specific information for each computer or user. When used with an UAF, the UDF eliminates the need for any user input during installation. To use a metaphor, if the answer file were the form file, the UDF would be the merge file.

The UDF can replace sections in, or otherwise re-organize, the UAF during the GUI-driven part of the Windows 2000 setup process. During installation, the UAF can handle most of the setup process, while certain elements that are unique to certain computers can be handled by the UDF.

The UDF is divided into two sections: *unique IDs* and *unique ID parameters*. The unique ID portion identifies which parts of the answer file will be modified or replaced. It also establishes which users or machines will receive the unique information specified in the answer file. The unique ID parameters section holds the data that will be merged into the answer file, such as computer names or time zone information.

For each individual environment, you should make one UAF. This is the best way to use the UAF and the UDF together. You should also write at least one UDF to set the unique IDs of every machine that will be installed.

The name and path to the UDF is set with the /udf switch when starting the setup process from the command line. The UDF should be located on a distribution server with the other Windows 2000 Professional installation files.

WORKING WITH SYSDIFF

Windows 2000 might not be the only software you will need to install on a workstation. Where application installations are needed as well, you can use the SYSDIFF utility to install any software that does not support a scripted installation.

SYSDIFF serves an entirely different function from the UAF. Whereas the UAF and UDF install the operating system, SYSDIFF comes in afterward and installs the applications. You can use it with an unattended installation to fully automate the entire installation.

SYSDIFF takes a *snapshot* of a system after a standard installation and before any alterations. It then makes a *difference file* that tracks each change from the standard installation to the finalized installation. This allows you to trace the changes between a standard installation and one that you have tailored to your computing environment.

The following three steps are involved here:

1. Making a snapshot file
2. Making a difference file
3. Applying the difference file

SYSDIFF can also be used to make an Initialization File (INF) and to delete the contents of a difference file (defined further on).

CREATING A SNAPSHOT • To create the snapshot file, you first must install Windows 2000 Professional on a master computer with a hardware configuration consistent with those of target computers. You must also use the same method of installation that you plan to use on your system. Besides having the same hardware platform, the Windows 2000 root directory must be the same on both the reference system and the machines that will ultimately have Windows 2000 installed. Once you have installed the operating system, you can use SYSDIFF to take a snapshot of the standard installation with a command in the following format:

```
sysdiff /snap [/log:<log_file>] <snapshot_file>
```

In this command, "log_file" is the name of the optional log file created by SYSDIFF and "snapshot_file" is the name of the file containing the snapshot of the system. The command makes the snapshot file, which can be called the original configuration. The original configuration becomes the standard system against which you can compare the altered system.

CREATING A DIFFERENCE FILE • Once the snapshot has been taken, you can install the applications that you want on the master system. The difference file is created with another command in the following format:

```
Sysdiff /diff [/c:<title>] [/log:<log_file>] <snapshot_file>
<difference_file>
```

In this command, "title" is the path name for the difference file and "log_file" is the name of an optional file log that SYSDIFF can create. In addition, "snapshot_file" is the file that contains the snapshot of the system. This file must be created from the same snapshot file created with the /snap switch previously described. If you create it from a file from another system, SYSDIFF will not run. "Difference_file" is the file that lists the changes made to the snapshot to turn it into the current system configuration.

USING A DIFFERENCE FILE • There is one last step in the SYSDIFF process. The difference file must be applied to a new installation as part of the unattended setup. This is done with the following command:

```
sysdiff /apply /m [log:<log_file>] <difference_file>
```

In this command, "/m" takes the changes made to the menu structure and routes them to the default user profile structure instead of to the user currently logged on (with the local user profile). Otherwise, the changes would affect only the current user, and the system would not change. "Log_file" is an optional file in which SYSDIFF writes information regarding the process. If the process fails for some reason, the log file is a good source of information for finding out why. "Difference_file" is the file you created with the command described previously. The Windows 2000 root directory must be in the same location as that of the system that created the difference file.

This command can be run during the unattended installation or any time once Windows 2000 Professional has been installed.

This difference file can be truly gigantic. After all, it does contain all the files and all the Registry settings for the applications you installed. Applying such a large component during installation can drag out the process. However, you can reduce the time by creating an INF from the difference file.

WORKING WITH INFS • Rather than containing all the information that the difference file does, the Initialization File (INF) only has the initialization file commands and the Registry. The command to start the INF part of installation is:

```
Sysdiff /inf /m [/u] <sysdiff_file> <oem_root>
```

In this command, the "/m" switch takes the changes made to the menu structure and routes them to the default user profile structure instead of the current user. The "/u" switch overrides the default and cues for the INF to be created as a Unicode text file. Otherwise, the INF would be created using the system ANSI codepage. "Sysdiff_file" denotes the path to the file created through the "/diff" process (described previously). "Oem_root" is the path of a directory. This creates the \OEM directory required by the INF in which the INF and files from the difference file package are placed. If you are installing x86 machines, you should create this directory under the \I386 directory on the distribution server.

The first portion of the Windows 2000 Professional installation cannot copy directories with path names longer than 64 characters because it is

DOS-based, so you need to watch the length of the subdirectory path names under the \OEM directory.

To use the INF once it is created, you need to trigger it. You do this by adding the following line to the file "CMDLINES.TXT" under the \OEM directory:

```
RUNDLL32 syssetup,SetupInfObjectInstallAction section 128 inf
```

In this command, "section" names the section in the INF. "Inf" sets the name of the file in a relative path.

DUMPING THE DIFFERENCE FILE • If you want to read the difference file as text so that you can edit it, you can do so with the "/dump" command in the following format:

```
Sysdiff /dump <difference_file> <dump_file>
```

In this command, "difference file" establishes the name of the difference file to edit. "Dump_file" sets the name for the dump file. You can edit the dump file by opening it with a text editor.

WORKING WITH UNATTEND.TXT

The contents of the UNATTEND.TXT answer file are organized into section headings, parameters, and values modifying the parameters, as shown in Figure 1.11.

Figure 1.11 *Contents of an UNATTEND.TXT file.*

These parameters may include the following:

- **Unattend.** Used during text mode setup. It can be customized only by editing the answer file, as there is no entry in the UDF. This section indicates to the setup application that this installation is unattended. It also enables settings such as installation (upgrade or new), installation path, and file system type (NTFS/FAT).
- **OEMBootFiles.** Displays Original Equipment Manufacturer (OEM) boot file names for the HAL and SCSI driver. Like the Unattend section, it can be specified only in the UAF.
- **MassStorageDrivers.** Describes the hard drive drivers to be loaded by the text mode setup process.
- **OEM_Ads.** Modifies the default user interface of the Setup program. It is used to modify the background bitmap and logo used during the GUI-driven portion of the setup process.
- **GuiUnattended.** Specifies settings for the GUI-driven portion of setup. It indicates the time zone and hides the Administrator password dialog box.
- **UserData.** Provides user-specific data such as user name, organization name, computer name, and product ID.
- **Networking.** Specifies network settings such as those for network adapters, services, and protocols. If this section is missing, networking will not be installed. This section specifies the domain or workgroup to join, and creates a computer account in the domain.
- **Display.** Indicates specific settings for the display adapter card's installation. These settings must be correct and must be supported by the adapter.
- **Components.** Specifies the components that should be installed along with Windows 2000 Professional, such as the Internet Information Server (IIS) Web server or the all-important Pinball game.

STARTING THE UNATTENDED INSTALLATION

Once you have created UNATTEND.TXT, the uniqueness database, and the SYSDIFF file, you can begin the setup process. To begin setup from the command line, launch it from Windows 95, 98, or NT 4.0 with a command in the following format:

```
F:\i386\winnt32.exe /s:<source_path>u:v:\unattend.txt /
UDF:user1;v:\udf.txt
```

The command for launching the setup from Windows 3.1 or MS-DOS would look like the following:

```
F:\i386\winnt.exe /s:<source_path> /u:v:\unattend.txt /
UDF:user1;v:\udf.txt
```

In these commands, "F:\" is the drive mapped to your installation CD-ROM or network share. "<source_path>" is the path pointing to the \I386 directory of the distribution files. "v:\" is the drive mapped to the directory containing your UNATTEND.TXT file and UDF.

USING SETUP MANAGER

The graphical Setup Manager Wizard lets you create an UAF more easily. It provides you with three options on launch: build a new answer file, build an answer file based on your current computer's configuration, or modify an existing answer file. With it, you can forgo many of the previously described procedures by simply installing a pristine version of Windows 2000 Professional on your perfectly configured master computer and using the second option to duplicate its settings. Create fully automated installations by answering all of the wizard's questions, or create partially unattended installations by bypassing some wizard options.

After you choose to create a new answer file, the Setup Manager Wizard asks whether you wish to create an answer file for your own scripted installation or for use with the previously described disk duplication methods, as shown in Figure 1.12.

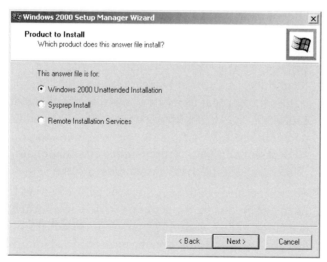

Figure 1.12 *Choosing purpose of answer file.*

Next, you are asked to choose between creating an UAF for Windows 2000 Professional or Windows 2000 Server, and then to define the level of user interaction that Setup permits, as shown in Figure 1.13.

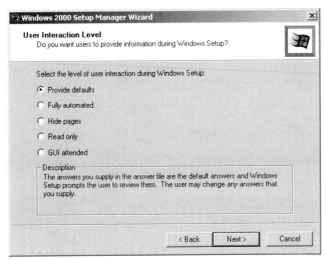

Figure 1.13   *Choosing the level of user interaction.*

The options here are as follow:

- **Provide defaults.** Use this option to pre-define default settings that can be amended by users as necessary.
- **Fully automated.** Use this option to leave the user out of the process entirely.
- **Hide pages.** Use this option to permit users to enter data in only those windows that contain settings that you chose not to preconfigure in the UAF. Windows that relate to areas you did preconfigure will not be seen.
- **Read only.** This option works in much the same way as the previous option, except that users are allowed to see all windows whether you preconfigured their settings or not. They are only allowed to enter data into those windows that you skipped, however.
- **GUI attended.** This option limits automation to just the second phase (text-based) of the installation process.

Next, the Setup Wizard presents you with windows that mirror many questions that arise during the setup process. These include setting the user and organization names, computer name (or import it from a UDF, or generate it automatically based on organization name), Administrator password, display settings, network settings, workgroup or domain, and time zone. You may also add additional settings for such options as printer, telephony, regional, language, and browser settings. Finally, you are asked about the manner in which you intend to distribute Windows 2000 Professional, as shown in Figure 1.14.

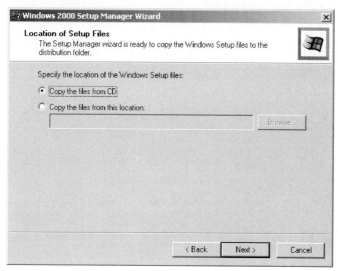

Figure 1.14   *Choosing the setup files locations.*

For remote installations, you may wish to create a distribution folder on a file server share that contains all of the setup files needed, including the UAF. Choose the Copy the files from CD radio button to move the necessary setup files to this location, as shown in Figure 1.15.

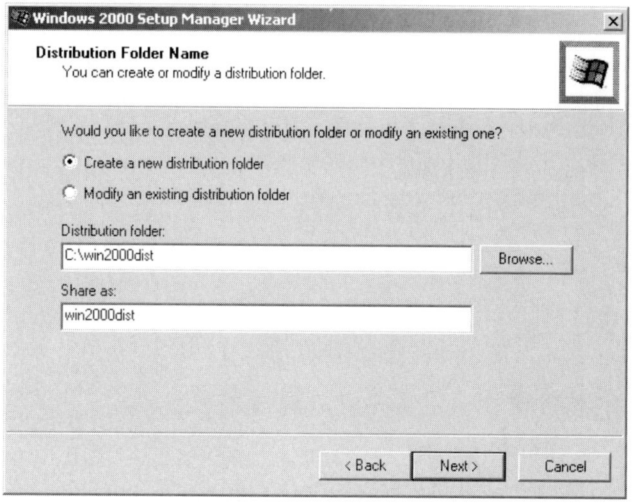

Figure 1.15   *Choosing the distribution folder location.*

Additional windows prompt you for more esoteric information, such as additional storage devices, specific HALs, and OEM branding art. You may also identify commands that will be run in addition to setup, including a "run-once" command that launches when the user first logs on, and specifies additional folder and files to be copied as part of the installation.

Finally, you are prompted to supply the UAF's name or except the default of "unattend.txt, as shown in Figure 1.16.

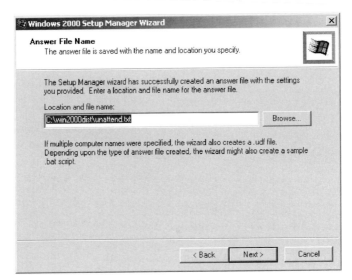

Figure 1.16   *Renaming the "unattend.txt" file.*

You should avail yourself of this opportunity, for if you do not rename the file, Setup Manager copies installation files onto the distribution volume that include a sample "unattend.txt" *which will overwrite yours.*

Once it has your information, Setup Manager creates the UAF and distribution folder, copies the setup files, and exits.

To launch the setup process using your new UAF, enter a command in the following format from the command line:

```
F:\i386\winnt[32] /s:f:\i386 /unattend:C:\myunattend.txt
```

Here the "F:" drive is the CD-ROM or mapped network share containing the distribution files, and "myunattend.txt" is the UAF.

Study Break

Create a Setup Manager Installation

Practice what you have learned by creating a scripted installation using the Setup Manager Wizard.

First, install Windows 2000 Professional on a master computer, as described in the previous section. Next, run the Setup Manager Wizard to create an UAF. Note the options that are presented in the various windows. Allow the wizard to create a distribution folder on the hard drive of the master computer or on network share. Once completed, open the "unattend.txt" file — whatever you renamed it — and review the settings that have been created. If appropriate, use your scripted installation package to install Windows 2000 Professional on additional machines remotely.

MCSE 1.3 Upgrading

You may upgrade any computer running Windows 95, 98, NT 3.51 or NT 4.0 to Windows 2000 Professional by simply inserting the installation CD-ROM in the drive and following the Setup Wizard's instructions. As shown in Figure 1.17, the CD-ROM's Autorun screen gives you the option of upgrading when it detects one of these operating systems.

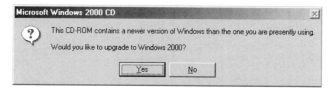

Figure 1.17 *Installation CD-ROM upgrade prompt.*

The upgrade process differs from the clean installation in that it overwrites the computer's existing system. The advantage is that it keeps most of the computer's setting preferences and applications.

When upgrading a Windows 95 or 98 machine, you might be required to create a previously unnecessary computer account for it so that it may be a member of a domain. In addition, you are prompted to upgrade the hard drive from FAT or FAT32 to NTFS. When upgrading a Windows NT 3.51 or 4.0 machine, you are prompted to upgrade your hard drive's NTFS to version 5. Other than that, installation proceeds with little user input required.

If the computer is running Windows NT 3.1 or 3.5, you must upgrade to Windows 3.51 or 4.0 and then upgrade again to Windows 2000 Professional.

If the computer is running the old Windows 3.1 or Windows for Workgroups 3.11, the relatively new Windows Me, or the new Windows XP, you must perform a clean installation.

It is not necessary to apply service packs to older Windows operating systems prior to upgrading.

Applying Update Packs

It might not be possible to run applications that work fine under the current operating system after you upgrade to Windows 2000 Professional. You should check with the Windows 2000 Product Compatibility Web site (*www.microsoft.com/windows2000/compatible*) for information on required software upgrades. In some cases, updates may be available from the software's' manufacturer that should be applied to your critical applications. You are given the opportunity to include update packs during the upgrade process.

Preparing Computers for Upgrade

Do not assume that if a system is running a previous version of Windows NT it automatically becomes a candidate for upgrade. The minimum system requirements for Windows NT 4.0 were much less: A 66 MHz 486 processor, 12 MBs of RAM, and 110 MBs of free hard disk space. To run Windows 2000 Professional, your computer should have at least a 133 MHz Pentium processor (or equivalent), 32 MBs of RAM, and 650 MBs of free hard disk space.

Even if your computer's hardware meets the minimum requirements, it may still contain components that are not supported by Windows 2000. The Setup program automatically runs the Hardware Compatibility tool during the installation process to verify this, but you are better off identifying and resolving such incompatibilities ahead of time. One way to do this is to run the WINNT32.EXE program with the /checkupgradeonly switch, as previously described. With any luck, you are presented with the results shown in Figure 1.18.

If problems are found, you can use the Details button to determine exactly which hardware or software components are incompatible, then either replace them or upgrade them according to their manufacturers' instructions. The report can also be saved as a text file.

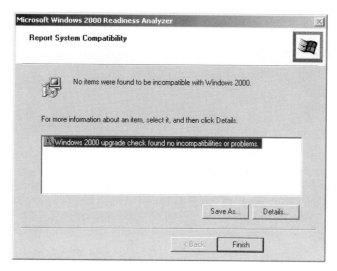

Figure 1.18 *Successful run of the Hardware Compatibility tool.*

Because of known incompatibility issues between Windows NT Workstation 3.51 or 4.0 and Windows 2000 Professional, Microsoft recommends that you remove the following software before upgrading:

- Third-party networking protocols and client applications that are not included in the I386\WINNTUPG folder of the installation CD-ROM.
- All anti-virus and disk quota software. This is necessary because of the changes in NTFS between version 4 (NT 4.0) and version 5 (Windows 2000).
- Custom power management utilities. These are replaced under Windows 2000 by built-in Advanced Configuration and Power Interface (ACPI) and Advanced Power Management (APM) features.

Study Break

Perform an Upgrade Precheck

Practice what you have learned by running the WINNT32.EXE program with the "/checkupgrade-only" switch, as previously described, on a potential computer.

If the tool detects incompatibilities, save the report as a text file. Use the report to locate the incompatible hardware or software by vendor and check with them for available Windows 2000 compatibility updates.

MCSE 1.4 Deploying Service Packs

Another step that should be added to the setup process is the installation of the latest Windows 2000 Professional Service Pack, which can be downloaded from the Microsoft Web site (as shown in Figure 1.19) or ordered on CD-ROM.

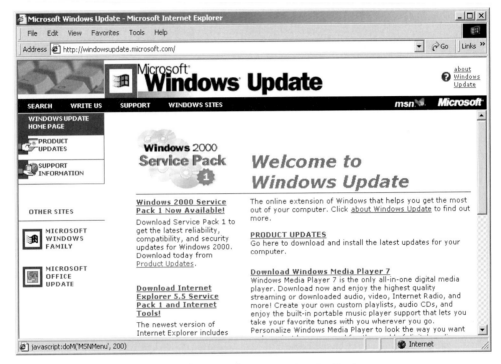

Figure 1.19 *Downloading Windows 2000 Service Pack.*

Service Packs are free updates from Microsoft that contain bug fixes, security enhancements, drivers, tools, components, and just general improvements made to the operating system since it shipped originally.

Windows 2000 makes it easy to find the latest Service Packs. Just connect to the Internet and select the Windows Update command from the Start menu to be directed to the Microsoft update site. Windows 2000 also makes it easy to determine which version of a Service Pack is currently installed.

Simply run the "winver" command from the Run dialog box to open the About Windows dialog box shown in Figure 1.20.

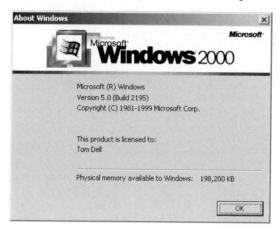

Figure 1.20   *Viewing the Windows version and build.*

To be blunt, installing Service Packs under Windows NT 4.0 was a pain in the posterior. If you added components from the installation CD-ROM, you always had to reinstall one or more Service Packs, often more than doubling your installation time. Under Windows 2000, you use the UPDATE.EXE utility to install Service Packs. Windows 2000 keeps track of which files were added or replaced, and when you add or remove a component thereafter, it automatically retrieves any necessary files from the Service Pack. Install the Service Pack once, and you are done!

One problem with Service Packs that has not gone away is the fact that they might sometimes contain changes that conflict with other software on your computer, making a previously solid workstation unstable. Since Microsoft cannot predict the effects of adding a Service Pack to every environment in the field, your best recourse is to always install a Service Pack on a test machine first, verifying its compatibility before deploying it throughout your organization.

Microsoft lets you include Service Packs in a distribution image process through slipstreaming. Under this process, the original installation files are overwritten by Service Pack files, giving you the latest installation image possible. To create this distribution, use the UPDATE.EXE command with the "/slip" switch.

Study Break

Install Service Packs

Practice what you have learned by installing a Service Pack.

First, run the "winver" command to determine whether any Service Packs have been applied on the computer to which you installed Windows 2000 Professional in previous study breaks. (Unless you have been skipping ahead, the answer will be "no.") Next, download the latest Service Pack from the Microsoft Web site using the Windows Update command. Use the UPDATE.EXE utility to install the Service Pack. Test the machine before installing the Service Pack on additional workstations.

MCSE 1.5   Troubleshooting Installations

One of Microsoft's objectives in the MCSE exam is to ensure that you know how to resolve installation problems. Some common installation problems and solutions, as identified by Microsoft, are as follows:

- **There is a problem with the installer disks.** If you encounter media errors on the Windows 2000 Professional Installation CD-ROM, you can request a replacement from Microsoft Sales at (800) 426-9400. A new set of installation floppy disks can be created from the CD-ROM. Open the Command Prompt program and switch to the CD's BOOTDISK directory (see Figure 1.2). Next, insert a blank 1.44 MB floppy disk in the disk drive and type the command: MAKE-BOOT A: (where A: is the floppy disk drive). Follow the directions to create four setup disks.

- **There is insufficient disk space for installation to take place.** If there is not enough disk space on the server, you can make some room by deleting unnecessary files and folders, especially those found in "temp" directories or Web browser caches. If you have NTFS drives, you can compress them. You can reformat partitions or re-partition a disk drive to make more space available. Finally, you can add an additional disk drive for use as the boot drive. (Consider that you will need space not only for the \WINNT directory, but for the paging file as well.)

- **The CD-ROM drive does not work.** If Windows 2000 does not recognize the adapter used by your CD-ROM drive, you might try booting from another operating system that does recognize it, such as

Windows Me. You may then run the Setup application from the CD-ROM. Alternately, you might try installing over the network. Finally, you might replace the adapter or CD-ROM drive with one that is listed on the HCL.

- **A dependency service does not start.** In this situation, first make sure the computer has a unique name on the network. Next, check to see that the necessary network protocols are installed and configured properly.
- **An error occurs in assigning a domain name.** In this situation, make sure there are no other identical domain or computer names on the network.
- **A computer cannot access a domain controller.** In this situation, first make sure that the correct user name, password, and domain were typed into the logon dialog box. Next, check the Primary Domain Controller to make sure it is online and functioning properly, and verify that its protocol and adapter configurations are correct. Also make sure that your network's DNS service is functioning properly. If all else fails, simply make the computer a member of a workgroup until you can resolve the domain logon issue.

Viewing Logs

The following log files, which can be invaluable in the troubleshooting process, are created during the installation process:

- **Setupact.log.** The Action log file chronologically lists the actions that were performed during installation, such as copying files and creating Registry keys.
- **Setuperr.log.** The Error log file lists installation errors that occurred, as well as their severity. If necessary, this file is automatically opened at the end of the setup process.
- **Setupapi.log.** The Application Programmer's Interface (API) log lists device drivers that were copied during installation, including warning and error messages. It logs an entry for each line in an INF.
- **Setuplog.txt.** The Setup log file also lists details about device driver installations.
- **Comsetup.log.** The Component Setup Log file lists details on the installation of Optional Component Manager and Com + elements.
- **Mmdet.log.** The Multimedia Detection log file lists multimedia devices, their ports and address ranges.
- **Netsetup.log.** The Network Setup log file lists activity for joining a workgroup or domain.

These logs can be opened from the \WINNT directory using Notepad, as shown in Figure 1.21.

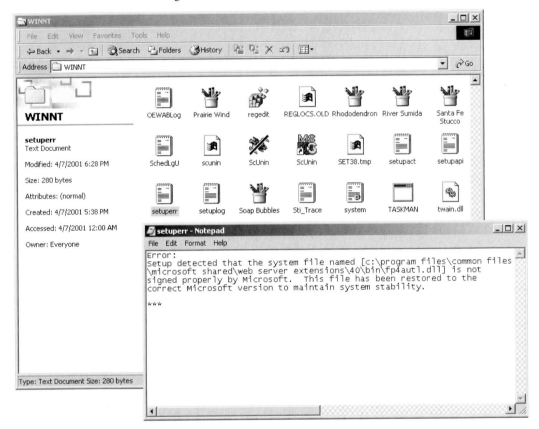

Figure 1.21 *Viewing the "Setuperr.log" file.*

Getting the Latest News

To review the latest release notes and updated information for Windows 2000, see the Microsoft Knowledge Base on the Microsoft Personal Online Support Web site at http://*support.microsoft.com/support/*.

Study Break

Review Installation Logs

> Practice what you have learned by opening the log files created in the \WINNT folder during Windows 2000 Professional.
>
> Open each log to familiarize yourself with its contents. Pay particular attention to the error and setup logs. If any problems are listed, be sure that these have been resolved.

■ Summary

In this chapter, we considered various Windows 2000 Professional installation topics including planning, attended and unattended installations, upgrades, Service Packs, and troubleshooting.

Installation Planning

Prior to installing Windows 2000 Professional, you should ensure that your hardware and software is compatible and meets or exceeds Microsoft's minimum system requirements. Then you may determine whether you will be upgrading an existing operating system or starting afresh, as well as consider how you will partition the computer's hard disk, and which file system format(s) it will use. Also be sure to back up your important files, and record network information. If the computer targeted for the installation will participate in a Microsoft Networking domain, also make sure that either a computer account has been created for it, or that you have the administrative permissions to do so.

Windows 2000 Professional's minimum system requirements are at least a 133 MHz. Pentium processor (or equivalent), 32 MBs of RAM, and 650 MBs of free hard disk space. Microsoft recommends 64 MBs of RAM and 2 GBs of free hard disk space. You can also use dual-processors.

You may upgrade any computer running Windows 95, 98, NT 3.51 or NT 4.0 to Windows 2000 Professional. If the computer is running Windows NT 3.1 or 3.5, you must upgrade to Windows 3.51 or 4.0 and then upgrade again to Windows 2000 Professional. If the computer is running Windows 3.1, Windows for Workgroups 3.11, Windows Me or XP, you must perform a clean installation.

In selecting a disk drive configuration, you should first decide if you plan to run additional operating systems on the computer—perhaps both Windows Me and Windows 2000. If so, then you must format all of the partitions that you wish to have accessible from multiple operating systems as FAT or FAT32. If you want to get the most from Windows 2000 in terms of performance, safety and security, you should format server disk drive partitions as NTFS. If you are unsure, you should format the drive as FAT initially. It is easy to convert a FAT drive to NTFS later.

Attended Installations

Microsoft breaks the process of installing Windows 2000 Professional manually on a single computer into the steps of running the Setup program, running the Setup Wizard, installing Windows networking components, and completing the Setup program. Setup can be launched from the installation CD-ROM, boor floppy disks, or a network share. Among the important decisions you must make is whether to join a network domain or workgroup.

Unattended Installations

The first methodology that can be applied to unattended installations is disk duplication, also know as disk cloning or disk imaging. At its simplest, disk duplication involves performing a clean install of Windows 2000 Professional on a master computer, then creating a disk image of the hard drive that can be redistributed to other similar machines. Microsoft provides the System Preparation (Sysprep) tool for this purpose, which is used to create images that can be distributed by third party applications. Alternately, networks that host a Windows 2000 Server can employ Remote Installation Services (RIS), which creates images that can be distributed from a distribution server. The caveats are that you may only perform clean installs, and it works best with identically configured workstations.

The second methodology that can be applied to unattended installations is scripting. Here you create an unattended answer file to automatically provide answers to the questions that you would ordinarily be prompted for if you were sitting in front of the computer while running Setup from a remote server. This method can be used for both clean installs and upgrades. Microsoft provides the Setup Manager to help you create answer files, although they can also be created with any text editor using the proper syntax.

The Setup program can be launched from the command line as "winnt.exe" or "winnt32.exe" using a number of switches helpful in unattended installation.

Upgrading

You may upgrade any computer running Windows 95, 98, NT 3.51 or NT 4.0. If the computer is running Windows NT 3.1 or 3.5, you must upgrade to Windows 3.51 or 4.0 and then upgrade again to Windows 2000 Professional. When upgrading a Windows 95 or 98 machine, you might be required to create a previously unnecessary computer account for it so that it may be a member of a domain. In addition, you will be prompted to upgrade the hard drive from FAT or FAT32 to NTFS. When upgrading a Windows NT 3.51 or 4.0 machine, you will be prompted to upgrade your hard drive's NTFS to version 5.

Before upgrading, you should ensure that your computer's hardware and software is compatible with Windows 2000 by running the Setup program from the command line with the /checkupgradeonly switch.

Deploying Service Packs

Service Packs are free updates from Microsoft that contain bug fixes, security enhancements, drivers, tools, components, and just general improvements made to the operating system since it shipped originally. To get the latest Service Pack, connect to the Internet and select the Windows Update command from the Start menu to be directed to the Microsoft update site. Use the UPDATE.EXE utility to install Service Packs. Windows 2000 keeps track of which files were added or replaced and when you add or remove a component, thereafter, it automatically retrieves any necessary files from the Service Pack.

Microsoft lets you include Service Packs in a distribution image process through slipstreaming. Under this process, the original installation files are overwritten by Service Pack files, giving you the latest installation image possible.

Troubleshooting Installations

Problems that can arise during installation include media errors on the Windows 2000 Professional Installation CD-ROM, insufficient disk space on the target computer, incompatible CD-ROM drives, dependency services that will not start, errors in assigning a domain name, and failure to access a domain controller. Additional problems can be detected by viewing the log files created during installation, particularly the Setup Errors log.

▲ CHAPTER REVIEW QUESTIONS

Here are a few questions relating to the material covered in the Installing Windows 2000 Professional section of Microsoft's Installing, Configuring, and Administering Microsoft Windows 2000 Professional exam (70-210).

1. *Where can you find out if a computer's hardware is compatible with Windows 2000 Professional? Select all that apply:*

    A. The ReadMe file on the installation CD-ROM

    B. The HCL

    C. The Microsoft Web site

    D. Various hardware manufacturer's Web sites

2. *Windows NT Server can be installed in which of the following ways? Select all that apply:*

    A. From floppy disks

    B. From CD-ROM

    C. From a network share

    D. From the Microsoft Web site

3. *If you format a disk drive as NTFS, you can convert it to FAT later without reinstalling data or Windows NT.*

    A. True

    B. False

4. *Which of the following operating systems require that you perform only a clean installation of Windows 2000? Select all that apply:*

    A. Windows for Workgroups 3.11

    B. Windows 95

    C. Windows NT 3.5

    D. Windows Me

5. *It is only possible to install Windows 2000 from CD-ROM if the target computer's CD-ROM drive recognizes the Autorun screen.*

    A. True

    B. False

6. *Which of the following are true of (NetBIOS) computer names? Select all that apply:*

   A. Can be as long as 14 characters

   B. Can be as long as 15 characters

   C. Must not be the same as the Administrator logon password

   D. Are case sensitive

7. *If you do not choose to join a domain name when installing Windows 2000, Setup will choose what name for the domain by default? Select only one:*

   A. DOMAIN

   B. My Network

   C. WORKGROUP

   D. None

8. *Which of the following tools can be applied to a scripted unattended installation? Select all that apply:*

   A. RIPrep

   B. Update.exe

   C. Sysprep

   D. UAF

9. *Which of the following network services must be properly configured to work with RIS? Select all that apply:*

   A. DNS

   B. DHCP

   C. Active Directory

   D. HAL

10. *Which of the following are limitations of the RIS installation process? Select all that apply:*

    A. You can only apply distribute images by CD-ROM

    B. You can only duplicate the active partition

    C. You cannot duplicate the Windows 2000 Server operating system

    D. You can only remote boot from PCI-based network adapters

11. *The System Preparation tool can prepare images for distribution by which of the following utilities. Select all that apply:*

    A. Symantec Norton Ghost

    B. Microsoft RIS

C. Microsoft Sysprep

D. PowerQuest DriveImage

12. *Which of the following are components of the System Preparation tool. Select all that apply:*

A. Sysprep

B. Sysdiff

C. Mini-Setup Wizard

D. Sysprep.inf

13. *Setup Manager can be used to create which of the following? Select all that apply:*

A. UAFs

B. UDFs

C. Distribution folders

D. Remote boot floppies

14. *Which of the following switches must be used when running a Setup Manager-created installation from the command line? Select only one:*

A. /unattend

B. /uaf

C. /udf

D. /sysman

15. *If you have Windows 95, 98, or NT 4.0 on a computer, you must upgrade them if you wish to run Windows 2000 Professional on the same workstation.*

A. True

B. False

16. *Application update packs are available for download from Microsoft.*

A. True

B. False

17. *Application update packs must be applied prior to Windows 2000 Professional installation.*

A. True

B. False

18. *Which of the following command is used to generate a hardware and software compatibility report? Select all that apply:*

A. update.exe /checkupgradeonly

B. winnt32.exe /checkupgradeonly

C. winnt32.exe /hcl

D. winver

19. *Which of the following should be removed from the target computer before upgrading to Windows 2000 Professional? Select all that apply:*

A. Some third-party networking software

B. Anti-virus software

C. Disk quota software

D. Power management software

20. *Service Packs must be deployed after the Windows 2000 Professional installation process has completed.*

A. True

B. False

21. *Which of the following are methods of obtaining the latest Service Packs? Select all that apply:*

A. From the Microsoft Web site

B. From the Update Windows command

C. On CD-ROM

D. They are installed automatically when available.

22. *If you are unable to logon to a domain during installation, you must quit Setup and try the installation again after you have resolved the problem.*

A. True

B. False

23. *Which of the following are logs useful to the troubleshooting process. Select all that apply:*

A. unattend.txt

B. setuperr.log

C. setuplog.log

D. winsetup.log

Administering Windows 2000 Professional Resources

▲Chapter Syllabus

MCSE 2.1 File and Folder Access

MCSE 2.2 Shared Folder Access

MCSE 2.3 Working with Print Devices

MCSE 2.4 Working with File Systems

In this chapter, we examine the some of the administration topics covered in the *Implementing and Conducting Administration of Resources* section of Microsoft's *Installing, Configuring, and Administering Microsoft Windows 2000 Professional* exam (70-210).

The following material is designed to make you comfortable with establishing file and folder access, as well as sharing files and folders on a local network or the Web. Similarly, you will know how to connect to and share printers. You must also understand how administration differs between file systems.

MCSE 2.1   File and Folder Access

In this section, we look at issues surrounding file and folder access, including moving and copying, naming, compression, permissions, and optimization.

Copying Files vs. Moving Files

Under Windows 2000 Professional, you can either *copy* or *move* files. These commands are accessible on any folder menu bar and from the Edit menu bar item, as shown in Figure 2.1.

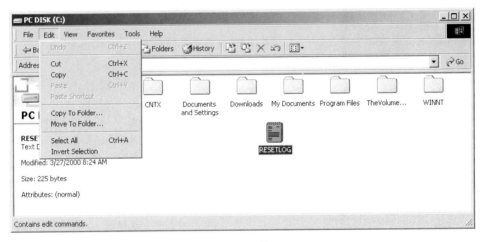

Figure 2.1   *Selecting to move or copy files.*

When you use the Copy command to move files within or between partitions, new files are created that inherit the security characteristics and compression status of the *destination parent directory.* When you use the Move command to move files between partitions, the same thing occurs. The only difference is that the original files are then deleted. When you use the Move command to move files within partitions, however, the files are not altered, and so they retain their original security and compression characteristics.

Naming Folders and Files

Windows 2000 supports file names that do not adhere to the limitations of the old DOS 8.3 naming convention (e.g., eight characters plus a three-character extension). This so-called *long file name support* is available under both the NTFS and FAT32 file systems.

Windows 2000 also provides an algorithm to convert long files to the 8.3 naming convention standard to accommodate operating systems that do not provide long file name support. The first six characters of the name, minus any spaces, remain the same. The seventh character becomes the tilde character (~). The eighth character becomes a numeric increment to accommodate for files that have the same first six characters.

After the first four iterations in a volume, however, Windows 2000 changes its tack and no longer converts with the numeric increment. Instead, it keeps only the first two characters, and then inserts five random characters (see Table 2.1).

Table 2.1 *Truncated File Names*

Original Long file names	file names After the 8.3 Conversion
file tid leans 24.xls	fileti~1.xls
file tid leans 25.xls	fileti~2.xls
file tid leans 26.xls	fileti~3.xls
file tid leans 27.xls	fileti~4.xls
Long file name after four iterations	**Truncated file name After Four Iterations**
file tid leans 28.xls	filitts1.xls
file tid leans 29.xls	filitts2.xls
file tid leans 30.xls	filitts3.xls
file tid leans 31.xls	filitts4.xls

You should be aware of this if you plan to share files and folders with computers running other operating systems, such as MS-DOS.

Working with File Compression

Windows 2000 Professional provides file and folder compression on NTFS formatted partitions. Compression is allowed for individual files and folders, as well as whole volumes. Any NTFS formatted disk or folder has the ability to contain both compressed and noncompressed files.

Window 2000 file compression can provide up to 2:1 compression. Once enabled, compression takes place automatically and is transparent to both applications and users. NTFS can compress all files in the partition, including hidden and system files (except NTLDR and Pagefile.sys).

Besides being automatic, NTFS compression is optimized for performance. When you select a file to compress, NTFS first determines how much disk space will be saved and compares that to the resources it will take to do the compression. If NTFS decides it is not worth the effort, it does not compress the file. In addition, NTFS compression ratios are not as dramatic as those achieved by other utilities, but neither is performance compromised.

CONFIGURING FILE COMPRESSION

To enable this feature, select a file that you wish to compress, then right-click and select the Properties command to open the Properties dialog box, as shown in Figure 2.2.

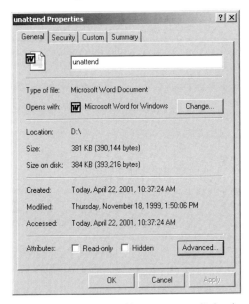

Figure 2.2 *NTFS file Properties dialog box.*

Here, select the Advanced button to open the Advanced Attributes button, as shown in Figure 2.3.

Next, enable the Compress contents to save disk space checkbox. You may choose to compress entire folders, in which case you are asked if subfolders should be compressed too. You can also compress entire partitions. In truth, however, you are compressing the files within partitions and folders rather than the partitions and folders themselves.

If you enable compression for a folder, then all new files created in that directory are also compressed.

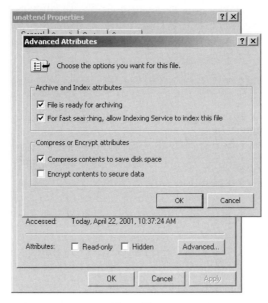

Figure 2.3 *Enabling file compression.*

COMPRESSION FROM THE COMMAND LINE • You can also enable compression from the command prompt using the COMPACT.EXE utility. It reports compression status, ratio, and file size for compressed files in the file list. It can also be used with a number of switches in the format:

```
COMPACT /<switch> file/folder_name
```

The possible switches include the following:

/C Compresses files

/U Uncompresses files

/S Compresses all files in a directory (and subdirectories)

/I Continues compression after errors have occurred

/F Forces compression on all files, even if already compressed

/A Compresses hidden and system files

MANAGING FILE COMPRESSION

The previously mentioned difference between the Copy and Move commands becomes evident when working with compressed files. If you create a file in a compressed directory, it becomes a compressed file. If you use the Copy command to move the file to an uncompressed directory, then the file becomes uncompressed. This is because a new instance of the file has been created that adopts the characteristics of its parent directory.

When the Move command is used, however, a file created in a compressed directory and moved to an uncompressed directory remains compressed. This is because the Move command does not actually move anything, it only directs the source and destination directories to swap pointers, making it appear to move. Since the file does not change, it does not lose its original characteristics.

There is an exception. When relocating a file in another partition, the Move command is unable to play its little trick with directory pointers and must instead copy the file (deleting it from the source partition thereafter). Consequently, a file that is moved from a compressed directory on one partition to an uncompressed directory on another partition would be uncompressed.

There is a major difference in the way copying files between computers over the network is handled by Windows 2000 Professional vs. Windows NT 4.0. Under Windows NT 4.0, a file would be decompressed on the server computer before being sent over the network. Under Windows 2000 Professional, a file is copied over the network then decompressed on the client machine. This change makes it faster to copy compressed files over the network.

VIEWING COMPRESSED FILES • You may change the display of your compressed file and folders to an alternate color, making it easier to differentiate between compressed and uncompressed data. To do this, select the Folder Options command from the Tools menu bar item to open the Folder Options dialog box, as seen in Figure 2.4.

Under the View tab, enable the Display compressed files and folders with alternate color checkbox.

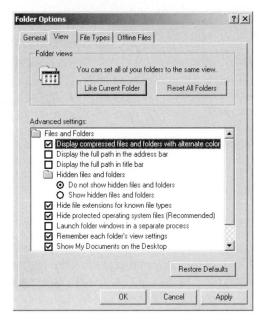

Figure 2.4 *Changing compressed file display colors.*

TROUBLESHOOTING FILE COMPRESSION

Note that only NTFS compression is available under Windows 2000 Professional. You cannot use Microsoft's DriveSpace as you can under Windows 9x/Me, for example.

Note also that Windows 2000 Professional supports file encryption, which cannot be used with file compression. You may compress files or encrypt files, but not both.

Working with Permissions

How you control access to your computer's files and folders depends on whether you intend to share them over a network. If you do, share permissions come into play, as described further on. If you do not, you need only be concerned with *local security*. This restricts access to anyone sitting down at your machine and logging on directly. With local security, you can determine which of your files and folders others may manipulate.

Local security does not exist on FAT-formatted volumes. You have no control over what others do with your data beyond requiring a user name/

password log-on. This is scant protection because anyone savvy enough to boot from a system floppy disk could bypass the Windows 2000 Professional log-on and gain direct access to a FAT partition.

Local security under NTFS is quite another matter. First, the only way to access an NTFS partition is through Windows 2000, so the log-on cannot be bypassed. Second, the data that can be viewed after using a given log-on is subject to a wide range of possible permissions controls. In addition, NTFS permissions can be applied to a user who is accessing either a local resource or a shared network resource.

SPECIAL NTFS PERMISSIONS

The following NTFS special permissions can be applied to any file or folder:

- **Traverse Folder/Execute File.** Users with this permission may browse through various folders to locate other folders and files, as well as launch applications.
- **List Folder/Read Data.** Users with this permission may see folder and subfolder names. They may also view the contents of files.
- **Create Folders/Append Data.** Users with this permission may create folders within a folder, as well as add new data to a file, as long as it does not change existing data.
- **Create Folders/Write Data.** Users with this permission may create folders within a folder, as well as add new data to a file that may overwrite existing data.
- **Delete Subfolders and Files.** Users with this permission may delete subfolders and files.
- **Delete.** Users with this permission may delete folders and files.
- **Read Attributes.** Users with this permission may view the system-generated attributes associated with a folder or file.
- **Read Extended Attributes.** Users with this permission may view the program-generated extended attributes associated with a folder or file.
- **Write Attributes.** Users with this permission may change the system-generated attributes associated with a folder or file.
- **Write Extended Attributes.** Users with this permission may change the program-generated extended attributes associated with a folder or file.
- **Read Permissions.** Users with this permission may view file and folder permissions.
- **Change Permissions:** Users with this permission may view and modify file and folder permissions.

- **Take Ownership:** Users with this permission may take ownership of files and folders.
- **Synchronize.** Permits threads to synchronize with other threads.

STANDARD NTFS FILE PERMISSIONS

To apply the standard NTFS file permissions, select a file that you wish to secure, then right-click and select the Properties command to open the Properties dialog box. Next, switch to the Security tab, as shown in Figure 2.5.

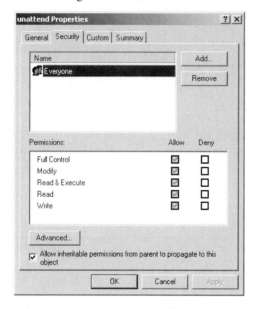

Figure 2.5 *Setting NTFS file permissions.*

NTFS file permissions combine several NTFS special permissions that can be allowed or denied in the following categories:

- Full Control
- Modify
- Read & Execute
- Read
- Write

The special permissions associated with each standard file permission are listed in Table 2.2.

Table 2.2 *Standard vs. Special NTFS Permissions*

Special Permission	Full Control	Modify	Read & Execute	Read	Write
Traverse Folder/Execute File	Yes	Yes	Yes	No	No
List Folder/Read Data	Yes	Yes	Yes	Yes	No
Read Attributes	Yes	Yes	Yes	Yes	No
Read Extended Attributes	Yes	Yes	Yes	Yes	No
Create Files/Write Data	Yes	Yes	No	No	Yes
Create Folders/Append Data	Yes	Yes	No	No	Yes
Write Attributes	Yes	Yes	No	No	Yes
Write Extended Attributes	Yes	Yes	No	No	Yes
Delete Subfolders and Files	Yes	No	No	No	No
Delete	Yes	Yes	No	No	No
Read Permissions	Yes	Yes	Yes	Yes	No
Change Permissions	Yes	No	No	No	No
Take Ownership	Yes	No	No	No	No

NTFS file permissions can be set individually for each file. If you do, the file permissions override NTFS folder permissions that differ.

STANDARD NTFS FOLDER PERMISSIONS

To apply standard NTFS folder permissions, select a folder that you wish to secure, then right-click and select the Properties command to open the Properties dialog box.

Next, switch to the Security tab, as shown in Figure 2.6.

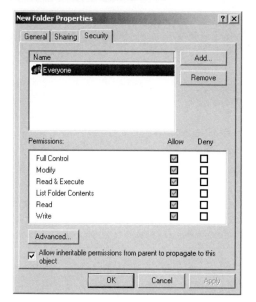

Figure 2.6   *Setting NTFS folder permissions.*

NTFS folder permissions are also combinations of NTFS special permissions, categorized as follows:

- Full Control
- Modify
- Read & Execute
- List Folder Contents
- Read
- Write

The only difference is the addition of the List Folder Contents permission.

The special permissions associated with each standard folder permission are listed in Table 2.3.

Table 2.3 *Standard vs. Special NTFS Folder Permissions*

Special Permission	Full Control	Modify	Read & Execute	List Folder Contents	Read	Write
Traverse Folder/ Execute File	Yes	Yes	Yes	Yes	No	No
List Folder/Read Data	Yes	Yes	Yes	Yes	Yes	No
Read Attributes	Yes	Yes	Yes	Yes	Yes	No
Read Extended Attributes	Yes	Yes	Yes	Yes	Yes	No
Create Files/Write Data	Yes	Yes	No	No	No	Yes
Create Folders/ Append Data	Yes	Yes	No	No	No	Yes
Write Attributes	Yes	Yes	No	No	No	Yes
Write Extended Attributes	Yes	Yes	No	No	No	Yes
Delete Subfolders and Files	Yes	No	No	No	No	No
Delete	Yes	Yes	No	No	No	No
Read Permissions	Yes	Yes	Yes	Yes	Yes	No
Change Permissions	Yes	No	No	No	No	No
Take Ownership	Yes	No	No	No	No	No

By default, the Full Control permission is granted to the Everyone group when a folder is created. If the default has been changed, or for whatever reason your account no longer has the Full Control permission, you must either be given Change Permissions or Take Ownership permissions, which includes the right to Change Permissions, to be able to reassign Full Control to yourself. You must either be the creator of the file or folder in question or have Full Control or Change Permissions granted to alter permissions on NTFS partitions.

ADVANCED NTFS PERMISSIONS

Although these standard permissions should cover must security scenarios that you are likely to encounter, you are not restricted to them. To apply advanced NTFS file and folder permissions individually, select an object that you wish to secure, then right-click and select the Properties command to open the Properties dialog box. Next, switch to the Security tab (see Figure 2.6). In the lower left, click the Advanced button to open the Access Control Settings dialog box, as shown in Figure 2.7.

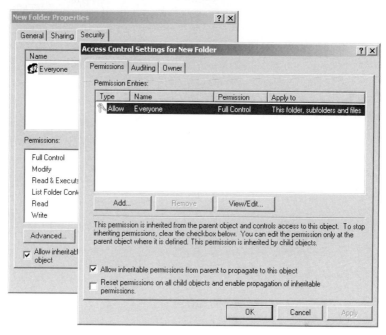

Figure 2.7 *Viewing advanced access control.*

Double-click any group account in the Access Control Settings window to view and edit special permissions, as shown in Figure 2.8.

File permissions are applied file by file. Folder permissions, however, can be applied to a folder, a folder plus all of its subfolders, or a folder, its subfolders, and all of the files in that folder and subfolders.

You may select the level of security you prefer from the Apply onto drop-down menu in the Permission Entry dialog box (see Figure 2.8).

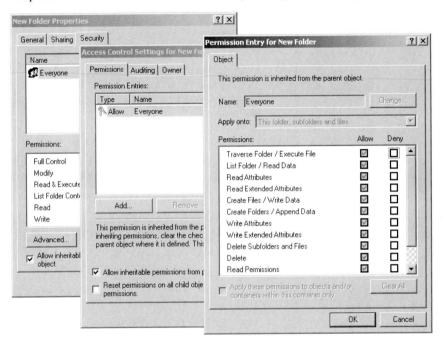

Figure 2.8 *Viewing special permissions.*

Optimizing Access

Unless you explicitly change them, files and folders inherit permissions from their parent objects. For example, if you create a "Downloads" folder at the root level of your computer's hard drive (e.g., C:), then copy the file "MCSE.HTM" into that folder, the file adopts the same permissions as the root. In short, \Downloads inherits its permissions from C:\ and MCSE.HTM in turn inherits its permissions from \Downloads.

You may change this behavior by simply deselecting the Allow inheritable permissions from parent to propagate to this object check box in the Properties dialog box (see Figure 2.6) or Access Control Settings dialog box (see Figure 2.7). This enables the previously described Apply onto drop-down menu.

It also opens the Security dialog box shown in Figure 2.9, in which you may choose to forgo inheritance in favor of your own explicit permissions scheme. Choose with care, for you might make data inaccessible to the system or other users that you should have left alone.

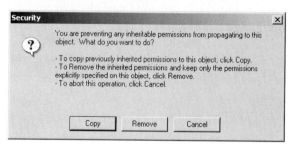

Figure 2.9 *Choosing to bypass permissions inheritance.*

You can tell that a file or folder is inheriting its permissions if the permissions check boxes are grayed out, or the Remove button is unavailable (see Figure 2.6).

If your account has Full Control over a folder, you have the power to delete subfolders and files within that folder regardless of the permissions assigned to those subfolders and files individually.

COMBINED PERMISSIONS

Users and groups can both be granted NTFS permissions. Sometimes a user is a member of multiple groups that have different access levels to a resource through NTFS permissions. In such a case, that user's combined permissions, including the least restrictive level granted by these associations, is the effective permission level. The exception comes into play if the user or one of the groups of which the user is a member has been assigned the Deny permission. The Deny permission overrules any other combination of permissions that user might have otherwise been granted.

TAKING OWNERSHIP

You can assign the NTFS permission to take ownership of files or folders through special permissions. By default, the creator of a file or folder is its owner and has Full Control over it. In order for another user to take ownership, that user must be given that right through NTFS permissions. If the owner has removed every user but himself, only an Administrator can take ownership. (An Administrator always has this access.)

You can give a user permission to use a resource, but you cannot give away ownership. When an Administrator makes himself owner of a resource, he remains owner until someone else that he permits takes ownership, or takes *back* ownership. This way, an unsuspecting user cannot be made to look like he made changes to someone else's files or folders. It will be apparent that the administrator has ownership.

You can give someone the right to take ownership by granting Take Ownership or Change Permissions special permissions, or Full Control standard permission.

DENYING PERMISSIONS

Choosing to Deny a permission overrides all other permissions for all users and groups except Administrators. For instance, a user that is a member of Group One, which has Full Control, will be able to Change Permissions. However, if the user is also a member of Group Two, which has been denied Change Permissions, the user is restricted.

MOVING OR COPYING FILES

Copying a file from one folder to another applies the permissions of the new host folder to that file. The original file is deleted, and a new one is created in the new folder. Moving a file between folders allows the file to retain its original permissions. The file stays in the same physical location on the disk. In the target folder, a new pointer to the file is created. If a move is made across partitions, however, the file is actually deleted and recreated in the new folder, thus assuming the permissions of the new folder.

Study Break

Assign Special Permissions

Practice what you have learned by assigning special permissions to folders and files.

First, create a folder at the root level of your computer's hard drive (e.g, C:). Next, drag a file into this folder. Open the file's Properties dialog box and switch to the Security tab. De-select the Allow inheritable permissions from parent to propagate to this object check box to access the grayed out checkboxes. Experiment with assigning various standard and special permissions.

MCSE 2.2   Shared Folder Access

Users can access the folders resident on your computer if you make them available over the network via *sharing*. You can share folders regardless of the file system under which they are stored: FAT, FAT32, NTFS, Compact Disk File System (CDFS) or DVD's Universal Disk Format (UDF). Like local folders created under NTFS, access to shared folders is controlled through permissions. Unlike with NTFS however, share permissions only affect those accessing a folder over the network. NTFS permissions always apply in either case.

Only members of the Administrators, Server Operators, Power Users, or Users groups can create network shares.

Creating Shared Folders

Sharing cannot be done at the individual file level. It can be done only at the folder level. The share access level of each parent folder is automatically passed on to the subfolders within it. Therefore, you must be careful to not place a folder with strictly limited access under a parent folder with open access, or vice versa. Keep security in mind.

SHARING A FOLDER LOCALLY

When you share a folder locally, you are logged onto the workstation on which the folder that you want to share exists.

To begin, select the folder, right-click, then select the Sharing command to open the Properties dialog box, as shown in Figure 2.10. The following choices are listed under the Sharing tab of the Properties dialog box:

- **Share this folder.** This radio button shares the resource across the network.
- **Do not share this folder.** This radio button stops sharing the resource.
- **Share name.** In this field you can enter the name users will see when they are browsing the resources that your computer is advertising on the network. This network name need not match the folder's local name. If you will have DOS or Windows 3.x users, you must use the 8.3 naming convention.
- **Comment.** When users are browsing the resources on the machine, they will see the comment you enter in this field next to the share. This is a handy place to describe your share's purpose or physical location.

- **User limit**. These radio buttons allow you to limit the number of inbound connections for performance reasons. Windows 2000 Professional has a built-in limit of 10 inbound networking connections, so really you may limit users to 10 or less here.

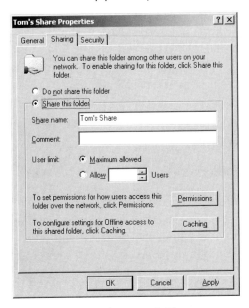

Figure 2.10 *Sharing a folder.*

- **Permissions**. This button allows you to set individual user and group permissions for access to the share. All subfolders inherit the same permissions.
- **Caching**. This button permits a remote user to download a copy of the share to his local computer for access when your share is unavailable, such as when the remote user is offline or your computer is shut down. After clicking this button to open the Caching Settings dialog box, you may choose to permit either the automatic or manual caching of documents and programs, as shown in Figure 2.11.

The Automatic Caching for Documents setting downloads every file that a user opens from your shared folder for that user's offline access. The Automatic Caching for Programs setting applies to the contents of shares that do not change. The Manual Caching for Documents setting, the default, only caches those files specifically selected by the remote user. If you wish to retain all versions of cached files, assign only the Read permission to them.

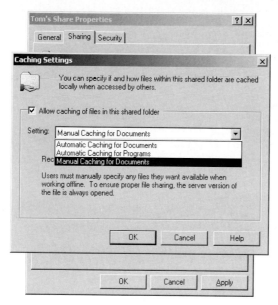

Figure 2.11 *Enabling shared folder caching.*

Removing Shared Folders

To stop sharing a shared folder, perform the following steps:

1. Right-click the folder and select Sharing.
2. Click the Do not share this folder radio button.

If you want to add a level of security, you can go beyond disabling your shared folders to disabling your computer's ability to share files at all.

To do this, simply open the Services Control Panel application and turn off the Server service, as shown in Figure 2.12.

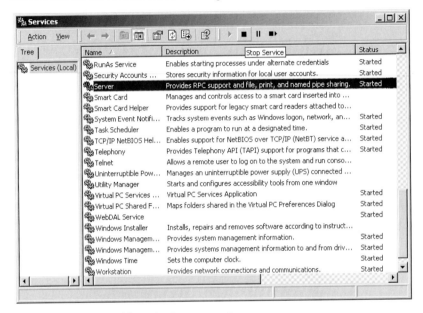

Figure 2.12 *Disabling the Server service.*

Working with Permissions

Click the Permissions button in the share Properties dialog box to establish share permissions, as shown in Figure 2.13. You can allow or deny the following three levels of access in Windows 2000:

- **Read**. This allows users or groups to use programs contained within shared folders, and to view documents. They cannot make changes to the documents, however.
- **Change**. This permission allows all the permissions included with the Read access level. In addition, it allows users and groups to add files or subfolders to the share, and to add or delete information from existing files and subfolders.

- **Full Control**. This is the default permission given by Windows 2000 when a share is created. A user or group with Full Control permissions can perform all tasks allowed by the Change permission, as well as modify file permissions and take ownership of files.

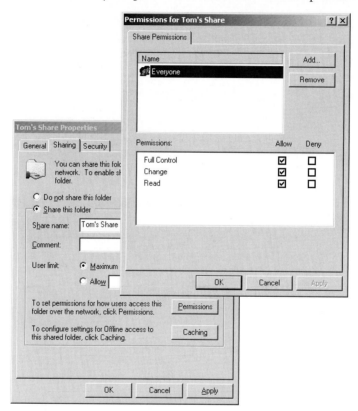

Figure 2.13 *Setting share permissions.*

Click the Add button to change the default permissions and explicitly add additional users and groups, as shown in Figure 2.14. Next, choose the access level you want to assign to that user or group. The default is Read access. To further secure the share, you may remove the Full Control permission granted to Everyone by default.

To set up permissions on shared directories effectively and responsibly, you have to know what those permissions really mean across the network. Because users and groups can each be given varied share permissions, a user could potentially have different share permissions than his group. The potential problem is exaggerated if the user belongs to more than one group.

When users and groups have different share permissions, Windows 2000 defaults to the least restrictive one. Therefore, a user with Read permissions who is also a member of a group with Full Control access is granted Full Access permissions.

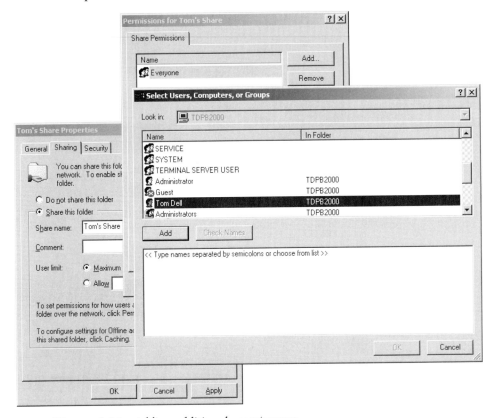

Figure 2.14 *Adding additional users/groups.*

The one exception to this rule comes into play when permissions are explicitly denied. A user with a denied permission is not granted the restricted access to a shared resource even if he is a member of a group with greater access.

A user with a certain level of access who is a member of a group with no specified access maintains his specific permission level. This makes the following true where User A is member of Group B:

- If User A is allowed Read access and Group B is allowed Full Control access, then User A is allowed Full Control access.
- If User A is allowed Change access and Group B is allowed Read access, then User A is allowed Change access.

- If User A is denied Full Control access and Group B is allowed Full Control access, User A is still denied Full Control access.
- If User A is allowed Change access and Group B is denied Change Access, then User A is denied Change access.
- If User A is allowed Read access and Group B has no defined permissions, then User A is still allowed Read access.
- If User A has no defined permissions and Group B is allowed Change access, then User A is allowed Change access.

The tasks that can be performed with each standard share permission are listed in Table 2.4. (These tasks are file system-specific, so you cannot perform the Take Ownership or Change Permissions tasks unless you are working from an NTFS partition.)

Table 2.4 *Tasks Performed Using Share Permissions*

Task	Full Control	Change	Read
Traverse folder	Yes	Yes	Yes
View file/subfolder names	Yes	Yes	Yes
View data in files/run programs	Yes	Yes	Yes
Change data in files	Yes	Yes	No
Add files/subfolders to share	Yes	Yes	No
Delete subfolders and files	Yes	Yes	No
Take ownership	Yes	No	No
Change permissions	Yes	No	No

You can get a quick view of the folders currently shared on your computer by launching the Microsoft Management Console (MMC) through the Computer Management shortcut in the Administrative Tools program group. Select the Shared Folders item in the Tree pane, as shown in Figure 2.15.

Here you may view the shares you create, as well as "hidden" administrative shares used by the operating system (e.g., C$, etc.) that do not appear shared in My Network Places or My Computer.

You may also see which users have initiated sessions with your server and which files they have open.

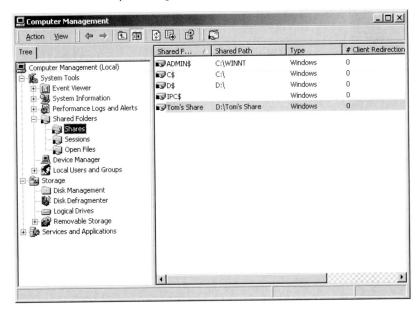

Figure 2.15 *Viewing all shares.*

SHARE VS. NTFS PERMISSIONS

When folders have NTFS permissions that differ from folder share permissions, Windows 2000 grants the most restrictive of the two. If a user has Read access to a share, that user will have Read access when opening the folder over the network even if the user has Full Control access when opening the folder locally on the workstation.

Connecting to Shared Folders

Finding and using resources on remote machines is a fundamental element of networking. The *Universal Naming Convention (UNC)* allows you to follow a path to a computer and a resource, and the My Network Places allows you to see a list of the computers on the network.

USING MY NETWORK PLACES

The Network Neighborhood icon appears on your desktop if your workstation has a network adapter installed. When you double-click the icon, it gives you the option of establishing a shortcut to regularly used resources with the Add Network Place wizard or browse the entire network, as shown in Figure 2.16.

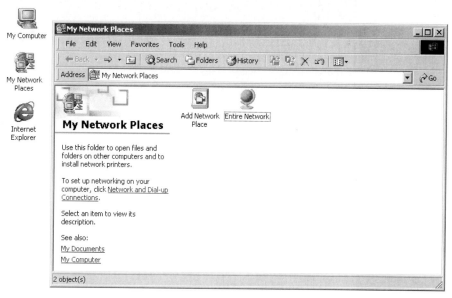

Figure 2.16 *Opening My Network Places.*

Select the Entire Network icon, and you are given the choice to search for networked computers, file and folders, or see the network's entire contents. Choose the latter, then click the Microsoft Windows Network icon to view a graphical representation workgroups, domains, and workstations in the *browse list*, as shown in Figure 2.17.

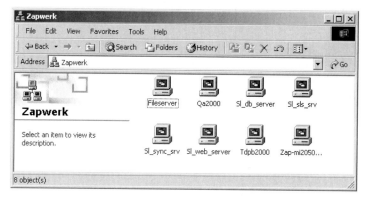

Figure 2.17 *Viewing the Microsoft Windows Network browse list.*

The browse list is maintained by the network computer that has been designated as Master Browser. The browse list is constantly kept up-to-date because every computer on the network with an active Server service registers its name with the Master Browser.

Click on a remote computer's icon to see the folders it has shared, as shown in Figure 2.18.

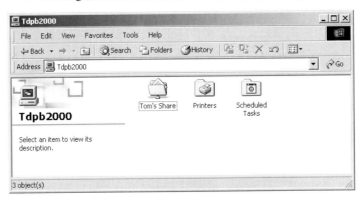

Figure 2.18   *Viewing remote shares.*

If you plan to access a networked share regularly, you can make it appear as a local hard drive by right clicking and choosing the Map Network Drive command. The share then appears with its own drive letter.

USING THE UNIVERSAL NAMING CONVENTION

You can also use the UNC to specify a share name on a specific computer, such as through the shown in Figure 2.19.

Figure 2.19   *Locating a resource by UNC path.*

A connection made through a UNC path takes place immediately and does not need a drive letter. The UNC path looks like this:

`\\server_name\share_name`

UNC connections can also connect to network printers. The format is:

`\\server\printer`

If a share name has a dollar sign at the end of it, the share becomes *hidden* and does not appear in listings, although you can still access it through its UNC name.

If you are using a 16-bit application, it may not work with UNC paths. In this case, you have to either map a drive letter to the share or connect a port to a network printer.

You also use the Command Prompt to access the browse list or assign network resources. The NET VIEW command, for example, accesses the current browse list, as shown in Figure 2.20.

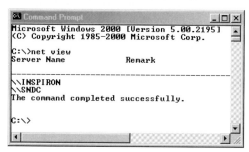

Figure 2.20 *Using the NET VIEW command.*

The NET USE command and the UNC path of the resource assign network resources to drive letters. To connect a drive letter to a share on a server, the command format is:

`NET USE <drive_letter>:\\SERVER\SHARE`

The NET USE command can also connect clients to network printers. To connect a port to a network printer on a server, the command format is:

`NET USE <port>:\\SERVER\PINTER`

To disconnect the network resources from a drive letter or port, use the /d switch:

`NET USE <drive_letter>: /d`

Working with NetWare Shares

Windows 2000 Professional can run Novell NetWare connectivity services and access NetWare networks easily, although you must install some additional software.

If your computer has NWLink IPX/SPX/NetBIOS Compatible Transport (NWLink for short) installed, it can establish client/server connections. If you want to access files or printers on a NetWare server, you also have to install the Microsoft Client Services for NetWare (CSNW) service.

CSNW allows Windows 2000 Professional to access files and printers on NetWare servers running NetWare 2.15 or later. CSNW installs an additional network redirector.

When you install NWLink, your computer obtains the following benefits:

- It gets a new network redirector compatible with the NetWare Core Protocol (NCP). NCP is the standard Novell protocol for file and print sharing.
- It gets the ability to use long file names, if the NetWare server is so configured.
- It gets Large Internet Protocol (LIP) to automatically negotiate and determine the largest possible frame size to communicate with NetWare servers.

NWLink and CSNW allow the workstation to access files and printers on a NetWare server running NetWare Directory Services (NDS). However, it does not support administration of NDS trees.

Windows 2000 Professional can access files and printers on a NetWare server without CSNW by connecting through a Windows NT Server or Windows 2000 Server configured with Gateway Services for NetWare (GSNW).

Once NWLink and CSNW are installed, you can access your network's NetWare servers without any special procedures.

- **Browsing.** You can browse the NetWare or Compatible Network when you double-click on Entire Network in the My Network Places.
- **Map.** Right-click on My Network Places and select Map Network Drive from the Shortcut menu to reassign any drive letter to any shared directory on a NetWare server.

• **Command Prompt.** Use the UNC to locate NetWare resources with commands in the following format:

```
NET USE drive_letter: \\UNC_name\NetWare_name
```

Working with FTP shares

Windows 2000 Professional can access Transmission Control Protocol/Internet Protocol (TCP/IP)-based File Transfer Protocol (FTP) shares through My Network Places, the Add Network Place Wizard, Internet Explorer, or its built-in command line utility, as shown in Figure 2.21.

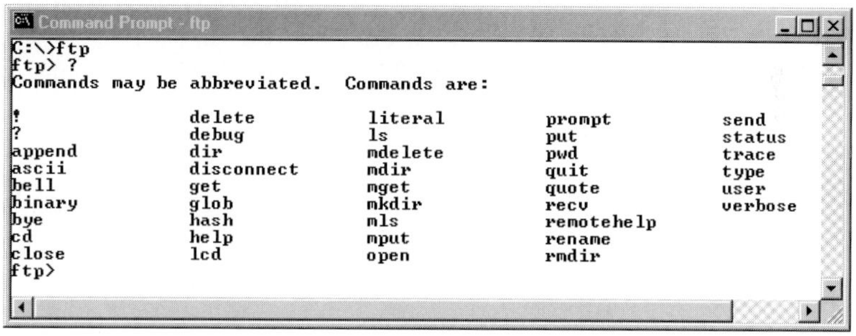

```
C:\>ftp
ftp> ?
Commands may be abbreviated.  Commands are:

!              delete        literal      prompt      send
?              debug         ls           put         status
append         dir           mdelete      pwd         trace
ascii          disconnect    mdir         quit        type
bell           get           mget         quote       user
binary         glob          mkdir        recv        verbose
bye            hash          mls          remotehelp
cd             help          mput         rename
close          lcd           open         rmdir
ftp>
```

Figure 2.21   *Commands for the built-in FTP utility.*

Windows 2000 Professional can share files and folders if you install the Internet Information Service (IIS), as described in the next section.

Working with Web Server Resources

To share files and folders on the Web, you must install Windows 2000 Professional's IIS 5.0, giving it the ability to act as both an FTP and HyperText Transfer Protocol (HTTP) server. To do so, select the Install Add-on Components link in the installation CD-ROM's Autorun screen to open the Windows Components Wizard, as shown in Figure 2.22.

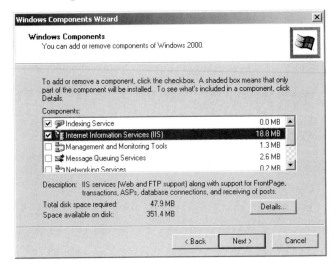

Figure 2.22 *Installing IIS 5.0.*

Enable the IIS checkbox and click the Next button to proceed. With IIS installed, a Web Sharing tab appears in the dialog box (see Figure 2.23).

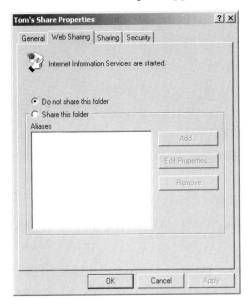

Figure 2.23 *IIS-enabled folder properties.*

Enable the Share this folder radio button to open the Edit Alias dialog box, as shown in Figure 2.24.

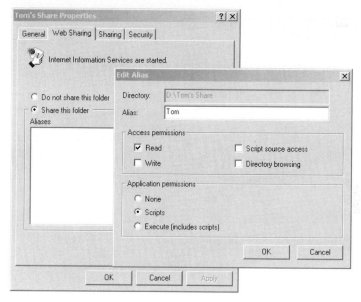

Figure 2.24   *Creating an Internet alias.*

An alias might be needed to make your share's name legal for access of the Web. To be valid on the Internet, folder names must not contain spaces of the following characters:

```
!#$%&'*+-/=?{}|^`~.
```

To be accessible from a Web browser, for example, "Tom's Share" would need to become something like "tom."

In most cases, you may keep the default Access permissions of Read only. Enable Write access only if you wish to permit Web users to upload Web pages to your machine. Likewise, do not enable Script source access unless you wish to allow users to modify scripting that is established in your Web folder. Enable Directory browsing to permit users to see the files in the Web folder and choose among them (rather than being restricted to an "index" page).

Enable Applications permissions if your Web folder's Web pages use scripting or are designed as Active Server pages (ASPs).

To access your shared folder, users may enter a Universal Resource Locator (URL) through a the Add Network Place Wizard or Internet Explorer in the following format:

```
http://server_name/alias_name
```

Figure 2.25 shows such a folder with Directory browsing enabled.

Figure 2.25 *Viewing contents of a shared Web folder.*

MANAGING WEB SERVER RESOURCES

Once installed, you can manage your Web server resources using the IIS snap-in to the MMC, as shown in Figure 2.26.

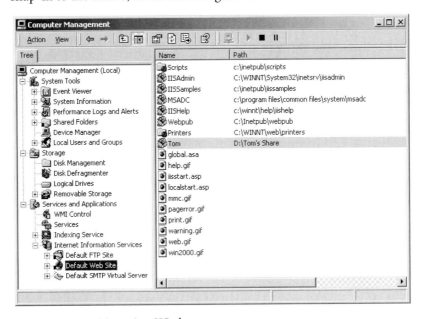

Figure 2.26 *Managing IIS shares.*

With the IIS snap-in, you can perform the following tasks:

- Find and list all Peer Web Services (Windows NT Workstation 4.0) and IIS (Windows NT Server, Windows 2000) servers on the network.
- Connect to servers and view their installed services.
- Start, stop, or pause any service.
- Configure service properties.

You can learn how to set-up your IIS server through Internet Explorer by entering the following URL:

`http://localhost/`

This brings up the Web page shown in Figure 2.27 (if IIS has been enabled as described above).

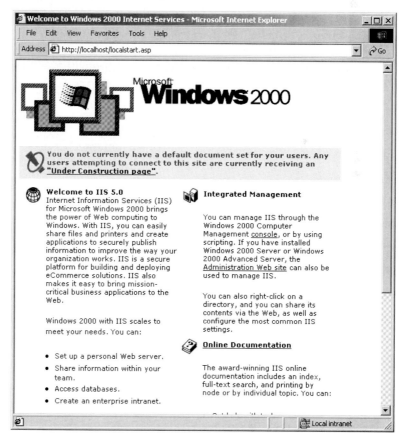

Figure 2.27 *Setting up IIS through Internet Explorer.*

IIS 5.0 can also be managed locally or remotely through the Command Prompt using a command in the following format:

```
iisreset server_name
```

Some important switches that can be added to this command include the following:

/RESTART Stops and restarts all Internet services.

/START Starts all Internet services.

/REBOOT Reboot the computer.

/REBOOTONERROR Reboots the computer when errors occur starting, restarting, or stopping Internet services.

/NOFORCE Do not forcefully terminate Internet services if attempting to stop gracefully fails.

/TIMEOUT:<seconds> Specify the number of seconds to wait for a successful stop of Internet services. Upon expiration, the computer may be rebooted if used in conjunction with the /REBOOTONERROR parameter. Default values are 20 seconds for restart, 60 seconds for stop, and 0 seconds for reboot.

/STATUS Provides status of all Internet services.

/DISABLE Prevents restarting of Internet services on the local system.

/ENABLE Permits restarting of Internet services on the local system.

TROUBLESHOOTING WEB SERVER RESOURCES

Most problems associated with Web resource access are associated the use of erroneous URLS and misconfigured TCP/IP. If remote users fail to access your shared folders, verify the following:

- Remote users have TCP/IP properly configured. One quick way to tell is if they can access resources other than yours.
- You computer has TCP/IP properly configured. Make sure you can access Web resources with Internet Explorer.
- IIS is running properly. Type the URL "http://localhost/" to bring up your index page (see Figure 2.27).

More complicated problems can be detected by viewing the Event Viewer logs in the MMC, as shown in Figure 2.28.

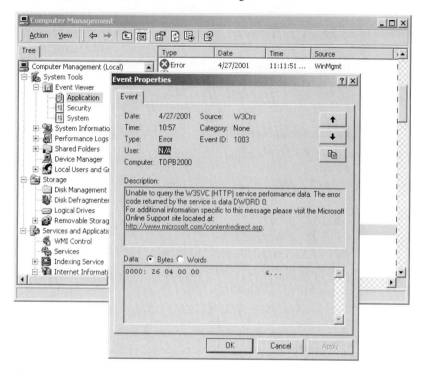

Figure 2.28 *Viewing IIS errors in Event Viewer.*

Create a Shared Folder

Practice what you have learned by creating a shared folder.

Create a folder at the root level of the hard drive under a name such as "share." Next, enable sharing for the folder, giving it a different share name, such as "My Share," and adding a comment. Click the Permissions button to establish access rights, and the Caching button to set offline behavior. Use the MMC to review your configuration. Attempt to locate, connect with, and transfer a file into your shared folder from a remote computer.

MCSE 2.3   Working with Print Devices

Windows 2000 Professional computers can print to one or more printers attached to them directly, printers shared from other computers, and printers that stand alone on the network. They can also print using variety of protocols, including TCP/IP, IPX/SPX, DECnet, DLC, and AppleTalk.

Understanding Windows Printing

In common usage, a *printer* is the hardware device that outputs hard copy. In Windows NT/2000 terminology, however, these are *printing devices*. Microsoft defines a printer as software that controls printing devices. Similarly, the term *print queue* means different things to different vendors. To Microsoft, *print queue* means a list of documents that are waiting to be printed.

To understand the Windows NT printing architecture (as required by the MCSE exam), you should understand a few more terms.

PRINTER DRIVERS

At the beginning of any Windows 2000 print job, the operating system identifies the printer driver version on the client computer to ensure it is current with the print server. If the print server has a newer version, it downloads it to the client computer automatically. It is important, therefore, that you select all of the hardware and operating systems of print client computers when installing or managing your printer (see Figure 2.38).

Windows 2000 printer drivers have two parts. The first part is composed of two Dynamic Link Libraries (DLLs). The *Printer Graphics Driver DLL* is the driver's rendering mechanism, which is called by the Graphics Device Interface during printing. The *Printer Interface Driver DLL* is the driver's user interface, which you call on to configure the printer.

The second part of the Windows 2000 printer driver, which is called on by both DLLs as needed, is the *Characterization File*. This configuration file contains printer-specific information about RAM, fonts, resolution, paper size, paper orientation, and other characteristics.

PRINT SPOOLER SERVICE

The Windows 2000 printing process is managed in the background by the Print Spooler service, which must be running on both server and client. Its general purpose is to save print jobs to disk, or *spool*, and then dole them out at a speed the printing device can handle while permitting the user to work on other things. Print jobs are saved in the following directory (by default):

```
WINNT\system32\spool\PRINTERS
```

PRINT PROCESSOR

Rendering is the process of converting data into a form that a printing device can understand and reproduce on paper. The *print processor* is responsible for this process. Windows 2000's main print processor is WINPRINT.DLL. Its tasks vary with the type of data it is passed from the printer driver. These types include:

- **Raw data**. This data is already rendered by the printer driver that need only be passed to the printing device.
- **Enhanced Metafile (EMF).** This is a standard file format supported by many printing devices. Windows NT EMF is generated by the Graphical Device Interface prior to spooling.
- **Text**. This is the most basic type, used by printing devices that do not support ASCII text. It includes only minimal formatting.

PRINT ROUTER

The print router passes print jobs from the spooler to the appropriate print processor.

PRINT MONITOR

As the name implies, *print monitors* watch the status of printing devices and report back to the spooler, which in turn displays information through the user interface. Among its specific duties are detecting error conditions, such as "out of paper" or "low toner," as well as printing errors that require the job to be restarted. Another duty is end of job notification, wherein the print monitor notifies the spooler that the last page has been imaged and the print job can now be purged.

Windows 2000's standard print monitors are:

- **LOCALMON.DLL**. Used for output to the LPT and COM ports, as well as shared printers.
- **HPMON.DLL**. Used for output to Hewlett-Packard printing devices via the Data Link Control (DLC) network protocol.
- **DECPSMON.DLL**. Used for output to Digital Equipment Corp. (DEC) network printers via TCP/IP or DECnet network protocols. (DECnet must be obtained separately from DEC).

- **LPRMON.DLL**. Used for output to Line Printer (LPR) printing devices, such as those supported by TCP/IP and UNIX Line Printer Daemon (LPD) print servers.
- **PJLMON.DLL**. Used for output to Printer Job Language (PJL) printing devices.
- **SFMMON.DLL**. Used for output to Apple's PostScript printers via AppleTalk.

Connecting to Local Print Devices

Only Administrators and Power Users have the right to install or create a printer. Such users may use the Add Printer Wizard from the Printers program group in the Start menu's Settings program group to install either a local print device or network print server, as shown in Figure 2.29.

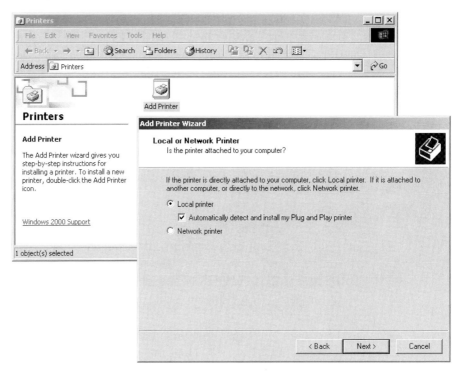

Figure 2.29 *Launching the Add Printer Wizard.*

The option to install locally connects the print device directly to your machine by a parallel port. This connection may be configured using Plug and Play, or failing that, manually, as shown in Figure 2.30.

In the Select the Printer Port window, choose the local port that physically attaches to the printer. Alternately, you may click on the Create a new port radio button if the printer is really a network printer and will be attached to a different port..

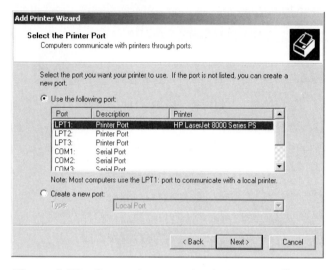

Figure 2.30 *Connecting to a print device manually.*

Next, you are asked to select the appropriate drivers, as shown in Figure 2.31.

Figure 2.31 *Choosing printer drivers.*

If you do not see your printer's manufacturer and/or model here, you can click the Windows Update button to query the Microsoft Web site for new drivers, or click the Have Disk button to locate drivers supplied to you by the manufacturer. Next, you are asked to name the printer as it should appear in the Printers program group, as shown in Figure 2.32.

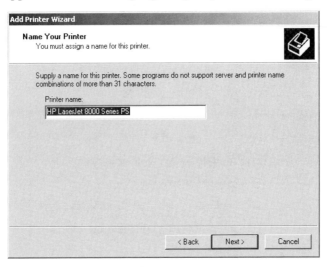

Figure 2.32 *Naming the printer.*

Similarly, if you choose to share the printer, you are asked to supply an 8.3-compatible share name after enabling the Share as radio button, as shown in Figure 2.33.

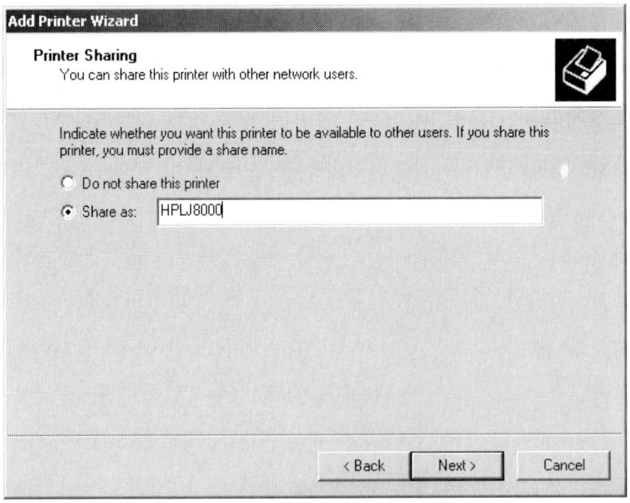

Figure 2.33 *Sharing the printer.*

In the last two steps, you are asked whether you wish to print a test page (always a good idea), then are given a summary of your configuration choices, as shown in Figure 2.34.

Figure 2.34 *Viewing installation options.*

Connecting to Internet Printers

To connect to a TCP/IP-enabled Internet or intranet-based printing device, launch the Add Printer Wizard again. This time when prompted to choose between a local and network printer (see Figure 2.29), choose the latter to open the Locate Your Printer window, as shown in Figure 2.35.

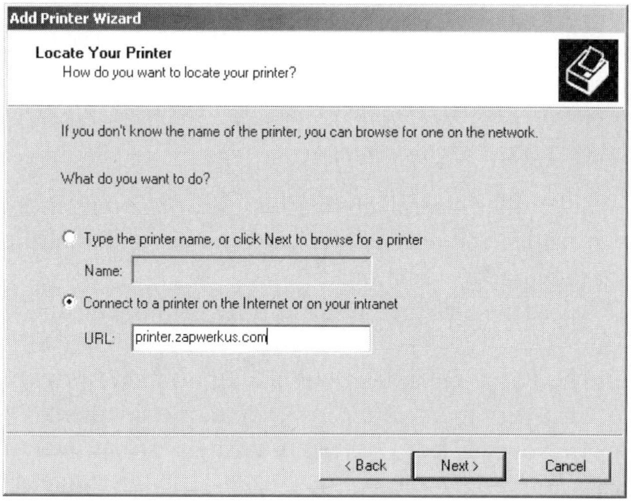

Figure 2.35 *Selecting an Internet printer.*

The Name radio button/field is used to locate Microsoft Networking-enabled printers. To attach an Internet printer, you would enable the URL radio button/field and type in the printer's domain name or IP address.

Configure additional options as prompted by the Add Printer Wizard.

Many printers have specific methods for making their print devices available. You should therefore consult the printer manufacturer's installation instructions where possible.

Managing Printers and Print Jobs

To manage a printer's configuration options, select it in the Printers program group. Right click, then select the Properties command to open the Properties dialog box shown in Figure 2.36.

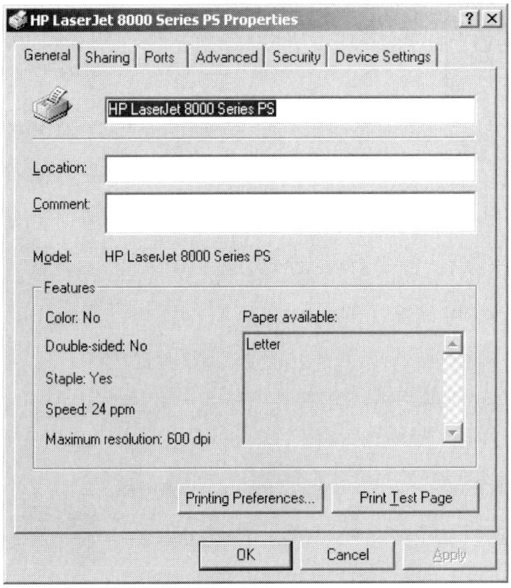

Figure 2.36 *Viewing printer properties.*

Select the General tab to access printing preferences, such as layout and paper quality. You may also add a comment and a location to further define the printer and its function.

Select the Sharing tab to set a network name and turn printer sharing on or off.

The Ports tab shows you which ports have printers and print devices associated with them, and allows you to modify them. By changing the port, you save yourself from having to create a new printer. This tab also allows you to set additional ports, delete ports, and configure existing ports. You can also enable bidirectional support from printers so that the printer can return a status update, such as an empty paper tray or a successfully completed print job.

Printer pooling connects one printer to more than one print device. Thus, as print jobs are received, they are routed to free printers to speed the process for the entire network. Check the Enable printer pooling option under the Ports tab and choose the ports that participate in the pool.

Select the Advanced tab to configure most of a printer's management functions, as shown in Figure 2.37.

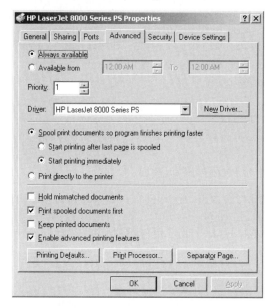

Figure 2.37   *Printer's advanced management properties.*

For example, you may choose a separator page, alternate between print processors, change printer drivers, and establish printing defaults.

Separator pages, sometimes called banners, print the name of the user who sent the print job and the time of the print job between each printed page. The banners can also switch the mode of the printer, or perform other functions. However, banner pages that serve no real purpose are just a nuisance and a waste of paper, especially if the printer is shared and other people are waiting for it.

Also under the Advanced tab, you may schedule print jobs. The first option allows you to set when the printer is available for use, limiting congestion by staggering printers. You can also set printer priorities, which staggers multiple printers by priority rather than by time. This way, relatively insignificant print items do not interfere with potentially company-saving reports, and a 50-page report does not hold up someone's one-page print-out.

The Advanced tab also enables you to set spool settings on each printer, including the following:

- **Spool print documents so program finishes faster.** Documents will spool. You can set them to store the documents until they have all spooled and then print them all, or to start printing immediately.
- **Print directly to the printer.** This turns off spooling, which works only if there is only one printer device attached to the printer.
- **Hold mismatched documents.** This prevents documents that do not match the printer's configurations from printing.
- **Keep printed documents.** This keeps documents in the spooler even after printing.

The last tab in the printer's Properties dialog box is Device Settings. It enables you to set specific options like color, resolution, and paper tray selection.

WORKING WITH PRINT SPOOLER

In Windows 2000, the Print Spooler service controls the print spooling process. If documents have been queued for printing but no printer is available, the print items may be lost, unable to be printed, or deleted. In such a case, you may need to stop the Print Spooler service and then restart it using the Services control panel application. The queued print jobs are then allowed to print.

While print jobs are spooling, they are started on the hard disk in a location called the spool directory. If the hard disk is having a hard time sending print documents, or if those documents are simply not reaching a printer, you may have insufficient space in the partition holding the spool directory. The partition should have at least 5 MBs of free for the spool directory. If you cannot free up enough space, you will have to move the spool directory somewhere else.

Working With Printer Permissions

You can share an existing printer by using the option under the Sharing tab of the printer's Properties dialog box. Under the Sharing tab, you can enter a share name and choose the appropriate operating system drivers that should be loaded, as shown in Figure 2.38.

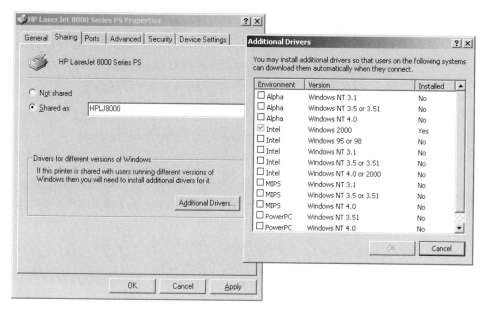

Figure 2.38 *Sharing a printer and choosing download drivers.*

Long share names are supported under Windows NT/2000 and Windows 9x/Me only.

Click the Additional Drivers button if there are non-Windows 2000 computers printing to your workstation's shared printer. Pick the operating systems from the list, and you receive a prompt for the location of the drivers for each system. This way, the drivers for each operating system selected can be downloaded when a user prints to your printer.

You can set permissions for the printer from the Security tab of the printer's Properties dialog box, as shown in Figure 2.39.

There are three types of printer permissions:

- **Print.** Users with this permission can print documents; pause, resume, restart, and cancel the their own documents; and connect to a printer.
- **Manage Documents.** Users with this permission can manage documents; pause, resume, restart and cancel their own documents; connect to a printer; and pause, restart and delete all documents.
- **Manage Printer.** Users with this permission can print documents, pause, resume, restart, and cancel their own documents; connect to a printer, control job settings for all documents, pause, restart and

delete all documents; share a printer, change printer properties, delete printers, and change printer permissions.

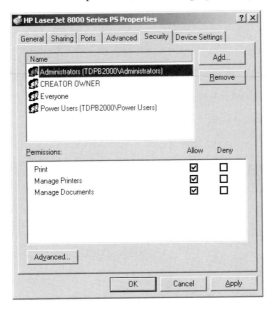

Figure 2.39   *Setting printer access permissions.*

Each user is given Print access by default, and the Creator/Owner is given permission to Manage Documents. Administrators and Power Users have Manage Documents and Manage Printer permissions.

As with NTFS and folder share permissions, Users with a Deny permission cannot do anything with a given permission level.

Study Break

Share a Local Printer

Practice what you have learned by connecting to and sharing a local printer.

First, attach a printer to your computer and run the Add Printer Wizard to connect to it. In so doing, designate the printer as shared under a name of your choice, and print a test page. Open the Properties dialog box to view and, if necessary, reset such options as spooling behaviors, downloadable drivers, and permissions. Finally, test your configuration by printing to your printer from a remote workstation.

MCSE 2.4   Working with File Systems

The first opportunity you have to consider the appropriate uses of disk file systems arises when running the Setup Wizard, which is why we spent so much time describing it in Chapter 1, *Installing Windows 2000 Professional*. After installation, Microsoft gives you several utilities for configuring file systems, which we describe in this section.

Configuring File Systems

The options you have in configuring your computer's disk file systems depends upon their format(s). These can be of three varieties.

FAT

You can only use FAT with partitions of 2 GBs or less. Microsoft recommends that you use FAT only when using these smaller disk drives, and when dual-booting with older operating systems such as MS-DOS, Windows 3.1, or Windows 95.

FAT32

You can use FAT32 with partitions larger than 2 GBs, and it is faster than FAT (16). Microsoft recommends that you use it when dual-booting with Windows 98 or Me, the only other two Windows versions that support it.

NTFS

NTFS is the recommended choice for Windows 2000. Its primary advantages are as follow:

- It provides strong security with both file and folder-level permissions and encryption.
- It supports hard drives as large as 2 TBs without the corresponding loss in performance characteristic of FAT.
- It has efficient built-in compression capabilities.

You can determine the type of file system under which a hard drive is formatted by right-clicking it in My Computer and selecting the Properties command to open the Properties dialog box. Besides being labeled as either "FAT" or "NTFS" under the General tab, you may note that an NTFS drive has Security and Quota tabs unavailable to FAT-formatted drives, as shown in Figure 2.40.

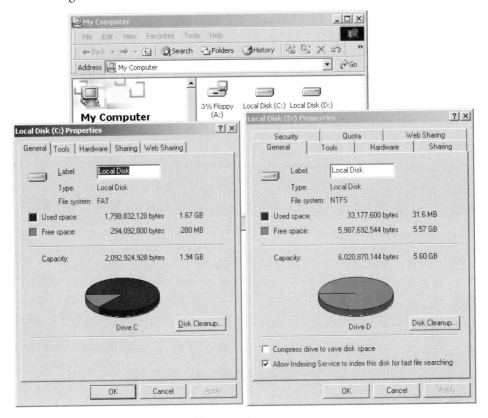

Figure 2.40 *FAT vs. NTFS properties.*

Regardless of file system, you can configure hard drives on your system using the Storage snap-in to the MMC, as shown in Figure 2.41.

Using the utilities accessible here you can perform such tasks as creating and deleting partitions, formatting, changing drive letter designations, marking active partitions, restoring previous disk configurations (from backup info), and defragmenting.

Converting File Systems

You can convert a FAT or FAT32 partition to an NTFS partition any time without reformatting. To do so, launch the Command Prompt and use the following command:

```
CONVERT <drive_letter>: /FS:NTFS
```

It is wise to back-up your hard drive first, just in case problems arise.

You cannot convert an NTFS partition back to a FAT or FAT 32 partition without reformatting.

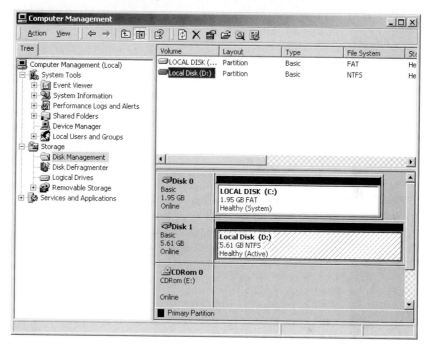

Figure 2.41 *Configuring file systems with the MMC.*

Study Break

Convert a FAT drive

Practice what you have learned by converting a FAT drive.

First, back up the data on your FAT-formatted hard disk to guard against mishaps. Next, view the FAT drive's Properties dialog box. Note the options present. Next, run the CONVERT.EXE utility to convert the disk drive to NTFS. View the newly formatted drive's expanded options in the Properties dialog box. Also view the configuration options present through the Storage snap-in of the MMC.

■ Summary

In this chapter, we considered various Windows 2000 Professional administration topics including securing and sharing files and folders, connecting to print devices, and configuring file systems.

File and Folder Access

On the local computer, file and folder access is controlled through the use of NTFS permissions. Standard NTFS file permissions are Full Control, Modify, Read & Execute, Read, and Write. Standard NTFS folder permissions are the same, with the additional inclusion of List Folder Contents. These standard permissions are each composed of several NTFS special permissions that control a user's ability to Traverse Folders/Execute Files, List Folders/Read Data, Create Folders/Read and/or Append Data, Delete Folders and/or Subfolders and Files, Read and/or Write Attributes and/or Extended Attributes, Read and/or Change Permissions, or Take Ownership.

Permissions can be set explicitly, file-by-file and folder-by-folder, or implicitly through file/folder inheritance. Users may be granted multiple permissions levels depending upon their group memberships.

Where permissions overlap, NTFS assigns the least restrictive. The exception occurs when the Deny setting is applied, in which case it overrides all other access levels.

Besides providing a strong security, NTFS supports the use of built-in disk compression. FAT supports neither security nor built-in compression.

Share Folder Access

On computers accessed over a network, folder access is controlled through the use of share permissions. Standard share folder permissions are Full Control, Change, and Read. These standard permissions control a user's ability to Traverse Folders, View File/Subfolder Names, View Data in Files/Run Programs, Change Data in Files, Add Files and Subfolders to Shares, Delete Subfolders and Files, Take Ownership, and Change Permissions. Share permissions can be applied to either FAT or NTFS drives, and differ from NTFS permissions. Where share and NTFS permissions conflict, Windows 2000 applies the most restrictive of the two.

Only members of the Administrators, Server Operators, Power Users, or Users groups can create network shares.

Windows 2000 computers can share folders using Microsoft Networking, NetWare networking, FTP, and the Web.

Administering Print Devices

You may configure access to local and remote printing devices using the Add Printer Wizard. When connecting to a local printing device, you must name it, install drivers for it, choose whether or not to share it, and test its printing. You can connect to an Internet or intranet-based printing device as easily as to a local device by supplying the correct domain name or IP address.

Three permission levels can be assigned to shared printers: Full Control, Manage Documents, and Manage Printer. Only members of the Administrators or Power Users groups may install printers.

Administering File Systems

The options you have in configuring your computer's disk file systems depend upon their format(s). Microsoft recommends that you use FAT only when using disk drives of 2 GBs or less, and when dual-booting with older operating systems such as MS-DOS, Windows 3.1, or Windows 95. Although you can use FAT32 with partitions larger than 2 GBs and it is faster than FAT, Microsoft recommends that you use it only when dual-booting with Windows 98 or Me. NTFS, the recommended choice for Windows 2000, provides strong security with both file and folder-level permissions and encryption, supports hard drives as large as 2 TBs without a corresponding loss in performance, and has efficient built-in compression capabilities.

Disk drives can be managed from the Properties dialog box or the Storage snap-in of the MMC. You can convert FAT/FAT32 drives to NTFS without reformatting using the CONVERT.EXE utility. You cannot convert from NTFS to FAT/FAT32 without reformatting, and therefore erasing, the disk drive.

▲ CHAPTER REVIEW QUESTIONS

Here are a few questions relating to the material covered in the *Installing Windows 2000 Professional* section of Microsoft's *Installing, Configuring, and Administering Microsoft Windows 2000 Professional* exam (70-210).

1. *When you move files between partitions, new files are created there that inherit the security characteristics and compression status of the parent folder.*

   A. True

   B. False

2. *Which of the following files cannot be compressed using built-in NTFS file compression? Select all that apply:*

   A. Default.htm

   B. Pagefile.sys

   C. NTLDR

   D. Config.sys

3. *File compression can be enabled from the command line using the CON-VERT.EXE utility.*

   A. True

   B. False

4. *Which of the following are standard NTFS permissions? Select all that apply:*

   A. Full Control

   B. Change Permissions

   C. Read

   D. Read & Execute

5. *Which of the following are standard NTFS permissions that only apply to folders? Select all that apply:*

   A. Traverse Folder

   B. List Folder Contents

   C. Read & Execute

   D. Modify

6. *If you want to apply the same permissions used in a folder to its subfolders, you must explicitly designate them.*

   A. True

   B. False

7. *When a user's share permission access levels and NTFS permissions levels clash, Windows 2000 applies the NTFS permissions.*

   A. True

   B. False

8. *Share folders may be accessed using either UNC or URL naming conventions.*

   A. True

   B. False

9. *Which of the following types of users may create shared folders? Select all that apply:*
   A. Administrators
   B. Creator/Owners
   C. Power Users
   D. Server Administrators

10. *Once a folder has been shared, the only way to "unshare" it is to remove its contents and delete it.*
    A. True
    B. False

11. *If User A is a member of Group B, then which of the following are true of his folder access permissions? Select all that apply:*
    A. If User A is allowed Read access and Group B is allowed Full Control access, then User A is allowed Full Control access.
    B. If User A is allowed Change access and Group B is allowed Read access, then User A is allowed Change access.
    C. If User A is allowed Read access and Group B is denied Full Control access, then User A is allowed Full Control access.
    D. If User A is allowed Read access and Group B is denied Full Control access, then User A is allowed Read access.

12. *If you share folders for access via NetWare, Microsoft Networking, and FTP, you will need to configure NTFS permissions for three different configurations.*
    A. True
    B. False

13. *Which of the following must you install to enable share folder access over the Web? Select all that apply:*
    A. CSNW
    B. FTP
    C. IIS
    D. Peer Web Services

14. *For users to see the contents of a shared Web folder, you must create a "home" page and add links to files for them.*
    A. True
    B. False

15. *Windows 2000 Professional supports Plug and Play printing devices.*

    A. True

    B. False

16. *To connect to an Internet printing device, you must know its UNC path.*

    A. True

    B. False

17. *You cannot disable a printer's spooling behavior.*

    A. True

    B. False

18. *Which of the following permissions can be applied to printers? Select all that apply:*

    A. Full Control

    B. Modify

    C. Manage Printer

    D. Manage Documents

19. *NTFS permissions might affect printer access.*

    A. True

    B. False

20. *Internet printers might or might not be enabled for TCP/IP access.*

    A. True

    B. False

21. *Internet printers are configured as local printers:*

    A. True

    B. False

22. *Local printers may be connected to either LPT or COM ports.*

    A. True

    B. False

23. *Local printers cannot be shared, as network printers can.*

    A. True

    B. False

24. *Which of the following are file systems supported by Windows 2000. Select all that apply:*
    A. FAT
    B. FAT32
    C. NTFS 4.0
    D. NTFS 5.0

25. *You may use the MMC to convert a FAT file system to NTFS.*
    A. True
    B. False

26. *You may use the MMC to convert an NTFS file system to FAT:*
    A. True
    B. False

27. *When should you consider using FAT? Select all that apply:*
    A. If the hard disk is 512 MBs.
    B. If security is required.
    C. If compression is required.
    D. If you must dual-boot with Windows 95

28. *The MMC can be used to manage hard disks formatted with NTFS only.*
    A. True
    B. False

T H R E E

Managing Windows 2000 Professional Devices

▲ Chapter Syllabus

MCSE 3.1 Working with Disk Drives

MCSE 3.2 Working with Display Devices

MCSE 3.3 Working with Mobile Computer Hardware

MCSE 3.4 Working with I/O Devices

MCSE 3.5 Updating Drivers

MCSE 3.6 Working with Multiple Processing Units

MCSE 3.7 Working with Network Adapters

In this chapter, we examine the some of the hardware topics covered in the *Implementing, Managing, and Troubleshooting Hardware Devices and Drivers* section of Microsoft's *Installing, Configuring, and Administering Microsoft Windows 2000 Professional* exam (70-210). The following material is designed to ensure that you can install, manage, and troubleshoot hardware drivers, as well as disk devices, display devices, mobile computer hardware, Input/Output (I/O) devices, and network adapters. We also take a look at multiple processing units.

After you physically install new hardware devices, you may have to configure the computer to recognize them. Windows 2000 normally detects newly installed Plug and Play hardware devices during startup, or when they are physically installed (e.g., PC Cards). It then automatically installs driver software and configures the hardware settings.

If Windows 2000 Professional does not automatically detect a hardware device, you must install it using the Add/Remove Hardware application in the Control Panel program group. This launches the Add/Remove Hardware Wizard (see Figure 3.1).

Use the following steps to install undetected hardware:

- After the Add/Remove Hardware Wizard searches for Plug and Play hardware, it prompts you to search for hardware that is not Plug and Play compatible. Select Yes when prompted.
- Windows 2000 Professional searches for new hardware devices that are not Plug and Play compatible, and then installs and configures any it locates. If Windows 2000 does not locate the device you want to install, select the Next button.
- Select the hardware type, and then select the device's manufacturer and model from the lists. If your device is not on the list, supply a path to a third-party driver on media provided by the manufacturer by pressing the Have Disk button.

Microsoft digitally signs all drivers included with Windows 2000 Professional. If a driver is digitally signed, it has passed testing done by Windows Hardware Quality Labs (WHQL). Windows 2000 can check this digital signature when you install a driver. If it does not check out, you have the option of blocking the installation.

The Win32 Driver Model provides a common set of drivers that work in Windows 98, Me and Windows 2000. The model helps hardware developers create device drivers for their products by letting them develop a driver that functions in multiple operating systems. Before the WDM, device drivers included hooks for a certain operating system in addition to the elements necessary to interact with a specific piece of hardware.

The Win32 Driver Model supports such technologies as Universal Serial Bus (USB), Firewire (e.g., IEEE 1394), OnPower Management, Digital Video Disk (DVD), and digital audio.

To find out whether a device that you have or intend to purchase is supported by Windows 2000 Professional, consult the Hardware Compatibility List (HCL).

When installing hardware, you should be logged on to the computer as a member of the Administrators group.

MCSE 3.1   Working with Disk Drives

In this section, we describe installing, configuring, and troubleshooting storage devices such as CD-ROM drives, hard disks, and removable media drives.

Working with DVD and CD-ROM Devices

Compact Disk-Read Only Memory (CD-ROM) drives, and their hybrid variation Digital Video Disks (DVDs), are standard equipment on many Windows 2000 Professional workstations.

The typical CD-ROM, the media of choice for most software distributors, stores about 650 MBs of data. Windows 2000 supports a wide-range of CD-ROM device drivers, as well as the Compact Disk File System (CDFS) used to both read and write CD-ROMs. Windows 2000 will also boot from CD-ROM drives that are El Torito compatible.

Windows 2000 supports DVD-ROM drives as both storage and playback devices. In a storage capacity, Windows 2000 supports the Universal Data Format (UDF), and will therefore treat a DVD-ROM disk as any other mass storage media. In a playback capacity, Windows 2000 includes a DVD-ROM driver and DVD Player application used to present movies and other video. The DVD-ROM driver supports streaming data types, MPEG-2, and Dolby Digital.

Windows 2000 makes CD-ROM devices easy to install, manage, and configure through Plug and Play technology and the Device Manager snap-in to the MMC. Windows 2000 Professional's support of Plug and Play is an improvement over Windows NT 4.0.

INSTALLING DVD AND CD-ROM DEVICES

To install a CD-ROM drive, or any other devices for that matter, simply install the hardware and restart the computer. Log in as Administrator. If the new device adheres to the Plug and Play standard, the Add/Remove Hardware Wizard opens, as shown in Figure 3.1. Windows attempts to locate and install the appropriate driver for it, and/or asks you to provide media that contains the manufacturer's drivers.

Figure 3.1 *The Add/Remove Hardware Wizard.*

If the device is not Plug and Play compatible, you can launch the Add/Remove Hardware Wizard manually by right-clicking My Computer and choosing the Manage command in the MMC.

In the MMC, select the Disk Management snap-in (see Figure 3.2).

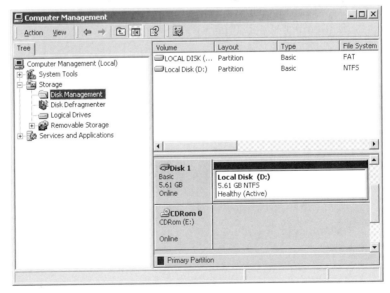

Figure 3.2 *Scanning for a CD-ROM in the MMC.*

Next, select the Rescan Disks command from the Action menu. The new device should appear in the lower right of the window.

CONFIGURING DVD AND CD-ROM DEVICES

To configure a CD-ROM or DVD-ROM drive, switch to the MMC's Device Manager snap-in, as shown in Figure 3.3.

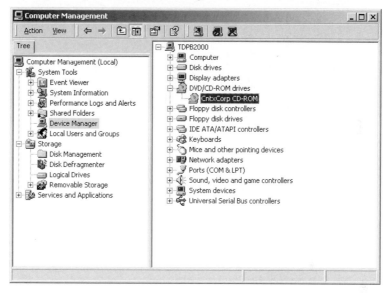

Figure 3.3 *Choosing a CD-ROM device in the MMC.*

Expand the DVD/CD-ROM drives item to view the available devices and drivers.

Next, select a device and click the Properties button to open the Properties dialog box, as shown in Figure 3.4.

Figure 3.4 *Viewing CD-ROM device properties.*

If the device has been properly installed and configured, Windows 2000 tells you so via the Device status field.

If not, an error message is displayed. If there is a problem, you can click the Troubleshooter button to bring up context-sensitive Microsoft Help, as shown in Figure 3.5.

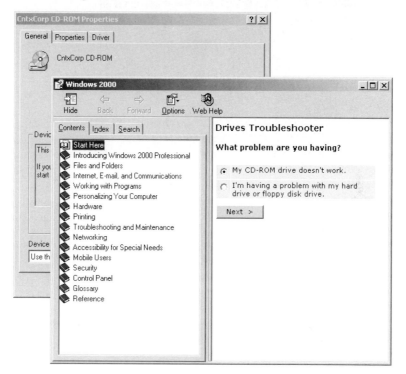

Figure 3.5 *Viewing troubleshooting help.*

You may also enable and disable the use of the device from the Device usage drop-down menu.

Even if no problems are listed under the General tab, you might wish to install a driver different from the one chosen by Plug and Play, to access special features or improve performance. To do so, switch to the Driver tab, as shown in Figure 3.6.

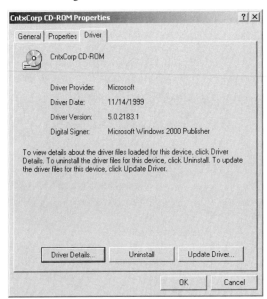

Figure 3.6   *Viewing driver information.*

Such useful data as driver manufacturer, date, and version are displayed.

Details about the actual files that comprise the driver can be viewed by clicking the Driver Details button, as shown in Figure 3.7.

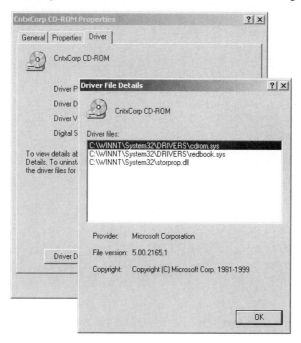

Figure 3.7 *Viewing driver details.*

If you know there is a newer or better driver available, such as from the hardware manufacturer, you can replace Microsoft's default choice by clicking the Update Driver button to launch the Update Device Driver Wizard, as shown in Figure 3.8.

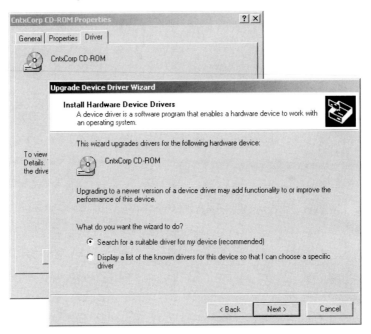

Figure 3.8 *Changing an installed driver.*

As with the Add/Remove Hardware Wizard, you may choose from a list of Microsoft drivers or specify the media on which a manufacturer's driver is stored.

MANAGING DVD AND CD-ROM DEVICES

CD-ROM and DVD drives can be managed through several interfaces. For example, you can access a master volume setting that applies to audio CD playback by switching to the Properties tab of the MMC's CD-ROM drive Properties dialog box, as shown in Figure 3.9.

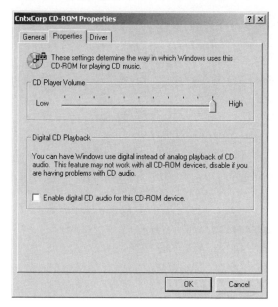

Figure 3.9 *Managing device settings.*

Here you can also determine whether the drive uses digital or analog playback, depending on its capabilities. These properties are also accessible through the Sounds and Multimedia Control Panel application.

The playback of CD content can be controlled more directly through such applications as Media Player, CD Player, and DVD Player, all found in the Entertainment program group.

When working with CD-ROMs as storage media, you can manage them as you would any other mass storage device. For example, right-click on a CD-ROM disk in My Computer and select the Properties command to open the Properties dialog box, as shown in Figure 3.10.

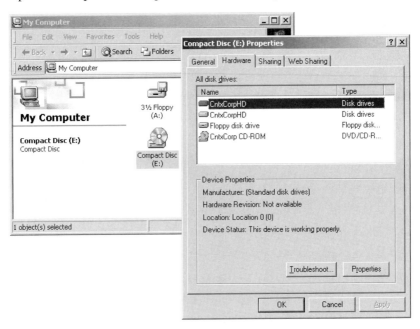

Figure 3.10   *Configuring properties for CD-ROM media.*

Here you can access the same device driver properties accessible through the MMC's Device Manager, as well as share CD-ROMs on a LAN or the Internet, and view content statistics.

Working with Hard Disks

Windows 2000 Professional lets you configure and manage one or more disk drives through its MMC Disk Management snap-in. This tool replaces the Disk Administrator application used under Windows NT 4.0. Another improvement over Windows NT 4.0 is the introduction of basic and dynamic disk types.

MONITORING HARD DISKS

The Disk Management snap-in, with the top window pane in Disk List view and bottom pane in Graphical View, provides a logical display of your computer's disk drives (see Figure 3.11).

Disk type, capacity, free space, status, controller type, and file system are all listed here, as well as an indication of health.

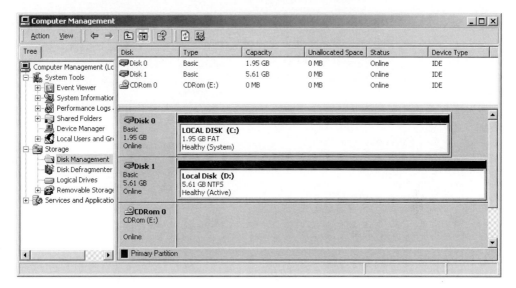

Figure 3.11   *Disk Management snap-in, viewed by Disk List.*

To monitor or configure a hard disk, select it (e.g., "Disk0") and choose from the commands in the Action menu to upgrade a basic disk to a dynamic disk or open the properties dialog box and access another set of tools, as shown in Figure 3.12.

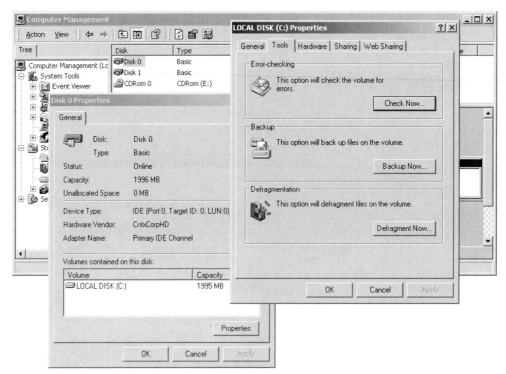

Figure 3.12   *Accessing properties via the MMC.*

Alternately, select a volume on a hard disk in Graphical View (e.g., "Local Disk (C:)") and choose from the commands in the Action menu to format, delete, and mark partitions as active, or change drive letter paths.

Overall, you can perform the following tasks via the Disk Management snap-in:

- Initialize hard disks.
- View disk information.
- Create basic disk *partitions*.
- Create dynamic disk *volumes*.
- Format disk partitions or volumes as FAT, FAT32, or NTFS.
- Manage basic and dynamic disks.
- Manage *simple*, *spanned*, and *striped* volumes.
- Manage hard disks on remote computers.

CONFIGURING HARD DISKS

New to Windows 2000 Professional is the concept of basic disks vs. dynamic disks. On a computer with a single hard drive, you may choose to use one or the other. On multiple disk systems, you may create both basic and dynamic disks.

CONFIGURING BASIC DISKS • The basic disk is the traditional format familiar and common to all Windows operating systems. The default storage type for Windows 2000 Professional, basic disks are fixed in size, can be divided into primary and extended partitions, and contain logical drives.

Under MS-DOS, disk drive partitioning was a relatively cumbersome process requiring the FDISK utility. The Disk Management snap-in can do more, and do it more quickly and easily. When creating basic disks, remember the following rules:

- Each disk drive can contain as many as four primary partitions, each of which may contain a bootable operating system.
- A primary partition cannot be further partitioned.
- Extended partitions are used in addition to one or more primary partitions.
- Only one extended partition can reside on a single disk drive. It can be subdivided into multiple logical partitions, each with its own letter designation (e.g., "D:, E:, F:," etc.).
- Logical drives are created within an extended partition.

To create a primary or extended partition, first select the free space on a new or existing drive in Disk Management's Graphical View pane, as shown in Figure 3.13.

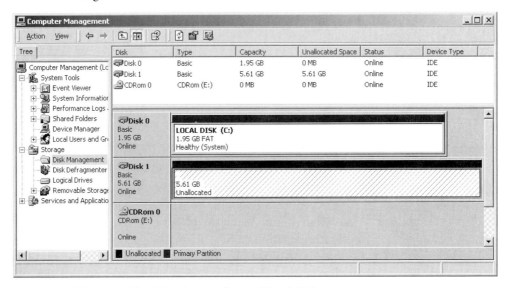

Figure 3.13   *Selecting unallocated hard disk space.*

Next, select the Create partition command from the Action menu to launch the Create Partition Wizard, as shown in Figure 3.14.

Figure 3.14   *Launching the Create Partition Wizard.*

After clicking the Next button, you must decide whether to create a primary or extended partition, as shown in Figure 3.15.

Figure 3.15   *Choosing partition types.*

When configuring a new disk, you should choose the Primary partition option.

Next, you must decide how much of the unallocated space the primary partition occupies, as shown in Figure 3.16.

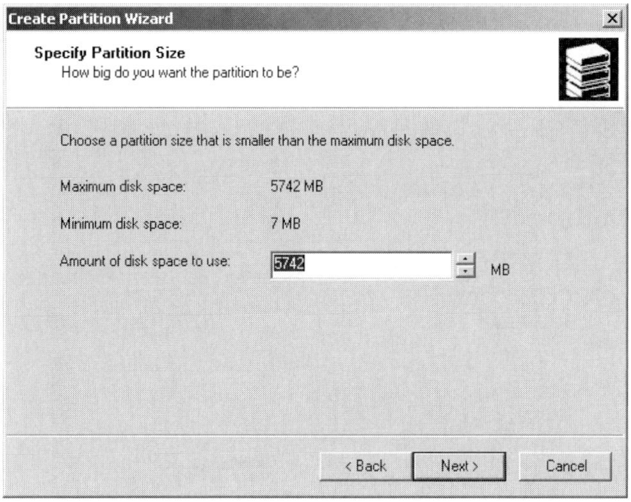

Figure 3.16   *Choosing partition size.*

You can create a single partition by using all available space, or leave room for additional partitions by selecting a fraction of the available space.

Next, you may choose a drive letter for the new partition, as shown in Figure 3.17.

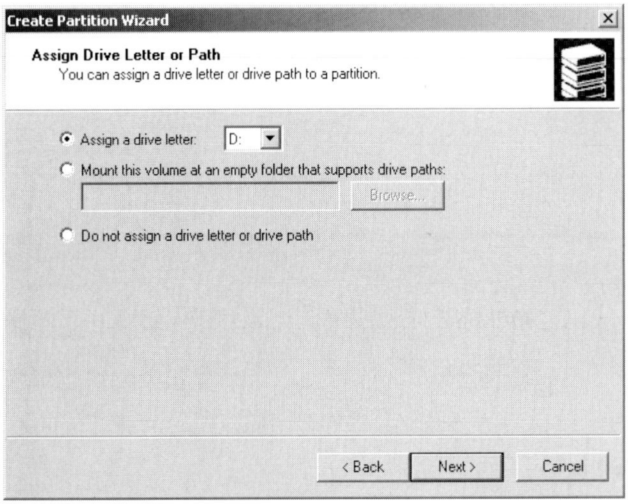

Figure 3.17   *Selecting a drive letter.*

Finally, you may choose to format the partition as FAT, FAT32, or NTFS and name it, as shown in Figure 3.18.

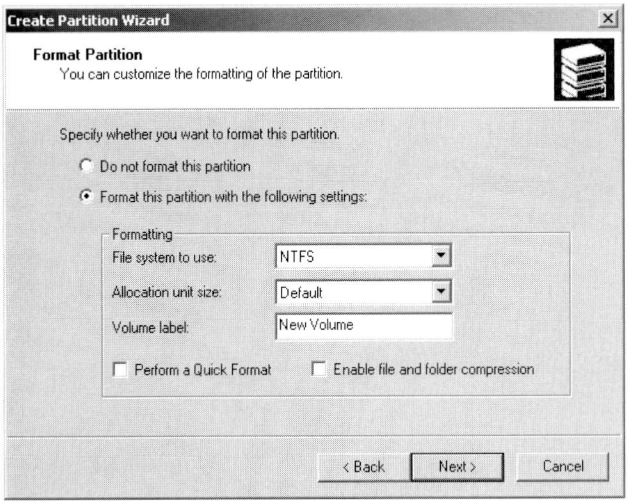

Figure 3.18   *Selecting a file system format.*

For additional information on working with basic disks, review Chapter 1, "Installing Windows 2000 Professional."

CONFIGURING DYNAMIC DISKS • If you do not intend to dual-boot with any other operating systems, you have the option of configuring your disk drives as dynamic disks, which are only supported by Windows 2000. Dynamic disks can be resized without reformatting, and in most cases, without rebooting the computer. Basic disks can be converted to dynamic disks.

When creating dynamic disks, remember the following rules:

- Dynamic disks can consist of one partition, multiple partitions on a single disk drive, or multiple partitions on multiple disk drives.
- Dynamic disks support the creation of simple, spanned, and striped volumes.
- Dynamic disks should not be configured with sector sizes greater than 512 bytes.
- Dynamic disks must have at least 1 MB of free space at the end of the disk.
- Dynamic disks do not support removable media or portable computer volumes.

To upgrade a basic disk to a dynamic disk, select the basic disk in the Disk Management snap-in and choose the Upgrade to Dynamic Disk command from the Action menu. If you are working on a multiple-disk system, you are prompted to confirm which disk(s) should be upgraded. You are also warned that only Windows 2000 can be used with dynamic disks. If the disk you are upgrading is a system disk, you are prompted to reboot.

Either way, the new disk can be viewed in the Disk Management snap-in as "dynamic" once the process is complete (see Figure 3.19).

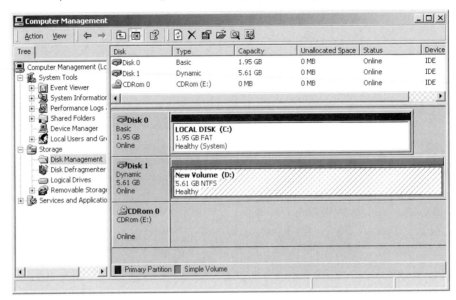

Figure 3.19 *Viewing a newly created dynamic disk.*

You can turn a dynamic disk back into a basic disk by selecting the Restore basic Disk Configuration command from the Action menu. This erases all data residing on the disk, however.

MONITORING VOLUMES

The Disk Management snap-in, with the top window pane in Volume List view and bottom pane in Graphical View, provides a logical display of your computer's disk drives from a volume-specific perspective (see Figure 3.20).

Volume name, layout, type, file system status, capacity, and space usage are listed here.

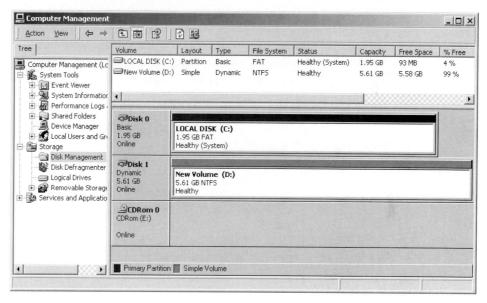

Figure 3.20 *Disk Management snap-in, viewed by Volume List.*

For more specific information about a volume, right-click it in the Graphical View pane to open the Properties dialog box (see Figure 3.21).

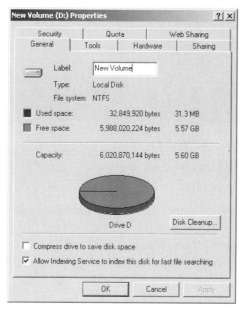

Figure 3.21 *Disk volume Properties dialog box.*

Under the General tab, you can view the volume's label, type, file system, and available space. On NTFS volumes, you may choose to enable disk compression and file indexing. You can also launch the Disk Cleanup utility to get rid of unnecessary files.

In addition to the settings under the Security, Sharing, and Web Sharing tabs — described in Chapter 2, "Administering Windows 2000 Professional"— the following options are available:

TOOLS PROPERTIES • Under this tab you can launch utilities for error checking, backup, and disk defragmentation, as shown in Figure 3.22.

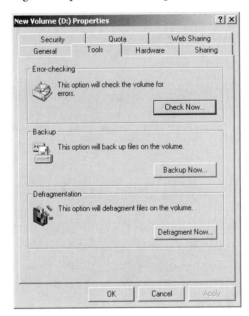

Figure 3.22 *The volume properties Tools tab.*

Click the Check Now button to scan the disk drive for file system and physical errors and fix them automatically (wherever possible). Click the Backup Now button to open the Backup and Restore Wizard or to create an Emergency Repair Disk (ERD). Click the Defragment Now button to analyze and/or defragment a volume.

HARDWARE PROPERTIES • Under this tab you can determine the drivers under which the hard disk is running. If the device has been properly installed and configured, Windows 2000 will tell you so via the Device status field. If not, an error message is displayed. If there is a problem, you can click the Troubleshooter button to bring up context-sensitive Microsoft Help (see Figure 3.5).

QUOTA PROPERTIES • Under this tab, you can enable quotas to restrict the amount of disk space available to each of the computer's users, as shown in Figure 3.23.

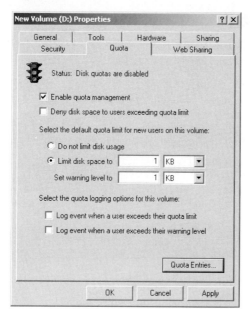

Figure 3.23 *Enabling disk quotas.*

You only see this tab if you are logged on as an administrator.

CONFIGURING VOLUMES

Several types of volume can be created on Windows 2000 Professional basic and dynamic hard disks. Only dynamic disks support dynamic volumes, however. When configuring the following volume types, you must be logged on as an administrator.

SIMPLE VOLUMES • A *simple volume* is a dynamic volume composed of disk space from single disk drive.

To create a simple volume from unallocated space, select the Create Volume command from the Action menu to open the Create Volume Wizard.

The volume creation process is similar to that already described for running the Create Partition Wizard, except that you are prompted to choose a volume type rather than a partition type, as shown in Figure 3.24.

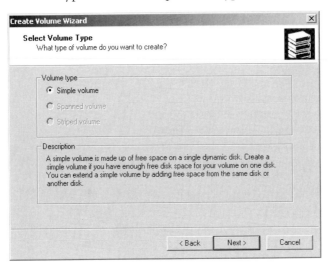

Figure 3.24 *Choosing to create a simple volume.*

To upgrade a basic disk to a dynamic disk, select the basic disk in the Disk Management snap-in and choose the Upgrade to Dynamic Disk command from the Action menu (see Figure 3.19).

A simple volume may be extended on its original dynamic disk or onto additional dynamic disks (creating a spanned volume) if it contains no file system or is formatted as NTFS.

Simple volumes cannot contain partitions or logical drives, and are inaccessible from any operating system except Windows 2000.

SPANNED VOLUMES • A *spanned volume*, also known as a volume set when applied to basic disks, is composed of disk space from between two and 32 dynamic disks. Data is written to each sequentially.

You may expand a simple volume into a spanned volume by choosing the Extend Volume command from the Action menu.

When running the Create Volume Wizard thereafter, you may choose to add space from at least two additional dynamic disks on your computer (see Figure 3.25).

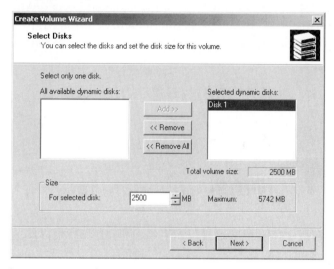

Figure 3.25 *Selecting space from additional dynamic disks.*

The following rules apply to spanned volumes:

- You may only extend simple volumes that were created on dynamic disks. You cannot extend simple volumes that were created by upgrading basic disks.
- You can only extend simple volumes that contain no file system, or were formatted as NTFS.
- You cannot extend system or boot volumes.

In Microsoft terminology, the system partition contains the files necessary to boot the operating system. The boot partition contains the Windows NT/2000 operating system. They might or might not be the same partition.

- You cannot extend striped or mirrored volumes, nor can you stripe or mirror spanned volumes.
- Once a spanned volume is created, deleting any portion of it deletes the entire spanned volume.

STRIPED VOLUMES • A *striped volume*, called a *stripe set* when applied to basic disks, is similar to a spanned volume in that it contains free space from multiple dynamic disks (between from two to 32). The main difference is that it applies the Redundant Array of Independent Disks (RAID) Level 0 technique of *striping*. In striping, data is written to and read from each disk drive in the set in 64 kB blocks, disk after disk and row after row, as illustrated in Figure 3.26.

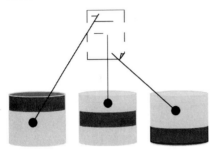

Figure 3.26 *Data is written to multiple disks simultaneously.*

The advantage is in speed, because if each disk drive has its own controller, the server can read and write to multiple drives simultaneously.

Think carefully before creating a striped volume under Windows 2000 Professional. While it can provide performance gains, it lacks RAID Level 5 fault tolerance, known as striping with parity, available under Windows 2000 Server. Consequently, the failure of any of a striped volume's member disk drives destroys the striped volume and its data.

To create a striped volume, select unallocated space from one dynamic disk, then choose the Create Volume command from the Action menu. When running the Create Volume Wizard thereafter, select the stripped volume option rather than the simple volume option (see Figure 3.24).

You may only upgrade a stripe set (basic disk) to a striped volume (dynamic disk) by first upgrading each of the stripe set's member disks from basic to dynamic.

MIRRORED VOLUMES • RAID Level 1, also known as *disk mirroring*, involves the use of two disk drives. Under this fault tolerance scheme, data is written to both disks so that if one fails, the other is still available to carry on, as illustrated in Figure 3.27. Because Windows 2000 must write to two hard disks simultaneously, this method results in somewhat slower write operations. The speed of read operations is increased, however, because Windows 2000 can read from both disks simultaneously.

Under a basic disk mirroring scenario, a single disk controller writes to both the primary and the mirror (redundant) disk drive (collectively called the mirror set when working with basic disks and a mirrored volume when working with dynamic disks). Should one of the two disks fail, operations can continue without interruption. If the disk controller fails, however, both the primary and the mirrored disk become inaccessible. True fault tolerance, then, requires that the computer be equipped with two disk drives and two disk controllers, a method called disk duplexing. In addition, because the two controllers act independently, *disk duplexing* does not incur the same performance degradation in write operations that disk mirroring does.

Mirrored volumes can only be created using Windows 2000 Server.

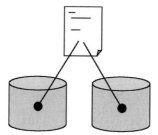

Figure 3.27 *Under RAID Level 1, data is written to two disks simultaneously.*

Table 3.1 summarizes the terminology used configuring either basic or dynamic disk volumes.

Table 3.1 *Basic Disk vs. Dynamic Disk Volume Types*

Purpose	Basic Disks	Dynamic Disks
Divide disk space	Primary partition	Simple volume
Divide disk space	Extended partition	Unallocated space/volume
Contains boot files	System partition	System volume
Contains system files	Boot partition	Boot volume
Contains bootable OS	Active partition	Active volume
Has own drive letter	Logical drive	Simple volume
Combines multiple disks	Volume set	Spanned volume
Stripes multiple disks	Stripe set	Striped volume
Mirrors disks	Mirror set	Mirrored volume

You should be aware of the following limitations when working with dynamic disks:

- Cannot install Windows 2000. You cannot install Windows 2000 on a dynamic volume that has been created from the unallocated space on a dynamic disk. The Setup program only recognizes dynamic volumes that contain partition tables, and these only appear in basic volumes or dynamic volumes created by updating basic volumes.
- Cannot extend boot volumes. If you install Windows 2000 on a dynamic volume, you are not able to extend the volume.

TROUBLESHOOTING VOLUMES

When encountering problems with hard disks, you should first attempt to determine if the cause is software or hardware related. Microsoft provides several tools for dealing with either.

CHECKING FOR ERRORS • Whether your volumes are set up as basic or dynamic, you may troubleshoot them using the Disk Check tool that is accessible through the Check Now button in the Properties dialog box (see Figure 3.22). The utility gives you the option of automatically fixing file system errors, addressing the volume's software structure, and scan for and recover from bad sectors, addressing the disk's physical structure (see Figure 3.28).

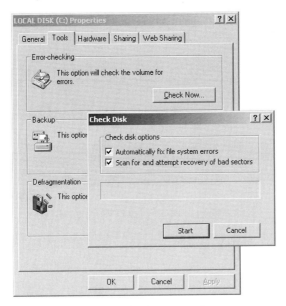

Figure 3.28 *Troubleshooting volumes.*

TROUBLESHOOTING BOOT FAILURES • If any one of the hard disk's boot files is missing or corrupt, Windows 2000 fails to boot. You must then employ the emergency repair process to reinstall the corrupted or missing files.

During the installation process, you were given a chance to create an emergency repair directory and emergency repair floppy diskette. These contain backup copies of the Registry that can be used to repair a faulty Windows 2000 system. Both the \WINNT\REPAIR directory and Emergency Repair Disk are computer-specific. They contain the following files:

- **SETUP.LOG.** This read-only text file contains the names of each Windows 2000 installation file and its checksum. If they become corrupted, the emergency repair process is capable of detecting this by using the checksum information.
- **SYSTEM.** This is the Windows 2000 control set collection, a compressed version of the Registry SYSTEM hive.
- **SAM.** This is the Windows 2000 user and groups database, a compressed version of the Registry's Security Accounts Manager (SAM) hive.
- **SECURITY.** This is the Windows 2000 security setup, a compressed version of the Registry SECURITY hive.
- **SOFTWARE.** This is the Windows 2000 software configuration collection, a compressed version of the Registry SOFTWARE hive.
- **DEFAULT.** This is a compressed version of the default system profile.
- **CONFIG.NT.** This is a version of the MS-DOS CONFIG.SYS file used by the Virtual DOS Machine (VDM).
- **AUTOEXEC.NT.** This is a version of the MS-DOS AUTOEXEC.BAT file used by the VDM.
- **NTUSER.DAT.** This is a copy of NTUSER.DAT file, which contains user profiles.

Neither the Emergency Repair Disk nor the \REPAIR directories are updated after their creation. You must do this manually whenever you make a change to the system or install a Service Pack. This can be done using the Backup program that is accessible through the Backup button in the Properties dialog box (see Figure 3.22). Among its options is Emergency Repair Disk, as shown in Figure 3.29.

The first step in the emergency repair process is to boot the computer. This cannot be done from the Emergency Repair Disk. Rather, it must be done by loading the Setup floppy diskettes used during the installation process or booting from the installation CD-ROM. The Setup application offers you the choice of installing Windows 2000 or repairing a faulty installation. Choose the latter. At this point, the Setup application attempts to locate the computer's disk drives. It then asks if you want to use an Emergency Repair Disk or if the Setup application should search for the \REPAIR directory.

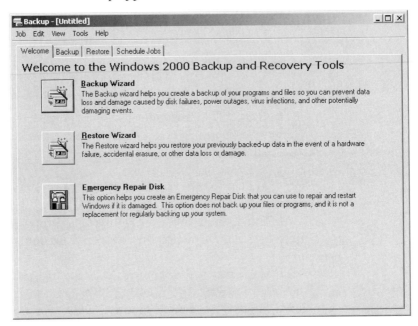

Figure 3.29 *Creating an Emergency Repair Disk in Backup.*

The Setup application examines your system to find problems, offering a number of repair options.

- **Inspect Registry Files.** Should the Registry be corrupt, you can choose to repair a combination of the SYSTEM, SOFTWARE, DEFAULT, SECURITY, and SAM Registry hives from the backup Registry. This information is computer-specific, so only an Emergency Repair Disk created for your server works here.
- **Inspect Startup Environment.** Should any of the boot files go missing or become corrupt, you can use this option to reinstall them.
- **Verify Windows 2000 System Files.** You can use this option to determine if any files are missing or corrupt. Each file in the Windows 2000 directory tree is inspected and compared to the checksum values in the SETUP.LOG file. Any that are faulty can be replaced from the installation CD-ROM.
- **Inspect Boot Sector.** Should you find that your computer no longer boots from Windows 2000, it is probable that the boot sector has been corrupted or replaced. This commonly happens after you install

a new version of MS-DOS or Windows Me in a dual-boot partition. You may use this option to repair it.

CHECKING THE MASTER BOOT RECORD • Viruses that replace the Master Boot Record (MBR) can produce such start-up errors as "invalid partition table," "missing operating system," and "error loading operating system." To help address this issue, Microsoft includes the "AVBoot" program on the installation CD-ROM, which can scan for and remove viruses from the MBRs on any of the computer's hard drives.

If the volume is inaccessible, or appears as an "unknown volume" when viewed from the Disk Management snap-in, it may be that either the boot sector or the Master File Table (MFT) is corrupt. On NTFS volumes, it might be that the permissions have changed.

In the past, you could overcome boot sector problems by running the FDISK utility with the /MBR switch. Microsoft no longer recommends this.

Working with Removable Media Devices

Removable media devices include any drives that contain removable storage media, such as read/write CD-ROM drives, Digital Audio Tape (DAT) drives, and Iomega Zip drives. Among the popular device types supported by Windows 2000 are the following:

SCSI DEVICES • The Small Computer Serial Interface (SCSI) is commonly used with Quarter-Inch Cartridge (QIC), DAT, and Digital Linear Tape (DLT) drives, as well as the Iomega Jaz drive.

FIREWIRE DEVICES • The Firewire, or International Electrical and Electronic Engineers (IEEE) 1394, bus standard is designed for high-throughput PC devices. Firewire currently supports bus speeds of 98,304 Mbps, 196,608 Mbps, and 393,216 Mbps, with a 800 Mbps rate under development. The IEEE 1394 specification accommodates different transfer rates simultaneously on the same bus. Firewire also supports both asynchronous and isochronous communication across the bus.

Firewire is implemented in a daisy chain topology (e.g., with one component linked to the next, and so on). The maximum distance between devices is 4.5 meters, and the maximum hop count is 16.

Firewire is composed of four primary components. An I/O device, such as a computer or tape drive, is attached to the bus. These devices have two or more connectors that allow them to be daisy-chained. A splitter provides flexibility in designing and implementing the IEEE 1394 topology by providing extra ports. A bridge isolates data traffic within a specific area of the bus.

A repeater extends the distance between devices by retransmitting data signals across the bus.

Firewire is fully Plug-and-Play compatible, so you can add devices without rebooting the computer. If a Firewire device is added while data is being transmitted through an isochronous channel across the bus, the channel being used is reallocated so that no data is lost. The following events occur during the addition of a device:

- A bus initialize signal is broadcast, forcing all nodes into a suspended state.
- A tree identity process designates one node as the root and the rest as either a parent node, attached directly to the root node, or a child node, attached indirectly.
- A self-identity process runs during which each node selects one of 63 zero-based bus IDs.
- The bus is reactivated.

UNIVERSAL SERIAL BUS DEVICES • The Universal Serial Bus (USB) is designed to provide fast support for peripherals such as storage and I/O devices. USB supports two data transfer rates, which depend on the amount of bus throughput a peripheral device requires. A 1.5 Mbps transfer rate supports devices that do not require much bandwidth (such as mouse devices). A 12 Mbps isochronous transfer rate supports high-bandwidth devices such as disk drives.

USB devices are described in greater depth later in this chapter.

CONFIGURING REMOVABLE MEDIA DEVICES

As with CD-ROM/DVD drives and hard disks, removable media devices can be configured from the MMC by selecting the Removable Storage item under Storage in the tree, as shown in Figure 3.30.

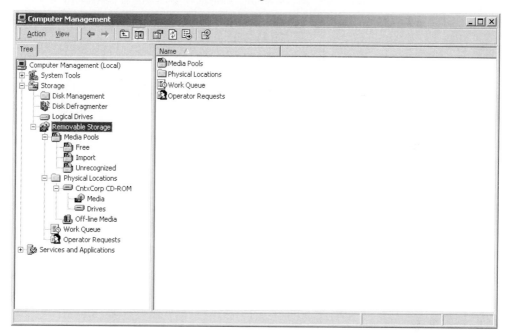

Figure 3.30 *Working with removable media drives in the MMC.*

MONITORING REMOVABLE MEDIA DEVICES

To monitor removable media drives from the MMC, expand the Physical Locations item to see a list of devices. Expand a device, then right-click the drive name in the main window and choose the Properties command to open the Properties dialog box, as shown in Figure 3.31.

Under the General tab, you can view the state and type of the media inserted in the drive, as well as mount and cleaning statistics. Under the

Device Information tab, you can view driver data, such as manufacturer and version, and device address (where applicable).

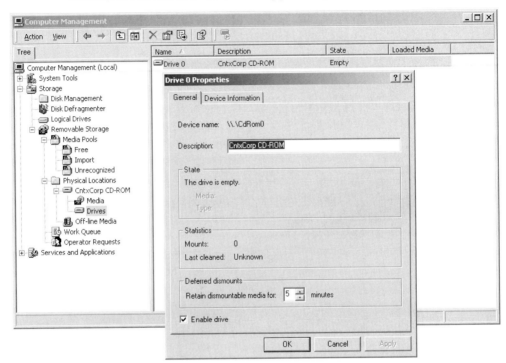

Figure 3.31 *Monitoring removable media devices.*

Upgrade a Basic Disk

Practice what you have learned by upgrading a basic disk to a dynamic disk.

First, launch the MMC and select the Disk Management branch to view the computer's drive configurations. Select a drive for conversion. Next, launch the Disk Check program from the Properties dialog box. Upon completion, upgrade the basic disk to a dynamic disk. Note the differences that then appear as seen from the MMC.

| MCSE 3.2 | **Working with Display Devices** |

The Display Control Panel application can be used to configure Windows 2000 Professional's visual settings, as shown in Figure 3.32.

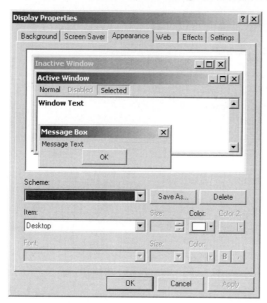

Figure 3.32   *The Display control panel dialog box.*

Among the tasks that may be performed here are changing the GUI's colors, fonts, and icons, enabling desktop wallpapers and Active Desktop, and enabling a screen saver. The application's most significant controls are found under the Settings tab, as shown in Figure 3.3.

Under the Settings tab, you can select display color depth and screen area. Click the Troubleshoot button to view content-specific Microsoft Help..

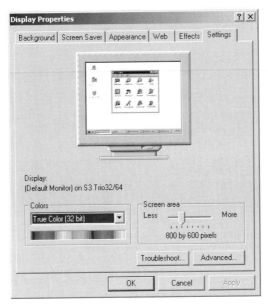

Figure 3.33   *Viewing display settings properties.*

Click the Advanced button to change settings under the following tabs:

- **General.** Select the GUI's default font size here. In addition, decide whether the computer will be restarted after you apply new display settings. Only displays and drivers that are Plug and Play compatible can be configured without requiring a restart.
- **Adapter.** Here you may view information about the currently selected display driver, such as manufacturer and version. You may also click the Properties button to view adapter status or to select a new driver. Click the List All Modes button to choose from supported color, desktop area, and refresh frequency options.
- **Monitor.** Here you may view information relating to installed monitor hardware and choose among supported refresh frequency rates.
- **Troubleshooting.** Here you may increase or lower the effect of display hardware acceleration until you find a level that works reliably.

Missing from Windows 2000 Professional is the Test button that allowed you to try out such changes as color depth and screen area before applying them under Windows NT 4.0. Instead, Windows 2000 simply warns you that it will apply your new settings for the next 15 seconds. During this time, you may choose the option of accepting the changes ... if your changes have not made you unable to see the dialog box shown in Figure 3.34.

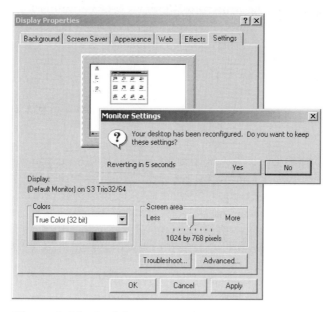

Figure 3.34 *Applying new monitor settings.*

Unless you explicitly accept the changes, the settings revert to their original state.

Gone also is the VGA option in the Windows NT 4.0 Boot Loader menu that let you force your video card into 16-color standard VGA mode so that you could experiment with the Display Properties dialog box again. Instead, you are given the option of pressing F8 after restarting, then selecting the option "Enable VGA Mode" from the Advanced Options menu.

Configuring Multiple Display Support

Windows 2000 Professional has multiple display support for several graphics adapter cards running as many as nine monitors at the same time. Multiple display support modifies the desktop to span several monitors, regardless of size or position. You can modify the resolution and color depth for each display individually, however, thanks to the Microsoft Win32 Application Programmer's Interface (API) set. Most applications do not need to be modified to run with Windows 2000 multiple display support.

Multiple display uses primary and secondary displays. All applications running in a window may be viewed on any display. In addition, the Taskbar and Desktop icons may be moved to any display. Only full-screen MS-DOS applications are restricted to the primary display.

When configuring your Windows 2000 computer for multiple displays, you must ensure that all display adapters meet specific hardware requirements. All of the display adapters must be Peripheral Component Interconnect (PCI) or Accelerated Graphics Port (AGP) devices. Even so, a display adapter that functions as a primary display may not always work as a secondary device.

Installing Video Adapters

After installing secondary display adapter hardware, you can identify the primary display monitor by rebooting the computer. The primary display shows the Power On Self Test (POST) information while the secondary display remains black. As Windows 2000 Professional starts up, a message appears on the secondary display indicating that its display adapter has initialized. Generally, the system BIOS picks the primary VGA device based on the PCI slot order.

You can also open the Display Control Panel application and switch to the Settings tab to show a numbered frame for each installed monitor. If you click and hold onto frame 1, the primary monitor will respond by displaying a number "1" on its screen.

When working with display adapters that are built into the logic board (as with a laptop), the on-board adapter becomes the secondary adapter only if it is multiple-display compatible. In addition, you must completely set up Windows 2000 before installing the additional adapter. Otherwise, Windows 2000 Setup will disable the on-board adapter during setup when the add-on adapter is detected.

A VGA device cannot be "suspended." This is an important consideration when working with docking units. Some laptop computers disable their built-in displays when "hot-docked." Multiple display support does not function with these configurations, however, unless multiple adapters are attached to the docking station.

CONFIGURING VIDEO ADAPTERS

Once you have installed the adapters, you can configure multiple display devices in the Display Control Panel application (see Figure 3.33).

Perform the following steps to configure multiple display support:

1. Under the Settings tab, numbers in the framed areas indicate monitors configured for the system. Frame "1" is for the primary and frames "2" through "9" are for secondary displays.
2. Select the display adapter for the primary display. Select its color depth in the Color field and its resolution in the Screen area field.
3. Click on frame 2 to select the secondary monitor. Select its adapter in the Display field. Enable the Extend my Windows desktop onto this monitor checkbox. Select its color depth in the Color field and its resolution in the Screen area field.
4. You can change the monitor positioning on the virtual desktop by dragging the frames around, thus reflecting the relative positions of the displays to each other.

TROUBLESHOOTING VIDEO ADAPTERS

If you experience problems with multiple display support, try fixing them with the procedures listed in Table 3.2.

Table 3.2 Multiple Display Troubleshooting

Problem	Solutions
You cannot see output on the secondary display.	Confirm that the device has been activated through the Display Control Panel application. Confirm that the correct video driver is selected for the secondary adapter. Confirm that the secondary display has been initialized. If not, check the MMC's Device Manager snap-in for its status. Physically switch the order of the adapters in the PCI slots (if the primary display can also act as a secondary display).
The Extend my Windows desktop onto this monitor option is disabled.	Confirm that the secondary display is highlighted in the Display Control Panel application. Confirm that the secondary display adapter is supported. Confirm that the secondary display has been detected.
You have problems running a program under multiple displays.	Run the program on the primary display. Run the program full screen (MS-DOS) or maximized (Windows). Disable the secondary display to see if the issue is specific to multiple display support.

Adjust Display Settings

Practice what you have learned by adjusting display settings.

First, open the Display Control Panel application and switch to the Settings tab. Modify a display settings variable, such as color depth or screen area. Click the Apply button. If your changes are acceptable, approve the changes before the 15-second countdown dialog box finishes. If problems occur thereafter, restart the computer in VGA mode and reverse the changes in the Display Control Panel application.

MCSE 3.3   Working with Mobile Computer Hardware

In this section, we consider issues most relevant to users or mobile computers, such as power management and working with PC Card devices.

Configuring Advanced Power Management

At it simplest, power management controls how a computer powers down various components during idle times, a real must for laptop users who are trying to squeeze every available ounce of power from their batteries. Mobile computers have a couple of options for doing this, depending on their age.

The older of the two power management technologies is Advanced Power Management (APM). Computers compliant with this standard can put various hardware components into low power consumption modes after specified intervals of inactivity, spinning down hard drives, turning off monitors, and so on. These computers remain in a "sleep" mode until re-activated by a key combination or other user activity, such as mouse movement. Not a bad system, but not ideal, because what APM might consider system inactivity might not agree with what users think. For example, if you do not touch the mouse or keyboard for several minutes because you are waiting for the completion of a 50-MB download, APM will likely suspend your computer, consequentially killing your modem connection.

Enter the Advanced Power Configuration Interface (APCI). This more modern multi-vendor specification is implemented throughout the entire system — hardware and software — making it more intelligent. For example, your computer might sleep after a period of relative inactivity, but be awakened to answer an incoming modem call. After completing the telecommunications transaction, it would then power down again.

Whether a computer uses APM, APCI, or no power management methodologies is determined by their BIOS. Before attempting to employ power management, you should make sure that its features are enabled through BIOS and that they do not conflict with those of Windows 2000.

CONFIGURING POWER SCHEMES

Windows 2000 Professional comes with preset power management configurations called Power Schemes. If none of the preconfigured schemes is appropriate to your system, you can either change the properties of an existing scheme or create a completely new one. This is done through the Power Options Control Panel application, as shown in Figure 3.35.

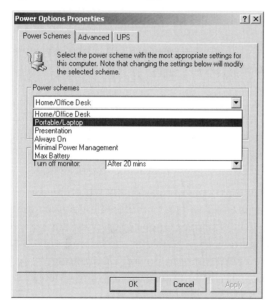

Figure 3.35 *Selecting Power Schemes.*

If your computer is capable of advanced power management, you may adjust the settings for the system standby, turning off the monitor, and spinning down hard disks through these properties. For example, you may select whether you want the computer to alert you if the battery reaches a critically low level under the Alarms tab. Under the Advanced tab, choose whether to show the power meter on the Taskbar or to have the computer prompt you for a password as it comes out of standby. There might be a Hibernate tab as well if your computer supports a hibernation mode.

USING ONNOW POWER MANAGEMENT • The OnNow design initiative encompasses overall system power management including BIOS support, specifications for peripheral devices, and the design of applications that allow the system to go into a low power state. OnNow requires changes in the Windows 98 and Windows NT operating systems, device drivers, hardware, and applications. The initiative also relies on the changes defined in the ACPI Revision 1.0 specification.

Under the initiative, the operating system works with Win32 Driver Model to control the power management of individual devices. Peripheral devices must be constructed to specifications such as those for USB and Firewire if they are to work in the OnNow structure.

In general, applications assume that the computer is always on. When these applications are inactive, they can prevent the system from entering a lower power state. In addition, applications that assume that the computer is always on might stop responding when the computer wakes up. Although the operating system performs most of the work for OnNow, applications must be designed for power management and Plug and Play to make the process transparent to the user.

The ACPI specification is a set of BIOS-level instructions with which Windows 2000 can interact. It defines a hardware interface that provides a standard way to integrate power management features throughout a system. This allows the computer to automatically turn on and off standard devices like CD-ROM drives and printers.

OnNow power management features include the following:

- The computer is ready immediately when the user "wakes" it.
- The computer appears to be off when not in use, but responds to wake-up events such as a device receiving data.
- Software adjusts its behavior in accordance with power state changes.
- All devices participate in power management, whether they are part of the original configuration or were added later.

Working with Card Services

Windows 2000 Professional card services manage any "PC Card" devices, which are about the size of credit cards, that can be inserted into a computer's Personal Computer Memory Card International Association (PCMCIA) bus. Their small size and Plug and Play design make them an effective mobile computer replacement for desktop devices and buses that would be too large and draw too much power. Typical PC Card devices include modems, network adapters, SCSI controllers, and memory storage devices.

In most cases, PC Cards can be added to and removed from a Windows 2000 system without requiring a reboot.

CONFIGURING CARD SERVICES

To add a PC Card device to a Windows 2000-based mobile computer, first log in as administrator. Windows 2000 normally detects newly installed Plug-and-Play hardware devices during startup, or when they are physically installed. Windows 2000 then automatically installs driver software and configures the hardware settings. If it does not, launch the Add/Remove Hardware Wizard and navigate through its screens (as previously described) to add the new hardware and its drivers.

To uninstall a PC Card device, you should also use the Add/Remove Hardware Wizard to inform Windows 2000 that it is no longer available. In this case, choose the Uninstall/Unplug A Device option when prompted, as shown in Figure 3.36.

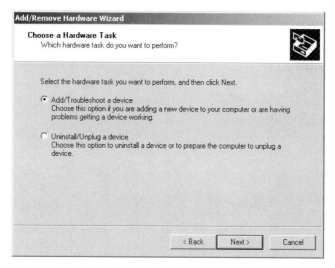

Figure 3.36 *Unplugging a PC Card device.*

Subsequently, the wizard provides you with a list of possible devices to unplug, from which you may choose. Complete the wizard to disable the device, then remove it from the PCMCIA bus when Windows 2000 Professional informs you that it is safe to do so.

The wizard also gives you the option of displaying an Unplug/Eject icon on the Taskbar that provides you with faster access to these features.

As with the other devices described so far, the PCMCIA bus can be managed from the MMC's Device Manager snap-in, as shown in Figure 3.37.

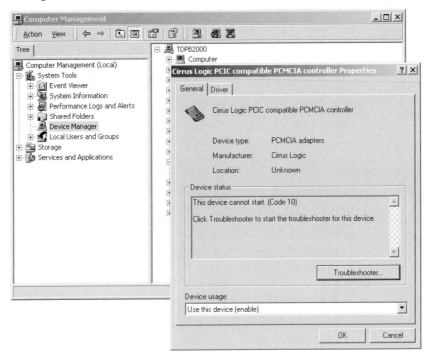

Figure 3.37 *Managing PC Card devices.*

Study Break

Enable Power Schemes

Practice what you have learned by creating a Power Scheme for your computer.

First, open the Power Options Control Panel application. Here you can determine the type of power management your computer is capable of based on the available tabs. Choose from among the available schemes in the drop-down menu. Adjust one or more power time-out settings, such as system standby, turning off the monitor, or turning off the hard drive.

Working with I/O Devices

Input/Output (I/O) devices include keyboards, pointing devices (e.g., mice), scanners, smart card readers, digital cameras, game controllers, microphones, speakers, video cameras, and modems.

Regardless of the type of I/O device involved, it can usually be configured from one centralized location, the Device Manager snap-in to the MMC, as shown in Figure 3.38.

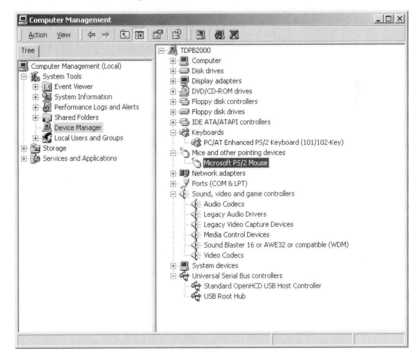

Figure 3.38 *Viewing I/O devices in the MMC's Device Manager.*

Double-click any device in the Device Manager list to open its Properties dialog box, where you may modify many device-specific settings, such as the mouse settings shown in Figure 3.39.

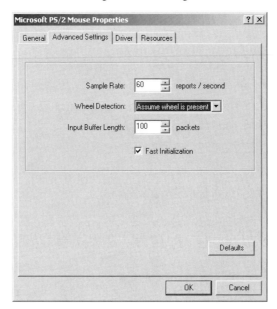

Figure 3.39   *Configuring mouse properties.*

The Device Manager snap-in also lets you monitor devices, displaying informational or error messages when hardware fails to respond to operating system queries or conflicts occur (yellow exclamation point icons appear on problem devices in the list).

In troubleshooting, you may use the Status field of the Properties dialog box to locate device problems and the Resources tab to spot and compensate for device conflicts. While all Properties displays are similar, how there settings are applied is device-specific.

Working with Multimedia Devices

Microsoft groups the Properties for audio, video, and CD music devices within the Sounds and Multimedia Control Panel application, as shown in Figure 3.40.

Figure 3.40 *Viewing multimedia device properties.*

Click the Advanced tab for a given device to configure its operational settings, such as for the sound card shown in Figure 3.41.

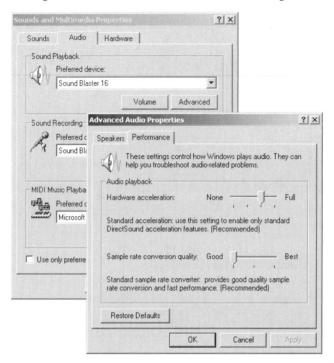

Figure 3.41 *Configuring advanced audio properties.*

Switch to the Hardware tab to monitor the device drivers and codecs that are in use.

A coder/decoder (codec) is used to convert audio or video signals between analog and digital forms, or to compress and decompress audio and video data.

When troubleshooting, click the Properties button under the Hardware tab to verify appropriate driver usage and resource settings.

Working with Modems

Microsoft groups the Properties for modems and other telephony devices within the Phone and Modem Options Control Panel application, as shown in Figure 3.42.

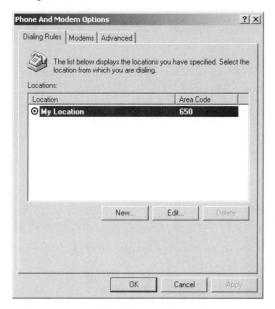

Figure 3.42   *The Phone and Modem Options Control Panel application.*

INSTALLING MODEMS

Most modems fall into one of the following categories: Internal, external, PCMCIA, or portable. Modems have a variety of attributes and features, such as error correction, compression, and flow control. Perhaps the most important attribute is the speed at which the modem can transfer data over the telephone line in bits per second.

Windows 2000 Dial-Up Networking supports modems that can use the miniport driver. This includes modems that use the standard AT command set. Some of the advanced modem features that Dial-Up Networking supports include MNP 5 and v.42bis compression and error controls. It also includes RTS/CTS and XON/XOFF software flow control.

Flow control regulates data traffic between communication devices and is a key component to implementing data compression and error correction. Flow control is supported in Windows for Workgroups 3.11 and Windows NT/2000.

If you have a modem installed in your computer, the Windows 2000 Setup program attempts to detect the modem brand and speed, and then install the proper driver files. If it fails to detect the modem, you must install the driver files manually using the manufacturer's provided software, as previously described.

To install a new modem in Windows 2000 Professional, press the Add button in the Modems Properties dialog box of the Phone and Modems Control Panel application. This launches the Add/Remove Hardware Wizard to guide you through the process, as shown in Figure 3.43.

Figure 3.43 *Adding a new modem.*

In subsequent screens you may proceed by specifying the manufacturer and model name of the modem (which installs the proper modem drivers), port number, and other information.

CONFIGURING MODEMS

Modems transfer data to and from your computer's main logic board through communication (COM) ports. The Windows 2000 Setup program automatically detects your COM ports and attempts to configure any devices (such as modems, printers, game devices, etc.) attached to them. Windows 2000 then attempts to communicate with the COM port and creates the computer files and connections necessary to allow data to flow from the computer to the device.

To manually configure a COM port (without a modem attached), launch the MMC and select the Device Manager branch, as shown in Figure 3.44.

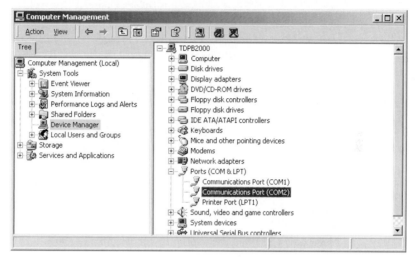

Figure 3.44   *Managing COM ports in the MMC.*

A list of the devices in your computer is displayed. Double-click on the COM port you want to configure.

A Communications Port Properties dialog box with several tabs appears, including Port Settings (see Figure 3.45).

You can configure the port to any specifications you need, such as port settings, device driver setup, and resource allocation information.

You can also open the Properties dialog box for specific modems from the Device manager snap-in.

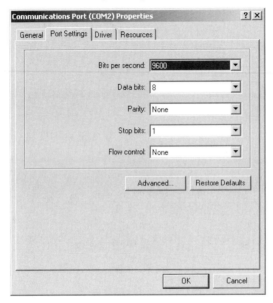

Figure 3.45 *Configuring a COM port.*

MANAGING MODEMS

To diagnose connection problems, Windows 2000 provides command logging when you use Telephone Application Programming Interface (TAPI)-compliant communication software. The modem log records all AT commands sent to the modem and logs the responses.

To view this log, switch to the Diagnostics tab in the modem's Properties dialog box and press the View Log button to open the log text file, as shown in Figure 3.46.

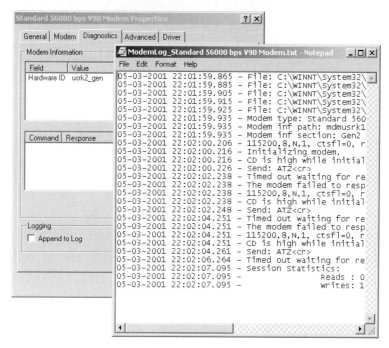

Figure 3.46 *Logging a modem connection.*

Such a log file can be used to troubleshoot modem initialization problems, slow connections, and to determine which computer (the host or the guest) is dropping a connection.

CONFIGURING DIALING RULES • Using a modem's Dialing Rules, you can define calling locations by specifying area code, country code, and in-house dialing parameters. You can also enable calling card rules. You can access these settings from the Dialing Rules tab in the Phone and Modem Options Control Panel application, as shown in Figure 3.47.

Figure 3.47 *Managing dialing rules.*

After you install and configure a modem, you must specify such properties. These properties control the manner in which the modem dials the various numbers used to connect to other services, such as remote computers using Dial-Up Networking.

Working with Wireless Devices

Windows 2000 Professional provides support for wireless communications, such as Infrared (IR) and Radio Frequency (RF).

INSTALLING AND CONFIGURING WIRELESS DEVICES

You can configure and manage IR and RF devices through either the Device Manager snap-in or the Wireless Link Control Panel application. Wireless Link can be configured to search for wireless devices, such as other IR-enabled computers. If the infrared receiver of an infrared device is lined up with the infrared receiver of the computer, within about three to nine feet, they should be able to communicate. If the device is Plug-and-Play enabled, you should not need to install any software.

MANAGING IR DEVICES

In Windows 2000 Professional, Infrared Data Association (IrDA) protocol (version 3.0) supports invisible infrared communications links. With it, the same technology that permits you to switch TV channels with a remote control is used to let your computer do things like access a printer or mouse without serial cables.

If infrared communications are interrupted, check for one of the following causes:

- Excessive direct light.
- Too great a distance between the computer and the device.
- The device was moved out of line.
- Dirt or grease on one of the infrared receivers.

Working with USB Devices

The Universal Serial Bus (USB) is designed to provide fast support for peripherals, including mouse devices, joysticks, scanners, digital cameras, and keyboards. Although not commonly implemented, USB is supported by the Win32 Driver Model.

USB supports both isochronous and asynchronous data transfer. The isochronous connection transfers data at a fixed rate. This is required to support the demands of multimedia applications and devices.

MANAGING USB DEVICES

USB supports two data transfer rates, which depend on the amount of bus throughput a peripheral device requires. A 1.5 Mbps transfer rate supports devices that do not require much bandwidth (such as mouse devices). A 12 Mbps isochronous transfer rate supports high-bandwidth devices such as modems, speakers, scanners, and monitors. The USB host determines the bus transfer rate as well as the priority assigned to a data stream.

The USB host controls traffic on the bus and functions as a hub. The hub provides a point of attachment. It detects devices that are attached or detached from the bus and provides power management services. Hubs are powered either from the bus or from an external supply.

USB devices are the I/O devices that are attached to the bus. They have a single connector type, which means any device can be used in any port.

USB devices may also function as hubs, and they can draw their power either from the bus or from an external source.

USB allows up to 127 devices to be attached at one time. Each device can be up to five meters from the hub.

INSTALLING USB DEVICES

USB is an external bus that supports Plug-and-Play, so you can add or remove devices from the bus while the computer is on. On most Windows 2000-compatible computers, the host is built into the motherboard. If it is not, you can install an adapter card:

- When a device is added to the bus, the following occurs:
- The hub notifies the host controller that a new device is present.
- The device is assigned a unique address.
- The operating system loads the device driver.
- The device is configured.
- The device driver is initialized.

CONFIGURING USB DEVICES

USB devices do not really require configuration. In addition, resource settings cannot cause a USB device to malfunction or fail. If problems do occur, the following steps should resolve them:

- Check the host controller's firmware version by viewing the host controller's properties in Device Manager. A version number of 000 indicates the controller is using the unsupported A-1 stepping chip, and should be replaced
- If only one device is failing, try the device in another USB port. If the device works there, the original port might have failed. If the device does not work there, the device might have failed.
- Plug the device directly into the host controller (bypassing any hubs). If the device is bus powered, it might be that it is drawing too much power when plugged into a hub.
- If you are using cascading hubs (one hub plugged into another hub), make sure that the USB bus follows the necessary guidelines. A bus-powered hub cannot be plugged into another bus-powered hub, for example. Bus-powered hubs can support no more than four downstream ports. Bus-powered hubs cannot support bus-powered devices that draw more than 100 milliamps. Hub cascades cannot exceed five tiers.

• Remove the USB host controller from Device Manager and restart the computer to allow the entire bus to be redetected and reinstalled.

Study Break

Install and Configure a Hardware Device

Practice what you have learned by installing—or reinstalling—a hardware device, such as a modem. If you have a new device available that has not set been detected by Windows 2000 Professional's Plug and Play, use it. Otherwise, remove a device from the computer and reinstall it. Follow the screens of the Add/Remove Hardware Wizard for both Plug-and-Play and unsupported devices. Review the device properties for the device through Device Manager, and troubleshoot any problems that arise.

MCSE 3.5 Updating Drivers

You may update drivers for various hardware devices using the Device Manager MMC snap-in. Right-click a device to select the Properties command. In the device Properties dialog box, switch to the Driver tab (see Figure 3.48).

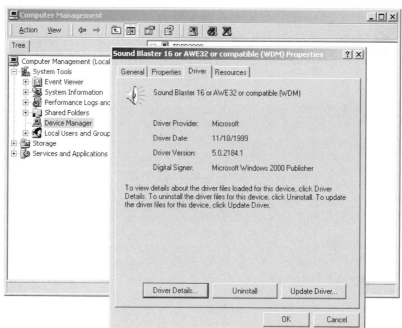

Figure 3.48 *Opening device driver properties.*

Click the Update Driver button to open the Upgrade Device Driver Wizard.

Similar to the Add/Remove Hardware Wizard, you are prompted to either let the wizard search for the driver for you, or display a list of known drivers from which you may choose. If you choose the former, the wizard prompts you to extend the search to several media types and the Microsoft update Web site, as shown in Figure 3.49.

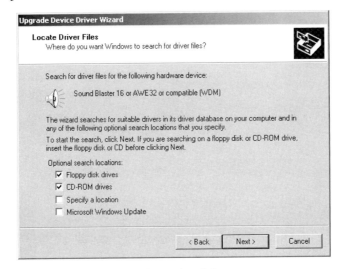

Figure 3.49 *Searching for updated drivers.*

Continue to let the wizard locate suitable new drivers and install them.

Study Break

Update Device Driver

Practice what you have learned by installing an updated device driver.

Obtain an updated device driver from a hardware manufacturer from which you previously used an older driver, or a generic Microsoft driver. Next, launch the MMC and access the device's driver properties through the Device Manager. Through the Update Driver button, launch the Update Device Driver Wizard to locate and install the new wizard.

MCSE 3.6 # Working with Multiple Processing Units

Most modern operating systems have the ability to divide their workload into smaller units and to control the way in which these units are passed on to the processor. This process of *multitasking* takes on two forms.

Under *cooperative multitasking*, all applications and the operating systems share the processor, with neither having a particular priority. If an application freezes before it can release the processor for the next application in line, the system crashes and the computer must be rebooted.

Under *preemptive multitasking*, the operating system kernel takes control of the processor. It schedules processor use for each application, while reserving the highest priority for its itself (preempting other applications). This gives the kernel the ability to force applications to wait for the next processor cycle when they are slow to respond, or to remove stopped processes from the processor queue altogether. A program that freezes is simply dumped from memory, affecting no other processes and leaving the system stable.

It is Windows 2000's preemptive multitasking that gives it the ability to schedule processor use for more than one processor. Under Windows 2000 Professional, two processors can be used. Windows 2000 Server supports as many as four, Windows 2000 Advanced Server supports as many as eight, and Windows 2000 Datacenter Server supports as many as thirty-two. Windows 2000 only supports Intel or compatible processors.

Multiple processors can be monitored using the Task Manager application, which can be launched by right-clicking the Taskbar and choosing the Task Manager command. Under the Performance tab, the CPU usage and CPU Usage History graphs tell you how busy each processor is, while Windows 2000 automatically load balances between them. Switch to the Processes tab to see which processors are running and what percentage of processor time they are using. Switch to the Applications tab to see programs that are requiring processor time, and to end any that are not responding.

Study Break

View Multiprocessor Workload

If you have a multi-processor system, practice what you have learned by viewing processing statistics. Launch the Task manager application and make note of processor workloads when the computer is idle. Next, launch some operations, such as a network file transfer and a print job, and watch how Windows 2000 distributes the work across the two CPUs.

MCSE 3.7 Working with Network Adapters

A network adapter creates a physical connection to a network type, media, and protocol. Windows 2000 Professional supports several network types including Ethernet, Token Ring, Attached Resource Computer Network (ARCNet), Fiber Distributed Data Interface (FDDI), Asynchronous Transfer Mode (ATM), and wireless technologies (such as Infrared).

Installing Network Adapters

Network adapters can be installed via the Add/Remove Hardware Wizard in the same manner as previously described for other hardware components.

Configuring Network Adapters

You can configure network adapters via the Properties dialog box available through the Device Manager snap-in, as shown in Figure 3.50.

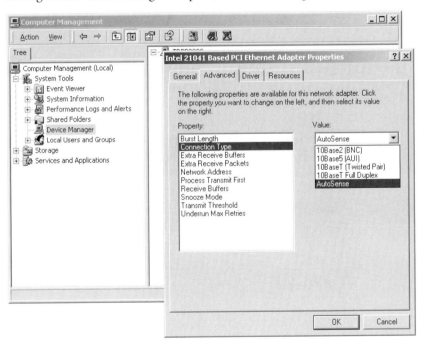

Figure 3.50 *Configuring a Network Adapter.*

TROUBLESHOOTING NETWORK ADAPTERS

Network adapters must be properly configured for IRQ, I/O port, I/O base address, and DMA channels, as visible under the Resources tab. Most likely, these settings have been picked up during Plug and Play installation, but you should verify this.

If the network adapter has been properly installed and configured but still does not work, look for a problem in the network's physical cabling.

- **Token Ring.** This networking scheme uses segments of twisted-pair (e.g., like telephone) cabling to connect each computer to a central Media Access Unit (MAU). The network is powered by the MAU, so its failure will cause a network outage. When troubleshooting a Token Ring network, check for loose cable connections, improperly crimped ends, or problems with the MAU. Token Ring networks can support speeds of either 4 Mbps or 16 Mbps.
- **Thinnet.** 10Base2 Ethernet, commonly called Thinnet, makes use of segments of coaxial (e.g., VCR-like) cables that are daisy chained together. The network is powered by its Ethernet transceivers. If the computers at either end of the chain are not properly terminated, the entire network will fail. In addition, if the daisy chain's connectors become separated anywhere along the network's length, the network will fail. A Thinnet network should be used to support no more than 30 computers, and its total length should be about 600 feet. Thinnet has a speed of 10 Mbps.
- **Twisted-Pair Ethernet.** 10BaseT Ethernet uses segments of Unshielded Twisted-Pair (UTP) cabling to connect each computer to a central hub. The network is powered by the hub, and you can tell if the connection is functional by looking for the "link status" light on the network adapter card. If it is not illuminated, check for loose connections, improperly crimped ends, or problems with the hub. A 10BaseT network can support more than 1,000 computers, and each cabling run should be no more than about 325 feet. 10BaseT has a speed of 10 Mbps. A variant on the 10BaseT standard is 100BaseT, or Fast Ethernet. This system works in the same manner as does 10BaseT, except that its cabling requirements are more stringent and it provides much faster performance (100 Mbps). Faster still is Asynchronous Transfer Mode (ATM), which also requires stringent adherence to cabling requirements to achieve speeds of 155 Mbps. If problems occur on these types of networks, it is a good idea to have the cabling plant tested with a certified "Category 5" cable scanner.

- **Fiber.** 10BaseF, or Fiber Distributed Data Interface (FDDI), networks make use of fiber optic cabling that transmits data using light instead of electricity. It is impervious to electromagnetic interference and so can be run for great distances (e.g, miles). Its cables are very fragile, however, so when an error occurs here first look for bent or broken cables, especially patch cords running from the computer to the wall.

Never "look into" a fiber optic cable; doing so can cause permanent eye damage.

Study Break

Verify Network Adapter Settings

Practice what you have learned by inspecting network adapter settings.

First, launch the MMC and open a network adapter's properties dialog box from the Device Manager snap-in. Next, switch to the Resources tab and verify that no conflicts are reported. If there is a device conflict, adjust such settings as the IRQ, I/O port, or I/O base address to resolve the problem.

■ Summary

In this chapter, we considered various Windows 2000 Professional hardware topics including hardware device drivers, various devices such as disk drives, displays, and network adapters, and multiple processing units.

Working with Disk Devices

CD-ROM, DVD, hard drives, and removable media devices may be installed, managed, and configured through Plug and Play technology and the Device Manager snap-in to the MMC.

Windows 2000 Professional supports the configuration of either basic or dynamic disks. A simple volume is a dynamic volume composed of disk space from single disk drive. A spanned volume, also known as a volume set when applied to basic disks, is composed of disk space from between two and 32 dynamic disks. A striped volume, called a stripe set when applied to basic disks, is similar to a spanned volume in that it contains free space from multiple dynamic disks (between from two to 32). The difference is that it applies the Redundant Array of Independent Disks (RAID) Level 0 technique of striping, wherein data is written to and read from each disk drive in the set in 64 kB blocks, disk after disk and row after row. The MMC's Disk Management snap-in provides a logical display of your computer's disk drives, and can be used to configure and manage them.

Removable media devices include any drives that contain removable storage media, such as read/write CD-ROM drives, QIC, DAT and DLT drives, and Iomega Zip drives. Among the popular device types supported by Windows 2000 are SCSI devices, Firewire (IEEE 1394) devices, and USB devices. Removable media devices can be configured from the MMC by selecting the Removable Storage item under Storage in the tree.

Working with Display Devices

You can configure and manage display settings through the Display Control Panel application. Windows 2000 Professional has multiple display support for several graphics adapter cards running as many as nine monitors at the same time. Multiple display support modifies the desktop to span several monitors, regardless of size or position. When configuring your Windows 2000 computer for multiple displays, you must ensure that all display adapters are PCI or AGP compliant.

Working with Mobile Computer Hardware

Mobile computers are particularly dependent on power management, of which two technologies are supported. Computers compliant with the APM standard can put various hardware components into low power consumption modes after specified intervals of inactivity, spinning down hard drives, turning off monitors, and so on. Computers compliant with the APCIs standard are more intelligent and can awaken computer components as demanded by hardware or software input. Power Management can be configured and managed through the Power Options Control Panel Application.

Windows 2000 Professional card services manage any credit-card sized "PC Card" devices that can be inserted into a computer's PCMCIA bus. Typical PC Card devices include modems, network adapters, SCSI controllers, and memory storage devices.

In most cases, PC Cards can be added to and removed from a Windows 2000 system without requiring a reboot. PC Cards can be removed from the system by running the Add/Remove Hardware Wizard.

Working with I/O Devices

Input/Output (I/O) devices include keyboards, pointing devices (e.g., mice), scanners, smart card readers, digital cameras, game controllers, microphones, speakers, video cameras, and modems. Regardless of the type of I/O device involved, it can usually be configured from the Device Manager snap-in to the MMC. In addition, properties for audio, video, and CD music devices can be managed within the Sounds and Multimedia Control Panel application. Properties for modems and other telephony settings can be managed within the Phone and Modem Options Control Panel application. Wireless devices, such as Infrared, can be managed through the Wireless Link application.

Windows 2000 supports USB, which is designed to provide fast support for peripherals, including mouse devices, joysticks, scanners, digital cameras, and keyboards.

Updating Drivers

You may update drivers for various hardware devices using the Device Manager snap-in to the MMC to open the Update Device Driver Wizard. This process works in much the same way as using the Add/Remove Hardware Wizard, in that you are prompted to supply the location of the new driver, such as on a hard drive, removable media, or the Microsoft update Web site.

Working with Multiple Processing Units

Windows 2000 Professional supports as many as two Intel or compatible processors on a single system through preemptive multitasking. These processors can be monitored and managed somewhat through the Task Manager application.

Working with Network Adapters

A network adapter creates a physical connection to a network type, media, and protocol. Windows 2000 Professional supports several network types including Ethernet, Token Ring, Attached Resource Computer Network (ARCNet), Fiber Distributed Data Interface (FDDI), Asynchronous Transfer

Mode (ATM), and wireless technologies (such as Infrared). Network Adapters can be installed using the Add/Remove Hardware Wizard. They can be configured through the MMC's Device Manager snap-in.

▲ CHAPTER REVIEW QUESTIONS

Here are a few questions relating to the material covered in the *Implementing, Managing, and Troubleshooting Hardware Devices and Drivers* section of Microsoft's *Installing, Configuring, and Administering Microsoft Windows 2000 Professional* exam (70-210).

1. When a device driver is digitally signed, it has been tested by Microsoft and verified as Windows 2000 compatible.

    A. True

    B. False

2. Windows 2000 supports which of the following CD-ROM/DVD file systems? Select all that apply:

    A. UFS

    B. UDF

    C. CDFS

    D. NTFS

3. To configure a CD-ROM drive's settings, you may access its properties through the MMC's Disk Management snap-in.

    A. True

    B. False

4. Which of the following tasks can be performed using the MMC's Disk Management snap-in? Select all that apply:

    A. View disk information

    B. Format CD-ROMs

    C. Manage volume sets, stripe sets, and mirror sets

    D. Manage simple volumes, spanned volumes, and striped volumes

5. Which of the following are found on basic disks? Select all that apply:

    A. Logical drives

    B. Primary partitions

    C. Extended partitions

    D. Volume sets

6. *Dynamic volumes are viable on dual-boot systems so long as both operating systems are Windows NT-based (e.g., Windows NT Workstation and Windows 2000 Professional).*

   A. True

   B. False

7. *Which of the following must be true in order for you to extend a simple volume into a spanned volume? Select all that apply:*

   A. You must be working with a dynamic disk.

   B. There must be no file system present, or be NTFS.

   C. It must be extended to dynamic disks.

   D. It cannot be extended from volumes created through upgrading to a dynamic disk.

8. *Removable media drives are meant to be configured using the Disk Management snap-in to the MMC.*

   A. True

   B. False

9. *Which of the following are common bus types for removable media? Select all that apply:*

   A. Firewire

   B. USB

   C. SCSI

   D. IEEE 1394

10. *Windows 2000 may support different displays through separate configurations, but not two displays at the same time.*

    A. True

    B. False

11. *Which of the following can be used to detect or recover from a display misconfiguration? Select all that apply:*

    A. The Test button in the Display Control Panel application.

    B. The 15-second countdown in the Monitor settings dialog box.

    C. The F8 key.

    D. The Boot Loader menu's VGA option.

12. *Only display adapters that are PCI or AGP-compliant may be used in multiple display support.*
    A. True
    B. False

13. *When you reboot a computer with multiple monitors attached, the POST process should appear on all of them if multiple display support is working properly.*
    A. True
    B. False

14. *When working with display adapters that are built into the logic board, the on-board adapter will not function as a secondary display unless the computer is multiple display compatible.*
    A. True
    B. False

15. *Which of the following are power management standards? Select all that apply:*
    A. AGP
    B. APM
    C. BIOS
    D. APCI

16. *A computer running APCI is likely to be less modern than a computer running APM.*
    A. True
    B. False

17. *Microsoft's version of the APCI standard is a subset known as Power Scheme.*
    A. True
    B. False

18. *"Card services" refer to Windows 2000 support of card reader devices, which might be connected via USB or Firewire buses.*
    A. True
    B. False

19. *Card devices can be removed from a Windows 2000 system by simply unplugging them.*

   A. True

   B. False

20. *Which of the following are classed as I/O devices? Select all that apply:*

   A. Keyboards

   B. Digital cameras

   C. Modems

   D. Scanners

21. *Most I/O devices can be configured via their own Control Panel applications.*

   A. True

   B. False

22. *Yellow exclamation points designate problem devices within Device Manager.*

   A. True

   B. False

23. *Multimedia devices can be configured via the Sounds and Multimedia Control Panel application or the Device Manager MMC snap-in.*

   A. True

   B. False

24. *Resource conflicts can be detected via the Sounds and Multimedia Control Panel application:*

   A. True

   B. False

25. *Modem devices can be configured via the I/O Hardware Control Panel application or the Device Manager MMC snap-in.*

   A. True

   B. False

26. *Connection logging can help you troubleshoot modem problems.*

   A. True

   B. False

27. *Wireless devices can be configured via the Wireless Link Control Panel application or the Device Manager MMC snap-in.*
- A. True
- B. False

28. *Line of sight is unimportant when working with IR devices.*
- A. True
- B. False

29. *Which of the following are true of IR connections? Select all that apply:*
- A. Excessive direct light can interfere.
- B. Devices should be within three and nine feet of each other.
- C. Devices should have clean receivers.
- D. Devices should be IrDA compliant.

30. *Which of the following are classed as IR devices? Select all that apply:*
- A. IR
- B. USB
- C. IEEE 1394
- D. RF

31. *How many USB devices can be attached to a Windows 2000 computer? Select only one:*
- A. 2
- B. 4
- C. 10
- D. 127

32. *USB buses require extensive configuration under Windows 2000.*
- A. True
- B. False

33. *You may update drivers for various hardware devices using via the Device Manager snap-in to the MMC:*
- A. True
- B. False

34. *Updating device drivers is a significantly different process from that of adding new hardware.*

   A. True

   B. False

35. *Multiprocessing relies on cooperative multitasking:*

   A. True

   B. False

36. *Windows 2000 Professional supports how many processors? Select only one:*

   A. Two

   B. Four

   C. Eight

   D. 32

37. *Network adapters create a physical connection to a network type, media, and protocol.*

   A. True

   B. False

38. *Network adapters can be configured via the Network Control Panel application or the Device Manager MMC snap-in.*

   A. True

   B. False

Optimizing Windows 2000 Professional Devices

▲Chapter Syllabus

MCSE 4.1 Working with Driver Signing

MCSE 4.2 Using Task Scheduler

MCSE 4.3 Offline File Synchronization

MCSE 4.4 Optimizing the Desktop

MCSE 4.5 Managing Hardware Profiles

MCSE 4.6 Recovering System State and User Data

In this chapter, we examine some of the performance and system stability topics covered in the *Monitoring and Optimizing System Performance and Reliability* section of Microsoft's *Installing, Configuring, and Administering Microsoft Windows 2000 Professional* exam (70-210).

The following material is designed to ensure that you can manage and troubleshoot such features as driver signing, Task Scheduler, offline files, and hardware profiles, as well as optimize desktop memory, processor, disk, network, and application performance. You must also know how to restore the Windows 2000 Professional system to its original state after problems occur, and restore user data.

MCSE 4.1   Working with Driver Signing

Microsoft digitally signs all drivers included with Windows 2000 Professional. A digitally signed driver has passed testing by Windows Hardware Quality Labs (WHQL). Windows 2000 can check for this digital signature when you install a new driver, as shown in Figure 4.1.

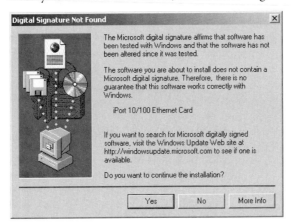

Figure 4.1 *Warning of new digital signature.*

As an administrator, you can decide to ignore driver signing, in which case you have no guarantee that a given driver will work properly with your computer. You can accept Windows 2000's habit of informing you whenever it encounters a driver that is not signed (the default), making your decisions selectively. Finally, you can block the installation of any driver that is not digitally signed.

Managing Driver Signing

Driver Signing can be configured and managed from the System Properties dialog. Right-click My Computer and select the Properties command to open the dialog box, then click the Driver Signing button to open the Driver Signing Options dialog box shown in Figure 4.2.

You may choose to apply one of the following settings as the system default:

- **Ignore.** This radio button disables driver checking.
- **Warn.** This radio button enables driver checking. As a result, a message warns users if they try to install a driver that fails the signature check.

Block. This radio button prohibits the installation of drivers that fail the signature check.

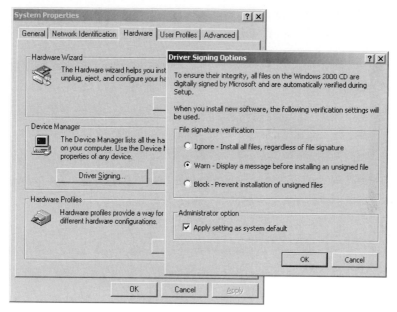

Figure 4.2 *Configuring driver signing.*

Troubleshooting Driver Signing

You may verify digital signatures by using the File Signature Verification tool, which can be launched from the System32 folder of the WINNT folder using the command line or Run dialog box, as shown in Figure 4.3. Click the Advanced button to direct the application to search for unsigned system files only, or to search for any unsigned drivers of the file type and in the location that you specify.

Switch to the Logging tab to record the tool's observations, including file name, modification date, version number, location, and whether it is signed.

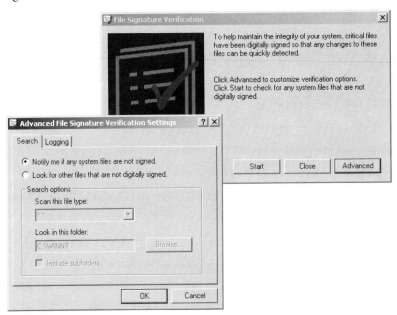

Figure 4.3 *The File Signature Verification tool.*

Click the Start button to run the verification scan. Any drivers found to be unsigned are displayed, as shown in Figure 4.4.

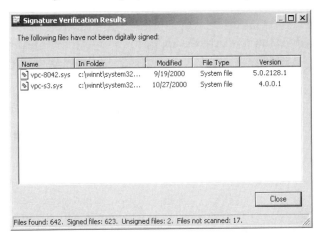

Figure 4.4 *Viewing unsigned drivers.*

If you encounter unsigned drivers, attempt to determine if they support any devices with which you have been experiencing problems. You may wish to check with their manufacturers to see if any Microsoft-approved drivers have since been released.

USING SYSTEM FILE CHECKER • During the course of work on your computer, system files can become corrupted. You are not likely to discover them except in an unpleasant and surprising way when an application crashes. To prevent this, Windows 2000 Professional allows you to check for corrupt system files by verifying their digital signatures with the System File Checker utility.

System file problems can occur in several ways. For example, system file problems occur when applications overwrite important system files, disk errors corrupt them, or users inadvertently delete them. System File Checker is used to troubleshoot and repair system file problems. It scans operating system files looking for incorrect version numbers, file corruption, and missing data. If any of these problems are identified, System File Checker prompts you to restore the original files.

You may launch the System File Checker (see Figure 4.5) from the command line using the following options:

- /scannow Scans all system files immediately.
- /scanonce Scans at system files once, at reboot.
- /cancel Stops scanning of system files.
- /enable Scans for system files that have incorrect versions and prompts the user to replace them from the installation CD-ROM.
- /quiet Scans for and replaces system files that have incorrect versions from the installation CD-ROM without prompting the user.

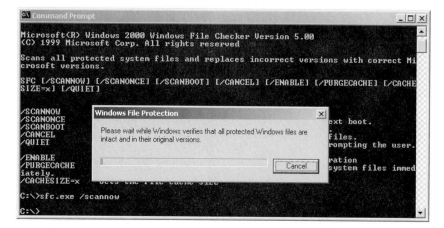

Figure 4.5   *Running the System File Checker tool.*

Study Break

Verify System Files

> Practice what you have learned by using System File Checker to verify system files with the /
> enable switch. If you find any that are corrupted, replace them from Windows 2000 Professional
> installation media as prompted.

MCSE 4.2   ## Using Task Scheduler

It can be difficult to remember when to monitor your computer and run diagnostic tasks on it. Windows 2000 Professional provides multiple tools for scheduling and automating tasks that help keep your computer running smoothly.

CONFIGURING TASK SCHEDULER

Task Scheduler is an application used for scheduling other programs to run at specific times. With it, you can schedule the launch of useful maintenance utilities such as Disk Cleanup, Disk Defragmenter, and Backup, to run at regular intervals and at times when there is little demand on computer resources. You can also run other nonmaintenance applications, such as Outlook Express or Media Player.

Launch the Task Scheduler (Scheduled Tasks) program from the System Tools program group. The Scheduled Tasks window has an icon for each task you schedule, as shown in Figure 4.6.

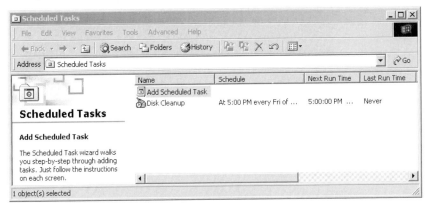

Figure 4.6   *The Scheduled Tasks window.*

You can create a task schedule by double clicking the Add Scheduled Task item to open the Scheduled Task Wizard and selecting the applications to be run, as shown in Figure 4.7.

Figure 4.7 *Selecting an application in Scheduled Task Wizard.*

Next, name the task and choose a timing interval (see Figure 4.8).

Figure 4.8 *Selecting task name and interval.*

Next, define start time, frequency, and days, as shown in Figure 4.9. A subsequent window prompts you for administrator-level account information. The next window summarizes your settings and gives you the option of opening advanced schedule settings.

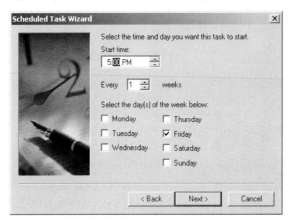

Figure 4.9 *Setting time and day.*

MANAGING TASK SCHEDULER

Once a task has been created, you may modify its settings by double clicking its listing in the Scheduled Tasks window to open the advanced settings dialog box, as shown in Figure 4.10.

Figure 4.10 *Viewing Advanced settings.*

Most of these options you have already set by running the wizard. Some new options are provided under the Settings tab, however, where you can limit the duration of time in which the task may run, specify that a task only be run during idle times, and prevent the task when running in battery mode.

You can manage Task Scheduler overall by choosing among the following settings under the Advanced menu bar item:

- **Stop Using Task Scheduler.** Disables tasks from running. Task Scheduler does not launch at reboot.
- **Pause Task Scheduler.** Tasks do not run until the next scheduled event.
- **Notify Me of Missed Tasks.** Displays a dialog box when tasks are not completed.
- **AT Service Account.** In the AT Service Account Configuration dialog box, select either the System Account, or the name and password for a user account that has sufficient permissions to perform the task (see Figure 4.11).
- **View Log.** Review the past task sessions..

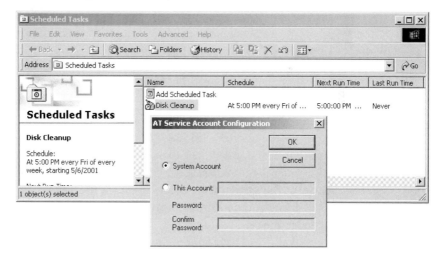

Figure 4.11 *Specifying the AT service account.*

Tasks can be shared between computers. Right-click a task to copy and paste it in a location from which it can be distributed, such as a network share. It will be saved under the ".job" extension. To install it, users need only drag and drop it into the Scheduled Tasks window. This file does not include the security settings, however.

TROUBLESHOOTING TASK SCHEDULER

Troubleshoot Task Scheduler by viewing the log file, as shown in Figure 4.12.

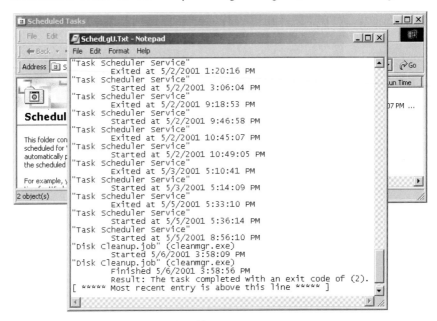

Figure 4.12 *Task Scheduler log file.*

Here you can determine which tasks ran, when, and whether they were completed successfully.

If tasks are not being completed successfully, check the following:

- Is the service running? If not, the command Start Task Scheduler appears under the Advanced menu. Also make sure that Task Scheduler is not paused.
- Is the system time correct? Check the system clock to make sure the time and date are accurate.
- Is the AT account valid? Make sure that the AT accounts selected are valid and have sufficient permissions to perform the tasks.

Schedule a Task

> Practice what you have learned by using Task Scheduler to set the time at which a maintenance task, such as running Disk Cleanup, should be run. Verify your work by ensuring that the task does occur when scheduled.

MCSE 4.3   Offline File Synchronization

You can direct Windows 2000 Professional to store copies of documents that reside on network shares locally. This ensures that your mobile computer always has access to vital documents, and that the documents you have are up-to-date.

As described in Chapter 2, "Administering Windows 2000 Professional," you can establish offline file synchronization when you set up a shared folder under Windows 2000. Press the Caching button in the shared folder's Properties dialog box to open the Caching Settings dialog box, in which you may choose to permit either the automatic or manual caching of documents and programs. The Automatic Caching for Documents setting downloads every file that you open from the shared folder for offline access. The Automatic Caching for Programs setting lets you store networked applications and run them locally, which saves time and network bandwidth. The default Manual Caching for Documents setting only caches those files you specifically select.

You can establish offline file synchronization with any file server that supports Server Message Block (SMB) file sharing. That includes Windows 2000 Server, as well as Windows NT, Windows for Workgroups, some UNIX servers, Apple's AppleShare IP, and many others.

Configuring Offline File Synchronization

To configure offline file synchronization, first map a shared volume as a network drive. Next, open the share and choose the Folder Options command from the Tools menu to open the Folder Options dialog box. Switch to the Offline Files tab, as shown in Figure 4.13.

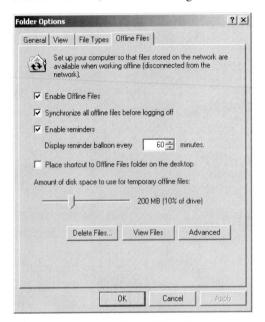

Figure 4.13 *Enabling offline files.*

Click the Enable Offline Files checkbox to activate the options. Select the Synchronize all offline files before logging off checkbox to make sure local and networked data are synchronized before you log off the server. Select the Enable reminders checkbox to make sure you are reminded of your connection status after the given interval.

Determine what you will be notified of, such as the loss of a network connection, by clicking the Advanced button, as shown in Figure 4.14.

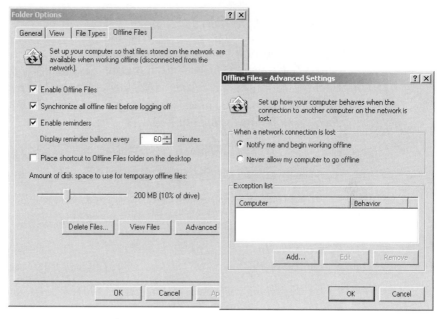

Figure 4.14 *Configuring connection loss behaviors.*

Use the level to choose the amount of disk space you are willing to allocate to file storage (see Figure 4.13). Finally, enable the Place shortcut to Offline Files folder on desktop checkbox to provide you with faster access to locally stored offline files (similar to the Briefcase) as shown in Figure 4.15.

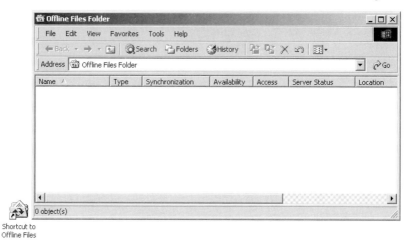

Figure 4.15 *Viewing the Offline Files shortcut.*

From the Offline Files Folder you can determine the synchronization status, location, and availability of offline files at a glance.

Managing File Synchronization

Depending on how you configured your offline folder connection, its contents will be synchronized automatically. Alternately, you can engage the Synchronization Manager manually by choosing the Synchronize command from the Offline Files Folder's Tools menu to open the Items to Synchronize Dialog box, as shown in Figure 4.16.

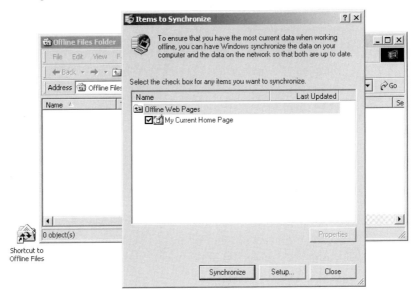

Figure 4.16   *Engaging Synchronization Manager.*

To manage the events that trigger synchronization, click the Setup button to open the Synchronization Settings dialog box, as shown in Figure 4.17.

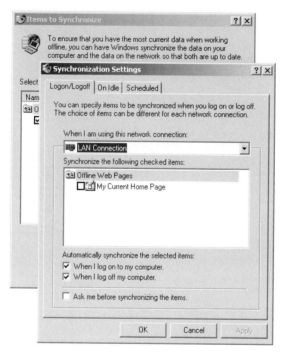

Figure 4.17 *Managing synchronization settings.*

Under the Logon/Logoff tab, direct Synchronization Manager to update files when you log on and/or when you log off. You can also decide which items will be synchronized, and whether you will be prompted. Switch to the On Idle tab and enable the checkbox to permit synchronization only when the computer is idle. Switch to the Scheduled tab and click the Add button to launch the Scheduled Synchronization Wizard to set the exact times and intervals in which synchronization should occur.

In addition to network shares, you can synchronize Web pages by adding them to Internet Explorer's Favorites and choosing to make them available offline through the Organize Favorites dialog box (see Figure 4.18).

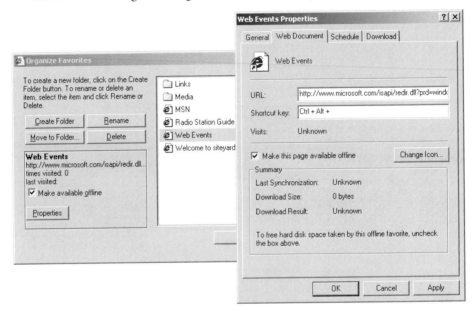

Figure 4.18 *Synchronizing Web Pages in Internet Explorer.*

Click the Properties button to view information about the Web pages' size and most recent update.

Remember that Synchronization Manager is designed to do just that: Synchronize offline files. Setting up offline file folders must be done through the Windows Explorer as described.

Troubleshooting File Synchronization

After Synchronization Manager has updated your local file copies, it should inform you of its success.

If it does not, you will note an error message, as shown in Figure 4.19.

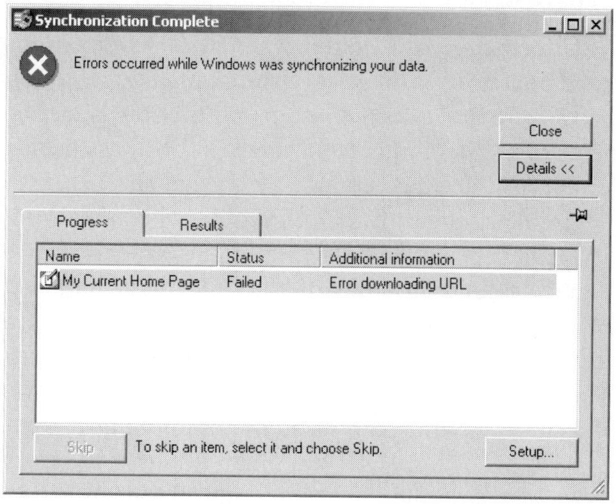

Figure 4.19 *Synchronization failure.*

Such an error is generated if Synchronization Manager was unable to open or maintain a connection with the share or Web server. If this occurs, you can troubleshoot your network connection as described In Chapter 6, "Networking Windows 2000 Professional."

Study Break

Enable File Synchronization

Practice what you have learned by enabling offline file synchronization. First, enable offline file synchronization on a network share, such as that of a Windows 2000 Server computer, and permit the automatic update of files.

Next, map the share as a local network drive on your working computer. Configure Folder Options properties to enable offline synchronization and create a desktop shortcut. Then, open a file from the share.

Open the Offline Files folder and manually initiate synchronization. When completed, you should be bale to view the status of the offline file in the Offline Files Folder window.

MCSE 4.4   Optimizing the Desktop

Optimal performance is achieved when your workstation's hardware and software are operating at the best of their capabilities. Optimal performance is not necessarily the same as acceptable performance, however. Because components in a system interact, it might not be possible to achieve the performance that you deem acceptable for a given task because one component is not as capable as the others. For example, the fastest processor available, lots of RAM, and speedy disk drives cannot compensate for a network made slow by faulty cabling. The network then becomes a bottleneck.

Optimization is the process of measuring and analyzing the resource demands of a given task to see if there is anything that can be done to make it faster. In some cases, the results of this analysis might lead you to reconfigure your workstation. In other cases, you might find it necessary to replace components altogether. Alternately, you might find that the workstation is delivering optimal performance, and you might decide that this performance is acceptable. Whatever the conclusion, no educated decision can be arrived at in the absence of data. This is why baselining and continuous logging is important.

For the most part, Windows 2000 Professional tunes itself by evaluating resource demands and responding to them. Optimization beyond this requires manual intervention. The MCSE exam requires that you know how to monitor your computer's most important resources: Processor, disk drive, network, and memory. You must analyze usage data for these resources to determine how best to optimize your computer's performance. You can obtain the performance data you require in the following ways:

- **Create baselines.** These are snapshots of your computer's normal activity over a regular interval of time. These should be created shortly after installation when all components are in use. You should have baselines for both individual components and the computer system as a whole.
- **Monitor activity.** Examine your computer's activity regularly and take special note when it deviates from the baseline. This is a sign that your network environment has changed, which might mean reconfiguration is appropriate, or that failures are occurring, in which case repairs might be needed.
- **Find Bottlenecks.** Look for signs that the computer is not working as well it might, and pinpoint the causes of less-than-optimal performance.

- **Optimize.** Determine whether server configurations and usage can be altered to achieve optimal performance.
- **Upgrade.** Determine whether more capable software components or hardware should be added to achieve acceptable workstation performance.

One of the utilities that enable you to make such determinations is the System Monitor application, a snap-in to the Performance MMC found in the Administrative Tools program group, as shown in Figure 4.20.

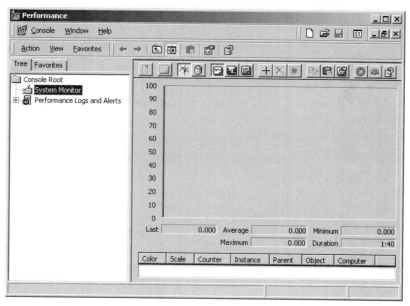

Figure 4.20 *The System Monitor tool.*

This tool replaces the Performance Monitor utility found in Windows NT 4.0.

Working with System Monitor

The System Monitor application lets you establish a wide range of statistical measurements for most of the computer's hardware and software components. These measurements are referred to as counters. Hardware and software components are referred to as objects.

System Monitor's primary objects are shown in Table 4.1.

Table 4.1 *Primary Objects in System Monitor*

Object	Description
Cache	Physical memory that contains recently requested data.
LogicalDisk	Divisions of disk space, such as partitions.
Memory	RAM, contains code and data.
Objects	System software.
Paging File	File containing Virtual Memory code and data.
PhysicalDisk	Disk drive or RAID array.
Process	Running software programs.
Processor	Central Processing Unit (CPU), executes instructions.
Redirector	Workstation service.
System	Computer hardware and software.
Thread	Part of a program that uses the processor.

Some objects, such as PhysicalDisk, can apply to more than one component. Each component is referred to as an instance. A total instance comprises all occurrences of an object. For example, a computer with two disk drives has two instances of the PhysicalDisk object.

In some cases, an object is dependent on another object. These are referred to as child objects that are dependent on parent objects.

Threads are the parts of programs that access the processor to execute instructions. A process may execute multiple threads concurrently. Some threads may be dependent on other threads, becoming child objects to parent objects.

Overall, System Monitor can be used to:

- Monitor objects on multiple computers simultaneously.
- Log data pertaining to objects on multiple computers over time.
- Analyze the effects of changes to a system.
- Launch programs and send notifications when thresholds are reached.
- Export data for analysis in spreadsheet or database applications.
- Save counter and object settings for repeated use.
- Create reports for use in analyzing performance over time.

The objects that provide the greatest indicators of server health and performance pertain to the processor, memory, disk drive, and network resources.

SYSTEM MONITOR VIEWS

The System Monitor window displays a Toolbar that contains the following buttons:

- ▫ **New Counter Set.** Clears counters and data.
- ▫ **Clear Display.** Clears data.
- ✳ **View Current Activity.** Presents live data.
- ▫ **View Log File Data.** Presents data from a log file.
- ▫ **View Chart.** Presents data in a chart format.
- ▫ **View Histogram.** Presents data is a histogram format.
- ▫ **View Report.** Presents data in a report format.
- ＋ **Add.** Adds object counters.
- ✕ **Delete.** Removes object counters.
- ♀ **Highlight.** Highlights a counter.
- ▫ **Copy Properties.** Copies counter data.
- ▫ **Paste Counter List.** Pastes counter data.
- ▫ **Properties.** Views System Monitor properties.
- ◉ **Freeze Display.** Stops collecting data.
- ▫ **Update Data.** Collects data sample.
- ▫ **Help.** Gets help.

To see the counters and objects that System Monitor is capable of tracking, select the Add button. This opens the Add Counters dialog box, as shown in Figure 4.21.

Enable the Use local computer counters or Select counters from computer radio buttons to choose either a local or remote computer to monitor. Use the Performance object drop-down menu to choose the objects that can be tracked. Use the Select counters from list field to establish which statistics will be measured.

In the instance list field, choose between multiple occurrences of the same object (e.g., multiple disk drives). The Explain button opens the Explain Text window, as seen at the bottom of Figure 4.21.

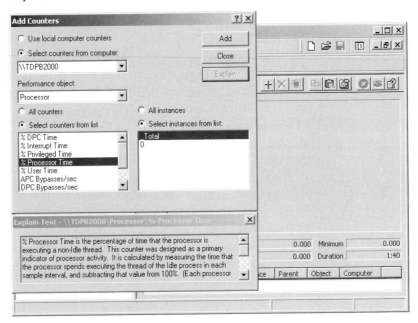

Figure 4.21 *Add Counters dialog box.*

Data can be displayed in one of three ways, but only one at a time.

CHART VIEW • System Monitor's default view is the chart. To highlight an individual line in the chart, select the line at the bottom of the window and click the Highlight button. This makes the line wider than the others and changes its color to white. The highlight can be moved from line to line with the mouse or arrow keys, and disabled with the Highlight button (or Ctrl-H), as shown in Figure 4.22.

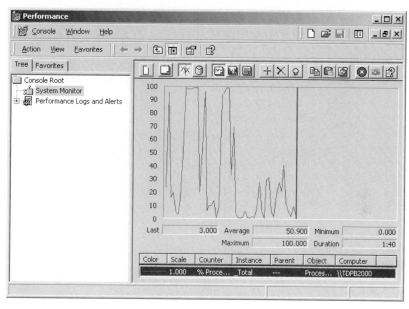

Figure 4.22 *System Monitor in Chart view.*

REPORT VIEW • You may also have data listed in a simple report, as shown in Figure 4.23.

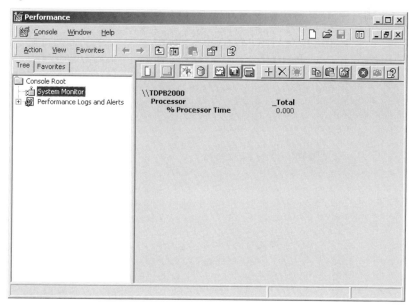

Figure 4.23 *System Monitor in Report view.*

To do this, select the View Report icon to switch to the Report view window. View data live, or choose the View Log File Data button to open a log file for viewing.

HISTOGRAM VIEW • Select the View Histogram icon to switch to the Histogram view window, as shown in Figure 4.24.

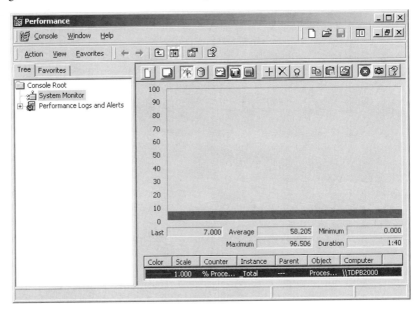

Figure 4.24 *System Monitor in Histogram view.*

PERFORMANCE LOGGING

In addition to its ability to track specific events in real time, System Monitor is also able to track events historically for your review. To do this, expand the

Performance Logs and Alerts branch and select the Counter Logs item, as shown in Figure 4.25.

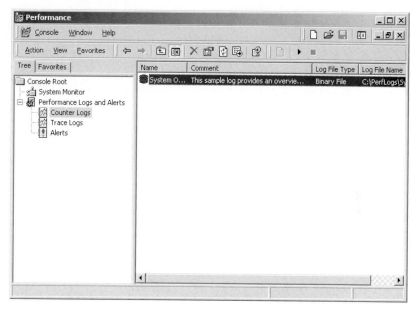

Figure 4.25 *System Monitor log views.*

Next, right click in the main window and select the New Log Settings command. You are prompted to name your new log. Click the OK button to open a namesake properties dialog box, as shown in Figure 4.26. Under the General tab, select one or more counters to log by clicking the Add button to open the Add Counters dialog box (see 4.21). Also determine the logging interval, in seconds, minutes, hours, or days.

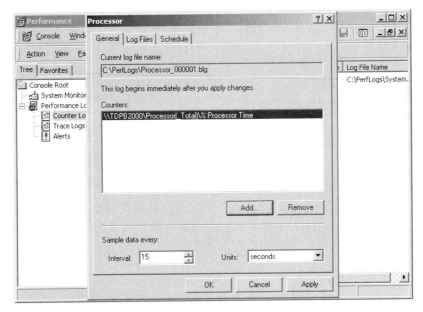

Figure 4.26 *Adding counters to a log file.*

Next, switch to the Log Files tab, as shown in Figure 4.27.

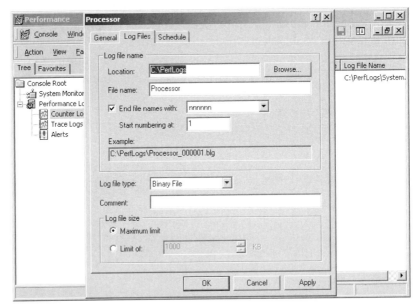

Figure 4.27 *Naming the log file.*

Change the log's name and location, establish an incremental numbering scheme, and add a descriptive comment. You may also choose to save the log as binary, binary circular file, comma-delimited text, or tab-delimited text. Finally, you may limit the file's size.

Next, switch to the Schedule tab to specify an automatic launch and stop time, as shown in Figure 4.28.

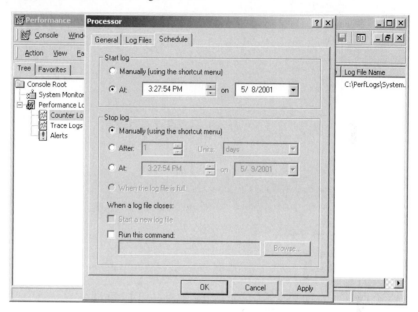

Figure 4.28 *Scheduling logging.*

Alternately, you may choose to initiate and/or stop logging manually from the System Monitor console. You may also choose to create a new file when one is closed, or to execute a command.

When you are ready to view the log, press the View Log File Data button in the System Monitor window.

Right click and choose the Properties command to determine how log data is presented, as shown in Figure 4.29.

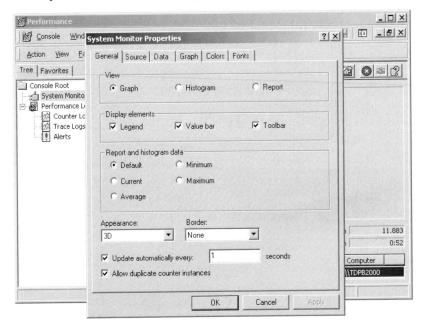

Figure 4.29   *Choosing viewing options in the Properties dialog box.*

Switch to the data tab to add or remove counters from the log's presentation. You might have logged everything associated with the object, but here you can decide what you really want to view.

Note that the logged data, once charted, is static. It is a snapshot of your workstation's history. To focus on a particular period, switch to the Source tab to establish a time range, as shown in Figure 4.30.

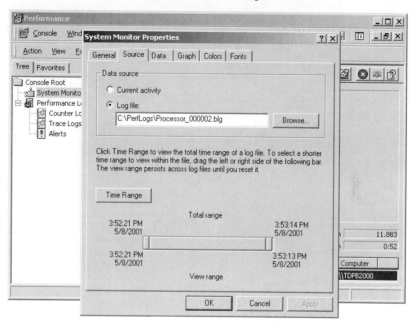

Figure 4.30 *Choosing a time range.*

Establish a beginning and an end to the interval that you wish to examine using the gray slide bars.

SETTING ALERTS

In addition to using System Monitor for establishing baselines and analyzing performance, you can use it as an early warning system. To do this, expand the Performance Logs and Alerts branch and select the Alerts item (Figure 4.25). Next, right click in the main window and select the New Alert Settings command. You are prompted to name your new alert.

Click the OK button to open a properties dialog box, as shown in Figure 4.31.

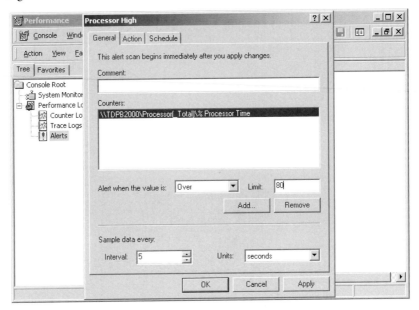

Figure 4.31 *Adding counters to monitor.*

Under the General tab, select one or more counters to monitor by clicking the Add button to open the Add Counters dialog box (see Figure 4.31). Next, define an event that should trigger an alert, such as the counter going over or under a specified limit. Also determine the logging interval.

Next, switch to the Action tab to tell System Monitor what to do when the alert is triggered, as shown in Figure 4.32.

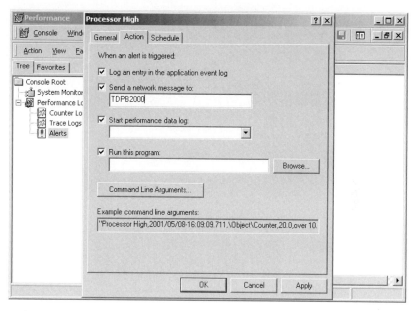

Figure 4.32 *Establishing an alert action.*

In addition to logging an entry in the application event log, you may choose to send a network message to another computer, begin recording to a performance log, or run a program.

Next, switch to the Schedule tab to specify an automatic or manual launch and stop time, as shown in Figure 4.33.

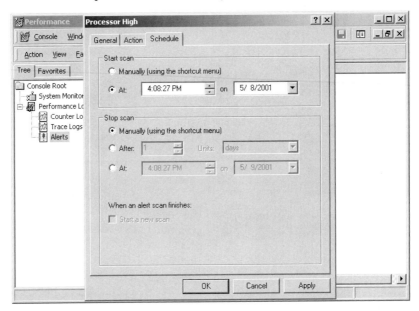

Figure 4.33 *Scheduling alerts.*

TROUBLESHOOTING SYSTEM MONITOR

System Monitor is designed to affect Windows 2000 Professional performance minimally. Nevertheless, it still has some impact. For the most accurate measurements, you should monitor a workstation from a different computer whenever possible. The exception is the case of network performance, which should be monitored locally.

Several factors can affect System Monitor performance. If readings are collected at too short an interval, the log file becomes overly large. If readings are collected at too long an interval, major events can be missed. If readings are collected too often, the processor registers an increased burden. You might need to experiment to find the right settings for each object.

If you begin monitoring too soon after startup, data is skewed by component initialization sequences. Be sure to let the workstation "settle down" before beginning performance analysis.

Baselining

All of the previously described counters are relatively useless without a frame of reference. That reference, or baseline, is a snapshot of your computer's normal activity over a regular interval of time. Save this data for comparison. Any deviation from the baseline is an indicator that the way the computer or network is being used has changed, or that a problem has arisen. Either way, you will have a basis for isolating a bottleneck or error and responding.

Several methods can be used to create a baseline. One of the most common is to monitor a newly installed computer with all of its components running for a week. This gives you an overview of its initial performance, at various times of the day, to which later samplings can be compared. It is also useful to create baselines component by component, as this provides a basis for comparison if you change a component or its configuration later.

Baselines should always include the processor, memory, disk drive, and network components. In addition, it is useful to monitor the Cache, Logical Disk, Memory, Network Adapter, Network Segment, Physical Disk, Processor, Server, and System objects. You must use System Monitor's Performance Logs and Alerts functions to create baselines, as this is the only way to log data.

The following is a good baselining strategy:

- Create an initial baseline during a one-week period soon after the workstation is installed. Be sure to capture different times of day, have all components running, and wait until initialization sequences have completed.
- Create baselines for individual components, especially the processor, memory, disk drive, and network.
- Create a new baseline whenever a component is added or changed. Create a baseline for the individual component and the system as a whole. This tells you what the effects of the change are.
- Using the same settings established in the initial baseline (which can be saved in System Monitor), log computer and network performance at regular intervals. Log files can grow large, so save them to a partition with sufficient free space.
- Create a database or spreadsheet that contains information from the original baseline as well as subsequent measurements to aid you in making comparisons.

BOTTLENECKS

Bottlenecks are those components in systems that slow the performance of other components. If you have performed sufficient baselining, you can usually spot bottlenecks and determine when they occur to eliminate them. The component that takes the most time to complete a task is typically the culprit.

Several counters are useful in analyzing the performance of the server's main component: Processor, memory, disk drive, and networking. The values these counters record can point you to a number of solutions to alleviate the problem.

Optimizing Memory Performance

Memory resources include both physical memory (SIMMs, DRAM, and so on) and Virtual Memory (paging). The more physical memory that is installed in a computer the better, for Virtual Memory uses a disk drive-based paging file. This makes it slower and a drain on disk drive performance. How much Virtual Memory is being used in relation to physical memory is an important performance indicator.

Technically, a Windows 2000 Professional computer need never run out of memory. When insufficient physical (or nonpaged) memory is unavailable, Windows 2000 Professional resorts to using virtual (or paged) memory. nonpaged memory resides in fast RAM chips, while paged memory resides on comparatively slow disk drives. You can keep enlarging the paging files on a computer's disk drives to increase memory practically without limit. You will find out, however, that it does not take long for the workstation to slow to unacceptable performance after you do. The easiest way to improve system performance is to install more RAM. You should especially do this when memory becomes a bottleneck.

The following counters are useful in identifying memory bottlenecks:

PAGES/SEC. • This counter, found under the Page Fault object, is used to measure the number of times a page was loaded into memory or written out to the disk drive. This pertains to the memory accessible by applications. Be concerned when this counter hits sustained levels of about 20.

AVAILABLE BYTES • This counter, found under the Page Fault object, is used to measure the usable amount of physical memory. Higher levels of paging occur when physical memory falls below 4 MBs.

COMMITTED BYTES • This counter, found under the Page Fault object, is used to measure the amount of RAM in the nonpaged pool area used by the operating system. When the number exceeds the amount of physical RAM in the system, a RAM upgrade is needed.

TROUBLESHOOTING MEMORY PERFORMANCE

The primary method of addressing a memory bottleneck is to add more RAM. Some of the options here include:

- **Increase physical RAM.** The more RAM your server has, the less often it must rely on Virtual Memory, paging to and from the much slower disk drives.
- **Use faster RAM.** Some computers accept RAM chips of varying speeds. Always use the fastest RAM possible.
- **Upgrade the cache.** Most server computers are equipped with a RAM cache that holds commonly accessed data. The size of this cache can often be increased.
- **Disable ROM BIOS shadowing.** Many computers use the feature of "shadowing" ROM information in RAM to improve performance. This feature does not improve performance under Windows 2000, however, and should therefore be disabled using the computer's ROM BIOS utility.

REMOVE UNNECESSARY PROGRAMS • Windows 2000 Professional can be configured with many device drivers, network protocols, and services that you might not need. For example, if all the workstations on your network are using TCP/IP, do you really need any other protocols? If there is no UPS being managed from your workstation, do you really need the UPS service? These types of unnecessary components can be removed.

Alternately, many services can be "turned off." You might wish to use IIS' FTP server capability but prefer to set its Web server functionality to "manual" in the MMC's Services snap-in, for example. This frees up RAM as well as relieve the processor of unnecessary threads. Just be sure you know that what you are disabling is not a necessary component or one on which other services depend.

OPTIMIZE VIRTUAL MEMORY • Virtual Memory refers to the paging file that Windows 2000 creates on the boot drive to use in lieu of physical RAM. Theoretically, there is no limit to the amount of Virtual Memory that can be used with Windows 2000. Large amounts make the workstation run more slowly, however, since disk I/O is much slower than RAM I/O.

You can alter the way Windows 2000 Professional uses Virtual Memory. From the Advanced tab of the System Control Panel application, click the Performance Options button to open the Performance Options dialog box.

Next, open the Virtual Memory properties dialog box by pressing the Change button (as shown in Figure 4.34).

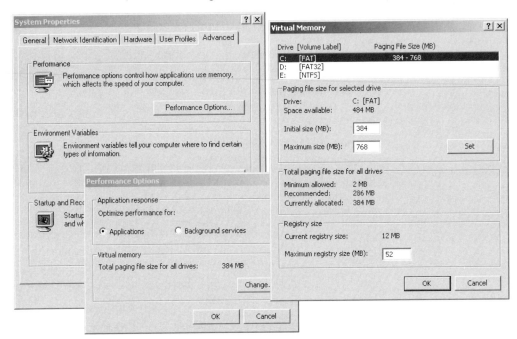

Figure 4.34 *Virtual Memory dialog box.*

If you have multiple disk drives and controllers in your server, spreading the paging file across these disks should improve performance. If you have multiple disk drives but one controller, putting the paging file on the disk drive that sees the least activity can improve performance.

Optimizing Processor Utilization

Windows 2000 Professional can support as many as two processors, and other flavors of Windows 2000 can support many more. In single processor systems, the speed of the chip (e.g., MHz) affects workstation performance. In multiple processor computers, the speed and number of processors affects performance.

The following counters are useful in identifying processor bottlenecks:

PERCENT PRIVILEGED TIME • This counter, found under the Processor object, is used to monitor the amount of time a processor is handling operating system services. The processor is likely to be a bottleneck if this value averages greater than 75 percent.

PERCENT USER TIME • This counter, found under the Processor object, is used to monitor the amount of time a processor is responding to desktop applications and other user services. The processor is likely to be a bottleneck if this value averages greater than 75 percent.

PERCENT PROCESSOR TIME • This counter, found under the Processor object, is used to measure the amount of time the processor spends executing active threads. It is derived from adding the Percent Privileged Time value to the Percent User Time value. The processor is likely to be a bottleneck if this value averages greater than the range of 75-80 percent. This can be caused by applications that require more powerful CPU resources.

INTERRUPTS/SEC. • This counter, found under the Processor object, is used to monitor the number of interrupts from hardware devices and software handled by the processor every second. Excessive interrupts can be caused by faulty disk drives or network components.

PROCESSOR CUE LENGTH • This counter, found under the System object, is used to measure the number of threads waiting in queue for processor time. More than two generally signals low processor performance.

Do not worry about the processor spiking the 100 mark on these counters, so long as it does not do so regularly for sustained periods of activity.

TROUBLESHOOTING PROCESSOR UTILIZATION

There are several methods for addressing a processor bottleneck.

REDISTRIBUTE WORKLOAD • Whenever you have multiple workstations, it is wise to distribute processor intensive applications evenly among them. They make the best use of processors on all systems.

RESCHEDULE TASKS • Performance can benefit from task scheduling. For example, running a backup or database update late at night when everyone has gone home has less impact than doing it during the business day. Running two processor intensive operations at different times rather than together is also wise.

UPGRADE THE PROCESSOR • Many server computers permit you to upgrade the Intel processor. Some of the options here include:

- **Upgrade processor speed.** Faster processors are released to the marketplace regularly, and you might be able to swap your workstation's current chip for one that can work considerably faster.
- **Upgrade the cache.** Throughput can often be improved by adding or upgrading the size of a processor's secondary cache.
- **Use multiple processors.** Some computers are designed to accept multiple processors, of which Windows 2000 Professional is able to take advantage. This is particularly helpful when running programs capable of multithreading.

Optimizing Disk Performance

In considering disk drive performance, a number of factors are involved, as follow:

- **Controller Type.** There are a number of disk drive controllers available, including IDE, EIDE, PCI, SCSI, Fast SCSI, and Fast-Wide SCSI. Each has greater or lesser performance characteristics.
- **Number of Controllers.** If multiple disk drives are served by a single controller, performance will be less than if they are served by multiple controllers. In addition, the use of busmaster controllers that have built-in processors for handling read/write requests can make a big difference in a system's main processor performance.
- **Drive Specifications.** As with controllers, some disk drives have higher access and rotation speeds than do others, with larger disk drives tending to be faster. In addition, it is important that disk drives of a certain specification always be paired with a controller of the same capabilities (e.g., Fast-Wide SCSI with Fast-Wide SCSI, and so on).
- **RAID Usage.** The use of mirroring (RAID Level 1) can slow disk drive performance, unless duplexing (multiple controllers) is also used. Striping (RAID Level 0) can improve performance.
- **Caching.** Read/write performance is improved when onboard memory is available to store requested data.
- **File System.** FAT 32 and NTFS are more efficient on disk drives in excess of 400 MBs than is FAT.
- **Drive Usage.** How the computer is used (e.g., light word processing vs. heavy calculations) determines how much that its components are used and how quickly it responds.

Two objects measure disk drive performance. The LogicalDisk object keeps track of logical partitions and monitors the requests made by applications and services. The PhysicalDisk object keeps track of each disk drive as a whole.

Windows 2000 Professional only enables the PhysicalDisk performance counters by default. You may enable or disable additional counters using the following commands in Command Prompt:

- `diskperf -y` Enable counters on local system.
- `diskperf -yd` Enable PhysicalDisk counters.
- `diskperf -yv` Enable LogicalDisk counters.
- `diskperf -nd` Disable PhysicalDisk counters.
- `diskperf -nv` Disable LogicalDisk counters.
- `diskperf -y \\<computer_name>` Enable counters on remote system.
- `diskperf -n` Disable counters on a local system.

The following counters are useful in identifying memory bottlenecks.

PERCENT DISK TIME • This counter, found under the PhysicalDisk object, is used to measure the amount of time a disk drive spends reading and writing data. That should be about 50 percent of the time. If this counter reaches levels of 90 percent or more, you have an indication of problems.

AVG. DISK QUEUE LENGTH • This counter, found under the PhysicalDisk object, is used to measure the average number of read/write requests made before the disk drive was able to accept them. An upgrade is needed when this value equals or exceeds two.

AVG. DISK BYTES/TRANSFER • This counter, found under the PhysicalDisk object, is used to measure the average number of bytes transferred to and from the system when reading from and writing to the disk drive.

DISK BYTES/SEC. • This counter, found under the PhysicalDisk object, is used to measure the speed at which bytes are read from and written to the disk drive.

TROUBLESHOOTING DISK PERFORMANCE

There are several methods for addressing a disk drive bottleneck:

- **Allow more free space.** Use disk drives that are large enough so that you are not forced to resort to file compression. Although Windows 2000's compression algorithms are optimized for efficiency, there is still a performance penalty.
- **Install more RAM.** The more physical memory available on a system, the larger the cache it can create.

- **Use fast drives.** Disk drives are not created equal. Some disk drives are much faster at locating and moving data than are others, so choose carefully. In addition, large disk drives tend to be faster than smaller ones.
- **Use fast controllers.** The speed of your disk drives is also determined by the speed of their controller cards, as well as their ability to cache recently requested information. The SCSI interface is faster than the IDE interface, for example.
- **Use NTFS.** NTFS or FAT32 is more efficient than FAT on disk drives larger than 400 MBs.
- **Use separate disk drives.** It is often helpful to isolate I/O intensive applications on their own disks and controllers.
- **Use striping.** As previously mentioned, RAID Level 0 striping techniques increase disk drive read/write access. Using RAID Level 1 mirroring with a single controller slows performance, however, as the controller must write the same data to different disk drives.

USE DISK DEFRAGMENTER • As Windows 2000 reads data from and writes data to a disk drive, files are stored in noncontiguous clusters that fragment the hard disk. It takes much longer for the computer to read and write fragmented files than nonfragmented files. The disk defragmentation process moves these clusters into one contiguous area on the hard disk, reducing their access times. You can defragment both compressed and uncompressed drives.

When an application starts, it typically reads a file with the .EXE extension and any supporting .DLL files. If the application must read noncontiguous portions of these files when it opens, it must locate each portion of each file on the disk separately. Meanwhile, you wait. Disk Defragmenter tries to place disk clusters in the order they are read. Besides decreasing applications' launch times, this can improve your system's overall performance.

To run Disk Defragmenter, open the utility from the System Tools program group, select a disk drive, and click the Defragment button, as shown in Figure 4.35.

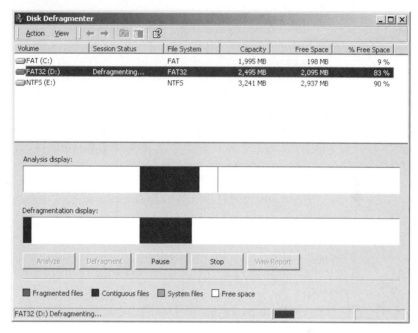

Figure 4.35 *Running Disk Defragmenter.*

The one file you cannot defragment is the paging file. The only way to defragment this file is to move it to a new volume. Microsoft recommends that you give the paging file its own volume, in fact, although you should leave at least a small paging file on the boot volume for recovery purposes.

You must be logged in with Administrator-level permissions to run Disk Defragmenter.

Disk Defragmenter takes longer to defragment your hard disk if you run it with details showing. For quickest performance, minimize the Disk Defragmenter window while it is running.

Optimizing Network Performance

In considering network performance, a number of factors are involved, as follow:

- **Topology.** Different networking schemes have different inherent performance characteristics. Token Ring, for example, is commonly deployed in either 4 Mbps or 16 Mbps varieties. Ethernet is commonly deployed in either 10 Mbps or 100 Mbps varieties.
- **Network design.** The way in which an extended network is designed affects network throughput. A network properly divided into multiple collision domains is "faster" than one that is not. Networks that make use of such devices as switches and routers perform better than "flat" networks.
- **Network adapter.** The specifications of and bus used by the Network Interface Card (NIC) can affect actual system throughput.

It is useful to evaluate network performance in terms of the Open Systems Interconnection (OSI) model. It is comprised of seven layers that provide an abstract way of representing the specific components that enable communications to take place on a network. The OSI layers break down as follows:

- **Application Layer.** At Layer 7, the languages and syntax that programs use to communicate with each other are defined. Most of the commands needed to open, read, write, transfer and close files over the network are exchanged at this level.
- **Presentation Layer.** The encoding of data so that it can be exchanged between different computer systems is managed at Layer 6. For example, the encryption and decryption for security applications occurs at this level.
- **Session Layer.** It is the job of Layer 5 to maintain an orderly process of communications. Among the things that are determined here are whether communications are one-way (half duplex) or two-way (full duplex) and how that dialog is managed so that it can be recovered in the event of a connection failure. System Monitor's Browser, Redirector, Server, and Server Work Queues for NBT Connection objects work at these layers.
- **Transport Layer.** The responsibility for maintaining integrity of a transmission overall rests with Layer 4. If a 1 MB file is sent from a server, it is the job of Layer 4 to ensure an identical 1 MB file is received by a workstation. System Monitor's AppleTalk, NetBEUI for NetBIOS, TCP, and UDP objects apply here.

- **Network Layer.** At Layer 3, the route over which the sending and receiving computers communicate is established. Where a network is segmented, these routes can become quite complicated as data hops across routers. System Monitor's Network Segment, IP, and NWLink IPX/SPX objects work at this level.
- **Data Link Layer.** The division of data bits into frames for node-to-node transmission takes place at Layer 2. A process of error checking and retransmission is used to ensure that all the necessary data is eventually transferred, even if a few frames go missing in Cyberspace.
- **Physical Layer.** Layer 1 is responsible for the electrical and mechanical signaling that moves data bits from one computer to another. You can use System Monitor's Network Interface object to troubleshoot these last two layers.

A mnemonic phrase to help you remember these layers, from bottom to top, is "People Don't Need Those Stupid Protocols Anyway."

When monitoring the performance of the OSI model, it is best to start at the lowest level and work your way up to layer 7.

The following counters are useful in identifying network bottlenecks:

PERCENT NETWORK UTILIZATION • This counter, found under the Network Segment object, is used to monitor the amount of network activity, sometimes referred to as "bandwidth," on the local segment. On the typical Ethernet network, bandwidth utilization in access of 30 percent usually results in throughput-depleting collisions. Results for other topologies vary.

BYTES SENT/SEC. • This counter, found under the Network Interface object, is used to monitor the number of bytes sent over a given adapter.

BYTES TOTAL/SEC. • This counter, found under the Network Interface object, is used to monitor the number of bytes sent and received over a given adapter.

TROUBLESHOOTING NETWORK PERFORMANCE

Network optimization can generally be divided into two areas: Physical, which includes hardware and cabling; and data, which includes network transactions and control traffic. They can be addressed as follows:

- **Use a fast bus.** Get a NIC that uses the fastest possible bus on your workstation computer. Replace 16-bit network adapters with 32-bit NICs.
- **Install a faster network.** Although it requires special cabling, NICs, and hubs, your organization might benefit by upgrading a 10 Mbps Ethernet network to a 100 Mbps "Fast Ethernet" network. Similarly, a 4 Mbps Token Ring network can often be upgraded to a 16 Mbps Token Ring scheme. Still faster choices are available as well, such as Asynchronous Transfer Mode (ATM) at 155 Mbps.
- **Segment your network.** You can improve network performance by segmenting it into multiple collision domains with switched hubs or multiple network segments with routers.
- **Turn off unused protocols.** If there are protocols that do not need to be supported on your network, turn them off. Each has its own control traffic, however slight. For example, it might not be necessary to support both NetBEUI and NWLink IPX/SPX-Compatible Transport if your network's computers can use either. In addition, you might be able to consolidate protocols. If you have been using DLC to print to Hewlett-Packard printers, you could probably use the printer's built-in NetWare or TCP/IP support instead. If your network is connected to the Internet, so that you must deploy TCP/IP, you might as well make that the network's standard protocol.

Optimizing Application Performance

In preemptive multitasking, Windows 2000 Professional uses a system of 32 priority levels to establish which application has access to the processor. The default priority level for every application is eight. The system adjusts the priority level as necessary to give the process or thread with the highest priority access to the processor, and a shorter response time, based on the following factors:

- Windows 2000 randomly boosts the priority for lower-priority threads, allowing low-priority threads to run that would otherwise not have enough memory space. This also allows a lower-priority process to access to a resource when a higher-priority resource might otherwise monopolize it.
- Windows 2000 raises the priority level of any thread that has been waiting voluntarily. The increase is determined by the resource's wait time.
- Priority levels 0 through 15 are used by dynamic applications that can be written to the Windows 2000 page file. By default, this includes

user applications and operating system functions that are nonessential.

- Priority levels 16 through 31 are used by real-time applications that cannot be written to the Windows 2000 page file, such as executive services and the Windows NT kernel.

You can change the default priority level from Normal by using the command prompt to start an application or, by using the Task Manager for an open application. You can set four separate priority levels by using the following command lines:

- Low (4):

```
Start /low executable.exe
```

- Normal (8):

```
Start /normal executable.exe
```

- High (13):

```
Start /high executable.exe
```

- Realtime (24):

```
Start/realtime executable.exe
```

After an application is running, you can use the Task Manager to change the base priority by following these steps:

1. Right-click the Taskbar and choose Task Manager.
2. Select the Process tab to view all running processes.
3. Right-click a given process in the Process list.

4. Select Set Priority, then click the desired priority (see Figure 4.36).

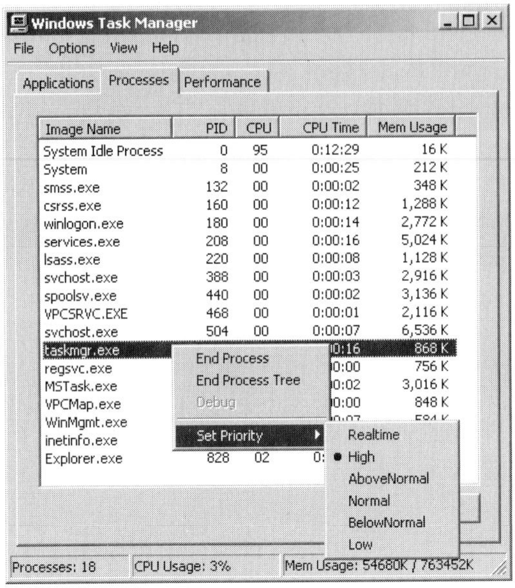

Figure 4.36 *Changing the Priority level.*

By default, the foreground application is given a priority boost of two levels over background applications. For example, a normally prioritized application would be raised from eight to 10. If you want to change that level, follow these steps:

1. Launch the System application in the Control Panel program group.
2. Open the Performance Options dialog box from the Advanced tab (see Figure 4.34).
3. Select one of two radio buttons in the Performance Options dialog box to raise the priority level of the foreground application over background applications.

TROUBLESHOOTING APPLICATION PERFORMANCE

In addition to permitting you to set priorities for applications, Task Manger can also be used to kill processes that have gone awry. Simply switch to the Processes tab, click on the errant process, and click the End Process button. Fortunately, Task Manager does not let you end a process that is critical to Windows 2000 operations.

Study Break

Optimize the Disk Drive

> Practice what you have learned by using System Monitor and Disk Defragmenter to baseline and optimize your hard drive. First, run System Monitor to create a baseline of hard drive performance during normal operations. Next, run Disk Defragmenter to organize file data. Baseline the disk drive again thereafter. Compare the performance of disk operations afterward with their previous performance. Be aware of the fact that this process can take a long time and cannot occur while other applications are making calls to the disk drive, so do this when your computer is not in demand.

MCSE 4.5   Managing Hardware Profiles

Most settings for hardware and software are configured dynamically and automatically in Windows 2000 Professional. However, it is sometimes necessary to manually add, delete, or modify configuration settings. Generally, the Control Panel program group is used for this. Should you want to keep a record of a specific hardware configuration, however, you may want to create a hardware profile for it.

A hardware profile is a record of a specific configuration of hardware in the computer. For instance, a mobile user's computer has one configuration when it is on the road. When the user plugs the portable computer into a docking station in the office that includes a CD-ROM drive or a monitor, however, another hardware configuration comes into play.

When you need to establish several hardware configurations for a single computer, Windows 2000 uses hardware profiles to determine which drivers to load when the system hardware changes. Windows 2000 automatically creates one profile for a portable computer in a docking station and a second profile for it when it is standalone. Windows 2000 detects the status of the computer during startup and configures itself accordingly.

Creating Hardware Profiles

You can create and modify hardware profiles (other than the one you have currently booted from) through the System Control Panel application. Switch to the Hardware tab and click the Hardware Profiles button. In the

Hardware Profiles dialog box, all existing profiles are listed, as shown in Figure 4.37.

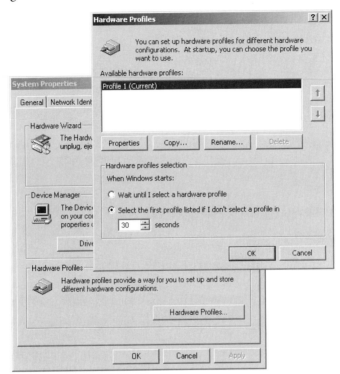

Figure 4.37 *Selecting hardware profiles.*

To create a new profile, select the current configuration and press the Copy button to rename it. Next, reboot the computer. When you restart the computer, Windows 2000 prompts you to select which hardware profile to load.

To configure a new profile, open the System Control Panel application, switch to the Hardware tab, and click the Device Manager button to view all installed hardware devices, as shown in Figure 4.38.

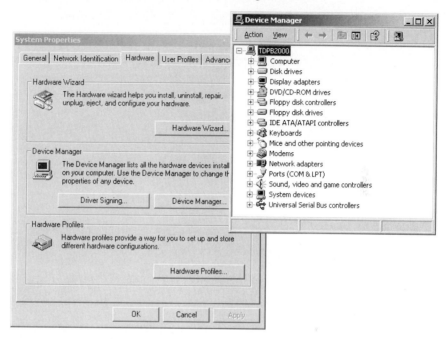

Figure 4.38   *Viewing devices in hardware profile.*

Select a device that you want to disable or remove from this profile and press the Properties button to open the Properties dialog box, as shown in Figure 4.39.

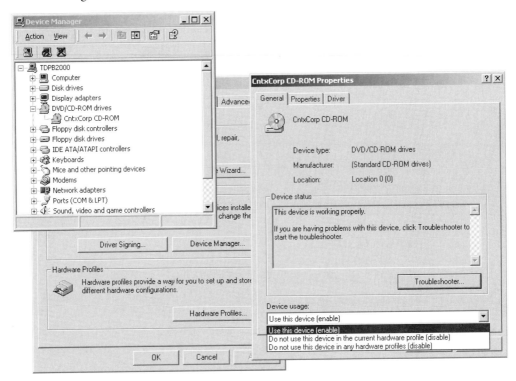

Figure 4.39 *Disabling a hardware device.*

Under the General tab of the device Properties dialog box are the following Device usage options:

- **Use this device.** This option enables the use of the hardware.
- **Do not use this device in the current hardware profile.** This option prevents the drivers for the given device from being loaded during startup for this hardware profile only.
- **Do not use this device in any hardware profiles.** This option prevents the drivers for the given device from being loaded during startup for any hardware profile you choose.

You should use hardware profiles only to indicate different hardware configurations. Identical profiles serve no purpose, and it slows the startup process because you have to select a profile to load.

Create a Hardware Profile

Practice what you have learned by creating a new hardware profile. First, select the current configuration in the System Control Panel application and press the Copy button to duplicate it. Rename this second hardware profile, then reboot the computer. When Windows 2000 prompts you to select a hardware profile to load, select the new hardware profile. Configure the new profile through the System Control Panel application's Device Manager window by adding or removing a hardware device. To verify your work, reboot the computer and switch back and forth between the hardware profiles, noting the differences.

MCSE 4.6   Recovering System State and User Data

In this section, we describe how you can create backups to protect your important data, as well as how to return your workstation to its previously reliable state after hardware or software malfunctions.

Using Backup

Learning to use the Backup application is one of the most important things a user of a Windows 2000-based computer can do. This is made easy by the Backup Wizard, as shown in Figure 4.40.

The wizard walks you through the configuration process. You can access Backup from the System Tools program group.

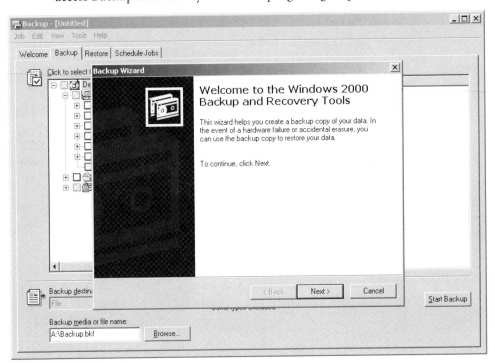

Figure 4.40 *Launching the Backup utility and Wizard.*

Your first decision is to back up an entire hard drive, just selected files and folders, or just system state data, as shown in Figure 4.41. Whenever possible, it is best to stick with the default and backup everything. This ensures that in the event of a complete hard drive failure, you can restore operating system files, applications, and documents and get back to work fast. If your operating system remains static after you have created a complete backup, you can use the Backup selected files, drives, or network data option to update it with just the new documents that you have created. Finally, you can choose to back up system data only, a wise thing to do before installing new hardware or system-level software. This options backs up boot files, COM+ Class Registration Database, and the Registry.

(You can also create an Emergency Repair Disk, as described in Chapter 3, "Managing Windows 2000 Professional.")

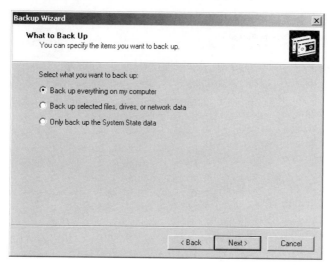

Figure 4.41 *Choosing what to back up.*

If you choose to back up selected files, you are asked to tell the wizard which ones, as shown in Figure 4.42.

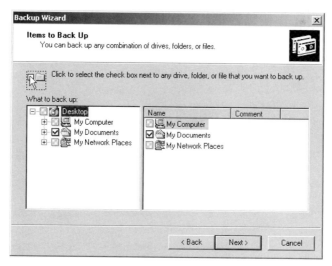

Figure 4.42 *Selecting folders to backup.*

Files can reside locally or on network shares. Be forewarned, however, that backing up data from network shares is often prohibitively slow.

Next, you must tell the utility where the backed up files will go, as shown in Figure 4.43.

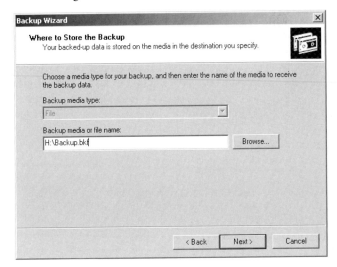

Figure 4.43 *Choosing a backup destination.*

You may choose to backup to a local disk (somewhat defeating the purpose), a network share, or most appropriately, removable media. Backup supports the following devices and media types:

- DAT
- DLT
- DC 6000
- TR1, 2, 3, and 4
- 8mm
- QIC 80, 3010, and 3020
- QIC 80-Wide, 3010-Wide, and 3020-Wide
- Other removable media (floppy disks, Iomega, SyQuest, read/write CD-ROM)

Backup jobs are created as .bkf files.

Next, you are presented with a completion window and its settings summary, as shown in Figure 4.44.

Figure 4.44 *Wizard completion window.*

You might be far from ready for backing up, however. Many important settings, such as the type of backup shown in Figure 4.45, are only configured after you click the Advanced button.

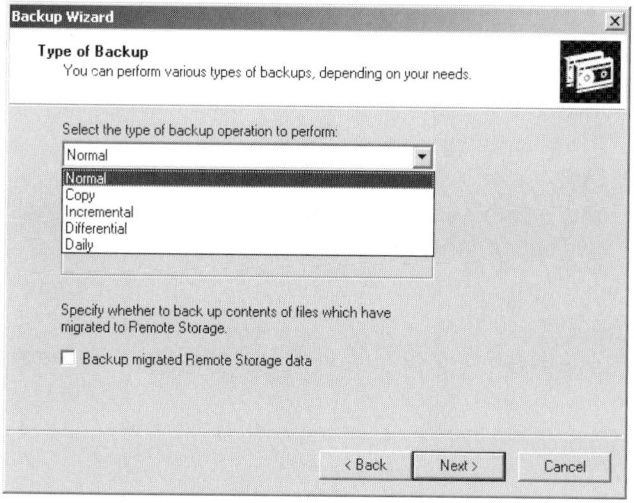

Figure 4.45 *Choosing the backup type.*

Backup supports five specific backup types:

- **Normal.** Used to back up all selected files and then reset the archive attribute off to signal that the files are part of a back up. This option, also called a full backup, backs up all files regardless of whether they have changed since the last job was run. It takes the longest amount of time, but it also makes complete recovery possible.
- **Incremental.** Used to back up only those files within a selected group of files that have the archive attribute set to on. The archive attribute on these files is reset to off thereafter. This option only backs up files that have changed since the last normal or incremental job was run. It takes less time to back up using this option. It takes more time to restore, however, as you must first restore the last normal backup and then move sequentially through each preceding incremental backup.
- **Differential.** Used to back up only those files within a selected group of files that have the archive attribute set to on. The archive attribute on these files is not reset thereafter. This option only backs up files that have changed since the last normal or incremental job was run. As with incremental backups, it takes less time to back up using this option. It takes more time to restore than full backups but less time to restore than incremental backups, because the latest differential backup contains all files that have changed since the last normal backup. You must first restore the last normal backup and then the last differential backup.
- **Copy.** Used to back up all selected files without resetting the archive attribute. This option permits you to run selective backups that do not affect the normal or incremental routines you have set up. You might use this option to copy a few files to portable media before going on a trip, for example.
- **Daily.** Used to back up files that have the archive attribute set to on and which were modified on the day of the backup. The archive attribute on these files is not reset thereafter.

In addition, you may choose to backup remote storage. Remote storage is a Windows 2000 options that archives seldom used files on a network share, from which they can be retrieved when users require them.

After choosing the type of backup, you may choose the way in which it will be performed, as shown in Figure 4.46.

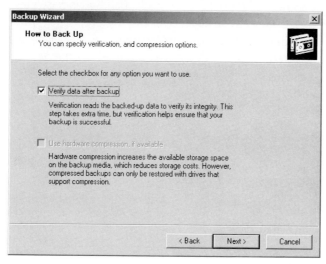

Figure 4.46 *Choosing verification and compression.*

It is a good idea to enable the Verify data after backup option checkbox. Verification makes the back up process take longer, but it is also the only way you can be assured that the files you backed up and really be restored. If your backup device supports it, you can also enable hardware compression, which provides more space on backup media.

Next, you are prompted to either let Backup append the job to existing jobs already on the media, or replace any previous jobs (see Figure 4.47).

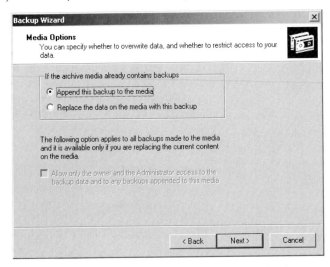

Figure 4.47 *Appending or replacing previous backups.*

Initially, it is wise to backup up an entire hard drive. Thereafter, you can append selective backups for only changed data. Only use the replace option when you wish to reclaim media from backups that are too old to be useful.

Next, you are prompted to label the backup job and its associated media, as shown in Figure 4.48.

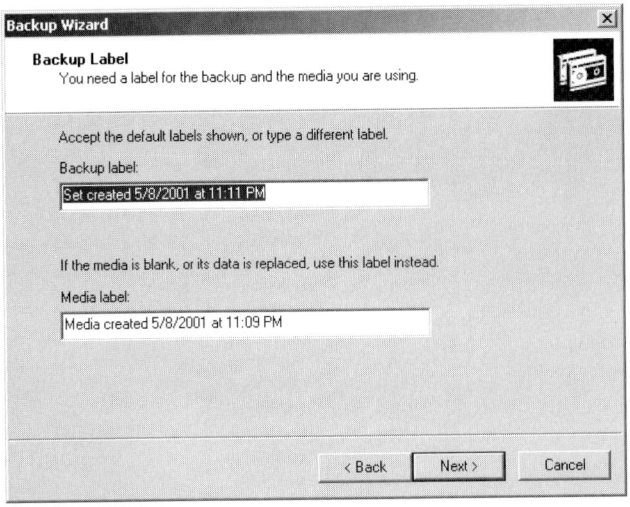

Figure 4.48 *Labeling the backup.*

Next, you may determine when the job will be run. Choose the Now radio button to begin after the wizard is completed. Choose the Later radio button to set a time in the future, or recurring intervals. You are prompted to provide logon information for an account that has appropriate permissions to run the job in the future, as shown in Figure 4.49.

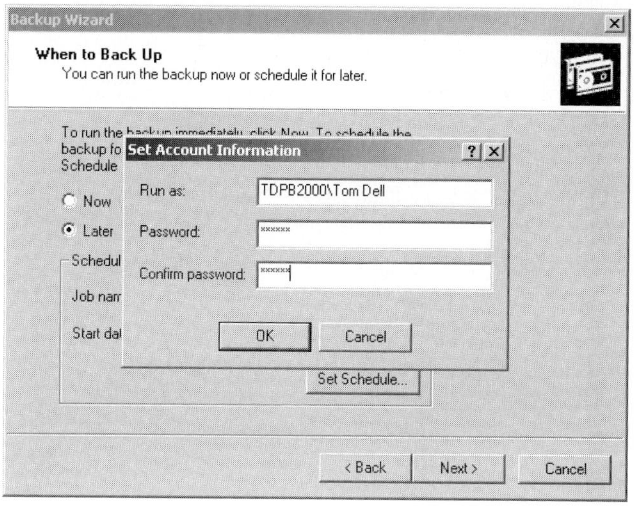

Figure 4.49   *Choosing when to back up.*

You can only back up those files that you own, or those files for which you have Read, Read and Execute, Modify, or Full Control permissions. If you are a member of the Administrators or Backup Operators groups, however, you can back up everything.

If you chose to run the job later, you may set the timing options by clicking the Set Schedule button, as shown in Figure 4.50.

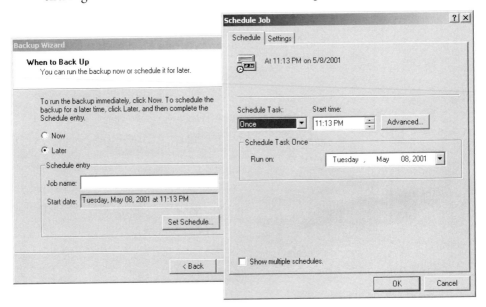

Figure 4.50 *Scheduling times.*

You may choose the run the job once, at system startup, at logon, when idle, weekly, or monthly in the Schedule task drop-down menu. Choose a start time and start date. If you wish to make the schedule recurring, click the Advanced button to select both start and end dates and choose an interval and duration for repeating the job (e.g., every 12 hours between June 1 and June 30 until 8 a.m.). Click the Show multiple schedules checkbox to add a drop-down menu to the dialog box in which you can create additional schedules that can be applied to the same job.

Switch to the Settings tab to tell Backup when the job should not run, as shown in Figure 4.51.

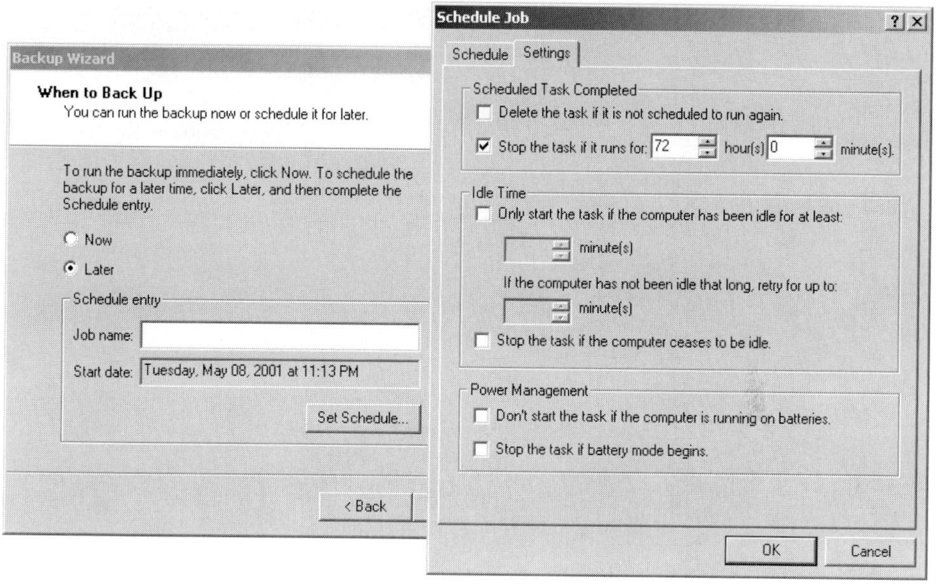

Figure 4.51   *Setting restrictions.*

Limit the backup job to idle times or when not running on batteries. You can also set a time to stop the job when no such restriction has been set up elsewhere.

After setting up the advanced options, you are returned to the backup wizard's completion window (see Figure 4.44).

The backup job then runs immediately after you click the Finish button, or at the future time you established, as shown in Figure 4.52.

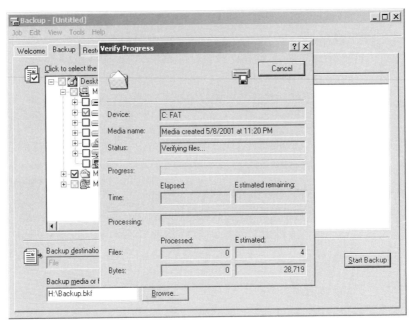

Figure 4.52 *Running the backup job.*

BACKUP STRATEGIES

The backup strategy you employ are chosen because of a number of different factors. Two of the foremost considerations are how long the backup takes to perform and how much data can be stored on the removable media drive. Three common strategies involve daily normal backups, weekly normal backups with daily differential backups, and weekly normal backups with daily incremental backups.

DAILY FULL BACKUPS • Unless the data on your workstation is of little value or can be recreated easily, it should be backed up no less than once a day. The easiest way to do this is to perform a normal backup daily. This works best when the data on your workstation can be accommodated by the storage capacity of your backup device, such as a DAT drive, and completed within an acceptable period of time, such as overnight. Under this scenario, the backup is usually contained on a single tape that can be restored in a single step.

On larger backups, other strategies are used to address the fact that additional backup storage capacity is needed or shorter backup times are required.

WEEKLY FULL/DAILY DIFFERENTIAL BACKUPS • When using another backup strategy, a normal backup is created once a week. Because this takes the longest, it is often performed on a Friday so that the backup can run over the weekend, if necessary. On other days of the week, differential backups are performed. As this process backs up only those files that have changed since the normal backup was run, it requires less storage space and takes less time. Under this scenario, the backup must be restored first from the normal backup and then from the differential backup.

WEEKLY FULL/DAILY INCREMENTAL BACKUPS. • Under yet another backup strategy, a normal backup is created once a week. On other days of the week, incremental backups are performed. Under this scenario, the backup must be restored first from the normal backup and then from each incremental backup.

RESTORING BACKUPS

To restore data from a backup, you essentially reverse the backup process using the Restore Wizard. You can choose to restore the entire backup, or select files and folder within the job. Next, you may choose to restore data it its original location. You may also restore to an alternate location, such as a folder or volume you specify, while maintaining the backup's hierarchical folder structure. Finally, you may restore to a single folder without regard to the original folder structure (e.g., all files in one place).

If you choose to restore files to the original location and some of these files already exist, you can specify whether Backup replaces all of these files or only those that are older than the copies in the backup. Other options let you choose to restore folder permission settings, the removable storage database, and hard disk/data junction points.

If you backup an NTFS volume, be sure to restore to an NTFS volume. Otherwise, you may lose permissions and disk quota settings. You might also lose data if, for example, you try to restore encrypted files (which are not supported under FAT).

You can only restore those files for which you have Write, Modify, or Full Control permissions, unless you are a member of the Administrators or Backup Operators groups, in which case you can restore any files.

RESTORING FROM THE EMERGENCY REPAIR DISK • When you use the Emergency Repair Disk to repair a damaged Windows 2000 Professional workstation, the procedure essentially reinstalls the sections of the operating system that are required for your particular setup. The data that you copied to the Emergency Repair Disk from the Registry determines which files need to be replaced, and how the configuration should be reestablished. The Emergency Repair Disk handles many tasks, including running CHKDSK to determine the validity of the partition containing the system files, and replacing the SAM hives.

You should have your Windows 2000 Professional Setup floppy disks with you whenever you attempt to restore your system. You need to boot from these, then provide the Emergency Repair Disk when prompted to either install or repair Windows 2000. You have four main repair options in the recovery process:

- **Inspect Registry files:** This option can use the Emergency Repair Disk to repair corrupt portions of the Registry. You can repair any combination of the Default, Security/SAM, Software, and/or System hives.
- **Inspect Startup environment:** This option can inspect boot files. If necessary, a boot file will be rejected. Any Emergency Repair Disk can be used to replace startup files.
- **Verify Windows 2000 system files:** This option compares any system file in the Windows 2000 directory and subdirectories and verifies them against the checksum values in the setup.log file. You need the installation CD-ROM to replace these files.
- **Inspect boot sector:** This option uses an Emergency Repair Disk and installation CD-ROM to repair the boot sector if it becomes invalid.

Using Safe Mode

When problems occur that interfere with Windows 2000 operations or startup, you can troubleshoot after starting the computer in "safe mode." Safe mode launches only the necessary drivers and services, such as the Event Log, mouse, keyboard, standard VGA, CD-ROM and disk controllers. You can then troubleshoot the network configuration, protected mode disk drivers, video drivers, and third-party virtual device drivers. Try disabling or removing suspect drivers or services. Restart the computer in Normal mode when you have located and resolved the problem.

To engage safe mode, press the F8 key when Windows 2000 starts up to open the Advanced Options menu, as shown in Figure 4.53.

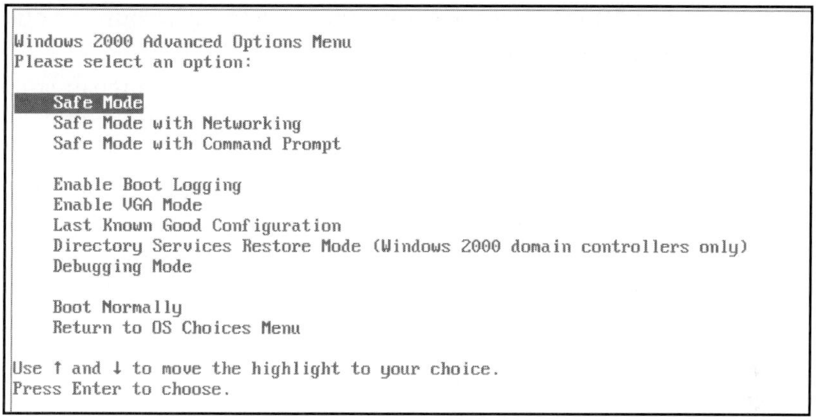

```
Windows 2000 Advanced Options Menu
Please select an option:

    Safe Mode
    Safe Mode with Networking
    Safe Mode with Command Prompt

    Enable Boot Logging
    Enable VGA Mode
    Last Known Good Configuration
    Directory Services Restore Mode (Windows 2000 domain controllers only)
    Debugging Mode

    Boot Normally
    Return to OS Choices Menu

Use ↑ and ↓ to move the highlight to your choice.
Press Enter to choose.
```

Figure 4.53 *Choosing to Boot in safe mode.*

You are given the option of booting up in safe mode with or without network support, or from the command prompt only.

LAST KNOWN GOOD RECOVERY • In case of an error in the boot process, the Last Known Good Control Set allows you to revert to your last system setup. To boot to the Last Known Good Control Set, press the F8 key when Windows 2000 starts up to open the Advanced Options menu, then select the Last Known Good Configuration option.

Windows 2000 automatically defaults to the Last Known Good Configuration when it finds a serious system error. However, if basic operating files are damaged, you must reboot using a boot floppy disk or the Windows 2000 Professional installation CD-ROM and recover the system.

Using the Recovery Console

A powerful Administrator-level tool that can also help you restore the state of a system that does not boot normally is the Recovery Console. This command-line utility bypasses the Windows 2000 Command prompt and lets you access your FAT, FAT32, or NTFS volumes directly. It can be run after booting the system from the Windows 2000 Professional installation CD-ROM or setup diskettes. Alternately, you can install it on the hard drive by running the following command from the installation CD-ROM's \i386 directory:

```
Winnt32.exe /cmdcons
```

Recovery Console gives you access to the following commands:

- **ATTRIB.** Sets the attributes of files.
- **BATCH.** Runs one or more commands from a text file.
- **CD.** Changes directory.
- **CHKDSK.** Runs Check Disk to verify and repair volumes.
- **CLS.** Clears the screen.
- **COPY.** Copies files. Wildcard characters (e.g., "*.*") cannot be used. As a security precaution, you cannot copy files to floppy disks. You can copy files from other media.
- **DELETE.** Deletes files. Wildcard characters cannot be used.
- **DIR.** Views files and subdirectories.
- **DISABLE.** Disables a service or driver.
- **DISKPART.** Adds or deletes partitions.
- **ENABLE.** Enables a service or driver.
- **EXIT.** Closes Recovery Console and reboots.
- **EXPAND.** Expands cabinet (.cab) files. Wildcard characters cannot be used.
- **FIXBOOT.** Rewrites the boot sector.
- **FIXMBR.** Rewrites the Master Boot Record (MBR).
- **FORMAT.** Formats a disk as FAT, FAT32, or NTFS.
- **HELP.** Displays Recovery Console commands.
- **LISTSRV.** Lists services.
- **LOGON.** Displays all available Windows NT/2000 installations that you may log on to and prompts you for the Administrator password. Three failed attempts exits Recovery Console and reboots. This security protects the system from unauthorized intrusion.
- **MAP.** Displays information on logical drives.
- **MKDIR.** Makes a directory.
- **TYPE.** Displays contents of a text file.
- **RMDIR.** Removes a directory. Wildcard characters cannot be used.
- **RENAME.** Renames a directory. Wildcard characters cannot be used.
- **SET.** Displays and lets you modify Recover Console settings.
- **SYSTEMROOT.** Changes directory to that of the system (e.g., \WINNT).

Recovery Console is particularly handy for restoring the Registry. By backing up the System State using Backup, you copy the Registry into the \WINNT\REPAIR\REGBACK directory. Should the Registry become corrupted, you can use the Recovery Console to replace it with the good back up copy.

STARTUP AND RECOVERY OPTIONS • You can establish several Windows 2000 startup behaviors through the System Control Panel application. Switch to the Advanced tab and click the Startup and Recovery button. In the Startup and Recovery dialog box are listed all bootable operating systems from which you may choose from, as shown in Figure 4.54.

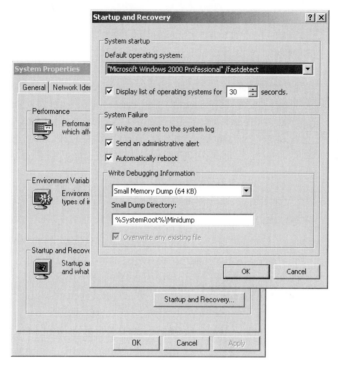

Figure 4.54 *Selecting startup and recovery behaviors.*

Select the operating system that you wish boot from by default, and set the amount of time that elapses before the Boot Loader menu is closed.

You can also specify what Windows 2000 Professional should do in the event of a "system error" — an event that cause all processes to stop — in other words, the dreaded "blue screen of death." You can opt to have Windows 2000 note the event in the System log, inform an Administrator, and reboot. Further, you can collect debugging information that might help pinpoint the cause of the problem later. You may choose a Small Memory Dump, creating a 6 kB file; a Kernel Memory Dump, creating a 50-800 MB file (depending on RAM); and a Complete Memory Dump, creating a file that is equal to the size of the system's RAM plus 1 MB.

Perform a Milestone Backup

> Practice what you have learned by configuring Backup. Prior to and after installing any significant hardware or software, it is wise to perform a milestone backup. The point of this procedure is to take a recoverable "snapshot" of the computer's condition immediately before a change, or before an installation has been affected by future events and alterations. For example, if you create a milestone backup that records the state of the computer just after the installation of Windows 2000 Professional, you will have preserved the state of the computer at a time before alterations and reconfigurations have been made. Should some of these alterations later prove problematic, you can always revert using the backup. In this case, select all files when you run Backup. Also enable verification, to be sure the data is sound, and that a backup report can be referred to as necessary in the future.

■ Summary

In this chapter, we considered various Windows 2000 Professional optimization topics including improving processor, memory, disk, network, and application performance. We also described maintenance tasks such as using driver signing, Task Scheduler, offline files, and restoring system state and user data.

Working with Driver Signing

Microsoft digitally signs all drivers included with Windows 2000 Professional so that you can be assured that they have passed WHQL testing for compatibility and reliability. By configuring signature checking, you can specify that Windows 2000 Professional accept drivers that are not signed, alert you when you attempt to install an unsigned driver, or prohibit the installation of unsigned drivers. Drivers can be checked for digital signing using the File Signature Verification tool or System File Checker utilities.

Working with Task Scheduler

Task Scheduler lets you schedule other programs, such as Disk Cleanup, to run at specific times or recurring intervals. The tasks you specify can be managed from the Scheduled Tasks window. Tasks can be saved as ".job" files and distributed to other Windows 2000 computers.

Offline File Synchronization

Windows 2000 Professional lets you store copies of files that reside on network volumes locally, making them available when your computer is offline or moved to a new location. Offline files can be synchronized automatically or manually through the Offline Files Folder, which is similar to the Briefcase. Web pages can also be synchronized.

Optimizing the Desktop

Optimal performance is achieved when your workstation's hardware and software are operating at the best of their capabilities. Optimization is the process of measuring and analyzing the resource demands of a given task to see if there is anything that can be done to make it faster. This involves creating baselines, monitoring activity, finding bottlenecks, optimizing processor, disk drive, memory, network, and application resources, and upgrading components where necessary.

The System Monitor application lets you establish a wide range of statistical measurements for most hardware and software components. These components are referred to as objects, and their measurements as counters. Data can be viewed in charts, histograms, reports, or logs. Data can also be used to trigger alerts and subsequent reactions. System Monitor is a vital tool in baselining and troubleshooting.

Bottlenecks are those components in systems that slow the performance of other components. Among the things you can do to alleviate memory bottlenecks are increase the amount of physical RAM, use faster RAM, upgrade the cache, disable ROM BIOS shadowing, remove unnecessary programs, and optimize Virtual Memory. To alleviate a processor bottleneck, you can redistribute the workload, upgrade to a faster processor, upgrade the cache, or employ multiple processors. To alleviate bottlenecks in disk access, you can allow more free space, install more RAM, use faster drives, use faster controllers, use NTFS over FAT or FAT32, employ multiple disk drives, use striping, and run Disk Defragmenter. Network bottlenecks can be overcome by using faster NICs, installing a faster network, segmenting the network, and turning off unused protocols. Task Manager can be used to overcome some application performance issues by permitting you to change process priorities.

Managing Hardware Profiles

A hardware profile is a record of a specific configuration of hardware in the computer. When you need to establish several hardware configurations for a single computer, Windows 2000 uses hardware profiles to determine which drivers to load when the system hardware changes. You can create and modify hardware profiles through the System Control Panel application.

Recovering System State and Data

You may use the Backup utility to back up and restore all hard drive data, selected files and folders, and/or System State data. Backup's Normal option backs up all files regardless of whether or not they have changed since the last job was run. The Incremental option backs up files that have changed since the last normal or incremental job was run. The Differential option backs up files that have changed since the last normal or incremental job was run, but contains all files that have changed since the last normal backup. The Copy option permits you to run selective backups that do not affect the normal or incremental routines you have set up. The Daily lets you back up files that were modified on the day of the backup.

When problems occur that interfere with Windows 2000 operations or startup, you can troubleshoot after starting the computer in "safe mode." Safe mode launches only the necessary drivers and services, such as the Event Log, mouse, keyboard, standard VGA, CD-ROM and disk controllers.

If Safe Mode does not work, you can use the Recovery Console command-line utility to bypass the Windows 2000 Command prompt and access your disk volumes directly.

You can establish several Windows 2000 startup behaviors, such as default boot operating system and memory dumps, through the System Control Panel application's Startup and Recovery dialog box.

▲ CHAPTER REVIEW QUESTIONS

Here are a few questions relating to the material covered in the *Monitoring and Optimizing System Performance and Reliability* section of Microsoft's *Installing, Configuring, and Administering Microsoft Windows 2000 Professional* exam (70-210).

1. *Unfortunately, you only know that a system file is corrupted if your system crashes, and then it is difficult to determine which one.*

   A. True

   B. False

2. *Which of the following are valid driver signing options? Select all that apply:*

    A. Ignore

    B. Disable

    C. Warn

    D. Block

3. *Tasks you schedule are only run during idle times.*

    A. True

    B. False

4. *Which of the following are intervals at which tasks may be scheduled? Select all that apply:*

    A. Once only

    B. Daily

    C. Monthly

    D. At shutdown

5. *Which of the following are displayed in the Offline Files Folder window? Select all that apply:*

    A. Synchronization status

    B. Availability

    C. Location

    D. Server status

6. *Synchronization Manager can be used to configure folders for shared folder for offline access and to synchronize files with remote shares.*

    A. True

    B. False

7. *Which of the following are vital components in desktop performance optimization? Select all that apply:*

    A. Processor

    B. Memory

    C. Power

    D. Applications

8. *Paged memory is faster than nonpaged memory.*

    A. True

    B. False

9. *When should you be concerned about the amount of usable physical memory displayed by the Available Bytes counter? Select only one:*

   A. When it exceeds 4 MBs.

   B. When it falls below 4 MBs.

   C. When it exceeds the amount of Virtual Memory.

   D. When it falls below the amount of Virtual Memory.

10. *The processor is likely a bottleneck when the Percent Privileged Time counter exceeds 50 percent.*

    A. True

    B. False

11. *Multiprocessing is supported under Windows 2000 Professional.*

    A. True

    B. False

12. *Disk Performance counters are not enabled by default under Windows 2000 Professional.*

    A. True

    B. False

13. *A disk drive should spend about 50 percent of its time and reading and writing data, as indicated by the Percent Disk Time counter.*

    A. True

    B. False

14. *It is unnecessary to turn off unused protocols to save on network overhead, because by definition, they are unused.*

    A. True

    B. False

15. *When troubleshooting network performance in terms of the OSI model, one should start at the top layer and work down.*

    A. True

    B. False

16. *How many processor priority levels does Windows 2000 professional assign? Select only one:*

   A. 2

   B. 4

   C. 8

   D. 32

17. *Task Manager cannot be used to end a process, but it can be used to change its priority to relatively infrequent.*

   A. True

   B. False

18. *Hardware profiles can be used to exclude certain hardware components.*

   A. True

   B. False

19. *You should use hardware profiles only to indicate different hardware configurations.*

   A. True

   B. False

20. *Which of the following utilities are useful in recovering user data and System State? Select all that apply:*

   A. File Signature Verification

   B. Recovery Console

   C. Backup

   D. Safe Mode

21. *You can only back up all files on a hard disk that you have ownership permissions for.*

   A. True

   B. False

22. *Both back up and restorations jobs involving Normal backups take the longest to perform.*

   A. True

   B. False

23. *You must be an Administrator to access a desktop via Safe Mode.*

   A. True

   B. False

24. *There is no networking support for Safe Mode.*
   A. True
   B. False

25. *The Recovery Console can compromise system security by permitting its user to copy files from the hard drive via the command line.*
   A. True
   B. False

26. *Recovery Console is particularly useful in restring the Registry.*
   A. True
   B. False

Configuring Windows 2000 Professional Environments

▲ Chapter Syllabus

MCSE 5.1   Working with User Profiles

MCSE 5.2   Supporting Multiple Languages and Locations

MCSE 5.3   Working with Windows Installer Packages

MCSE 5.4   Working with Desktop Settings

MCSE 5.5   Working with Fax Support

MCSE 5.6   Working with Accessibility Services

In this chapter, we will look at material covered in the *Configuring and Troubleshooting the Desktop Environment* section of Microsoft's *Installing, Configuring, and Administering Microsoft Windows 2000 Professional* exam (70-210).

In the following pages you will learn to configure and manage user profiles, multiple languages, multiple locations, desktop settings, fax support, and accessibility services. You will also work with Windows Installer packages.

Working with User Profiles

Windows 2000 Professional automatically creates a user profile when a user logs on. The user profile controls the settings for the user's local environment, such as wallpaper, screen saver, and desktop shortcuts. You can access the user profile in the System Properties dialog box, as shown in Figure 5.1.

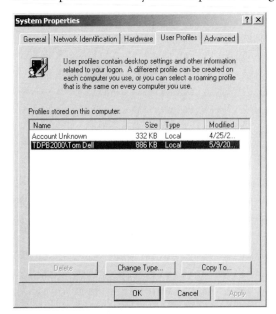

Figure 5.1 *User Profiles in the System control panel.*

A user profile exists mainly for convenience, but an administrator can use it to control a user's local environment. The user profile can be stored either locally on the user's workstation or on the server so that it can be accessed from anywhere on the network.

Information stored in the user profile includes:

- **Accessories.** User-selected add-on applications, such as Accessibility tools, Calculator, Address Book, and Notepad.
- **Control Panel.** User-defined settings defined within the Control Panel program group, including icons, display and cursor properties, and email and fax properties.
- **Printers.** Workstation-to-network-printer connections.
- **Start menu.** Personal program groups and their properties, including the Documents folder.
- **Taskbar**. Properties associated with the Taskbar (but for some reason, not its icons).

- **Windows Explorer.** User-specific settings for Windows Explorer, such as whether to view the Toolbar, show large or small icons, which icons to show, and how the icons are arranged.

By default, user profiles are created on the local machine when users log onto a computer running Windows 2000 Professional. Users have folders bearing their user names and containing their profiles in the Documents and Settings folder of the Windows 2000 system volume, as shown in Figure 5.2.

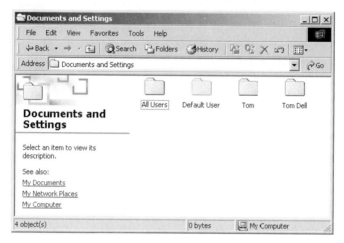

Figure 5.2   *Documents and Settings folder.*

Windows 2000 copies information from the Default User profile into the new folder and combines the settings from the All Users folder to create the initial profile. Any changes users make to their immediate environments, such as rearranging the Desktop icons or changing the wallpaper, are saved to their profiles when they log off. The next time they log on, Windows pulls the settings and shortcuts from their folders and the Desktop appears just as they left it, regardless of how many other users have logged on and moved things around immediately before.

Among the subfolders that exist within users' folders are the following:

- **Application Data.** This hidden folder contains data pertaining to applications. The contents of the folder vary depending by application.
- **Desktop.** This folder contains the Desktop items, including shortcuts and any folders or files that are stored on the Desktop.
- **Favorites.** This folder contains links to the user's favorite locations, such as URLs on the Internet.

- **NetHood.** This hidden folder contains shortcuts to My Network Places items.
- **My Documents.** This folder contains the items users store in the My Documents folder.
- **PrintHood**. This hidden folder contains shortcuts to printers.
- **Recent.** This hidden folder contains shortcuts to items used recently.
- **SendTo.** This hidden folder contains shortcuts to items in the SendTo menu. Items such as a printer or Calculator can be added to this folder.
- **Start Menu.** Includes shortcuts to the programs in the Start menu.
- **Templates.** This hidden folder contains shortcuts to template files.

The Desktop, My Documents, Favorites, and Start Menu folders are visible by default, but the others are displayed only if you enable the Show All Files option in the Folder Options dialog box, as shown in Figure 5.3.

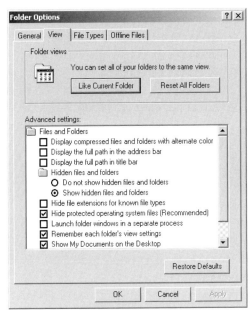

Figure 5.3 *Choosing to view hidden files and folders.*

The All Users folder contains all the Start menu shortcuts and program groups that apply to all users of the workstation. These settings are not added to a user profile because they are the property of the workstation rather than the users. Only an administrator can add or delete items from the All Users folder.

The Default User folder contains settings that new users inherit when they log on to the workstation. If the user has no preconfigured profile, the settings from the Default User folder are simply copied into his new profile folder. Any changes he makes while logged on are then saved in his user profile, leaving the Default User folder unchanged.

The idea here is permit users to customize the look and feel of their desktops without coming into conflict with the tastes and needs of other users working on the same machine. Of course, it is still the same machine, so should one user go in and delete data from another's user profile folder, there is still plenty of conflict to go around.

There are three types of user profiles:

LOCAL USER PROFILES • A local user profile is the default of Windows 2000. The first time a user logs onto a workstation, a local user profile is created and stored there. A local user profile is most effective if the user needs to change the settings of only the one computer.

MANDATORY USER PROFILES • Mandatory user profiles increase the administrator's control over users' environments. When a mandatory user profile is in place, the user can still make changes to the environment — such as screen saver or wallpaper — but when the user logs off, the changes are not saved.

ROAMING USER PROFILES • Users who jump or *roam* from workstation to workstation on the network are confronted with a different environment on each computer unless they have a roaming user profile. Roaming profiles are created only by the administrator and are stored on the server. Roaming profiles work only with Windows NT/2000. If the user makes a change to his roaming profile, those changes are stored on the server as well.

The administrator can choose to create a roaming mandatory profile, which can affect multiple users but only be modified by the administrator.

Configuring User Accounts

As an administrator, you can create a new user account — and subsequently a new user profile — through the Users and Passwords Control Panel application, as shown in Figure 5.4.

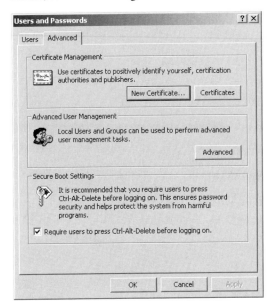

Figure 5.4 *The Users and Passwords Control Panel application.*

Switch to the Advanced tab and click the Advanced button to open the Local Users Manager snap-in to the MMC, as shown in Figure 5.5. Do not be alarmed to see accounts present here that you did not previously set up. Windows 2000 Professional creates several accounts on its own. One account you will recognize as yours, the Administrator-level account you used when installing Windows 2000. Also familiar should be the actual Administrator account, the password for which you set during setup. The Guest account, which has no associated password, is designed to give unknown, anonymous users access to your computer. If you just felt the hair rise on the back of your neck, relax. Windows 2000 only grants the Guest account limited rights, and disables it by default.

If you installed IIS, two accounts that serve similar functions are present as well: IUSR and IWAM.

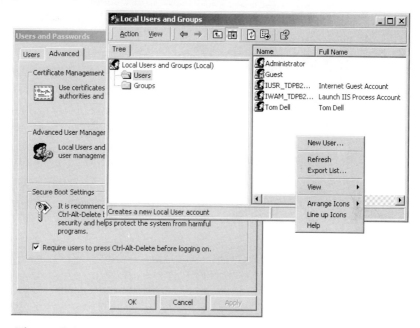

Figure 5.5   *Opening Local Users Manager.*

Next, select the Users branch in the left windowpane, right-click the right windowpane, and choose the New User command from the context menu.

This opens the New User dialog box, as shown in Figure 5.6.

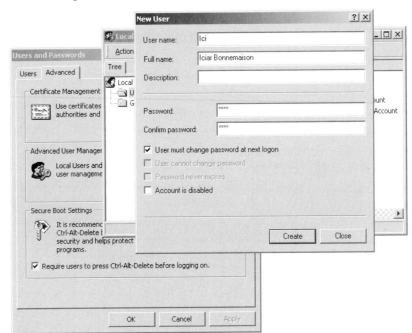

Figure 5.6 *Entering New User information.*

The two most important fields here are for User name and Password. The username is the user's identifier. It is not case sensitive and can be as long as 20 characters. It cannot include the following characters:

```
? " / : \ ; [ , ] + | = * < - >
```

The password is the heart of workstation security. It is case sensitive and can be as long as 127 characters. The password field can also be left blank, but this is not recommended as it defeats the purpose of having account security. An exception might be when the Users Must Change Password at Next Logon checkbox is selected (as it is by default). In this case, users must create their own passwords when they first log on with a username.

Other configuration options include the following:

- **Full name**. If you have used a simple name in the User name field (e.g., "Tom"), it might be helpful to have a user's complete name here (e.g., "Thomas R. Dell"). You can type anything you want into this field, however.

- **Description**. You can type whatever you want into this field. Useful information might be users' departments (e.g., "Accounting"), telephone extensions (e.g., x212), locations (e.g., Building 2, Room 222), or computer type (e.g., Celeron/Windows 2000).
- **User cannot change password**. This checkbox restricts password creation to administrators. This is useful for shared accounts and the Guest account.
- **Password never expires**. As a rule, it is a good idea to make passwords expire after a given time. However, you might wish to make some accounts, such as the Guest account, exempt from this rule.
- **Account is disabled**. This option "turns off," but does not delete, an account. When a person leaves your organization, it is wiser to disable the user's account than delete it. That way you can assign the same rights to the person's replacement by simply changing the user name and password. This is also useful for securing the accounts of users who are on leave, vacation, sabbatical, or temporary assignment elsewhere.

If an administrator has enabled the Account Lockout option through Account Policy, you have a fifth check box:

- **Account locked out:** This check box is enabled if the user reaches the preset limit of unsuccessful logon attempts. If the Lockout duration is set at Forever, the administrator must manually disable the check box before the user can access the account again.

Click the Create button when you are finished, which records the account data but does not dismiss the dialog box.

When the new user logs in, a new user profile is created in the Documents and Settings folder.

CONFIGURING LOCAL USER PROFILES

To configure additional user profile settings, double-click the user account in Local Users Manager to open the user Properties dialog box.

As shown in Figure 5.7, you see that new tabs have been added to the dialog box you were just working with, such as the Member Of tab.

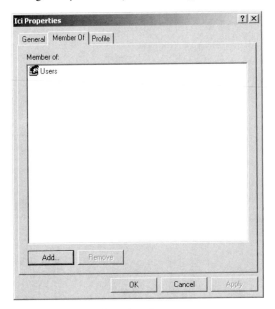

Figure 5.7 *Adding local users to groups.*

Next, click the Add button to open the Select Groups window, as shown in Figure 5.8. Select a group, then press the Add button to add a user to the group. When users become members of a group, they instantly inherit all of its rights and permissions.

If you select a member and then press the Remove button, you remove the member from the group and revoke those rights and permissions, effective with the next logon.

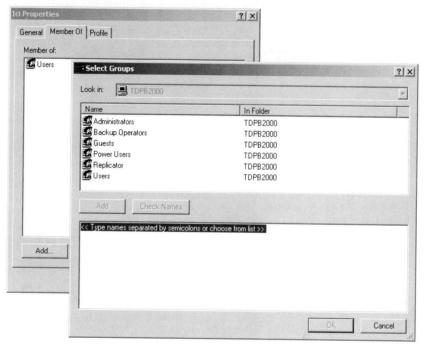

Figure 5.8 *Selecting groups for membership.*

Account *rights* define what a user can do, such as whether a user can log on locally or set the system time on the workstation. User *permissions* define where a user can do these things.

Users can be made members of the following groups:

- **Administrators**. Members of this group have complete administrative control over the computer. They can create users and can assign them to any group. They can create and manage network shares. They can gain access to any file, application, or resource on any computer on the network.
- **Power Users**. Members of this group can do many of the same things, but cannot fully administer the computer.
- **Users**. Members of this group are the default group for all new users. They have enough rights and permissions to productively operate their local computers.
- **Backup Operators**. Members of this group have sufficient access rights to all files and folders to control data backup and restoration.

- **Replicators.** Members of this group are part of the Windows 2000 service account used to perform directory replication.
- **Guests.** Members of this group occupy the bottom rung of the access ladder. The default Guest account is disabled during installation.

Next, switch to the Profiles tab, as shown in Figure 5.9.

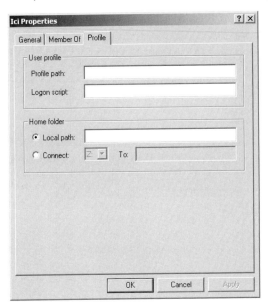

Figure 5.9 *Configuring advanced profile options.*

You may configure the following items:

- **Profile Path:** This setting specifies a path for a user profile that is centrally available on a server. It can also be used to assign a mandatory user profile. To use a roaming or mandatory user profile, create a share on a server, then specify the path to that share. The path name follows the syntax of the standard UNC (Universal Naming Convention):

```
\\servername\sharename\profile name
```

- **Logon Script:** This optional setting sets a logon script to be launched when the user logs on to the workstation. If the logon script is not in a subdirectory of the machine's logon script path, you must include the subdirectory in the logon script name. Logon scripts can have the extension .CMD, .BAT, or .EXE.

- **Home folder:** You can specify a home folder for a user's personal profile. You can configure two types of home folders: *local* and *remote*.
  A remote folder is always available to the user, regardless of where he logs on. If you choose to use a remote home folder, you must select a drive letter and specify the path to that remote share in a UNC format:

```
\\servername\users\Ici
```

A local home folder is always local to the machine that the user logs on to. If a user uses more than machine, he may not be able to access his local home folder from some computers. Local home folders should include the full path in the format:

```
C:\Documents and Settings\Ici
```

MODIFYING AND DELETING USER ACCOUNTS • Each user account created in Windows 2000 is created with its own Security Identifier (SID) that is unique to it, like a fingerprint. The SID is attached to the account itself and never changes, even if the attributes of the account are changed. Even renaming the account does not change its SID because the name is just another attribute of the account.

Deleting a user account is both permanent and irreversible. It also deletes the SID. For this reason, it is generally recommended that you simply disable the account until someone else can use it if someone has left a position that will be filled by someone else. However, if the account is for a position that is being eliminated and you are certain no one else will use it, then it is probably OK to delete it.

CONFIGURING REMOTE USER PROFILES

As an administrator, user profiles allow you to restrict users while allowing them to retain their own settings when they move from one machine to another. You can create a user profile if you have Administrator permissions by following these steps:

- Create a user account and log on as that user, thus placing a folder for that user under in the Documents and Settings folder.
- Configure the desktop environment as you desire for the new mandatory profile, then log off.

- Log back on as the Administrator and create a centralized location for storing user profiles on the server, then share that directory.
- Copy the user profile to the share.

If you want to make the profile mandatory, open the folder you made for the new user's roaming profile and rename the NTUSER.DAT file as "NTUSER.MAN." Next, open the new user's account in Local User Manager and type in the UNC path to the mandatory profile.

Remote user profiles are described in greater detail in future chapters.

Study Break

Create a User Profile

Practice what you have learned by creating a new user profile.

First, log on as Administrator and create a new user account. Next, log off and log back on as the new user. Note how the desktop may differ from that seen from your own account. Make some changes, such as saving a file to My Documents, adding a shortcut to the Desktop, or marking a Favorite URL in Internet Explorer. Log off and log back on with your own account. Navigate to the Documents and Settings folder, open the new user profile folder, and see how your changes have been stored within the folder structure.

MCSE 5.2   Supporting Multiple Languages and Locations

Many administrators find support challenging enough when their users reside in one building. The issues become more complicated when you have users in multiple locations, which might be geographically dispersed. Users still need to communicate with each other, send email, documents and so on, and they expect that their computer systems should let the do that regardless of distance and time zones. Fair enough. Windows is still Windows and English is still English. Assuming your users all speak English.

Consider the complexities that come into play when your users are spread across multiple countries. English is still English, but your users might speak French, German, Spanish, and Chinese. Windows is still Windows, but it is not the same Windows you use. Now what happens to communications?

Enter multiple language support, the goal of which is to permit humans to use their computers to communicate regardless of their native languages. In considering this issue, first be aware of the fact that computers could not care less about human language conventions. Computers care about ones and zeros, bits and bytes. To make computers accessible to people consistently, across platforms and operating systems, standards and methodologies had to be produced that mapped human language characters to the digits used by computers.

ASCII • Under the American Standard Code for Information Exchange (ASCII), characters are represented using 7 bits. This allows for the representation of 128 (2^7) characters, including punctuation, upper and lower case letters, and numbers. PCs have used this standard since their infancy (it was finalized in 1968). Each character has its own decimal code. For example, an "e" would be code "69." (Codes 0-31 are reserved for terminal control characters).

EBCDIC • Under the Extended Binary Coded Decimal Interchange Code (EBCDIC) standard, characters are represented using 8 bits. This allows for the representation of 256 (2^8) characters, such as the same upper and lower case letters, numbers, and punctuation, plus many more control characters. For example, an "e" would be code "133."

UNICODE • What if you want an "e" that is not pronounced like an "e" in English? For example, what if you speak French and want an "e" with an accent aigu, "é;" accent circumflex, "ê;" or accent grave, "è"? One could add to the EBCDIC character set to accommodate these variations, but when you take into account every character in all the known Roman languages, you would run out of decimal codes quickly. Then there are the non-Roman languages — such as Arabic, Greek, Hebrew, Japanese, Chinese, and Russian — that do not even use the same characters on which English is based. In the case of Chinese, a so-called "character" often represents a complete thought. The computer must, therefore, support not just mapping bits to characters, but mapping bits to entire words.

Despite the complexity, that is essentially what has been done, with scientists in each language field producing standards to map their own letters, numbers, and words with number codes. As with ASCII or EBCDIC in the

United States, these standards work well in their respective countries. The problem is that when a user in one country wishes to communicate in their native language with a user in another country, the recipient computer might not have any idea how to interpret the material it has received. This means that either the users who wish to communicate must have multiple computers, with at least one configured with their counterpart's language standards-enabled operating system, or single computers that have the ability to switch between standards and their associated character sets as needed.

So far, the best answer to this dilemma is the International Standards Organization (ISO) standard 10646, more commonly called *Unicode*. Under this standard, characters are represented using 16 bits. This allows for the representation of 65,536 (2^16) characters, including punctuation, upper and lower case letters, and numbers for all of the world's major languages. These include Chinese (Simplified), Chinese (Traditional), Czech, Danish, Dutch, English, Finnish, French, German, Hungarian, Italian, Japanese, Korean, Norwegian, Polish, Russian, Portuguese, Slovakian, Spanish, Swedish, and Turkish.

By default, Windows 2000 Professional uses the Unicode character set. This does not mean that if your users in Paris start sending documents to your users in Peking, they automatically make any sense to the recipients. The users at either end of the connection must still be able to read each others languages (or translate the documents before sending them). It does mean, however, that users on both continents see the same characters when they view the same documents.

This example brings to mind another issue worthy of mention: Right-to-Left Orientation (RTL). French speakers read left to right. Chinese speakers read right-to-left. This should not matter to you if you are sending documents to your users in China. Presumably, they are either translated or otherwise readable to them. It makes a difference if you need to distribute software to your Chinese users, however, because they read such things as Windows 2000 properties dialog boxes in a much different way than you would.

Fortunately, Microsoft addresses this issue in such programming environments as VBBasic (since version 6) with the bidirectional Application Programming Interface, more commonly called the RTL API. This API lets developers create interface elements that adhere to Microsoft's user interface guidelines while reformatting themselves to accommodate whichever version of Windows they are installed on. When programming your own applications or buying applications that are used in multiple countries, make sure they are developed using the RTL API and have Unicode support.

Enabling and Configuring Multiple-Language Support

Microsoft addresses regionally specific user interface issues by providing localized versions of Windows 2000 Professional in 24 languages. Microsoft deals with the representation of different character sets through Unicode support. If you are supporting users in multiple locations, first make sure they install the version of Windows 2000 Professional appropriate to their location, which gives them user interface elements such as dialog boxes, applications, and Help files in their own tongues. Next, install Windows 2000 Professional's support for different Locales, which allows all of your international users to communicate with each other.

As you might recall from Chapter 1, "Installing Windows 2000 Professional," you were given the chance to enable multiple language support when you installed the operating system (see Figure 1.7). You can install multiple language support thereafter by opening the Regional Options Control Panel application, as shown in Figure 5.10.

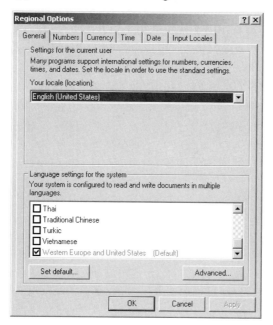

Figure 5.10 *Adding multiple language support.*

Under the General tab, you may use the scrolling list at the bottom of the dialog box to view the language groups currently installed on the workstation. What is selected here determines which Locales you can select from in the drop-down menu at the top of the dialog box. For example, the Western Europe and United States language group gives you the English (United States) Locale, as shown in Figure 5.10.

To add more languages and Locales, select the necessary language groups in the dialog box. You are prompted for the Windows 2000 Professional installation media and to reboot.

Configuring Local Settings for Multiple Locations

Language groups are composed of fonts, keyboard layouts, Input Method Editor (IME) files (which support text input from various sources including keyboard and speech), and National Language Support (.nls) files. *Locales* include user environmental preferences relating to the display of numbers, currencies, dates, and times, and the way these values are input.

While Locales are dependent on the installed language groups, they may differ from actual languages. For example, installing the Western Europe and United States language group gives you English. It also gives you French, German, and Spanish. Further, the Western Europe and United States language group does not just give you just American English, it also gives you British English, South African English, and Australian English, to name a few. By applying Locales you can compensate for regional and cultural differences within a language.

For example, a North American would choose dollars under the Currency tab, while a Brit would choose pounds (see Figures 11).

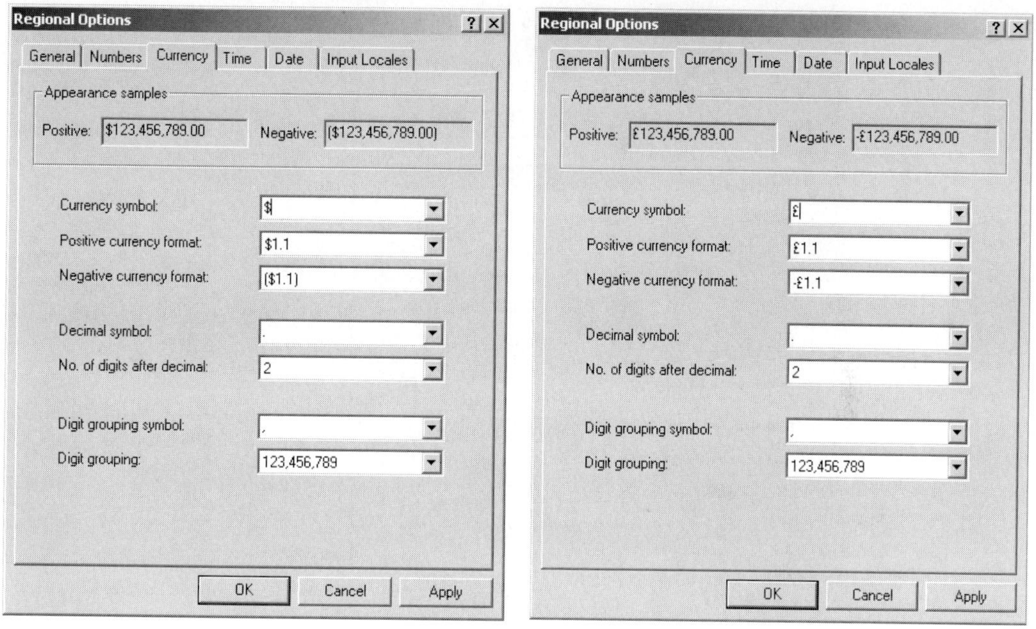

Figure 5.11 *U.S. vs. U.K Currency choices.*

After you have added a new language group, you can choose from additional Locales and input methods. For example, adding the Greek language group and choosing the Greek Locale lets you switch to Greek numbers, currency, time, and date conventions, and toggle between Greek or English keyboards from the dialog box or Taskbar, as shown in Figure 5.12.

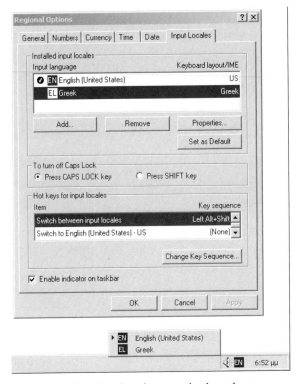

Figure 5.12   *Toggling between keyboards.*

 Microsoft also has a "MultiLanguage" version that supports all 24 languages and their associated Locales.

You can control language groups and Locales through group policy, as described further on in this chapter.

Configure New Locales

Practice what you have learned by installing a new language group.

For the sake of comparison, choose a language group that includes a non-Roman language, such as Arabic, Hebrew, or Chinese. Use the Regional Options Control Panel application to select environmental variables in the Locale, such as currency and dates. Next, open Notepad and enter a few characters using the newly added Input Locale.

MCSE 5.3   Working with Windows Installer Packages

Most applications that you need to deploy on Windows 2000 Professional workstations come with an installer application of some sort. In general, such utilities include a script, compressed program files, and a wizard that guides users through the installation. Should you be called upon to deploy some custom program throughout your organization, you can use Windows 2000 Professional's built-in installation technology to make your own installer application.

Windows 2000 Professional installer packages are composed of a single .msi file that contains program and support files, scripts, and instructions. Since it is self-contained, the installer package can be easily distributed. Other important features of the installation technology include the following:

- Installer packages can be scripted to avoid overwriting common system or application files.
- Installer packages can be "rolled back," returning the system to its preinstallation state in the event of problems during installation.
- Installer packages can log the installation process, which makes it possible to repair damaged or incomplete installations thereafter.
- Installer packages can work "silently," without user interaction.
- Installer packages can limit themselves to installing vital components when disk space is scarce, leaving other components to be installed only as needed.
- Installer packages can be completely uninstalled.

Creating Installer Packages

To use Windows 2000 Professional's installer technology, you need some program with which to script the process. Among the third party choices are InstallShield, WinINSTALL, and Wise. You can also find one such utility, Veritas Software's WinINSTALL Lite, on the Windows 2000 Professional installation CD-ROM in the following path:

```
F:\\VALUEADD\3RDPARTY\MGMT\WINSTLE
```

As with most of its counterparts, WinINSTALL takes "snapshots" of your system's condition before and after you install an application, then notes the differences to create an installation script. This is explained when you first launch the WinINSTALL Discover Wizard, as shown in Figure 5.13.

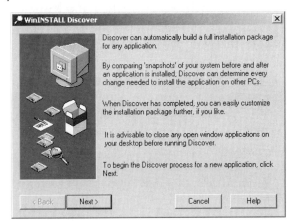

Figure 5.13 *Launching the WinINSTALL Lite Discover Wizard.*

First, you must name your installer package, as shown in Figure 5.14. (In this case, an updater for zapwerk Inc.'s siteyard Web content management tool).

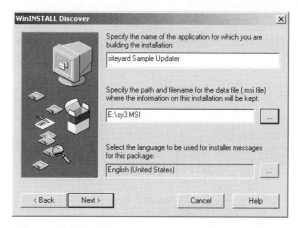

Figure 5.14 *Choosing a name and creation location.*

You must also tell the utility where the .msi file should be created and which language group should be applied. Along the same lines, the wizard's next window asks you to specify the location in which it should build the installation package, as shown in Figure 5.15. This location must have more available free space than is required by the application being installed.

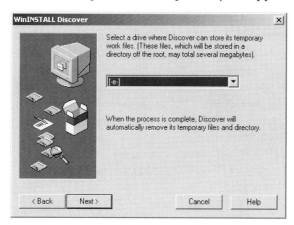

Figure 5.15 *Choosing a temporary directory.*

Next, you may choose to exclude any drives from the scanning process that is not affected by the software installation, as shown in Figure 5.16.

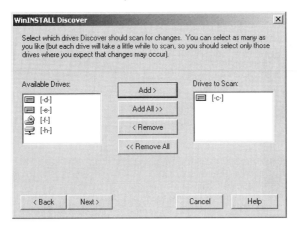

Figure 5.16 *Selecting drives to be scanned for differences.*

Then, you may choose to exclude specific folders and files from being scanned for differences. By default, WinINSTALL excludes such items as paging files and caches that change between snapshots, but which have nothing to do with the software that is being installed.

WinINSTALL Discover

For each drive to be scanned, select the files and/or directories to be excluded from the scan:

[-c-]   Files & Wildcard Entries

All Directories: Directories & Files to Exclude:
- c:\   Add >   *.SWP
- CNTX   Add All >>   *SPART.PAR
- Documents and...   _OFIDX*.FF?
- Inetpub   < Remove   c:\~secure.nt\
- My Documents   << Remove All   c:\catalog.wci\

☐ Enhanced Registry Scan

< Back   Next >   Cancel   Help

Figure 5.17 *Excluding unrelated folders and files.*

Next, WinINSTALL scans the selected hard drives to create the initial snapshot of its current state, as shown in Figure 5.18.

Figure 5.18   *Scanning current system state.*

The dialog box that appears when the scan is complete, shown in Figure 5.19, is important. If you choose the OK button here, WinINSTALL prompts you to identify any installers that accompany the program you are attempting to distribute. If yours is the only installer, you should choose the Cancel button instead so that you can make your changes manually.

Figure 5.19   *Choosing installer-driven or manual changes.*

At this point, WinINSTALL quits, giving you the opportunity to create folders, copy new files (such as .ini and .dll files) into the correct locations, change or add Registry keys, and provide shortcuts.

When you have finished, launch WinINSTALL again to resume the scripting process by creating a post-installation snapshot (see Figure 5.20).

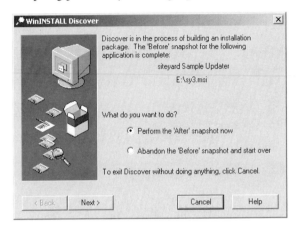

Figure 5.20 *Resuming the scripting process.*

Next, WinINSTALL scans the hard drive to identify changes, then creates the .msi file based on its comparison of the before and after snapshots. When completed, WinINSTALL prompts you with a dialog box like the one shown in Figure 5.21.

Figure 5.21 *Completing the after snapshot.*

Navigate to the location that you previously selected for the installer file's creation to find the new .msi file, as shown in Figure 5.22. Since your new package is contained within a single .msi file, it can be easily distributed—even sent via email—to your users. Recipients need only double-click the file to have its contents installed on their Windows 2000 Professional workstations.

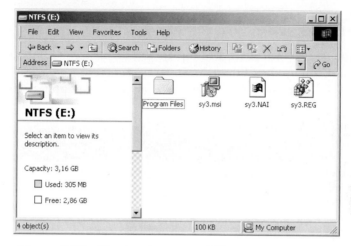

Figure 5.22   *Viewing the new .msi file.*

Study Break

Study Break

> Practice what you have learned by creating an installer package.
>
> First, identify some files that you might wish to install on multiple users' workstations. For example, you might choose to simply install a graphic file of your organization's logo in the My Pictures folder of each users' My Documents folder. Next, run the WinINSTALL Lite Discover Wizard to create before and after snapshots of your master computer, and produce a .msi file that can be distributed to users. Test the .msi installation on a target computer.

MCSE 5.4   Working with Desktop Settings

Windows 2000 Professional has many settings that can be altered to accommodate various user preferences, such as display size and resolution, wallpaper, color scheme, display fonts, and shortcuts. As an administrator, the way in which users rearrange the look and feel of their Desktops is of little concern to you in most cases. However, when user manipulation of the Desktop settings begins to cause problems in terms of support and security, most administrators find it useful to limit user access to certain configuration options. This is made possible throughout an organization by the implementation of group policies.

Configuring Desktop Settings

You can control users' desktop environments by setting group policy using the Group Policy Editor MMC snap-in. Typing "gpedit.msc" at the command line, as shown in Figure 5.23, launches this application.

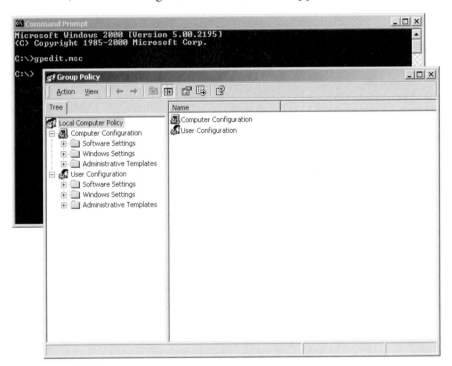

Figure 5.23 *Launching Group Policy Editor.*

Beneath the Local Computer Policy tree are configuration categories that pertain to both the computer and its users. Expand the Administrative Templates branch and select the Desktop item in the left pane to see a list of possible policies in the right pane, as shown in Figure 5.24.

Double-click a Desktop policy and choose the Enabled radio button under the Policy tab to apply it. Most policies are disabled by default.

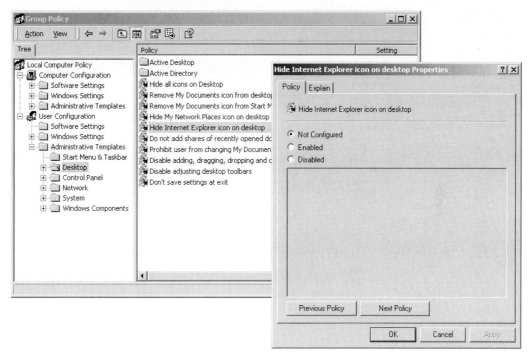

Figure 5.24   *Enabling a group policy.*

Switch to the Explain tab to see a description of the policy and its effects, as shown in Figure 5.25.

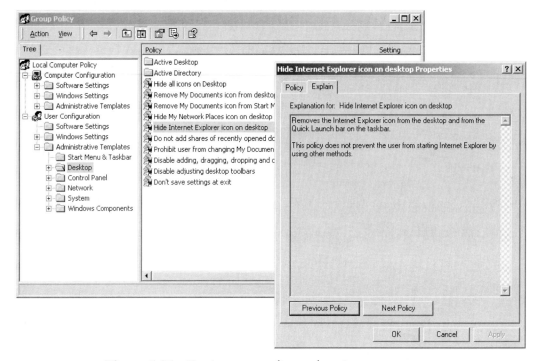

Figure 5.25 *Viewing group policy explanations.*

Among the Desktop settings you can control through group policy (found under the Active Desktop branch) are as follow:

- **Enable Active Desktop.** Users may set HTML or JPEG documents as wallpapers, but may not disable their use.
- **Disable all items.** Removes content from, but does not disable, Active Desktop.
- **Prohibit changes.** Users cannot enable or disable Active Desktop or change its settings.
- **Prohibit adding/deleting/editing/closing items.** Controls what users can do with Web content on their Active Desktops.
- **Add/delete items.** Adds and deletes specific Web content on users' Active Desktops.
- **Active Desktop wallpaper.** Forces the display of an Active Desktop background of your choosing.
- **Allow only bitmapped wallpaper.** Prevents the use of HTML or JPEG backgrounds.

Additional Desktop settings that you can control through group policy, found under the Start Menu & Taskbar branch, are as follow:

- **Remove user's folder from the Start menu.** User-created folders in the top section of the Start menu are hidden.
- **Disable and remove links to Windows Update.** Users are not permitted to access the Microsoft Web site to update system software on their workstations.
- **Remove common program groups from Start menu.** Users are not permitted to see the program group items that are included in the All Users user profile.
- **Remove Documents menu from the Start menu.** Users are not permitted to see the Documents folder in the Start menu, which contains recently used files.
- **Disable programs on Settings menu.** Users cannot open Control Panel, Printers, Network, or Dial-Up Connections applications.
- **Remove Network and Dial-Up Connections from Start menu.** Users cannot open Network or Dial-Up Connections applications.
- **Remove Favorites from Start menu.** Users cannot add Favorites to the Start menu.
- **Remove Search from the Start menu.** Users are not permitted to access the Search command from the Start menu, and some search functions are disabled.
- **Remove Help from the Start menu.** Users are not allowed to access Windows Help through the Start menu.
- **Remove Run from the Start menu.** Users are not allowed to launch applications from the Run Dialog box through the Start menu, nor through Task Manager's New Task button.
- **Add Logoff to Start menu.** Forces the presence of the logoff menu item in the Start menu.
- **Disable Logoff on the Start menu.** Forces the removal of the logoff menu item in the Start menu.
- **Disable and Remove the Shut Down command.** Users cannot shut down or restart Windows 2000.
- **Disable drag-and-drop context menus on the Start menu.** Users cannot remove or reorder Start menu items using drag-and-drop, and context menus are not displayed.
- **Disable changes to Taskbar and Start Menu Settings.** The Taskbar & Start Menu item is not displayed in the Settings program group, and users may not open the Taskbar Properties dialog box.
- **Disable context menus for the Taskbar.** Users cannot see context menus when they right-click Taskbar items.

- **Do not keep history of recently opened documents.** Shortcuts to recently used documents are not created.
- **Clear history of recently opened documents on exit.** Contents of the Documents menu are deleted on logoff.
- **Disable personalized menus.** Users see all menu items in a static listing rather than only those items they have used most recently.
- **Disable user tracking.** User actions, such as running a program or navigating a document path, are not recorded.
- **Add "Run in Separate Memory Space" checkbox to Run dialog box.** Users are permitted to run 16-bit legacy programs in their own Virtual DOS machine (VDM) process.
- **Do not use the search-based method when resolving shell shortcuts.** Users are not permitted to perform an exhaustive search in resolving shortcuts.
- **Do not use the tracking-based method when resolving shell shortcuts.** Users are not permitted to use NTFS tracking when resolving shortcuts.
- **Gray unavailable Windows Installer programs Start Menu shortcuts.** Users see partially installed programs in gray rather than black.

The group policies that you set here are universal to the system, affecting all of its users. If you wish to allow users to make changes to their own Desktop settings, changes should be made through the appropriate Control Panel applications.

Group policies do not disable Windows 2000 functionality, they simply control user access to them. Sophisticated users may still be able to work around your restrictions, perhaps by launching utilities from the Search window or Command Line.

Troubleshooting Desktop Settings

Should users report problems with their Desktop settings, check to make sure that what they perceive as a configuration problem is not a feature that you have made subject to group policy. If users report problems that turn out to be related to their own meddling with Desktop settings in the future, consider the use of group policies to limit their configuration choices and potential errors.

Configure Desktop Settings

Practice what you have learned by configuring a Desktop setting through group policy.

First, launch the Group Policy Editor from the command line. Familiarize yourself with the interface, its policy options, and the explanations for each policy that affects the desktop environment. Next, configure an obvious but relatively benign Desktop setting policy and observe its effects.

MCSE 5.5   ## Working with Fax Support

Windows 2000 Professional provides a convenient service that works with fax-capable modems.

Configuring Fax Support

To configure Windows 2000 fax support, launch the Fax Control Panel application, as shown in Figure 5.26.

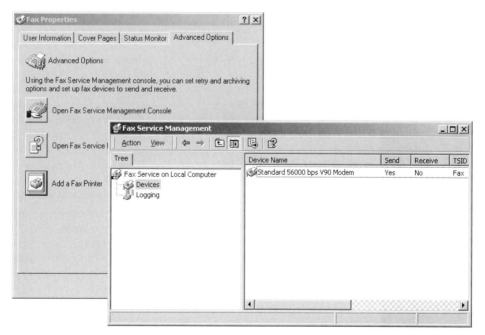

Figure 5.26   *Fax service management and the Fax Control Panel application.*

Under the User Information tab, identify yourself, the return fax number, and as much address information as you care to provide. Under the Cover Pages tab, select the New button to create a new cover page in the Fax Cover Page Editor, or the Add button to import a cover page created by someone else. Under the Status Monitor tab, choose such options as displaying status messages on the Taskbar and playing sounds when faxes are sent or received.

Windows 2000 Professional treats a fax modem as just another printing device, making it as easy to choose from an application menu as the local laser printer. As with printers, you can configure fax devices through a wizard—in this case, the Add a Fax Printer Wizard that can be launched from the Advanced tab.

Click the Open Fax Service Management Console button to configure more advanced settings (see Figure 5.26). By default, fax modems are configured to send only. To permit your workstation to receive faxes as well, select the Devices branch in the Tree pane and double-click the device name in the right pane to open its Properties dialog box, as shown in Figure 5.27. Click the Enable receive checkbox to direct the modem to answer incoming fax calls, and set the number of rings it should wait before picking up the line.

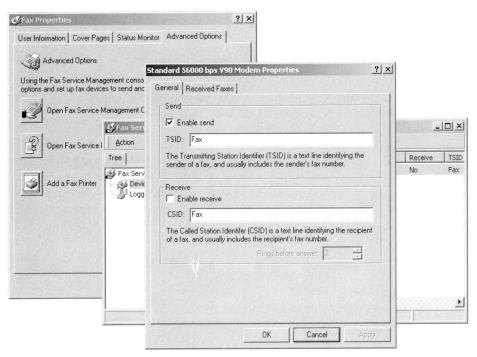

Figure 5.27 *Enabling incoming fax receiving.*

Troubleshooting Fax Support

To troubleshoot fax service connection problems, click the Logging branch in the Tree pane and review the information that was logged for failed communications. Double-click a log in the right pane to see statistics related to initialization or termination, outbound calls, inbound calls, or unknown errors. Right-click a log to set the level of logging detail from Medium to None, Minimum, or Maximum.

Study Break

Enable Fax Support

Practice what you have learned by enabling fax support.

Assuming your workstation has a fax-capable modem present, use the Add a Fax Printer Wizard to install fax support. Next, use the Fax Control Panel application to configure user information and display settings. Use the Fax Service Management MMC snap-in to enable fax receiving for your fax modem. Finally, test your fax service by sending, and if possible, receiving a fax. Review the logs to see how well the faxing process progressed.

MCSE 5.6   Working with Accessibility Services

Accessibility Services is the Windows 2000 Professional term for several utilities designed to help users with special vision, hearing, or input device needs. These services include Magnifier, Narrator, and On-Screen Keyboard utilities, as well as the Accessibility Wizard and Utility Manager tools used to configure and troubleshoot them.

Configuring Accessibility Services

To configure Accessibility Services, begin by opening the Accessibility Options Control Panel application, as shown in Figure 5.28.

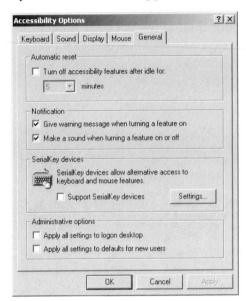

Figure 5.28   *Accessibility Options Control Panel application.*

Configuration options include the following:

- **Keyboard.** Under the Keyboard tab, enable options such as Filter-Keys, which directs Windows 2000 to be less sensitive in reacting to keystrokes; ToggleKeys, which plays sounds when the Caps Lock, Num Lock, or Scroll Lock keys are enabled; and StickyKeys, which modifies the selection of Shift, Ctrl, and Alt key combinations.

Press the Settings buttons to configure these options in greater detail, as shown in Figure 5.29.

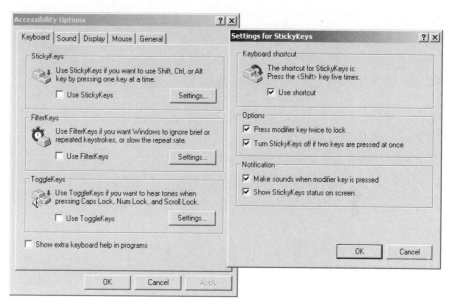

Figure 5.29 *Configuring StickyKey Options.*

- **Sound.** Under the Sound tab, enable SoundSentry to accompany audible messages with visual messages or ShowSounds to add captions to alerts and speech messages.
- **Display.** Under the Display tab, enable High Contrast to add greater differentiation to user interface elements and remove the typical Windows color and "chrome" theme.
- **Mouse.** Under the Mouse tab, enable MouseKeys to control the cursor by using the numeric keypad.

Under the General tab, you can specify when Accessibility Services should be activated, turned off, displayed, and applied to users.

ACCESSIBILITY WIZARD

For users who are unsure about how well Accessibility Services might meet their special needs, the Accessibility Wizard, shown in Figure 5.30, can be particularly helpful.

The wizard lets users choose from simple statements, such as "I am blind or have difficulty seeing things on screen," and then configures Windows 2000 accordingly.

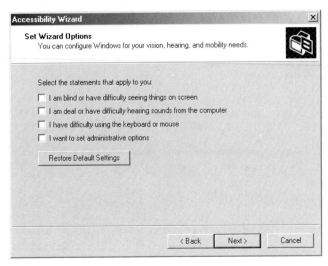

Figure 5.30 *Running the Accessibility Wizard.*

MAGNIFIER

The Magnifier utility can be used to enlarge the areas of the screen beneath the cursor, as shown in Figure 5.31.

Magnifier can be launched and configured from the Accessibility program group.

Figure 5.31 *Using Magnifier.*

NARRATOR

The Narrator utility, also available in the Accessibility program group, can be enabled to read dialog box messages, menu commands, and text aloud (see Figure 5.32).

Figure 5.32 *Enabling Narrator.*

ON-SCREEN KEYBOARD

For users who have trouble typing but can still maneuver a pointing device, you can enable the On-Screen Keyboard, as shown in Figure 5.33.

Figure 5.33 *Using On-Screen Keyboard.*

Troubleshooting Accessibility Services

If users report problems with their Accessibility Services, review the Accessibility Options Control Panel application and other utilities to make sure that they have not been inadvertently deactivated, or put to sleep by the Automatic Reset option.

When users are working with Magnifier, Narrator, or On-Screen Keyboard, you can make sure the tools are running by launching the Utility Manager from the Accessibility program group, as shown in Figure 5.34.

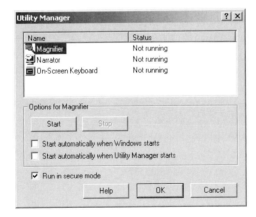

Figure 5.34 *Troubleshooting with Utility Manager.*

You can also enable options that launch accessibility programs at Windows 2000 startup or when you launch the Utility Manager itself.

Study Break

Enable Accessibility Options

> Practice what you have learned by enabling Accessibility Options.
>
> For example, enable the High Contrast display option to see the visual difference in the Windows user interface, or the Narrator utility to hear commands and messages recited.

■ Summary

In this chapter, we considered various options for configuring the Windows 2000 Professional user environment, such as managing user profiles, multiple languages and locations, custom software installations, desktop settings, fax support, and accessibility services.

Working with User Profiles

The user profile controls the settings for the user's local environment, such as wallpaper, screen saver, and desktop shortcuts. You can access your user profile in the System Properties dialog box. Three types of user profile can be created. Local user profiles are the default of Windows 2000. The first time a user logs onto a workstation, a local user profile is created and stored there. When a mandatory user profile is in place, the user can still make changes to the environment — such as screen saver or wallpaper — but when the user logs off, the changes are not saved. Roaming profiles are created only by the administrator and are stored on the server. These allow a user to access the same desktop environment from multiple machines. If the user makes a change to his roaming profile, those changes are stored on the server as well.

Supporting Multiple Languages and Locations

The goal of multiple language support is to permit humans to use their computers to communicate regardless of their native languages. Windows 2000 Professional supports ISO standard 10646, more commonly called *Unicode*. Under this standard, characters are represented using 16 bits, allowing for the representation of 65,536 (2^{16}) characters, including punctuation, upper and lower case letters, and numbers for all of the world's major languages. These include Chinese (Simplified), Chinese (Traditional), Czech,

Danish, Dutch, English, Finnish, French, German, Hungarian, Italian, Japanese, Korean, Norwegian, Polish, Russian, Portuguese, Slovakian, Spanish, Swedish, and Turkish. Windows 2000 language groups are composed of fonts, keyboard layouts, Input Method Editor (IME) files, and National Language Support (.nls) files. Locales include user environmental preferences relating to the display of numbers, currencies, dates, and times, and the way these values are input.

Working with Installer Packages

Windows 2000 Professionals built-in installer technology permits you to deploy custom software packages and files using a single .msi file that contains all programs, scripts, and instructions. A third-party application is required to create the installer package, such as WinINSTALL Lite (which can be found on the Windows 2000 Professional installation CD-ROM). Such utilities take snapshots of the system's condition before and after you add the necessary files, then compare the differences to create a script that can duplicate the installation procedure on other workstations.

Working with Desktop Settings

Users may modify their working Desktops in many ways For example, they might apply a Web page as an Active Desktop wallpaper, add shortcuts, or choose to hide certain features. As an administrator, you can enable or disable many Desktop settings and preferences through group policy. This permits you to enforce the use of features that have proven helpful or necessary to users or remove functions that should be inaccessible or have proven confusing.

Working with Fax Support

Windows 2000 Professional treats a fax modem as just another printing device, making it as easy to choose from an application menu as the local laser printer. As with printers, you can configure fax devices through a wizard—in this case, the Add a Fax Printer Wizard that can be launched from the Advanced tab of the Fax Control Panel application. You can manage fax devices through the Fax Service Management Console, which also provides logging options.

Working with Accessibility Services

Accessibility Services help users with special vision, hearing, or input device needs. These services include Magnifier, Narrator, and On-Screen Keyboard utilities, as well as the Accessibility Wizard and Utility Manager tools used to configure and troubleshoot them.

▲ CHAPTER REVIEW QUESTIONS

Here are a few questions relating to the material covered in the *Configuring and Troubleshooting the Desktop Environment* section of Microsoft's *Installing, Configuring, and Administering Microsoft Windows 2000 Professional* exam (70-210).

1. *New user profiles are created in a hidden PROFILES folder within the WINNT folder.*
   A. True
   B. False

2. *Which of the following can users customize through local user profiles? Select all that apply:*
   A. Desktop shortcuts
   B. A roaming profile
   C. A favorite URL
   D. My Network Places shortcuts

3. *Modern computers can interpret human language conventions inherently.*
   A. True
   B. False

4. *Which of the following are language encoding standards? Select all that apply:*
   A. ASCII
   B. RTL
   C. EBCDIC
   D. ISO

5. *Which of the following languages are supported by Unicode? Select all that apply:*

    A. English

    B. French

    C. Spanish

    D. Chinese

6. *When configuring non-Western languages, such as Chinese, you should enable Windows 2000s RTL user interface options.*

    A. True

    B. False

7. *Windows 2000 Professional can be purchased in 25 language versions.*

    A. True

    B. False

8. *Language groups can be added through the Add/Remove Software Control Panel application.*

    A. True

    B. False

9. *Which of the following are in the same language group as English (United States)? Select all that apply:*

    A. British English

    B. European Spanish

    C. Australian English

    D. South African English

10. *Adding language groups to Windows 2000 also adds possible locales.*

    A. True

    B. False

11. *Which best described how you would go about switching to an alternative language input method? Select only one:*

    A. Reboot Windows 2000 and select the alternate language group from the boot loader menu on restart.

    B. Switch between input methods from the Taskbar.

    C. Choose the alternate input method in the Keyboard Properties dialog box.

    D. You cannot change input methods.

12. *A vital component to an installer package is the step-by-step user guide, such as the wizard.*

 A. True

 B. False

13. *Which of the following are characteristic of Windows 2000 installer packages? Select all that apply:*

 A. They will always overwrite older system files.

 B. They can be rolled back in case of installation failure.

 C. They can install fewer components where disk space is scarce

 D. They can log the installation process.

14. *If you wish to permit some users on a workstation to have greater autonomy, you should make their user profiles exempt from local computer group policy.*

 A. True

 B. False

15. *By disabling a function through group policy, you make it inaccessible to users.*

 A. True

 B. False

16. *By default, the Fax service is configured to send faxes only.*

 A. True

 B. False

17. *When troubleshooting, you can review the initialization commands that took place prior to a fax session.*

 A. True

 B. False

18. *Which of the following utilities might help the visually impaired? Select all that apply:*

 A. Narrator

 B. Magnifier

 C. Utility Manager

 D. On-Screen Keyboard

19. *Narrator can be used to read document text.*

 A. True

 B. False

Networking Windows 2000 Professional

▲Chapter Syllabus

MCSE 6.1 Working with TCP/IP

MCSE 6.2 Working with Dial-Up Networking

MCSE 6.3 Connecting to Shared Resources

In this chapter, we look at material covered in the *Implementing, Managing, and Troubleshooting Protocols and Services* section of Microsoft's *Installing, Configuring, and Administering Microsoft Windows 2000 Professional* exam (70-210).

In the following pages, you learn to configure and troubleshoot TCP/IP and Internet Connection Sharing. You will also learn to connect computers through Dial-Up Networking, Virtual Private Networks (VPNs), and Remote Access Services (RAS). Finally, you learn to connect to shared resources on a Microsoft-based network.

MCSE 6.1   Working with TCP/IP

The Transmission Control Protocol/Internet Protocol (TCP/IP) is the language of the Internet, and Microsoft's 32-bit native implementation of it is the default protocol for Windows 2000 Professional networking. This routable, cross-platform protocol is the global industry-standard.

Configuring TCP/IP

TCP/IP is automatically installed with Windows 2000 Professional. Regardless if users are connecting to a TCP/IP-based network through a modem or network adapter, you can configure its settings through the Network and Dial-Up Connections program group. To configure TCP/IP LAN settings, for example, double-click the Local Area Connection application to open the Local Area Connection Status dialog box, as shown in Figure 6.1.

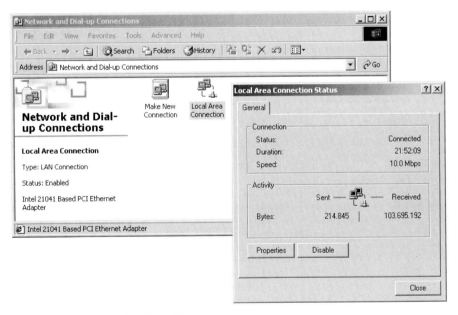

Figure 6.1 *Accessing Local Area Connection settings.*

Click the Properties button to open the Local Area Properties dialog box and select the TCP/IP protocol in the scrolling list (see Figure 6.2).

If it is not present, click the Install button to add it to the list.

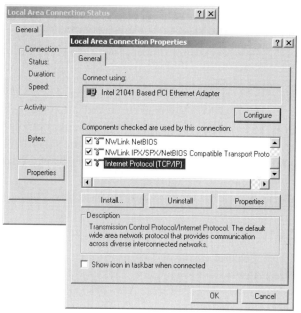

Figure 6.2   *Selecting a LAN protocol.*

Click the Properties button to open the Internet Protocol (TCP/IP) Properties dialog box, as shown in Figure 6.3.

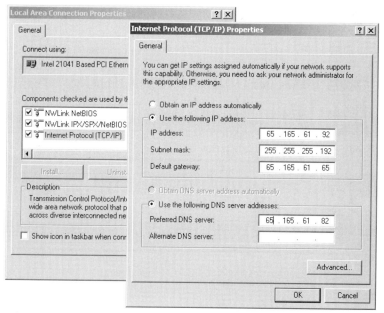

Figure 6.3   *Configuring General TCP/IP properties.*

GENERAL PROPERTIES

Depending on the design of and services running on the local network, you might need to select the Use the following IP address radio button to enable a static TCP/IP address configuration. In order to fill out the fields that this option makes active, you will need to know a little bit about how TCP/IP is configured on your network.

IP ADDRESS • In order to route packets to computers anywhere in the world, TCP/IP relies on a unique 32-bit binary number that serves as the address for each computer, or host, in the world. This number, the IP address, is mapped to the Media Access Control (MAC) layer or hardware address on each computer's network adapter, which is also unique.

A typical IP address looks like the following:

```
225.100.200.100
```

It is a designator composed of four octets, separated by periods. Each place can be a number between 0 and 255. This number is entered into the IP address field of the Internet Protocol (TCP/IP) Properties dialog box.

SUBNET MASK • TCP/IP also uses a subnet mask. Its purpose is designate part of the IP address as a network address and part of it as a host address. It does this by masking the network portion. For example, the previous address has a subnet mask:

```
255.255.255.0
```

This means that the first three octets are the address for a network, and only the last octet represents a host. This address is entered into Subnet mask field of the Internet Protocol (TCP/IP) Properties dialog box.

How much of the address is masked determines its class, as shown in Table 6.1. The class determines how many hosts can reside on a subnet.

Table 6.1 *IP Address Classes and Subnet Masks*

Class	Subnet Mask	Network Range	Hosts Possible
A	255.0.0.0	1.0.0.1-126.255.255.254	16,777,214
B	255.255.0.0	128.0.0.1-191.255.255.254	65,534
C	255.255.255.0	192.0.0.1-223.255.255.254	254

Smaller subnet divisions are possible. For example, a subnet mask of 255.255.255.128 would create two class C networks, one with a host range of 1-126 and the other with a host range of 129-254.

DEFAULT GATEWAY • If your network is connected to the Internet or another remote network, traffic is managed as it moves to and fro by a router. This can be either a hardware device or a computer configured with network interfaces to two or more networks and routing software (such as Windows 2000 Server's Multiprotocol Router (MPR)). The IP address for this service is entered in the Default Gateway field of the Internet Protocol (TCP/IP) Properties dialog box.

DNS SERVER ADDRESSES • To make IP addresses more accessible to humans, they can be mapped to Fully Qualified Domain Names (FQDNs). A typical domain name looks like this:

```
trd_pc.scionnet.com
```

Here the first part of the address, "trd_pc," refers to the host. The second part refers to a network's domain.

Each organization that holds a domain must also host a Domain Name System (DNS) server that aids computers in resolving host names with addresses. This server might reside on your network, or with your ISP. Enter the IP address for your DNS server in the Preferred DNS Server field of the Internet Protocol (TCP/IP) Properties dialog box.

OBTAINING IP ADDRESSES • IP addresses are generally obtained from an ISP or some authority within your organization. If your network is not connected to the Internet and there is no higher administrative authority, you can make them up. If you do, remember these rules:

- Each host address on a given TCP/IP network must be unique.
- Each network address in a given TCP/IP subnet must be the same.
- Host addresses should never be 0 or 255. The former refers to the network itself and the latter to a broadcast address.
- Network addresses should not begin with 127. These are loopback addresses used for diagnostics. Traffic directed to such an address is returned to the sender.
- Useful number schemes include those set aside especially for internal; networks, such as 192.168.*.*, a class C network; and 10.*.*.*, a class B network.

If there is a Dynamic Host Configuration Protocol (DHCP) server running on your network, you might choose to avoid all this effort by selecting the Obtain an IP address automatically radio button. Such a server loans your computer an address dynamically whenever TCP/IP service is needed. This is generally not done with servers, however, because this address can change from time to time. A dynamic address can make finding your computer difficult for client computers if when it is running IIS or TCP/IP-based printer sharing.

ADVANCED PROPERTIES

Additional configuration options are available when you click the Advanced button to open the Advanced TCP/IP Settings dialog box (see Figure 6.4).

IP SETTINGS • Choose the Edit button under the IP Settings tab to modify settings for multiple IP addresses, if present. Where static addressing is not being used, the IP address is replaced with "DHCP Enabled."

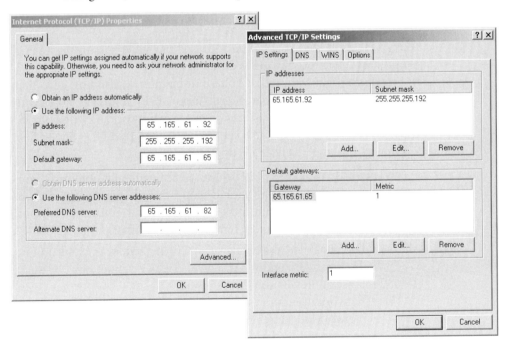

Figure 6.4 *Configuring the IP Settings tab.*

DNS • Enter the machine addresses for your network's DNS servers in the DNS server addresses field, in order of preference.

Enter the domain(s) for your network in the Append these DNS suffixes field, as shown in Figure 6.5.

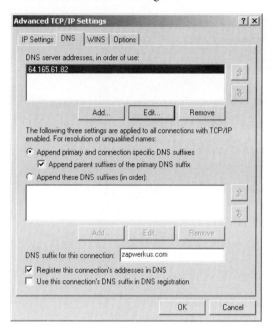

Figure 6.5 *Configuring the DNS tab.*

WINS • Windows Internet Name Service (WINS) is somewhat like DNS, except that it maps IP addresses to NetBIOS names instead of domain names. Configure the IP addresses of the servers that are running WINS for your network in the WINS addresses field under the WINS tab, as shown in Figure 6.6.

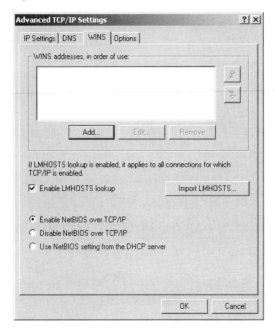

Figure 6.6   *Configuring the WINS tab.*

By default, the Enable LMHOSTS Lookup checkbox is selected. This permits the use of a text list of IP address-to-NetBIOS name mappings for computers outside the local subnet. If the Enable NetBIOS over TCP/IP radio button is selected (the default), Windows 2000 will look up NetBIOS names against a DNS server. Alternately, you can choose to obtain this information from a DHCP server.

IP SECURITY • Internet Protocol Security (IPSec) is a Windows 2000 networking safety feature that authenticates and encrypts (optionally) packet data. Configure IPSec use by double-clicking the IP security item under the Options tab to open the IP Security dialog box, as shown in Figure 6.7.

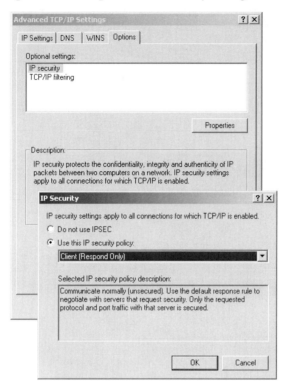

Figure 6.7   *Configuring IP Security under the Options tab.*

The following three security policies can be selected:

- **Client (respond only).** Your workstation will respond to other computers that request secure communications, or do not use IPSec.
- **Secure Server (Require Security).** Your workstation only uses secured communications.
- **Server (Request Security).** Your workstation requests, but does not require, secured communications.

The policy you choose will applies to all TCP/IP connections.

TCP/IP FILTERING • TCP/IP filtering allows you to specify which types of non-transit network traffic your workstation is allowed to process. Enable this feature by double-clicking the TCP/IP filtering item under the Options tab to open the TCP/IP Filtering dialog box, as shown in Figure 6.8.

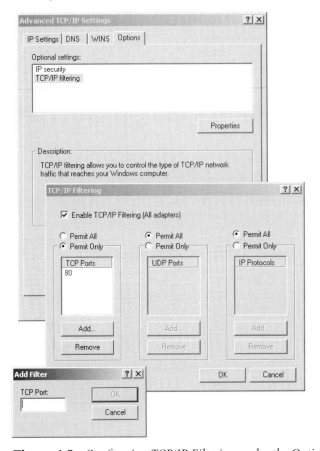

Figure 6.8 *Configuring TCP/IP Filtering under the Options tab.*

Ports can be configured for the following three protocols:

- **TCP.** A connection-oriented protocol, TCP is used for large data transfers
- **UDP (Datagram Delivery Protocol).** A connection-less protocol used for small data transfers.
- **IP.** A connection-less protocol that provides packet delivery for all other TCP/IP protocols.

Troubleshooting TCP/IP

Most of the problems encountered with TCP/IP pertain to its configuration, which as previously described can be done either manually or automatically (using DHCP). Fortunately, Windows provides many utilities helpful in troubleshooting TCP/IP configuration errors.

TROUBLESHOOTING MANUAL IP ADDRESSING

To verify manual TCP/IP configurations, select Internet Protocol (TCP/IP) in the Local Area Connections dialog box and click the Properties button to open the Internet Protocol (TCP/IP) Properties dialog box (see Figure 6.3). It is necessary for the number in the IP Address field to be unique on the network, and for the subnet mask and default gateway addresses to be correctly identified for the subnet on which the client is placed. Misconfiguration here is a common problem.

To test a manually configured computer's connectivity, you can use the Packet Internet Gopher (PING) utility to determine if the local client is capable of communicating with remote hosts, as described further on.

TROUBLESHOOTING WITH IPCONFIG

If the computer is configured to receive its addressing information from DHCP rather than through static addressing, you may employ the IPCONFIG utility in your troubleshooting. To determine which network settings a DHCP server has leased to a desktop, type the following command at the Command Line prompt:

```
IPCONFIG /all
```

Here you can verify the accuracy of TCP/IP information, including host name, physical address, IP address, subnet mask, and DHCP use, as shown in Figure 6.9.

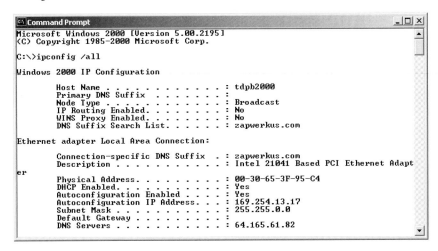

Figure 6.9   *Viewing the IP configuration.*

If there is a problem connecting to the DHCP server, you can probably see that the client computer has an invalid address, such as 255.255.255.255. In this case, you should release the client's IP address and try to lease a new one. To do this, type the following sequence of commands at a command prompt:

IPCONFIG /release

IPCONFIG /renew

If there is a DHCP server present on the network, the client should be granted a new lease for an IP address.

TROUBLESHOOTING WITH PING • The PING utility verifies a TCP/IP connection by sending Internet Control Message Protocol (ICMP) packets to remote hosts and listening for echo reply packets. PING waits up to one second for each packet sent, displaying the number of packets transmitted and received.

PING sends four packets by default, but you can change this behavior using command line switches (see Figure 6.10) to increase the duration where faulty physical links are suspected.

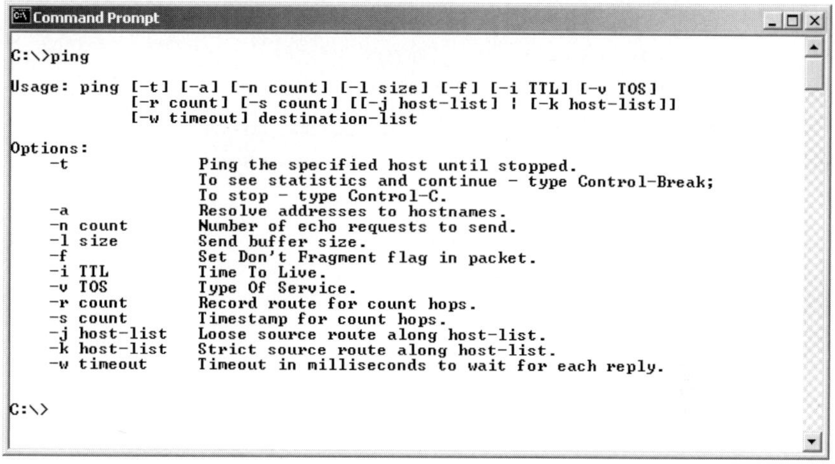

```
Command Prompt                                                    _ □ ×

C:\>ping

Usage: ping [-t] [-a] [-n count] [-l size] [-f] [-i TTL] [-v TOS]
            [-r count] [-s count] [[-j host-list] | [-k host-list]]
            [-w timeout] destination-list

Options:
    -t              Ping the specified host until stopped.
                    To see statistics and continue - type Control-Break;
                    To stop - type Control-C.
    -a              Resolve addresses to hostnames.
    -n count        Number of echo requests to send.
    -l size         Send buffer size.
    -f              Set Don't Fragment flag in packet.
    -i TTL          Time To Live.
    -v TOS          Type Of Service.
    -r count        Record route for count hops.
    -s count        Timestamp for count hops.
    -j host-list    Loose source route along host-list.
    -k host-list    Strict source route along host-list.
    -w timeout      Timeout in milliseconds to wait for each reply.

C:\>
```

Figure 6.10 *Viewing PING utility switches.*

To test a connection, use the PING command with an IP address, a host name, or a NetBIOS computer name. It is best to use the IP address initially to isolate the problem as related to connectivity vs. host name resolution (described further on).

To find out if the client's TCP/IP protocol stack is working properly, test the configuration of the computer by typing:

```
PING localhost
```

Localhost is a reserved host name that is mapped to a reserved IP address (127.0.0.1) that represents your computer. If pinging your local host is successful, you receive four replies from IP address 127.0.0.1 (see Figure 6.11).

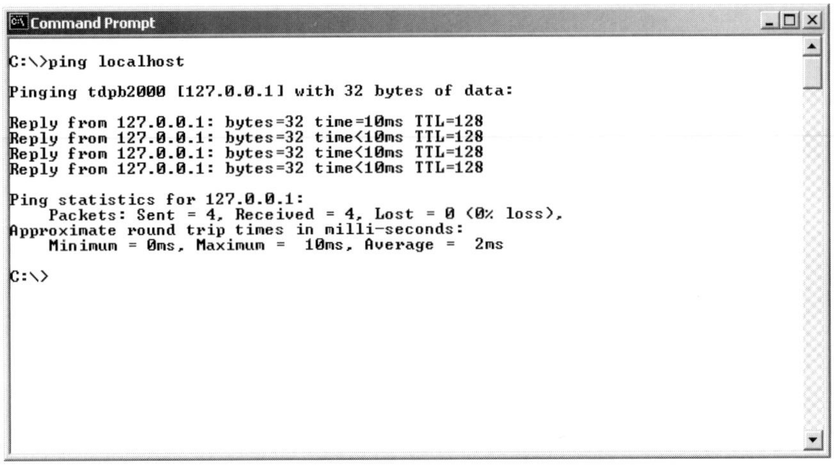

```
C:\>ping localhost

Pinging tdpb2000 [127.0.0.1] with 32 bytes of data:

Reply from 127.0.0.1: bytes=32 time=10ms TTL=128
Reply from 127.0.0.1: bytes=32 time<10ms TTL=128
Reply from 127.0.0.1: bytes=32 time<10ms TTL=128
Reply from 127.0.0.1: bytes=32 time<10ms TTL=128

Ping statistics for 127.0.0.1:
    Packets: Sent = 4, Received = 4, Lost = 0 (0% loss),
Approximate round trip times in milli-seconds:
    Minimum = 0ms, Maximum =  10ms, Average =  2ms

C:\>
```

Figure 6.11   *Successfully pinging a loopback address.*

If the PING command is unsuccessful, you receive a message telling you "localhost is unknown." If unsuccessful, make sure that the TCP/IP protocol is present on the computer, that the network adapter is properly installed, and that the TCP/IP protocol has been bound to the network adapter. Sometimes it is necessary to reboot the client computer to solve this problem. Another trick is to reinstall the TCP/IP protocol altogether.

You can further verify the configuration of the local host by using the PING command with the actual IP address of the local computer. If all is well, you should get immediate replies, as shown in Figure 6.12.

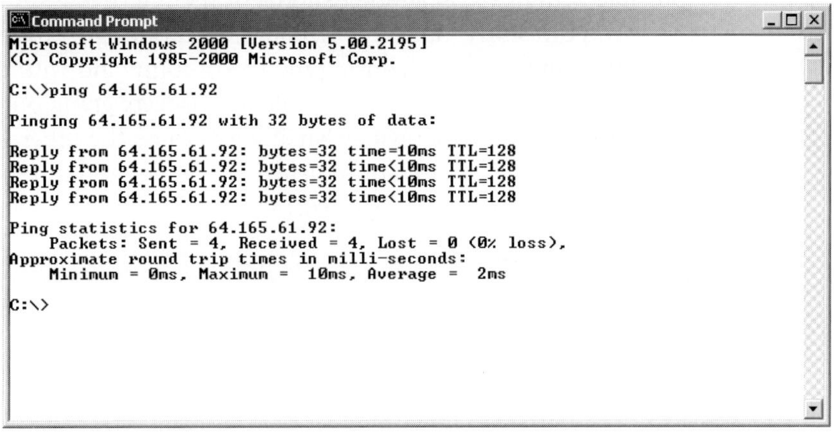

```
Command Prompt                                                    _ □ x
Microsoft Windows 2000 [Version 5.00.2195]
(C) Copyright 1985-2000 Microsoft Corp.

C:\>ping 64.165.61.92

Pinging 64.165.61.92 with 32 bytes of data:

Reply from 64.165.61.92: bytes=32 time=10ms TTL=128
Reply from 64.165.61.92: bytes=32 time<10ms TTL=128
Reply from 64.165.61.92: bytes=32 time<10ms TTL=128
Reply from 64.165.61.92: bytes=32 time<10ms TTL=128

Ping statistics for 64.165.61.92:
    Packets: Sent = 4, Received = 4, Lost = 0 (0% loss),
Approximate round trip times in milli-seconds:
    Minimum = 0ms, Maximum =  10ms, Average =  2ms

C:\>
```

Figure 6.12 *Successfully pinging the local address.*

If this test is unsuccessful, check to make sure that the correct IP address was either configured manually or received from the DHCP server. Because this test does not send packets out on the network, it does not tell you if the local host has proper network connectivity.

You can verify that network communications are possible between your computer and another host on your local subnet by using the PING command with the IP address of that other computer.

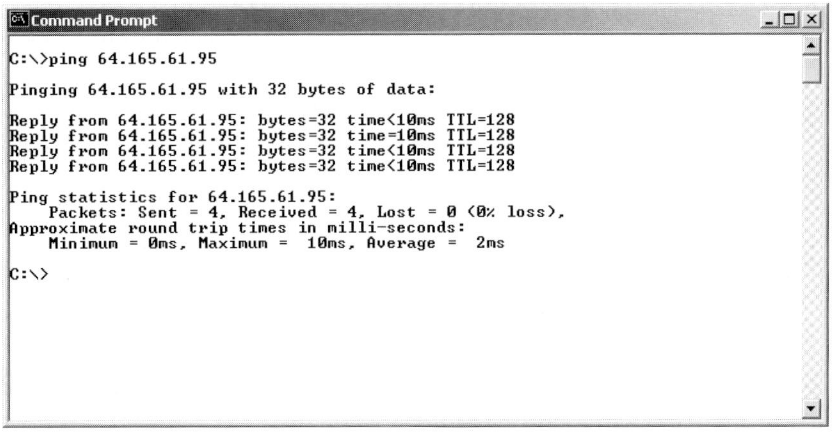

```
Command Prompt                                                    _ □ x
C:\>ping 64.165.61.95

Pinging 64.165.61.95 with 32 bytes of data:

Reply from 64.165.61.95: bytes=32 time<10ms TTL=128
Reply from 64.165.61.95: bytes=32 time=10ms TTL=128
Reply from 64.165.61.95: bytes=32 time<10ms TTL=128
Reply from 64.165.61.95: bytes=32 time<10ms TTL=128

Ping statistics for 64.165.61.95:
    Packets: Sent = 4, Received = 4, Lost = 0 (0% loss),
Approximate round trip times in milli-seconds:
    Minimum = 0ms, Maximum =  10ms, Average =  2ms

C:\>
```

Figure 6.13 *Successfully pinging a host on the local network.*

If all is well, you should see packets going out on and coming back over the network, as shown in Figure 6.13. If the test is unsuccessful, check to make sure that the proper IP addresses, subnet masks, and gateway addresses are configured on both hosts. This test only tells you if connectivity is possible on the local subnet, however. It does not tell you if communications are possible with hosts on another subnet or the Internet.

You can verify that network communications are possible between your computer and a router by using the PING command with the IP address of the gateway. If all is well, you should see packets going out on and coming back over the network, just as when you pinged the other host. If there is a problem, the packets are not returned in the required time and you see messages like those shown in Figure 6.14.

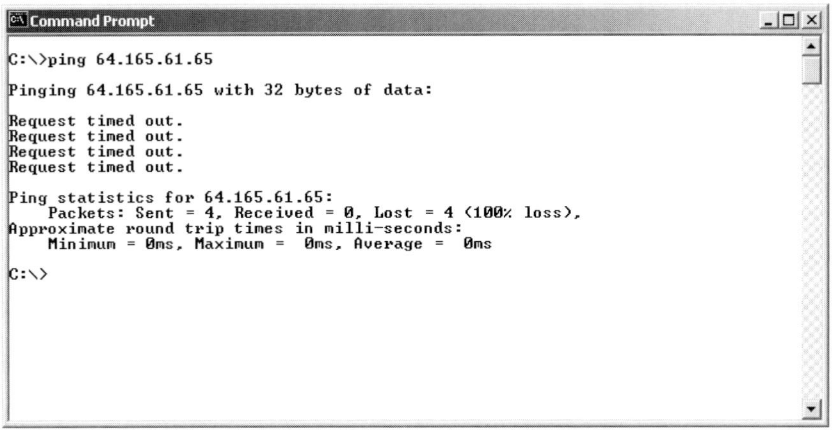

```
Command Prompt                                              _ □ ×

C:\>ping 64.165.61.65

Pinging 64.165.61.65 with 32 bytes of data:

Request timed out.
Request timed out.
Request timed out.
Request timed out.

Ping statistics for 64.165.61.65:
    Packets: Sent = 4, Received = 0, Lost = 4 (100% loss),
Approximate round trip times in milli-seconds:
    Minimum = 0ms, Maximum =  0ms, Average =  0ms

C:\>
```

Figure 6.14   *Unsuccessfully pinging the gateway.*

If the test is unsuccessful, you should first make sure the router is available (e.g., that it is powered up and connected to the network). Check again to make sure the local host is configured with the correct subnet mask and gateway addresses.

You might also need to verify that the router is configured properly. Routers have multiple IP addresses for the multiple subnets on which they reside. The port that is connected to the subnet on which your local host resides must have an IP address and subnet mask that is valid for your subnet. Other ports must have IP addresses and subnet masks that are valid for those subnets and/or the Internet. You can verify all of these ports by pinging each of their addresses.

You can verify that network communications are possible between your computer and a remote host on another subnet or the Internet by using the PING command with the IP address of that remote host. Again, if all is well, you should see packets going out on and coming back over the network via the gateway router. If there is a problem, the packets are not returned in the required time and you see time-out messages.

If the test is unsuccessful, and you have already performed the previous tests to determine that local connectivity is possible, then the problem might lie with routers or hosts beyond your network. This type of problem can often be tracked down using another utility: TRACERT.

TROUBLESHOOTING WITH TRACERT

If you can ping your default gateway but not a remote host, employ the TRACERT (Trace Route) utility next. It displays the domain name and IP address of each gateway along the route to a remote host. You can use TRACERT with either the host name or IP address of the remote computer, as shown in Figure 6.15.

```
Command Prompt                                                          _ |□| x|
Microsoft Windows 2000 [Version 5.00.2195]
(C) Copyright 1985-2000 Microsoft Corp.

C:\>tracert www.scionnet.com

Tracing route to www.scionnet.com [209.24.19.217]
over a maximum of 30 hops:

  1    10 ms   <10 ms    10 ms  64.165.61.65
  2    20 ms    10 ms    21 ms  64.164.203.229
  3    10 ms    10 ms    10 ms  edge1-ge1-0.snfc21.pbi.net [209.232.130.20]
  4    10 ms    10 ms    20 ms  sl-gw25-stk-8-3.sprintlink.net [160.81.16.21]
  5    10 ms    20 ms    10 ms  sl-bb20-stk-5-3.sprintlink.net [144.232.4.221]
  6    10 ms    20 ms    10 ms  sl-bb21-sj-6-0.sprintlink.net [144.232.8.190]
  7    20 ms    20 ms    30 ms  sl-gw8-sj-10-0.sprintlink.net [144.232.3.114]
  8    20 ms    20 ms    20 ms  p1-1-1-0.r02.snjsca01.us.bb.verio.net [129.250.9
.81]
  9    20 ms    10 ms    10 ms  p4-7-1-0.r06.plalca01.us.bb.verio.net [129.250.3
.121]
 10    10 ms    10 ms    20 ms  ge-1-0-0.a02.plalca01.us.ra.verio.net [129.250.1
5.16]
 11    10 ms    20 ms    10 ms  ge-2-0.a03.plalca01.us.ra.verio.net [129.250.15.
15]
 12    20 ms    30 ms    30 ms  p4-0-0.a05.mtvwca01.us.ra.verio.net [129.250.122
.70]
 13    20 ms    20 ms    10 ms  fa-2-1-0.a01.mtvwca01.us.ra.verio.net [129.250.1
22.195]
 14  fa-2-1-0.a01.mtvwca01.us.ra.verio.net [129.250.122.195]  reports: Destinati
on net unreachable.

Trace complete.
```

Figure 6.15 *Tracing a network path.*

Document the information that the TRACERT command returns when the remote host is available. Later, if the remote host becomes "unreachable," you can compare the information returned by TRACERT with the earlier results to determine which gateway is down.

TROUBLESHOOTING WITH PATHPING

New to Windows 2000, PATHPING is a hybrid of PING and TRACERT. Like PING, it sends packets to and receives packets back from remote routers. Like TRACERT, it lists the path taken by packets through various routers.

Unlike either, PATHPING can show you the percentage of packet loss occurring at each hop.

TROUBLESHOOTING WITH NETSTAT

The NETSTAT utility lists the TCP/IP ports that are in use during communications sessions, as shown in Figure 6.16. With it you can quickly determine if certain ports are not being accepted across the link, perhaps because they are being blocked at a firewall.

Figure 6.16   *Viewing active TCP/IP ports.*

If you find this is a problem, contact the administrator of the firewall to determine a solution.

TROUBLESHOOTING NAME RESOLUTION

If you have used PING and other utilities to determine that TCP/IP connectivity is functioning, but you are still unable to access a resource via a host name or computer name, it is time to troubleshoot name resolution. For example, you might successfully ping a host using the IP address, but fail when you attempt to use a host name, as shown in Figure 6.17.

```
Command Prompt                                                    _ □ ×

C:\>ping www.zapwerkus.com
Unknown host www.zapwerkus.com.

C:\>
C:\>
```

Figure 6.17   *Unsuccessfully resolving a host name.*

A proper resolution would match the host name with the IP address and successfully execute the PING command, as shown in Figure 6.18.

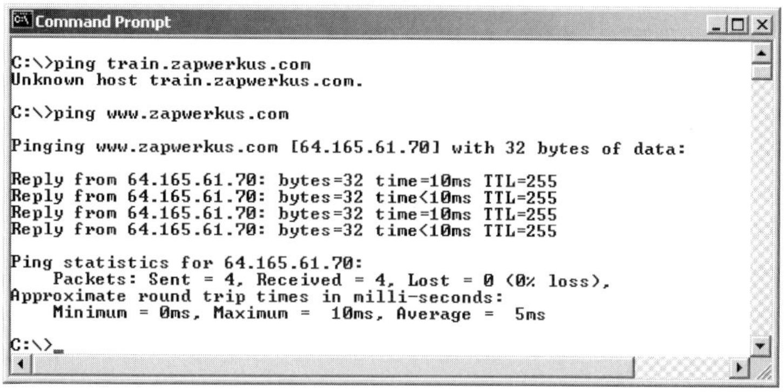

```
Command Prompt                                                    _ □ ×

C:\>ping train.zapwerkus.com
Unknown host train.zapwerkus.com.

C:\>ping www.zapwerkus.com

Pinging www.zapwerkus.com [64.165.61.70] with 32 bytes of data:

Reply from 64.165.61.70: bytes=32 time=10ms ITL=255
Reply from 64.165.61.70: bytes=32 time<10ms ITL=255
Reply from 64.165.61.70: bytes=32 time=10ms ITL=255
Reply from 64.165.61.70: bytes=32 time<10ms ITL=255

Ping statistics for 64.165.61.70:
    Packets: Sent = 4, Received = 4, Lost = 0 (0% loss),
Approximate round trip times in milli-seconds:
    Minimum = 0ms, Maximum =  10ms, Average =  5ms

C:\>_
```

Figure 6.18   *Successfully resolving a host name.*

Resolution refers to the process by which Windows maps host names (which make sense to humans) with IP addresses (which make sense to computers). Host name resolution for Windows-based computers occurs in a couple of ways. The TCP/IP host name (e.g., "laura_pc.mycompany.com") can be mapped to an IP address on the Internet or an intranet by a DNS server or a "HOSTS.SAM" file. On corporate networks, the NetBIOS computer name (e.g., "Laura's PC") can be mapped to an IP address on an intranet by a WINS server or "LMHOSTS.SAM" file.

You can use the HOSTNAME command to view the computer name of the local host.

TROUBLESHOOTING WINS RESOLUTION

You can use the NBTSTAT utility to view statistics relating to NetBIOS over TCP/IP parameters, as shown in Figure 6.19.

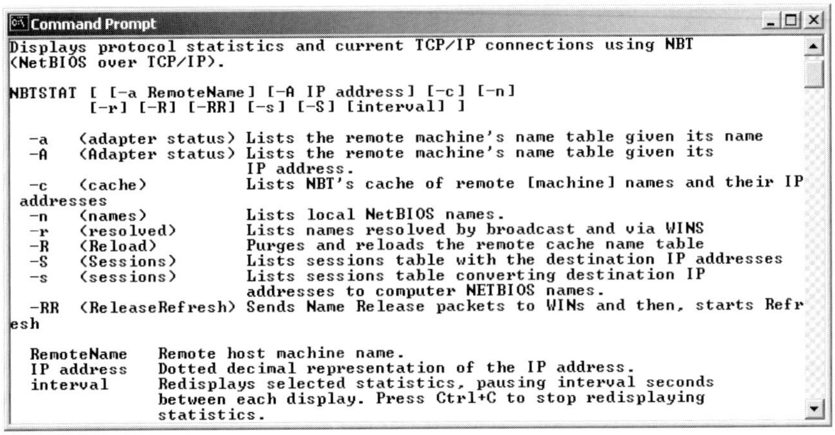

Figure 6.19   *Viewing NBTSTAT switches.*

Verify NetBIOS name resolution by establishing a session with another host. For example, you might map a drive or execute a Net Use command.

If you are unable to establish a session, check to see that both hosts are using the same NetBIOS scope IDs. The use of NetBIOS scopes permits the creation of logical TCP/IP networks that are invisible to one another. If your network is configured in this manner, you will need to configure the scope ID, as hosts can only communicate if they belong to the same NetBIOS scope. This requires a modification of the following Registry key:

```
HKEY_LOCAL_MACHINE\SYSTEM\CurrentControlSet\Services\NetBT\
Paramaters\ScopeID
```

Another area to check is the local name cache. Make sure that its entries are correct using the NBTSTAT utility with the –C switch. If there is incorrect data there, reload the cache (–R switch) and try the session again.

If there is no problem with the name cache, verify that the correct WINS server information has been configured on the client computer. This information can be viewed using IPCONFIG with the /all switch.

If there appears to be no problem with either the local name cache or WINS, take a look at the LMHOSTS file, as shown in Figure 6.20.

```
# Copyright (c) 1993-1999 Microsoft Corp.
#
# This is a sample LMHOSTS file used by the Microsoft TCP/IP for Windows.
#
# This file contains the mappings of IP addresses to computernames
# (NetBIOS) names.  Each entry should be kept on an individual line.
# The IP address should be placed in the first column followed by the
# corresponding computername. The address and the computername
# should be separated by at least one space or tab. The "#" character
# is generally used to denote the start of a comment (see the exceptions
# below).
#
# This file is compatible with Microsoft LAN Manager 2.x TCP/IP lmhosts
# files and offers the following extensions:
#
#      #PRE
#      #DOM:<domain>
#      #INCLUDE <filename>
#      #BEGIN_ALTERNATE
#      #END_ALTERNATE
#      \0xnn (non-printing character support)
#
# Following any entry in the file with the characters "#PRE" will cause
# the entry to be preloaded into the name cache. By default, entries are
# not preloaded, but are parsed only after dynamic name resolution fails.
#
```

Figure 6.20 *Viewing a sample LMHOSTS file.*

Problems can occur with the LMHOSTS file if it is moved. This file must be located in the system directory. Also make sure that the correct names and IP addresses are listed in the LMHOSTS file. If there are multiple entries for the same computer, only the first entry will be used.

TROUBLESHOOTING DNS RESOLUTION

Host name resolution is needed when clients make use of TCP/IP-based applications such as the Web, Gopher, FTP, Telnet, and IRC. Three components come into play during this process. When a client requests a host name-to-IP address mapping, it is acting as a domain name resolver. The service that receives the client's request is the domain name server. A local DNS server will know about the address mappings for the local network, but not for the rest of the world. Therefore, when a client requests an address that resides on the Internet, the local DNS server must pass the request on to the domain name space. This refers to a distributed database of unique IP address-to-host name mappings that resides on DNS servers worldwide.

When a Windows computer searches for a resource, it resolves the host name with an IP address by performing the following steps:

1. The client computer looks in its local name cache to see if the address mapping information is there.
2. If the address mapping information is not in the local name cache, it looks for it in the HOSTS file.
3. If the client computer cannot find address mapping information in the HOSTS file, and the client has been configured to use DNS, it queries the name server.
4. If the name server is not able to provide the address mapping information, and the client computer is configured to use WINS, it queries the WINS server.
5. If the WINS server is not able to provide the address mapping information, the client computer sends a broadcast query onto the local subnet (broadcast packets typically do not travel across routers).
6. If the client computer receives no response to its query, it looks for the address mapping information in the LMHOSTS file.

To determine if the local host is capable of resolving a domain name, you can use the NSLOOKUP utility. It can be launched from the Command Prompt with the following format:

```
NSLOOKUP <host_name>
```

If it works, the appropriate IP address will be returned, as shown in Figure 6.21.

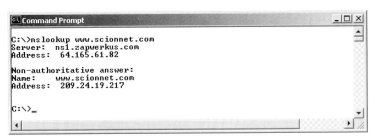

Figure 6.21   *Verifying name resolution.*

If not, verify that the correct DNS server information has been configured on the client computer. You should also verify the database on the name server.

If there appears to be no problem with the DNS server, take a look at the HOSTS file on the client computer, as shown in Figure 6.22.

```
# Copyright (c) 1993-1999 Microsoft Corp.
#
# This is a sample HOSTS file used by Microsoft TCP/IP for Windows.
#
# This file contains the mappings of IP addresses to host names. Each
# entry should be kept on an individual line. The IP address should
# be placed in the first column followed by the corresponding host name.
# The IP address and the host name should be separated by at least one
# space.
#
# Additionally, comments (such as these) may be inserted on individual
# lines or following the machine name denoted by a '#' symbol.
#
# For example:
#
#      102.54.94.97     rhino.acme.com          # source server
#       38.25.63.10     x.acme.com              # x client host

127.0.0.1       localhost
```

Figure 6.22   *Viewing a sample HOSTS file.*

Problems can occur if the HOSTS file is moved. It must be located in the \WINNT\system32\drivers\etc folder. Also make sure that the correct names and IP addresses are listed in the HOSTS file. Finally, ensure that the correct format is used for host name entries. As noted in Microsoft's sample file, each entry should be kept on an individual line. The IP address should be placed in the first column followed by the corresponding host name. The IP address and the host name should be separated by at least one space.

Additionally, comments may be inserted on individual lines or following the machine name and are denoted by a number (#) symbol.

Study Break

Check Your TCP/IP Settings

After you have configured TCP/IP on a workstation, it is a good idea to make sure your connection is working. One of the easiest ways to do this is simply to launch Internet Explorer and attempt to view a remote Web site. If this fails, however, IPCONFIG will tell you the TCP/IP settings with which your computer is configured. You can then review them for errors. Use the /ALL switch to see DHCP and WINS information as well.

PING tells you if a remote host is receiving your messages. Use the IP address of a properly configured local host. If your TCP/IP configuration is working, it responds. Then try the IP address of a remote host. If all is well with your network and router configurations, it should respond too.

TRACERT tells you how many routers are crossed as traffic moves from a local host to a remote host.

These are all DOS programs which can launched from Command Prompt.

MCSE 6.2   Working with Dial-Up Networking

All Dial-Up Networking connections can be configured using the Network Connection Wizard (see Figure 6.23) launched from Make New Connection icon in the Network and Dial-up Connections program group.

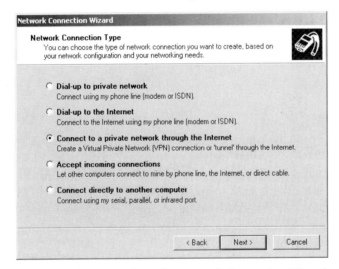

Figure 6.23 *Launching the Network Connection Wizard.*

You can configure the following types of connections:

- **Private network.** Connect to a corporate network remotely using an analog or Integrated Digital Services Network (ISDN) modem.
- **Internet.** Connect to an Internet Service Provider (ISP) using an analog or ISDN modem.
- **Virtual Private Network (VPN).** Connect to a corporate network by "tunneling" through the Internet.
- **Host.** Accept incoming connections from other computers via phone lines, the Internet, or a direct (non-network) cable.

- **Peer-to-Peer.** Initiate a connection to another computer using the serial, parallel, or Infrared ports.

Connecting to Private Networks

You can extend your network to far away locations through Remote Access Service (RAS) and Dial-up Networking. RAS servers and Dial-up Networking clients allow remote clients to access your LAN through ordinary analog telephone lines or higher-bandwidth technologies such as ISDN. Incoming connections to your LAN can be made through PPP Point-to-Point Protocol (PPP), the industry standard, or the more secure Point-to-Point Tunneling Protocol (PPTP) and Layer Two Tunneling Protocol (L2TP). Dial-up Networking also uses Serial Line Internet Protocol (SLIP) to make dialup connections to legacy SLIP servers.

Using PPP, PPTP, or L2TP, a client establishes a dialup connection to a RAS server. The client user is then authenticated on the local network and can take advantage of its services as if it was connecting locally through a LAN (although the connection will be slower).

USING LINE PROTOCOLS

Protocols such as NetBEUI, NWLink IPX/SPX/NetBIOS Compatible Transport, and TCP/IP are all designed for the characteristics of LANs. For this reason, they cannot be used with telephone-based connections unless they are enclosed in a line protocol.

SERIAL LINE INTERNET PROTOCOL • SLIP is an industry standard that supports TCP/IP connections made over serial lines. Unfortunately, SLIP has the following shortcomings:

- SLIP does not support encryption and sends authentication passwords as clear text.
- SLIP generally requires a script for logging on.
- SLIP supports TCP/IP, but it does not support either IPX or NetBEUI.
- SLIP does not support DHCP and requires static IP addresses.

RAS supports SLIP client connectivity, but it does not support operation as a SLIP server.

POINT-TO-POINT PROTOCOL • PPP was designed to overcome SLIP's shortcomings. By comparison, it has the following advantages:

- PPP supports TCP/IP, IPX, NetBEUI, and other protocols.

- PPP supports static or DHCP addresses.
- PPP supports encryption for authentication.
- PPP does not require a script for logging on.

POINT-TO-POINT TUNNELING PROTOCOL • PPTP, an extension to PPP, allows a Dial-up Networking client to establish secure communication sessions with a RAS server over the Internet. It has the following advantages:

- PPTP supports encryption for both communications and authentication.
- PPTP supports multi-protocol VPNs, allowing remote users to gain secure encrypted access to their corporate networks over the Internet.
- PPTP allows the Internet to be used as the transport for NWLink IPX/SPX/NetBIOS Compatible Transport and NetBEUI by encapsulating their packets.

Layer Two Tunneling Protocol

L2TP is similar in function to PPTP, creating a encrypted tunnel through the Internet. Unlike PPTP, however, it does not encrypt its sessions directly, relying instead such technologies as IPSec. It also differs from PPTP in the following areas:

- L2TP requires IPSec for tunnel encryption and authentication.
- L2TP supports such packet-oriented protocols as X.25, Frame Relay, UDP, and Asynchronous Transfer Mode (ATM). (PPTP is limited to IP.)
- L2TP does not support header compression, which is used to speed up network connections by reducing session overhead.

Configuring Dial-Up Network Connections

Select the Dial-up to private network radio button in the Network Connection Wizard to establish dialup settings for communications between your workstation and a corporate dialup server. First, you are prompted to specify the dialup server's telephone number, as shown in Figure 6.24.

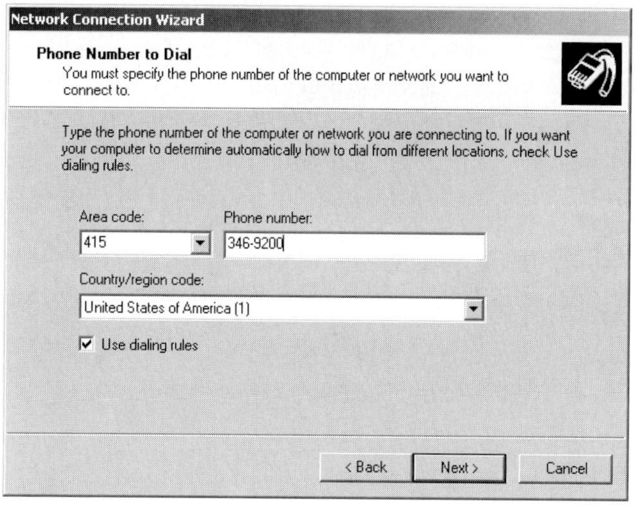

Figure 6.24 *Establishing the network's dialup number.*

Next, you are given the option of making your configuration available to all users (e.g., stored in the All Users profile), or only yourself (e.g., only accessible from your logon). Finally, you are prompted to name the connection and decide whether or not to put a connection shortcut on the Desktop.

Once completed, the wizard creates a connection icon in the Network and Dial-up Connections program group under the name you defined. Double-click this shortcut to open the Connect dialog box (see Figure 6.25).

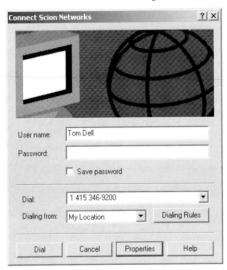

Figure 6.25 *Dial-Up Connection dialog box.*

Click the Properties button and switch to the Options tab to configure several connection behaviors, such as whether to be prompted for logon information and dialup telephone number, as shown in Figure 6.26.

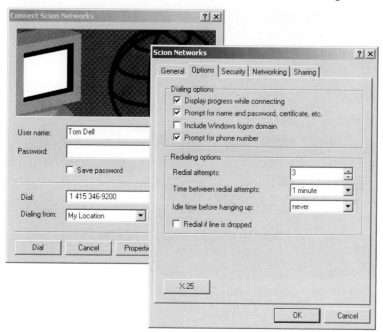

Figure 6.26   *Selecting connection options.*

Switch to the Networking tab to choose between SLIP or PPP line protocols, and to choose the LAN protocols supported by the network to which you are calling, as shown in Figure 6.27.

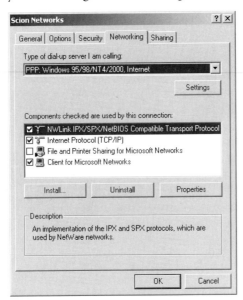

Figure 6.27 *Selecting protocols.*

Connecting to the Internet

Select the Dial-up to the Internet radio button in the Network Connection Wizard to establish dialup settings for communications between your workstation and an ISP. This launches the Internet Connection Wizard (which can also be launched from the Connect to the Internet shortcut on the Desktop).

First, you are prompted to specify whether you require an ISP, as shown in Figure 6.28.

Figure 6.28 *Choosing new or existing ISP.*

If you select the "I want to sign up for a new Internet account" radio button, the wizard detects your modem and uses an 800 number to dial-in to the Microsoft Internet Referral Service, from which you may sign-up for a local ISP account. If you already have an account with an ISP, select the "I want to transfer my existing Internet account to this computer" radio button, through which you may enter your existing ISP's dialup number and provide your username and password. If you already have an account with an ISP, you can also select the "I want to set up my Internet connection manually, or I want to connect through a LAN" radio button to configure your existing ISP's dialup number and provide your username and password. Alternately, you can choose to configure a LAN connection by supplying any necessary proxy server information and establishing email account settings.

Connecting via Virtual Private Networks (VPN)

Select the Connect to a Private network through the Internet radio button in the Network Connection Wizard to establish dialup settings for secure connections between your workstation and a corporate dialup server. First, you are prompted to specify the existing dialup connection that should be used, if any. Choose the Automatically dial this initial connection radio button and choose from the options in the drop menu, such as a previously configured private network or Internet connection (as just described). Alternately, create an entirely new connection by selecting the "Do not dial the initial connection" radio button.

Next, you are asked to supply the host name or IP address of the host to which you are connecting, such as a Windows 2000 Server computer. You are prompted to apply the connection to all user profiles or yours exclusively and to name the connection.

Once completed, the wizard creates a connection icon in the Network and Dial-up Connections program group under the name you defined. Depending on how you chose to initiate the connection, double-click to launch the previously created network connection or to open the new Connect dialog box (see Figure 6.29). Click the Properties button and switch to the Security tab to configure the connection's various security options, such as whether to encrypt data or authenticate logons using secured passwords, as shown in Figure 6.29.

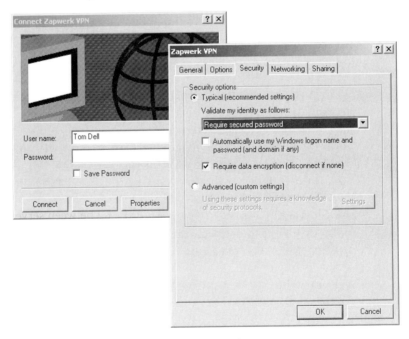

Figure 6.29 *Choosing VPN security settings.*

Enable the Advanced radio button and click the Settings button to a make available an extensive list of additional security protocol options, as shown in Figure 6.30.

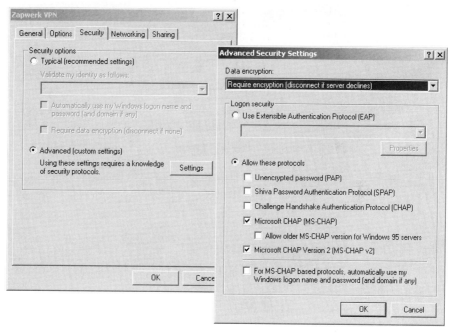

Figure 6.30   *Selecting Authentication options.*

In the Advanced Security Settings dialog box, you can specify that data encryption be required for all connections, be disabled for all connections, or be made optional depending on the dialup server's capabilities. Similarly, you can choose among various options for how your workstation encrypts authentication information, which may vary between servers. Enabling Password Authentication Protocol (PAP) would be the least secure. Enabling the Challenge Handshake Authentication Protocol (CHAP) would be the most secure.

Enable the Extensible Authentication Protocol (EAP) radio button to override traditional PAP or CHAP settings in favor of some other public key or certificate authentication method. Default options include Message Digest 5 (MD5)-CHAP and Smart Card or other Certificate. The latter implements Transport Level Security (TLS), supporting credit-card like devices that store user names and passwords. EAP supports third-party developers, so many other authentication schemes are possible. EAP is new to Windows 2000, and supports both PPTP and L2TP.

Switch to the Networking tab to choose between PPTP or L2TP line protocols, and to choose the LAN protocols supported by the network to which you are calling, as shown in Figure 6.31.

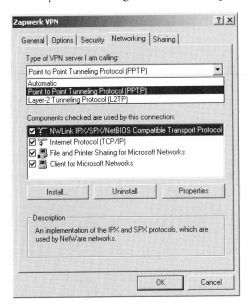

Figure 6.31 *Selecting protocols.*

Configuring Remote Access Server

Select the Accept incoming connections radio button in the Network Connection Wizard to turn your workstation into a Remote Access Server. In this capacity, Windows 2000 Professional can serve connections from dialup, VPN, or serial clients, although no more than 10 at one time.

First, the wizard will ask you to choose the type of connection it should serve, such as modem, serial port, or parallel port. Next, you are prompted to choose whether to enable VPN support, which may be used if your workstation maintains a static host name or IP address.

Next, you are asked which local users should be allowed to connect to the workstation and which of the available LAN protocols and services are supported. Select a user and click the Properties button to open a dialog box in which to establish "callback" behavior. This security feature can be used to disconnect a user when they first logon, then call them back at a specified phone number to reestablish the connection.

Finally, you are asked to name the connection. Once configured, you can modify your server's settings by double-clicking the incoming connections icon to open the Connection dialog box shown in Figure 6.32.

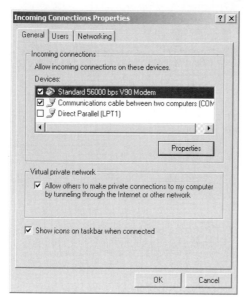

Figure 6.32 *Configuring Incoming Connection Settings.*

Under the General tab, choose among connection types and enable or disable VPN support. Click the Properties button to configure advanced connection parameters such as port speed, compression, flow control, data bits, stop bits, and parity.

Switch to the User tab to allow or deny access to local user accounts. You may also enable options that force users to secure passwords and data, and which permit password-less access to direct-connect devices such as handheld computers.

Switch to the Networking tab to enable and deny access through various protocols and configure their parameters. For example, select the Internet Protocol (TCP/IP) item and click the Protocol button to define client access through static or automatically assigned (DHCP) addressing, as shown in Figure 6.33.

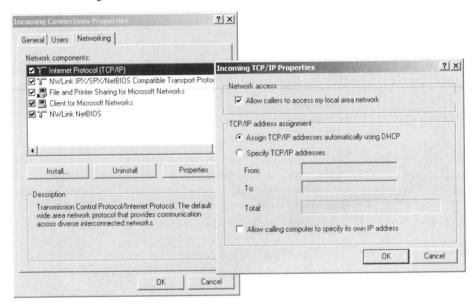

Figure 6.33 *Configuring TCP/IP options.*

You can also choose to limit dialup access to your workstation, or extend it to your local network.

Configuring Internet Connection Sharing

Internet Connection Sharing (ICS) allows you to make your workstation a gateway between the Internet and other workstations on a small local network, such as a home office. By enabling this feature, you can cut the costs that would be incurred by setting up multiple dialup lines and ISP accounts. It is particularly useful when you have a fast dialup connection, such as through Digital Subscriber Lines (DSL), ISDN, or broadband cable. All that is required on your workstation is dialup access to the Internet, such as through a modem, and a separate network adapter for access to your LAN. ICS then provides DHCP-based addresses for other computers on the network and makes it possible for them to access the Internet as if they were connected directly.

To enable, ICS, open your Internet connection's Properties dialog box and switch to the Sharing tab, as shown in Figure 6.34. Click the Enable Internet Connection Sharing for this connection checkbox.

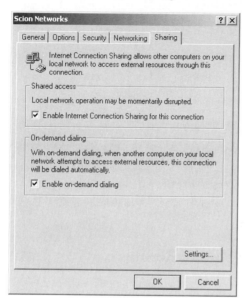

Figure 6.34 *Enabling ICS.*

You can also choose to enable on-demand dialing, which forces your workstation to dial up for a connection whenever any computer on the network requires an Internet-based resource.

Troubleshooting Internet Connection Sharing

A caveat to using ICS is the fact that it cannot be used on networks with pre-assigned static addresses, DNS servers, DHCP servers, and Internet routers (gateways), or domain controllers. Because ICS reconfigures your workstation's network adapter for its own addressing scheme, previously established connectivity is lost.

Other common problems and their solutions include the following:

- **The modem connection fails.** Troubleshoot the modem as described in Chapter 2, "Administering Windows 2000 Professional."
- **The network connection fails.** If you have multiple network adapters installed, make sure that you are sharing the one that is accessing the Internet connection (such as to a cable modem or DSL router).

- **TCP/IP fails.** Make sure that TCP/IP is properly installed on all client computers, and that they are configured to receive their addressing information automatically through DHCP.

Study Break
_____

Create and Share an Internet Connection

Practice what you have learned by creating and sharing an Internet dialup connection.

First, launch the Network and Dial-Up Connection Wizard or Internet Connection Wizard to establish a dialup connection to the Internet. Next, configure the connection to support ICS. Test ICS by connecting to the Internet through a networked client workstation. If unsuccessful, use the TCP/IP troubleshooting tools described earlier in this chapter to track down the problem.

MCSE 6.3   **Connecting to Shared Resources**

Finding and using resources on remote machines is a fundamental element of networking. The Universal Naming Convention (UNC) allows you to manually specify a path to a computer and a resource, and My Network Places allows you to see a list of the computers on the network.

Connecting Through My Network Places

The My Network Places shortcut appears on your Desktop if your workstation has a network adapter installed. When you double-click the icon, it brings a list of all the computers in your workgroup or domain, as shown in Figure 6.35.

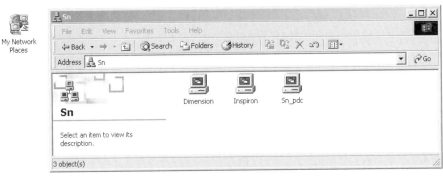

Figure 6.35 _Browsing the "SN" domain in My Network Places._

This list is actually a graphical representation of a browse list, which is maintained by the network computer that has been designated as Master Browser. The browse list is constantly kept up-to-date because every computer on the network with an active Server service registers its name with the Master Browser.

To connect to a shared resource, double-click a remote computer to see its list of available folders and printers, as shown in Figure 6.36.

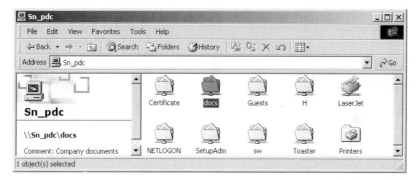

Figure 6.36   *Viewing shared resources.*

Double-click a folder to view its contents and copy files to and from your workstation. If you expect to work with the share often, you can choose the Map Network Drive command from the Tools menu to assign it a drive letter, thereafter treating it like another hard drive on your computer (assuming the host computer is turned on). Similarly, you can launch the

Add Network Place Wizard to locate a share (see Figure 6.37) and create a shortcut to it in My Network Places.

Figure 6.37 *Locating a share in the Add Network Place Wizard.*

Network places can include Microsoft-networking shares as well as FTP sites and Web folders.

Connecting With the Universal Naming Convention

You can also use the UNC instead of the Browse button (see Figure 6.37) to specify a share name on a specific computer. A connection made through a UNC path takes place immediately and does not need a drive letter. A UNC share path looks like the following:

```
\\computer_name\share_name
```

UNC connections can also connect to network printers using the following format:

```
\\server_name\printer_name
```

If a share name has a dollar sign at the end of it, the share becomes hidden and does not appear in listings. You can still access it through its UNC name, however, if you know that it exists.

The UNC can also be used from the command line, along with several other utilities. The NET VIEW command, for example, accesses the current browse list. The NET USE command and the UNC path of the resource assign network resources to drive letters. To connect a drive letter to a share on a server, the command would use the following format:

```
NET USE <drive_letter>:\\server_name\share_name
```

The NET USE command can also connect clients to network printers. To connect a port to a network printer on a server, the command would use the following format:

```
NET USE <port>:\\server_name\printer_name
```

To disconnect the network resources from a drive letter or port, use the /d switch as in the following command:

```
NET USE <drive_letter>: /d
```

Windows 2000 Professional as Microsoft Client

On a Microsoft network, you must have Client for Microsoft Networks installed in order to communicate with other Windows clients. You can allow other computers on the network to access shared data on your computer by enabling File and Print Sharing for Microsoft Networks.

Client for Microsoft Networks is a 32-bit protected-mode network client that provides network interoperability with Microsoft operating systems including Windows NT/2000, Windows 95/98/Me, Windows for Workgroups, Workgroup Add-on for MS-DOS, and LAN Manager. Client for Microsoft Networks can use any combination of NetBEUI, IPX/SPX-compatible, and TCP/IP network protocols.

If the Windows 2000 Setup program detects a network adapter during installation, it installs Client for Microsoft Networks by default.

Windows 2000 Professional as NetWare Client

Windows 2000 Professional can run Novell NetWare connectivity services and access NetWare networks easily, although you must install some additional software in order to access and share resources from a NetWare server.

NWLink IPX/SPX/NetBIOS Compatible Transport can establish peer-to-peer connections, but it does not enable access to files and printers on a NetWare server. If you want to access files or printers on a NetWare server, you have to install the Microsoft Client Services for NetWare (CSNW) service.

> **CSNW allows Windows 2000 Professional workstations to access files and printers on NetWare servers running bindery security or NetWare Directory Services (NDS). This is limited to NetWare versions 2.15 to 4.0. You cannot access a NetWare 5 server that is running pure IP using CSNW and IPX/SPX. In this case, use the Novell networking client instead.**

When you install NWLink IPX/SPX/NetBIOS Compatible Transport, you give your computer important benefits.

- It gets a new network redirector compatible with the NetWare Core Protocol (NCP). NCP is the standard Novell protocol for file and print sharing.
- It gets the ability to use long file names if the NetWare server is so configured.
- It gets Large Internet Protocol (LIP) to automatically negotiate and determine the largest possible frame size to communicate with NetWare servers.

NWLink and CSNW allow the workstation to access files and printers on a NetWare server running NDS. However, it does not support administration of NDS trees.

Although CSNW allows Windows 2000 Professional to access files and printers on a NetWare server, it does not allow NetWare clients to access files and printers on Windows 2000 computer. To enable this, you must also install Microsoft File and Print Services for NetWare (FPNW) on Windows NT Server.

A Windows 2000 Professional workstation can also access files and printers on a NetWare server without CSNW by connecting through a Windows 2000 Server configured with Gateway Services for NetWare (GSNW). GSNW can be installed only on a Windows 2000 Server computer.

You may install CSNW through the Local Area Connections Properties dialog box in the Network and Dial-Up Connections program group by adding Client software. After CSNW has been installed, you will need to enter some information about your NetWare account by clicking the Properties button to open the Select NetWare Logon dialog box, (see Figure 6.38).

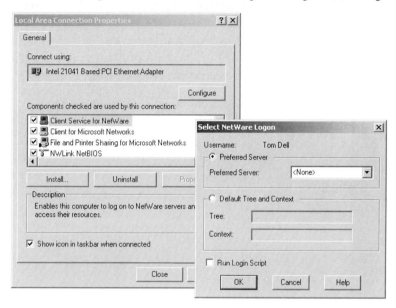

Figure 6.38 *Configuring NetWare logons.*

Enter the preferred server under NetWare version 2.15 or higher or version 3.x. Alternately, enter a default tree and context for NDS, the default for NetWare 4.x. Whenever the same user logs onto that machine, he automatically connects to the specified NetWare account as well as the Windows 2000 account. If users do not have NetWare accounts, they can specify None.

Once NWLink IPX/SPX/NetBIOS Compatible Transport and CSNW are installed, you can access your network's NetWare servers without any special procedures. You can browse either the Microsoft Windows network or the NetWare or Compatible Network when you double-click Entire Network in My Network Places. Right-click a folder in My Network Places and select Map Network Drive from the Shortcut menu to reassign any drive letter to any shared directory on a NetWare server.

CAPTURE, LOGIN, LOGOUT, and ATTACH are all NetWare commands that can cause problems if run from Windows 2000 Professional. You should only use them through other utilities supplied with Windows 2000.

Connecting to Shared Printers

You can create a connection to printing device shared from another workstation as easily is if it were connected directly to your own. As with local printers, launch the Add Printer Wizard from the Printers program group. Rather
than a selecting local printer, however, choose the Network printer radio
button when prompted, as shown in Figure 6.39.

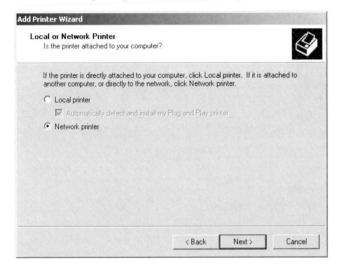

Figure 6.39 *Choosing to install a network printer.*

Next, you are prompted to enter the printer's name, if using Microsoft
or NetWare networking, or the printer's host name or IP address if connecting over TCP/IP.

Alternately, you can choose to browse the network for available printers, as shown in Figure 6.40.

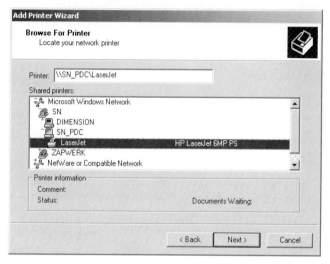

Figure 6.40 *Browsing for a network printer.*

If the printer resides on the network as a standalone device, rather than
being shared from a Windows workstation or server, you can connect to it by
creating a network port. In this case, select the Local printer option in the
Add Printer Wizard and disable the Plug and Play detection checkbox. Next,
choose the Create a new port radio button and choose the Standard TCP/IP
Port option from the Type drop-down menu, as shown in Figure 6.41.

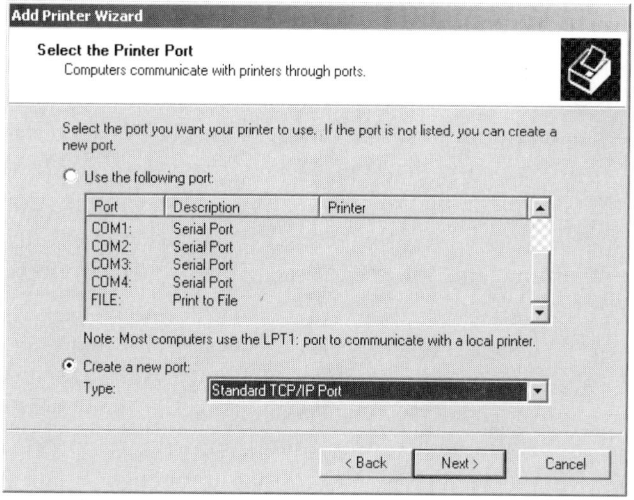

Figure 6.41 *Creating a new TCP/IP port.*

In subsequent steps, the Add Standard TCP/IP Port Wizard is launched to prompt you for such information as the printer's host name or IP address, and the name of the port (the same by default). Once completed, the printer is added as another shortcut within the Printers program group.

Study Break

Create a Network Place

Practice what you have learned by adding a shortcut to the My Network Places program group.

First, navigate through the various levels of My Network Places to locate a shared folder on a remote Microsoft networking client. Next, connect to the share and attempt to transfer a file to or from the folder. If you do not have sufficient permissions, either change your access level on the remote share or choose a different share for which you have better access. Finally, use the Map Network Drive command to map the remote folder as a drive letter, or the Add Network Place to create a network shortcut.

■ Summary

In this chapter, we described the configuration and troubleshooting of TCP/IP, setting up Dial-Up Networking connections, and connecting to shared resources.

Working With TCP/IP

To configure static TCP/IP connections, you must supply Windows 2000 Professional with IP address, subnet mask, and gateway addresses. In addition, the configuration of DNS server and WINS server addresses might be needed. To configure dynamic TCP/IP connections, you need only tell Windows 2000 Professional to obtain an IP address automatically. The operating system will then request the necessary networking parameters from a DHCP server. Among your options for securing TCP/IP connections are IPSec and IP filtering.

Several tools can be executed from the command line to help you troubleshoot TCP/IP connections. Use IPCONFIG to determine the current address of your workstation, as assigned statically or by a DHCP server. Use PING to determine if communication with remote hosts possible. Use TRACERT and/or PATHPING to map the network path between local and remote hosts and determine the point at which communication is failing.

Use NETSTAT to see which TCP/IP ports are open on your workstation for communications. Other issues that might require attention are DNS and WINS host name resolutions, to which you can apply such tools as NBT-STAT and NSLOOOKUP.

Working With Dial-Up Networking

Dial-Up Networking can be used to configure modem connections from your workstation to private networks, the Internet, or nearby computers using a serial cable. Among your connection options are VPNs, which use secure protocols such as PPTP or L2TP to "tunnel" through insecure networks, such as the public Internet. You can also configure your workstation to act as a Remote Access Server, accepting phone calls from other computers and connecting them to itself, and optionally, the rest of the network on which it resides.

Connecting to Shared Resources

You can connect your workstation to remote network shares on other Microsoft networking-based computers through My Network Places if you have a network adapter and Client for Microsoft Networks installed. Using My Network Places, you can locate resources from a network-wide browse list. You can also use UNC commands to attach remote resources from My Network Places or the command line. Your workstation can access NetWare-based resources just as easily if you install the IPX/SPX/NetBIOS Compatible Transport protocol and Client Services for NetWare. You can connect to shared printers by browsing for them through My Network Places or the Add Printer Wizard, or in the case of standalone devices, by creating a TCP/IP port connection to them using their host names or IP addresses.

▲ CHAPTER REVIEW QUESTIONS

Here are a few questions relating to the material covered in the *Implementing, Managing, and Troubleshooting Protocols and Services* section of Microsoft's *Installing, Configuring, and Administering Microsoft Windows 2000 Professional* exam (70-210).

1. Under TCP/IP, host addresses can never end in "0" or "255."

    A. True

    B. False

2. *Which of the following is not an IP security policy setting? Select all that apply:*

   A. Client responds to secure and insecure requests

   B. Client only works with insecure communications

   C. Client only works with secure communications

   D. Client requests but does not require secure communications

3. *Windows 2000 professional cannot support connections through SLIP.*

   A. True

   B. False

4. *Which of the following protocols directly support VPN implementations? Select all that apply:*

   A. PPP

   B. PPTP

   C. EAP

   D. L2TP

5. *Which of the following are advantages L2TP has over PPTP? Select all that apply:*

   A. Supports more packet-oriented protocols

   B. Supports tunnel authentication

   C. Supports header compression

   D. Supports tunnel encryption

6. *You can configure your workstation to support incoming connections of three types.*

   A. True

   B. False

7. *The number of simultaneous RAS connections supported by Windows 2000 Professional is limited mostly by available RAM.*

   A. True

   B. False

8. *You must establish an account with an ISP and have the settings that are provided handy before attempting to configure a dialup connection to the Internet.*

   A. True

   B. False

9. *Among the serial line protocols that can be used to connect to the Internet are SLIP and PPP:*

   A. True

   B. False

10. *ICS can only be enabled on networks that use pre-existing static IP addresses.*

    A. True

    B. False

11. *ICS' on-demand dialing forces your workstation to dial up for a connection whenever any computer on the network requires an Internet-based resource.*

    A. True

    B. False

12. *Client for Microsoft Networking is used in conjunction with only Microsoft's own protocol.*

    A. True

    B. False

13. *FalseWhich are ways in which you might access a shared folder? Select all that apply:*

    A. Through My Network Places

    B. Through a mapped network drive

    C. Through a UNC command

    D. Through the Add Network Place Wizard

S E V E N

Securing Windows 2000 Professional

▲Chapter Syllabus

MCSE 7.1 Encrypting Hard Disk Data

MCSE 7.2 Implementing Local Security Policy

MCSE 7.3 Implementing User Account Security

MCSE 7.4 Authenticating Local Users

MCSE 7.5 Implementing Security Configurations

In this chapter, we will look at material covered in the *Implementing, Monitoring, and Troubleshooting Security* section of Microsoft's *Installing, Configuring, and Administering Microsoft Windows 2000 Professional* exam (70-210).

In the following pages, you will learn to protect hard drive data through encryption, create security policies and configurations for your local workstation, and manage user accounts and authentication.

MCSE 7.1   Encrypting Hard Disk Data

Windows 2000 Professional implements the Encrypting File System (EFS) on NTFS-formatted drives. As described earlier in this book, EFS does not work with NTFS compression and does make accessing encrypted files somewhat slower. Beyond that, EFS is easy to enable and its operation is largely transparent to users.

Encrypted files are only easily accessible to the users who created them. To these users, opening a file is a simple matter of double-clicking. Other users are unable to open any encrypted files that they did not create, however, so EFS does not lend itself to file sharing.

Encrypting Files

EFS security is a two-tier strategy. At one level, Windows 2000 uses a symmetric encryption scheme wherein a randomly generated EFS key is used to encrypt and decrypt files. At another level, Windows 2000 uses an asymmetric private key/public key encryption scheme in which one key encrypts the EFS key and another key decrypts the EFS key. The process works as follows:

1. You choose to encrypt a file by right-clicking it to open the Properties dialog box. Next, you switch to the General tab and click the Advanced button to open the Advanced Attributes dialog box, as shown in Figure 7.1.

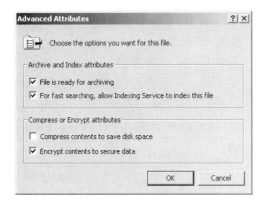

Figure 7.1   *Choosing to encrypt files.*

2. In the Advanced Attributes dialog box, you select the Encrypt contents to secure data check box. When you click OK, you are given the further

choice of additionally encrypting the folder that contains the file, as shown in Figure 7.2.

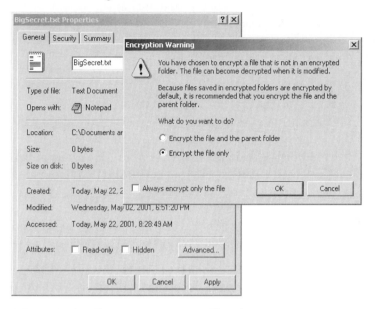

Figure 7.2 *Choosing to encrypt a file only.*

 Windows 2000 does not really encrypt a folder, it encrypts files that are added to the folder.

3. After you click OK in the Encryption Warning dialog box, EFS randomly generates a key that is used to encrypt and decrypt the file.
4. After being used to encrypt the file, the EFS key is itself encrypted using your public key.
5. To decrypt a file, you require a private key that can decrypt your public key and gain access to the EFS key. The private key is stored on your workstation, becoming available after your identity is validated by logon authentication.

Decrypting Files

Only the person who encrypted a file has access to it. To make the file available to others, the person who encrypted the file must decrypt it by reversing the process previously described, deselecting the Encrypt contents to secure data checkbox (see Figure 7.1).

Exporting and Importing Private Keys

It is possible to carry your private key away from the workstation by importing and exporting your security certificate. To make the key accessible when you are working from another system, you can set up a roaming user profile. Alternately, you can export your certificate to a floppy disk or (presumably secure) network share.

To export your private key, you will need to add the Certificates snap-in to the Group Policy Editor MMC. To do this, type "gpedit.msc /a" at the command line to open the Group Policy Editor in author mode, as shown in Figure 7.3.

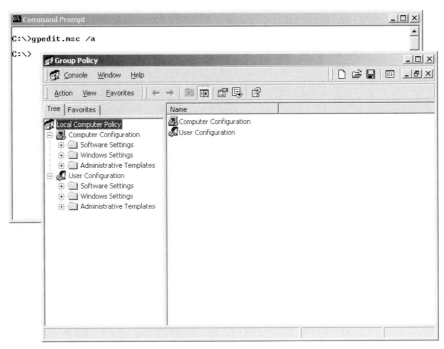

Figure 7.3 *Launching the Group Policy Editor MMC in author mode.*

Next, select the Add/Remove Snap-ins command from the Console menu to open the Add/Remove Snap-in dialog box. Click the Add button to add Certificates under the Local Computer Policy node, as shown in Figure 7.4. When prompted to apply the changes to the user, service, or computer account, choose the My User Account radio button.

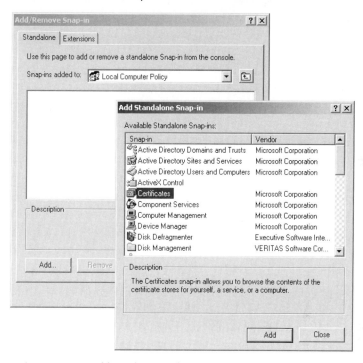

Figure 7.4 *Adding the Certificates snap-in.*

Once returned to the MMC, expand the Certificates node and navigate to the Personal/Certificates branch, as shown in Figure 7.5.

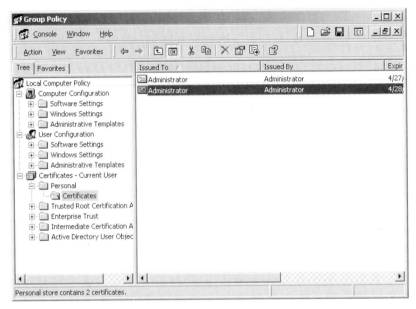

Figure 7.5 *Selecting a certificate.*

Select a certificate, then choose the Export command from the Action menu's All Tasks submenu. This will launch the Export Certificate Wizard.

In the Certificate Export Wizard, enable the Yes, export the private key radio button when prompted, as shown in Figure 7.6.

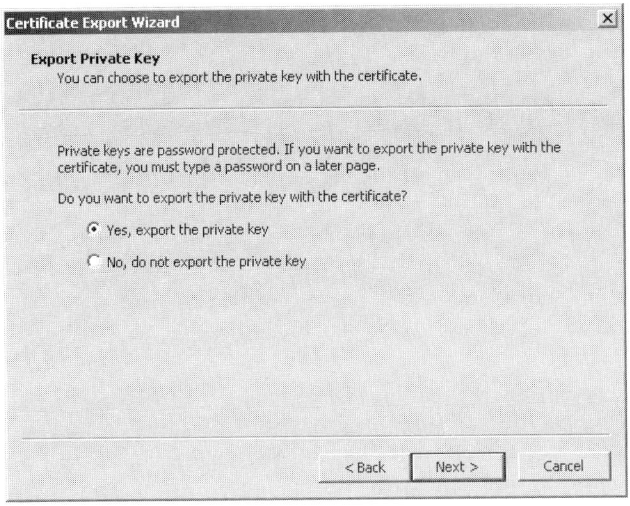

Figure 7.6 *Selecting to export the private key.*

Next, you will be prompted to choose the certificate's file format, as shown in Figure 7.7.

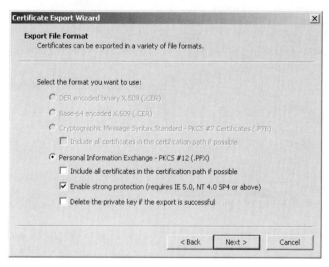

Figure 7.7 *Choosing a file format.*

Select the default .pfx format. Deselect the Enable strong protection checkbox if you will be using the certificate on a non-Windows 2000 system or a Windows NT 4.0 system without at least Service Pack 4.

The wizard will continue by asking you for a password, and then a file name and location to save the certificate. When complete, the wizard will create a small .pfx file that you can copy to a floppy disk or secure on a network share for use on other computers. When at another computer, simply reverse this process by choosing the Certificate snap-in's Import command.

Recovering Private Keys

Private keys are not impervious to the mechanisms that can destroy normal files (user deletions, hard disk failures, and so on). Once a private key has been destroyed, however, its loss has a far greater effect than the loss of most other files, because its owner can no longer access any of the files that were encrypted. Fortunately, Microsoft supplies a fail-safe in the form of Recovery Agents, special users with the power to decrypt files without having the creator's private or EFS keys.

Administrators can create Recovery Agents. To do this, navigate to the Encrypted Data Recovery Agents folder under the Local Computer Policy node, as shown in Figure 7.8.

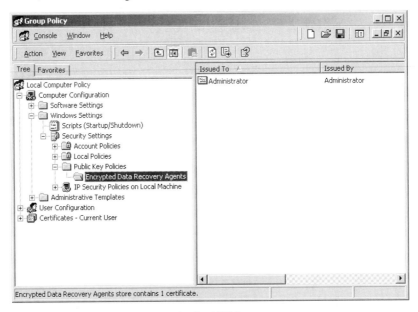

Figure 7.8 *Recovery Agents in the MMC.*

Next, choose the Add command from the Action menu to open the Add Recovery Agent Wizard. You will be prompted to locate a certificate by either browsing the Active Directory or selecting a .cer file on the local computer, as shown in Figure 7.9.

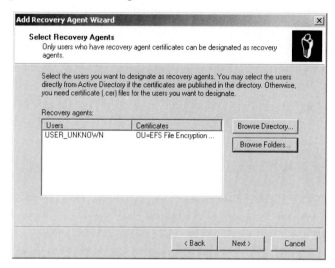

Figure 7.9 *Browsing for a certificate.*

To gain access to a local certificate, you must first save a copy of it as a .cer file. This is done by following the export procedure as previously explained, except that you must choose the No, do not export private key radio button and save the certificate under an X.509 .cer file format instead of the .pfx format (see Figures 7.6 and 7.7).

In addition to determining whether or not encrypted data can be recovered, Recovery Agents also determine whether or not EFS can be used at all! By default, Windows 2000 makes at least the Administrator a Recovery Agent. If you delete all accounts as Recovery Agents, including Administrator, EFS will be disabled for the entire system.

With the release of Service Pack 2, Microsoft upgraded EFS and its other services to 128-bit encryption. If your system is running under the earlier 56-bit encryption and you install Service Pack 2, you cannot revert back to 56-bit encryption, even if you uninstall the Service Pack. Other services affected by the change include Kerberos, RAS, RPC, SSL/TLS, CryptoAPI, Terminal Services RDP, and IPSec.

Using CIPHER

The CIPHER utility can be used to encrypt and decrypt files from the command line. Its options are as follow:

- **/e** Encrypt file.
- **/d** Decrypt file.
- **/s: dir** Perform operation on all subdirectories.
- **/a** Perform operation on all files of the specified name.
- **/i** Continue operation regardless of errors.
- **/f** Force encryption (even on encrypted files).
- **/q** Minimize reporting.
- **/h** Perform operation on hidden files.

Study Break

Encrypt a File

Practice what you have learned by encrypting a file.

First, create a file on the root level of an NTFS volume. Next, encrypt the file using the Administrator logon account. Next, log on with another account, such as your user account, and attempt to open the file.

MCSE 7.2 | Implementing Local Security Policy

Local security policy can be implemented by launching the Local Security Settings MMC shortcut found in the Administrative Tools program group, as shown in Figure 7.10.

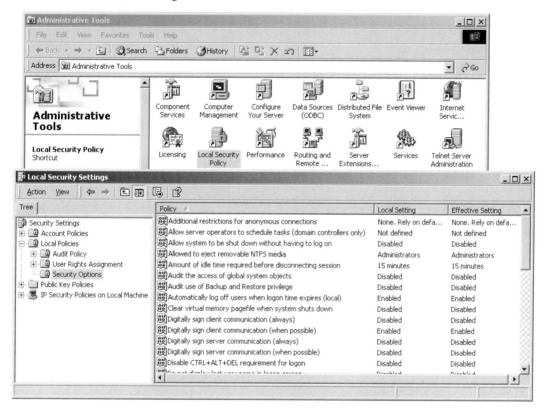

Figure 7.10 The Local Security Settings MMC.

You may configure settings under the Local Policies node for audit policies and user rights (both described further on in this chapter), as well as general security options.

Configuring Local Security Policy

To configure a local policy setting, double-click a policy document in the list to open a dialog box in which you can either select a Disable or Enable radio button or choose an option from a drop-down menu (see Figure 7.11).

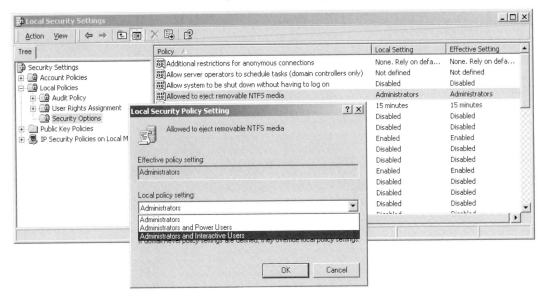

Figure 7.11 *Setting a local security option.*

Managing Local Security Policy

Among the policy settings of greatest interest are the following:

- **Allow system to be shut down without having to logon.** If enabled (the default), anyone can shut down your workstation whether or not they have the right to logon to begin with. If your workstation is running important processes when you are not around, you might wish to restrict this ability so that the workstation is not inadvertently turned off.
- **Clear Virtual Memory pagefile when system shuts down.** If enabled, Windows 2000 will purge the pagefile or residual data that might be otherwise open to unauthorized access.
- **Disable CTRL-ALT-DELETE requirement for logon.** If disabled (the default), this setting ensures that only Windows 2000 is accepting your logon information, rather than some Trojan horse program whose purpose is to steal that data. If security is no concern, this feature might be considered an annoyance.

- **Do not display last user name in logon screen.** If enabled, the next person to sit down at your computer will not see your logon user name—which puts them halfway through the authentication process, perhaps making it easier to guess your password—when they attempt to log on.
- **Recovery Console: Allow floppy copy and access to all drives and all folders.** If enabled, this policy could compromise security by permitting someone to navigate through a hard drive's directory structure and copy files from the Recovery Console command prompt. Recovery Console is still subject to Administrator logon authentication (unless you also disable that policy), so you might consider this change in policy useful for making last ditch efforts at file recovery.
- **Unsigned driver installation behavior.** By default, this policy is not defined. You can define a policy of Silently succeed, in which case all unsigned drivers are installed without prompting, Warn but allow installation, or Do not allow installation.

Troubleshooting Local Security Policy

If your workstation is a member of a domain, the policies you establish locally will not necessarily be the last word on the matter. Local policy settings are always overruled by domain-wide policy settings when conflicts occur. Should you find that a policy you set locally is having no effect, double-check the Local Security Settings MMC to make sure that the Local Setting listed matches the Effective Setting (e.g., the domain-wide setting).

Study Break

Establish Local Security Policy

Practice what you have learned by setting local security policy.

First, launch the Local Security Settings MMC and navigate to the policy documents in the Security Settings folder. Here, alter a setting, such as defining the Unsigned driver installation behavior option. Make sure your local settings do not conflict with effective (domain-wide) settings. Perform the action controlled by the policy setting to verify its effect.

MCSE 7.3 Implementing User Account Security

In order to use Windows 2000 Professional workstation resources, users must have rights and permissions to access them. These rights can be assigned explicitly, by a user's account characteristics, or implicitly, by a user's affiliation with a group and its account characteristics. User accounts grant rights to one person. Group accounts extend like rights to a collection of user accounts.

Working with Local Users and Groups

Administrators generally create user accounts. A user may have one or more accounts, each with different rights and group memberships. When prompted by the Windows logon dialog box, users enter the name assigned to their accounts and its associated password. Windows 2000 then validates the user accounts by checking its users and groups databases. Users must be validated for each Windows 2000 object for which they request access.

Windows 2000 Professional comes with a number of built-in accounts. These accounts have their own hard-coded characteristics that cannot be altered.

DEFAULT USER ACCOUNTS

Two user accounts are created by default, when you install Windows 2000 Professional.

ADMINISTRATOR • This is the account you choose a password for when installing Windows 2000 Professional and which has given you the rights needed to configure the workstation since. This account can be renamed, but it cannot be disabled or deleted. It is automatically a member of the Administrators group.

GUEST • This account is used to grant access to people who do not have user accounts on the workstation. The security implications of this should be immediately obvious. For maximum security, this account can be disabled, although it is otherwise permanent.

This account is automatically assigned to the Guests group. If properly used, both the account and group can be helpful. It is the resources to which the account is granted access that are of concern, so as long as you never assign "guest access" to sensitive areas, the account itself is relatively harmless.

DEFAULT GROUP ACCOUNTS

Practically speaking, a user account's affiliation with group accounts is what really provides it with access. As an administrator, you can assign user accounts to each resource implicitly, but it is much easier to designate the desired permissions for a group account and reuse that account for multiple resources.

User and group accounts are not prioritized. One account does not take precedence over any other account. Windows 2000 recognizes three groups.

LOCAL GROUPS

These groups have rights and permissions to resources on the local computer. Its members have access to mass storage and printers on the workstation itself, but not on other computers. Rules that apply to local groups include the following:

- A local group cannot be renamed.
- A local group cannot be disabled.

Workstations have seven built-in local group accounts.

ADMINISTRATORS • The most powerful group, this account has control over the entire computer and all of its resources. Members of this group may perform the following tasks:

- Modify user accounts.
- Delete user accounts.
- Create other Administrator accounts.
- Modify membership to built-in groups.
- Unlock workstations.
- Format disk drives.
- Upgrade the operating system.
- Back up directories and files.
- Restore directories and files.
- Modify security policies.
- Connect to Administrator-only share points.

USERS • All new user accounts are made part of the Users group by default. Members of this group may perform the following tasks:

- Manage directories and files.
- Use applications.
- Use printers.
- Connect to share points and printers.
- Save personal profiles.

The Users group does not have the right to share directories and files or to manage printers.

GUESTS • This group includes the previously described Guest account.

BACKUP OPERATORS • Any user who is not a member of this group can back up and restore directories and files to which they have access rights. Members of this group have the additional power to override security and back up or restore any directories and files using the Backup utility.

REPLICATOR • This group is used by the Directory Replicator service.

POWER USERS • This group has more power than Users but less power than Administrators. Members of this group may perform the following tasks:

- Share directories and files.
- Share printers.
- Turn off sharing.
- Create and manage printers.
- Create accounts (except for Administrators).
- Modify and delete accounts (that they created).
- Set a computer's date and time.
- Create program groups.

This group is useful for sharing some administrative duties with users, while at the same time restricting them from true Administrator-level access.

GLOBAL GROUPS

These groups are administered from domain controllers and have no specific rights until they are associated with local groups. They are used to contain a collection of user accounts for a given domain. Each user account is a member of a global group. When a Windows 2000 Professional computer joins a domain, the domain's global groups merge with corresponding local groups in the workstation's security database. This effectively extends access to resources for each user account to each member computer in the domain.

Some rules that apply to global groups are:

- A global group can only contain user accounts.
- A global group must be a member of a local group.
- A local group cannot be a member of a global group.
- A global group cannot be a member of another global group.
- Global groups can only be created and administered on domain controllers.

Domain controllers manage the following three built-in global groups:

DOMAIN ADMINS • This is a domain-wide group of Administrator accounts. As a default member of the Administrators local group, this group extends the rights of Administrators to every Windows 2000 computer in a domain.

DOMAIN USERS • This is a domain-wide group of User accounts. The domain's Administrator account and all new user accounts are added to this group by default.

DOMAIN GUESTS • This is a domain-wide group of Guest accounts.

SPECIAL GROUPS

These groups are used to extend system resource access to a predefined set of user accounts. They cannot be deleted or added, and include the following:

CREATOR/OWNER • This group contains the accounts of users that create or take ownership of resources.

EVERYONE • This group contains each user who accesses the server, whether locally or remotely.

INTERACTIVE • This group contains each user that accesses the server locally.

NETWORK • This group contains all users who connect to a resource via the network.

CREATING USER ACCOUNTS

On domain controllers, users and groups are managed through Active Directory.

On standalone servers and workstations, users and groups can be created and managed using the Computer Management MMC's System Tools node, as shown in Figure 7.12.

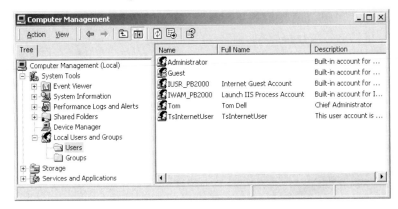

Figure 7.12 *Viewing local users and groups.*

To create a new user account, select the Users folder in the Tree pane, right-click the right windowpane, and choose the New User command from the context menu. This will open the New User dialog box, as shown in Figure 7.13.

Figure 7.13 *Creating a new user account.*

In the New User dialog box, fill in the following fields:

- **User name.** The user name is the user's logon identification. It need not have anything to do with a person's real name, although making some correlation is a good idea for convenience. It is not case sensitive and can be as long as 20 characters. It cannot include the following characters:

```
? " / : \ ; [ , ] + | = * < - >
```

  In addition, the user name cannot consist solely of periods or spaces, and must be unique from any other user or group name in the computer or domain.
- **Password.** Assuming you do not leave this field blank, what you type here is case sensitive and can be as long as 127 characters. The best passwords are at least eight characters long and include both upper and lower case characters mixed randomly with numerals. (Windows NT and 9.x only support passwords of 14 characters.)

> The toughest passwords we know of are created by a colleague of mine who takes German slang phrases, reverses them, and intersperses them with numbers. It is overkill, but it is also very effective.

- **Full name.** It is helpful to have a user's complete name here. However, you can type any description you want into this field.
- **Description.** Useful information to add to this field might be users' departments (e.g., "Information Services"), telephone extensions (e.g., "x101"), physical locations (e.g., "Washington Office"), or computer type (e.g., "Windows 2000 Pro laptop").
- **Users must change password at next logon.** This checkbox is selected by default. It forces users to create their own passwords when they first log on with the user name you provide. When enabled, it disables the next two checkboxes.
- **User cannot change password.** This checkbox restricts password creation to Administrators. This is useful when working with shared accounts and the Guest account, or when you do not trust users to create sufficiently difficult passwords.
- **Password never expires.** Old passwords are often about as good as no passwords. After a password has been hollered across a crowded room, written down on sticky notes, or emailed to co-workers often enough, it loses any real security. Because of this, Windows 2000

"times out" a password after a certain time has elapsed and forces users to create new ones. As a rule, this is a good idea. However, you might wish to make some accounts, such as the Guest account, exempt from this rule.

- **Account is disabled.** This option will "turn off," but not delete, an account. When a person leaves your organization, it is wiser to disable the user's account than delete it. That way you can assign the same rights to the person's replacement by simply changing the user name and password. This is also useful for securing the accounts of users who are on leave, vacation, sabbatical, or temporary assignment elsewhere.

Click the Create button when you are finished, which will record the account data but leave the cleared dialog box open so that you can create more accounts.

CREATING GROUP ACCOUNTS

To create a new group account, select the Groups folder in the Tree pane of the Computer Management MMC, right-click the right windowpane, and choose the New Group command from the context menu. This will open the New Group dialog box, as shown in Figure 7.14.

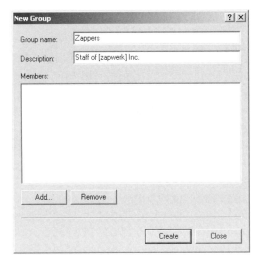

Figure 7.14 *Creating a new group account.*

Name and describe the group, then click the Add button to include members, as shown in Figure 7.15.

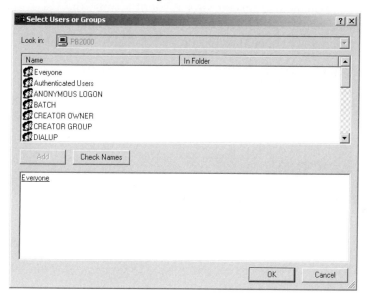

Figure 7.15 *Adding members to a new group.*

You may add user accounts, global group accounts, or both.

Once created, local groups can be managed like user accounts. They cannot be renamed or disabled, but they can be deleted (without deleting their member accounts).

MANAGING USERS AND GROUPS

Once created, user and group accounts can be managed through the Computer Management MMC. To change a user's account name, for example, right-click a user in the right windowpane to make the user name editable. To change a user account's password, select the Set password command from the Action menu. To configure account settings, double-click a user.

Implementing Account Settings

To implement a specific user account setting, the Users folder in the Tree pane of the Computer Management MMC, and double-click a user in the right pane to open the User Properties dialog box, as shown in Figure 7.16.

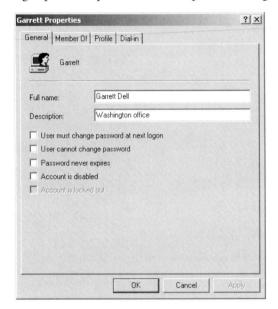

Figure 7.16   *Configuring General user account settings.*

CONFIGURING AND MANAGING ACCOUNT SETTINGS

You may reconfigure all of the account parameters you established when creating the user account, with the exception of user name and password, under the General tab. If an administrator has enabled the Account Lockout option through Account Policy, you will also see an active Account locked out check box.

Switch to Member Of tab to add or remove group memberships, as shown in Figure 7.17.

Figure 7.17 *Configuring user account group membership settings.*

Switch to Profile tab to configure several environmental variables, as shown in Figure 7.18. These settings are particularly useful in an enterprise environment when the items referred to are stored on a central server.

User profiles and home folders that are located in one place are easier to back up.

- **User Profile Path.** This field is used to specify the location on a server of a user profile file. Among other things, this file contains information about the user's Start menu, Desktop, and recently used documents. Specifying this path permits users to have their preferences follow them from workstation to workstation. The most common user profile path is:

  ```
  \\<server_name>\Profileshare\%username%
  ```

  Note that the local machine must be able to access the share on which the profile is stored for this to work. To reduce unnecessary routing traffic, this should be a server on the local subnet.

- **Logon Script Name.** This field is used to specify a .CMD or .BAT file containing scripted instructions, such as to map network drives or display a welcome message.
- **Home Folder.** These fields are used to specify the default location where users will store their work. This folder can be local or on a network share. If you create a user's home folder on an NTFS partition, the user is granted Full Control permissions and all other users are denied access by default.

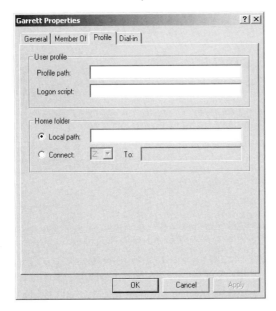

Figure 7.18 *Configuring user account profile settings.*

TROUBLESHOOTING ACCOUNT SETTINGS

Among the issues that can be addressed by troubleshooting account settings are the following:

- If a user is unable to access a resource, verify that the proper group memberships have been assigned.
- Should a user report repeated failures in logging on, check to see if an administrator has enabled the Account Lockout option through Account Policy. If so, you will see that the Account locked out check box is active in the user's account properties. It is triggered (enabled) when the user reaches the preset limit of unsuccessful logon attempts.

If the Lockout duration is set for a long time, then you must manually disable the check box so the user can access the account again.

- If users report problems with their environmental settings, verify that the path to their profile folders is still accurate.
- If users report they have problems logging on, verify that the settings in the login script are still valid (e.g., NET USE, etc.).
- If users cannot access their home folders, verify that the share on which they are stored is still accessible and that the path is still valid.

Implementing User Rights

User rights refer to what a user is allowed to do on a given computer. Resource permissions refer to the context in which user rights may be applied. Put simply, rights determine what can be done, and permissions determine where it can be done.

User rights can be implemented through the User Rights Assignment node of the Local Security Settings MMC, as shown in Figure 7.19.

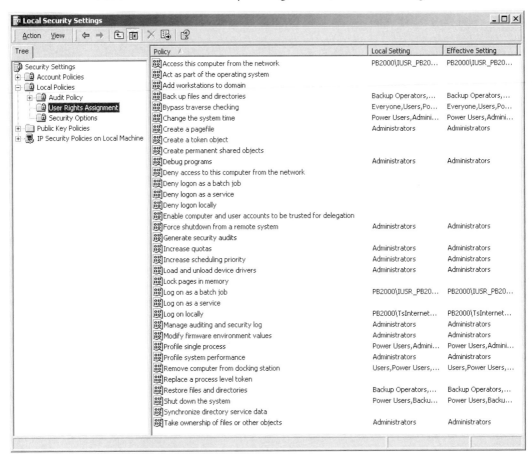

Figure 7.19 *User rights in the Local Security Settings MMC.*

User rights do not have to be explicitly assigned under Windows 2000. They are implemented automatically and stored in the account database. Table 7.1 describes several user rights as named in the Registry, their uses, and the groups to which they are initially assigned.

Table 7.1 *User Right Assignments*

User Right	Characteristics
Access this computer from the network	Users may connect via the network. Assigned to Everyone, Users, Power Users, Backup Operators, and Administrators.
Act as part of the operating system	Process may act as a secure part of the operating system. BackOffice applications are common examples. Not assigned to any groups initially.
Add workstations to the domain	Users may add workstations to the domain. Irrevocable right of Administrators and Server Operators. Not assigned to any groups initially.
Back up files and directories	Users may back up files and directories regardless of their permissions. Assigned to Administrators, Backup Operators, and Server Operators.
Bypass traverse checking	Users may traverse the directory structure regardless of its permissions. Assigned to Everyone, Users, Power Users, Backup Operators, and Administrators.
Change system time	Users may change the internal clock. Assigned to Administrators, Server Operators, and Power Users.
Create a pagefile	Users may create a Virtual Memory paging file. Assigned to Administrators.
Create a token object	Rights granted to create access tokens. Not assigned to any groups initially.
Create permanent shared objects	Users may create shared objects used within Windows 2000. Does not relate to printer or folder shares. Not initially assigned.
Debug programs	Users may debug low-level objects such as process threads. Assigned to Administrators.
Generate security audits	Processes may generate security audit logs. Not initially assigned.
Increase scheduling priority	Users may boost the execution priority of a process using the Task Manager. Assigned to Administrators.
Load and unload device drivers	Users may install and remove device drivers. Assigned to Administrators.

Table 7.1 *User Right Assignments (continued)*

Lock pages in memory	Users may lock pages into memory so that they cannot be paged out to the disk-based pagefile. Not initially assigned.
Log on as a service	Users may register as a service with the system. Granted to service accounts automatically, but not initially assigned otherwise.
Log on locally	Users may log on to the system by typing a username/password combination into the User Authentication dialog box. Assigned to local Guests, Users, Power Users, Backup Operators, and Administrators.
Manage audit and security log	Users may specify which files, groups, and printers to audit. Users may view and clear the Security Log in Event Viewer. Does not allow changes to audit policy. Assigned to Administrators.
Modify firmware environment variables	Users may modify system environment variables stored in nonvolatile RAM. Assigned to Administrators.
Profile single process	Users may perform performance sampling on processes. Assigned to Administrators and Power Users.
Profile system performance	Users may perform performance sampling on a computer. Assigned to Power users and Administrators.
Remove computer from docking station	Users may move mobile computers. Assigned to Users, Power Users, and Administrators.
Replace a process level token	Used by the system to modify a process's security access token. Used by the process of impersonation. Not initially assigned.
Restore file and directories	Users may restore backed-up files and directories regardless of their permissions. Assigned to Administrators, Backup Operators, and Server Operators.
Shut down the system	Users may shut down the computer. Assigned to Users, Administrators, Backup Operators, and Power Users.
Take ownership of files or other objects	Users may take ownership of any object, even those for which they do not have sufficient access permissions. Assigned to Administrators.

CONFIGURING USER RIGHTS

To configure a user right, double-click a policy document in the list to open a dialog box to which you can add group accounts, as shown in Figure 7.20.

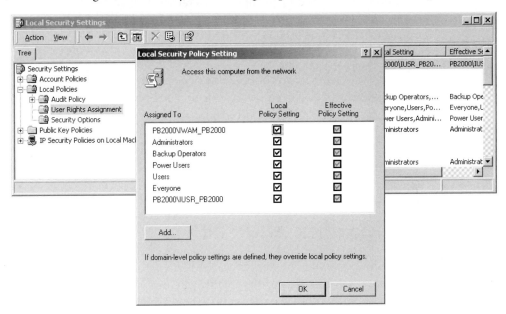

Figure 7.20   *Configuring user rights.*

The dialog box also provides you with a comparison of local policy settings vs. effective policy settings. As previously described, domain-wide (effective) permissions always override local permissions.

MANAGING USER RIGHTS

Of these user rights, a few are more powerful than others. The most powerful is the Act as part of the operating system user right, which grants the same level of access to a user that Windows 2000 itself has. Needless to say, it is unlikely that you will wish to grant a user group that much potential for mayhem!

Another powerful and potentially problematic user right is Take ownership of files or other objects. By default, owners have exclusive control over the resources they create. Not even Administrators have equal access. An Administrator can, however, take a resource away from an owner thanks to this user right. This is discretionary access to be used only under special circumstances. This cannot be done clandestinely, however, because no one who takes ownership of a resource can relinquish ownership! The only way to return ownership to original owners is to allow them to explicitly take it back. In short, ownership can only be taken, never granted.

Note that some user rights, such as Deny logon locally, can cause confusion because adding groups denies rather than allows the right.

TROUBLESHOOTING USER RIGHTS

In general, you do not want to change default user rights. A mistake here can render the workstation inoperable. There are sometimes exceptions to the rule, however. For example, the default membership of the Log on locally user right includes the Guest group. For better security, you might wish to remove this group's access.

If users report problems with their levels of system access, verify that they belong to the groups appropriate to the user rights they need. Also, be sure to verify that user rights you grant locally correspond to those of the domain at large, where applicable.

Implementing Auditing

Windows 2000 provides extremely powerful auditing capabilities. Any attempt to access a directory or file, whether or not it was successful, can be tracked and recorded in the Security Log (which can been examined in Event Viewer).

Auditing can be implemented through the Audit Policy node of the Local Security Settings MMC, as shown in Figure 7.21.

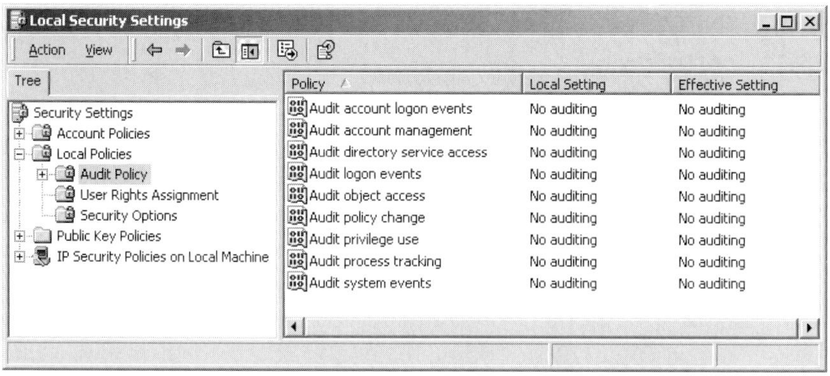

Figure 7.21 *Audit policies in the Local Security Settings MMC.*

CONFIGURING AUDITING

To configure an audit policy, double-click a policy document in the list to open a dialog box to which you can enable tracking for successes, failures, or both, as shown in Figure 7.22.

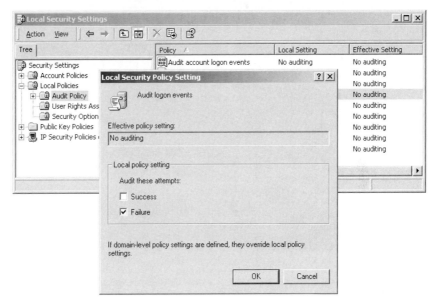

Figure 7.22   *Configuring audit policy.*

MANAGING AUDITING

When you enable auditing policy, what gets audited is up to you. For example, to monitor access to a particular folder, you would first enable the Successes checkbox for the Audit Object Access policy. Next, right-click the folder that you wish to monitor and select the Properties command to open the Properties dialog box. Next, switch to the Security tab and click the

Advanced button to open the Access Control Settings dialog box. Switch to the Auditing tab, as shown in Figure 7.23.

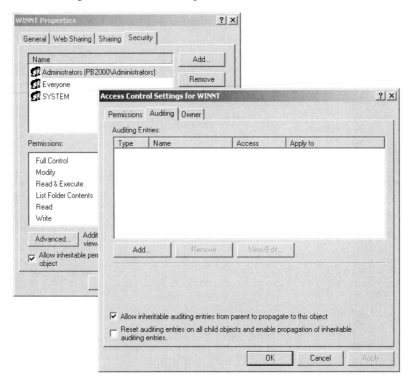

Figure 7.23 *Choosing auditing options.*

Next, click the Add button to select the groups whose access you wish to watch. Click the OK button and you will be given the opportunity to enable checkboxes to monitor the successes and failures of the group's activities by permission level, as shown in Figure 7.24.

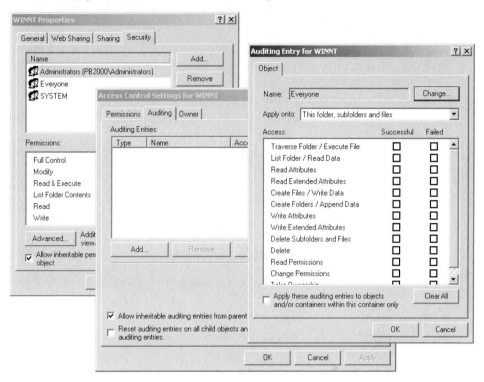

Figure 7.24   *Choosing access level for auditing.*

Administrators and any users or groups that are assigned the Manage auditing and security log user right can set directory and file auditing options. They may also view the status of successes and failures in the Security Log.

In enabling file auditing, you must first determine whom it is you want to audit. The Everyone group default is a catch-all, but if you know that a file is only accessible to a smaller group you may change this.

If you are auditing a folder (as shown in Figure 7.24), you will also need to decide if you will extend your auditing to subfolders and existing files. Next, you must decide what events will be audited. Among the questions these choices can answer are the following:

- **Read.** Who is trying to read a file?
- **Write.** Who is attempting to modify a file?
- **Execute.** Who is trying to execute a program?
- **Delete.** Who is trying to delete a file?

- **Change Permissions.** Who tried to change access to a directory or file?
- **Take Ownership.** Who attempted to take ownership of a directory or file?

Whether you audit for successes or failures will depend on what you are looking for. If someone keeps deleting an important file, for example, you should enable success auditing to see who it is the next time it happens. If you know your permissions are secure but you suspect someone of malicious intent, you should enable failure auditing to see who might be probing your security.

The latter case is every administrator's nightmare. If you fear that network security has been compromised and there are unauthorized users accessing your resources, enable logon and logoff auditing. Audit for both successes and failures. This will point you to the location of failed logon attempts and actual security breaches.

TROUBLESHOOTING AUDITING

If you find that your system is responding more slowly, be aware that auditing does increase performance degradation and should be used sparingly. Similarly, you might find that the Security Log is filling rapidly with auditing events. In this case, either reduce the number of auditing events or increase the size of the Security Log.

Implementing Account Policy

Under Windows 2000, account policies determine the circumstances under which users are permitted to log on. Account policies are implemented through the Password Policies and Account Lockout Policy subfolders of the

Account Policies folder under the Local Computer Policy node of the Group Policy Editor MMC, as shown in Figure 7.25.

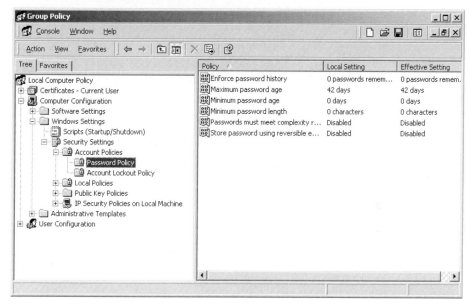

Figure 7.25   *Account policies in the Group Policy Editor MMC.*

CONFIGURING ACCOUNT POLICY

To configure an account policy, double-click a document in the Policy list to open a dialog box in which you can enable a rule or enforce a parameter, as shown in Figure 7.26.

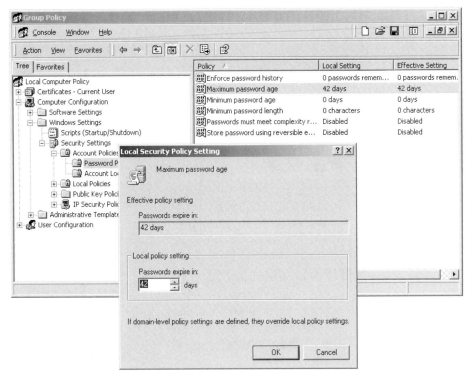

Figure 7.26   *Configuring account policy.*

The Password Policy folder contains group policy objects that let you require more secure passwords for all users. The Account Lockout Policy folder lets you cut off access to an account when password authentication has been repeatedly tried and failed.

MANAGING ACCOUNT POLICY

What keeps your workstation's data safe more than any other security factor is the strength of its passwords. You should therefore review and manage Password Policy carefully. Among the areas in which policies can be assigned are the following:

- **Maximum password age.** Passwords have a habit of falling into the hands of unauthorized persons. Users will unintentionally give their passwords away by writing them down on paper, which eventually ends up in dumpsters where the passwords can be retrieved by hackers (a process called "dumpster diving"). At other times, they are given to temporary employees who inadvertently jeopardize security after leaving (careless computer consultants, in particular). Some users even give their passwords away by yelling them out across a crowded room! One of the best ways to maintain password integrity is to keep them changing. This policy can be used to force users to pick new passwords after the specified interval.

- **Minimum password age.** Some users may attempt to bypass the purpose of the previous feature by setting a new password as required, then promptly switching back to a favorite password. If you accept the default setting of allowing changes immediately here, users can switch back to their favorite passwords whenever they want. Alternately, you can set an interval of between one and 999 days before they can change the new password to a previous one.
- **Minimum password length.** The longer the password, the more difficult it is to crack. With this field, you can require passwords of up to 14 characters in length. In general, passwords longer than four characters are considered reasonably secure, with eight characters being a common minimum.
- **Password uniqueness.** This setting can be used in conjunction with the Minimum Password Age field to keep users from reusing passwords. It will direct Windows 2000 to remember each user's last passwords and refuse to permit their reuse.

As previously described, the Account Lockout policies direct Windows 2000 to lock out an account that has been subject to a certain number of bad logon attempts in a given amount of time. Such occurrences are the usual sign of someone attempting to gain unauthorized access. One problem here is that once a hacker knows the number and interval by trial and error, the hacker will desist before triggering this action. The hacker will then try again later (a process known as "nibbling"). Be sure, then, to reset the counter only after a reasonably long time. You can also establish how long the account will be disabled. Make this interval long enough for you to become aware of the attempted breach and investigate.

TROUBLESHOOTING ACCOUNT POLICY

If it appears that your account policy settings are not being applied, make sure that the local settings are not working against the effective settings.

Group policies can be applied at the local, site, domain, or Organizational Unit (OU). All other levels have the strength to override what you set locally.

If your settings are in agreement, it might be that the policies have not yet had a chance to propagate. If necessary, you can force a refresh by executing the following command from the Run dialog box:

```
Secedit /refreshpolicy MACHINE_POLICY
```

Study Break

Secure User Accounts

Practice what you have learned by improving security for user accounts.

First, implement a local security policy, such as not permitting the installation of unsigned device drivers. Next, strengthen access security by limiting group access to user rights in critical areas. Next, set up an audit policy to track access failures to an important resource. Next, establish stronger password security and the account lock-out mechanism. Finally, create a new user account and verify that your new policies have been applied.

MCSE 7.4   Authenticating Local Users

Windows 2000 authentication is designed to ensure that only the appropriate users gain access to resources and data on your workstation or the network. Depending on the presence and configuration of your network environment, users may either log on to the workstation locally or to the domain of which the workstation is a member.

In the Windows 2000 security model, users are associated with resources and resources have permissions. Permissions assigned to directories and files become attributes of those resources, called the Access Control Lists (ACLs). ACLs contain Access Control Entries (ACEs), each of which references a user or group account Security Identifier (SID) and the type of access it is to be permitted.

When users log on to a system, processes they run during the logon session generate access tokens. These access tokens, which contain users' SIDs and a list of group memberships, serve as credentials during the logon session. Thereafter, when a user wishes to access a resource, these access tokens serve as security credentials.

When users request access to resources, their access tokens are compared to a resource's ACL. Its ACEs are sorted by access permission. If the user, or any groups of which the user is a member, has the Deny permission, access is denied. Otherwise the determination whether to grant or deny access is made as follows:

1. The ACEs are checked to see if the user, or any groups of which the user is a member, has matches to any entries for the type of access that is being requested. If such an entry is found, access is granted.
2. The ACL is evaluated to determine if the user's accumulated permissions are sufficient to allow the type of access that is being requested. If so, access is granted.
3. If no ACEs are present and accumulated permissions are insufficient for the type of access that is being requested, access is denied.

Once the user obtains successful access, a different process takes over. Instead of going through the ACL process every time the user attempts to do something with the object, a system creates a list of granted access rights that it can refer to. The user is also given a handle, which is used to identify them in reference to the object.

This security model has some drawbacks. Users' access tokens are generated at logon and used repeatedly thereafter, so any changes to users' group memberships will not be reflected in their ability to access resources unless they log on again. Similarly, a user's handle and granted access list are assigned when the user first accesses an object and are not updated until a completely new access request is made.

Remember that permissions differ from rights. NTFS permissions are embodied in the ACL attribute and are stored with a directory or file. User rights are stored with user account information in the Registry.

Configuring Local User Authentication

The local user authentication process works as follows:

1. The Log On To Windows dialog box prompts the user to enter a user name and a password, as shown in Figure 7.27.

Figure 7.27 *Local Windows 2000 logon authentication.*

2. Windows 2000 processes logon information through the local security subsystem, comparing it with the user information stored in the local security database.
3. Assuming the logon is verified, Windows 2000 creates an access token that serves as the user's identification for the local computer. The token contains the security settings that allow the user to gain access to resources and perform specific system tasks.

Windows 2000 reads from the local user profile to determine such user-specific settings as mapped network shares, shared printer connections, application preferences, personalized program groups, and the most recent documents. All subsequent changes that the user makes to the environment are saved to this profile, so when the user logs in again, Windows 2000 can recall their user-specific settings.

Troubleshooting Local User Authentication

When users cannot log on, try the following:

- Make sure they are using the right user name.
- Make sure they are using the right password.
- Make sure the Caps Lock is off. Passwords are case sensitive.
- Make sure that the local account database is selected in the drop-down menu at the bottom of the logon dialog box, if applicable.
- Try logging on from the workstation using another account, such as Administrator. If successful, recheck the user's account settings. Also

check Group Policy Editor MMC to see if restrictions are being applied to the user.

Configuring Domain User Accounts

The domain user authentication process works as follows:

1. The Log On To Windows dialog box prompts the user to enter a user name and a password. The user is given the option of logging on either locally or to a domain after clicking the Options button, as shown in Figure 7.28.

Figure 7.28 *Domain Windows 2000 logon authentication.*

2. The user is also given the option of dialing in to the network for authentication. Windows 2000 networks will employ one or more of the following security protocols for the exchange of user authentication information:

   • Password Authentication Protocol (PAP).
   • Challenge Handshake Authentication Protocol (CHAP).
   • Challenge Handshake Authentication Protocol (MS-CHAP).
   • Shiva Password Authentication Protocol (SPAP).
   • Point-to-Point Tunneling Protocol (PPTP).
   • Extensible Authentication Protocol (EAP).
   • Remote Authentication Dial-In User Service (RADIUS).
   • Internet Protocol Security (IPSec).
   • Layer Two Tunneling Protocol (L2TP).
   • Bandwidth Allocation Protocol (BAP).

3. The Windows 2000 workstation (which has its own domain account) contacts the designated network's domain controller, which then pro-

cesses user logon information through the network's Directory database.

4. On the network, the Kerberos protocol is Windows 2000's default authentication and security protocol.

5. Assuming the logon is verified, Windows 2000 creates an access token that serves as the user's identification throughout the domain.

After logging in, the workstation will also check to see if there is a roaming profile specified. If there is a roaming profile available, the workstation then compares this profile with any local profile to see which is more recent. If the local profile is more recent, the user is asked which of the versions should be used. Otherwise, Windows 2000 downloads the roaming profile.

A mandatory profile is a read-only roaming profile. To use one, first create a roaming profile folder. Next, launch the System Control Panel and use the Copy To button under the User Profiles tab to copy an appropriate profile into the folder. Rename the NTUSER.DAT file as "NTUSER.MAN," which will make the profile read-only. Now you can specify the path to the mandatory profile, using the Computer Management MMC or Active Directory Users and Computers MMC.

Troubleshooting Domain User Accounts

When users cannot log on, try the following:

- Make sure that the correct domain account database is selected in the drop-down menu at the bottom of the logon dialog box.
- Try logging on from the workstation using another account. If successful, recheck the user's settings in the Active Directory Users and Computers MMC. It may be that the user's group memberships have changed or that a change in group rights is restricting the user. You might also check system policy to see if restrictions are being applied to the user.
- If unsuccessful, try logging in from another workstation. If that fails, you might need to repair the user accounts database using the emergency repair procedure. First, however, check to see if the NetLogon, Server, and Workstation services are running properly. Also, check the networking properties to ensure that the services are bound to the right applications and adapters.

Verify Local and Domain Logons

Practice what you have learned by creating and testing local and domain logon authentication.

First, create a local user account through the Computer Management MMC. Log on to the local computer and verify that a user profile is created. Next, create a domain user account on a domain controller through the Active Directory Users and Computers MMC (either by yourself of with the aid of a domain administrator). Log on to the domain from the same computer and verify that you have access to local and networked resources.

MCSE 7.5 Implementing Security Configurations

Windows 2000 provides three MMC tools that let you configure security settings as well as analyze your system to verify or change them: the Security Configuration and Analysis snap-in; Security Templates snap-in; and Group Policy snap-in. Among the settings in a Windows 2000 security configuration are the following:

- Security policies (account policies and local policies).
- Access controls (services, files, and Registry).
- Event logs.
- Restricted group memberships.
- IP Security policies.
- Public key policies.

Configuring Security Configuration Tools

Because of the inherent security risks they impose, Windows 2000 does not go out of its way to make its security tools obvious. For example, you should recall from earlier in this chapter that the process for adding snap-ins to the Group Policy Editor MMC ("gpedit.msc") would probably not be stumbled across by the casual user. The same is true of the Security Configuration and Analysis snap-in.

To create an MMC based on the Security Configuration and Analysis snap-in, type "mmc" at the command line to open an empty console in author mode, as shown in Figure 7.29.

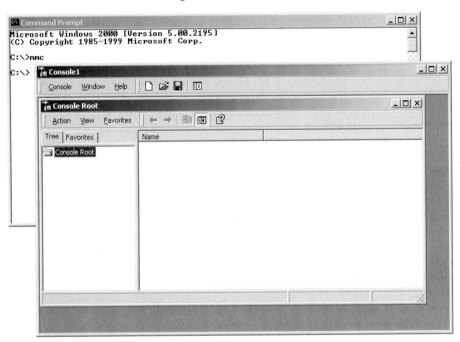

Figure 7.29 *Configuring the Security Configuration and Analysis MMC.*

Next, select the Add/Remove Snap-ins command from the Console menu to open the Add/Remove Snap-in dialog box. Next, click the Add button to include the Security Configuration and Analysis snap-in under the Console Root node, as shown in Figure 7.30.

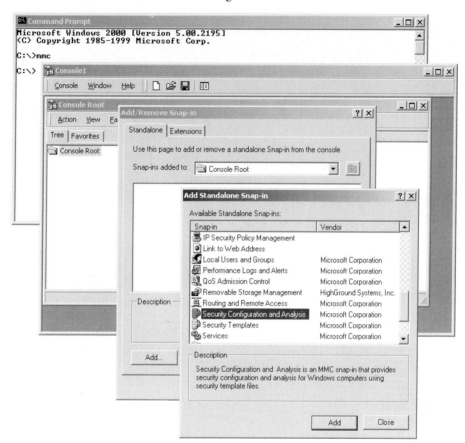

Figure 7.30   *Adding the Security Configuration and Analysis snap-in.*

Upon returning to the MMC, you will note that an empty Security Configuration branch has been added, as shown in Figure 7.31.

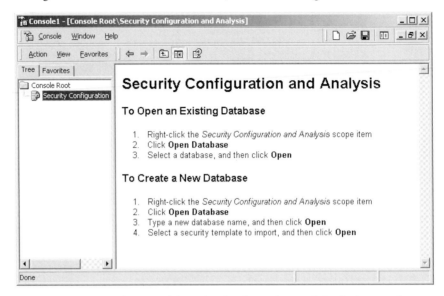

Figure 7.31 *Newly created Security Configuration and Analysis console.*

You can import templates into the Security Configuration and Analysis snap-in that can be used to configure local security by applying their settings to the group policy object (GPO) for the local workstation. Security templates are created using the Security Templates snap-in, so add it to the MMC as well.

Managing and Troubleshooting Security Configurations

You can manage your security configurations by using the Security Configuration and Analysis snap-in to analyze system settings and provide recommendations for changing them. Once analyzed, you can further use the snap-in to adjust security policy and detect potentially vulnerable areas. Overall, the Security Configuration and Analysis snap-in lets you perform the following tasks:

- Create a settings database.
- Import and export security templates.
- Analyze and review security.
- Configure security settings.

Once you have installed the Security Templates snap-in, expand the C:\WINNT\Security\Templates folder under the Security Templates node to see all of the defined templates and their explanations, as shown in Figure 7.32.

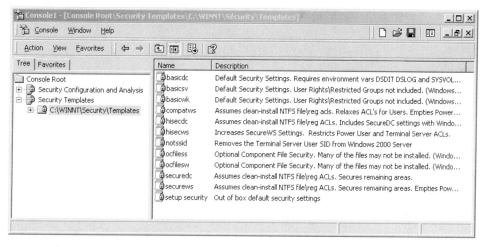

Figure 7.32 *Viewing templates in the Security Templates snap-in.*

Double-click a template document, such as the Windows 2000 Professional default template "basicwk," to view and modify its settings for Account Policies, Local Policies, Event Log, Restricted Groups, System Services, Registry, and File System.

To apply one of these templates, select the Security Configuration and Analysis node and choose the Import template command from the Action menu to open a file selection dialog box, as shown in Figure 7.33.

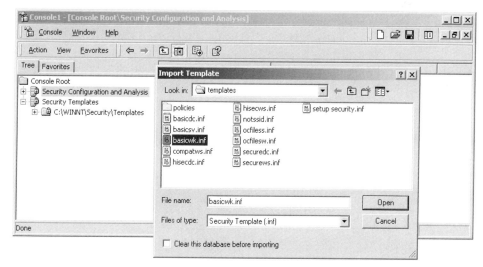

Figure 7.33 *Importing a security template.*

After the template is imported, a new database will be created and you will be able to browse and modify security settings, as shown in Figure 7.34.

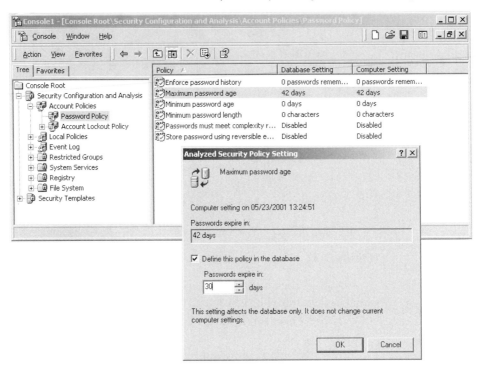

Figure 7.34 *Modifying the working security database.*

To analyze your system's settings, select the Security Configuration and Analysis node and choose the Analyze Computer Now command from the Action menu. This will open the Perform Analysis dialog box, in which is displayed the path and name of the error log. When you click the OK button, the utility will check the local security configuration against the template, displaying its progress in the Analyzing System Security dialog box, as shown in Figure 7.35.

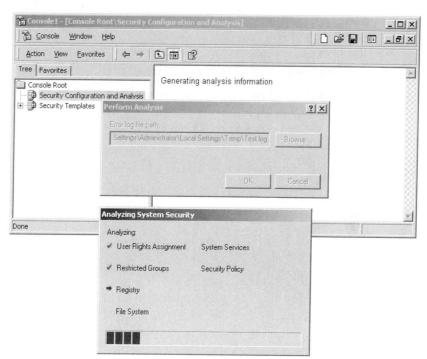

Figure 7.35   *Analyzing a security configuration.*

The settings in both the security template and system configuration are displayed for each policy. Any discrepancies appear with a red alert symbol, while consistent settings appear with green check marks in the center, as shown in Figure 7.36. Settings not appearing with one of these symbols are not specified in the template.

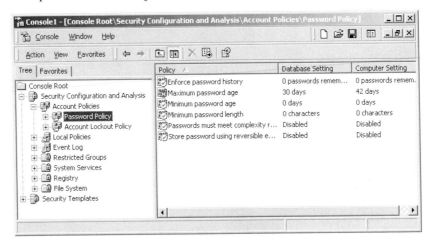

Figure 7.36 *Viewing analysis results.*

To synchronize the two policies, select the Configure Computer Now command from the Action menu to open the Configure System dialog box. After you click OK, the Configuring Computer Security dialog box will show you its progress. When it is complete, verify that the values under the Database Settings now match the values under the Computer Setting column.

Study Break

Analyze Security Configurations

Practice what you have learned by applying and analyzing a security configuration.

First, create a new MMC console that contains the Security Configuration and Analysis, and the Security Templates snap-in. Next, import a template and create a security database using the "basicwk" security template document. Next, make some changes to the security configuration. Finally, analyze the system and compare the results to see how your changes compare with the template.

■ Summary

In this chapter, we described encrypting data, as well as implementing, configuring, managing, and troubleshooting user and system security configurations.

Encrypting Hard Disk Data

Windows 2000 Professional implements EFS on NTFS-formatted drives. At one level of EFS strategy, Windows 2000 uses a symmetric encryption scheme wherein a randomly generated EFS key is used to encrypt and decrypt files. At another level, Windows 2000 uses an asymmetric private key/public key encryption scheme in which one key encrypts the EFS key and another key decrypts the EFS key. User keys can be exported in the form of certificate files. Only the person who encrypted a file has access to it, with the exception of specially designated Recovery Agents.

Implementing Local Security Policy

You may configure settings for audit policies and user rights, as well as general security options, by launching the Local Security Settings MMC shortcut found in the Administrative Tools program group.

Implementing User Account Security

In order to use Windows 2000 Professional workstation resources, users must have rights and permissions to access them. These rights can be assigned explicitly, by a user's account characteristics, or implicitly, by a user's affiliation with a group and its account characteristics. User accounts grant rights to one person. Group accounts extend like rights to a collection of user accounts.

Windows 2000 has several built-in accounts, such as groups for Administrators, Users, and Guests. Additional user and group accounts can be created through the System Tools node of the Computer Management MMC. Security settings that can be set include passwords and their associated policies.

User rights refer to what a user is allowed to do on a given computer. Resource permissions refer to the context in which user rights may be applied. User rights can be implemented through the User Rights Assignment node of the Local Security Settings MMC.

Windows 2000 provides extremely powerful auditing capabilities. Any attempt to access a directory or file, whether or not it was successful, can be tracked and recorded in the Security Log (which can been examined in Event Viewer).

Auditing can be implemented through the Audit Policy node of the Local Security Settings MMC. Administrators and any users or groups that are assigned the Manage auditing and security log user right can set directory and file auditing options. They may also view the status of successes and failures in the Security Log.

Account policies determine the circumstances under which users are permitted to log on. Account policies are implemented through the Password Policies and Account Lockout Policy subfolders of the Account Policies folder under the Local Computer Policy node of the Group Policy Editor MMC. The Password Policy folder contains group policy objects that let you require more secure passwords for all users. The Account Lockout Policy folder lets you cut off access to an account when password authentication has been repeatedly tried and failed.

Authenticating Local Users

Windows 2000 authentication is designed to ensure that only the appropriate users gain access to resources and data on your workstation or the network. Users may either log on to the workstation locally or to the domain of which the workstation is a member. When users log on to a system, processes they run during the logon session generate access tokens. These access tokens, which contain users' SIDs and a list of group memberships, serve as credentials during the logon session. Thereafter, when a user wishes to access a resource, these access tokens serve as security credentials.

Implementing Security Configurations

Windows 2000 provides three MMC tools that let you configure security settings as well as analyze your system to verify or change them: the Security Configuration and Analysis snap-in, Security Templates snap-in, and Group Policy snap-in. Among the settings in a Windows 2000 security configuration are security policies (account policies and local policies, access control (services, files, and Registry), event logs, group membership, IP Security policies, and public key policies. The Security Configuration and Analysis snap-in can be used to apply and modify security settings from predefined templates and analyze the system for compliance.

▲ CHAPTER REVIEW QUESTIONS

Here are a few questions relating to the material covered in the *Implementing, Monitoring, and Troubleshooting Security* section of Microsoft's *Installing, Configuring, and Administering Microsoft Windows 2000 Professional* exam (70-210).

1. *EFS cannot be used with NTFS compression.*

   A. True

   B. False

2. *If you delete all accounts as Recovery Agents, EFS will be disabled for the entire system.*

   A. True

   B. False

3. *Local policy settings always overrule domain-wide policy settings when conflicts occur.*

   A. True

   B. False

4. *Which of the following policies can be disabled through local security policy? Select all that apply:*

   A. Allow system shutdown without logon.

   B. Allow system startup without logon.

   C. Disable CTRL-ALT-DELETE for logon.

   D. Allow floppy copy and access from Recovery Console.

5. *Both user and group accounts are validated through password authentication.*

   A. True

   B. False

6. *When auditing is enabled, resource access successes and failures are reported in the Local Security Settings MMC policy pane.*

   A. True

   B. False

7. *Which of the following questions can be answered through file access auditing? Select all that apply.*

   A. Who is trying to read a file?

   B. Who is trying to modify a file?

   C. Who is trying to change file permissions?

   D. Who is trying to delete a file?

8. *Which of the following account settings can be used together? Select all that apply.*

   A. User must change password at next logon

   B. User cannot change password

   C. Password never expires

   D. Account is locked out

9. *Passwords are not case sensitive.*

   A. True

   B. False

10. *Account policies determine the circumstances under which users are permitted to access resources.*

    A. True

    B. False

11. *It is wise to "time out" passwords eventually, since old passwords are more likely to be compromised.*

    A. True

    B. False

12. *By default, Windows 2000 puts all users in the Guest group initially.*

    A. True

    B. False

13. *Which of the following are required for creating a new user account? Select all that apply:*

    A. User name

    B. Full name

    C. Password

    D. Group memberships

14. *User rights determine what can be done and permissions determine where it can be done.*

    A. True

    B. False

15. *Ownership can only be granted, never taken.*

    A. True

    B. False

16. *NTFS permissions and User rights are embodied in the ACL attribute and stored with user account information in the Registry.*

    A. True

    B. False

17. *Regardless of whether a user intends to work locally or as a member of a domain, the user's user name and password are always initially processed by the workstation's security database.*

    A. True

    B. False

18. *Local access tokens contain security settings that allow the user to gain access to resources and perform specific system tasks.*

    A. True

    B. False

19. *On a network, PAP is Windows 2000's default authentication and security protocol.*

    A. True

    B. False

20. *Renaming the NTUSER.DAT file as "NTUSER.MAN" will make the roaming profile read-only.*

    A. True

    B. False

21. *A shortcut to the Security Configuration and Analysis MMC can be found in the Administrative Tools program group.*

    A. True

    B. False

22. *Any discrepancies in the Security Configuration and Analysis MMC appear with a red alert symbol, while consistent settings appear with green check marks in the center.*

   A. True

   B. False

Windows 2000 Server

♦ In This Part

♦ **CHAPTER 8**: Installing Windows 2000 Server

♦ **CHAPTER 9**: Administering Windows 2000 Server Resource Access

♦ **CHAPTER 10**: Managing Windows 2000 Server Devices

♦ **CHAPTER 11**: Optimizing Windows 2000 Server

♦ **CHAPTER 12**: Administering Windows 2000 Server Storage

♦ **CHAPTER 13**: Networking Windows 2000 Server

♦ **CHAPTER 14**: Securing Windows 2000 Server

In this section we will cover material from MCSE exam 70-215, *Installing, Configuring, and Administering Microsoft Windows 2000 Server.* This will give you the knowledge necessary to install, configure, and manage networked Windows 2000 Server computers and support their Windows 2000-based clients. This section's topics include the following:

- **Installing.** Performing attended or unattended installations and upgrades, deploying service packs, and troubleshooting failed installations.

- **Administering resources.** Working with network services, file, folder, and printer access, and Web sites.

- **Devices.** Configuring and troubleshooting hardware and device drivers.

- **Optimizing.** Getting the most from system resources, processing, and disk performance while ensuring maximum system state and user data availability.

- **Administering storage.** Configuring and troubleshooting disks and volumes, disk compression, and disk quotas.
- **Networking.** Working with shared access, VPNs, network adapters, services, and protocols, remote access, and terminal services.
- **Securing.** Working with system policy, accounts, auditing, and overall security configurations.

Much of the material that is common to both Windows 2000 Professional and Windows 2000 Server was already covered in the first section of this book. We will not repeat it here other than to review it. Where there is overlap, we will present the material from a strictly server-oriented perspective. Where there is new material, we will cover it in depth.

Installing Windows 2000 Server

▲ Chapter Syllabus

Installation Planning

MCSE 8.1 Attended
Installations

MCSE 8.2 Unattended
Installations

MCSE 8.3 Upgrading

MCSE 8.4 Deploying Service
Packs

MCSE 8.5 Troubleshooting
Installations

In this chapter, we will examine the installation topics covered in the *Installing Windows 2000 Server* section of Microsoft's *Installing, Configuring, and Administering Microsoft Windows 2000 Server* exam (70-215).

The following material is designed to make you comfortable with installing the operating system on a single computer, multiple computers, and computers running under Windows NT Server.

Before installing Windows 2000 Server, you should go through the READ1ST.TXT file on the installation CD-ROM. It contains the latest information available at the time of the installation disk's pressing, including important preinstallation notes.

To locate it, click the Browse This CD link in the Windows 2000 Server installation CD-ROM Autorun screen that appears when you insert the disk, as shown in Figure 8.1.

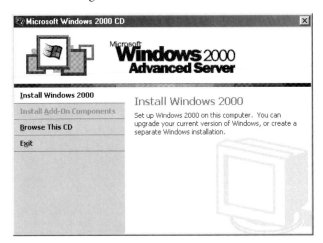

Figure 8.1 *The CD-ROM Autorun screen.*

Other important resources that come with your installation CD-ROM include README.TXT, which covers postinstallation and compatibility details; the SETUPTXT folder, the contents of which describe installation on a single computer; and HCL.TXT, which lists the systems and components that are known to be compatible with Windows 2000 Server.

Another useful reference is Microsoft's *Windows 2000 Server Resource Kit*.

Installation Planning

In this section, we will describe the process of installing Windows 2000 Server on a single computer or multiple computers. We first considered these issues in Chapter 1, "Installing Windows 2000 Professional," but there are a few new variables unique to the server operating system.

Choosing the Operating System Version

Windows 2000 ships in the following versions:

- **Windows 2000 Professional.** As you learned in this first section of this book, this is Microsoft's high-performance client desktop. It draws its technologies from both Windows 98 and Windows NT Workstation 4.0 while adding several improvements. It can also act as a peer-to-peer server in a limited capacity.
- **Windows 2000 Server.** This product includes all of the technologies in Windows 2000 Professional and adds robust application, file, print, terminal, and Web server capabilities. It is positioned to support workgroups, small- to medium-sized enterprise environments, or dedicated Web services. It replaces Windows NT Server 4.0.
- **Windows 2000 Advanced Server.** This product includes all of the capabilities of Windows 2000 Server, but is positioned to provide improved support for Internet services and Network Operations Systems (NOS). It supports larger memory configurations as well as clustering and load-balancing technologies, making it ideal for database applications.
- **Windows 2000 Datacenter Server.** The most powerful of all, this product is designed to support large data warehousing applications, econometric analysis, server consolidation, transaction processing, and scientific/engineering simulations. It is also ideal for large-scale Web hosting.

You should choose the version that will best meet your needs.

Considering Installation Methods

Once you have determined which version of Windows 2000 Server you need, you must decide whether to install it as a new operating system, such as on a new system, or as an upgrade to an existing Windows NT Server installation. Windows 2000 Server can also be installed in a dual-boot capacity with such operating systems as Windows Millennium Edition (Me) or MS-DOS.

PLANNING FOR UPGRADES

You may choose to upgrade if the target computer is running one of the following operating systems:

- Windows NT 4.0
- Windows NT 3.51

Upgrading will overwrite your existing system but keep most of your setting preferences and applications.

If the computer is running Windows NT 3.1 or 3.5, you must upgrade to Windows NT 4.0 and then upgrade again to Windows 2000 Server. Windows 2000 Professional, Windows NT Workstation, and Windows 9x/Me cannot be upgraded to Windows 2000 Server.

PLANNING FOR CLEAN INSTALLS

If the target computer has no operating system or one that Windows 2000 cannot replace, you must perform a clean install. This will require you to manually configure all of the operating system's preference settings and reinstall your applications. It will also permit you to install Windows 2000 alongside other operating systems in a multi-boot capacity, however.

If you are preparing the computer for multi-boot, the file system becomes especially important, as described further on.

CHOOSING INSTALLATION MEDIA

The easiest way to install Windows 2000 Server is from a CD-ROM or DVD drive. If your CD-ROM drive is not bootable, meaning that you cannot start the Setup program from the installation CD-ROM, you will also need a 3.5-inch High-Density floppy disk drive from which to launch boot disks. You can also install the operating system from a network share if the computer has a Windows 2000-compatible network adapter.

Verifying System Requirements

In order to run Windows 2000 Server, your computer must have at least the following components:

- A 133 MHz Pentium microprocessor (or equivalent). This includes the Pentium II, III, or 4 as well as the AMD K-6, K-6 II or III, and K-7 Athlon.

  Windows 2000 Server also supports four-way multiprocessing. (Windows 2000 Advanced Server supports as many as eight processors, and Windows 2000 Datacenter Server supports as many as 32 in some configurations.)

- You will need a minimum of 64 MBs for networking between one and five clients. Microsoft recommends 128 MBs in most circumstances. Windows 2000 Server will support a maximum of 4 GBs of RAM.

- 671 MBs of free hard disk space is the minimum required for a local, default installation. Microsoft recommends a minimum of 2 GBs. Installing over the network requires another 100–200 MBs more for driver files. Additional components require additional space as well.

If you are upgrading from Windows NT Server 4.0, you will need more space to import the Security Accounts Database (SAM).

- A VGA or better monitor capable of 640 by 480 resolution.
- A keyboard.
- A mouse.
- A CD-ROM or DVD drive, or a Windows 2000-compatible network adapter plus a 3.5-inch High-Density floppy disk drive, depending on the installation media you choose.

Verifying Hardware and Software Compatibility

Once you have verified that the target computer meets the necessary system requirements for such components as processor and RAM, make sure other components, such as ROM BIOS, controllers, and adapter cards, are also supported. To determine this, review the Hardware Compatibility List (HCL), which can be opened from the SUPPORT folder on the installation CD-ROM, as shown in Figure 8.2.

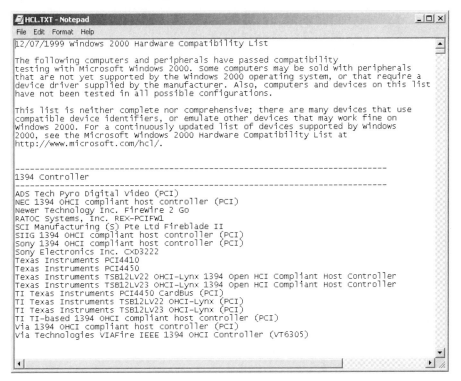

Figure 8.2 *Viewing the HCL.*

The most up-to-date version of the HCL can be found at the Microsoft Web site (*www.microsoft.com/hcl*).

If you are upgrading from Windows NT, you might also have pre-existing software installations that need to be verified. For this purpose, Microsoft includes the Application Compatibility tool that can be launched from the SUPPORT folder of the installation CD-ROM (see Figure 8.3).

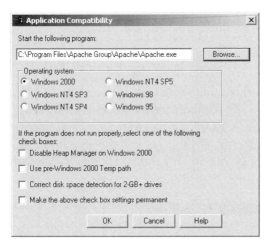

Figure 8.3 *Running the Application Compatibility tool.*

Also refer to the Windows 2000 Product Compatibility Web site at *www.microsoft.com/windows2000/compatible* for information on software compatibility. Consult the README.TXT file to determine which existing applications, if any, should be disabled during installation (e.g, anti-virus software, disk utilities, etc).

If you encounter hardware or software that is not listed, contact the manufacturer to obtain a Windows 2000 device driver or program update, if available.

Considering Partitions and File Systems

As described extensively in Chapter 1, you should plan for the physical and logical structure that is appropriate for your server's disk drive. On new disk drives—or existing disks on which you do not mind deleting existing data—this involves formatting. During this process you are given the opportunity to create partitions.

PLANNING FOR PARTITIONS

Under Windows NT and 2000, the system partition contains the files necessary to boot the operating system. Such files include NTLDR, NTDETECT.COM, and BOOT.INI. By definition, this will also be the active partition. The boot partition, which might or might not also be the system partition, contains the Windows NT/2000 operating system. This includes the Windows 2000 kernel and all the files in the WINNT folder (the default name of the system folder).

PLANNING FOR FILE SYSTEMS

Windows 2000 Server can be installed on a partition formatted with the File Allocation Table (FAT), FAT32, or New Technology File System (NTFS) file systems.

FAT • The FAT file system, also known as FAT16, was introduced with MS-DOS. The 16-bit FAT is supported by Windows 3.x, 95, 98, Me, NT, and 2000, as well as IBM's OS/2. Because it is the most universally supported file system, FAT is useful on computers from which you plan to boot multiple operating systems that must access the same partitions (not recommended).

FAT32 • The 32-bit version of FAT is an improvement over FAT16, but its capabilities fall far short of those possessed by NTFS and its usefulness on dual-boot computers is limited, because it is only supported by Windows 95 Release B, 98, Me, or 2000.

NTFS • Because of its inherent superiority to FAT in terms of performance and security, NTFS is the best choice for your server in most circumstances. You should use NTFS if your server requires file- and directory-level local security, disk compression, disk quotas, or file encryption. You must use NTFS if your server is to act as a domain controller, because only NTFS supports Active Directory.

ADDITIONAL CONSIDERATIONS

- **Dual-Boot.** Microsoft does not recommend dual-booting servers. Nevertheless, if you must dual-boot a computer with another operating system but require the functionality of NTFS, you could install the system partition under FAT/FAT32 but the boot partition under NTFS.
- **Compression.** Windows 2000 is not compatible with the DriveSpace or DoubleSpace file compression available under Windows 9x, so

decompress any such drives before installation. Windows 2000 is compatible with NTFS 4.0 file compression.

- **Mirroring.** When performing a clean install on a computer configured with Windows NT disk mirroring, disable it before installation. It can be re-enabled after setup. This is not required when upgrading.
- **Viruses.** Verify that your computer is not infected by a boot sector virus before installing Windows 2000 Server. To do this, create a scan disk by running the following utility on the installation CD-ROM:

```
\Valueadd\3rdparty\CA_antiv\Makedisk.bat
```

Use the floppy disk that is created to run a boot sector virus check.

- **Backup.** Back up your important files before installing Windows 2000 Server!

Recording Network Settings

If the computer on which you are installing Windows 2000 has already been participating in network services, record the following information:

- NetBIOS computer name.
- Name of workgroup or domain.
- IP address (if applicable).

Considering Licensing

Windows 2000 Server supports the following license modes:

- **Per Seat.** This license requires that each client accessing the server has a Client Access License (CAL).
- **Per Server.** This license requires that the server has as many CALs as will be needed for simultaneous client connections.

CALs are not required for HyperText Transfer Protocol (HTTP), File Transfer Protocol (FTP), or Telnet connections. So, for example, connections to Microsoft's Internet Information Server (IIS) are exempt. Additional licenses might be required for Microsoft BackOffice products.

In general, per server licensing is preferred where only one Windows 2000 Server is deployed. In an enterprise environment containing multiple servers, per seat licensing makes more sense. If you are unsure about how to proceed initially, go with per server licensing. You are given a one-time chance to convert the server to per seat licensing if it becomes necessary later, but the reverse is not true.

MCSE 8.1 **Attended Installations**

Microsoft breaks the process of installing Windows 2000 Server manually into the following steps:

- **Precopy phase.** In this step, installation files are copied to temporary directories on the local hard drive from either the installation CD-ROM or a network share.
- **Text mode.** In this step, Setup prompts you to approve the license agreement then select or create an installation partition and its file system.
- **GUI mode.** This step is broken down further into the following steps:
  1. Gathering information about your computer.
  2. Installing Windows 2000 Server networking.
  3. Completing Setup.

Running the Precopy Phase

You will need to boot from either your computer's CD-ROM drive or from a floppy disk drive using the Windows 2000 Server startup disks if the target computer has a newly formatted hard disk or is running an operating system that will not recognize the installation CD-ROM.

You can create installation floppy disks from the installation CD-ROM. Simply load the CD-ROM on a computer that is capable of reading it, open the Command Prompt program, and switch to the CD's BOOTDISK directory. Next, insert a blank 1.44 MB floppy diskette in the disk drive and type the command: MAKEBOOT A: (where A: is the floppy disk drive). Follow the directions to create four setup diskettes.

If the target computer is running an operating system that will recognize the CD-ROM, you can simply insert it and click the Install Windows 2000 link in the Autorun screen (see Figure 8.1) to launch the Setup Wizard. You will be given a chance to choose between an upgrade and a clean installation. If you choose the latter, you will be able to boot from either your old operating system or Windows 2000 after the installation.

In the next few screens, you will be prompted to read and approve the Microsoft licensing agreement, supply the license key code, and select options for languages and special accessibility. If you click the Advanced Options button, you will be presented with the Advanced Options dialog box in which you can specify the source of setup files, such as the \I386 directory on the CD-ROM or a network share, and the name of the destination system folder (\WINNT by default). You may also enable options that will copy all of the setup files to the hard drive for later convenience and permit you to choose the installation partition (further on).

Finally, the Setup Wizard will copy setup files to the hard disk and reboot the computer.

Running in Text Mode

The computer will restart with a minimal version of Windows 2000 loaded into memory. This will launch the text-based Setup program, as shown in Figure 8.4.

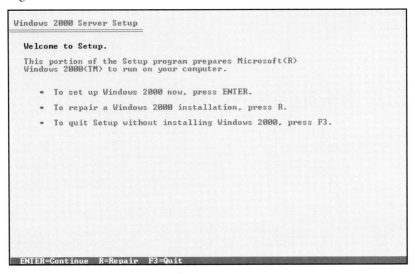

Figure 8.4 *Setup in text mode.*

Press the Enter key to continue, and you will be asked to choose a partition for the installation of Windows 2000 Server, as shown in Figure 8.5.

When performing a new installation, the Setup program will pick the active disk partition by default, although you can alter this choice through the Advanced Options button described previously. You can select an existing partition, create a new partition from unused disk space, or delete an existing partition so that you may reconfigure the drive. Microsoft recommends that you create only the partition on which you plan to install Windows 2000 Server at this point. Once the operating system is in place, you can use the Disk Management MMC snap-in to make further modifications.

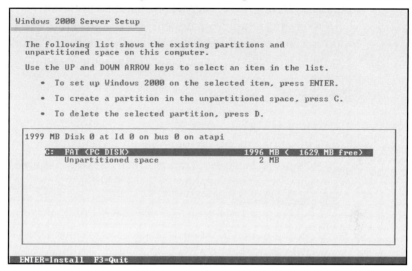

Figure 8.5 *Selecting a partition.*

Once you have created the installation partition, you will be asked to choose a file system with which to format it, as shown in Figure 8.6.

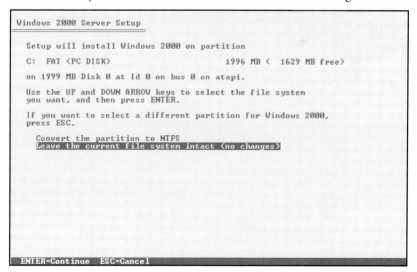

Figure 8.6 *Selecting a file system.*

As previously described, your best choice is NTFS. If a file system is already present, you can choose to leave it intact. If you choose FAT, 100–200 MBs of additional disk space will be required for setup.

Next, the Setup program will format the hard drive according to your choices, copy its installation files to the disk, and save its configuration information. It will then restart and launch the Setup Wizard.

Running the Setup Wizard

The Graphical User Interface (GUI)-based Setup Wizard will ask you the following questions about the computer and its environment:

- **Regional Settings.** Windows 2000 can be configured for multiple languages and regional preferences. Choose a language, locale, and keyboard layout here.
- **Name and Organization.** Identify the person who owns the copy of Windows 2000 Server that you are installing, and the organization with which that person is associated (optional).
- **Licensing Mode.** If you will be using the operating system in a per server capacity, enter the number of computers for which you have CALs, as shown in Figure 8.7. Otherwise, choose the Per seat radio button.

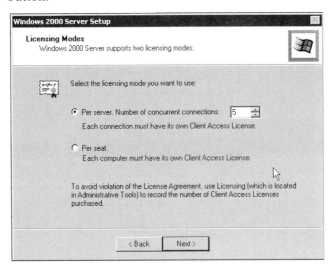

Figure 8.7 *Selecting a licensing mode.*

- **Computer Name and Administrator Password.** You must choose a name of between one and 15 characters that is unique from any other computer, domain, or workgroup name on the network. Windows

2000 will make up a name by default. The password you choose for the automatically created Administrator account grants you the administrative privileges necessary to fully configure and manage the computer. It can be left blank or made as long as 127 characters.

· **Windows 2000 Components.** Choose to install the server's default components, as shown in Figure 8.8.

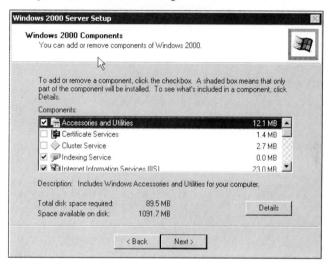

Figure 8.8 *Selecting additional components.*

Optionally, you can choose any additional components you know you will need. Table 8.1 provides a list of optional components and their functions.

Table 8.1 *Optional Server Components*

Component	Details
Certificate Services	Provides smart card, email, and Web service authentication support.
Internet Information Services (IIS)	Provides a host of Web site management tools, along with HyperText Transfer Protocol (HTTP), File Transfer Protocol (FTP), Simple Mail Transfer Protocol (SMTP), and Network News Transfer Protocol (NNTP) services.
Management and Monitoring Tools	Provides the Network Monitor packet analyzer application and Simple Network Management Protocol (SNMP). Also includes phone book management utilities for dialup services and a (Novell) NetWare Directory Services (NDS) to (Microsoft) Active Directory migration tool.

Table 8.1 *Optional Server Components (continued)*

Message Queuing Services	Supports messaging between distributed applications.
Microsoft Indexing Service	Indexes stored document for faster search and retrieval by content or properties.
Microsoft Script Debugger	Used in developing JScript or VBScript programs, such as for Web pages.
Networking Services	Provides support for the following: • COM Internet Services Proxy. Supports communications between distributed applications using HTTP. • Domain Name System (DNS). Supports IP address-to-host name mapping. • Dynamic Host Configuration Protocol (DHCP). Supports the dynamic allocation of client IP addresses. • Internet Authentication Service. Supports dialup user authentication. • QoS Admission Control Service. Controls application bandwidth allocations. • Simple TCP/IP Services. Provides Character Generator, Daytime Discard, Echo, and Quote of the Day. • Site Server ILS Service. In conjunction with IIS, supports such telephony applications as caller ID, audio and video conferencing, and faxing. • Windows Internet Naming Service (WINS). Provides IP address-to-NetBIOS name mapping.
Other File and Print Services	Supports file and print services for Mac OS and print services for UNIX.
Remote Installation Services	Supports remote installation and configuration of client computers.
Remote Storage	Supports the archiving of seldom used data to removable media.
Terminal Services	Supports terminal clients.
Terminal Services Licensing	Tracks terminal client licensing.
Windows Media Services	Supports multimedia services, such as Advanced Streaming Format (ASF) Internet applications.

- **Date and Time Settings.** You can establish the time, date, and resident time zone, if they have not already been read from the computer's BIOS. You can also choose automatic updates for daylight savings time.
- **Networking Settings.** The Setup program installs Client for Microsoft Networks, File and Printer Sharing for Microsoft Networks, and TCP/IP by default. You can either accept the default of automatic (e.g. DHCP) addressing, or choose to configure static addressing manually.
- **Workgroup or Computer Domain.** If a domain controller and DNS server exist on your network, you can choose to make your server part of the domain. If your network does not support domains, such as when all of the client workstations are running under non-Windows 2000 operating systems, you can add your server to a workgroup. If you are creating a domain and intend to make the server a domain controller, or if you are unsure about whether to select a workgroup or domain, go with the default of joining a workgroup named "WORKGROUP." You can address the issue again later.

In its final stage, the Setup Wizard installs Start menu items, registers the components, applies the settings that you selected, saves your configuration settings to the hard drive, deletes unnecessary installation files, and restarts the computer.

NETWORK INSTALLATIONS

The process of installing Windows 2000 Server over a network differs little from installing it locally, other than being slower.

To prepare for a network installation, you must first establish a distribution server by sharing a folder and copying the installation CD-ROM's I386 folder to it. The target computer must have at least 850 MBs of free disk space. If the target computer is unable to log on to the share through an exiting operating system, you will need to start the computer from a boot disk that contains the necessary network client software.

To perform a network installation, first connect to the distribution server share. If you are performing a clean install from MS-DOS or Windows 3x, launch the WINNT.EXE program from the share. If you are performing an installation from a computer that is already running Windows NT or Windows 9x/Me, launch the WINNT32.EXE program. This directs Setup to create and copy installation files into a temporary folder, "win_nt.bt," on the system partition. Restart the computer when prompted to begin the previously described installation process.

You can also modify the installation process somewhat through the use of command line switches. Table 8.2 describes several WINNT.EXE switches that can be used to launch clean installs on computers running MS-DOS or Windows 3.x.

Table 8.2 *WINNT.EXE Switches*

Command	Purpose
/a	Enable the Accessibility option.
/e: *command*	Execute command before Setup completion.
/I: *file_name*	Apply specified Setup information file.
/r: *folder_name*	Create specified folder within the system folder.
/rx: *folder_name*	Create specified folder within the system folder, then delete files before Setup completion.
/s: *source_path*	Specify path of installation files, using drive letter (e.g., "E:\I386") or Universal Naming Convention (UNC) path (e.g., "\\server_name\share\I386").
/t: *temp_path*	Specify path of temporary installation folder.
/u: *file_name*	Apply specified Unattended Answer File (UAF). It must be used in combination with /s switch.
/udf:id,*file_name*	Permits the application of an automatically generated computer name from an Uniqueness Database File (UDF).

Table 8.3 describes several WINNT32.EXE switches that can be used with either clean installations or when upgrading from a computer running Windows NT or 9x/Me.

Table 8.3 *WINNT32.EXE*

Command	Purpose
/copydir: *folder_name*	Creates a subfolder within the folder in which Windows 2000 files are installed that is not deleted after Setup completes. Use additional /r switches to install additional folders. This is handy for copying down third-party drivers for later installation.
/copysource: *folder_name*	Similar to the previous option, creates a subfolder within the folder in which Windows 2000 files are installed that is deleted after Setup completes.
/cmd: *command*	Executes a command just prior to Setup's final phase.
/cmdcons	Installs the files needed to restart the system in command line mode for the purpose of repair after a failed installation. It adds a Recovery Console item to the BOOT.INI file.
/syspart: *hard_drive*	Prepares a hard disk to be transferred to another computer by installing setup files and marking the partition as active. With it, you can put the installation files on a hard disk, remove the disk from the machine, install it in another machine, and complete the installation there. Use in conjunction with the /tempdrive switch.
/tempdrive: *hard_drive*	Specifies the drive to which Windows 2000 temporary files will be installed during setup.
/makelocalsource	Copies Windows 2000 source files to the target drive during setup, making it unnecessary to depend on a CD-ROM drive or network connection thereafter.
/noreboot	Prevents reboot after installation so that another command can be executed. You must then restart manually, after which time Setup will resume.
/checkupgradeonly	Checks the computer for incompatibilities that might interfere with a successful upgrade. This option will not actually launch the Setup program.
/unattend	Upgrades a previous version of Windows using unattended Setup mode that requires no user intervention. Settings are taken from the previous installation.
/unattend[#]:*file_name*	As described further on in this section, Setup can use an UAF to provide specific information about setup options that would otherwise be asked of the user. In addition, a number can be specified for a time delay before reboot using this switch.
/udf:id ,*file_name*	Permits the application of an automatically generated computer name from an UDF.

Note that several WINNT.EXE and WINNT32.EXE switches pertain to unattended installations, the topic of the next section.

Study Break

Install Windows 2000 Server Manually

Practice what you have learned by compiling the information you will need prior to installing Windows 2000, then following the description provided in this section to install the operating system as a clean install.

If you are unable to install Windows 2000 as a clean install because you must upgrade Windows NT Server, skip ahead and read Section 8.3, "Upgrading," before proceeding.

MCSE 8.2 Unattended Installations

Microsoft makes the unattended installation of Windows 2000 Server possible through the use of several unattended installation strategies. The first methodology is disk duplication, also know as disk cloning or disk imaging. Disk duplication involves performing a clean install of Windows 2000 Server on a master computer, then creating a disk image of its hard drive that can be redistributed to other similar machines. Microsoft's System Preparation (SysPrep) tool is used to create images that can be distributed by third-party applications. The Remote Installation Preparation (RIS) Wizard creates images that can be distributed over the network from a Windows 2000 Server. You can only perform clean installs using this method.

The second methodology that can be applied to unattended installations is scripting. Here you create an Unattended Answer File (UAF) to automatically provide answers to the questions that you would ordinarily be prompted for if you were sitting in front of the computer while running Setup. This method can be used for both clean installs and upgrades. Microsoft's Setup Manager can be used to create UAFs, as can any text editor, so long as you know the correct syntax.

Creating Unattended Answer Files

Unattended installations involve the use of Setup program (WINNT.EXE or WINNT32.EXE) command line switches, which determine how setup will handle the preinstallation phases. Thereafter, UAFs supply the answers to questions that arise during the latter GUI-based installation phases.

A well-written UAF ensures that you do not have to sit at each target computer on which Windows 2000 Server is to be installed and reply to every setup prompt that comes along. Since your servers are likely to be configured in much the same way, one UAF can often be applied to many computers. One drawback is that having a single text file limits all target computers to a single computer name, domain membership, and other applicable network information such as IP address. In order to automate these variables as well, different UAFs can be created for each computer—but this increases the time required for installation and the probability of human error. Alternately, you can call upon an Unattended Database File (UDF) to fill in unique information for individual computers, such as the computer name.

WRITING THE UAF

The Windows 2000 Server installation CD-ROM contains a sample UAF, the "unattend.txt" document located in the I386 folder. You can use the example, shown in Figure 8.9, as a template for your own UAF.

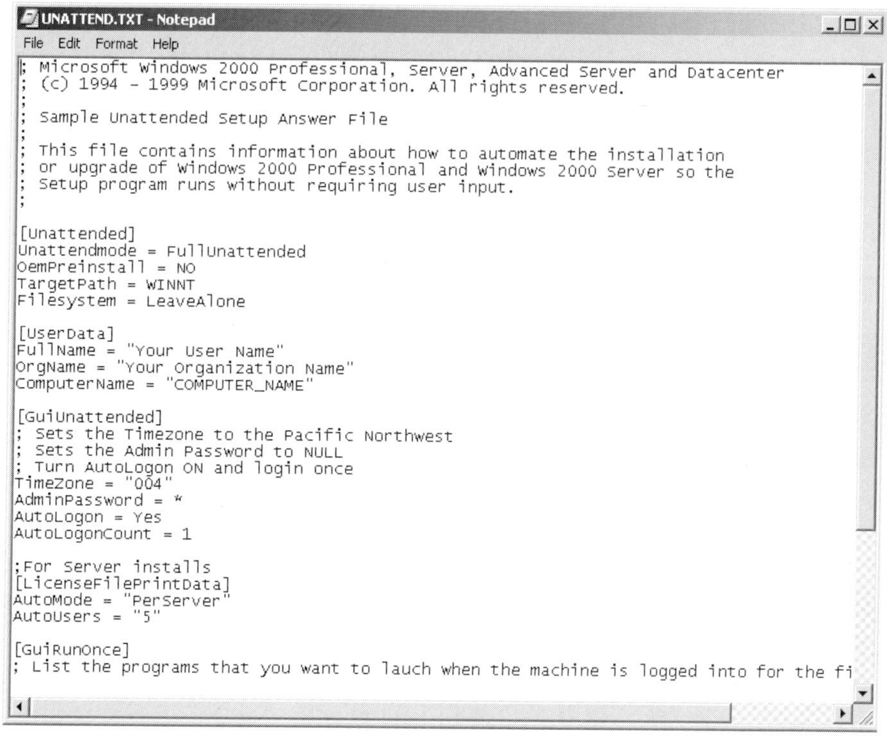

```
; Microsoft Windows 2000 Professional, Server, Advanced Server and Datacenter
; (c) 1994 - 1999 Microsoft Corporation. All rights reserved.
;
; Sample Unattended Setup Answer File
;
; This file contains information about how to automate the installation
; or upgrade of Windows 2000 Professional and Windows 2000 Server so the
; Setup program runs without requiring user input.
;

[Unattended]
UnattendMode = FullUnattended
OemPreinstall = NO
TargetPath = WINNT
Filesystem = LeaveAlone

[UserData]
FullName = "Your User Name"
OrgName = "Your Organization Name"
ComputerName = "COMPUTER_NAME"

[GuiUnattended]
; Sets the Timezone to the Pacific Northwest
; Sets the Admin Password to NULL
; Turn AutoLogon ON and login once
TimeZone = "004"
AdminPassword = *
AutoLogon = Yes
AutoLogonCount = 1

;For Server installs
[LicenseFilePrintData]
AutoMode = "PerServer"
AutoUsers = "5"

[GuiRunOnce]
; List the programs that you want to lauch when the machine is logged into for the fi
```

Figure 8.9 *Contents of the Unattend.txt file.*

The contents of an UNATTEND.TXT answer file are organized into section headings, parameters, and values modifying the parameters. These parameters may include the following:

- **Unattended.** Used during text mode setup, this parameter indicates to the setup application that this installation is unattended. It also enables settings such as unattend mode, target path, and file system type (NTFS, FAT or "LeaveAlone").
- **OEMBootFiles.** Displays Original Equipment Manufacturer (OEM) boot file names for the Hardware Abstraction Layer (HAL) and SCSI driver.
- **MassStorageDrivers.** Describes the hard drive drivers to be loaded by the text mode setup process.
- **OEM_Ads.** Modifies the default user interface of the Setup program. It is used to modify the background bitmap and logo used during the GUI-driven portion of the setup process.
- **GuiUnattended.** Specifies settings for the GUI-driven portion of setup. It indicates the time zone and hides the Administrator password dialog box.
- **UserData.** Provides user-specific data, such as user name, organization name, computer name, and product ID.
- **Networking.** Specifies network settings such as those for network adapters, services, and protocols. If this section is missing, networking will not be installed. This section specifies the domain or workgroup to join and creates a computer account in the domain.
- **Display.** Indicates specific settings for the display adapter card's installation. These settings must be correct and must be supported by the adapter.
- **Components.** Specifies the components that should be installed along with Windows 2000 Server, such as IIS.

You can also build an UAF using the graphical Windows 2000 Setup Manager Wizard, which is located on the Windows 2000 Server installation CD-ROM in the Support/Tools/Deploy.cab file (as described further on).

WRITING THE UDF

The UDF can replace certain parameters that are unique to certain computers in the UAF during the GUI-driven part of the Windows 2000 setup process. The UDF is divided into two sections: unique IDs and unique ID parameters. The unique ID portion identifies those parts of the answer file that will be modified or replaced, as well as establishing which users or machines will receive the unique information specified in the answer file. The unique ID parameters section holds the data that will be merged into the answer file.

The best way to use the UAF and UDF together is to create one UAF for each individual environment and at least one UDF to set the unique IDs of every machine that will be installed. The name and path to the UDF is set with the /udf switch when starting the setup process from the command line. The UDF should be located on a distribution server with the other Windows 2000 Server installation files.

USING SETUP MANAGER • The graphical Setup Manager Wizard provides you with the following options on launch:

- Build a new answer file.
- Build an answer file based on your current computer's configuration.
- Modify an existing answer file.

With it, you can forgo many of the previously described procedures by simply installing a pristine version of Windows 2000 Server on your perfectly configured master computer and using the second option to duplicate its settings. Create fully automated installations by answering all of the wizard's questions, or create partially unattended installations by bypassing some wizard options.

The Setup Manager Wizard performs the following steps after you choose to create a new answer file:

1. The Setup Manager Wizard asks you whether you wish to create an answer file for your own scripted installation or for use with a disk duplication method such as SysPrep or RIS (described further on).

2. You are asked to choose between creating an UAF for Windows 2000 Professional or Windows 2000 Server.

3. You are asked to define the level of user interaction that Setup will permit. The options here are as follow:

   - **Provide defaults.** Use this option to predefine default settings that can be amended by users as necessary.
   - **Fully automated.** Use this option to leave the user out of the process entirely.
   - **Hide pages.** Use this option to permit users to enter data in only those windows that contain settings that you chose not to preconfigure in the UAF.

- **Read only.** This option works in much the same way as the previous option, except that users are allowed to see all windows whether you preconfigured their settings or not. They are only allowed to enter data into those windows that you skipped, however.
- **GUI attended.** This option limits automation to just the second (text-based) phase of the installation process.

4. You are presented with windows that mirror the questions that arise during the setup process. These include setting the user and organization names, computer name (which can also be imported from a UDF or generated automatically based on organization name), Administrator password, display settings, network settings, workgroup or domain, and time zone. You may also add additional settings for such options as printer, telephony, regional, language, and browser settings.

5. You are asked about the manner in which you intend to distribute Windows 2000 Server. For remote installations, you will wish to create a distribution folder on a file server share that will contain all of the setup files needed, including the UAF. Choose the Copy the files from CD radio button to move the necessary setup files to this location. You may then specify this location in a following window.

6. Additional windows prompt you for such information as additional storage devices, specific HALs, and OEM branding art. You may also specify additional folders and files to be copied as part of the installation and identify commands that will be run in addition to setup, including a "run-once" command that will launch when the user first logs on.

7. You are prompted to supply the UAF's name or accept the default of "unattend.txt." If you do not rename the file, Setup Manager copies installation files onto the distribution volume that includes the sample "unattend.txt," which will overwrite your UAF if it has the same name!

Once it has your information, Setup Manager creates the UAF and distribution folder, copies the setup files, and exits.

Working with Automated Installations

How you perform the unattended installation will depend on whether or not you are employing the scripted or disk duplication method.

INSTALLING WITH THE UNATTENDED ANSWER FILE

Once you have created the UAF and UDF, you can begin the setup process from Windows 9x/Me or Windows NT with a command in the following format:

```
F:\i386\winnt32.exe /s:<source_path>u:v:\unattend.txt /
UDF:user1;v:\unattend.udf
```

Alternately, you could launch setup from Windows 3.1 or MS-DOS with a command in the following format:

```
F:\i386\winnt.exe /s:<source_path> /u:v:\unattend.txt /
UDF:user1;v:\unattend.udf
```

In these commands, "F:\" is the drive mapped to your installation CD-ROM or network share, "<source_path>" is the path pointing to the \I386 directory of the distribution files, and "v:\" is the drive mapped to the directory containing your UAF and UDF files.

Note that while similar, WINNT.EXE and WINNT32.EXE have some different options and syntax.

INSTALLING WITH REMOTE INSTALLATION SERVICES

Remote Installation Services (RIS) is an optional component of Windows 2000 Server that lets you install Windows 2000 Professional remotely on multiple computers of the same or differing configurations. Under RIS, you create a disk image of a properly configured Windows 2000 Professional workstation using any disk duplication tool, preferably the companion Remote Installation Preparation Wizard. This image is then distributed to additional workstations from the RIS server. The Remote Installation Preparation Wizard strips hardware-specific settings and the security identifier (SID) from the master image, making its duplicates useable by any workstation.

RIS can only be used to duplicate the Windows 2000 Professional operating system.

INSTALLING WITH THE SYSTEM PREPARATION TOOL

The System Preparation (SysPrep) tool can be applied to computers with identical hardware and software configurations only. This makes it limited if you have computers from many different manufacturers or with many differing software environments, since a disk image must be created to support each machine. If you have large numbers of computers from the same manufacturer with standardized software, however, it is a handy tool.

As with the Remote Installation Preparation Wizard, you must configure a master computer from which to create a disk image using the System Preparation tool. The image can then be burned on to CD-ROMs or shared from a server. Third-party utilities, such as Symantec's Norton Ghost or PowerQuest's DriveImage, must then be used to replicate the image to target computers.

You must have a volume licensing agreement for Windows 2000 Professional before employing the System Preparation tool. When creating an image, you must log on to the master computer with an Administrator account.

The SysPrep can be extracted to your hard drive or a floppy diskette from the following path on the Windows 2000 Server installation CD-ROM:

```
D:/SUPPORT/TOOLS/Deploy.cab
```

The System Preparation tool can be executed from the Run dialog box using a command in the following format:

```
Sysprep.exe [sysprep.inf] [-quiet] [-nosidgen] [-reboot]
```

Another component of SysPrep, the Mini-Setup Wizard, is used to regenerate the SIDs on target computers and to permit user input for the end-user license agreement, product key, user name, company name, Administrator password, network configuration, domain vs. workgroup selection, or date and time zone. Alternately, you can automate the selection of these parameters by creating a "sysprep.inf" answer file.

Table 8.4 provides a comparison of unattended installation methods.

Table 8.4 *Comparison of Unattended Installation Methods*

Capabilities	UAF	RIS	SysPrep
Install Windows 2000 Server	Yes	No	Yes
Install Windows 2000 Professional	Yes	Yes	Yes
Perform clean installs	Yes	Yes	Yes
Perform upgrades	Yes	No	No
Install on identical hardware	Yes	Yes	Yes
Install on differing hardware	Yes	Yes	No
Requires third-party applications	No	No	Yes

Study Break

Create an UAF Installation

Practice what you have learned by creating a scripted installation using Setup Manager.

First, install Windows 2000 Server on a master computer, as described in the previous section. Next, run the Setup Manager Wizard to create an UAF. Note the options that are presented in the various windows. Let the wizard create a distribution folder on a network share. Once completed, open the "unattend.txt" file and review the settings that have been created. Create an UDF if necessary. If appropriate, use your scripted installation package to install Windows 2000 Server on additional machines remotely.

MCSE 8.3   Upgrading

If you have Windows NT Servers deployed on your network, they will have been installed in one of the following roles:

- **Primary Domain Controller (PDC).** Where the domain model is used, a PDC is the first server installed in that domain. It hosts the master user database and is responsible for validating logons. User accounts are established and modified on this computer only. There is only one PDC in each domain.
- **Backup Domain Controller (BDC).** Where the domain model is used, there may be one or more BDCs. These host a copy of the domain's user account database and can share logon authentication duties with the PDC, even taking over if the PDC goes offline. BDCs synchronize their account databases with the PDC at regular intervals. A BDC cannot be installed unless there is already a PDC on the network. There can be multiple BDCs in a single domain.
- **Stand-alone or Member Server.** This type of server might or might not be a member of a domain, but does not participate in the domain. It does not host a copy of the user accounts database and cannot authenticate logon requests. Commonly used in the workgroup model, these computers may act as file, print, or application servers in the same way as domain controllers. There can be multiple member servers in a domain or workgroup.

Before attempting to upgrade your servers, you must first determine which role they were configured to play. If you have one or more standalone servers and are content with their operations in that role, upgrading is a relatively straightforward process of updating system software. If you are upgrading a domain, however, you will need to consider some differences between the way Windows NT and Windows 2000 handles networking. Fortunately, you do not need to upgrade all of your servers simultaneously. Windows 2000 Server can be configured to be backwards compatible with Windows NT Server, permitting you to make your server deployments cautiously and at your own pace.

Upgrading Domains

Windows NT domains can be upgraded to Windows 2000 domains in the following steps:

1. **Upgrade the PDC.** The Windows NT PDC is upgraded to a domain controller under Windows 2000.
2. **Upgrade BDCs.** Windows NT BDCs are upgraded to domain controllers or member servers under Windows 2000.
3. **Windows 2000 makes no distinction between a PDC and BDCs.** All domain controllers perform authentication through Active Directory.
4. **Upgrade standalone or member servers.** Windows NT standalone or member servers remain such under Windows 2000. Under Windows NT, you had to choose among domain controller and standalone/member server roles carefully during installation, because to change them thereafter required reinstalling the operating system. Windows 2000 lets you reassign roles after installation as needed.

Windows 2000's Active Directory is composed of domains, organizational units (OUs), trees, forests, and schema.

OUs group such objects as computers, user and group accounts, printers, and other OUs independently of domains. Multiple domains can be organized using their own OU structures.

Trees group one or more domains within a hierarchical structure that shares a common namespace. Domains within the tree all share resources within a single directory. Domains manage the users and groups within their own area of the directory, but their inclusion in the tree gives those users and groups global access to all of the tree's resources.

A forest is a group of one or more trees. The members of a forest do not share a common namespace. However, they do share a common configuration, directory schema, and global catalog. Despite their separation, all trees maintain a two-way transitive trust between root domains that permits them to share resources.

The intricacies of Active Directory are the subject of this book's fourth section. For our purposes here, you need only be aware of the following:

- The first domain controller you upgrade becomes the forest root domain. You cannot rename, change, or delete a root domain thereafter without completely rebuilding Active Directory, so choose among your servers carefully. You can choose to either make your existing domain the root domain or create a new domain that will act only as the root domain.
- Much of your existing domain configuration will be preserved when you upgrade to Windows 2000. At the same time, your domains will reap numerous benefits, such as more granular design, escape from the SAM database size limits, and easier management. You can also choose to restructure your domains, moving user accounts from one domain to another without affecting their SIDs and moving domain controllers from one domain to another without reinstalling Windows 2000.

Upgrading Windows NT Server

You may upgrade a computer running Windows NT Server 3.51, Windows NT Server 4.0, Windows NT Terminal Server 4.0, or a beta version of Windows 2000 Server by inserting the installation CD-ROM in the drive and following the Setup Wizard's instructions. The upgrade process differs from the clean installation in that it will overwrite the computer's existing system. The advantage is that it keeps most of the computer's setting preferences and applications. It is not necessary to apply service packs to Windows NT prior to upgrading.

Windows NT 4.0 Enterprise Edition can only be upgraded to Windows 2000 Advanced Server or Windows 2000 Datacenter Server.

Even if a system is running a previous version of Windows NT Server, it might not be a candidate for upgrade. The minimum system requirements for Windows NT Server 3.51 and 4.0 were much less. In order to run Windows 2000 Server, your computer should have at least a 133 Mhz Pentium processor (or equivalent), 64 MBs of RAM (128 MBs recommended), and 671 MBs of free hard disk space.

Even if your computer's hardware meets the minimum requirements, it might still contain components that are not supported by Windows 2000. The Setup program will automatically run the Hardware Compatibility tool during the installation process to verify this, but you would be wise to identify and resolve incompatibilities ahead of time. One way to do this is to run the WINNT32.EXE program with the /checkupgradeonly switch.

Because of known incompatibility issues between Windows NT Server 3.51 or 4.0 and Windows 2000 Server, Microsoft recommends that you remove the following software before upgrading:

- Third-party networking protocols and client applications that are not included in the I386\WINNTUPG folder on the CD-ROM.
- All antivirus and disk quota software. This is necessary because of the changes in NTFS between version 4 (NT 4.0) and version 5 (Windows 2000).
- Custom power management utilities. These are replaced under Windows 2000 by built-in Advanced Configuration and Power Interface (ACPI) and Advanced Power Management (APM) features.

UPGRADING A PDC

When upgrading domain controllers to Windows 2000 Server, the PDC must be upgraded first. Prior to upgrading a PDC, you should perform the following tasks:

- **Disable WINS.** If the WINS service is running, shut it down so that Windows 2000 can convert the database.
- **Disable DHCP.** Likewise, disable the DHCP service so that the database can be updated.
- **Synchronize BDCs.** Although the PDC will still communicate properly with BDCs after the upgrade, it is wise to make sure all domain controllers have up-to-date copies of the account database in case problems occur during installation.

When you upgrade the PDC, you will be prompted to choose between creating the first tree in a forest or a new tree in an existing forest, as well as choosing between a new domain or a child domain. You will also be asked to specify where tree files, such as user accounts, the system volume, and the log file, will be located. This should be an NTFS partition.

During the upgrade process, the Windows NT SAM database is copied to the Active Directory. Thereafter, the PDC will act as any other domain controller with regard to other Windows 2000 clients. At the same time, it will emulate a Windows NT 4.0 PDC with regards to existing BDCs, faithfully recording and replicating changes to user accounts as if nothing had occurred. This ability is referred to as Mixed Mode.

One good rollback strategy is to synchronize the database on a BDC, then take the machine offline until you are confident that the PDC has been upgraded successfully. If something should go wrong, you can put the reserve BDC back on line and promote it to PDC.

UPGRADING BDCS

The process of upgrading a BDC differs little from that of the PDC. Make sure that the upgraded former PDC is available on the network when upgrading BDCs, because this computer acts as a template to other domain controllers. There is no hurry to upgrade all of your BDCs at once, thanks to Mixed Mode.

While Mixed Mode is handy for backwards compatibility, it does hamper some Windows 2000 capabilities, such as group nesting and Kerberos authentication. Once you have upgraded all BDCs on your network, you can gain full Windows 2000 functionality by switching to Native Mode using the Active Directory Domains and Trusts MMC. After that, all domain controllers will use Active Directory for authentication exclusively. Although you can switch to Native Mode at any time, you cannot switch back to Mixed Mode thereafter.

UPGRADING MEMBER SERVERS

You can upgrade a member server at any time, without regard to the current configuration of existing domains. The local user accounts database remains local after the upgrade and is not subject to Active Directory. Should you later decide to promote a standalone or member server to a domain controller, you can easily do so using the Active Directory Installation Wizard.

Study Break

Perform an Upgrade

Practice what you have learned by upgrading a Windows NT Server computer to Windows 2000 Server (if possible).

Make sure that the target server has compatible hardware and software, and that it meets the necessary performance requirements. If possible, practice by upgrading a standalone or member server rather than a domain controller. If you must upgrade a domain controller, upgrade a PDC with great care, synchronizing a BDC ahead of time to provide the ability to roll back the upgrade.

MCSE 8.4   Deploying Service Packs

Windows 2000 Service Packs are free updates from Microsoft that contain bug fixes, security enhancements, drivers, tools, components, and just general improvements made to the operating system since it shipped originally. The latest Service Pack can be downloaded from the Microsoft Web site, by using the Update Windows command in the Start menu, or ordered on CD-ROM. To determine which version of a Service Pack (build) is currently installed on your server, run the "winver" command from the Run dialog box to open the About Windows dialog box.

Installing Service Packs under Windows NT Server 4.0 was often frustrating. Whenever you added components from the installation CD-ROM, you had to follow up by reinstalling one or more Service Packs. Windows 2000 keeps track of which files were added or replaced, and when you add or remove a component thereafter, it will automatically retrieve any necessary files from the Service Pack.

Whenever you install a Service Pack, it is always wise to select the option to backup original files, as shown in Figure 8.10.

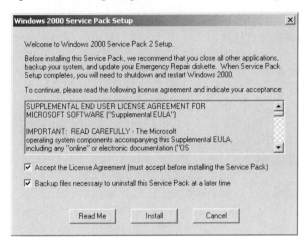

Figure 8.10   *Installing a Service Pack.*

Microsoft cannot guarantee the results of upgrading software in every situation, so selecting this option lets you roll back to your server's previous condition should problems arise. The backup might require more than 100 MBs of free disk space, however.

Study Break

Install Service Pack

Practice what you have learned by installing the latest Service Pack.

Download the latest Service Pack from the Microsoft Web site using the Windows Update command. Use the Backup files necessary to uninstall this Service Pack at a later time option. Test the machine before installing the Service Pack on additional servers or workstations.

MCSE 8.5   Troubleshooting Installations

Some common installation problems and solutions are as follows:

- **Faulty installer disks.** If you encounter media errors on the Windows 2000 Server Installation CD-ROM, you can request a replacement from Microsoft Sales at (800) 426-9400. A new set of installation floppy diskettes can be created from the CD-ROM.
- **Insufficient disk space.** If there is not enough disk space on the server, you can make some room by deleting unnecessary files and folders, especially those found in "temp" directories or Web browser caches. If you have NTFS drives, you can compress them. You can reformat partitions or repartition a disk drive to make more space available. Finally, you can add an additional disk drive for use as the boot drive. (Consider that you will need space not only for the \WINNT directory, but for the paging file as well.)
- **CD-ROM drive is inoperable.** If Windows 2000 does not recognize the adapter used by your CD-ROM drive, you might try booting from another operating system that does recognize it, such as Windows Me. You may then run the Setup application from the CD-ROM. Alternately, you might try installing over the network. Finally, you might replace the adapter or CD-ROM drive with one that is listed on the HCL. If Windows 2000 will not boot from the CD-ROM drive, begin the installation using the Setup boot diskettes.
- **Dependency service will not start.** Make sure the computer has a unique name on the network. Next, check to see that the necessary network protocols are installed and configured properly. Also, verify the compatibility of the network adapter.
- **An error occurs in assigning a domain name.** Make sure there are no other identical domain or computer names on the network.
- **A computer cannot access a domain controller.** First make sure that the correct user name, password, and domain were typed into the logon dialog box. Ensure that a PDC or Windows 2000 Server domain controller is online and functioning properly, and verify that its protocol and adapter configurations are correct. Also make sure that your network's DNS service is functioning properly. If all else fails, make the computer a member of a workgroup and resolve the logon issue later.

Viewing Logs

Windows 2000 creates the following useful log files during the installation process:

- **Setupact.log.** The Action log file lists, in chronological order, the actions that were performed during installation, such as copying files and creating Registry keys (see Figure 8.11).
- **Setuperr.log.** The Error log file lists installation errors, along with their severity. When errors occur, this file will open automatically at the end of the setup process.
- **Setupapi.log.** The Application Programmer's Interface (API) log lists device drivers that were copied during installation and includes warning and error messages.
- **Setuplog.txt.** The Setup log file lists details about device driver installations.
- **Comsetup.log.** The Component Setup Log file provides details on the installation of Optional Component Manager and COM + elements.
- **Mmdet.log.** The Multimedia Detection log file lists the multimedia devices that were installed, their ports, and their address ranges.
- **Netsetup.log.** The Network Setup log file documents the process that takes place when joining a workgroup or domain.

These logs can be opened from the \WINNT directory using a text editor, as shown in Figure 8.11.

Figure 8.11   *Viewing the "Setupact.log" file.*

<hr>

Study Break

Review Installation Logs

Practice what you have learned by opening the log files created in the \WINNT folder during Windows 2000 Server installation.

Open each log to familiarize yourself with its contents. Pay particular attention to the error, setup, and networking logs. If they list any problems, attempt to resolve them before placing any workload on the server.

■ Summary

In this chapter, we considered various Windows 2000 Server installation topics including planning, attended and unattended installations, upgrades, Service Packs, and troubleshooting.

Installation Planning

Prior to installing Windows 2000 Server, you should ensure that your hardware and software are compatible and meet or exceed Microsoft's minimum system requirements. You should then consider whether you will be upgrading from Windows NT Server or performing a clean install, how you will partition the hard disk, and which file system to use. You should also back up your important files and record network information.

Windows 2000 Server's minimum system requirements are at least a 133 Mhz Pentium processor (or equivalent), 64 MBs of RAM, and 671 MBs of free hard disk space. Microsoft recommends 128 MBs of RAM and 2 GBs of free hard disk space. You can also use four-way multiprocessing.

You may upgrade any computer running Windows NT Server 3.51 or NT 4.0 to Windows 2000 Server. If the computer is running Windows NT 3.1 or 3.5, you must upgrade to Windows NT 4.0 and then upgrade again to Windows 2000 Server. If the computer is running Windows 3.1, Windows for Workgroups 3.11, Windows 95, 98, Me, or XP, you must perform a clean installation.

To get the most from Windows 2000 in terms of performance, safety, and security, you should format server disk drive partitions as NTFS. If you must run additional operating systems on the same computer (not recommended), leave the partitions that you wish to have accessible from multiple operating systems formatted as FAT or FAT32.

Your network can be licensed as either per server or per seat. Under the former, you require CALs for as many workstations as will be supported by the server. Under the latter, the server can support as many logons as necessary but each workstation must have a CAL.

Attended Installations

An attended Setup can be launched from the installation CD-ROM, boot floppy diskettes, or a network share. Microsoft breaks the installation process into three steps. In the precopy phase, installation files are copied to temporary directories on the local hard drive from either the installation CD-ROM or a network share. In Text mode, Setup prompts you to approve the license agreement and then select or create an installation partition and its file system. GUI mode is broken down into the following steps: gathering information about your computer; installing Windows 2000 Server networking; and completing Setup. Among the important decisions you must make are which optional components to install, how to license clients, and whether to join a network domain or workgroup.

Unattended Installations

The first methodology that can be applied to unattended installations is disk duplication, which involves performing a clean install of Windows 2000 Server on a master computer, then creating a disk image of the hard drive that can be redistributed to other similar machines. Microsoft provides the System Preparation (SysPrep) tool for this purpose, which is used to create images that can be distributed by third-party applications. The caveats to disk duplication are that you may only perform clean installs and it works best with identically configured servers.

The second methodology that can be applied to unattended installations is scripting. Here you create an UAF to automatically provide answers to the questions that you would ordinarily be prompted for if you were sitting in front of the computer while running Setup from a remote server. This method can be used for both clean installs and upgrades. Microsoft provides the Setup Manager to help you create answer files, although they can also be created with any text editor using the proper syntax. Automated installations can be launched from the command line through WINNT.EXE and WINNT32.EXE using several switches.

Upgrading

You may upgrade a computer running Windows NT Server 3.51, Windows NT Server 4.0, Windows NT Terminal Server 4.0, or a beta version of Windows 2000 Server. When upgrading standalone or member servers, you may proceed as if you were upgrading a Windows 2000 Professional computer. When working with domain controllers, however, you must upgrade the PDC first. Thanks to Mixed Mode's backwards compatibility, you may upgrade BDCs thereafter at your leisure.

Deploying Service Packs

Service Packs are free updates from Microsoft that contain bug fixes, security enhancements, drivers, tools, components, and general improvements made to the operating system since it shipped. You can order the latest Service Pack on CD-ROM or download it by connecting to the Internet and selecting the Windows Update command from the Start menu. Windows 2000 keeps track of which files were added or replaced, and when you add or remove a component thereafter, it will automatically retrieve any necessary files from the Service Pack.

Troubleshooting Installations

Problems that can arise during installation include media errors on the Windows 2000 Server Installation CD-ROM, insufficient disk space on the target computer, and incompatible CD-ROM drives. Network problems can result in dependency services that will not start, errors in assigning domain names, and failure to access a domain controller. Most problems are recorded in the log files created during installation.

▲ CHAPTER REVIEW QUESTIONS

Here are a few questions relating to the material covered in the *Installing Windows 2000 Server* section of Microsoft's *Installing, Configuring, and Administering Microsoft Windows 2000 Server* exam (70-215).

1. *Which of the following operating systems can be directly upgraded to Windows 2000 Server? Select all that apply:*
   A. Windows NT Server 4.0
   B. Windows NT Workstation 4.0
   C. Windows NT Server 3.5
   D. Windows NT Enterprise Server 4.0

2. *If you are installing Windows 2000 Server into an enterprise environment, per server licensing makes the most sense.*
   A. True
   B. False

3. *Which of the following tools can be used in performing an unattended installation of Windows 2000 Server? Select all that apply.*
   A. WINNT.EXE
   B. SysPrep
   C. Setup Manager
   D. RIS

4. *Which of the following are parameters that can be specified in an UAF? Select all that apply:*

   A. file system

   B. user name

   C. IIS components

   D. computer name

5. *When automating Windows 2000 Server installation from Windows 9x, you should use WINNT.EXE command line switches.*

   A. True

   B. False

6. *Which of the following tools perform automated installations through scripting? Select all that apply:*

   A. SysPrep

   B. RIS

   C. Setup Manager

   D. WINNT32.EXE

7. *Which of the following tools can be used to perform automated upgrades? Select all that apply:*

   A. SysPrep

   B. RIS

   C. Setup Manager

   D. UAFs

8. *In a domain environment, which of the following severs should be upgraded first? Select only one:*

   A. PDC

   B. BDC

   C. Member server

   D. Stand-alone server

9. *After upgrading, a member server's account database is incorporated into Active Directory.*

   A. True

   B. False

10. *If you install optional server components after a Service Pack has been installed, you must go back and reinstall the Service Pack thereafter.*

   A. True

   B. False

11. *If you choose to back up affected files before installing a Service Pack, you will be able to roll back to the earlier configuration if problems arise.*

   A. True

   B. False

12. *If you cannot boot from the installation CD-ROM, you should try booting from the Setup floppy diskettes.*

   A. True

   B. False

13. *Which of the following logs is most useful in the troubleshooting the domain logon process? Select only one:*

   A. netsetup.log

   B. setuperr.log

   C. setuplog.log

   D. winsetup.log

Administering Windows 2000 Server Resource Access

▲Chapter Syllabus

MCSE 9.1 Network Services
Interoperability

MCSE 9.2 Working with Printer
Access

MCSE 9.3 Working with File
and Folder Access

MCSE 9.4 Working with Web
Site Access

In this chapter, we will examine topics covered in the *Installing, Configuring, and Troubleshooting Access to Resources* section of Microsoft's *Installing, Configuring, and Administering Microsoft Windows 2000 Server* exam (70-215).

The following material will teach you to install and configure network services that are critical for interoperability, review the process of sharing printers, files, and folders, and cover Web sharing in greater depth.

MCSE 9.1   Network Services Interoperability

Windows 2000 Server supports several network protocols and their related services, including the following:

- Asynchronous Transfer Mode (ATM)
- Internetwork Packet Exchange/Sequenced Packet Exchange (IPX/SPX)
- NetBIOS Enhanced User Interface (NetBEUI)
- AppleTalk
- Data Link Control (DLC)
- Infrared Data Association (IrDA)
- Transmission Control Protocol/Internet Protocol (TCP/IP)

The most important of these is TCP/IP, the world's most common and Windows 2000's default protocol. When implemented in a Microsoft networking environment, TCP/IP relies on three primary network services for interoperability:

- **Dynamic Host Configuration Protocol (DHCP).** In order to participate in services on a TCI/IP-based network, each computer (host) must have a unique IP address. These are composed of four numbers between 0 and 255 separated by decimal points (e.g., 255.255.255.255). Typically, these are static addresses that must be manually configured on each workstation, requiring a lot of effort on the part of network administrators. By using DHCP, administrators can avoid this effort by letting workstations obtain their addresses dynamically from a server that manages a range of available addresses, doling them out automatically when a workstation attempts to use a TCP/IP service. These addresses are "leased" for a limited time. When the time is up, they are returned to the server's pool of addresses and become available for use by other workstations. DHCP is covered extensively in Chapter 16, "Administering DHCP."
- **Domain Name Service (DNS).** In order to make IP addresses more accessible to humans, they can be mapped to domain names. A typical domain name looks like the following:

```
www.scionnet.com
```

It is the job of the DNS server to match any request for a connection to a domain name with the correct IP address so that communications between hosts can occur. The DNS server makes this determination either from its own database of IP address-to-domain name mappings, as in the case of local hosts, or by querying other Internet-based DNS servers that in turn consult their databases, as in the case of remote hosts. DNS is covered extensively in Chapter 15, "Administering DNS."

* **Windows Internet Naming Service (WINS).** This service works in much the same way as DNS except that it maps IP addresses to Network Basic Input/Output System (NetBIOS) names rather than domain names. NetBIOS names identify resources on Microsoft networks (as seen in My Network Places). NetBIOS names follow the Universal Naming Convention (UNC) format. You can use this convention to locate resources from the Windows 2000 command line as shown:

```
\\computername\sharename\path
```

Another difference is that WINS can create IP address-to-NetBIOS name mappings dynamically, while DNS must refer to a predefined table of IP address-to-domain name mappings. WINS is covered extensively in Chapter 19, "Administering DNS."

Installing Network Services for Interoperability

To install such network services as DNS, DHCP, and WINS, click the Install Add-On Components link in the installation CD-ROM Autorun screen. This will open the Windows Components window.

Choose the Networking Services item in the scrolling list and click the Details button to open the Networking Services window, as shown in Figure 9.1.

Figure 9.1 *Adding network services.*

Enable the checkboxes next to the DNS, DHCP, and WINS tabs, then click the OK button. Click the Next button in the Windows Components window to perform the installation.

It is important that the server on which you install these services has its own static IP address.

Configuring Network Services Interoperability

Once installed, network services can be enabled and disabled through the Services MMC snap-in, found in the Administrative Tools program group, as shown in Figure 9.2.

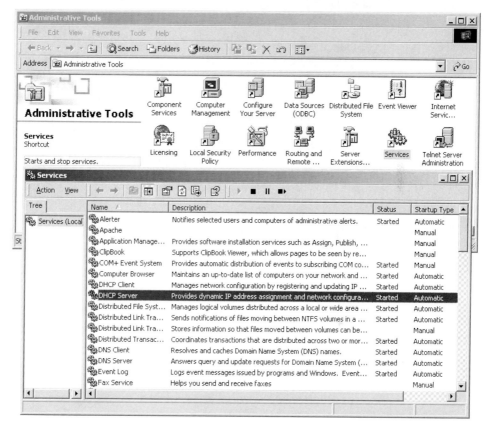

Figure 9.2 *The Services MMC snap-in.*

This snap-in contains all of the services that are running on your server. Its interface gives you the option of starting, stopping, pausing, and continuing a service. The Pause command differs from the Stop command in that the service will finish handling its current processing, but will not take on new requests until it is continued.

As shown in Figure 9.3, the Startup type drop-down menu lets you specify that the service will start automatically, manually, or not at all (disabled).

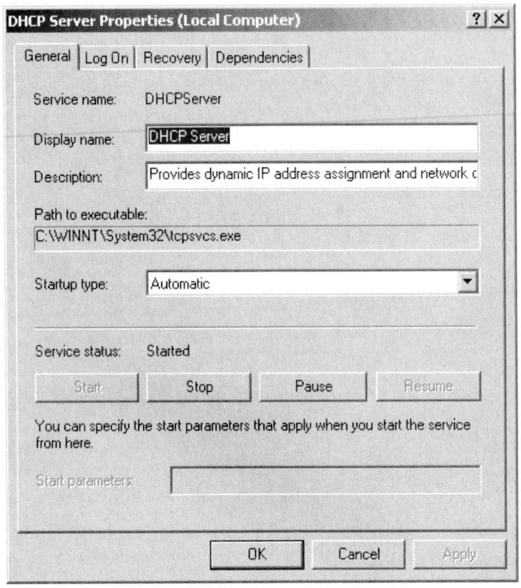

Figure 9.3 *Configuring service startup options.*

Logon security is provided for services under the Log On tab. An internal Windows 2000 system account provides access to both services and the operating system, as shown in Figure 9.4. Alternately, you can specify any account from the users database. In addition, you can associate services for specific hardware profiles.

Although many services are managed via the Services snap-in exclusively, others such as DHCP, DNS, and WINS are configured within their own interfaces. They can still be added, started, stopped, and paused through the Services snap-in, however.

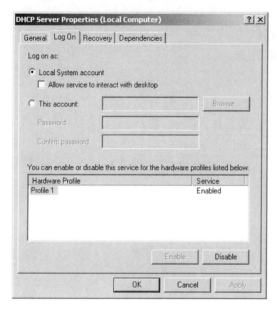

Figure 9.4 *Configuring service logon options.*

CONFIGURING DHCP

Once installed, the DHCP server can be configured through the Services and Applications snap-in of the Computer Management MMC, as shown in Figure 9.5.

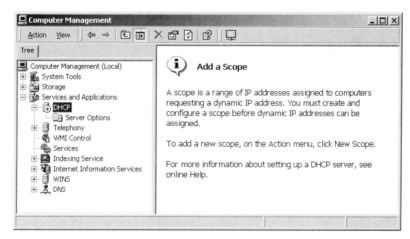

Figure 9.5 *Configuring the DHCP server.*

The first step is to create a "scope" of IP addresses that can be distributed to client computers. To do this, select the New Scope command from the Action menu to open the New Scope Wizard. Give the scope a name and description in the Scope Name window, as shown in Figure 9.6.

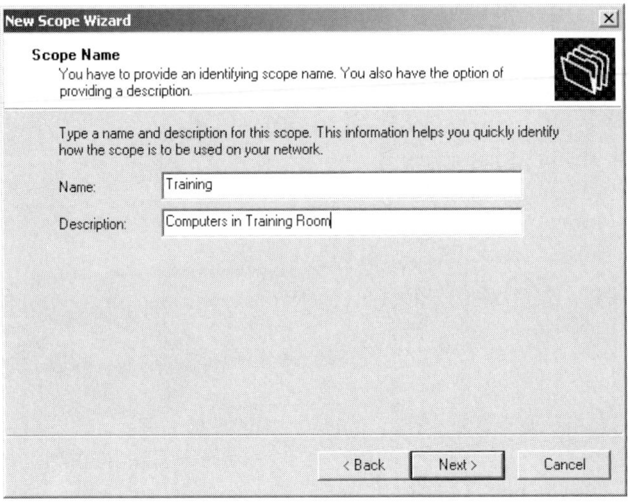

Figure 9.6 *Naming a new scope.*

Next, identify a range of contiguous IP addresses that will be managed by the DHCP server, as shown in Figure 9.7.

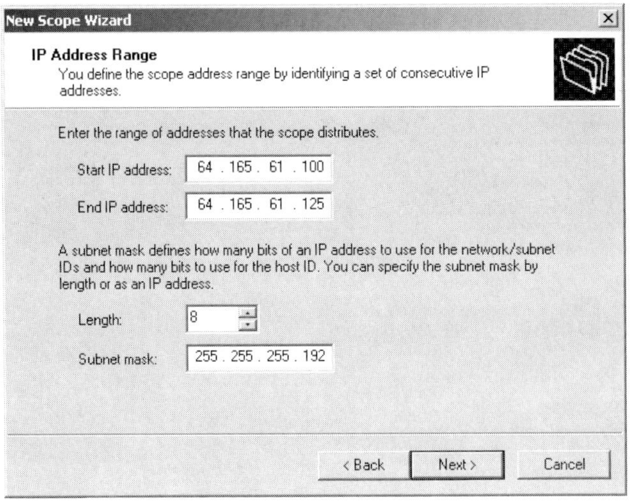

Figure 9.7 *Identifying the scope's IP address range.*

Make sure that these addresses do not overlap with those managed by any other DHCP servers. You will also need to specify the scope's subnet mask. The DHCP server need not be on the same subnet.

Optionally, identify any IP addresses within the scope that you wish to leave statically assigned, as shown in Figure 9.8.

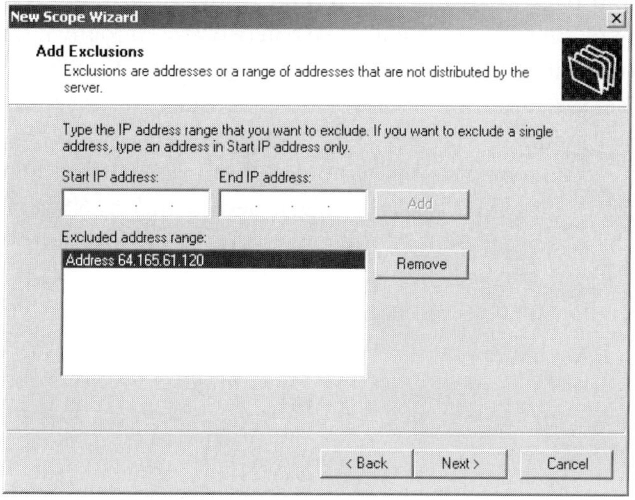

Figure 9.8 *Excluding IP addresses.*

This is handy if, for example, you have a server using one of the IP addresses assigned to the scope.

Next, set a lease duration, as shown in Figure 9.9.

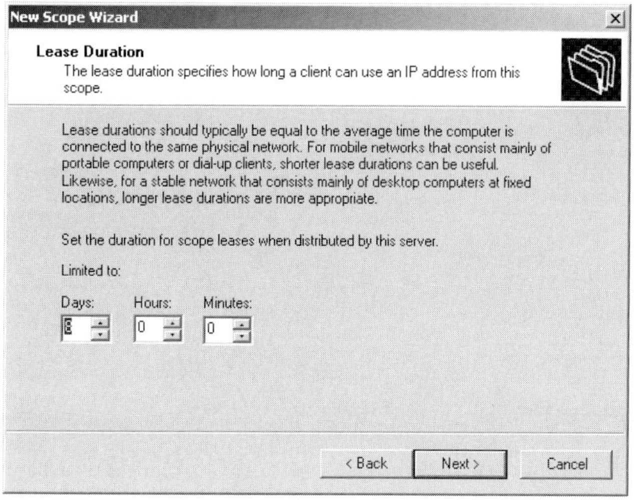

Figure 9.9 *Setting a lease duration.*

The value you set here determines how long an inactive client will be allowed to keep its address. This is particularly useful in "timing out" the IP addresses of mobile computers that have left the network, returning their settings to the scope for reassignment. If you have a relatively static network with plenty of IP addresses to go around, you can use a lease duration measured in days to reduce the amount of network traffic generated by clients renewing their leases. If you have a network with many mobile computers or with insufficient IP addresses to serve all clients at one time, you can configure the lease duration in hours to help ensure that every IP address assigned is being used.

Subsequent optional windows permit you to configure the IP address of the default router (gateway), DNS server, and WINS server that should be used by client computers. After you click the Finish button to complete the wizard, you will see the new scope listed under the MMC's DHCP branch (see Figure 9.10).

If you failed to input some necessary settings when running the wizard, you can still do so by selecting the Configure Options command from the Action menu to open the Server Options dialog box, as shown in Figure 9.10.

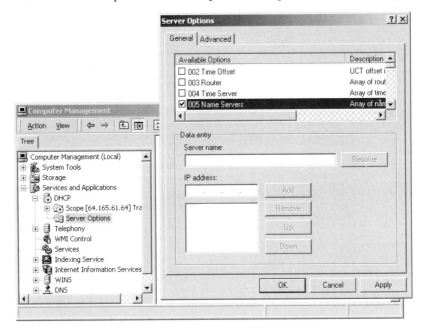

Figure 9.10 *Configuring DHCP Server options.*

If you do not configure these options, clients will be assigned the same settings used by the server computer. If these settings are manually configured on a client locally, they will override those assigned by the DHCP server.

Once configured, the new scope appears in the MMC with a red arrow indicating that it is not yet authorized in Active Directory. To authorize the scope, right-click and select the Activate command from the menu. The arrow icon will change to green.

In order to obtain an IP address, workstations will send out network broadcast packets to any available BOOTP/DHCP servers. Since one function of a router is to limit broadcast traffic to its network of origin, a workstation on one side of a router will often be unable to communicate with a DHCP server on the other side. To overcome this limitation, Windows 2000 provides the DHCP Relay Agent, which can be installed as a network service and will pass broadcast traffic directly to the DHCP servers you designate.

BOOTP, or Bootstrap Protocol, is an earlier UNIX technique for obtaining dynamic IP addresses. DHCP is based upon this earlier, more limited protocol. Because of this, DHCP servers can process requests from BOOTP clients as well.

CONFIGURING DNS

When the Internet began, a "Hosts" file was used to maintain the IP address-to-domain name mappings for member computers. As it grew, however, it became apparent that this file was becoming impossibly large to manage and distribute. In 1984, therefore, the Domain Name System (DNS) was created. Under this client-server model, administered by the Internet Network Information Center (InterNIC), multiple servers maintain the equivalent of multiple Hosts files and are in communication which each other. This distributes the database of IP address-to-host name mappings across the globe. Each DNS server needs only keep track of its local addresses. When addresses beyond the immediate location are called for, other DNS servers are queried.

Under DNS, domain names are arranged in a hierarchical tree-like directory structure. Common root-level domains, administered by the InterNIC, are listed in Table 9.1.

Table 9.1 *Root-Level Domains*

Domain name	Type of Organization
.com	commercial
.edu	educational
.org	organization (not-for-profit)
.net	network (ISPs)
.gov	government
.mil	military

Country codes are also common, such as "ca" for Canada or "es" for Spain.

When you obtain access to the Internet from an ISP, you obtain a local domain name that is assigned under one of the root-level domains. Part of your ISP's job is usually to direct querying computers to your local domain.

You can use your ISP or your own DNS server to map IP addresses to local host names. Domain names are processed left to right, so in the following domain name:

```
www.microsoft.com
```

… "com" refers to the root-level domain, "microsoft" is an example of a company's local domain, and "www" is the host. This is an example of a Fully Qualified Domain Name (FQDN), because it specifies the exact path to the host.

Although the break up of the Internet naming database into multiple domains lessens the administrative challenges and the burden on server machines, it is often necessary to subdivide large domains even further. This is done using zones. These are database files that contain manageable portions of the domain namespace and which can be replicated across multiple servers.

In some cases, you might know the IP address of a given host rather than its FQDN. To locate the resource, a reverse lookup is used. A FQDN is processed from right to left, with the leftmost designation being that of the host. An IP address, however, is processed from left to right with the rightmost octet being the host address. To be used with DNS, then, an IP address such as "64.165.61.121" must become "121.61.165.64." These reserve mappings are maintained in special zones that use the network portion of the address and the in-addr.arpa designator, as in the following example:

```
61.165.64.in-addr.arpa
```

You will need to apply this terminology in configuring your own DNS server. Microsoft first introduced its DNS server with the Resource Kit for Windows NT Server 3.51. This implementation is based on Internet Request For Comment (RFC) documents 974, 1034, and 1035.

The popular Berkeley Internet Name Domain (BIND), a UNIX-based DNS implementation, is not fully compliant with these RFCs. Therefore, the Microsoft DNS implementation does not support some features found in BIND. You can read these RFCs on the Internet at *http://ds.internic.net/ds/rfc-index.html.*

Under Windows 2000 Server, a DNS server can be deployed in one of several roles:

- **Primary.** A primary DNS server is responsible for maintaining the master database for a given zone. Addressing changes are made to this database only. The primary DNS server also caches recent name resolution requests to speed up future requests for the same host. The primary DNS server keeps track of the address mappings for Internet-based root domain servers. There can only be one primary DNS server.
- **Secondary.** Secondary DNS servers provide redundancy by hosting a read-only copy of the master zone database. This database is regularly updated with that of the primary DNS server during zone transfers. Secondary DNS servers respond to queries when the primary DNS server fails to respond because of a server failure or heavy workload. Multiple secondary servers can be deployed on a network to provide fault tolerance and load-balancing functions.
- **Caching-only.** Caching-only DNS servers speed up resource access by caching recent external queries. They do not maintain a copy of the zone database.
- **DNS Forwarder.** The DNS forwarder server resolves queries handed to it by another DNS server (forwarding server), rather than directly from a client.
- **Dynamic.** New to Windows 2000, the dynamic DNS server works closely with DHCP to update its database with the proper mappings whenever DHCP assigns an address.

The DNS server can be configured through the Services and Applications snap-in of the Computer Management MMC, as shown in Figure 9.11.

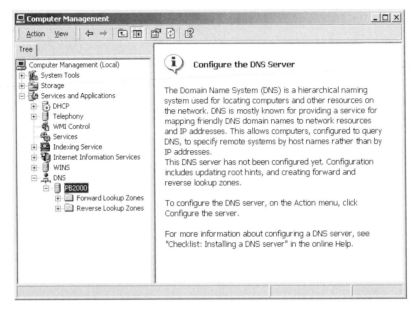

Figure 9.11 *Configuring the DNS server.*

Select the Configure the Server command from the Action menu to open the Configure DNS Server Wizard. If this will be the primary server, select the This is the first DNS server on this network radio button in the Root Server window, as shown in Figure 9.12.

Figure 9.12 *Creating a primary or secondary server.*

If you are creating a secondary DNS server, choose the other radio button and provide an IP address for an existing DNS server, preferably the primary DNS server.

Next, you will be asked whether or not you wish to create a forward lookup zone. During a forward lookup query, a client asks the DNS server for the IP address associated with a particular host name. The server either resolves this query from its own database or passes the request on up the line to the next DNS server. If you enable the creation of the forward lookup zone, the DNS server will create a database for local address resolution.

Next, you must choose to create a standard primary or secondary DNS server, or one that is integrated with Active Directory, as shown in Figure 9.13.

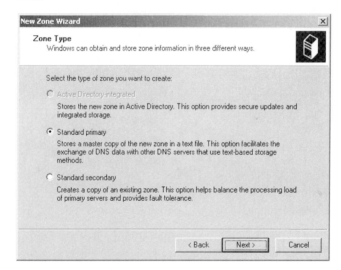

Figure 9.13 *Choosing DNS zone type.*

Since Windows 2000 domains require DNS and are based on DNS zones, it is best to select the Active Directory-integrated checkbox in most cases. This provides the benefits of Active Directory security and ease of management.   In addition, Active Directory permits all domain controllers to modify the zone and replicate updates to their peer domain controllers through the process of multimaster replication. This provides fault tolerance by eliminating a single point of update failure. This process is also quicker than zone transfers (which can still take place with standard secondary DNS servers), because only zone information changes are replicated.

Next, you will be prompted to name the zone in the following format:

mycompany.com

If you choose to create a standard primary or secondary DNS server, you will be prompted next to create a new zone file or select an existing one.

Next, you will be asked whether or not you wish to create a reverse lookup zone. As with the forward lookup zone, you will then be asked in the subsequent window whether or not the zone will be created under Active Directory or for a standard primary or secondary DNS server. You will also be asked to specify the Network ID portion of the zone's IP address range, as shown in Figure 9.14.

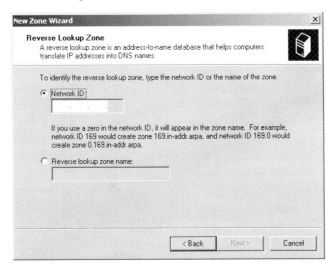

Figure 9.14 *Identifying the network ID.*

The wizard will automatically fill in the Reverse lookup zone name field based on the Network ID you supply.

If you choose to create a standard primary or secondary DNS server, you will again be prompted to create a new zone file or select an existing one.

After you complete the wizard, the new forward and reverse lookup zones will be available in the Computer Management MMC DNS snap-in. Initially, Start of Authority (SOA) and Name Server (NS) records are created.

Double-click a record to modify its configuration (see Figure 9.15).

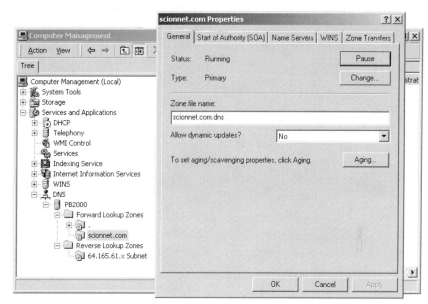

Figure 9.15 *Configuring a SOA record.*

To actually create a host record, choose the New Host command from the Action menu to open the New Host dialog box, as shown in Figure 9.16.

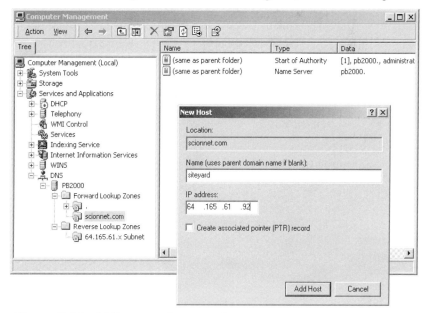

Figure 9.16 *Adding a new host record.*

Enter the host name and IP address, then click the Add Host button to add the new record to the database.

CONFIGURING WINS

WINS supports clients running under the following operating systems:

- Windows 2000
- Windows NT 3.5, 2.51, 4.0
- Windows 95, 98, Me
- Windows for Workgroups 3.11
- MS-DOS/LAN Manager 2.2c
- MS-DOS/Microsoft Network Client 3.0 (With real mode TCP/IP driver).

WINS servers can be installed on a standalone Windows 2000 Server or a domain controller, in either primary or secondary roles. Windows 2000 adds several improvements to WINS, including the following:

- **Dynamic database.** The WINS database is distributed and works in conjunction with DHCP to register and query dynamic NetBIOS names.
- **Burst mode.** WINS has an increased capability to handle a burst of NetBIOS registration requests, such as when computers are started at the beginning of the workday or after a power outage.
- **Tombstoning.** WINS records that are marked for deletion are tombstoned. Manual tombstoning permits a record's removal across all WINS servers, ensuring that a record that was not deleted on one server never gets propagated back to the rest of the system.
- **Persistent connections.** WINS servers can keep their connections between replicating partners open, saving time and overhead that would be generated by constantly opening and closing connections.

The WINS server can be configured through the Services and Applications snap-in of the Computer Management MMC, as shown in Figure 9.17.

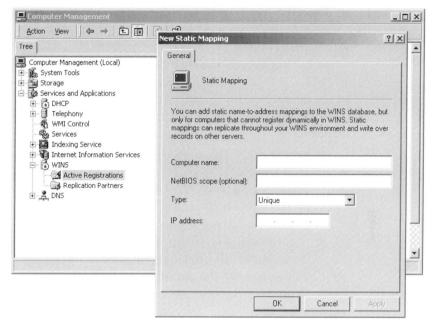

Figure 9.17   *Configuring the WINS server.*

Using the WINS snap-in, you can display records by name (NetBIOS) or owner (IP address), verify name records, and delete owners. You can also establish static mappings for computers that are not WINS clients (as shown in Figure 9.18).

Somewhat like DHCP Relay Agents, WINS Proxy Agents redirect requests for non-WINS network clients to a WINS server. WINS Proxy Agents can be configured by editing the Registry on WINS client computers.

Study Break

Create a DHCP Scope

Practice what you have learned by creating a DHCP scope.

Install the DHCP server. Next, find a range of unassigned IP addresses on your network. Assign this address range to a DHCP scope. Activate the DHCP server. Configure a client computer for automatic addressing and launch a TCP/IP program, such as a Web browser, to obtain an address from the DHCP server.

MCSE 9.2	**Working with Printer Access**

As described in Chapter 2, "Administering Windows 2000 Professional," Windows 2000 computers can output copy to print devices that are attached to them directly, shared from other computers, or that stand alone on the network. They can also print using variety of protocols, including TCP/IP, IPX/SPX, DECnet, DLC, and AppleTalk. In working with Windows 2000 Server, the emphasis is on shared printing.

The following terms are important to the Windows 2000 printing architecture:

- **Print device.** This is the hardware device that outputs hard copy. A local print device is connected to the server directly via a parallel, serial, or USB cable. A network print device is connected to the server by way of the network, such as via a built-in Ethernet interface card.
- **Printer.** To Microsoft, this is the software that controls print devices, not the hardware. The printer interface lets you determine the print device on which a document will be printed, when it will be printed, and with which job options.
- **Print queue.** This is a list of documents that are waiting to be printed.
- **Print server.** This is a computer that manages shared printing. Print servers can be dedicated, controlling multiple print devices and accepting numerous network connections, or nondedicated, sharing a print device as minor process among others.
- **Print driver.** This is software responsible for translating the output needs of a program into instructions that the print device can understand. At the beginning of any Windows 2000 print job, the operating system will identify the printer driver version on the client computer to ensure it is current with the print server. If the print server has a newer version, it will download it to the client computer automatically. It is important, therefore, that you select all of the hardware and operating systems of client computers when setting up a shared printer. This ensures that the platform-specific printer drivers will be installed on the print server and can be downloaded.

Windows 2000 print drivers have two parts. The first is composed of Dynamic Link Libraries (DLLs). The Printer Graphics Driver DLL is the driver's rendering mechanism, which is called by the Graphics Device Interface during printing. The Printer Interface Driver DLL is the driver's user interface, which you call on to configure the printer. The characterization file is called on by both DLLs as needed. It contains printer-specific information about RAM, fonts, resolution, paper size, paper orientation, and other characteristics.

- **Print Spooler.** This service, which must be running on both server and client, manages the printing process in the background. Its general purpose is to save print jobs to disk, or spool, and then dole them out at a speed the printing device can handle while permitting the user to work on other things.
- **Print Processor.** This software is responsible for rendering, the process of converting data into a form that a printing device can understand and reproduce on paper. Windows 2000's main print processor is WINPRINT.DLL. Its tasks vary with the type of data it is passed from the printer driver. These types include raw data, which is already rendered by the printer driver and needs only be passed to the printing device, Enhanced Metafile (EMF), a standard file format supported by many printing devices that is generated by the Graphical Device Interface prior to spooling, and text, a basic type used by printing devices that do not support ASCII and which includes only minimal formatting.
- **Print Router.** This software passes print jobs from the spooler to the appropriate print processor.
- **Print Monitor.** This software watches the status of print devices and reports back to the spooler, which in turn displays information through the user interface. Among its specific duties are detecting error conditions, such as "out of paper" or "low toner," as well as printing errors that require the job to be restarted. Another duty is end-of-job notification, wherein the print monitor notifies the spooler that the last page has been imaged and the print job can now be purged.

During a print job, all of these components work together as follows:

1. A client notifies the Windows 2000 print server that it has a print job.
2. The print server checks to see which version of the printer driver the client is running. If it is older than the one on the print server, the newer printer driver will be downloaded to the client.
3. The printer driver passes the print data to the Print Spooler service that is running on the client.
4. The client spooler writes the print data to a file, which it places in the spool folder.

5. The client spooler uses a Remote Procedure Call (RPC) to transfer the data to the spooler running on the print server.

6. The server spooler sends the data to the Local Print Provider.

7. The Local Print Provider routes the data to a print processor. If necessary, the Local Print Provider will send the data to a separator page processor as well.

8. The print processor renders the data in a format the printing device can understand.

9. The Local Print Provider passes the rendered data to the print monitor.

10. The print monitor forwards the rendered data through the correct printer port to the printing device.

11. The printing device images the data.

12. The print monitor sends an end-of-job notification back to the spooler, which then purges the finished print job.

Print jobs can be deleted from the spooler's print queue during the process. If a given print job cannot be deleted or purged by the administrator or print operator, the Print Spooler service can be stopped and restarted using the Services MMC snap-in.

SUPPORTING NETWARE PRINT CLIENTS

In order to permit Windows 2000 computers to print to NetWare-based printers via the server, Gateway (and Client) Services for NetWare (GSNW) must be installed. The Windows 2000 Server can also accept print jobs from NetWare-based clients.

SUPPORTING UNIX PRINT CLIENTS

The Windows 2000 Server can accept print jobs from UNIX hosts if the Print Services for UNIX service is installed. This service acts as a Line Printer Daemon (LPD) to remote UNIX Line Printer Remote (LPR) clients. Windows 2000 clients can also make use of LPR.

The Windows 2000 Server LPR service can be addressed with the following command:

```
lpr -S{server} -P{printer} -J{job} -C{class}

-O{option} -x -d{file name}
```

To display queue information, you can use the following command:

```
lpq -S{server} -P{printer}
```

SUPPORTING MAC OS PRINT CLIENTS

Macintosh computers print using the PostScript printer description language. Mac OS clients can print to Windows 2000 printers regardless of the language they support, however, if the Print Services for Macintosh (SFM) service is installed on the server. The SFM print processor (SFMPSPRT.DLL) supports the PSCRIPT1 data type, which processes Level 1 PostScript jobs for non-PostScript printers (PostScript printers use the RAW data type). These jobs are passed to SUM's built-in Microsoft TrueImage Raster Image Processor (RIP), which creates one-page bitmap renderings. The receiving non-Postscript printer can then image these bitmaps.

Mac OS clients can print to SFM printers over their native AppleTalk protocol. Windows 2000 Server can also print to and "capture" AppleTalk-based print devices, such as Apple LaserWriters.

Configuring Printer Access

To share a printer, select it in the Printers program group. Right click, then select the Properties command to open the Properties dialog box. Switch to the Sharing tab to set a network name and turn printer sharing on or off, as shown in Figure 9.18.

Long share names are supported under Windows NT/2000 and Windows 9x/Me only. Click the Additional Drivers button to select all of the appropriate operating system drivers that should be loaded from the Additional Drivers list (see Figure 9.18).

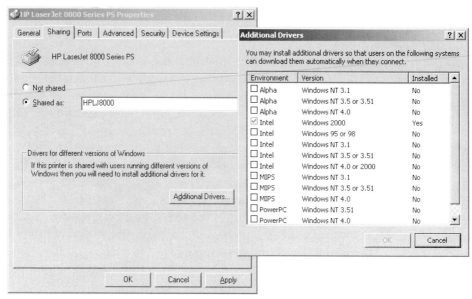

Figure 9.18 *Enabling printer sharing properties.*

Select the Advanced tab to configure most of a printer's management functions, as shown in Figure 9.19.

Figure 9.19 *Printer's advanced management properties.*

For example, you may change printer drivers and establish printing defaults. You may schedule print jobs and specify when the printer will be available for use, limiting congestion by staggering printers. You can also set printer priorities, which staggers multiple printers by priority rather than by time.

Separator pages are used to separate one print job from another, something Windows 2000 does not do by default. In order to use this feature, you must select a separator file using the Separate Page button.

The Print Processor button lets you specify the print processor and data type used to render print jobs.

The Advanced tab also enables you to set spool settings on each printer, including the following:

- **Spool print documents so program finishes faster.** You can store documents until they have all spooled and then print them all or have them start printing immediately.
- **Print directly to the printer.** This turns off spooling, which works only where there is only one printer device attached to the printer.
- **Hold mismatched documents.** This prevents documents that do not match the printer's configurations from printing.
- **Keep printed documents.** This keeps documents in the spooler even after printing.

Printer pooling connects one printer to more than one print device. Thus, as print jobs are received, they are routed to free printers to speed the process for the entire network.

Check the Enable printer pooling option under the Ports tab and choose the ports that will participate in the pool, as shown in Figure 9.20.

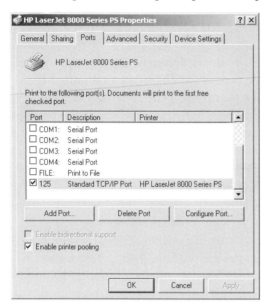

Figure 9.20 *Enabling printer pooling.*

When you share a printer using the Add Printer Wizard, it is listed in Active Directory by default. You can remove it by disabling the List in the Directory check box under the Sharing tab of the printer Properties dialog box. When listing printers in Active Directory, keep the following points in mind:

- Printers appear in Active Directory as printQueue objects. These can be found in the print server's computer object.
- Print servers publish information for their own printers. If a printer is updated on the print server, its Active Directory information is updated automatically and propagated throughout the system.
- When a print server goes offline, its printers are removed from Active Directory lists.

Once a printer has been shared, clients can locate it by using the Add Printer Wizard, through the Windows 2000 Search application, through My Network Places, by URL, or by UNC path. You can also configure printers to work in conjunction with the Internet Information Server (IIS) to make them available through a Web browser using a URL in the following format:

```
http://<servername>/printers
```

CONTROLLING PRINTER ACCESS

Access to shared printers can be controlled through permissions. These can be set under the Security tab of the printer's Properties dialog box, as shown in Figure 9.21.

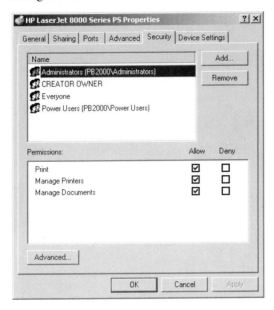

Figure 9.21   *Setting printer access permissions.*

There are three types of printer permissions:

- **Print.** Users with this permission can print documents; pause, resume, restart, and cancel the their own documents; and connect to a printer.
- **Manage Documents.** Users with this permission can manage documents; pause, resume, restart and cancel their own documents; connect to a printer; and pause, restart and delete all documents.
- **Manage Printers.** Users with this permission can print documents; pause, resume, restart, and cancel their own documents; connect to a printer; control job settings for all documents; pause, restart and delete all documents; share a printer; change printer properties; delete printers; and change printer permissions.

Each user is given Print access by default, and the Creator/Owner is given permission to Manage Documents. Administrators and Power Users have Manage Documents and Manage Printers permissions. Users with a Deny permission cannot do anything with a given permission level.

Monitoring Printer Access

Beyond providing printer access, you should be prepared to monitor print jobs that pass through your print server to ensure that the process is as smooth and error-free as possible. To monitor the activity on a shared printer, double-click its icon in the Printers folder to open the print queue window, as shown in Figure 9.22.

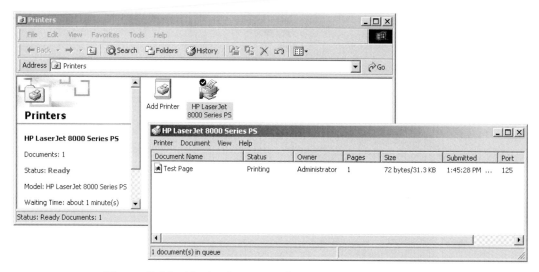

Figure 9.22   *Monitoring print jobs.*

In addition to the names, sizes, and originators of print jobs, you can quickly determine the status of documents in the queue. If the status is listed as "waiting" or "printing," all is well. If an error is listed, however, you will need to troubleshoot.

By default, all print jobs are given the same low priority, printing on a first come first serve basis. When queues are long and some print jobs are needed more quickly than others, you can alter a print job's priority by double-clicking its listing in the queue and adjusting the Priority lever upward, as shown in Figure 9.23.

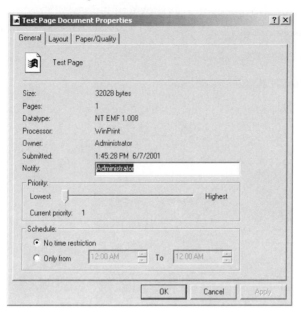

Figure 9.23   *Adjusting print priorities.*

For particularly large jobs of relative unimportance, you might use the Schedule radio buttons to print at a time when printer demand is low, such as after business hours.

The print queue can be managed overall from the Printer menu, where you can pause or cancel printing, adjust printer preferences, and configure printer properties, as shown in Figure 9.24.

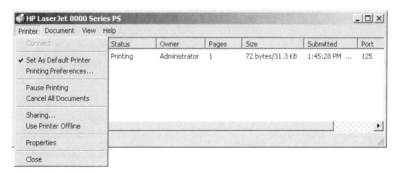

Figure 9.24   *Managing print queues.*

The print server can be managed by selecting a printer in the Printers folder, then selecting the Server Properties command to open the Print Server Properties dialog box, as shown in Figure 9.25.

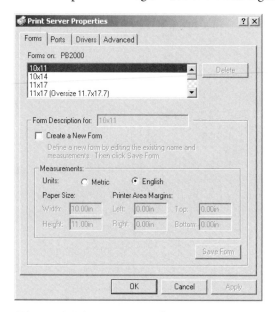

Figure 9.25 *Managing the print server.*

Troubleshooting Printer Access

When printing problems occur, it is often useful to follow this basic trouble-shooting procedure:

1. Check to see that the printing device is properly attached to the print server or network port. Make sure that it is turned on, online, and that all status indicators are normal (no paper jams, etc.). Finally, make sure that the print device has paper in the paper tray.

2. Go to the print server and use the Print Test Page button in the printer's Properties dialog box. If the page does not print correctly, the print driver might be corrupt or parts of it might be missing. You should then reinstall the print driver. If the page does print correctly, also try printing from a basic word processor; such as Notepad or WordPad. If this page also prints correctly, the problem might lie in whichever application is not able to print.

3. Also on the print server, check to see that all the necessary print drivers for various operating systems are enabled under the Sharing tab of the

Properties dialog box (see Figure 9.19). This is required by the print driver autodownloading feature.

4. Check to see that the proper permissions have been enabled under the Security tab of the printer Properties dialog box (see Figure 9.22). Remember that a single Deny setting disables an entire permission level.

Other common printing problems and solutions are as follow:

- **Printer is offline.** This situation might be caused by a user pressing a button and taking the printing device offline, perhaps while fixing a paper jam. It is often caused by a loose or faulty cable connection between the server and printing device, or the network and a printing device.

- **Printing is incorrect.** In this situation, verify that the correct printer driver has been installed and that the correct driver is available for download to the client. If all else fails, reinstall the printer. Another idea is to print to a file, then download the file to the printer port directly. If this works, the problem is likely to be in data transfer or spooling. If this does not work, the problem is likely to be the application or print driver.

- **Application cannot print.** In this situation, make sure that there is a valid default printer selected in the Printer folder or in the application's print dialog box. Another idea is to print from another application. If this works, the problem is most likely application-specific.

- **Print job will not spool.** In this situation, make sure there is enough disk drive space available. By default, spooled print jobs reside in the \WINNT\System32\spool\PRINTERS folder until imaged. You can change the default spool directory to a different partition via the

Advanced tab of the Print Server Properties dialog box, as shown in Figure 9.26.

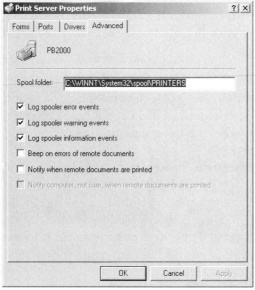

Figure 9.26 *Managing print spooling.*

If the hard disk is having a hard time sending print documents, or if those documents are simply not reaching a printer, you may have insufficient space in the partition holding the spool directory. The partition should have at least 5 MBs of free disk space for the spool directory. If you cannot free up enough space, you will have to move the spool directory somewhere else.

Also check the spool directory to see if anything is in it. Two files are created there for each print job. The file with the .SPL extension is the actual print file. The file with the .SHD extension, a "shadow" file, contains information about the job, such as owner and priority. If the computer crashes, such files may be left over from jobs that were waiting in the queue. These should be processed immediately when the spooler service restarts. If these files become corrupted, however, they might not be deleted automatically, and you might need to do it manually.

• **The Print Spooler service controls the print spooling process.** If documents have been queued for printing but no printer is available, the print items may be lost, unable to be printed, or deleted. In such a case, you may need to stop the Print Spooler service and then restart it using the Services MMC snap-in application. The queued print jobs are then allowed to print.

Share a Network Printer

Practice what you have learned by connecting to and sharing a network printer.

First, attach a printer to your server and run the Add Printer Wizard to connect it. In so doing, designate the printer as shared under a name of your choice. Open the Properties dialog box to view and, if necessary, reset such options as spooling behaviors, downloadable drivers, and permissions. Finally, test your configuration by locating the printer and printing a test page from a remote workstation.

MCSE 9.3 Working with File and Folder Access

In this section, we will review issues surrounding file and folder access first described in Chapter 2. In addition, we will introduce issues surrounding the management of Windows 2000's Distributed File System (DFS).

Administering Local File and Folder Security

How your server's files and folders are secured depends on which file system the partition on which they reside has been formatted with and whether or not you intend to share them over a network. If you do not intend to share a given folder, you need only be concerned with local security in determining which of your files and folders others may manipulate. This restricts access to anyone sitting down at the server and logging on directly.

FAT-formatted volumes do not support local security. You have no control over what others do with your data beyond requiring a user name/password logon. Under NTFS, the data that can be viewed after using a given logon is subject to a wide range of possible permissions controls.

CONFIGURING LOCAL SECURITY

To apply standard NTFS file permissions, select a file that you wish to secure, then right-click and select the Properties command to open the Properties dialog box. Next, switch to the Security tab, as shown in Figure 9.27.

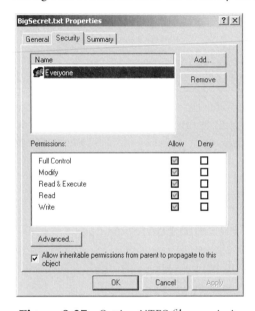

Figure 9.27 *Setting NTFS file permissions.*

NTFS file permissions combine several NTFS special permissions that can be allowed or denied in the following categories:

- Full Control
- Modify
- Read & Execute
- Read
- Write

The following NTFS special permissions can be applied to any file or folder:

- **Traverse Folder/Execute File.** Users with this permission may browse through various folders to locate other folders and files, as well as launch applications. This special permission is included in the Full Control, Modify, and Read & Execute standard permissions.
- **List Folder/Read Data.** Users with this permission may see folder and subfolder names. They may also view the contents of files. This special permission is included in the Full Control, Modify, Read & Execute, and Read standard permissions.

- **Create Folders/Append Data.** Users with this permission may create folders within a folder, as well as add new data to a file, so long as it does not change existing data. This special permission is included in the Full Control, Modify, and Write standard permissions.
- **Create Folders/Write Data.** Users with this permission may create folders within a folder, as well as add new data to a file that may overwrite existing data. This special permission is included in the Full Control, Modify, and Write standard permissions.
- **Delete Subfolders and Files.** Users with this permission may delete subfolders and files. This special permission is included in the Full Control standard permission.
- **Delete.** Users with this permission may delete folders and files. This special permission is included in the Full Control and Modify standard permissions.
- **Read Attributes.** Users with this permission may view the system-generated attributes associated with a folder or file. This special permission is included in the Full Control, Modify, Read & Execute, and Read standard permissions.
- **Read Extended Attributes.** Users with this permission may view the program-generated extended attributes associated with a folder or file. This special permission is included in the Full Control, Modify, Read & Execute, and Read standard permissions.
- **Write Attributes.** Users with this permission may change the system-generated attributes associated with a folder or file. This special permission is included in the Full Control, Modify, and Write standard permissions.
- **Write Extended Attributes.** Users with this permission may change the program-generated extended attributes associated with a folder or file. This special permission is included in the Full Control, Modify, and Write standard permissions.
- **Read Permissions.** Users with this permission may view file and folder permissions. This special permission is included in the Full Control, Modify, Read & Execute, Read, and Write standard permissions.
- **Change Permissions.** Users with this permission may view and modify file and folder permissions. This special permission is included in the Full Control standard permission.
- **Take Ownership.** Users with this permission may take ownership of files and folders. This special permission is included in the Full Control standard permission.

- **Synchronize.** Permits threads to synchronize with other threads. This special permission is included in the Full Control, Modify, Read & Execute, Read, and Write standard permissions.

NTFS file permissions can be set individually for each file. If you do, the file permissions override NTFS folder permissions that differ.

To apply standard NTFS folder permissions, select a folder that you wish to secure, then right-click and select the Properties command to open the Properties dialog box. Next, switch to the Security tab, as shown in Figure 9.28.

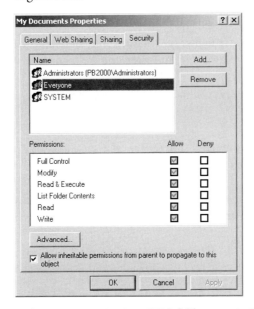

Figure 9.28 *Setting NTFS folder permissions.*

NTFS folder permissions are also combinations of NTFS special permissions, categorized as follows:

- Full Control
- Modify
- Read & Execute
- List Folder Contents
- Read
- Write

The only difference is the addition of the List Folder Contents permission. It applies to the Traverse Folder/Execute File, List Folder/Read Data, Read Attributes, Read Extended Attributes, Read Permissions, and Synchronize special permissions.

CONTROLLING LOCAL SECURITY

By default, the Full Control permission is granted to the Everyone group when a folder is created. If the default has been changed, or for whatever reason your account no longer has the Full Control permission, you must either be given Change permissions or Take Ownership permissions, which includes the right to Change permissions to be able to reassign Full Control to yourself. You must either be the creator of the file or folder in question or have Full Control or Change permissions granted to alter permissions on NTFS partitions.

You are not restricted to standard NTFS permissions, although they should cover most security scenarios that you are likely to encounter. To apply advanced NTFS file and folder permissions individually, select an object that you wish to secure, then right-click and select the Properties command to open the Properties dialog box. Next, switch to the Security tab and click the Advanced button to open the Access Control Settings dialog box, as shown in Figure 9.29.

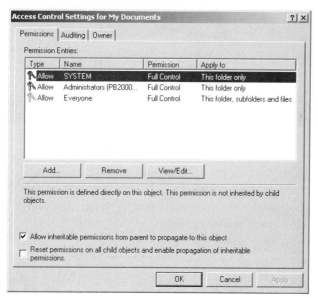

Figure 9.29 *Configuring advanced access control.*

Double-click any group account in the Access Control Settings window to view and edit special permissions, as shown in Figure 9.30.

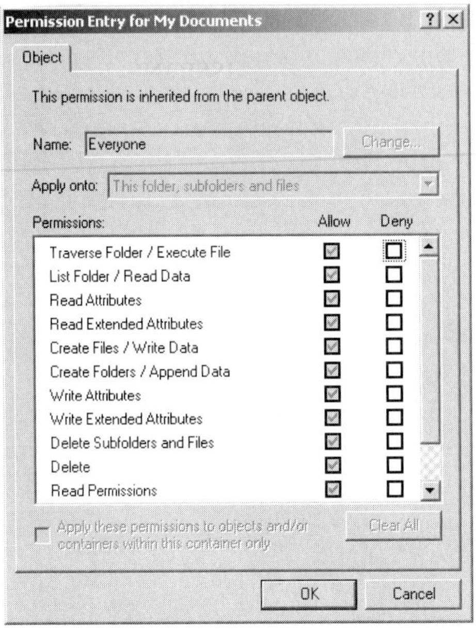

Figure 9.30 *Viewing special permissions.*

Files and folders inherit permissions from their parent objects unless you explicitly change them. For example, if you create a "share" folder at the root level of your server's hard drive (e.g., C:), then copy the file "file.txt" into that folder, the file will adopt the same permissions as the root. In short, \share inherits its permissions from C:\ and file.txt inherits its permissions from \share. You may change this behavior by deselecting the Allow inheritable permissions from parent to propagate to this object check box in the Properties dialog box or Access Control Settings dialog box. This enables the Apply onto drop-down menu.

File permissions are applied file by file. Folder permissions, however, can be applied to a folder, a folder plus all of its subfolders, or a folder, its subfolders, and all of the files in that folder and subfolders. You may select the level of security you prefer from the Apply onto drop-down menu. You can tell that a file or folder is inheriting its permissions if the permissions check boxes are grayed out or the Remove button is unavailable.

You may opt to forgo inheritance in favor of your own explicit permissions scheme. Choose with care, for you might make data inaccessible to the system or other users that you should have left alone.

If your account has Full Control over a folder, you have the power to delete subfolders and files within that folder regardless of the permissions assigned to those subfolders and files individually.

COMBINING AND DENYING PERMISSIONS

Users and groups can both be granted NTFS permissions. When a user is a member of multiple groups that have different access levels to a resource, that user's combined permissions—including the least restrictive level granted by these associations—is the effective permission level. An exception applies when the user or one of the groups of which the user is a member has been assigned the Deny permission.

Choosing to Deny a permission overrides all other permissions for all users and groups except Administrators. For instance, a user that is a member of group one, which has Full Control, will be able to Change permissions. However, if the user is also a member of group two, which has been denied Change permissions, the user will be restricted.

TAKING OWNERSHIP

By default, the creator of a file or folder is its owner and has Full Control over it. In order for another user to take ownership, that user must be given the Take Ownership special permission. If the owner has removed every user but himself, only an Administrator can take ownership. (An Administrator always has this access.)

You can give a user permission to use a resource, but you cannot give away ownership. When an Administrator makes himself owner of a resource, he remains owner until someone takes back ownership. This way, an unsuspecting user cannot be made to look like he made changes to someone else's files or folders. It will be apparent that the administrator has ownership.

You can give someone the right to take ownership by granting Take Ownership or Change permissions special permissions, or Full Control standard permission.

MONITORING LOCAL SECURITY

One of Windows 2000's most powerful features lets you monitor file and folder access by auditing permission levels by groups. To apply auditing controls, select an object that you wish to monitor, then right-click and select the Properties command to open the Properties dialog box. Next, switch to the Security tab and click the Advanced button to open the Access Control Settings dialog box. Switch to the Auditing tab, then click the Add button to select a user or group and audit access by successes or failures, as shown in Figure 9.31.

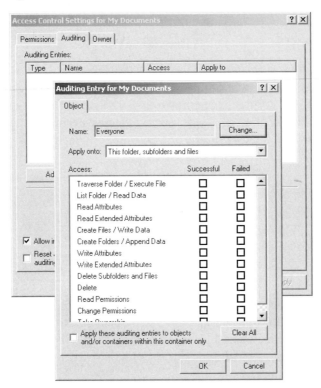

Figure 9.31 *Monitoring group resource access.*

TROUBLESHOOTING LOCAL SECURITY

Troubleshooting local security usually requires a straightforward review of the pertinent permissions to determine why a user or group is or is not accessing a given file or folder.

A typical problem can occur when files and folders are relocated. Copying a file from one folder to another applies the permissions of the new host folder to that file. The original file is deleted, and a new one is created in the new folder. Moving a file between folders allows the file to retain its original permissions. The file stays in the same physical location on the disk. In the target folder, a new pointer to the file is created. If a move is made across partitions, however, the file is actually deleted and recreated in the new folder, thus assuming the permissions of the new folder.

Administering Shared File and Folder Access

Client computers can access the folders you share from the server's hard drive regardless of the file system under which they are stored: FAT, FAT32, NTFS, Compact Disk File System (CDFS), or DVD's Universal Disk Format (UDF). Like local folders created under NTFS, access to shared folders is controlled through permissions. Unlike with NTFS, however, share permissions only affect those accessing a folder over the network (and NTFS permissions still apply).

CONFIGURING SHARE ACCESS

Although commonly referred to as file sharing, resource sharing cannot actually be done at the individual file level. It can be done only at the folder level. The share access level of each parent folder is automatically passed on to the subfolders within it. Therefore, you must be careful to not place a folder with strictly limited access under a parent folder with open access, or vice versa.

Members of the Administrators, Server Operators, Power Users, or Users groups can create network shares. To create a share locally, log on to the server and select the folder, right-click, then select the Sharing command to open the Properties dialog box. The following choices are listed under the Sharing tab:

- **Share this folder.** This radio button shares the resource across the network.
- **Do not share this folder.** This radio button will stop sharing the resource.
- **Share name.** In this field you can enter the name users will see when they are browsing the resources that your computer is advertising on the network. This network name need not match the folder's local name. If you will have DOS or Windows 3.x users, you must use the 8.3 naming convention.
- **Comment.** When users are browsing the resources on the machine, they will see the comment you enter in this field next to the share. This is a handy place to describe your share's purpose or physical location.
- **User limit.** These radio buttons allow you to limit the number of inbound connections for performance reasons.
- **Permissions.** This button allows you to set individual user and group permissions for access to the share. All subfolders will inherit the same permissions.

- **Caching.** This button permits a remote user to download a copy of the share to his local computer for access when your share is unavailable, such as when the remote user is offline or your computer is shut down.

Alternately, you can establish shares through the Computer Management MMC. Expand the Shared Folder branch of the System Tools snap-in and chose the Shares folder. Next, select the File Share item from the Action menu's new command to open the Create Shared Folder Wizard, as shown in Figure 9.32.

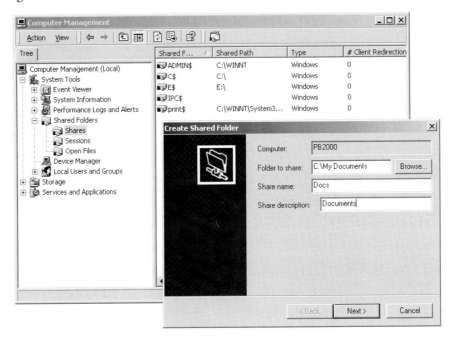

Figure 9.32 *Configuring a file share.*

CONTROLLING SHARE ACCESS

You can allow or deny the following three levels of share access in Windows 2000:

- **Read.** This allows users or groups to use programs contained within shared folders and to view documents. They cannot make changes to the documents, however.
- **Change.** This permission allows all the permissions included with the Read access level. In addition, it allows users and groups to add files or subfolders to the share and to add or delete information from existing files and subfolders.

- **Full Control.** This is the default permission given by Windows 2000 when a share is created. A user or group with Full Control permissions can perform all tasks allowed by the Change permission, as well as modify file permissions and take ownership of files.

By default, new shares grant all users Full Control.

The tasks that can be performed with each standard share permission are listed in Table 9.2.

Table 9.2 *Tasks Performed Using Share Permissions*

Permission	Full Control	Change	Read
Traverse Folder	Yes	Yes	Yes
View Names	Yes	Yes	Yes
View Data	Yes	Yes	Yes
Change Data & Run Programs	Yes	Yes	No
Add Files & Folders	Yes	Yes	No
Delete Files & Folders	Yes	Yes	No
Take Ownership	Yes	No	No
Change Permissions	Yes	No	No

These tasks are file system-specific, so you cannot perform the Take Ownership or Change permissions tasks unless you are working from an NTFS partition.

Because users and groups can each be given varied share permissions, a user can have share permissions that differ from those of a group. When users and groups have different share permissions, Windows 2000 defaults to the least restrictive one. Therefore, a user with Read permissions who is also a member of a group with Full Control access will be granted Full Access permissions. An exception applies when permissions are explicitly denied. A user with a denied permission will not be granted the restricted access to a shared resource even if he is a member of a group with greater access.

When folders have NTFS permissions that differ from folder share permissions, Windows 2000 grants the most restrictive of the two. If a user has Read access to a share, that user will have Read access when opening the folder over the network even if the user has Full Control access when opening the folder locally on the workstation.

MONITORING SHARE ACCESS

You can monitor the folders shared from the server through the Computer Management MMC. Select the Shares folder under the Shared Folders item in the System Tools branch (see Figure 9.33). You may view the shares you create, as well as "hidden" administrative shares used by the operating system (e.g., C$, etc.) that do not appear shared in My Network Places or My Computer. Click the Sessions folder to see which users have initiated sessions with your server. Click the Open Files folder to see which documents users are reading.

TROUBLESHOOTING SHARE ACCESS

When users are denied access to shared resources, a failure either in logon authentication or resource permissions is involved.

TROUBLESHOOTING LOGONS • Problems with logons generally have simple solutions. When users cannot log on, try the following:

- Make sure they are using the right user name.
- Make sure they are using the right password.
- Make sure the Caps Lock is off. Passwords are case sensitive.
- Make sure that the correct account database is selected in the drop-down menu at the bottom of the logon dialog box. (Users can log on to either the domain or to the workstation's local account database.)
- Try logging on from the workstation using another account. If successful, recheck the user's account settings. It might be that the user's group memberships have changed or that a change in group rights is restricting the user.

TROUBLESHOOTING PERMISSIONS • Denial of resource access not attributable to the network logon process is due to either insufficient share permissions or insufficient NTFS permissions.

There are several issues to consider in both establishing and troubleshooting share permissions:

- Share permissions are assigned at the folder level, so whatever permissions a user has for a folder are the same for any of its subfolders.
- Share permissions are not assigned to files.
- Share permissions are the only security controls applied to FAT partitions. NTFS partitions, however, have another level of security.
- New shares give Full Control access to the Everyone group by default. This group contains both users and guests. For better security, you should replace this group with the Users group.

- Share permissions do not apply to resources accessed locally. They only apply to resources accessed over the network.

NTFS permissions can be applied to both folders and files that reside on NTFS partitions. Issues to consider in troubleshooting NTFS permissions pertain to how permissions may change when a file is relocated.

- If a file is copied to a folder on an NTFS partition, the file will assume the NTFS permissions of the destination folder.
- If a file is moved to a folder on the same NTFS partition, the file will retain its original NTFS permissions.
- If a file is moved to a directory on another NTFS partition, the file will assume the NTFS permissions of the destination folder.
- If a file is copied or moved to a FAT partition, it will lose its NTFS permissions.

Problems commonly occur when share and NTFS permissions are combined. For example, NTFS and share permissions might both allow users access to a directory, but then NTFS permissions might restrict their access to files. Since NTFS permissions are the most restrictive, a good rule is to always set share permissions to match the highest level of access permitted by NTFS permissions. That way you need only worry about troubleshooting NTFS permissions, which are more restrictive, and not both.

Administering File and Folder Web Access

In order to share files and folders on the Web, you must install Windows 2000 Server's IIS 5.0, giving it the ability to act as both a File Transfer Protocol (FTP) and HyperText Transfer Protocol (HTTP) server.

CONFIGURING WEB ACCESS

Once IIS is installed and running, a Web Sharing tab is added to the folder Properties dialog box, as shown in Figure 9.33.

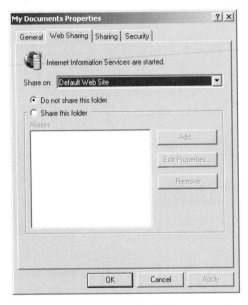

Figure 9.33   *IIS-enabled folder properties.*

To configure Web access, enable the Share this folder radio button to open the Edit Alias dialog box, as shown in Figure 9.34.

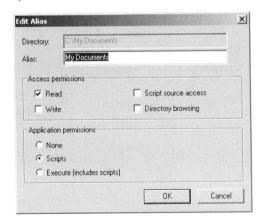

Figure 9.34   *Assigning Web access permissions.*

An alias might be needed to make your share's name legal for access to the Web. In order to access your shared folder, users may enter a URL through a the Add Network Place Wizard or Internet Explorer in the following format:

```
http://server_name/alias_name
```

CONTROLLING WEB ACCESS

Like share permissions, HTTP permissions function independently of NTFS permissions. The default access permission enabled in the Edit Alias dialog box is Read only. Enable Write access only if you wish to permit Web users to upload files to your machine. Likewise, do not enable Script source access unless you wish to allow users to modify scripting that is established in your Web folder. Enable Applications permissions if your Web folder's contents use scripting or are designed as Active Server Pages (ASPs).

Enable Directory browsing to permit users to see the files in the Web folder and choose among them.

These and other security options are provided by viewing the Web folder through the Computer Management MMC's Internet Information Services branch, as shown in Figure 9.35.

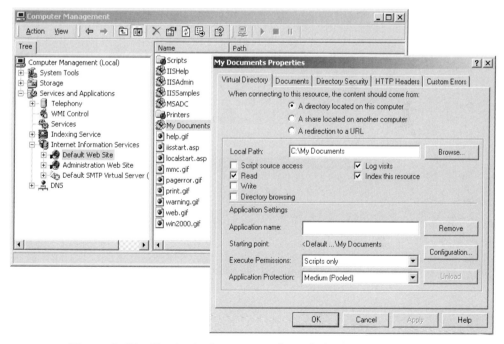

Figure 9.35 *Viewing Web properties through the Computer Management MMC.*

Public Web sites make use of anonymous access to permit Web page viewing without requiring users to submit usernames and passwords. This behavior can be altered for private Web folders, however, by enabling user and group authentication. To enable authenticated Web access, switch to the Directory Security tab, as shown in Figure 9.36.

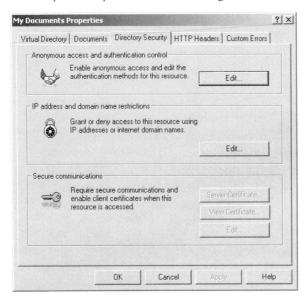

Figure 9.36 *Setting directory security properties.*

Next, select the Edit button in the Anonymous access and authentication control field. This will open the Authentication Methods dialog box, as shown in Figure 9.37.

Figure 9.37 *Enabling authenticated Web access.*

If you enable the Allow Anonymous Access checkbox (the default), browsers will be able to access the Web folder's contents without submitting user names or passwords. Pressing the Edit button permits you to choose an account other than the IUSR account used by default. If you disable anonymous access and enable the Basic authentication checkbox, a valid user name and password will be required to permit browsers to access your Web folder. The user name/password combinations must correspond to those found in the NTFS Access Control List (ACL). The logon information will be sent across the network in clear text, so this option should only be used in environments with minimal security requirements.

If you disable anonymous access and enable the Integrated Windows authentication checkbox, a valid user name and password will also be required to permit browsers to access your Web site. Here too, the user name/password combinations must correspond to those found in an NTFS hard drive's ACL. Logon information will be encrypted before being sent across the network, however. This provides higher security, and so is the default. It requires Internet Explorer version 2.0 or greater, or a compatible browser, and is slightly slower than a clear text logon.

The Digest authentication option can be used within Windows 2000 domains only, and only Internet Explorer 5 or later supports it. It works in much the same way as basic authentication, except that authentication credentials are passed through a more secure hashing process.

Further access controls are implemented by granting or denying access to certain hosts or domains and/or by requiring secure communications protocols and certificates (as described further on).

MONITORING WEB ACCESS

You can determine which of your server's folders are shared on the Web by viewing the Computer Management MMC's Internet Information Services branch (see Figure 9.36). You can monitor Web folder activity by enabling the Log Visits check box under the Virtual Directory tab of the Web folder's Properties dialog box.

TROUBLESHOOTING WEB ACCESS

Most problems associated with Web resource access are associated with the use of erroneous URLS and misconfigured TCP/IP. If remote users fail to access the server's shared Web folders, verify the following:

- **Clients have TCP/IP properly configured.** One quick way to tell is if they can access other Web sites.

- **The server has TCP/IP properly configured.** Make sure you can access Web sites from the server with Internet Explorer.
- **IIS is running properly.** Type the URL "http://localhost/" in Internet Explorer to bring up the server's default index page.
- **Authentication is properly enabled.** If you alter the default anonymous access, make sure that you have properly assigned user and group access. Also make sure that you have not enabled digest authentication if you have users that are not running Windows 2000 and at least Internet Explorer 5.

Administering Distributed File Systems

The DFS model lets you create and manage network resources through a logical hierarchical structure. Instead of requiring users to remember which share on which server contains the resource they require, DFS lets users view resources as nodes on a tree. Instead of creating multiple network drive mappings for each server share, users see all resources as part of the single tree hierarchy.

In addition to making navigation easier for users, DFS simplifies the administrator's job and provides greater service reliability. For example, should an administrator need to take down a server that is sharing a heavily used resource, the resource can first be duplicated on another server and then remapped under DFS. User access to the resource is uninterrupted and transparent. This methodology can provide both fault tolerance and load balancing.

DFS is automatically installed with Windows 2000 Server. It can be configured through the Distributed File System MMC, which has a shortcut in the Administrative Tools program group. When establishing DFS, you create roots that contain nodes representing the network's individual resources. DFS roots can be either standalone or domain-based.

CONFIGURING STAND-ALONE DFS

Information for standalone roots is recorded within the Registry of the server on which they are based. As such, they are not fault tolerant, as they have no inherent replication or backup capabilities. They are limited to one level of nodes.

Both Windows NT 4.0 Server and Windows 2000 Server computers can host standalone DFS roots.

To configure a standalone root, choose the New Dfs root command from the Distributed File System MMC's Action menu to open the New Dfs Root Wizard, as shown in Figure 9.38.

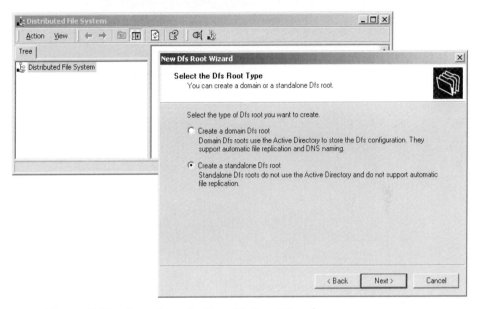

Figure 9.38   *Launching the New Dfs Root Wizard.*

First, you will be prompted to choose the DFS root type (see Figure 9.38). Next, you will be prompted to identify the Windows 2000 Server that will host the DFS root.

Next, choose an existing folder share to act as the new root or create a new share, as shown in Figure 9.39.

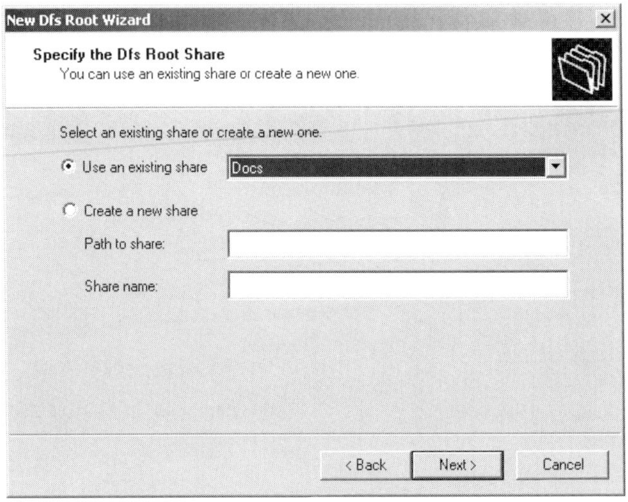

Figure 9.39 *Choosing a share to act as root.*

Next, you will be given the chance to rename the tree and provide a description of its purpose.

In the last step, verify the configuration, as shown in Figure 9.40.

Figure 9.40 *Verifying the DFS root settings.*

The New DFS root will now appear in the Distributed File System MMC, as shown in Figure 9.41.

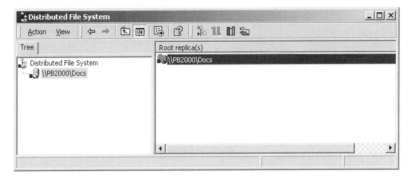

Figure 9.41 *Newly created DFS root.*

A client can now access its contents through a UNC command in the following format:

```
\\domain\DFS_root_name
```

Alternately, client computers can map the path to the root share as a network drive.

DFS client version 5.0 is included with Windows 2000. Windows NT 4.0/Service Pack 3 and Windows 98 computers support client versions and 4.x and 5.0, and can interact with standalone DFS roots. Client versions 4.x and 5.0 can be downloaded for Windows 95.

CONFIGURING DOMAIN-BASED DFS

Domain-based DFS roots are configured in the same manner as standalone DFS roots. They differ in that they are fault tolerant, existing in Active Directory and drawing upon multiple servers to answer requests for DFS-based resources. Since changes to the DFS tree are automatically synchronized and published under Active Directory, there is no single point of failure. Domain-based DFS roots cannot always be extended to all of your network users, however. Only Windows 2000 workstations have the built-in ability to access them, and only Windows 2000 Servers with NTFS drives can host them.

MANAGING DFS

Once you have established a DFS root, you can add additional shares by selecting the Distributed File System MMC and choosing the New Dfs link command from the Action menu, as shown in Figure 9.42.

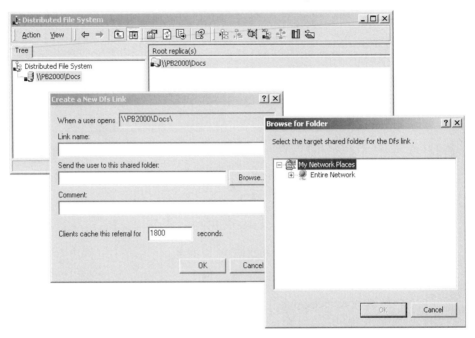

Figure 9.42 *Creating new DFS links.*

Name the link, and use the Browse button to locate the appropriate folder share. You may also add a comment.

Add as many links as you like. When completed, all of the shared folders will appear as subfolders in the DFS root folder, regardless of their true locations.

TROUBLESHOOTING DFS

Periodically, you should check the DFS root's status by selecting it and choosing the Check Status command from the Action menu. If a green check mark is displayed, all links are accessible. If not, one or more of the shared folders was not found and you should begin troubleshooting. Look at the shared folder's properties to determine its physical location, then find out why the connection has failed. Chances are good that the server is down.

Study Break

Create A Share

Practice what you have learned by creating a shared folder.

Create a folder at the root level of the hard drive under a name such as "share." Next, enable network sharing for the folder, giving it a different share name, such as "Public," and adding a comment. Click the Permissions button to establish access rights and the Caching button to set offline behavior. Make the folder accessible from the Web. Use the MMC to review your configuration. Attempt to locate, connect with, and transfer a file into your shared folder from a remote computer. For added experience, use the shared folder as a node in a DFS root.

MCSE 9.4 | Working with Web Site Access

As described in the last section, you must install IIS in order to share files and folders on the Web. Once installed, a default Web site is installed that is configured through the Computer Management MMC's Internet Information Services branch.

Configuring Web Site Access

To configure your server's default Web site access, select the Web site item and open the Default Web Site Properties dialog box, as shown in Figure 9.43.

Each user that transfers a file from your server's Web directories uses a portion of processor, memory, hard disk, and network bandwidth. To avoid the resulting server performance degradation, you might wish to limit the number of concurrent connections that the Web server will accept under the Web Site tab. If you have a powerful server that is dedicated to only the Web service, you can probably leave the Unlimited radio button (the default) enabled. Otherwise, you should set a number in the Limited To X connections field that is appropriate for your server's level of performance. The default is 1,000 connections.

The Connection Timeout field is used to establish an interval after which idle connections are dropped. The default is 900 seconds (15 minutes). A common setting here is 300 seconds (five minutes). If you do not want idle users dropped, fill the field with nines.

As originally designed, a Web server opens a connection to a Web browser that requests a document and then closes that connection as soon as the document has been delivered. While this quickly frees up resources on the server, it results in a longer wait for Web browsers as every document request requires a new connection. You can alter this behavior by enabling keep-alives, which maintain Web browser connections. To enable keep-alives, select the HTTP Keep-Alives Enabled checkbox.

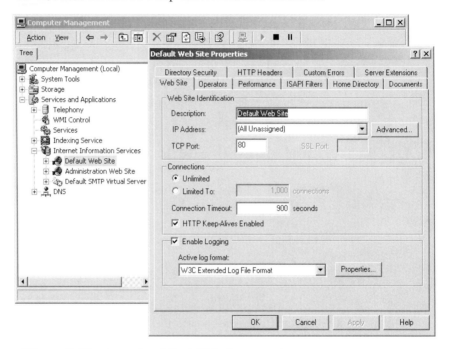

Figure 9.43 *Accessing default Web site properties.*

Most Web browsers expect to find the WWW service at port address 80. As with FTP, you can change this port number to another that is beyond the reserved range of up to 1024. You can change the WWW port setting by changing the number in the TCP Port field. Because Web browsers default to port number 80, users will have to specify the new port number in order to access your site.

If the Web server is not the only service running on your server, you might wish to enable bandwidth throttling. By enabling this feature, you can control the amount of network bandwidth used by the Web server (site by site) so that there will be network bandwidth available to other services, such as FTP, email, and news.

To enable bandwidth throttling, switch to the Performance tab and select the Enable bandwidth throttling checkbox, as shown in Figure 9.44.

Figure 9.44   *Enabling bandwidth throttling.*

You can establish how much of the network connection will be reserved for Web server use in the Maximum network use X KB/S field. Naturally, what you enter here will depend on what your network bandwidth is. The default setting (1,024) might be reasonable for an server residing on a T1 Internet connection (1.5 Mbps), but too conservative for an intranet server residing on a local Ethernet (10 Mbps or 100 Mbps).

Similarly, you can control the amount of processor time the Web server is allowed to monopolize through processor throttling.

When users access your site with a Web browser, they are presented with a default home page that usually contains links to other pages within the directory structure. This page is presented when users enter your Web site's URL without specifying a document.

To select the default Web page, switch to the Documents tab, as shown in Figure 9.45.

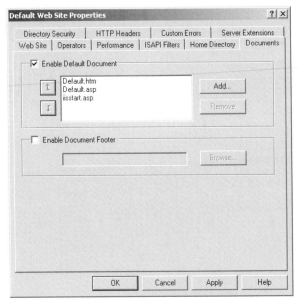

Figure 9.45 *Selecting a default Web page.*

Here you can use the Add button to select several HTML documents. The first document in the list will be the default Web page. The second document will be presented if the first document is missing, and so on. You can use the arrow keys to change the order of documents. If you disable the Enable Default Document checkbox, users will be required to submit a document name as part of the URL when accessing your site. If you enable the Enable Document Footer checkbox, the Web server will insert the HTML footer file that you specify into all documents. This is useful for repetitive information such as copyright notices or Webmaster mail links.

IIS supports HTTP 1.1. Among the features of this protocol is the use of host header names that permit multiple host names to be associated with a single IP address. This permits you to host multiple virtual Web sites from one IIS computer. The feature is supported by Internet Explorer 3.0 and newer and Netscape Navigator 2.0 and newer. To enable host header names for multiple Web sites, switch to the Web Site tab and click the Advanced button to open the Advanced Multiple Web Site Configuration dialog box, as shown in Figure 9.46.

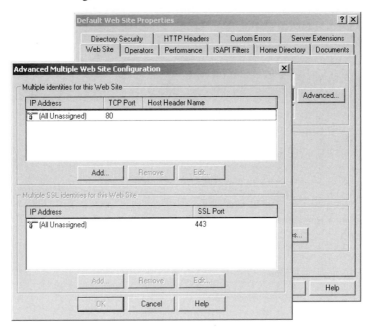

Figure 9.46 *Configuring multiple virtual Web sites.*

Click the Add button to open the Advanced Web Site Identification dialog box, in which you may add the Web server address in the IP Address field, specify a port number in the TCP Port field, and enter a valid FQDN in the Host Header Name field.

Controlling Web Site Access

As described in the previous section, you can enable Web site access to a group of registered users or open it up to unknown users. No user can access your Web site without being given permission to do so. You can grant that permission to a specific user or group in the SAM database, or to anyone in the world by using anonymous access. You can also enable encrypted logon authentication for greater security.

The Secure Socket Layer (SSL) protocol lets your server establish private, encrypted connections with client applications. Using certificates, it authenticates both registered and anonymous users. When enabled, only those clients possessing a valid personal certificate are permitted access.

On the server side, certificates can be used to support user authentication and secure communications with Web clients. Servers can present clients with server authentication certificates from trusted authorities that verify their identities. The same is true of clients, such as Internet Explorer, which can present their own trusted certificates to servers. The exchange of certificates between clients and servers is done using a secure transmission protocol, such as SSL.

Using SSL, secure, encrypted connections can be created between the server and client using the public key encryption system. This type of security should be used whenever private data, such as credit card information, is passed over the Internet.

SSL has two protocol layers. The first layer, the SSL Handshake Protocol, is used at the beginning of the client-server communications process to establish the encryption algorithm. The second layer, the SSL Record Protocol, is used to handle the encapsulation of data communicated over TCP and other higher-level protocols. This capability allows SSL to operate independent of applications, services, and data types.

In a typical Web server-to-browser connection, SSL works as follows:

1. The Web browser requests a URL for a secured resource on the server, initiating the communications process.
2. The server sends a certificate to the Web browser. This contains the Web site's unique digital identification. It might also request a certificate from the Web browser.
3. The Web browser sends a certificate to the server, if requested.
4. The Web browser attempts to verify the server's certificate with a public key. If the certificate is verified, the Web browser requests an encryption specification, called the session key, from the server. This is encrypted using the Web browser's private key.
5. The Web server attempts to verify the Web browser's certificate with a public key, if requested.
6. The Web server receives the session key, which it decrypts using the Web browser's public key. It then modifies its encryption specification to match that requested by the Web browser.
7. The Web server and Web browser begin normal communication over the encrypted connection.

If any of these steps is executed incorrectly, SSL communications will fail. It is mandatory for both the client and server to be able to supply the correct encryption, certificates, and other information.

SSL 2.0 supports server authentication only. SSL 3.0, TLS 1.0, and PCT 1.0 support both client and server authentication.

The highest-possible level of security is afforded by the use of Server Gated Cryptography (SGC). This encryption method enables a 128-bit server with an SGC certificate, such as IIS 3.0 or newer, to communicate securely with Internet Explorer 4.0 or newer using 128-bit SSL encryption. If your organization requires such a high level of security, perhaps to support financial transactions, you could make use of it with a 128-bit SSL Windows 2000-based Internet server and Internet Explorer.

Monitoring Web Site Access

It is possible to monitor the actions of your Web server connection by connection through logging, which can be enabled under the Web Site tab. You may choose from the following logging formats:

- **Microsoft IIS Log Format.** Used to record such basic information as user name, request time, client IP address, bytes received, and HTTP status in a comma-delimited ASCII file.
- **NCSA Common Log File Format.** Used to record such information as remote host name, user name, request type, bytes received, and HTTP status in a space-delimited ASCII file using the format developed by the National Center for Supercomputing Applications (NCSA).
- **ODBC Logging.** Used to record such information as client IP address, user name, request date, request time, HTTP status, bytes received, bytes sent, action carried out, and the target.
- **W3C Extended Log File Format.** Used to record such information as request date, request time, client IP address, server IP address, server port, and HTTP status in a space-delimited ASCII file format developed by the World Wide Web Consortium (W3C). This is the default setting.

If you select the W3C Extended Log File Format option, several additional options become available when you click the Properties button to open the Extended Logging Properties dialog box, as shown in Figure 9.47.

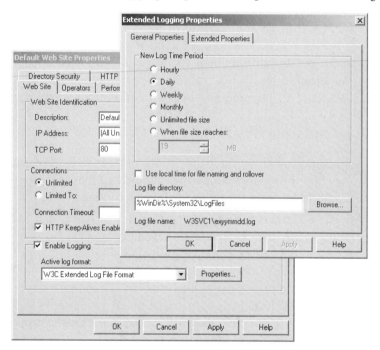

Figure 9.47 *Enabling general logging properties.*

Under the General Properties tab, you can establish the time interval or size restrictions that will trigger new log file creation. Each new log is named in a format that includes the date (e.g., "ex990104.log").

You should use the Log file directory field to establish the Log file directory on a partition that has plenty of space. Log files commonly grow to 100 MBs or more.

Figure 9.48 *Enabling extended logging properties.*

Under the Extended Properties tab, as shown in Figure 9.48, you can establish which items will be logged. These are described in Table 9.3.

Table 9.3 *W3C Extended Logging Options*

Option	Result
Date	Logs the date on which an action occurred.
Time	Logs the time at which an action occurred.
Client IP Address	Logs the IP addresses of computers that access the server.
User Name	Logs the names of people who access the server.
Service Name	Logs the names of clients' Internet services.
Server Name	Logs the name of the server on which logging is enabled.
Server IP	Logs the IP address of the server on which logging is enabled.
Server Port	Logs the IP ports that clients are accessing.
Method	Logs the actions that clients perform.
URI Stem	Logs the resources clients are accessing, such as Web pages.
URI Query	Logs the search strings clients are attempting to match.
HTTP Status	Logs the status of client actions, using HTTP terminology.

Table 9.3 *W3C Extended Logging Options (continued)*

Win32 Status	Logs the status of client actions, using Windows NT terminology.
Bytes Sent	Logs the amount of data sent by the server.
Bytes Received	Logs the amount of data received by the server.
Time Taken	Logs the amount of time that elapses in performing requested actions.
User Agent	Logs the name of the client Web browser.
Cookie	Logs the contents of cookies sent or received by the server.
Referrer	Logs the URL from which the user was directed to the server.

Study Break

Disable Anonymous Web Access

Practice what you have learned by disabling anonymous access to your Web site and establishing user and group authentication.

First, create a group called "IIS Users." Grant this group the right to Log on Locally. Make your user account part of this group. Make sure that you have assigned the group sufficient permissions to read the Web server's default pages.

Next, disable anonymous access and enable Integrated Windows authentication.

Finally, launch a browser, such as Internet Explorer, from a workstation on the network and log on to the Web site. If you are able to see the default Web page after entering your user name and password in the authentication dialog box, then you have set up the server correctly. This is a good configuration for intranet sites.

■ Summary

In this chapter, we considered various Windows 2000 Server administration topics including configuring network services for interoperability, connecting to print devices, securing and sharing files and folders, and configuring Web access.

Network Services Interoperability

When implemented in a Microsoft networking environment, TCP/IP relies on three primary network services for interoperability. By using DHCP, administrators can avoid the effort of assigning IP addresses manually by letting workstations obtain their addresses dynamically from a server that manages a scope of available addresses, doling them out automatically when a workstation attempts to use a TCP/IP service. It is the job of the DNS server to match any request for a connection to a host name with the correct IP address so that communications between hosts can occur. The DNS server makes this determination either from its own database of IP address-to-domain name mappings, as in the case of local hosts, or by querying other Internet-based DNS servers who in turn consult their databases, as in the case of remote hosts. WINS works in much the same way as DNS except that it maps IP addresses to NetBIOS names rather than domain names. NetBIOS names identify resources on Microsoft networks, as seen in My Network Places.

Working with Printer Access

Access to local and remote printing devices is configured using the Add Printer Wizard. When sharing a printing device, you must name it, install downloadable drivers for the client operating systems that will use it, enable access permissions, and test its printing. Shared printers can be managed through the Printers program group. Full Control, Manage Documents, and Manage Printer permission levels can be assigned to shared printers.

Working with File and Folder Access

Local file and folder access is controlled through the use of NTFS permissions. Standard NTFS file permissions are Full Control, Modify, Read & Execute, Read, and Write. Standard NTFS folder permissions are the same, with the additional inclusion of List Folder Contents. These standard permissions are each composed of several NTFS special permissions.

Permissions can be set explicitly, file by file and folder by folder, or implicitly through file/folder inheritance. Users may be granted multiple permissions levels depending upon their group memberships. Where permissions overlap, NTFS assigns the least restrictive. The exception occurs when the Deny setting is applied, in which case it will override all other access levels.

Shared folder access is controlled through the use of share permissions. Standard share folder permissions are Full Control, Change, and Read. Share permissions can be applied to either FAT or NTFS drives, and differ from NTFS permissions. Where share and NTFS permissions conflict, Windows

2000 applies the most restrictive of the two. Only members of the Administrators, Server Operators, Power Users, or Users groups can create network shares.

Shared folders can also be shared on the Web, either through anonymous access or Windows authentication. Web permissions are simply Read and Write, and are overridden by NTFS permissions.

Under traditional sharing scenarios, resources are shared by server and folder paths. You also have the option of deploying DFS, however, under which resources are seen as existing within a single root accessible through a single network path, regardless of their actual physical location. DFS roots can be either standalone, in which case they have no fault tolerance, or domain-based, in which case they are integrated with Active Directory and provide fault tolerance and load balancing.

Working with Web Site Access

You must install Windows 2000 Server's IIS 5.0 in order to share files and folders on the Web. Once installed, a default Web site is installed that be configured through the Computer Management MMC's Internet Information Services branch. Among the access features that are configured are the number of simultaneous connections, port number, keep-alives, and virtual directories. You can grant access permissions to a specific user or group in the SAM database, or to anyone in the world by using anonymous access. You can also enable encrypted logon authentication for greater security. You can monitor Web site access through logging, which tracks such information as client IP address, user name, request date, request time, HTTP status, bytes received, and bytes sent.

▲ CHAPTER REVIEW QUESTIONS

Here are a few questions relating to the material covered in the *Installing, Configuring, and Troubleshooting Access to Resources* section of Microsoft's *Installing, Configuring, and Administering Microsoft Windows 2000 Server* exam (70-215).

1. TCP/IP network services are installed along with Windows 2000 Server by default.

    A. True

    B. False

2. *Which of the following are network services important in supporting cross-platform client-server interoperability? Select all that apply:*

   A. DNS

   B. DFS

   C. DHCP

   D. WINS

3. *In Microsoft terminology, a "printer" is a hardware device that outputs hard copy, while a "print queue" is a list of documents waiting to be printed.*

   A. True

   B. False

4. *Which of following permissions can be applied to printer access? Select all that apply:*

   A. Full Control

   B. Print

   C. Manage Printers

   D. Change Permissions

5. *File and folder permissions differ under FAT from this of NTFS.*

   A. True

   B. False

6. *Stand-alone DFS can be configured under Windows NT 4.0 Server.*

   A. True

   B. False

7. *Stand-alone DFS supports fault-tolerance when deployed on multiple partitions.*

   A. True

   B. False

8. *Domain-based DFS supports fault-tolerance when DFS roots are replicated on multiple servers.*

   A. True

   B. False

9. *Which of the following clients can participate in domain-based DFS? Select all that apply:*

   A. Windows 95

   B. Windows 98

C. Windows NT 4.0 SP3

D. Windows 2000

10. *You can apply either NTFS standard permissions or NTFS special permissions to local security, but not both.*

   A. True

   B. False

11. *Local security assigned to a file overrides the security assigned to its enclosing folder.*

   A. True

   B. False

12. *Share permissions cannot be applied at the file level.*

   A. True

   B. False

13. *When share permissions differ from NTFS permissions, Windows applies the least restrictive of the two:*

   A. True

   B. False

14. *Web folders adopt share permissions.*

   A. True

   B. False

15. *Web folders adopt anonymous access by default.*

   A. True

   B. False

16. *Bandwidth throttling determines how much bandwidth IIS can steal from other processes during peak activity.*

   A. True

   B. False

17. *If SSL connections are to succeed, both client and server must supply the right encryption and certificate information.*

   A. True

   B. False

Managing Windows 2000 Server Devices

▲ Chapter Syllabus

MCSE 10.1 Configuring Hardware Devices

MCSE 10.2 Configuring Driver Signing

MCSE 10.3 Updating Device Drivers

MCSE 10.4 Troubleshooting Hardware Problems

In this chapter, we will examine hardware issues covered in the *Configuring and Troubleshooting Hardware Devices and Drivers* section of Microsoft's *Installing, Configuring, and Administering Microsoft Windows 2000 Server* exam (70-215).

Much of this material was addressed in Chapter 3, "Managing Windows 2000 Professional Devices," so we will not look too deeply into the common issues here. In order to pass the exam, you will need to know how to install, manage, and troubleshoot such devices as disk drives, displays, Input/Output (I/O) devices, network adapters, and processors, as well as their device drivers.

MCSE 10.1   Configuring Hardware Devices

When installing devices on your server, you should perform the following steps:

- Determine whether or not they are present on the HCL. If not, contact the device's manufacturer to determine whether or not a Windows 2000-compatible driver is available.
- Determine whether or not you have the latest device drivers, again by consulting with the manufacturer or the Microsoft update site.
- Obtain as much information about the device's current settings as possible, such as Interrupt Request (IRQ), DMA (Direct Memory Access), and I/O settings.

Unlike Windows NT 4.0 (and like Windows 9x/Me), Windows 2000 detects newly installed hardware devices that are Plug-and-Play compatible during startup. It then automatically installs driver software and configures the hardware settings. If Windows 2000 Professional does not automatically detect a hardware device, you must install it manually in two steps. First, install the necessary device drivers. Next, configure the resource settings.

When installing hardware, you must be logged on to the computer as a member of the Administrators group.

The procedure for installing non-Plug-and-Play devices is as follows. First, launch the Add/Remove Hardware application in the Control Panel program group to start the Add/Remove Hardware Wizard, as shown in Figure 10.1.

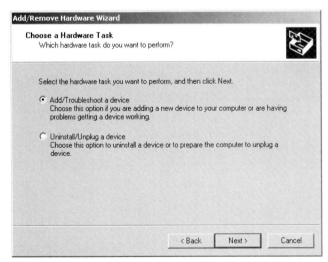

Figure 10.1   *Adding a device through the Add/Remove Hardware Wizard.*

Select the Add/Troubleshoot a device radio button, then continue to select the appropriate device type, as shown in Figure 10.2.

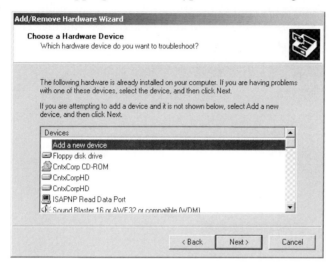

Figure 10.2 *Identifying a new device type.*

Choose the Add a new device option in the list of currently installed hardware.

Next, you will be prompted to decide how Windows 2000 will locate the device, as shown in Figure 10.3.

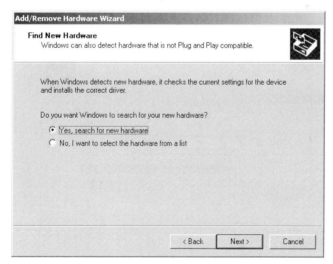

Figure 10.3 *Choosing hardware detection options.*

Choose the Yes radio button in most cases, allowing Windows 2000 to search for and detect the device (even when it is not Plug-and-Play compatible). Choose the No radio button if your know Windows 2000 detection will fail. If Windows 2000 fails to detect the device, you may choose its hardware category, as shown in Figure 10.4, to proceed.

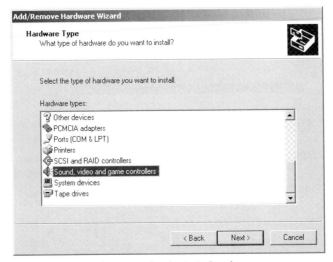

Figure 10.4 *Choosing the device's hardware type.*

Depending upon the hardware type that was detected or that you specified, Windows 2000 will present you with a list of known vendors and device drivers, as shown in Figure 10.5.

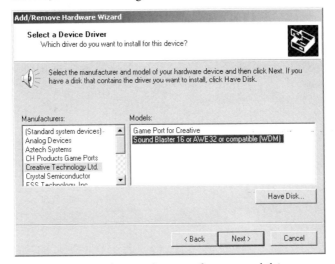

Figure 10.5 *Selecting the manufacturer and driver.*

Choose the listing that best describes the hardware you are installing, or direct Windows 2000 to search for the appropriate drivers on media that you supply by clicking the Have Disk button.

In subsequent windows, the wizard reaffirms your selection and prompts you to install the necessary software. Thereafter, you are presented with the final wizard window, as shown in Figure 10.6.

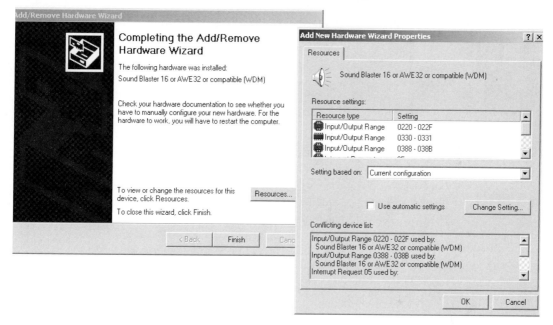

Figure 10.6 *Completing the wizard and configuring resource properties.*

Windows 2000 will dynamically assign resource settings for the device. You may verify that these settings do not conflict with other devices by clicking the Resources button to select the Set Configuration Manually button, which will open the Properties dialog box shown in Figure 10.6. You may alter these settings where necessary.

Microsoft recommends that you leave these settings alone. When such resource assignments are fixed through manual installation, they restrict the ability of Windows 2000 to dynamically assign resources to new Plug-and-Play devices. If you must make manual adjustments, first disable the Use automatic settings checkbox to enable the Settings based on drop-down menu and Change Setting button. The settings most likely to require manual adjustment are the following:

- **IRQ.** The IRQ, or *Interrupt Request*, refers to when the CPU will process the data passed on from the device. This is denoted by numerical value in the range of zero to 15, with zero having the highest priority. IRQ's can also be set through hardware switches on the device or via a manufacturer's configuration software.

- **I/O address.** The I/O, or Input/Output address, pertains to the device's unique logical location within the system. It is to this address that device instructions are sent.

 If you disable Plug-and-Play devices, resources such as IRQ and DMA are made available for other devices automatically. If you disable a non - Plug-and-Play device, however, those resources are still considered in use unless you remove the device from the hardware list in Device Manager and physically remove it from your computer

Another way to control the configuration of hardware devices is through hardware profiles. As described in Chapter 3, "Managing Windows 2000 Professional Devices," these are records of a specific configuration of hardware in the computer. When you need to establish several hardware configurations for a single computer, Windows 2000 uses hardware profiles to determine which drivers to load when the system hardware changes.

Study Break

Configure a Device Manually

Practice what you have learned by installing a hardware device manually.

You may do this by installing a new piece of hardware or by using the Add/Remove Hardware Wizard to first remove and then reinstall an existing device. First, make sure that you have the latest device drivers by consulting with the manufacturer or the Microsoft update site. Next, install the necessary device drivers using the Add/Remove Hardware Wizard. Next, verify and/or configure the resource settings. Remember that you must be logged on to the computer as a member of the Administrators group.

MCSE 10.2   Configuring Driver Signing

To ensure that only high-quality device drivers are used by your Windows 2000 Server, Microsoft promotes its driver signing, or code signing, technology. If a driver is digitally signed, it has passed testing done by Windows Hardware Quality Labs (WHQL) and is thought to be free from problems that would lead to system instability. Windows 2000 can check this digital signature when you install a driver by reading the catalog driver file (.CAT), as directed by the driver information (.INF) file.

To configure how Windows 2000 Server handles the presence or lack of digital signing when installing drivers, launch the System Control Panel application and switch to the Hardware tab, as shown in Figure 10.7. Click the Driver Signing button to open the Driver Signing Options dialog box.

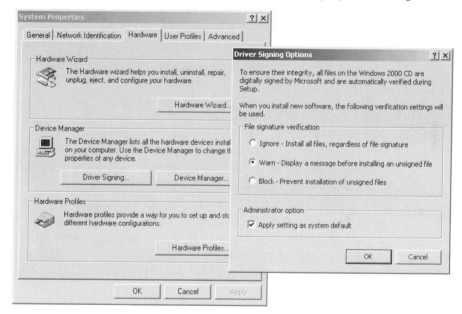

Figure 10.7 *Configuring driver signing properties.*

All files on the Windows 2000 installation CD-ROM are digitally signed. You may choose among the following options for verifying the signatures of newly installed drivers:

- **Ignore.** Install all driver files, whether digitally signed or not. This effectively disables driver signing.
- **Warn.** Install all driver files, but first warn the user that the driver is not signed and might therefore be unreliable. The user may optionally halt the installation. This option is the default, ensuring that important driver updates not yet passed by the WHQL may still be used.
- **Block.** Install no drivers that are not digitally signed.

Any user may change these options from Ignore to Warn or Warn to Block. To change these settings from Block to Warn or Warn to Ignore, however, requires an Administrator.

Study Break

Review Driver Signing Options

Practice what you have learned by reviewing driver signing options.

First, launch the System Control Panel application and switch to the Hardware tab, then click the Driver Signing button to open the Driver Signing Options dialog box. If the Ignore option is selected, change it back to the Warn option. If you wish to ensure the most stable server operation possible, select the Block option.

MCSE 10.3 Updating Device Drivers

The device driver you install initially, whether approved by the WHQL or not, may not be the last one you need to install for a given device. Device manufacturers update their drivers all the time to correct newly discovered problems, implement new standards and features, or take advantage of new Windows improvements. As with Windows NT 4.0 Server, you may update drivers for various hardware devices using the Device Manager, as shown in Figure 10.8. It is accessible as a snap-in to the MMC, through the System Control Panel application, or from the My Computer properties dialog box.

Figure 10.8 *Viewing devices by type in Device Manager.*

Use the View menu to list devices or resources by type (see Figure 10.8, the default) or connection. To see non-Plug-and-Play devices, choose the Show hidden devices command.

To view details for a given device, select it in the window and right-click to select the Properties command. In the device Properties dialog box, switch to the Driver tab, as shown in Figure 10.9.

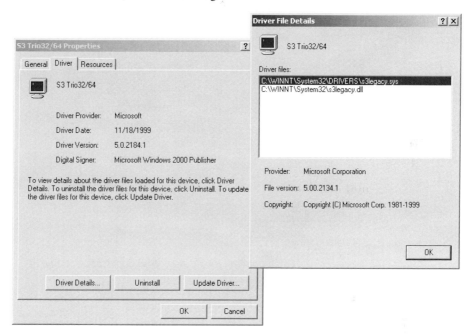

Figure 10.9 *Viewing device driver properties.*

You may view digital signature information here. Click the Driver Details button to see the actual files that comprise the driver and their installed locations.

To update a driver, click the Update Driver button to open the Upgrade Device Driver Wizard. You will be prompted to either let the wizard search for the driver for you or display a list of known drivers from which you may choose, as shown in Figure 10.10.

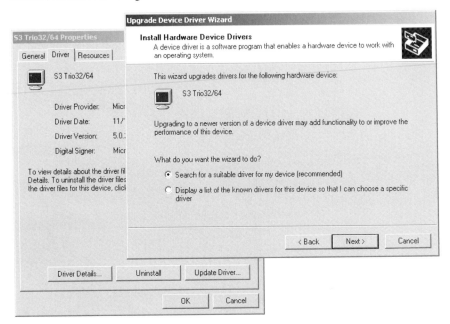

Figure 10.10   *Searching for updated device drivers.*

If you choose the former, the wizard will prompt you to extend the search to several media types and the Microsoft update Web site. Continue to let the wizard locate suitable new drivers and install them.

Removing Devices

An issue similar to updating a device driver is removing it when the hardware for which it was installed is no longer in the system. For Plug-and-Play devices, simply removing or disconnecting the hardware is enough to trigger the removal of the driver. For non Plug-and-Play devices, you can either click the Uninstall button in the Device Manager's device properties dialog box (see Figure 10.10) or follow the steps in the Add/Remove Hardware Wizard.

However you choose to remove a device, its drivers will remain of your system's hard drive thereafter. This can be handy should you ever need to reinstall the hardware device.

Disabling Devices

If for some reason you do not wish your system to have access to a hardware device, but you do not wish to remove it, Windows 2000 gives you the option of disabling it. To do so, select it in the window and right-click to select the Properties command. In the device Properties dialog box, switch to the General tab, as shown in Figure 10.11.

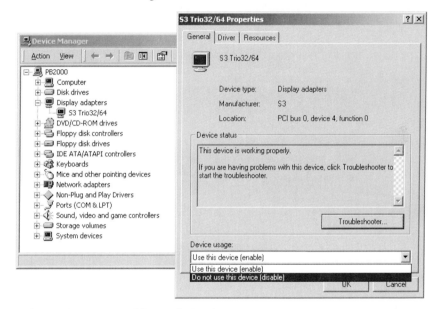

Figure 10.11 *Disabling a device driver.*

Next, select the Do not use this device (disable) option from the Device usage menu.

Study Break

Update Device Driver

Practice what you have learned by updating a device driver.

First, obtain a new device driver through a hardware manufacturer from which you previously used a generic Microsoft driver. Next, launch Device Manager. Use the Update Driver button to launch the Update Device Driver Wizard. Follow the steps to install the new wizard.

Troubleshooting Hardware Problems

Windows 2000 Server provides two primary tools for identifying problem hardware: Device Manager and the System Information tool. Both are accessible through the Computer Management MMC. They differ primarily in the amount of information they present, in how much detail it is presented, and in the fact that only Device Manager can be used to make changes to device settings.

To locate a faulty device in Device Manager, look for the yellow exclamation point, such as shown on the highlighted sound card in Figure 10.12.

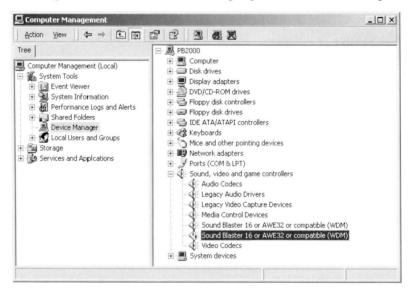

Figure 10.12 *Identifying a problematic sound card in Device Manager.*

To locate a faulty device in System Information, select the Problem Devices subfolder of the Components folder, as shown in Figure 10.13.

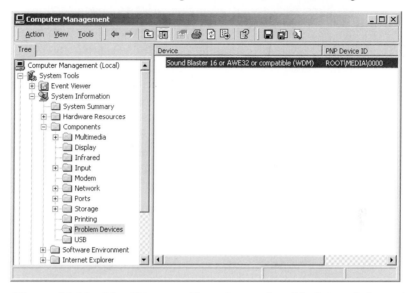

Figure 10.13   *Identifying a problematic sound card in System Information.*

When you encounter a faulty device, open its Properties dialog box in Device Manager to view its condition, as shown in Figure 10.14.

Figure 10.14   *Viewing a device error condition.*

The Device status pane provides a description of the problem and an error code. In many cases, you will be told what must be done to fix the problem, such as performing one of the following actions:

- **Reinstall the driver.** This will often solve the problem if parts of the driver have been deleted or if it was not completely installed to begin with.
- **Update the driver.** This will often solve the problem when the driver is corrupt, misconfigured, or fails to start.
- **Restart.** This will solve the problem if the computer has not yet been rebooted so that changes made to the driver can take effect.
- **Use Troubleshooter.** This might solve the problem when further information about the problem is needed.

If directed to launch the Windows 2000 Troubleshooter, click the Troubleshooter button. This will open the Windows Help window, as shown in Figure 10.15.

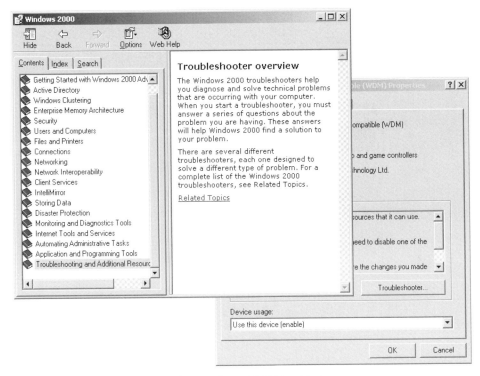

Figure 10.15 *Viewing the Windows 2000 Troubleshooter.*

The Troubleshooter will direct you to respond to questions that will help you narrow down the problem's possible causes.

Using Safe Mode

If device failures interfere with Windows 2000 Server startup, you can troubleshoot after starting the computer in "safe mode." Safe mode launches only the necessary drivers and services, such as the Event Log, mouse, keyboard, standard VGA, CD-ROM, and disk controllers. You can then troubleshoot the network configuration, protected mode disk drivers, video drivers, and third-party virtual device drivers.

To engage safe mode, press the F8 key when Windows 2000 Server starts up to open the Advanced Options menu. You will be given the option of booting up in safe mode with or without network support, or from the command prompt only. Try disabling or removing suspect drivers or services. Restart the computer in Normal mode when you have located and resolved the problem.

Using Last Known Good Recovery

The Last Known Good control set allows you to revert to your last functional system setup. To boot to the Last Known Good control set, press the F8 key when Windows 2000 starts up to open the Advanced Options menu, then select the Last Known Good Configuration option.

Windows 2000 automatically defaults to the Last Known Good configuration when it finds a serious system error. However, if basic operating files are damaged, you will have to reboot using a boot floppy disk or the Windows 2000 Professional installation CD-ROM and recover the system.

■ Summary

In this chapter, we considered various Windows 2000 Server hardware topics, including configuring devices, managing driver signing, updating device drivers, and troubleshooting hardware problems.

Configuring Hardware Devices

Windows 2000 detects newly installed hardware devices that are Plug-and-Play compatible during startup. It then automatically installs driver software and configures the hardware settings. If Windows 2000 Professional does not automatically detect a hardware device, you must install it manually in two steps. First, install the necessary device drivers using the Add/Remove Hardware Wizard. Next, configure the resource settings. You must be logged on to the computer as a member of the Administrators group to do this.

Configuring Driver Signing

Microsoft's driver signing technology can ensure that your Windows 2000 Server uses only high-quality device drivers. If a driver is digitally signed, it has passed testing done by WHQL and is thought to be free from problems that would lead to system instability. You can establish your system's acceptance of signed or nonsigned drivers through the System Control Panel application.

Updating Device Drivers

You can update a device driver by clicking the Update Driver button in a Device Manager Properties dialog box to open the Upgrade Device Driver Wizard. You will be prompted to either let the wizard search for the driver for you, such as on removable media, or display a list of known drivers from which you may choose. Similarly, you may choose to remove a device from the system or disable the use of a device through Device Manager.

Troubleshooting Hardware Problems

Windows 2000 Server provides two primary tools for identifying problem hardware: Device Manager and the System Information tool. They differ in the amount of information they present and in how much detail it is presented. Only Device Manager can be used to make changes to device settings. In addition, the Windows 2000 Troubleshooter will direct you to respond to questions that will help you narrow down a problem's possible causes. If device failures interfere with Windows 2000 Server startup, you can troubleshoot after starting the computer in "safe mode." Safe mode launches only the necessary drivers and services, such as the Event Log, mouse, keyboard, standard VGA, CD-ROM, and disk controllers. In addition, the Last Known Good control set allows you to revert to your last functional system setup.

▲ CHAPTER REVIEW QUESTIONS

Here are a few questions relating to the material covered in the *Configuring and Troubleshooting Hardware Devices and Drivers* section of Microsoft's *Installing, Configuring, and Administering Microsoft Windows 2000 Server* exam (70-215).

1. *Only device drivers found on the Windows installation CD-ROM can be added to the Windows 2000 Server system.*

   A. True

   B. False

2. *Which of the following actions can be performed using the Device Manager? Select all that apply:*

   A. Install a Plug and Play device

   B. Install a non-Plug-and-Play device

   C. Remove a device

   D. Disable a device

3. *You should never use drivers that are not digitally signed.*

   A. True

   B. False

4. *Which are digital signature file verification options? Select all that apply:*

   A. Block

   B. Warn

   C. Administrator Only

   D. Ignore

5. *When a device is removed using Device Manager, its driver files remain on the hard drive.*

   A. True

   B. False

6. *When a device is disabled using Device Manager, its driver files remain on the hard drive.*

   A. True

   B. False

7. *Which of the following could be used to diagnose and edit faulty resource settings? Select all that apply:*

    A. Add/Remove Hardware Wizard

    B. Device Manager

    C. Safe mode

    D. System Information tool

8. *The Windows 2000 Troubleshooter is accessible through the System Information tool.*

    A. True

    B. False

Optimizing Windows 2000 Server

▲ Chapter Syllabus

MCSE 11.1 Managing System Resources

MCSE 11.2 Managing Processes

MCSE 11.3 Optimizing Disk Performance

MCSE 11.4 Optimizing System State and User Data

MCSE 11.5 Recovering System State and User Data

In this chapter, we will examine some of the performance and reliability topics covered in the *Managing, Monitoring, and Optimizing System Performance, Reliability, and Availability* section of Microsoft's *Installing, Configuring, and Administering Microsoft Windows 2000 Server* exam (70-215).

The following material is designed to ensure that you can manage and optimize system resources, such as memory, processor, storage, and networking. You must also know how to ensure the best possible Windows 2000 Server system state reliability and user data availability.

Windows 2000 Server is largely self-tuning, evaluating resource demands and reconfiguring itself to meet them. Complete optimization, however, might require some manual intervention.

MCSE 11.1 Managing System Resources

As described in Chapter 4, "Optimizing Windows 2000 Professional," optimization is the process of measuring and analyzing the resource demands of a given task to see if it can be made more efficient. In some cases, the results of this analysis might lead you to reconfigure your server or replace some of its components. Alternately, you might decide that the server is running optimally and make no changes. No conclusion can be made, however, without the data gleaned from an initial baseline and continuous logging.

Monitoring System Resources

Optimizing your server requires that you know how to monitor your computer's most important resources: processor, disk drive, network, and memory. To help you in this effort, Windows 2000 provides the System Monitor application, a snap-in to the Performance MMC found in the Administrative Tools program group, as shown in Figure 11.1.

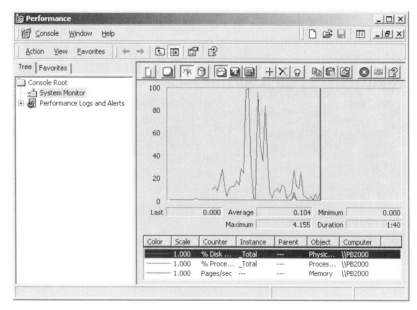

Figure 11.1 *The System Monitor tool in the Performance MMC.*

Replacing the Performance Monitor utility found in Windows NT Server 4, System Monitor can be used to perform the following tasks:

- Monitor system resources on multiple computers simultaneously.
- Log data pertaining to system resources on multiple computers over time.

- Analyze the effects of changes to a system.
- Launch programs and send notifications when thresholds are reached.
- Export data for analysis in spreadsheet or database applications.
- Save analysis settings for repeated use.
- Create reports for use in analyzing performance over time.

System Monitor refers to your server's hardware and software components as objects. These include such local system variables as Cache (disk), Memory (physical and virtual), Paging file, Physical disk, Process, Processor, Server, System, and Thread. They also include services such as DHCP, WINS, IAS, HTTP indexing, and RAS. System Monitor's statistical measurements of these objects are referred to as counters.

Some objects apply to multiple components. Multiple components are referred to as instances. For example, a computer with two disk drives will have two instances of the PhysicalDisk object. The total instance comprises all occurrences of an object.

Objects that are dependent on other objects are child objects that are dependent on parent objects.

Threads are the parts of programs that access the processor to execute instructions. A process may execute multiple threads concurrently. Some threads may be dependent on other threads, becoming child objects to parent objects.

System Monitor's controls can be accessed through the Toolbar, which contains the following buttons:

- **New Counter Set.** Clears counters and data.
- **Clear Display.** Clears data.
- **View Current Activity.** Presents live data.
- **View Log File Data.** Presents data from a log file.
- **View Chart.** Presents data in a chart format (see Figure 11.1). To highlight an individual line in the chart, select the line at the bottom of the window and click the Highlight button. This makes the line wider than the others and changes its color to white. The highlight can be moved from line to line with the mouse or arrow keys, and disabled with the Highlight button (or Ctrl-H).
- **View Histogram.** Presents data is a histogram format.
- **View Report.** Presents data in a report format. View data live or choose the View Log File Data button to open a log file for viewing.
- **Add.** Adds object counters.
- **Delete.** Removes object counters.
- **Highlight.** Highlights a counter.

- ▣ **Copy Properties.** Copies counter data.
- ▣ **Paste Counter List.** Pastes counter data.
- ▣ **Properties.** Views System Monitor properties.
- ⊙ **Freeze Display.** Stops collecting data.
- ▣ **Update Data.** Collects data sample.
- ▣ **Help.** Gets help.

To see the counters and objects that System Monitor is capable of tracking, select the Add button. This will open the Add Counters dialog box, as shown in Figure 11.2.

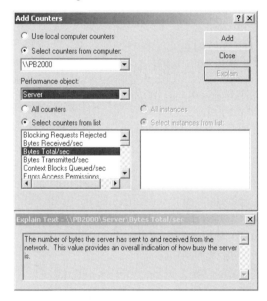

Figure 11.2 *Add Counters dialog box.*

Use the Performance object drop-down menu to choose the objects that will be tracked. Use the Select counters from list field to establish which statistics will be measured. In the instance list field, choose between multiple occurrences of the same object (e.g., multiple disk drives). The Explain button opens the Explain Text window.

Enable the Use local computer counters or Select counters from computer radio buttons to choose either a local or remote computer to monitor.

Data is displayed in one of the following three ways: Chart; Histogram; or Report. Only one view can be used at a time.

CREATING LOGS

In addition to its ability to track specific events in real time, System Monitor is also able to track events historically for your review. To do this, perform the following steps:

1. Expand the Performance Logs and Alerts branch and select the Counter Logs item.
2. Right-click in the main window and select the New Log Settings command. You will be prompted to name your new log. Click the OK button to open a namesake properties dialog box.
3. Select one or more counters to log under the General tab by clicking the Add button to open the Add Counters dialog box. Also determine the logging interval.
4. Switch to the Log Files tab to change the log's name and location, establish an incremental numbering scheme, and add a descriptive comment. You may also choose to save the log as binary, a binary circular file, comma-delimited text, or tab-delimited text, as well as limit the file's size.
5. Switch to the Schedule tab to specify an automatic launch and stop time. Alternately, you may choose to initiate and/or stop logging manually from the System Monitor console. You may also choose to create a new file when one is closed, or to execute a command.

When you are ready to view the log, press the View Log File Data button in the System Monitor window.

CREATING ALERTS

In addition to using System Monitor for analyzing performance, you can use it as an early warning system. To do this, perform the following steps:

1. Expand the Performance Logs and Alerts branch and select the Alerts item.
2. Right-click in the main window and select the New Alert Settings command. You will be prompted to name your new alert. Click the OK button to open a properties dialog box.
3. Select one or more counters to monitor under the General tab by clicking the Add button to open the Add Counters dialog box.
4. Define an event that should trigger an alert, such as the counter going over or under a specified limit. Also determine the logging interval.
5. Switch to the Action tab to tell the System Monitor what to do when the alert is triggered, such as log an entry in the application event log, send a

network message to another computer, begin recording to a performance log, or run a program.

6. Switch to the Schedule tab to specify an automatic or manual launch and stop time.

CREATING BASELINES

A baseline is a snapshot of your computer's normal activity over a regular interval of time. Save such data for comparison. Any deviation from the baseline is an indicator that the way the computer or network is being used has changed or that a problem has arisen. In this way, capturing a baseline provides a basis for isolating a bottleneck or error and responding.

One of the most common ways to create a baseline is to monitor the server with all of its components and services running during a typical week. This will give you an overview of its usual performance at various times of the day, to which later samplings can be compared. It is also useful to create baselines component by component and service by service, as this will provide a basis for comparison if you change a configuration later.

Baselines should always include the processor, memory, disk drive, and network components. In addition, it is useful to monitor the Cache, Logical Disk, Memory, Network Adapter, Network Segment, Physical Disk, Processor, Server, and System objects. You must use System Monitor's Performance Logs and Alerts functions to create baselines, as this is the only way to log data.

You should create the following baselines:

- An initial baseline during a one-week period, preferably just after the server has first been deployed. Log performance at different times of day, with all components running.
- Individual component baselines, especially for the processor, memory, disk drive, and network.
- New baselines whenever a component is added or changed, for both the individual component and the system as a whole.
- Update baselines at regular intervals, using the same settings established in the initial baseline (which can be saved in System Monitor).

From this data, create a database or spreadsheet that contains information from the original baseline, as well as subsequent measurements, to aid you in making comparisons. This should allow you to quickly spot any bottlenecks. Bottlenecks are those components in systems that slow the performance of other components. The component that takes the most time to complete a task is typically the culprit.

Optimizing System Resources

A few counters are especially useful in analyzing the performance of the server's main components: processor, memory, disk drive, and networking. The values that these counters record can point you towards making changes that will improve server performance and alleviate bottlenecks.

OPTIMIZING MEMORY RESOURCES

Memory resources include both physical memory (SIMMs, DRAM, etc.) and Virtual Memory (pagefiles). Technically, a Windows 2000 Server computer will not run out of memory. When insufficient physical (or nonpaged) memory is unavailable, Windows 2000 Server will supplement it by using virtual (or paged) memory. How much Virtual Memory is being used in relation to physical memory is an important performance indicator.

Nonpaged memory resides in fast RAM chips, while paged memory resides on comparatively slow disk drives. You can keep enlarging the paging files on a computer's disk drives to increase memory practically without limit. You will find out, however, that it does not take long for the server to slow to a crawl.

The following counters are useful in identifying memory bottlenecks:

AVAILABLE BYTES • This counter measures usable physical memory. Higher levels of paging occur when physical memory falls below 4 MBs.

COMMITTED BYTES • This counter measures the amount of RAM in the non-paged pool area used by the operating system. When the number exceeds the amount of physical RAM in the system, a RAM upgrade is advisable.

PAGES/SEC. • This counter measures the number of times a page was loaded into memory or written out to the disk drive, as pertains to the memory accessible by applications. Be concerned when this counter hits sustained levels of about 20.

The primary method of optimizing memory resources is to add more RAM. Additional options include the following:

- **Use faster RAM chips.** Some computers accept RAM chips of varying speeds. Always use the fastest RAM possible.
- **Upgrade the RAM cache.** Most server computers are equipped with a RAM cache that holds commonly accessed data. The size of this cache can often be increased.
- **Disable ROM BIOS shadowing.** Many computers use the feature of "shadowing" ROM information in RAM to improve performance. This feature does not improve performance under Windows 2000,

however, and should therefore be disabled using the computer's ROM BIOS utility.

- **Remove unnecessary programs and services.** Windows 2000 Server can be configured with many device drivers, network protocols, and services that you might not need. For example, if all the workstations on your network are using TCP/IP, do you really need IPX/SPX and AppleTalk? If there is a DHCP-capable router running on your network, do you really need the DHCP Server service? These types of unnecessary components can be removed or "turned off." This will free up RAM, as well as relieve the processor of unnecessary threads. Just be sure you know that what you are disabling is not a necessary component or one on which other services depend.

- **Optimize Virtual Memory.** You can alter the way Windows 2000 Server uses Virtual Memory. If you have multiple disk drives and controllers in your server, spreading the paging file across these disks should improve performance. If you have multiple disk drives but one controller, putting the paging file on the disk drive that sees the least activity can improve performance.

OPTIMIZING PROCESSOR RESOURCES

Windows 2000 Server can support more than one processor. In single processor systems, the speed of the chip (e.g., Mhz) affects server performance. In multiple processor computers, the speed and number of processors affects performance.

The following counters are useful in identifying processor bottlenecks:

PERCENT PRIVILEGED TIME • This counter measures the amount of time a processor is handling operating system services. The processor is likely to be a bottleneck if this value averages greater than 75 percent.

PERCENT USER TIME • This counter measures the amount of time a processor is responding to desktop applications and other user services. The processor is likely to be a bottleneck if this value averages greater than 75 percent.

PERCENT PROCESSOR TIME • This counter measures the amount of time the processor spends executing active threads. It is derived from adding the Percent Privileged Time value to the Percent User Time value. The processor is likely to be a bottleneck if this value averages greater than the range of 75–80 percent.

INTERRUPTS/SEC. • This counter measures the number of interrupts from hardware devices and software handled by the processor every second. Excessive interrupts can be caused by faulty disk drives or network components.

PROCESSOR CUE LENGTH • This counter measures the number of threads waiting in queue for processor time. More than two generally signals low processor performance.

Methods for optimizing the processor include the following:

- **Redistribute Workload.** Distribute processor-intensive applications evenly among multiple servers. This will make the best use of processors on all systems.
- **Reschedule Tasks.** Running a backup operation or database update late at night when everyone has gone home will have less impact than doing it during the business day. Running two processor-intensive operations at different times rather than together is also wisest.
- **Upgrade processor speed.** Faster processors are released to the marketplace regularly, and you might be able to swap your server's current chip for one that can work considerably faster.
- **Upgrade the cache.** Throughput can often be improved by adding or upgrading the size of a processor's secondary cache.
- **Use multiple processors.** Some computers are designed to accept multiple processors, and Windows 2000 Server is able to take advantage of this. This is particularly helpful when running programs capable of multithreading.

Additional processor optimization strategies will be described later in this chapter.

OPTIMIZING DISK RESOURCES

Two objects measure disk drive performance:

LOGICALDISK • This object keeps track of logical partitions and monitors the requests made by applications and services.

PHYSICALDISK • This object keeps track of each disk drive as a whole.

Windows 2000 Server enables the PhysicalDisk performance counters by default. You may enable or disable additional counters from the command line using the following commands:

- **diskperf –y.** Enable counters on local system.
- **diskperf -yd.** Enable PhysicalDisk counters.
- **diskperf –yv.** Enable LogicalDisk counters.
- **diskperf -nd.** Disable PhysicalDisk counters.

- **diskperf –nv.** Disable LogicalDisk counters.
- **diskperf -y \\<computer_name>.** Enable remote system counters.
- **diskperf -n.** Disable counters on a local system.

The following counters are useful in identifying memory bottlenecks:

PERCENT DISK TIME • This counter measures the amount of time a disk drive spends reading and writing data. That should be about 50 percent of the time. If this counter reaches levels of 90 percent or more, you have an indication of problems.

AVG. DISK QUEUE LENGTH • This counter measures the average number of read/write requests made before the disk drive was able to accept them. An upgrade is needed when this value equals or exceeds two.

AVG. DISK BYTES/TRANSFER • This counter measures the average number of bytes transferred to and from the system when reading from and writing to the disk drive.

DISK BYTES/SEC. • This counter measures the speed at which bytes are read from and written to the disk drive.

Disk drive optimization strategies will be described further on in this chapter.

OPTIMIZING NETWORK RESOURCES

Among the factors involved in network performance are the following:

- **Topology.** Different networking schemes have different inherent performance characteristics. Ethernet, for example, is commonly deployed in either 10 Mbps or 100 Mbps varieties. Wireless is commonly deployed in 11 Mbps implementations.
- **Network design.** The way in which an extended network is designed affects network throughput. A network properly divided into multiple collision domains will have better throughput than one that is not. Networks that make use of such devices as switches and routers perform better as well.
- **Network adapter.** The specifications of and bus used by the Network Interface Card (NIC) can affect actual system throughput.

The following counters are useful in identifying network bottlenecks:

PERCENT NETWORK UTILIZATION • This counter measures the amount of network activity, sometimes referred to as "bandwidth," on the local segment. On the typical Ethernet network, bandwidth utilization in excess of 30 percent will usually result in throughput-depleting collisions. Results for other topologies vary.

BYTES SENT/SEC. • This counter measures the number of bytes sent over a given adapter.

BYTES TOTAL/SEC. • This counter measures the number of bytes sent and received over a given adapter.

Network optimization can generally be divided into two areas: physical, which includes hardware and cabling; and data, which includes network transactions and control traffic. They can be addressed in the following ways:

- **Use a fast bus.** Get a NIC that uses the fastest possible bus on your workstation computer. Replace 16-bit network adapters with 32-bit NICs.
- **Install a faster network.** Although it requires special cabling, NICs, and hubs, your organization might benefit by upgrading a 10 Mbps Ethernet network to a 100 Mbps "Fast Ethernet" network. Still faster choices are available as well, such as Asynchronous Transfer Mode (ATM) at 155 Mbps.
- **Segment your network.** You can improve network performance by segmenting it into multiple collision domains with switched hubs or multiple network segments with routers.
- **Turn off unused protocols.** If there are protocols that do not need to be supported on your network, turn them off. Each has its own control traffic, however slight. For example, it might not be necessary to support both NetBEUI and NWLink IPX/SPX-Compatible Transport if your network's computers can use either. In addition, you might be able to consolidate protocols. If you have been using DLC to print to Hewlett-Packard printers, you could probably use the printer's built-in NetWare or TCP/IP support instead. If your network is connected to the Internet, so that you must deploy TCP/IP, you might as well make that the network's standard protocol.

Create a Server Baseline

Practice what you have learned by creating server baselines.

First, use System Monitor to create a baseline of normal server activity over a week. Next, add a service, such as the IIS Web server. Create a new baseline with the new service running. Compare the first and second baselines to determine the effect of adding the new service.

MCSE 11.2   Managing Processes

Windows 2000 Server's pre-emptive multitasking uses a system of 32 priority levels to establish which application has access to the processor.

Priority levels zero through 15 are used by dynamic applications that can be written to the Windows 2000 page file. By default, this includes user applications and operating system functions that are nonessential.

Priority levels 16 through 31 are used by real-time applications that cannot be written to the Windows 2000 page file, such as executive services and the Windows NT kernel.

The default priority level for every application is eight.

The system adjusts the priority level as necessary to give the process or thread with the highest priority access to the processor, and a shorter response time, based on the following factors:

- Windows 2000 randomly boosts the priority for lower-priority threads, allowing low-priority threads to run that would otherwise not have enough memory space. This also allows a lower-priority process to access to a resource when a higher-priority resource might otherwise monopolize it.
- Windows 2000 raises the priority level of any thread that has been waiting voluntarily. The increase is determined by the resource's wait time.

Setting Priorities

You can use the Task Manager to change the base priority of a running application. To do so, select the Process tab and right-click a given process in the

Process list. Select Set Priority, then click the desired priority as shown in Figure 11.3.

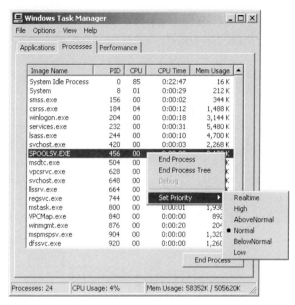

Figure 11.3 *Changing the process Priority level.*

By default, the foreground application is given a priority boost of two levels over background applications. For example, a normally prioritized application would be raised from eight to 10.

To change that level, launch the System application from the Control Panel program group, switch to the Advanced tab, and click the Performance Options button to open the Performance Options dialog box, as shown in Figure 11.4.

Select the Applications radio button to raise the priority level of foreground applications over background applications.

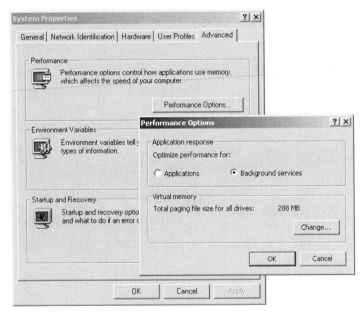

Figure 11.4 *Changing the application response level.*

Starting Processes

You can change the default priority level via the command prompt when you start an application by using the following command lines:

- Low (4):

```
Start /low executable.exe
```

- Normal (8):

```
Start /normal executable.exe
```

- High (13):

```
Start /high executable.exe
```

- Realtime (24):

```
Start/realtime executable.exe
```

Stopping Processes

Task Manger can be used to kill processes that have gone awry or applications that stop responding. To do so, switch to the Processes tab, click on the errant process, and click the End Process button, as shown in Figure 11.5.

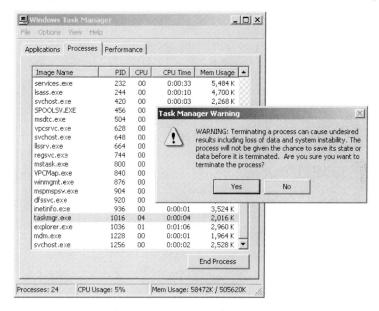

Figure 11.5   *Ending a process in Task Manager.*

Task Manager will not let you end a process that is critical to Windows 2000 operations.

The End Process Tree command, available when you right-click the target process, kills the selected process and all related processes.

On multiprocessor servers, the SET AFFINITY command lets you assign a process to run on the processor you choose.

Study Break

End a Process

Practice what you have learned by ending a nonessential process.

First, launch a process that is not critical to Windows operations, such as the Calculator application (CALC.EXE). Next, launch Task Manager, locate the process in the process list, and end its execution using the End Process button.

MCSE 11.3   Optimizing Disk Performance

The following factors are involved in disk drive performance:

Disk Controllers

There are a number of disk drive controllers available, including IDE, EIDE, SCSI, Fast SCSI, and Fast-Wide SCSI. Each has greater or lesser performance characteristics. One way to improve disk performance is to install faster bus/drive combinations. The SCSI interface is faster than the IDE interface, for example.

Another factor is the number of controllers used. If multiple disk drives are served by a single controller, performance will be less than if they are served by multiple controllers. In addition, the use of busmaster controllers that have built-in processors for handling read/write requests can make a big difference in a system's main processor performance.

It is often helpful to isolate I/O intensive applications on their own disks and controllers.

Drive Specifications

As with controllers, some disk drives have higher access and rotation speeds than do others, with larger disk drives tending to be faster. In addition, it is important that disk drives of a certain specification always be paired with a controller of the same capabilities (e.g., Fast-Wide SCSI with Fast-Wide SCSI, etc.).

Caching

Read/write performance is improved when onboard memory is available to store requested data. Try installing more RAM. The more physical memory available on a system, the larger the cache it can create.

File System

FAT 32 and NTFS file systems are more efficient on disk drives in excess of 400 MBs than is FAT. Unless you absolutely must share server hard drives with an operating system that does not support it (not recommended), NTFS will give you the best performance and security.

Drive Usage

How the server is used (e.g., occasional data requests vs. heavy file sharing read/writes) determines how often the drives are accessed and therefore how quickly it responds. If your server is bogged down by multiple disk intensive tasks, try to redistribute some of the tasks to other servers.

Compression

Use disk drives that are large enough so that you are not forced to resort to file compression. Although Windows 2000's compression algorithms are optimized for efficiency, there is still a performance penalty.

RAID

The use of Redundant Array of Independent Disks (RAID) striping can improve performance. Mirroring can slow disk drive performance, unless duplexing (multiple controllers) is also used.

Fragmentation

As Windows 2000 reads data from and writes data to a disk drive, files are stored in noncontiguous clusters that fragment the hard disk. It takes much longer for the computer to read and write fragmented files than nonfragmented files. The disk defragmentation process moves these clusters into one contiguous area on the hard disk, reducing their access times. You can defragment both compressed and uncompressed drives using the Disk Defragmenter tool.

USING DISK DEFRAGMENTER

When an application starts, it typically reads a file with the .EXE extension and any supporting .DLL files. If the application must read noncontiguous portions of these files when it opens, it must locate each portion of each file on the disk separately. Meanwhile, you wait. Disk Defragmenter tries to place disk clusters in the order they are read. Besides decreasing applications' launch times, this can improve your system's overall performance.

To run Disk Defragmenter, open the utility from the System Tools program group, select a disk drive, and click the Analyze button. If defragmentation will be beneficial, Windows 2000 will tell you, as shown in Figure 11.6.

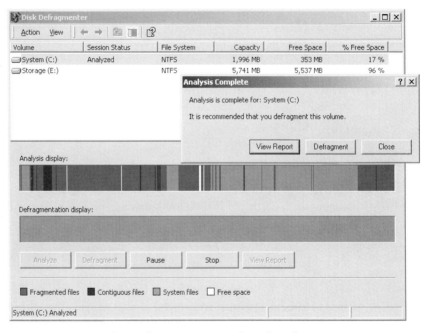

Figure 11.6 *Analyzing fragmentation with Disk Defragmenter.*

Click the View Report button to get details on how fragmented files, folders, free space, the Master File Table (MFT), and paging files have become, as shown in Figure 11.7.

Since servers are commonly subject to a great deal of user file storage and deletion, they must be defragmented more often than workstations. When analysis shows that defragmentation is necessary, schedule it for off-peak times as the process puts a heavy load on server resources.

Disk Defragmenter takes longer to defragment your hard disk if you run it with details showing. For quickest performance, minimize the Disk Defragmenter window while it is running.

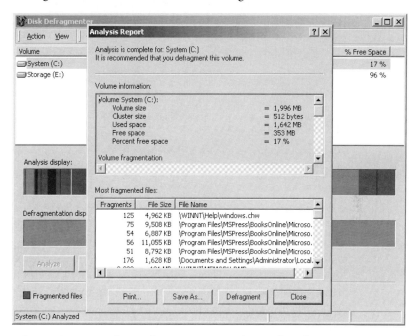

Figure 11.7 *Analyzing fragmentation with a Disk Defragmenter report.*

You must be logged in with Administrator-level permissions to run Disk Defragmenter. Disk defragmentation must be performed manually. It cannot be scheduled as an automated task.

The one file you cannot defragment is the paging file. The only way to defragment this file is to move it to a new volume. Microsoft recommends that you give the paging file its own volume, in fact, although you should leave at least a small paging file on the boot volume for recovery purposes.

Analyze Fragmentation

Practice what you have learned by running Disk Defragmenter to analyze disk fragmentation.

First, select a server disk drive and click the Analyze button to determine how fragmented the drive has become. Once analysis is complete, click the View Report button to see the disk drive's condition in greater detail. If necessary, defragment the target disk drive.

MCSE 11.4   Optimizing System State and User Data

Basically, you can consider your server's system state and user data availability to be optimized if the server is always there! If your server is prone to software crashes or boot failures, you have some work to do with regards to its system state. Maintaining user data availability is a bit trickier, as it requires that you ensure against both catastrophic disk failures and user error. In both areas, Windows 2000 Server provides tools that can help you ensure that your server has the maximum possible "uptime."

Managing and Optimizing System State Availability

Managing and optimizing system state availability requires that you know how to work with Windows 2000 Server's startup and recovery options, safe mode, Recovery Console, and Emergency Repair Disk (ERD) procedure.

MANAGING STARTUP AND RECOVERY OPTIONS

You can establish several Windows 2000 startup behaviors through the System Control Panel application by switching to the Advanced tab and clicking the Startup and Recovery button. In the Startup and Recovery dialog box are listed all bootable operating systems from which you may choose and the time delay before which the default is selected, as shown in Figure 11.8.

You can specify what Windows 2000 Server should do after the dreaded "blue screen of death," a system error that causes all processes to stop. You can opt to have Windows 2000 note the event in the System log, inform an Administrator, and reboot.

The Automatically reboot option is particularly important, for it ensures that the server will not remain in a "hung" state unable to respond to user requests.

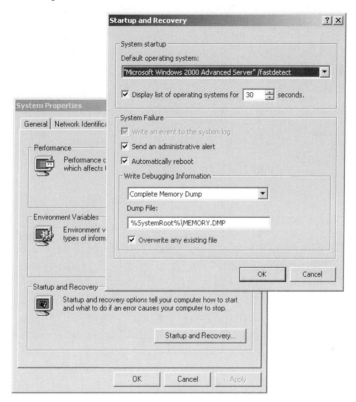

Figure 11.8 *Selecting startup and recovery options.*

You can also collect debugging information that might help pinpoint the cause of the problem later. Choose a Small Memory Dump, creating a 6 kB file; a Kernel Memory Dump, creating a 50–800 MB file (depending on RAM); or a Complete Memory Dump, creating a file that is equal to the size of the system's RAM plus 1 MB.

USING SAFE MODE

When problems occur that interfere with Windows 2000 operations or startup, you can troubleshoot after starting the computer in "safe mode." Safe mode launches only the necessary drivers and services, such as the Event Log, mouse, keyboard, standard VGA, CD-ROM, and disk controllers. You can then troubleshoot the network configuration, protected mode disk drivers, video drivers, and third-party virtual device drivers. The proper use of safe mode options will be described in later in this chapter.

INSTALLING THE RECOVERY CONSOLE

Another powerful Administrator-level tool that can also help you restore the state of a system that will not boot normally is the Recovery Console. This command line utility bypasses the Windows 2000 Command prompt and lets you access your FAT. FAT32, or NTFS volumes directly. It can be run after booting the system from the Windows 2000 Server installation CD-ROM or setup diskettes. Alternately, you can install it on the hard drive by running the following command from the installation CD-ROM's \i386 directory:

```
Winnt32.exe /cmdcons
```

CREATING AN ERD

The Emergency Repair Disk (ERD) contains all of the Registry's hardware and software configuration items, and the security account database. A backup copy of these files is stored in two locations, one on the ERD floppy disk and one in the \WINNT\REPAIR subfolder. You were given a chance to create an ERD when you first installed Windows 2000 Server. Thereafter, you can create or update the ERD using the Backup utility (as described in Chapter 3, "Managing Windows 2000 Professional").

The ERD floppy diskette can be used to restore a corrupted Registry, as described later in this chapter.

Managing and Optimizing User Data Availability

Managing and optimizing user data availability requires that you know how to work with the Windows Backup utility and RAID fault tolerance.

BACKING UP USER DATA

One of the most important tasks any server administrator can perform is backing up the disk drives. Windows makes this process easy by providing a Backup Wizard to walk you through the process. You can access Backup from the System Tools program group.

The Backup Wizard gives you the option of backing up an entire hard drive, just selected files and folders, or just system state data (as described in Chapter 4, "Optimizing Windows 2000 Professional"). In most cases, it is best to back up everything. This ensures that in the event of a complete hard drive failure, you can restore operating system files, applications, and documents and get the server back online quickly.

You can automate backup jobs to occur at regular intervals using many types of removable media devices. Backup supports several backup types that support different backup strategies.

NORMAL BACKUPS • This option backs up all selected files. It then resets (turns off) the archive attribute to signal that the files are part of a backup job. Also called a full backup, this setting backs up all files regardless of whether or not they have changed since the last job was run.

This option takes the longest amount of time, but it also makes complete recovery possible.

Unless the data on your server is of little value or can be recreated easily, it should be backed up no less than once a day. The easiest way to do this is to perform a normal backup daily. This works best when the data on your server can be accommodated by the storage capacity of your backup device, such as a DAT drive, and completed within an acceptable period of time, such as overnight. Under this scenario, the backup is usually contained on a single tape that can be restored in a single step. On larger backups, other strategies are used to address the fact that additional backup storage capacity is needed or shorter backup times are required.

INCREMENTAL BACKUPS • This option backs up only those files within a selected group of files that have the archive attribute set to on. The archive attribute on these files is reset to off thereafter. This setting only backs up files that have changed since the last normal or incremental job was run.

This option takes less time to perform a backup. It takes more time to restore, however, as you must first restore the last normal backup and then move sequentially through each preceding incremental backup.

Under a weekly full/daily incremental backup strategy, a normal backup is created once a week. On other days of the week, incremental backups are performed. Under this scenario, the backup must be restored first from the normal backup and then from each incremental backup.

DIFFERENTIAL BACKUPS • This option backs up only those files within a selected group of files that have the archive attribute set to on. The archive attribute on these files is not reset thereafter. This setting only backs up files that have changed since the last normal or incremental job was run.

As with incremental backups, it takes less time to back up using this option. It takes more time to restore than full backups but less time to restore than incremental backups, because the latest differential backup contains all files that have changed since the last normal backup. You must first restore the last normal backup and then the last differential backup.

Under a weekly full/daily differential backup strategy, a normal backup is created once a week. Because this takes the longest, it is often performed on a Friday so that the backup can run over the weekend, if necessary. On other days of the week, differential backups are performed. As this process backs up only those files that have changed since the normal backup was run, it requires less storage space and takes less time. Under this scenario, the backup must be restored first from the normal backup and then from the differential backup.

COPY • This option backs up all selected files without resetting the archive attribute. This option permits you to run selective backups that do not affect the normal or incremental routines you have set up. You might use this option to copy a few files to portable media for archiving.

DAILY • This option backs up files that have the archive attribute set to on and which were modified on the day of the backup. The archive attribute on these files is not reset thereafter.

REMOTE STORAGE • This option archives seldom used files on a network share, from which they can be retrieved when users require them.

The backup strategy you employ will be chosen because of a number of different factors. Two of the foremost considerations will be how long the backup takes to perform and how much data can be stored on the removable media drive.

By default, the Backup Files and Directories and Restore Files and Directories rights are assigned to Administrators, Backup Operators, and Server Operators. Users can back up and restore files and folders that they own, as well as Backup files and folders for which they have Read and Execute, Modify, or Full Control permissions. To restore files and folders, users need Write, Modify, or Full Control permissions.

EMPLOYING FAULT TOLERANCE SCHEMES

Enterprise servers exhibit fault tolerance when they are able to compensate for a hardware failure without losing data or disrupting operations. Because of the vital importance of the disk-drive-to-server operations, they are perhaps the most important targets for fault tolerance methods.

Disk drive fault tolerance schemes are embodied in the various levels of the Redundant Array of Independent Disks (RAID) standards. Windows 2000 Server offers support for three RAID standards, two of which are fault tolerant.

RAID LEVEL 0: STRIPING • In striping, data is written to and read from multiple disk drives in 64 kB blocks, disk after disk and row after row. This provides greater I/O speed, because if each disk drive has its own controller, the server can read and write to multiple drives simultaneously. Striping does not provide fault tolerance, however. The failure of any of a stripe set's member disk drives will destroy the stripe set and its data.

RAID LEVEL 1: MIRRORING • RAID Level 1, also known as disk mirroring, involves the use of two disk drives. Under this scheme, data is written to both disks so that if one fails, the other is still available to carry on with the redundant copy of data. Because Windows 2000 must write to two hard disks simultaneously, this method results in somewhat slower write operations.

Under a basic disk mirroring scenario, a single disk controller writes to both the primary and the mirror (redundant) disk drive (collectively called the mirror set). Should one of the two disks fail, operations can continue without interruption. If the disk controller fails, however, both the primary and the mirrored disk become inaccessible. True fault tolerance, then, requires that the server be equipped with two disk drives and two disk controllers, a method called disk duplexing. Because the two controllers act independently, disk duplexing does not incur the same performance degradation in write operations that disk mirroring does.

Mirroring is the most expensive form of fault tolerance, for two hard disks are required to contain one set of data. Mirror sets can contain system and boot partitions.

RAID LEVEL 5: STRIPING WITH PARITY • RAID Level 5 refers to disk striping with parity. As with RAID Level 0, data is written across an array of disks. Because data is written to and read from multiple disks simultaneously, this increases performance. Data is not duplicated across disks as is done with RAID Level 1. Instead, parity information is written to each disk, so that should one disk drive fail, its data can be recreated from other disks.

Windows 2000 can stripe across from three to 32 disk drives. When data is written to a stripe set with parity, it is laid down in rows across the component disk drives. For each of these rows, or stripes, a parity stripe block is also written on one of the disks for use in recreating the data should one of the disks fail.

Striping is more efficient than disk mirroring, but write operations take three times as much RAM when using a stripe set with parity, because Windows NT must perform the parity calculations with each write. Striping is also cheaper than mirroring. System and boot partitions cannot be included in stripe sets, however.

SECTOR SPARING • Sector sparing, or hot fixing, verifies each data write and will automatically move data to another sector on the disk drive if the verification fails. This is supported by Windows 2000 Server RAID 1 or RAID 5 arrays formatted as NTFS.

HARDWARE RAID 5 ARRAYS • The most efficient implementation of RAID fault tolerance is provided by hardware RAID arrays. These are cabinets that contain multiple disk drives, multiple controllers, and often, multiple power supplies. They usually support the ability to hot swap hard disks, removing and replacing them from the cabinet without interrupting server operations. They can often contain system and boot partitions, because Windows 2000 sees the array unit as a single physical disk. All striping is handled by hardware.

While expensive, the ultimate in fault tolerance is probably the deployment of two hardware RAID 5 arrays that are mirrored.

The characteristics of the various RAID methods are summarized in Table 11.1.

Table 11.1 *Features of RAID Methods*

RAID Level 0	RAID Level 1	RAID Level 5
Fast read	Moderate read	Fast read
Fast write	Moderate write	Moderate write
No fault tolerance	Data duplication	Data regeneration
2–32 disks	2 disks	3–32 disks
100% utilization	50% utilization	Utilization varies, higher with more disks
No system/boot partition	System/boot partition ok	No system/boot partition

Study Break

Plan a Backup Strategy

> Practice what you have learned by preparing a backup strategy for your server.
>
> First, determine how important the availability of your user data is, and therefore how often it should be backed up. In most cases, user data will be dynamic and important enough to require at least daily backups. Next, determine how much can be backed up to your removable media drive and how long it will take. You might need to create an initial full backup to determine this. Next, choose a regularly scheduled backup strategy based on these considerations. In addition, consider any need for and advantages of employing a fault tolerance method.

MCSE 11.5   Recovering System State and User Data

If you are lucky and your server is well-configured, you will never need to employ a recovery strategy. If problems do occur, however, the training and planning you put into system and data recovery issues can quickly make up for failed luck.

Restoring Data with Backup

To restore data from a backup, reverse the backup process using the Backup program's Restore Wizard, in which you must make the following choices:

- Choose to restore the entire backup, or select files and folders within the job.
- Choose to restore data it its original location. You may also restore to an alternate location, such as a folder or volume you specify, while maintaining the backup's hierarchical folder structure. Alternately, choose to restore to a single folder without regard to the original folder structure (e.g., all files in one place).
- If you choose to restore files to the original location and some of these files already exist, specify whether Backup will replace all of these files or only those that are older than the copies in the backup.
- Choose to restore folder permission settings, the removable storage database, and hard disk/data junction points.

If you back up an NTFS volume, you may lose permissions and disk quota settings if you do not restore to an NTFS volume. You might also lose data if you try to restore encrypted files (which are not supported under FAT).

Users can only restore those files for which they have Write, Modify, or Full Control permissions. Members of the Administrators or Backup Operators groups can restore any files.

RESTORING SYSTEM DATA

If you included system data in your backup plan, as previously described, your backup jobs will include at least the system Registry database, COM+ Class registration database, and system startup files. Depending on the configuration of your server, it might also include the Certificates Server database, Active Directory and SYSVOL folder, and Cluster Services database. You can use the Restore Wizard to restore these files should they become damaged. This can be done on local servers only, and only by a domain administrator.

RESTORING ACTIVE DIRECTORY SERVICES • Before restoring Active Directory data, you must first decide whether or not the restored server will be authoritative or nonauthoritative. By default, restoration is for nonauthoritative servers, which do not replicate data to other domain controllers. For authoritative restorations, you must run the "nydsutil" tool after restoring the system data.

RESTORING FROM THE ERD • Using the ERD to repair a damaged Windows 2000 system essentially reinstalls the sections of the operating system that are required for your particular setup. The data that you copied to the ERD from the Registry determines which files need to be replaced and how the configuration should be reestablished.

Have your Windows 2000 Server Setup floppy disks handy whenever you attempt to restore your system. You will need to boot from these, then provide the ERD when prompted to either install or repair Windows 2000.

The ERD handles many tasks, including running CHKDSK to determine the validity of the partition containing the system files and replacing the SAM hives. It lets you chose between the following repair options:

- **Inspect Registry files.** This option uses the ERD to repair corrupt portions of the Registry. You can repair any combination of the Default, Security/SAM, Software, and/or System hives.
- **Inspect Startup environment.** This option inspects boot files. If necessary, a boot file will be rejected. Any ERD can be used to replace startup files.

- **Verify Windows 2000 system files.** This option compares any system file in the Windows 2000 directory and subdirectories and verifies them against the checksum values in the setup.log file. You will need the installation CD-ROM to replace these files.
- **Inspect boot sector.** This option uses an ERD and installation CD-ROM to repair the boot sector if it becomes invalid.

Troubleshooting in Safe Mode

To engage safe mode, press the F8 key when Windows 2000 starts up to open the Advanced Options menu, as shown in Figure 11.9.

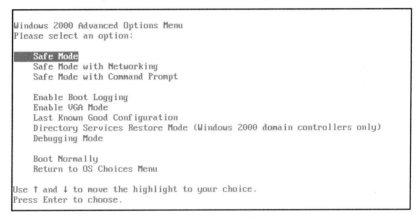

```
Windows 2000 Advanced Options Menu
Please select an option:

   Safe Mode
   Safe Mode with Networking
   Safe Mode with Command Prompt

   Enable Boot Logging
   Enable VGA Mode
   Last Known Good Configuration
   Directory Services Restore Mode (Windows 2000 domain controllers only)
   Debugging Mode

   Boot Normally
   Return to OS Choices Menu

Use ↑ and ↓ to move the highlight to your choice.
Press Enter to choose.
```

Figure 11.9   *Choosing to Boot in safe mode.*

The basic troubleshooting strategy is to disable or remove suspect drivers or services, then restart the computer in Normal mode to see if your changes have an effect. Depending on the level of difficulty the server is having, and whether or not you have an idea of what the problem might be, you can pick from the following startup options:

- **Safe Mode.** Launches Windows 2000 with only the most basic drivers and system files, such as keyboard, mouse, display, CD-ROM, and disk drives. Network support is not available, and display resolution is limited to 640 by 480 pixels in 16 colors. Use this mode when you are unsure about the problem or when you think the problem is in a component other than the basic display and I/O devices. This mode will also give you access to analysis and repair utilities based on removable media.
- **Safe Mode With Networking.** Launches Windows 2000 with basic drivers and system files as well as networking drivers and protocols.

Use this mode when you know the problem is not caused by networking components and when you need access to the network, such as to move important data to another server quickly.

- **Safe Mode With Command Prompt.** Launches Windows 2000 with only the most basic drivers and system files, allowing you to boot into the command line rather than the Windows Desktop. Use this option to work directly with command line utilities and to watch the parade of drivers load at startup.

- **Enable Boot Logging.** Launches Windows 2000 in normal mode, but records all startup events in a log file. The log includes all drivers that load successfully and unsuccessfully. The log file, "ntbtlog.txt," can be opened from a text editor. Use this option to track down the offending driver upon reboot.

- **Enable VGA Mode.** Launches Windows 2000 with only basic display support. As with the other safe mode options, display resolution is limited to 640 by 480 pixels in 16 colors. Use this mode when you know the problem resides with the video driver.

- **Last Known Good Recovery.** The Last Known Good control set allows you to revert to the Registry settings from the system's last, presumably trouble-free, start-up. Use this option if you made a critical configuration mistake. It will not help, however, if driver files have been deleted or damaged.

- **Directory Services Restore Mode.** Used on domain controllers only, this option can be used to restore the Active Directory and SYSVOL directory.

- **Debugging Mode.** To use this option, you must connect to the problem computer from another computer using a serial cable. Debugging data is then sent to the monitoring computer. Consider this option when all else fails. It requires that you enable several sophisticated troubleshooting utilities, and is of the greatest use to software engineers.

TROUBLESHOOTING STOP SCREEN ERRORS

Blue screen, or stop, errors occur when the operating system is unable to start up or stops working suddenly because of a faulty component. Sometimes restarting the computer will overcome the problem (at least temporarily). When it does not, you must use the information provided by the blue screen or debugging log to isolate the faulty component or driver.

When a system drops into the blue stop screen, you are presented with five items of information that can help you determine how the problem occurred.

DEBUG PORT STATUS INDICATORS • The current operational status of the serial port, used in debugging, is indicated here. (This is described further on.)

BUGCHECK INFORMATION • The error code, as well as any additional information included by the developer, is indicated here. This is the most useful item of information, for the cause of the ABEND (Abnormal End) error is often what is displayed here. There might also be a pointer to the instruction that caused the crash. This can direct you to the driver that issued the instruction.

DRIVER INFORMATION • The drivers that were loaded when the error occurred are listed here. One item displays the memory location in which the driver was residing. Another item shows the time the driver was created. (This is listed as an offset from January 1, 1970, in seconds. It can be made readable by the CVTIME.EXE utility.) Finally, the name of the driver is listed.

KERNEL BUILD NUMBER/STACK DUMP • The code's current build number and the dumps of the last instructions to be executed are listed here.

DEBUG PORT INFORMATION • The data rate and other communications settings for the serial port that is being used in debugging are indicated here.

DEBUGGING

Sometimes troubleshooting a stop error requires that you debug the system. This can be done either by configuring a dump file than can be analyzed after the error occurs or by using a kernel debugger on another computer to analyze problems as they occur. Debugging software is available on the Windows 2000 Server installation CD-ROM.

The BOOT.INI file can be modified with several switches to enable debugging. If you use the /DEBUG switch, the system will load the debugger code on startup and be set up for interactive debugging, should it become necessary. If you use the /CRASHDEBUG switch, debugging will only be enabled after a stop error occurs. The /DEBUGPORT and /BAUDRATE switches are used in enabling communication between two computers for the purposes of interactive debugging.

The process of interactive debugging involves two computers. The target computer is the one that is being analyzed, and the host computer is the one that is running kernel-debugging software. Setting up interactive debugging involves several steps.

SETTING UP THE DEBUGGER • In order for the host and target computers to communicate through their serial ports, you must connect them with a null modem cable. The debugging null modem cable contains pin-outs that are different from those found in most null modem cables, so you will probably need to make your own. The pin-outs for both 9-pin and 25-pin cables are listed in Tables 11.2 and 11.3.

Table 11.2 *Pin-Outs for 9-Pin Null Modem Cable*

Target End	Host End	Signal Type
3	2	Transmit Data
2	3	Receive Data
7	8	Request to Send
8	7	Clear to Send
6, 1	4	Data Set Ready/Carrier Detect
5	5	Signal Ground
4	6, 1	Data Terminal Ready

Table 11.3 *Pin-Outs for 25-Pin Null Modem Cable*

Target End	Host End	Signal Type
3	2	Transmit Data
2	3	Receive Data
4	5	Request to Send
4	4	Clear to Send
6, 8	20	Data Set Ready/Carrier Detect
7	7	Signal Ground
20	6, 8	Data Terminal Ready

The host computer is also referred to as the calling system, and the target computer is referred to as the remote host.

Next, you must configure the target computer. As previously described, you must enable the /DEBUGPORT, /BAUDRATE, and either /CRASHDE-BUG or /DEBUG switches in the target computer's BOOT.INI file. You must also make sure that the Automatically Reboot option in the Startup and Recovery properties dialog box is not enabled. If it is, the computer will reboot when a stop error occurs without giving you a chance to run the debugger.

You must also configure the host computer. First, copy the debugging tools to the host computer's hard drive. Part of this software is the symbol directory, which provides information about what the code is doing. The version of the symbol directory on the Windows 2000 Server installation CD-ROM will not work if you have installed a Service Pack or are working with anything other than a single processor HAL. In either of these events, you must create a new symbol set. In the case of Service Packs, copy the symbols distributed with them onto the host computer's hard drive in the same order in which the Service Packs were applied. On multiprocessor systems, rename the NTOSKRNL.DBG file as NTKRNLMP.DBG and HAL.DBG as HALMP.DBG.

Next, use the SET command to enable a number of environmental variables:

- **_NT_DEBUG_PORT.** Used to identify the serial port that is in use.
- **_NT_DEBUG_BAUD_RATE.** Used to identify the data rate of the serial port.
- **_NT_SYMBOL_PATH.** Used to identify the path to the symbols directory.
- **_NT_LOG_FILE_OPEN.** Used to identify the name of an optional log file.

The easiest way to do this is by creating a batch file.

Before you begin debugging, you must restart the target and host computers.

RUNNING THE DEBUGGER • The debugger is run from the command line on the host computer. It is invoked using the Ctrl-C key combination. In using the debugger, you can employ a number of commands and switches, as described in Table 11.4.

Table 11.4 *Kernel Debugging Switches and Commands*

Switch/ Command	Action
-b	Send breakpoint (stopping execution as soon as possible).
-c	Request communications resync.
-m	Watch modem control (placing the debugger in terminal mode when no Carrier Detect).
-n	Load symbols immediately (vs. deferred mode).
-v	Activate verbose mode.
-x	Force break on exception.
G	Release target computer.
!reload	Reload symbol files.
!trap	Dump state when trap frame occurs.
!errlog	Display error log.
!process	Show currently running processes.
!thread	Show currently running threads.
!drivers	Show currently loaded drivers.
!vm	Show virtual memory usage.
.reboot	Restart target computer.

SAVING AND ANALYZING MEMORY DUMPS

An alternative to using interactive debugging is save a dump file that you can analyze yourself or in conjunction with Microsoft technical support. With the option configured, the data that was in memory at the time a stop error occurred is written to the paging file on the boot partition. When the computer is restarted, the data in the paging file is then saved to a dump file.

In order for this to work, there must be a paging file on the boot partition that is larger than the amount of physical RAM installed in the server. In addition, there must be enough hard drive space on the disk drive to which the dump file will be saved to accommodate a file the same size as the server's physical RAM.

Use of the dump file is enabled via Startup and Recovery properties, as previously described.

Windows 2000 comes with three utilities that can be used to analyze the dump file. The DUMPCHK program verifies the addresses in the dump file as well as listing system information and errors. The DUMPEXAM program creates a text file containing the same information that was displayed on the blue screen when the stop error occurred. Finally, the DUMPFLOP program compresses the dump file and backs it up to multiple floppy diskettes so that it can be shipped to Microsoft for analysis.

Recovering Data with Recovery Console

The Recovery Console can be used to boot a Windows 2000 computer that is having trouble starting up, repair a damaged Master Boot Record (MBR), and start and stop services and drivers. It can also provide limited access to disk partitions—FAT, FAT32, or NTFS—so that you can overwrite damaged files, and format partitions.

Recovery Console gives you access to the following commands:

- **ATTRIB.** Sets the attributes of files.
- **BATCH.** Runs one or more commands from a text file.
- **CD.** Changes directory.
- **CHKDSK.** Runs Check Disk to verify and repair volumes.
- **CLS.** Clears the screen.
- **COPY.** Copies files. Wildcard characters (e.g., "*.*") cannot be used. As a security precaution, you cannot copy files to floppy diskettes. You can copy files from other media.
- **DELETE.** Deletes files. Wildcard characters cannot be used.
- **DIR.** Views files and subdirectories.
- **DISABLE.** Disables a service or driver.
- **DISKPART.** Adds or deletes partitions.
- **ENABLE.** Enables a service or driver.
- **EXIT.** Closes Recovery Console and reboots.
- **EXPAND.** Expands cabinet (.cab) files. Wildcard characters cannot be used.
- **FIXBOOT.** Rewrites the boot sector.
- **FIXMBR.** Rewrites the Master Boot Record (MBR).
- **FORMAT.** Formats a disk as FAT, FAT32, or NTFS.
- **HELP.** Displays Recovery Console commands.
- **LISTSRV.** Lists services.
- **LOGON.** Displays all available Windows NT/2000 installations that you may log on to and prompts you for the Administrator password. Three failed attempts exits Recovery Console and reboots. This security protects the system from unauthorized intrusion.
- **MAP.** Displays information on logical drives.
- **MKDIR.** Makes a directory.
- **TYPE.** Displays contents of a text file.

- **RMDIR.** Removes a directory. Wildcard characters cannot be used.
- **RENAME.** Renames a directory. Wildcard characters cannot be used.
- **SET.** Displays and lets you modify Recover Console settings.
- **SYSTEMROOT.** Changes directory to that of the system (e.g., \WINNT).

Recovery Console is particularly handy for restoring the Registry. By backing up the System State using Backup, you copy the Registry into the \WINNT\REPAIR\REGBACK directory. Should the Registry become corrupted, you can use the Recovery Console to replace it with the good backup copy.

Study Break

Boot Into Safe Mode

Practice what you have learned by booting using safe mode.

Reboot your server using safe mode's various options. Note the differences between each, and pay attention to the level of access you have to various resources and utilities. Reboot in normal mode when finished.

■ Summary

In this chapter, we considered various Windows 2000 Server optimization topics including monitoring and optimizing system resources, system state, and user data availability.

Managing System Resources

Windows 2000 Server is largely self-tuning. Nevertheless, bottlenecks may arise in one or more components that will require your intervention. To determine where manual adjustments might be necessary, use the System Monitor utility to create baselines for important server components, such as memory, storage, networking, and processors, as well as the server overall. When bottlenecks are detected, take steps to alleviate them by reconfiguring or replacing components or adjusting their workloads.

Managing Processes

Windows 2000 Server's pre-emptive multitasking uses a system of 32 priority levels to establish which application has access to the processor. The default priority level for every application is eight. The system adjusts the priority level as necessary to give the process or thread with the highest priority access to the processor, and a shorter response time. You can also make manual adjustments from the command line or by using Task Manager. Processes can also be monitored and stopped using Task Manager.

Optimizing Disk Performance

Among the factors that contribute to disk drive performance, or lack thereof, are a drive's specifications, controller type, file system, use of compression, use of caching, fragmentation level, and general purpose (e.g., determining heavy or light read/write access). Beyond replacing your server's drives with faster hardware, you can improve performance by defragmenting disks regularly using the Disk Defragementer utility.

Optimizing System State and User Data

Managing and optimizing system state availability requires that you know how to work with Windows 2000 Server's startup and recovery options, safe mode, Recovery Console, and ERD procedure. Managing and optimizing user data availability requires that you know how to work with the Windows Backup utility and RAID fault tolerance.

Recovering System State and User Data

Problems that make the system unstable can be located through the process of elimination or from debugging logs. Where a problem is due to faulty device drivers, such tools as safe mode, the Recovery Console, and ERD can help you restore a server to stability. Where system or user data loss or corruption occurs, you can use the Backup utilities Restore functions to replace files from the most recent backup jobs. On domain controllers, the restoration of system data also involves the restoration of Active Directory.

▲ CHAPTER REVIEW QUESTIONS

Here are a few questions relating to the material covered in the *Managing, Monitoring, and Optimizing System Performance, Reliability, and Availability* section of Microsoft's *Installing, Configuring, and Administering Microsoft Windows 2000 Server* exam (70-215).

1. *You can monitor the status of your server's system resources using the Performance Monitor utility.*
   A. True
   B. False

2. *Which of the following are useful baselining strategies? Select all that apply:*
   A. Monitor your server when first deployed, with no load
   B. Monitor your server under a normal load
   C. Monitor your server after installing a new component
   D. Monitor your server when problems arise

3. *Windows 2000 boosts the priority of lower-level threads randomly.*
   A. True
   B. False

4. *Which of the following are priority levels at which applications can be started from the command prompt? Select all that apply:*
   A. Low
   B. Medium
   C. High
   D. Realtime

5. *Which of the following are Task Manager commands that can be run on processes? Select all that apply:*
   A. Kill process
   B. End process tree
   C. Pause process
   D. Set affinity

6. *Adding RAM to your server will improve disk performance.*
   A. True
   B. False

7. *Which of the following are can be upgraded to improve disk performance? Select all that apply:*

    A. Controllers

    B. Caching

    C. File system

    D. Compression

8. *Optimally, your server's data and services should always be available to users.*

    A. True

    B. False

9. *Which of the following are useful in managing user data availability? Select all that apply:*

    A. Recovery Console

    B. Backup Wizard

    C. Restore Wizard

    D. Safe mode

10. *System data and user data must be backed up using different processes and tools.*

    A. True

    B. False

11. *The Backup program can be scheduled to backup system data at regular intervals.*

    A. True

    B. False

12. *Additional steps are required in restoring Active Directory to an authoritative domain controller vs. a nonauthoritative domain controller.*

    A. True

    B. False

13. *An unfortunate effect of running a server in safe mode is the loss of network access.*

    A. True

    B. False

14. *Booting into safe mode can compromise server security by bypassing the authentication login.*

    A. True

    B. False

15. *You can access FAT partitions using the Recovery Console, but not FAT32 or NTFS partitions.*

    A. True

    B. False

16. *Recovery Console will permit you to perform which of the following actions? Select all that apply:*

    A. Repair the MBR

    B. Copy files from the disk drive

    C. Overwrite damaged files on the disk drive

    D. Format the disk drive

Administering Windows 2000 Server Storage

▲ Chapter Syllabus

MCSE 12.1 Working with Disks and Volumes

MCSE 12.2 Configuring Data Compression

MCSE 12.3 Working with Disk Quotas

MCSE 12.4 Recovering from Disk Failures

In this chapter, we will look at material covered in the *Managing, Configuring, and Troubleshooting Storage Use* section of Microsoft's *Installing, Configuring, and Administering Microsoft Windows 2000 Server* exam (70-215).

To meet the exam's objectives, you will need to know how to create and configure (pre-Windows 2000) basic and (Windows 2000-only) dynamic disks and volumes, NTFS data compression and disk quotas, and recover from disk failures.

MCSE 12.1 Working with Disks and Volumes

As previously described in Chapter 3, "Managing Windows 2000 Professional Devices," you can configure and manage multiple disk drives using the Disk Management MMC snap-in. This tool supersedes the Disk Administrator utility found in Windows NT Server 4.0.

Configuring Disks and Volumes

Your first taste of disk configuration comes when you install Windows 2000 Server. At that time, you might have chosen to upgrade the file system from FAT to NTFS, for example. Thereafter, server disk configuration might become a recurring issue, as you add hardware to meet growing needs and configure special volume types to increase performance or reliability. Conveniently, most disk-related configuration can be performed with the Disk Management MMC snap-in, as shown in Figure 12.1.

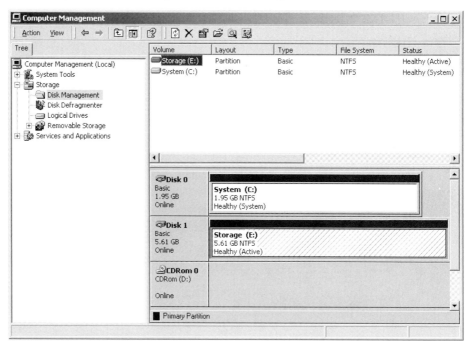

Figure 12.1 *Working with the Disk Management MMC snap-in.*

The Disk Management snap-in supports both basic and newer dynamic disk types. On a computer with a single hard drive, you may choose to use one or the other. On multiple-disk systems, you may create both basic and dynamic disks.

Overall, you can perform the following tasks via the Disk Management snap-in:

- View disk information.
- Create and manage basic disk partitions and dynamic disk volumes.
- Initialize hard disks and format disk partitions or volumes.
- Manage hard disks on remote computers.

CONFIGURING BASIC STORAGE

The basic disk is the traditional format familiar and common to all Windows operating systems. The default storage type for Windows 2000, basic disks are fixed in size. When working with basic storage, you can format hard disks as single drives or subdivide hard disks into multiple partitions. Although each partition resides on the same physical hard disk, each has its own drive letter designation and can be addressed by the operating system as if it was a separate drive. On a server, this method is helpful with large disk drives, because users find it easier to navigate a smaller directory structure. It is also a useful security technique to create different partitions for the operating system and shared data, keeping them separate.

PARTITIONING BASIC DISKS • When formatting a new hard disk under the basic storage model, you may define the following partition types:

- **Primary.** These partitions can support a bootable operating system. Each disk drive can contain as many as four primary partitions, but a primary partition cannot be further partitioned.
- **Extended.** These partitions will not support a bootable operating system. On single disk drive systems, they are used in addition to one or more primary partitions. An extended partition can be subdivided into multiple logical partitions, each with its own letter designation (e.g., "D," "E," "F," etc.), but only one extended partition can reside on a disk drive.

There can be no more than four partitions on a disk drive altogether, so if an extended partition is established, only three primary partitions can be used.

It is necessary to mark one primary partition as active. This is the partition from which the computer will boot on startup. Computers with disk drives containing multiple operating systems are typically formatted with a primary partition for each operating system. Computers with disk drives containing a single operating system are commonly formatted with either a single primary partition, or one primary partition and one extended partition.

Under Windows NT and 2000, the system partition contains the files necessary to boot the operating system. By definition, this will also be the active partition. Paradoxically, the boot partition contains the Windows NT/2000 operating system, but not the actual boot files.

You can create, delete, and repartition basic disks under Windows 2000, even those created under the older MS-DOS, Windows 9x, or Windows NT 4.0 operating systems.

To create a primary or extended partition in the Disk Management MMC snap-in, perform the following steps:

1. Select the free space on a new or existing drive in Disk Management's Graphical View pane.
2. Select the Create partition command from the Action menu to launch the Create Partition Wizard.
3. Choose to create a primary or extended partition. When configuring a new disk, you should choose the Primary partition option.
4. Specify the amount of unallocated space the primary partition will occupy. You can create a single partition by using all available space or leave room for additional partitions by selecting a fraction of the available space.
5. Specify a drive letter for the new partition.
6. Name and format the partition.

CONFIGURING BASIC DISK SETS • If you have upgraded a server previously configured under Windows NT Server 4.0, you might encounter one of the following basic disk sets:

- **Volume Set.** This disk set is a variation of the logical drive. It is one logical volume composed of as many as 32 portions of free space from one or more disks. Volume sets formatted under NTFS can grow, as you can add portions of free space to them. The reverse is not true. You cannot reclaim disk space from a volume set. Also, should one of the disks that contains part of the volume set crash, you will lose your entire volume set! System and boot partitions cannot be part of a volume set.
- **Stripe Set.** This disk set is similar to a volume set, in that it contains free space from multiple disk drives (between 2 and 32). The main difference is that it applies the Redundant Array of Independent

Disks (RAID) Level 0 technique of striping. In striping, data is written to and read from each disk drive in the set in 64 kB blocks, disk after disk and row after row. This improves speed when each disk drive has its own controller, because the server can read and write to multiple drives simultaneously. Another difference is that volume sets can be composed of unequal portions of free space, while stripe sets must be composed of equal portions of free space. Most of the same advantages and disadvantages that apply to volume sets apply to stripe sets. Stripe sets are not fault tolerant and cannot contain system or boot partitions.

- **Mirror Set.** Mirroring, enabled by RAID Level 1 fault tolerance, involves writing a redundant copy of one disk drive's data to another. A disadvantage to mirror sets is that they can degrade performance by requiring the server to do twice as much work. The advantage is that the loss of one disk in the mirror set will not result in a loss of data.
- **Stripe Sets with Parity.** Under striping with parity, enabled by RAID Level 5, data is written across an array of disks, just as with RAID Level 0. Because data is written to and read from multiple disks simultaneously, this greatly increases performance. Data is not duplicated across disks, however. Instead, parity information is written to each disk so that, should one disk drive fail, its data can be recreated from other disks.

Windows 2000 can stripe across from three to 32 disk drives in a stripe set. When data is written to a stripe set with parity, it is laid down in rows across the component disk drives. For each of these rows, or stripes, a parity stripe block is also written on one of the disks for use in recreating the data should one of the disks fail, as illustrated in Figure 12.2. Because only a parity stripe block is written, this is more efficient than disk mirroring (which writes a complete, redundant copy of data).

The formula for determining how much disk space will be available for data storage in a stripe set is as follows:

```
% Utilization = (no. of disks — 1) /

(no. of disks) X 100%
```

For example, if you were to stripe five disks, 80 percent of the stripe set would be available as free space. Obviously, the most storage you will ever get from a mirror set is 50 percent. Striping is therefore more efficient than disk mirroring. One caveat: Write operations take three times as much RAM when using a stripe set with parity because Windows 2000 must perform the parity calculations with each write.

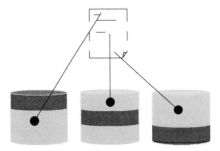

Figure 12.2 *Under RAID Level 5, data is written to three or more disks simultaneously, along with a parity stripe (represented in black).*

Your Windows 2000 Server will recognize and let you work with any of the pre-existing basic disk sets. It will not, however, permit you to create new basic disk sets.

CONFIGURING DYNAMIC STORAGE

If you do not intend to dual-boot with any other operating systems, you have the option of configuring your disk drives as dynamic disks, which are only supported by Windows 2000. Dynamic disks are especially useful on a server because they can be resized without reformatting, and in most cases, without rebooting the computer. In this they are somewhat similar to the basic volume set.

CONFIGURING DYNAMIC DISKS • Dynamic disks have the following characteristics:

- They can consist of one partition, multiple partitions on a single disk drive, or multiple partitions on multiple disk drives. Partitions are referred to as volumes and can be created without limit (other than the physical size of the disk).
- They support simple, spanned, and striped volume types.
- Basic disks can be converted to dynamic disks.
- They should not be configured with sector sizes greater than 512 bytes. This is one of the options you are given when creating or upgrading a dynamic volume.
- Dynamic disks must have at least 1 MB of unallocated space at the end of the disk. Here Windows 2000 stores volume information for the disk. In the case of multidisk systems, each dynamic disk stores

information for all other disks in the system as well as its own (for as many as 512 disks). Should the information be lost or corrupted on one disk, the correct information is automatically replicated from the others.

- Dynamic disks do not support removable media or laptop drives.

To upgrade a basic disk to a dynamic disk, select the basic disk in the Disk Management snap-in and choose the Upgrade to Dynamic Disk command from the Action menu. You will be prompted to choose the disk to update, as shown in Figure 12.3.

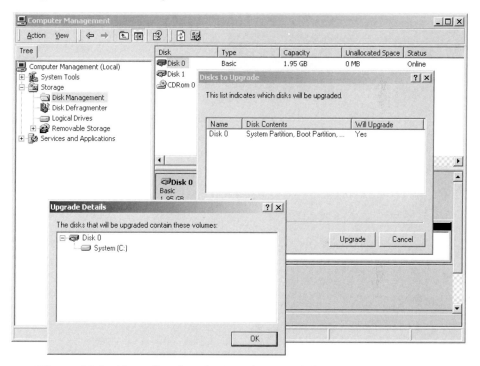

Figure 12.3 *Upgrading from basic to dynamic disks.*

After rebooting the server, you will be presented with the Write Signature and Disk Upgrade Wizard, as shown in Figure 12.4.

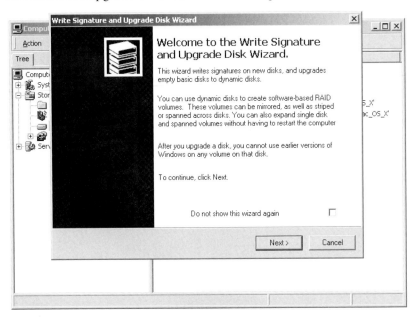

Figure 12.4 *Write Signature and Disk Upgrade Wizard.*

The Disk Management snap-in uses the unique signature to identify the disk drive accurately even when it has been renamed or used with a different controller. If you do not permit the signature, the Disk Management snap-in will list the drive as offline.

Once upgraded, the updated disk will appear in the Disk Management snap-in, as shown in Figure 12.5.

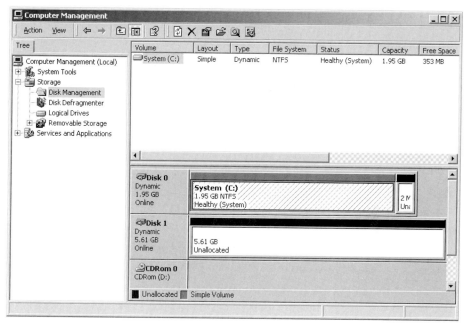

Figure 12.5 Viewing the upgraded dynamic disk.

You can turn a dynamic disk back into a basic disk by selecting the Restore Basic Disk Configuration command from the Action menu. This will erase all data residing on the disk.

CONFIGURING DYNAMIC DISK SETS • Dynamic disks can be configured as the following volume types:

- **Simple Volume.** This dynamic volume is composed of disk space from a single disk drive.

  To create a simple volume from unallocated space, select the Create Volume command from the Action menu to open the Create Volume Wizard. To upgrade a basic disk to a dynamic disk, select the basic disk in the Disk Management snap-in and choose the Upgrade to Dynamic Disk command from the Action menu, as previously described.

  A simple volume may be extended into unallocated space on its original dynamic disk or onto additional dynamic disks (creating a spanned volume) if it contains no file system or is formatted as NTFS. Simple volumes cannot contain partitions or logical drives, and are inaccessible from any operating system other than Windows 2000.

- **Spanned Volume.** This dynamic volume is similar to the basic volume set. It is composed of disk space from between two and 32 dynamic disks.

  You may expand a simple volume into a spanned volume by choosing the Extend Volume command from the Action menu. When running the Create Volume Wizard thereafter, you may choose to add space from additional dynamic disks.

  You may only extend simple volumes that were created on dynamic disks, and only those that contain no file system or were formatted as NTFS. You cannot extend simple volumes that were created by upgrading basic disks, nor extend system or boot volumes. You cannot extend striped or mirrored volumes, nor can you stripe or mirror spanned volumes. Once a spanned volume is created, deleting any portion of it will delete the entire spanned volume.

- **Striped Volumes.** This dynamic volume is like the basic stripe set. As with the spanned volume, it contains free space from multiple dynamic disks (between two and 32). Unlike the spanned volume, it applies RAID Level 0 striping.

  To create a striped volume, select the striped volume option rather than the simple volume option when running the Create Volume Wizard. You may only upgrade a Windows NT 4.0 stripe set (basic disk) to a striped volume (dynamic disk) by first upgrading each of the stripe set's member disks from basic to dynamic.

- **Mirrored Volumes.** Like basic mirror sets, this dynamic volume employs RAID Level 1 fault tolerance. Under this scheme, data is written to both disks so that if one fails, the other is still available to carry on.

To create a mirrored volume, choose the Add Mirror command from the Action menu, then select unallocated space from another dynamic disk, as shown in Figure 12.6.

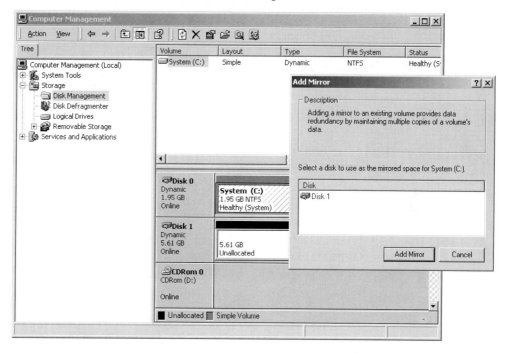

Figure 12.6   *Creating mirror volumes.*

Windows NT Server 4.0 mirror sets can also be migrated to Windows 2000 Server.

- **RAID 5.** This dynamic volume employs RAID Level 5 striping with parity. To create a striped volume, select unallocated space from one dynamic disk, then choose the Create Volume command from the Action menu. Windows NT Server 4.0 stripe sets can also be migrated to Windows 2000 Server.

Only dynamic disks support dynamic volumes. You cannot install Windows 2000 on a dynamic volume that has been created from the unallocated space on a dynamic disk. The Setup program only recognizes dynamic volumes that contain partition tables, and these only appear in basic volumes or dynamic volumes created by updating basic volumes. In addition, if you install Windows 2000 on a dynamic volume, you will not be able to extend the volume.

When configuring volume types, you must be logged on as an Administrator.

CONFIGURING FILE SYSTEMS

Windows 2000 Server supports three main file systems: File Allocation Table (FAT), FAT32, and New Technology File System (NTFS).

FAT • The FAT file system, or FAT16, was introduced with MS-DOS. The 16-bit FAT is supported by Windows 3.x, 95, 98, Me, NT, and 2000. It is the most universally supported file system, and must be used with multiboot computers that host multiple operating systems that do not recognize FAT32 or NTFS (if one is to access that partition from all of them). FAT is not well suited to servers, however, for the following reasons:

- FAT works most efficiently with small partitions (400 MBs or less). FAT32 and NTFS take less time to find and open files on partitions greater than 200 MBs.
- FAT cannot support file, directory, and partition sizes in excess of 4 GBs (2 GBs on early versions).
- NTFS offers a higher level of security.
- FAT can become corrupted with crosslinked files or orphan clusters in the event of a power loss. NTFS is more tolerant.
- FAT supports file names of only eight characters plus a three character extension (the 8.3 convention), no more than 512 files in a root directory, and no more than 65,535 files in a nonroot directory.

FAT32 • The original FAT was superseded with FAT32, or VFAT, with the introduction of Windows 95 Release B. Like FAT16, FAT32 is limited to 512 files in a root directory, but it supports file names of up to 255 characters, unlimited files in a nonroot directory, and a partition size of 32 GBs. FAT32 can also relocate the root directory and use backup copies of the file system, reducing the risk of crashes.

Although FAT32 is superior to FAT in many respects, it still cannot provide file-level security like NTFS.

NTFS • NTFS can take advantage of all of Windows 2000's capabilities. If you plan to run Windows 2000 alone on the disk drive, you will almost certainly want to choose the NTFS format for its increased performance and its inherent safety. For example, NTFS is capable of sector sparing on Small Computer Serial Interface (SCSI) drives. Should a hard disk sector fail on an NTFS-formatted SCSI drive partition, NTFS will attempt to write the data from RAM to a good sector and then automatically map out the bad sector so that it will not be used again.

NTFS also supports far greater security. An NTFS-formatted disk drive supports both directory-level and file-level permissions. The Windows 2000 version, NTFS 5, also supports disk quotas, file encryption, and sparse files.

You can convert a FAT or FAT32 partition to an NTFS partition any time without reformatting. To do so, launch the Command Prompt and use the following command:

```
CONVERT <drive_letter>: /FS:NTFS
```

You cannot convert an NTFS partition back to a FAT or FAT 32 partition without reformatting.

Monitoring Disks and Volumes

In addition to configuring various volumes, the Disk Management snap-in can provide you with an indication of disk health. Its Disk List view and Graphical View provides a logical display of your computer's disk types, capacity, free space, status, controller type, and file system. The Volume List view provides a logical display of your computer's disk drives from a volume-specific perspective, including volume name, layout, type, file system status, capacity, and space usage.

To perform further monitoring of a disk or volume, select it and open the Properties dialog box. Under the General tab, you can view the volume's label, type, file system, and available space, as shown in Figure 12.7.

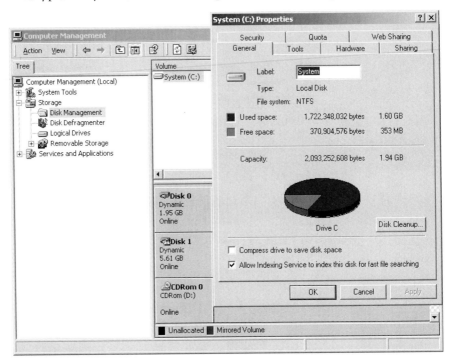

Figure 12.7 *Disk volume Properties dialog box.*

On NTFS volumes, you may choose to enable disk compression and file indexing. You can also launch the Disk Cleanup utility to get rid of unnecessary files.

Under the Tools tab you can launch utilities for error checking, backup, and disk defragmentation, as shown in Figure 12.8.

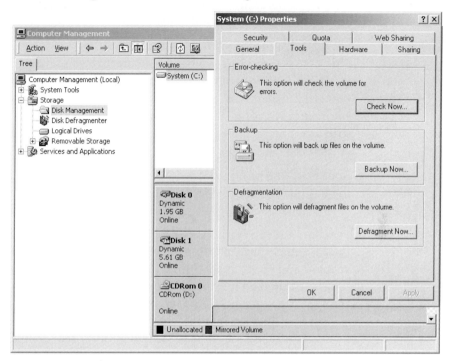

Figure 12.8 *The volume properties Tools tab.*

Click the Backup Now button to open the Backup and Restore Wizard or to create an Emergency Repair Disk (ERD). Click the Defragment Now button to analyze and/or defragment a volume. Click the Check Now button to scan the disk drive for file system and physical errors and fix them automatically.

Under the Hardware tab you can determine the drivers under which the hard disk is running. If the device has been properly installed and configured, Windows 2000 will tell you so via the Device status field. If not, an error message will be displayed. If there is a problem, you can click the Troubleshooter button to bring up context-sensitive Microsoft Help.

Under the Quota tab, you can enable quotas to restrict the amount of disk space available to each of the computer's users, as described further on in this chapter.

Troubleshooting Disks and Volumes

When encountering problems with hard disks, you should first attempt to determine if the cause is software or hardware-related using Windows 2000's built-in tools.

CHECK DISK • You can troubleshoot both basic and dynamic volumes using the Disk Check tool that is accessible through the Check Now button in the Properties dialog box (see Figure 12.8). The utility gives you the option of automatically fixing file system errors, addressing the volume's software structure, and scanning for and recovering from bad sectors, addressing the disk's physical structure (see Figure 3.28).

BOOT FAILURES • Should Windows 2000 fail to boot, it might be that one of the hard disk's boot files is missing or corrupt. You must then employ the emergency repair process to reinstall the corrupted or missing files.

STARTUP ERRORS • Viruses that replace the Master Boot Record (MBR) can produce such start-up errors as "invalid partition table," "missing operating system," and "error loading operating system." You may use the "AVBoot" program, found on the installation CD-ROM, to scan for and remove viruses from the MBRs on any of the server's hard drives.

If the volume is inaccessible, or appears as an "unknown volume" when viewed from the Disk Management snap-in, it may be that either the boot sector or the Master File Table (MFT) is corrupt. On NTFS volumes, it might be that the permissions have changed.

In the past, one could overcome boot sector problems by running the FDISK utility with the /MBR switch. Microsoft no longer recommends this.

Study Break

Convert a Basic Disk

Practice what you have learned by converting a basic disk into a dynamic disk.

First, select the basic disk in the Disk Management snap-in and choose the Upgrade to Dynamic Disk command from the Action menu. Follow the steps as presented by the wizard. After the conversion is complete, note that unallocated space has been added to the end of the volume, as seen from the Disk Management snap-in. Should you wish to turn the dynamic disk back into a basic disk, select the Restore basic Disk Configuration command from the Action menu. Remember that this will erase all data residing on the disk.

MCSE 12.2   Configuring Data Compression

Window 2000 Server can provide up to 2:1 compression of files and folders on NTFS-formatted partitions. Once enabled, compression takes place automatically and is transparent to both applications and users. Compression is allowed for individual files and folders, as well as whole volumes. NTFS can compress all files in the partition, including hidden and system files (except NTLDR and Pagefile.sys). Any NTFS formatted disk or folder has the ability to contain both compressed and noncompressed files.

NTFS compression is also optimized for performance. When you select a file to compress, NTFS will first determine how much disk space will be saved and compare that to the resources it will take to do the compression. If NTFS decides it is not worth the effort, it will not compress the file.

To enable file compression, perform the following steps:

1. Select a file that you wish to compress, then right-click and select the Properties command to open the Properties dialog box.
2. Select the Advanced button to open the Advanced Attributes dialog box.
3. Next, enable the Compress contents to save disk space checkbox.

You may choose to compress entire folders this way as well, in which case you will be asked whether subfolders should be compressed too. If you enable compression for a folder, then all new files created in that directory will also be compressed.

You may change the display of your compressed file and folders to an alternate color, making it easier to differentiate between compressed and uncompressed data. To do this, select the Folder Options command from the Tools menu bar item to open the Folder Options dialog box. Under the View tab, enable the Display compressed files and folders with alternate color checkbox.

Use the COMPACT.EXE utility to enable compression from the command prompt. It will report compression status, ratio, and file size for compressed files in the file list. It can also be used with a number of switches in the following format:

```
COMPACT /<switch> file/folder_name
```

The possible switches include the following:

- /C. Compresses files.
- /U. Uncompresses files.
- /S. Compresses all files in a directory (and subdirectories).

- **/I**. Continues compression after errors have occurred.
- **/F.** Forces compression on all files, even if already compressed.
- **/A.** Compresses hidden and system files.

You should be aware of the following facts when working with file compression:

- You can compress entire partitions. This is file-level compression, however, so you are only ever really compressing files.
- If you create a file in a compressed directory, it will be a compressed file. If you use the Copy command to move the file to an uncompressed directory, then the file will be uncompressed. This is because a new instance of the file has been created that will adopt the characteristics of its parent directory.
- When the Move command is used, a file created in a compressed directory and moved to an uncompressed directory will remain compressed. This is because the Move command does not actually move anything, it only directs the source and destination directories to swap pointers, making it appear to move. Since the file does not change, it does not lose its original characteristics.
- When relocating a file in another partition, the Move command is unable to play its little trick with directory pointers and must instead copy the file (deleting it from the source partition thereafter). Consequently, a file that is moved from a compressed directory on one partition to an uncompressed directory on another partition would be uncompressed.
- Under Windows 2000 Professional, a file is copied over the network, then decompressed on the client machine. This change makes it faster to copy compressed files over the network. Under Windows NT 4.0, a file would be decompressed on the server computer before being sent over the network.
- Only NTFS compression is available under Windows 2000 Server. You cannot use Microsoft's DriveSpace as you can under Windows 9x/Me, for example.
- Windows 2000 Server supports file encryption, which cannot be used with file compression. You may compress files or encrypt them, but not both.

Study Break

Compress a File

> Practice what you have learned by compressing a file.
>
> First, locate a large file, such as a lengthy document. Note its original file size. Next, enable file compression for the file. Note its new file size. Also examine the behavior of the file when you copy or move it between various folders and volumes.

MCSE 12.3 Working with Disk Quotas

When it comes to server storage, too much is not enough. It is a computing truism that no matter how much hard disk space you have, you will fill it up! Often new storage media are required, but sometimes the chronic problem can be alleviated by better use of the existing storage space. Disk quotas allow you to restrict the amount of hard drive space users can take up with the files they own, helping to ensure that only the most necessary data is stored on your server.

Configuring Disk Quotas

To enable a disk quota on an NTFS volume, select it and open the Properties dialog box. Under the Quota tab, enable the Enable quota management check box, as shown in Figure 12.9.

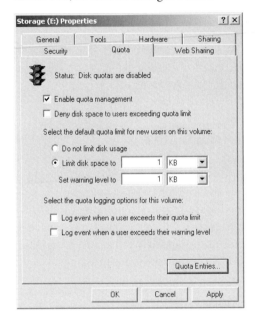

Figure 12.9 *Enabling quota management.*

As an administrator, you should decide on a quota management policy that is either friendly or restrictive. Under a friendly policy, set the Limit disk space to field to an appropriate level, and the Set warning level to field at a reasonable percentage of the previous field, such as 10 percent. Under a restrictive policy, do the same, but also enable the Deny disk space to users exceeding quota limit checkbox to force compliance.

To manage disk quotas on a per user basis, click the Quota Entries button to open the Quota Entries window, as shown in Figure 12.10.

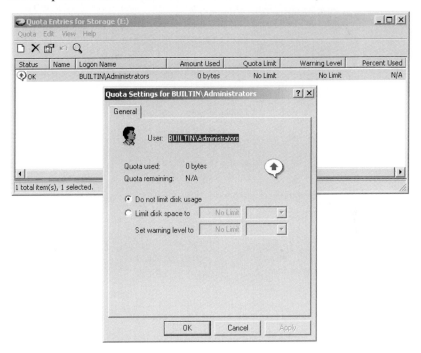

Figure 12.10 *Enabling per user quota management.*

Double-click a user entry to open the Quota Settings dialog box, in which you may enable the Limit disk space to radio button to establish a quota limit.

To add entries, select the New Quota Entry command from the Quota menu bar item to open the Select Users window, from which you may add users, as shown in Figure 12.11.

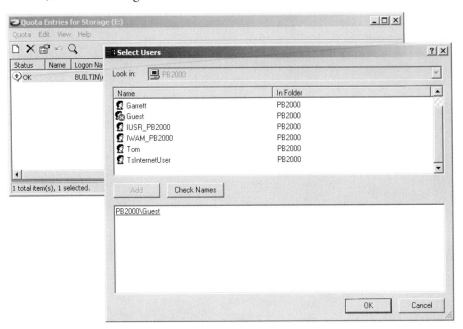

Figure 12.11   *Selecting users.*

You may then enable disk usage limits for each user.

Monitoring Disk Quotas

To monitor disk quotas, enable the logging options in the volume properties dialog box so that you can evaluate the needs of users who repeatedly reach the limit and perhaps adjust it upward. This will also tell you which users are ignoring the warnings, and therefore your quota management policy.

Some additional disk quota considerations include the following:

- Disk quotas can be set for all users, or individual users.
- Disk quotas are set per volume, not per folder, file, or physical disk.
- Where spanned or striped volumes are employed, disk quotas apply to the entire volume, not to each member disk.
- Usage is calculated when users create, copy, save, or take ownership of files.
- Disk quotas are applied to uncompressed file sizes, regardless of whether or not file compression is being employed on a volume.

Configure Disk Quotas

> Practice what you have learned by enabling disk quota management.
>
> Select a volume on which user data is stored and enable disk quotas. Next, use the Quota Entries window to locate and enable a limit for your own user account. Observe the effects of disk quota management as you save and copy files to the volume under various scenarios.

MCSE 12.4 **Recovering from Disk Failures**

Your first line of defense against data loss is a regular backup to removable media, such as DAT. Where more up-to-the-minute protection is needed, fault tolerance methods such as mirroring/duplexing or striping with parity can be employed. Used together, fault tolerance and backup strategy can reduce the chances of data loss to insignificance.

When all is well, the Disk Management snap-in will report your disk drives' status as "online" and "healthy." Other status levels are indications that you must perform one of the following recovery procedures.

Recovering Mirrored Drives

When a mirrored volume resides on a faulty disk, it will be removed from the mirror and become an orphan. This is not necessarily an urgent situation. If Windows 2000 lists the disk as "offline" but still displays its name, try right-clicking the disk in the Disk Management snap-in and selecting the Reactivate command. This should regenerate the mirror volume and return it to "online" status. Failing this, also try the Repair Volume and Resynchronize Mirror commands, which fix problems in the volume's file structure.

Should the system drive in a mirrored server fail, you will need to reassign the mirrored drive by modifying the BOOT.INI system file so that you can reboot your server. This file, which provides the options listed in the Boot Loader menu, can be modified to include a number of switches. The file is written using the Advanced RISC Computer (ARC) format, a cross-platform standard. It contains the following parameters:

- **scsi(x)/multi(x).** This is a zero-based parameter used to identify a hardware adapter (e.g., the first drive is "0," the second is "1," etc.). The multi(x) parameter is used most often, even for SCSI controllers. You will only see the scsi(x) parameter if the controller's BIOS is turned off. In that case, the NTBOOTDD.SYS file will load a SCSI device driver.
- **disk(x).** This is a zero-based parameter is used to identify the SCSI bus number, if a SCSI controller is present. It is always zero when used with the multi(x) parameter.
- **rdisk(x).** This is a zero-based drive number for use with the multi(x) parameter. It is ignored when used with the scsi(x) parameter.
- **partition(x).** This is a one-based parameter used to identify logical partitions (e.g., the first partition is "1," the second is "2," etc.).

Although some of these parameters are ignored, they must still be present in the path. For example, the following is a valid ARC path even though the disk(x) parameter, used with SCSI drives, is ignored:

```
multi(0)disk(0)rdisk(0)partition(l)
```

BOOT.INI is an editable text file. It is read-only, however, so you must remove the read-only attribute from in its Properties dialog box before editing it. When you open BOOT.INI, you will see that it has two sections. The "boot loader" section of BOOT.INI specifies the operating system that will be loaded if you do not make a selection within the time defined, in seconds; as the time-out. If you set the time-out to 0, the default loads immediately without giving you time to choose. If you set the time-out to -1, BOOT.INI will wait forever for a decision. The default parameter specifies the path to the operating system's directory.

The "operating systems" section refers to each OS available in the Boot Loader menu. You can also add switches that customize the Windows 2000 environment here. These include:

- **/basevideo.** Used to load a driver for a standard 16-color 640 by 480 VGA screen rather that the one optimized for the video controller card. This is useful for getting around display problems.
- **/sos.** Used to list each driver as it loads during boot up (rather than just showing dots as previously described). This is useful when you wish to see which driver is hanging the boot process.
- **/noserialmice.** Used in the format /noserialmice=[COMx | COMx,y,z_], this switch tells NTDETECT to forgo a search for serial mice. Sometimes when the operating system does this, it mistakes

other devices (such as modems) for serial mice, making the port unavailable for the real device.

- **/crashdebug.** Used to enable Startup and Recovery. This can also be added via the System Control Panel application.
- **/maxmem:x.** Used to track memory parity errors by specifying a specific amount of usable memory for Windows 2000.
- **/scsiordinal:x.** Used to assign values to multiple SCSI controllers.

Once you have replaced the faulty hard disk, use the Add Mirror command to re-establish your server's fault tolerance.

Recovering RAID 5 Drives

As with a mirror volume, when a volume fails under striping with parity, it becomes an orphan. I/O requests are redirected to the remaining partitions in the set so that it can be reconstructed. This data is stored in RAM using the parity, so you might notice a performance hit on the server until the set is regenerated. This feature will permit you to keep using the RAID array until it is repaired.

To regenerate a stripped volume, use the Disk Management snap-in's Reactivate Volume command. The information from the existing volumes in the stripe will be written to the orphan member.

Recovering Non–Fault Tolerant Drives

If your server is not configured for fault tolerance and you are unable to repair a disk problem using Windows 2000's built-in tools, your only recourse is to install a new or reinitialized drive and restore data from the latest backup job, as described elsewhere in this book.

Study Break

Prepare for Disk Failure

Practice what you have learned by preparing for a disk failure.

If you are using RAID fault tolerance, use the Disk Management snap-in to verify that your server's volumes are "online" and "healthy." Familiarize yourself with the Recover Volume, Reactivate, and Resynchronize Mirror commands.

Even if you have your Windows 2000 Server up and running with RAID Level 1 or Level 5 fault tolerance, do not assume its data will be safe and secure. The data might be safe if one of the disk drives in the computer crashes, but what if something destroys the entire computer? Businesses that survive fires, floods and earthquakes are not saved by their servers' fault tolerance systems. They are saved by the regular, systematic use of a backup system. In planning for server deployment, one of the most important considerations is what type of backup system it has. Whether it uses Digital Audio Tape (DAT) or some other type, it should make use of removable media. Copies of server data can then be kept offsite. Office buildings have been known to burn down, and fault tolerant server hardware tends to burn right along with them.

■ Summary

In this chapter, we explored the issues surrounded mass data storage, including volume types, compression, quotas, and fault tolerance.

Working with Disks and Volumes

Windows 2000 Server lets you configure and manage disk drives using the Disk Management MMC snap-in. This tool supersedes the Disk Administrator utility found in Windows NT Server 4.0 and can be used to view disk information, create and manage disk partitions or volumes, initialize and format disks, partitions, and volumes, and manage hard disks on remote computers. The basic disk is the traditional format familiar and common to all Windows operating systems. The default storage type for Windows 2000, basic disks are fixed in size. When working with basic storage, you can format hard disks as single drives or subdivide hard disks into multiple partitions. If you do not intend to dual-boot with any other operating systems, you have the option of configuring your disk drives as dynamic disks, which are only supported by Windows 2000, and which can be resized without reformatting. In addition, dynamic disks can consist of one partition, multiple partitions on a single disk drive, or multiple partitions on multiple disk drives. Partitions are referred to as volumes and can be created without limit (other than the physical size of the disk). Basic disks can be converted to dynamic disks.

Configuring Data Compression

Window 2000 Server provides up to 2:1 compression of files and folders on NTFS-formatted partitions. Once enabled, compression takes place automatically and is transparent to both applications and users. Compression is allowed for individual files and folders, as well as whole volumes. Any NTFS formatted disk or folder has the ability to contain both compressed and noncompressed files. Windows 2000 Server file encryption cannot be used with file compression.

Working with Disk Quotas

Disk quotas allow you to restrict the amount of hard drive space users can take up with the files they own, helping to ensure that only the most necessary data is stored on your server. Disk quotas can be set for all users, or individual users, on a per volume basis. Usage is calculated when users create, copy, save, or take ownership of files. Disk quotas are applied to uncompressed file sizes, regardless of whether or not file compression is being employed on a volume.

Recovering from Disk Failures

Your first line of defense against data loss is a regular backup to removable media. Where more up-to-the-minute protection is needed, fault tolerance methods such as mirroring/duplexing or striping with parity can be employed. When all is well, the Disk Management snap-in will report your disk drives' status as "online" and "healthy." Other status levels are indications that you must perform recovery procedures, such as reactivating or regenerating a mirrored or striped volume.

▲ CHAPTER REVIEW QUESTIONS

Here are a few questions relating to the material covered in the *Managing, Configuring, and Troubleshooting Storage Use* section of Microsoft's *Installing, Configuring, and Administering Microsoft Windows 2000 Server* exam (70-215).

1. *Dynamic disks can only be recognized by older operating systems, such as Windows 98, if formatted as FAT.*
    A. True
    B. False

2. *Striped Volumes provide better performance as well as fault tolerance:*
    A. True
    B. False

3. *Data compression achieves the lowest ratios when used in conjunction with encryption.*
   A. True
   B. False

4. *Data compression achieves the lowest ratios when used on FAT volumes.*
   A. True
   B. False

5. *Disk quotas can be applied to which of the following? Select all that apply:*
   A. Physical disks
   B. Volumes
   C. Groups
   D. Users

6. *Users can often avoid a disk quota limit by compressing files.*
   A. True
   B. False

7. *If a mirrored system volume fails, one can boot from the remaining mirror volume automatically.*
   A. True
   B. False

8. *Failed volumes on both mirror and RAID 5 volumes are called orphans.*
   A. True
   B. False

Networking Windows 2000 Server

▲Chapter Syllabus

MCSE 13.1 Working with Shared Access

MCSE 13.2 Working with Network Protocols

MCSE 13.3 Working with Network Services

MCSE 13.4 Working with Remote Access Services

MCSE 13.5 Working with Virtual Private Networks

MCSE 13.6 Working with Terminal Services

MCSE 13.7 Working with Network Adapters

In this chapter, we will look at material covered in the *Configuring and Troubleshooting Windows 2000 Network Connections* section of Microsoft's *Installing, Configuring, and Administering Windows 2000 Server* exam (70-215).

In the following pages, you will learn to install and configure various Windows 2000-supported network protocols, adapters, and services. You will also learn to configure file-sharing services for Windows and non-Windows based desktops, and resource access through Routing and Remote Access Services (RRAS) and Terminal Services.

You were first introduced to some of this material in the first section of this book, *Windows 2000 Professional*. This material will also serve as a foundation for topics covered in the third section of this book, *Windows 2000 Network Infrastructures*.

603

MCSE 13.1   Working with Shared Access

What distinguishes the Windows 2000 Server machine from other flavors of Windows more than anything is its ability to share access to its resources. Windows 2000 Server makes available the following resource sharing services:

- **File and Printer Sharing for Microsoft Networks.** This service supports clients running under Windows NT/2000, Windows 9x/Me, Windows for Workgroups, Workgroup Add-On for MS-DOS, and LAN Manager. Paired with Client for Microsoft Networks, it can use NetBEUI, IPX/SPX/NetBIOS-Compatible Transport, and TCP/IP network protocols.

- **Gateway (and Client Services) for NetWare (GSNW).** GSNW gives Windows 2000 Server direct access to Novell NetWare's file and print services over NWLink IPX/SPX/NetBIOS Compatible Transport while providing a gateway between Windows clients and NetWare servers. In this capacity, it permits Windows 9x/Me, Windows for Workgroups, and Windows NT/2000 computers to access NetWare resources using Microsoft Networking's native Server Message Block (SMB) protocol instead of requiring NetWare client software. The gateway does not support a large volume of traffic (there is only one connection to a NetWare server), but it does provide a low volume access solution that does not require the purchase of additional NetWare licenses.

  NetWare networking infrastructure takes two basic forms. NetWare Directory Services (NDS) uses a distributed database system to map network resources. It is associated primarily with NetWare 4.x and newer. An older system, the NetWare bindery, is primarily associated with NetWare 3.x. GSNW supports both systems. GSNW also supports NetWare Core Protocol (NCP) and Large Internet Protocol (LIP).

- **Internet Information Services (IIS).** Including both File Transfer Protocol (FTP) and HyperText Transfer Protocol (HTTP), this service technically supports UNIX-based clients, such as Linux and Sun Solaris desktops. Practically speaking, it supports clients from just about every operating system over the nearly ubiquitous TCP/IP. Windows 2000 Server also has services to support UNIX-based printing clients.

- **File Server for Macintosh (SFM).** SFM is a useful but scantly documented enterprise feature of Windows 2000 Server. With it, Mac OS computer users can access the same directories and files as do Windows users, but through their native file sharing architecture. SFM includes AppleTalk, the network protocol that supports native Mac OS-based file sharing and printing. SFM also supports an AppleTalk-TCP/IP hybrid protocol used for file sharing: AppleTalk File Protocol (AFP)/TCP.

Installing Shared Access

Windows 2000 Server's file and printer sharing abilities are installed in several different ways.

INSTALLING MICROSOFT FILE AND PRINTER SHARING

In order to support traditional file and print sharing from Windows 2000 Server, you must have the Client for Microsoft Networks and File and-Printer Sharing for Microsoft Networks services installed.

When the Setup program detects a network adapter during setup, it installs these services by default. You can verify their presence by clicking the Local Area Connection icon in the Network and Dial-Up Connections folder. In the Local Area Connection Status dialog box, click the Properties button to open the Local Area Connection Properties dialog box, as shown in Figure 13.1.

You can install, uninstall, and configure properties for these and additional services in the Local Area Connection Properties dialog box by clicking the appropriate buttons.

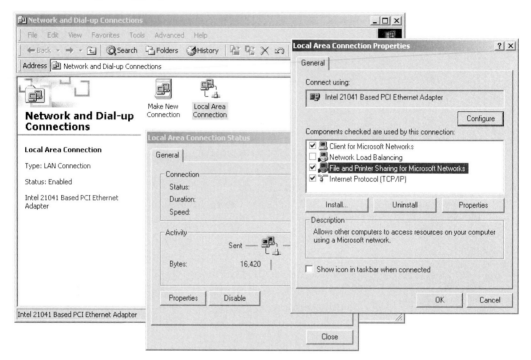

Figure 13.1 *Viewing installed file services.*

INSTALLING GSNW

To install GSNW, click the Install button to open the Select Network Component dialog box. Next, select Client and click the Add button to open the Select Network Client dialog box.

Select Gateway (and Client) Services for NetWare and click the OK button, as shown in Figure 13.2.

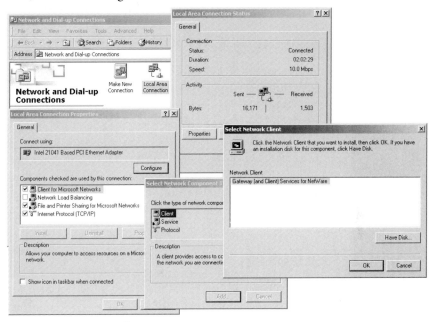

Figure 13.2   *Installing GSNW.*

You will have to restart the server. Upon boot up thereafter, you will be prompted with NetWare client logon choices, as shown in Figure 13.3.

Figure 13.3   *Initial NetWare Settings.*

You may enter a preferred server for NetWare version 2.15 or higher, or version 3.x. Alternately, you can enter default trees and context for NDS, which is the default for NetWare 4.x and higher. If you do not have a NetWare client account, click the Cancel button.

Once back in Windows 2000, note that a new GSNW icon is added to the Control Panel program group. In addition, the NWLink IPX/SPX/NetBIOS Compatible Transport and NWLink NetBIOS protocols are installed.

INSTALLING IIS

In order to share files and folders using FTP or HTTP, you must install Windows 2000 Internet Information Services (IIS). To do so, select the Install Add-On Components link in the installation CD-ROM's Autorun screen to open the Windows Components Wizard. Enable the IIS checkbox and click the Next button to proceed. This process was described in Chapter 2, "Administering Windows 2000 Professional Resources."

To install Print Services for UNIX, select Other Network File and Print Services from the Windows Components Wizard's scrolling list and click the Details button. Enable the Print Services for UNIX checkbox and click OK to continue.

INSTALLING SFM

In order to share files and printers using AppleTalk, you must install both File Services for Macintosh and Print Services for Macintosh. To do so, select the Install Add-On Components link in the installation CD-ROM's Autorun screen to open the Windows Components Wizard.

Next, select Other Network File and Print Services from the scrolling list and click the Details button.

Enable the File Services for Macintosh and Print Services for Macintosh checkboxes and click OK to continue, as shown in Figure 13.4.

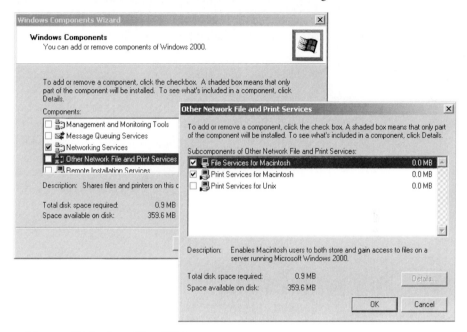

Figure 13.4   *Installing SFM.*

The AppleTalk protocol will be automatically installed as well.

Configuring Shared Access

The configuration of shared folders and printers was described in Chapter 9, "Administering Windows 2000 Server Resources." In addition to this information, there are some server-specific variables that you should know about.

CONFIGURING MICROSOFT FILE AND PRINTER SHARING

To configure File and Printer Sharing for Microsoft Networks, select its listing in the Local Area Connection Properties dialog box and click the Properties button to open the dialog box shown in Figure 13.5.

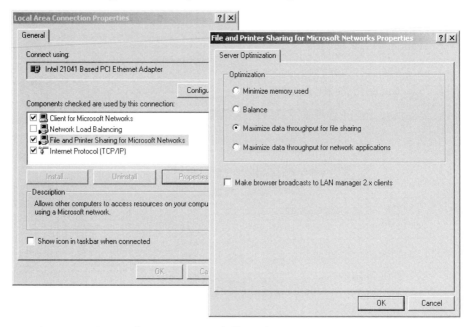

Figure 13.5 *Configuring Microsoft file and print server.*

Windows 2000 Server can be configured to give priority to one of the
following server roles:

- **Minimize Memory Used.** Best applied to servers supporting no more
  than 10 connections.
- **Balance.** Best applied to servers supporting no more than 64 connections.
- **Maximize Throughput for File Sharing.** Best suited to dedicated file
  and print servers supporting more than 64 connections. It creates a
  large file cache.
- **Maximize Throughput for Network Applications.** Best suited to
  dedicated application servers and domain controllers supporting
  more than 64 simultaneous connections.

You can also enable network-browsing support for legacy LAN Manager clients.

With File and Printer Sharing for Microsoft Networks installed, enable sharing for any folder through its Properties dialog box. Alternately, you can share folders from the Computer Management MMC's System Tools branch (Shared Folders) by selecting the Create New File Share menu bar button to open the Create New Shared Folder Wizard (see Figure 13.6).

Figure 13.6 *Choosing a folder in the Create New Shared Folder Wizard.*

Use the Browse button to locate the folder that will be shared. Next, name the share and optionally provide a description of its purpose. After clicking the next button, you may establish permissions for the share, as shown in Figure 13.7.

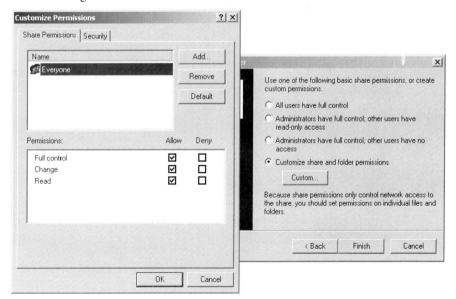

Figure 13.7 *Establishing share permissions.*

You may accept the default of giving everyone full control, the least secure state, limit write and control access to Administrators, or set up your own access list by clicking the Custom button.

CONFIGURING GSNW

In order to configure GSNW, you must give it access to a NetWare server. This requires that you have Supervisor or equivalent rights under NetWare. Once logged in to NetWare, create a group called "NTGATEWAY" on the NetWare server using the SYSCON utility. Next, create a user account that will be used by the gateway and add it to the NTGATEWAY group.

Returning to the Windows 2000 Server, double-click the GSNW icon in the Control Panel program group to open the Gateway Service for NetWare dialog box shown in Figure 13.8.

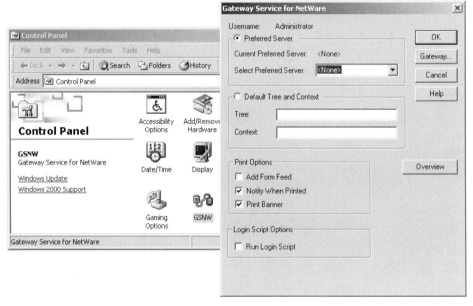

Figure 13.8 *Configuring GSNW.*

First, you will need to configure NetWare client access information, if you did not already do so after you first rebooted the server. Enter the information for preferred servers, default tree and context, print options, and login script.

Next, press the Gateway button to open the Configure Gateway dialog box (as shown in Figure 13.9.

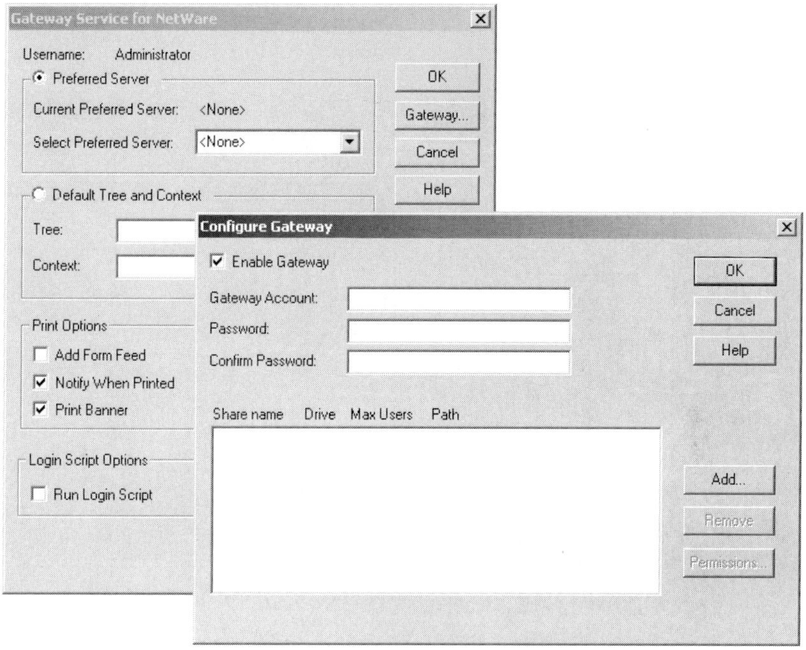

Figure 13.9   *Configuring Gateway.*

Select the Enable Gateway checkbox. Enter the user account that you created on the NetWare server in the Gateway Account field, and beneath it, the password.

Next, you must create Windows 2000 shares for each NetWare volume or directory that you wish to make available to Windows users. To do this, press the Add button. You will be asked to type in a NetWare network path and a share name, along with a drive letter. Use the Permissions button to set access permissions.

To Windows users, the NetWare share appears to be another share on the Windows 2000 server. As with File and Printer Sharing for Microsoft Networks, use the Browse button to locate the folder that will be shared in the Create Shared Folder Wizard. Next, name the share and optionally provide a description of its purpose. In addition, however, enable the Novell NetWare checkbox. After clicking the Next button, you may establish permissions for the folder, just as you would for a File and Printer Sharing for Microsoft Networks share.

CONFIGURING IIS

You may configure IIS' FTP and Web server components using the Computer Management MMC, as shown in Figure 13.10.

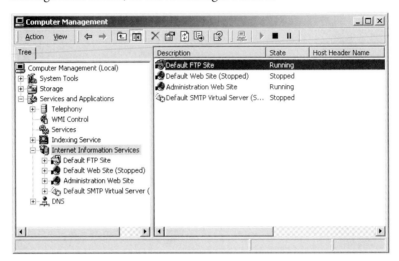

Figure 13.10 *Configuring IIS through the Computer Management MMC.*

To configure your FTP server, select it under the Internet Information Services branch in the Computer Management MMC and right-click to choose the Properties command from the pop-up menu. You can address most issues using the tabs of the Default FTP Site Properties dialog box (see Figure 13.9).

CONFIGURING FTP BANDWIDTH • Each user that transfers a file to or from your server's FTP directories uses a portion of processor, memory, hard disk, and network bandwidth. When there are a large number of concurrent connections, overall server performance can degrade. To minimize this, you might wish to limit the number of concurrent connections that the FTP server will accept.

To set a limit on concurrent user connections, select the FTP Site tab, as shown in Figure 13.11.

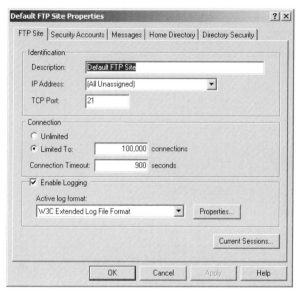

Figure 13.11 *Limiting concurrent FTP connections to preserve bandwidth.*

If you have a powerful server that is dedicated to only the FTP Service, as some e-commerce servers are, you might risk enabling the Unlimited radio button here. Otherwise, you should set a number in the Limited to X connections dialog box that is appropriate for your server's level of performance.

The Connection Timeout field is used to establish an interval after which idle connections are dropped. The default is 900 seconds (15 minutes).

CONFIGURING FTP LOGON AUTHENTICATION • You can enable FTP access to a group of registered users, which is useful in an intranet setting, or open it up to unknown users, which is useful in some Internet settings. You can also restrict the number of users who may log on.

No user can access your FTP site without being given permission to do so. You can either grant that permission to a specific user or group in the Windows 2000 SAM database, or to anyone in the world by using anonymous access.

To enable FTP access, switch to the Security Accounts tab in the FTP Site Properties dialog box, as shown in Figure 13.12.

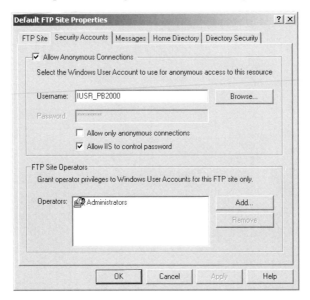

Figure 13.12 *Enabling FTP access.*

If you enable the Allow Anonymous Connections checkbox here, unknown users will be able to access your site using the name "anonymous" and an email address as a password. The IUSR account appears in the User-name field by default. This is the special account through which anonymous access is enabled. It can be changed using the Browse button should you wish to use the permissions of another account in the Windows 2000 users and groups database. You must then also set the chosen account's corresponding password or select the Allow IIS to control password checkbox to copy it from the user and group database automatically, which is useful when you do not know the password for the account that you wish to use.

If you select the Allow only anonymous connections checkbox, then only "guest" access is permitted. This ensures that only those permissions assigned to the anonymous account can be used, instead of whatever permissions a given user's account might have.

You may establish which users and groups will be allowed to administer the service in the FTP Site Operators section (e.g., Administrators).

CONFIGURING FTP PORT SETTINGS • Although not usually visible to a user, each TCP/IP-based service is associated with a port number that is part of the IP address used by a client to find it. For FTP services, that port number is 21. Most Web browsers and other FTP clients expect to find the FTP service at this port address. However, you can change this port number, perhaps to increase security, by using a different port number beyond 1024. (1024 and lesser ports are in the reserved range.)

To change the FTP port setting, switch to the FTP Site tab in the FTP Site Properties dialog box (see Figure 13.9). Here, change the number in the TCP Port field.

Because FTP clients default to port number 21, they will have to be configured with the new port number in order to access your site. So, for example, if you changed the port number to "1025," you would give users a URL in the format: "ftp://ftp.my-company.com:1025."

CONFIGURING FTP DIRECTORY LISTINGS • FTP directories can be viewed using two different styles. The first follows the MS-DOS convention:

```
C:\InetPub\ftproot\files
```

The second follows the UNIX convention:

```
/c/inetpub/ftproot/files
```

The UNIX convention is most compatible with Internet applications, such as Web browsers, and with non-PC platforms. You can choose the convention that you wish to use with the radio buttons in the Directory Listing

Style section under the Home Directory tab of the FTP Site Properties dialog box, as shown in Figure 13.13.

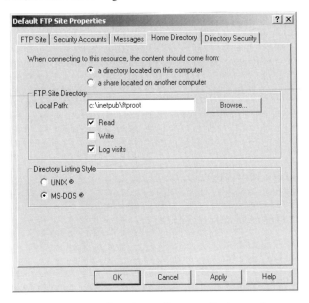

Figure 13.13   *Choosing a directory listing style.*

CONFIGURING VIRTUAL FTP DIRECTORIES AND SERVERS • When you install IIS, it creates a home directory (e.g., \InetPub\ftproot) by default. This is the server's primary location for download files, and the directory structure FTP clients see when they log on to your server. You can change this directory, however, by switching to the Home Directory tab in the FTP Site Properties dialog box (see Figure 13.13).

The actual path to the FTP site's directory structure is specified in the Logical Path field of the FTP Site Directory section. This path can be on the local server, or it can be on a share located on another networked computer (assuming the server connection to the remote computer is available and stable). These options are specified in the When Connecting to This Resource, the Content Should Come from section. Local directories are entered in standard syntax (e.g., \directory\subdirectory), while remote network shares are listed using the Universal Naming Convention (UNC) instead (e.g., \\server\files).

Note that you can also specify two levels of access to the home directory in the FTP Site Directory field. Read access permits users to download files from the home or virtual directory. Write access permits users to upload files to the home or virtual directory. Use this option with care, for you never know what or how much data someone will upload to your server. Log access enables the tracking of users to the home or virtual directory.

Microsoft does not enable Write access by default. This is because malicious users might upload fake, corrupted, or virus-infested files to your server, often replacing valid existing files. Others might upload huge amounts of garbage data to your server in an effort to fill the hard drive or overwhelm available bandwidth in a denial of service attack. At best, your site might become a staging area for pirated software and pornography—probably not the use you intended. If Write access is not required, you should not enable it. If Write access is required, you should monitor the home directory after enabling it. You might be amazed how fast hackers can find an "open" site.

CONFIGURING HTTP BANDWIDTH • As with FTP, each user that transfers a file from your server's Web directories uses a portion of server resources. Although these file transfers are generally smaller than those of FTP, there are usually more of them. To avoid the resulting server performance degradation, you might wish to limit the number of concurrent connections that the Web server will accept.

To set a limit on concurrent user connections, open the Web Site Properties dialog box and select the Web Site tab, as shown in Figure 13.14.

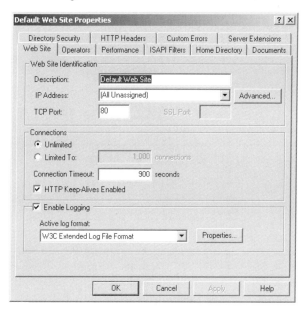

Figure 13.14 *Limiting concurrent connections to preserve bandwidth.*

If you have a powerful server that is dedicated to only the Web service, you can probably leave the Unlimited radio button enabled here (the default). Otherwise, you should set a number in the Limited to X connections dialog box that is appropriate for your server's level of performance and primary use. The default is 1,000 users.

The Connection Timeout field is used to establish an interval after which idle connections are dropped. The default is 900 seconds (15 minutes). A common setting here is 300 seconds (five minutes). If you do not want idle users dropped, fill the field with nines.

If the Web server is not the only service running on your server, you might wish to enable bandwidth throttling. By enabling this feature, you can control the amount of network bandwidth used by the Web server (site by site) so that there will be network bandwidth available to other services such as FTP, email, and newsgroups.

To enable bandwidth throttling, switch to the Performance tab and select the Enable bandwidth throttling checkbox, as shown in Figure 13.15.

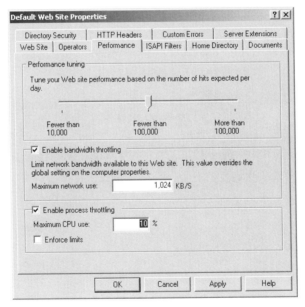

Figure 13.15 *Enabling bandwidth throttling.*

You can establish how much of the network connection will be reserved for Web server use in the Maximum network use X KB/S field. Naturally, what you enter here will depend on what your network bandwidth is. The default setting (1,024) might be reasonable for an server residing on a T1 Internet connection (1.5 Mbps), but too conservative for an intranet server residing on a local Ethernet (10 Mbps or 100 Mbps).

CONFIGURING HTTP LOGON AUTHENTICATION • As with FTP, no user can access your Web site without being given permission to do so. You can either grant that permission to a specific user or group in the SAM database, or to anyone in the world by using anonymous access. You can also enable encrypted logon authentication for greater security.

To enable authenticated Web access, switch to the Directory Security tab, as shown in Figure 13.16. You can also right-click on an individual directory or file (under NTFS) to access it alone.

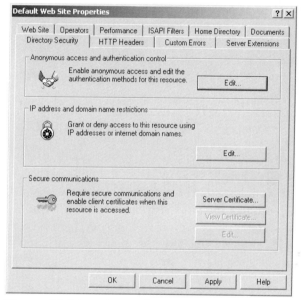

Figure 13.16   *Opening the Web Site Properties dialog box.*

Next, select the Edit button in the Anonymous access and Authentication Control section under the Directory Security tab. This will open the Authentication Methods dialog box, as shown in Figure 13.17.

If you enable the Allow anonymous access checkbox (the default), Web browsers will be able to access the site's pages without submitting usernames or passwords via the IUSR account. This account has Log on Locally permissions. Pressing the Edit button permits you to choose another account.

If you disable anonymous access and enable the Basic Authentication checkbox, a valid username and password will be required to permit Web browsers to access your site. The username/password combinations must correspond to those found in an NTFS disk drive's ACL. The logon information will be sent across the network in clear text, so this option should only be used in environments with minimal security requirements. Pressing the Edit button permits you to choose a default logon domain.

Figure 13.17 *Enabling authenticated WWW access.*

If you disable anonymous access and enable the Integrated Windows authentication checkbox, a valid username and password will also be required to permit browsers to access your Web site. Here too, the username/password combinations must correspond to those found in an NTFS hard drive's ACL. Logon information will be encrypted before being sent across the network, however. This provides higher security, and so is the default. It requires Internet Explorer version 2.0 or greater and compatible Web browsers, and is slightly slower than a clear text logon.

If you have installed the Certificate Server, you can also employ SSL in authenticating logons. This will be described in Chapter 21, "Administering Certificate Services."

These controls can be set directory by directory or file by file on volumes formatted under NTFS.

If you disable the Allow Anonymous Access checkbox or fail to specify an anonymous access account such as IUSR, then Windows authentication will be required for Web site access. If you enable the Basic Authentication checkbox or the Integrated Windows authentication checkbox but do not disable the Allow Anonymous Access checkbox, anonymous access will still be used.

CONFIGURING HTTP PORT SETTINGS • Most Web browsers expect to find the HTTP service at port address 80. As with FTP, you can change this port number to another that is outside the reserved range of 1—1024.

To change the HTTP port setting, switch to the Web Site tab in the Web Site Properties dialog box (see Figure 13.15). Change the number in the TCP Port field.

Because Web browsers default to port number 80, users will have to specify the new port number in order to access your site. So, for example, if you changed the port number to "1025," you would give users a URL in the format: "*http://www.my-company.com:1025.*"

CONFIGURING DEFAULT WEB PAGES • When users access your site with a Web browser, they are presented with a default home page that usually contains links to other pages within the directory structure. This page is presented when users enter your Web site's URL without specifying a document.

To select the default Web page, switch to the Documents tab in the Web Site Properties dialog box, as shown in Figure 13.18.

Figure 13.18 *Selecting a default Web page.*

Here you can use the Add button to select several HTML documents. The first document in the list will be the default Web page. The second document will be presented if the first document is missing, and so on. You can use the arrow keys to change the order of documents.

If you disable the Enable Default Document checkbox, users will be required to submit a document name as part of the URL when accessing your site.

If you enable the Enable Document Footer checkbox, the Web server will insert the HTML footer file that you specify into all documents. This is useful for repetitive information such as copyright notices or Webmaster mail links.

CONFIGURING HTTP HOST HEADER NAMES • IIS supports HTTP 1.1. Among the features of this protocol is the use of host header names that permit multiple host names to be associated with a single IP address. This permits you to host multiple virtual Web sites from one IIS computer. The feature is supported by Internet Explorer 3.0 and newer and Netscape Navigator 2.0 and newer.

To enable host header names for multiple Web sites, switch to the Web Site tab and press the Advanced button to open the Advanced Multiple Web Site Configuration dialog box, as shown in Figure 13.19.

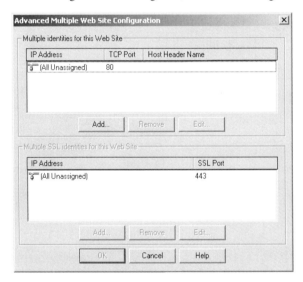

Figure 13.19   *Configuring multiple virtual Web sites.*

Here press the Add button to open the Advanced Web Site Identification dialog box, as shown in Figure 13.20.

Select the Web server address in the IP Address field. Specify a port number in the TCP Port field. Enter a valid domain name in the Host Header Name field.

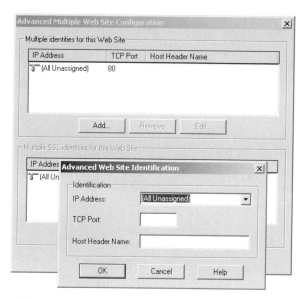

Figure 13.20 *Configuring multiple host header names.*

CONFIGURING HTTP KEEP-ALIVES • As originally designed, Web servers open a connection to a Web browser that requests a document and then close that connection as soon as the document has been delivered. While this quickly frees up resources on the server, it results in a longer wait for Web browsers as every document request requires a new connection. You can alter this behavior by enabling keep-alives, which maintain Web browser connections. To enable keep-alives, switch to the Web Site tab in the Web Site Properties dialog box (see Figure 13.15). Here select the HTTP Keep-Alives Enabled checkbox.

CONFIGURING SFM

Some of the features installed with SFM include the following:

- **AppleShare.** Mac OS users access Apple servers via the AppleShare client. Windows 2000 Server supports any AppleTalk Filing Protocol (AFP) version 2.0-compliant AppleShare client, which makes it compatible to with Macintosh clients running anything between System 6.0.8 and Mac OS X (10). Access is transparent to Mac OS users, as they log on to the Windows 2000 Server in the same manner as they would to native AppleShare servers.

- **One User/One Account.** In keeping with the Microsoft strategy, Mac OS user accounts are part of the SAM; therefore, one account serves a user who logs on from a PC, a Macintosh, or both.
- **Crossplatform printing.** Windows 2000 Server can recognize Apple-Talk-compatible printing devices on the network, such as Apple LaserWriters, and make them part of print spooling just as if they were PC-native printers. Macintosh users are able to access shared PC-native printers as well. SFM has a built-in Raster Image Processor (RIP) that permits Mac OS computers to print to PC printers running the Printer Control Language (PCL) and that enables PCs to print to Apple PostScript printers.
- **AppleTalk Routing.** Windows 2000's Routing and Remote Access (RRAS) supports AppleTalk Phase II routing. RRAS can serve as a seed or nonseed router, and will establish AppleTalk zones.

With the advent of AFP version 2.2, Apple introduced an AppleTalk-TCP/IP hybrid protocol used for file sharing: AFP/TCP. Mac OS computers equipped with AppleShare client version 3.7 or above can connect to AppleShare IP servers (version 5.0 and newer) via either AppleTalk or the new hybrid. Windows NT Server 4.0 only supported AppleTalk connectivity. Windows 2000 Server supports both.

You may configure SFM from the Computer Management MMC's System Tools branch (Shared Folders) by selecting the Configure File Server for

Macintosh command from the Action menu to open the Properties dialog box shown in Figure 13.21.

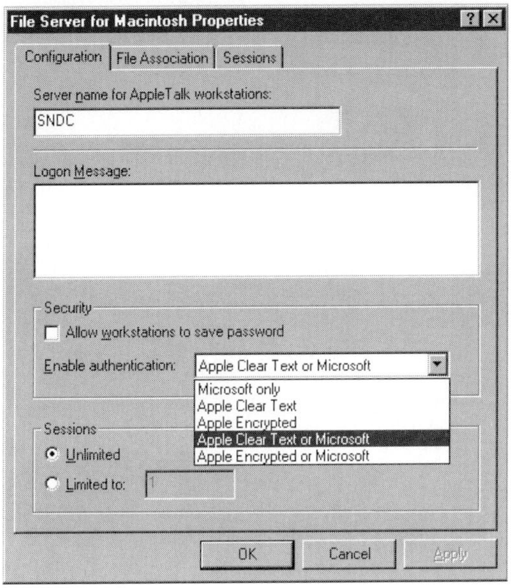

Figure 13.21 *Configuring SFM.*

You can change the name of the server as it appears to Mac OS users to something other than its default NetBIOS computer name, as well as enter a logon message. You may limit the number of Macintosh users who may log on. Of some importance here, you can enable users to save their passwords for automatic logons and enable the requirement for Microsoft authentication. If you enable the later checkbox, make sure all Macintosh clients have the Microsoft User Authentication Method (UAM) properly installed or they will not be able to log on.

The Sessions tab provides information about the current number of AppleTalk sessions, open file forks, and file locking (see Figure 13.22).

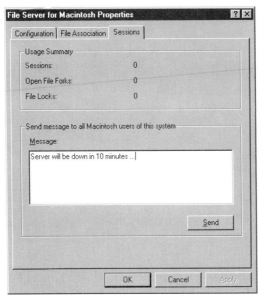

Figure 13.22 *Viewing SFM sessions.*

It also provides a one-way network communications tool that permits you to send messages to all Mac OS users.

When SFM is installed, it creates a default folder that is immediately available to all Mac OS users: "Microsoft UAM Volume." In it is a folder (and instructions) that can be used to upgrade the Mac OS' built-in AppleShare User Authentication Method (UAM) software to the optional Microsoft UAM.

Mac OS users cannot access existing Windows 2000 Server folders beyond the Microsoft UAM Volume directory until they are explicitly shared as Macintosh-accessible volumes. You can share such folders from the Computer Management MMC's System Tools branch (Shared Folders) by select-

ing the Create New File Share button from the menu bar to open the Create
New Shared Folder Wizard, as shown in Figure 13.23.

Figure 13.23   *Choosing a folder in the Create New Shared Folder Wizard.*

As with File and Printer Sharing for Microsoft Networks, use the
Browse button to locate the folder that will be shared. Next, name the share
and optionally provide a description of its purpose. In addition, however,
enable the Apple Macintosh checkbox and provide a Macintosh share name.

Both Windows- and MacOS-accessible volumes appear when you select
the Shares folder under the System Tools Shared Folders branch, as shown in
Figure 13.24.

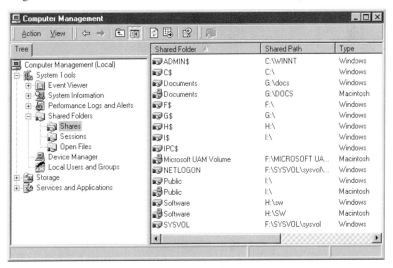

Figure 13.24   *Viewing Windows- and Macintosh-accessible volumes.*

Right-click a Macintosh volume and choose the Properties command to open the Properties dialog box shown in Figure 13.25.

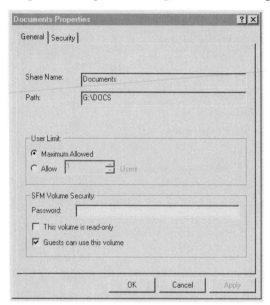

Figure 13.25 *Mac OS volume properties dialog box.*

If you wish to enable folder-specific password security, you may. You may also restrict the number of users who can access the volume and exclude Guests.

Note that you may restrict the volume to read-only. This is an NTFS permission, which overrides AppleShare privileges that might be set from the Macintosh desktop. As with Windows 2000, AppleShare allocates access to users and groups. In a Mac OS file sharing dialog box, you can give the Owner, another User or Group, and Everyone (including Guests) the same or varied levels of access.

Troubleshooting Shared Access

Problems with resource access are usually easy to solve. When users cannot log on, for example, first try the following:

- Make sure they are using the right user name.
- Make sure they are using the right password.
- Make sure the Caps Lock is off. Passwords are case sensitive.

- Make sure that the correct account database is selected in the drop-down menu at the bottom of the logon dialog box. (Users can log on to either the domain or to the workstation's local account database.)

Try logging on from the workstation using another account. If successful, recheck the user's account settings. It might be that the user's group memberships have changed or that a change in group rights is restricting the user. You might also check your security policies to see if restrictions are being applied to the user.

If unsuccessful, try logging in from another workstation. If that fails, you might need to repair the user accounts database using the emergency repair procedure. First, however, check the Computer Management MMC to see if the NetLogon, Server, and Workstation services are running properly. Also, check the network settings to ensure that the services are bound to the right applications and adapters.

Another useful resource for troubleshooting resource access is the MMC's Event Viewer snap-in Security Log. In order to use the Security Log, you must enable auditing. Once enabled, two types of events are tracked in the security log.

- **Success.** Indicated with a key symbol, this denotes successful resource access.
- **Failure.** Indicated with a padlock symbol, this denotes unsuccessful security access.

Numerous failures are an indication that a user might have reconfigured their logon settings, obviously without success.

If you see the error message "cannot connect to a domain controller" when you try to log on from a Windows workstation, first try changing its hardware configuration or network settings. There can be a number of causes, some of which can be resolved if you do the following:

- Making sure the account name you are using is listed in the SAM on the domain controller.
- Making sure the computer account has been added to the SAM.
- Making sure that the network bindings are properly installed.
- Making sure the computer does not have a duplicate computer name or IP address, incorrect subnet mask, or incorrect gateway address.

Where users report problems with NetWare access, make sure they have CSNW properly installed, have logged in to the correct preferred server or default tree and context, and have NWLink IPX/SPX/NetBIOS Compatible Transport protocol properly configured. If the GSNW is involved, make sure the Windows 2000 Server still has connectivity to the NetWare server.

When users report problems with Macintosh access, make sure they are looking for the server in the proper zone (if any are available) and that they have the correct authentication method configured (e.g., Microsoft UAM).

In any of these cases, verify that the appropriate client access types were configured for the folder in question to begin with (e.g., Microsoft, NetWare, Macintosh) using the Computer Management MMC.

Study Break

Create a Multiplatform Share

Practice what you have learned by creating a file share accessible to Microsoft Networking, NetWare, and Mac OS client access.

Install and configure GSNW and SFM. Next, use the Computer Management MMC to create a new share via the Create Shared Folder Wizard. Enable the checkboxes for Microsoft Windows, Novell NetWare, and Apple Macintosh client access. Customize access permissions. Verify your work by logging in from all three client types.

MCSE 13.2   Working with Network Protocols

Network protocols are the rules and procedures that govern communications between networked computers. They can be compared to human languages in that, as with humans, two computers must know the same language if communication is to take place between them. More precisely, they can be compared to human etiquette, such as parliamentary procedure. Unless computers adhere to rules, such as which of them may talk when, communication becomes garbled.

Windows 2000 Server makes the following network protocols available for use in a variety of situations:

- **TCP/IP.** The Transmission Control Protocol/Internet Protocol (TCP/IP) is the language of the Internet and Windows 2000 Server's default protocol. This easily routable, heterogeneous protocol is a global industry standard and is particularly useful in enterprise and WAN environments. Most computers can communicate with TCP/IP, including Windows clients, NetWare clients, UNIX and DEC workstations, IBM mainframes, and Apple Macintoshes—basically, any system that can be connected to the Internet. TCP/IP is, however, the most difficult protocol to administer.

Windows 2000 Server comes with three services that can be used to implement TCP/IP on an enterprise network. The Dynamic Host Configuration Protocol (DHCP) server manages a range of available addresses that it doles out automatically when a workstation attempts to use a TCP/IP service. The Domain Name Services (DNS) server lets an administrator map the names of local resources, such as servers and printers, to IP addresses. The Windows Internet Naming Service (WINS) server maps IP addresses to NetBIOS names. Finally, IIS supports HTTP and FTP services.

DNS, DHCP, WINS, and IP routing will be described in greater detail in the third section of this book, "Windows 2000 Networking."

- **NWLink IPX/SPX/NetBIOS Compatible Transport.** Microsoft's NetWare Link (NWLink) Internetwork Packet Exchange (IPX)/ Sequenced Packet Exchange (SPX)/NetBIOS Compatible Transport protocol was designed to make Windows 2000-based servers compatible with NetWare networks. Although used almost exclusively for this purpose, it is a complete network protocol in its own right and can be used instead of TCP/IP to support local connectivity.

  A Windows 2000-based computer can connect to client/server applications on a NetWare server using NWLink IPX/SPX/NetBIOS Compatible Transport protocol. In order to connect to file and print services on a NetWare server, Windows 2000 Server must be running both NWLink IPX/SPX/NetBIOS Compatible Transport protocol and GSNW. Windows 2000 Professional workstations must run NWLink IPX/SPX/NetBIOS Compatible Transport protocol and Client Services for NetWare (CSNW).

- **NetBEUI.** NetBIOS Enhanced User Interface (NetBEUI) is Windows' fastest protocol. It is useful only on nonextended LANS (and therefore generally small LANs) because it cannot be routed, except on Token Ring networks.

  (Routers are used to pass network communications between different networks or network segments. One can bridge NetBEUI network segments if necessary, however. Bridges connect multiple network segments while treating them all as one logical network. This is really only useful in increasing the size of a LAN).

  Designed by IBM in 1985, NetBEUI was the default network protocol for earlier Microsoft products such as Windows for Workgroups 3.1 and LAN Manager. Windows 2000 is capable of using it and can therefore communicate with computers running these earlier systems.

NetBEUI has some advantages over more robust protocols. It is self-configuring, self-tuning, and incurs little RAM overhead. On the downside, it generates a large number of network broadcasts that degrade network performance on large LANs. NetBEUI supports no more than 200 computers on a LAN.

- **DLC.** The Data Link Control (DLC) protocol was designed to enable communication between IBM mainframe systems and AS400 servers. Microsoft's Systems Network Architecture (SNA) server uses DLC as its underlying protocol to connect to IBM servers. More commonly, however, DLC is used with Hewlett-Packard LaserJet printers that are equipped with JetDirect NICs. These printing devices can also support TCP/IP, however, so that protocol is often used instead.

- **AppleTalk.** The native networking protocol of the Apple Macintosh, AppleTalk is installed in Windows 2000 Server as part of Services for Macintosh (SFM). It gives Mac OS users connectivity to Windows 2000 servers similar to that of Apple's AppleShare IP line of servers. It also permits Mac OS users to access Windows 2000-based print services. Like NetBEUI, AppleTalk is a self-configuring protocol that requires practically no maintenance. Unlike NetBEUI, it can be routed and supports large numbers of computers per network segment. It is therefore scalable to an enterprise environment.

The author of this book was among the team that created the Apple Certified Server Engineer (ACSE) program for Apple Computer. If you find yourself administering Mac OS-based workstations as well as Windows desktops, you might be interested in another book from this author titled *AppleShare IP* (ISBN: 0-12-208866-2). In addition to a wealth of information on AppleTalk network management, the book contains useful material on Mac-to-PC integration issues.

Network protocols will be described in greater detail in Chapter 18, "Administering Network Protocols."

Installing Network Protocols

You can install a network protocol by clicking the Local Area Connection icon in the Network and Dial-Up Connections folder. In the Local Area Connection Status dialog box, click the Properties button to open the Local Area Connection Properties dialog box. Click the Install button to open the Select

Network Component dialog box, and choose Protocol from the list. Click the Add button to open the Select Network Protocol dialog box, as shown in Figure 13.26.

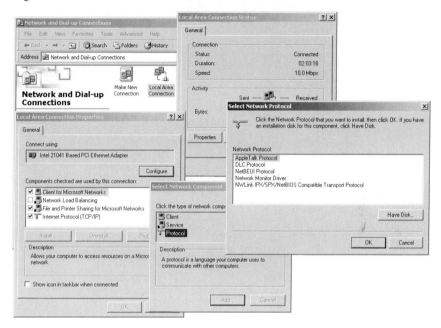

Figure 13.26 *Installing network protocols.*

If you do not see the protocol you wish to install, it might be that it was already installed as part of a file sharing service (e.g., GSNW, SFM). Select the appropriate protocol and click the OK button. You will then be prompted to restart the server.

Configuring Network Protocols

The configuration of network protocols varies in complexity from the easiest, NetBEUI, to the hardest, TCP/IP.

CONFIGURING TCP/IP

To configure TCP/IP LAN settings, double-click the Local Area Connection application to open the Local Area Connection Status dialog box. Click the Properties button to open the Local Area Properties dialog box and select the

TCP/IP protocol in the scrolling list. Click the Properties button to open the Internet Protocol (TCP/IP) Properties dialog box, as shown in Figure 13.27.

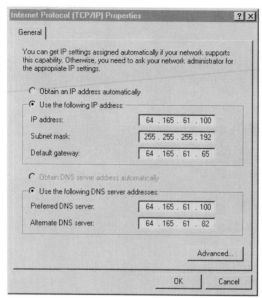

Figure 13.27 *Configuring General TCP/IP properties.*

GENERAL PROPERTIES • Since servers are expected to reside at the same address at all times, you will need to enable the Use the following IP address radio button to enable a static TCP/IP address configuration. In order to fill out the fields that this option makes active, you will need to know how TCP/IP works and is configured on your network, as was described in Chapter 6, "Networking Windows 2000 Professional."

Type in the appropriate numbers for IP address, subnet mask, default gateway, and DNS servers.

ADVANCED PROPERTIES • Additional configuration options are available when you click the Advanced button to open the Advanced TCP/IP Settings dialog box, as shown in Figure 13.28.

Choose the Edit button under the IP Settings tab to modify settings for multiple IP addresses and default gateways, if present.

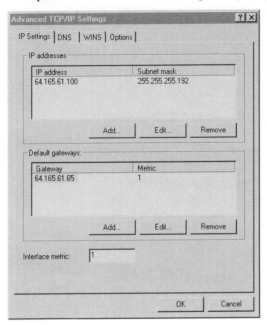

Figure 13.28 *Configuring the IP Settings tab.*

Enter the machine addresses for your network's DNS servers in the DNS server addresses field, in order of preference.

Also, enter the domain(s) for your network in the Append these DNS suffixes field (see Figure 13.29).

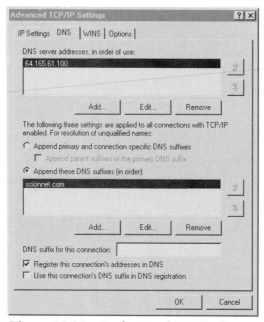

Figure 13.29 *Configuring the DNS tab.*

Configure the IP addresses of any servers that are running WINS in the WINS addresses field under the WINS tab (see Figure 13.30).

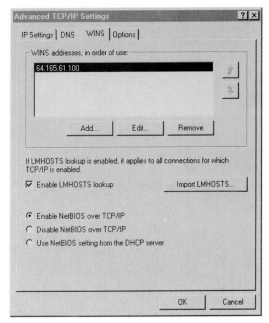

Figure 13.30 *Configuring the WINS tab.*

By default, the Enable LMHOSTS lookup checkbox is selected. This permits the use of a text list of IP address-to-NetBIOS name mappings for computers outside the local subnet. If the Enable NetBIOS over TCP/IP radio button is selected (the default), Windows 2000 will look up NetBIOS names against your DNS server.

To configure Internet Protocol Security (IPSec), a Windows 2000 networking safety feature that authenticates and encrypts packet data, double-click the IP security item under the Options tab, as shown in Figure 13.31, to open the IP Security dialog box.

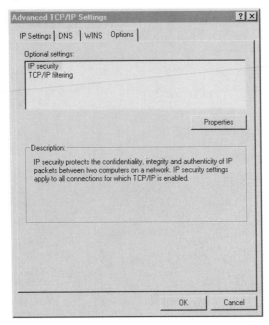

Figure 13.31 *Configuring IP Security under the Options tab.*

The following three security policies can be selected:

- **Client (respond only).** Your server will respond to other computers that request secure communications or do not use IPSec.
- **Secure Server (Require Security).** Your server will only use secured communications.
- **Server (Request Security).** Your server will request, but not require, secured communications.

The policy you choose will apply to all TCP/IP connections.

TCP/IP filtering allows you to specify which types of nontransit network traffic your server will be allowed to process. Enable this feature by double-clicking the TCP/IP filtering item under the Options tab to open the TCP/IP Filtering dialog box. Ports can be configured for the following three protocols:

- **TCP.** A connection-oriented protocol, TCP is used for large data transfers
- **UDP (Datagram Delivery Protocol).** A connectionless protocol used for small data transfers.

- **IP.** A connectionless protocol that provides packet delivery for all other TCP/IP protocols.

CONFIGURING IPX/SPX/NETBIOS COMPATIBLE TRANSPORT

As previously explained, NWLink IPX/SPX/NetBIOS Compatible Transport is Microsoft's implementation of the protocol that permits a Windows-client to connect to Novell NetWare servers and other network resources. To configure its settings, double-click the Local Area Connection application to open the Local Area Connection Status dialog box. Click the Properties button to open the Local Area Properties dialog box and select the NWLink IPX/SPX/NetBIOS Compatible Transport protocol in the scrolling list. Click the Properties button to open the Properties dialog box shown in Figure 13.32.

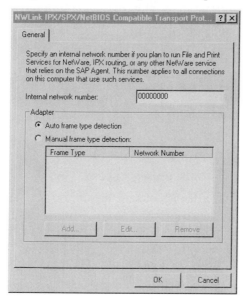

Figure 13.32 *Configuring the NWLink protocol.*

The first field under the General tab is for the Internal Network Number. This is somewhat like a TCP/IP subnet address. NetWare uses it to determine which servers are on the local network and which are on remote networks. It is important to add a number here whenever you intend to run file and print services, IPX routing, or any service that depends on a Service Advertising Protocol (SAP) agent.

The second field under the General tab is for Frame Type. Protocols divide data that is destined to move across the network into packets. These are passed to the NIC, which encapsulates them in frames. The types of frames used on your network will depend on both its physical media and the networking software deployed on it. The possibilities include:

- Ethernet 802.2
- Ethernet 802.3
- Ethernet II
- Ethernet SNAP

The details of this are beyond the scope of this section, but suffice it to say, you wish to have NWLink IPX/SPX/NetBIOS Compatible Transport protocol configured to use the same frame types that other servers are using. For example, modern servers running NetWare 3.12 or 4.x, Windows NT Server 3.5x or 4.0, or Windows 2000 Server commonly use the Ethernet 802.2 frame type. Older servers running NetWare 2.x or 3.11, or Windows NT Server 3.1 commonly use the Ethernet 802.3 frame type. The use of an incorrect frame type greatly degrades network performance.

The Institute of Electrical and Electronic Engineers (IEEE) 802.2 and 802.3 standards are different technologies, not different versions of the same technology. Novell's application of the word "Ethernet" to both standards is somewhat misleading, as all IEEE LANs support 802.2, including Token Ring, which is actually defined under standard 802.5! These standards all take their names from the time in which the IEEE's LAN standardization project began: 1980 (80), February (2).

Windows 2000 will attempt to detect the frame types used on your network automatically by sending out a Routing Information Protocol (RIP) query as NWLink IPX/SPX/NetBIOS Compatible Transport protocol is initialized. If it receives no response, it maintains its Ethernet 802.2 default setting. If it does receive a response, it uses that frame type and makes it the default for next time. If it receives multiple responses, it chooses the first frame type that comes up in the previous list. The Frame Type field under the General tab lets you change this behavior by manually setting the correct frame type.

Windows 2000 can also be configured for multiple frame types.

When NWLink IPX/SPX/NetBIOS Compatible Transport protocol is installed, the NWLINK NetBIOS component is installed alongside it. You cannot configure it, but you can disable it by deselecting its checkbox in the Local Area Connections Properties dialog box. When enabled, Windows 2000 sends its file and printer sharing information using NetBIOS over IPX. When disabled, these messages are sent over IPX directly (a process called direct hosting). This can be handy for pure NetWare environments.

CONFIGURING NETBEUI, DLC, AND APPLETALK

Configuring NetBEUI and DLC is easy—you don't. To configure AppleTalk's settings, double-click the Local Area Connection application to open the Local Area Connection Status dialog box. Click the Properties button to open the Local Area Properties dialog box and select the AppleTalk protocol in the scrolling list. Click the Properties button to open the properties dialog box shown in Figure 13.33.

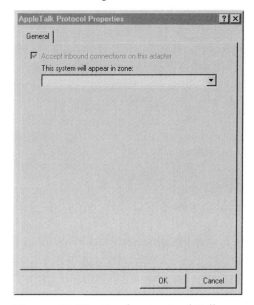

Figure 13.33 *Configuring AppleTalk.*

If your network has an AppleTalk router residing on it, the server will be placed in a default AppleTalk zone. A zone is a logical collection of Apple-Talk devices used to make browsing for computers easier. Like domains, they are commonly named for departments (e.g., "Accounting"), locations, (e.g., "San Francisco"), or services (e.g., "Servers"). You may choose to put the server in a different zone using the pop-up menu.

Troubleshooting Network Protocols

Most clients will use TCP/IP, NWLink IPX/SPX/NetBIOS Compatible Transport, NetBEUI, or some combination of these to connect to the server. Although each network protocol has its own characteristics, all rely on the NetBIOS Computer Name. No two Computer Names can be alike. When a client starts up, it will query the network for Computer Names. If there is a conflict, the client's networking services will not start up. This error can be detected in the Event Viewer snap-in and is solved by simply making sure all networked computers have different Computer Names.

Other problems are unique to each protocol.

TROUBLESHOOTING TCP/IP

Most of the problems encountered with TCP/IP pertain to its configuration at either the server or client end. Windows provides many utilities helpful in troubleshooting TCP/IP configuration errors.

TROUBLESHOOTING WITH PING • The Packet Internet Gopher (PING) utility verifies a TCP/IP connection by sending Internet Control Message Protocol (ICMP) packets to remote hosts and listening for echo reply packets. PING waits up to one second for each packet sent, displaying the number of packets transmitted and received. It sends four packets by default, but you can change this behavior using command line switches to increase the duration where faulty physical links are suspected.

To test a connection, use the PING command with an IP address, a host name, or a NetBIOS computer name. It is best to use the IP address initially to isolate the problem as related to connectivity vs. host name resolution (DNS).

You can use the following procedures to help locate the cause of TCP/IP problems:

- **Ping the local host.** To find out if the client's TCP/IP protocol stack is working properly, test the configuration of the computer by typing:

```
PING localhost
```

Localhost is a reserved host name that is mapped to a reserved IP address (127.0.0.1) that represents your computer. If pinging your local host is successful, you will receive four replies from IP address 127.0.0.1. If the PING command is unsuccessful, you will receive a message telling you "localhost is unknown."

If the test is unsuccessful, make sure that the TCP/IP protocol is present on the computer, that the network adapter is properly installed, and that the TCP/IP protocol has been bound to the network adapter.

You can further verify the configuration of the local host by using the PING command with the actual IP address of the local computer. If all is well, you should get immediate replies. If this test is unsuccessful, check to make sure that the correct IP address was configured.

- **Ping a nearby host.** You can verify that network communications are possible between your computer and another host on your local subnet by using the PING command with the IP address of that other computer. If all is well, you should see packets going out on and coming back over the network. If the test is unsuccessful, check to make sure that the proper IP addresses, subnet masks, and gateway addresses are configured on both hosts.

- **Ping the gateway.** You can verify that network communications are possible between your computer and a router by using the PING command with the IP address of the gateway. If all is well, you should see packets going out on and coming back over the network, just as when you pinged the other host. If there is a problem, the packets will not be returned in the required time and you will see error messages. If the test is unsuccessful, you should first make sure the router is available (e.g., that it is powered up and connected to the network). Check again to make sure the local host is configured with the correct subnet mask and gateway addresses.

    You might also need to verify that the router is configured properly. Routers have multiple IP addresses for the multiple subnets on which they reside. The port that is connected to the subnet on which your local host resides must have an IP address and subnet mask that is valid for your subnet. Other ports must have IP addresses and subnet masks that are valid for those subnets and/or the Internet. You can verify all of these ports by pinging each of their addresses.

- **Ping a remote host.** You can verify that network communications are possible between your computer and a remote host on another subnet or the Internet by using the PING command with the IP address of that remote host. You should see packets going out on and coming back over the network via the gateway router. If there is a problem, the packets will not be returned in the required time and you will see timeout messages.

    If the test is unsuccessful, and you have already performed the previous tests to determine that local connectivity is possible, then the problem might lie with routers or hosts beyond your network.

TROUBLESHOOTING WITH PATHPING • New to Windows 2000, PATHPING is a hybrid of PING that adds the functionality of the TRACERT (Trace Route) utility. If you can ping your default gateway but not a remote host, employ this utility next. It displays the domain name and IP address of each gateway along the route to a remote host, along with the percentage of packet loss occurring at each hop. You can use PATHPING with either the host name or IP address of the remote computer.

Document the information that the PATHPING command returns when the remote host is available. Later, if the remote host becomes "unreachable," you can compare the information returned by PATHPING with the earlier results to determine which gateway is down.

TROUBLESHOOTING WITH NETSTAT • The NETSTAT utility lists the TCP/IP ports that are in use during communications sessions, so that you can determine if certain ports are not being accepted across the link. This is commonly brought about because the ports are being blocked at a firewall. If you find this is a problem, contact the administrator of the firewall to determine a solution.

TROUBLESHOOTING DNS NAME RESOLUTION • If you can successfully ping a host using the IP address but fail when you attempt to use a host name, it is time to analyze DNS name resolution. A proper resolution would match the host name with the IP address and successfully execute the PING command.

A TCP/IP host name (e.g., "my_pc.mycompany.com") can be mapped to an IP address on the Internet or an intranet by a DNS server or a "HOSTS.SAM" file. On corporate networks, the NetBIOS computer name (e.g., "My PC") can be mapped to an IP address on an intranet by a WINS server or "LMHOSTS.SAM" file.

You can use the HOSTNAME command to view the computer name of the local host. To determine if the local host is capable of resolving a domain name, you can use the NSLOOKUP utility. It can be launched from the Command Prompt with the following format:

```
NSLOOKUP <host_name>
```

If it works, the appropriate IP address will be returned. If not, verify that the correct DNS server information has been configured on the server and verify the database on the name server.

TROUBLESHOOTING WINS NAME RESOLUTION • Use the NBTSTAT utility to view statistics relating to NetBIOS over TCP/IP parameters. Verify NetBIOS name resolution by establishing a session with another host. If you are unable to establish a session, verify that both hosts are using the same NetBIOS scope IDs. (NetBIOS scopes permit the creation of logical TCP/IP networks that are invisible to one another.) If your network is configured in this manner, you will need to configure the scope ID, as hosts can only communicate if they belong to the same NetBIOS scope.

Also check the local name cache. Make sure that its entries are correct using the NBTSTAT utility with the –C switch. If there is incorrect data there, reload the cache (–R switch) and try the session again. If there is no problem with the name cache, verify that the correct WINS server information has been configured on the server.

TROUBLESHOOTING WITH NETWORK MONITOR

A valuable tool for the general troubleshooting of network protocols is Network Monitor, which can be installed as a network service. To use it, launch it from the Administrative Tools program groups, select the network adapter connected to the network you wish to monitor, and then choose the Start command under the Capture menu. The utility will begin displaying network statistics in four windowpanes, as shown in Figure 13.34.

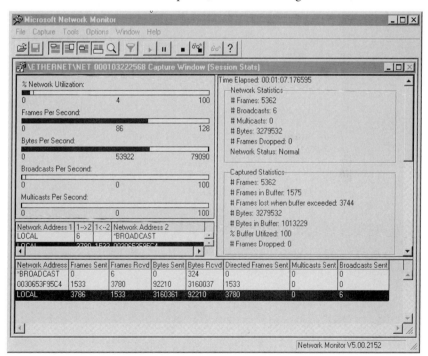

Figure 13.34 *Network Monitor window.*

The Graph pane (upper left) displays the current network activity in five bars: % Network Utilization, Frames Per Second, Bytes Per Second, Broadcasts Per Second, and Multicasts Per Second.

The Session Statistics pane (lower left) shows the exchange of information between nodes on the network, including the amount of data exchanged and its direction of travel, per session. Network Monitor will track up to 128 sessions.

The Total Statistics pane (upper right) displays information about overall network activity. This statistics are listed in five categories:

NETWORK STATISTICS •

- • # Frames
- • # Broadcasts
- • # Multicasts
- • # Bytes
- • # Frames Dropped
- • Network Status

CAPTURED STATISTICS •

- • # Frames
- • # Frames in Buffer
- • # Frames lost when buffer exceeded
- • # Bytes
- • # Bytes in Buffer
- • % Buffers Utilized
- • # Frames Dropped

PER SECOND STATISTICS •

- • # Frames/second
- • # Bytes/second
- • # Broadcasts/second
- • # Multicasts/second
- • % Network Utilization

NETWORK CARD (MAC) STATISTICS •

- • # Frames
- • # Broadcasts
- • # Multicasts
- • # Bytes

NETWORK CARD (MAC) ERROR STATISTICS •

- • Cyclical Redundancy Check (CRC) Errors
- • # Frames Dropped (No Buffers)
- • # Frames Dropped (Hardware)

The Station Statistics pane (lower right) displays information about each workstation's activity on the network. These can be sorted by Network Address, Frames Sent, Frames, Bytes Sent, Bytes Received, Directed Frames Sent, Multicasts Sent, and Broadcasts Sent.

The nuances of protocol analysis are beyond the scope of this section. However, some things to look out for here include dropped frames and high, sustained networked utilization. Also look for nodes that "ghost," disappearing and then reappearing. These are most often signs of bad network cabling.

Network protocols will be described in greater detail in Chapter 18, "Administering Network Protocols."

Study Break

Install and Configure Protocols

Practice what you have learned by installing and configuring a protocol other than the default TCP/IP.

For example, install NWLink IPX/SPX/NetBIOS Compatible Transport protocol and configure its network number. Also install its file and printer sharing components (GSNW). Similarly configure a workstation, and verify that access is possible between client and server. You might decide to use the new protocol instead of TCP/IP for LAN communications.

MCSE 13.3   Working with Network Services

Windows 2000 comes with a few network services that can be vital in some circumstances.

Installing and Configuring Network Services

You can install a network service by clicking the Local Area Connection icon in the Network and Dial-Up Connections folder. In the Local Area Connection Status dialog box, click the Properties button to open the Local Area Connection Properties dialog box. Click the Install button to open the Select

Network Component dialog box, and choose Service from the list. Click the Add button to open the Select Network Service dialog box, as shown in Figure 13.35.

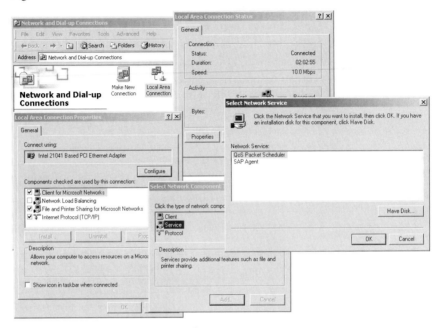

Figure 13.35   *Installing network services.*

Other network services can be installed by selecting the Install Add-On Components link in the installation CD-ROM's Autorun screen to open the Windows Components Wizard.

In addition to the software described elsewhere, you can install the following network services:

- **Quality of Service (QoS) Packet Scheduler.** Installed via the Select Network Service dialog box, this service provides network traffic control functions and is used in conjunction with the QoS Admission Control component.
- **SAP Agent.** Installed via the Select Network Service dialog box, this service supports the network advertising of NetWare resources.
- **Connection Manager Components.** Installed via the Windows Components Wizard, this component installs the Connection Manager Administration Kit (CMAK) and Phone Book Service.
- **Simple Network Management Protocol (SNMP).** Installed via the Windows Components Wizard, this component provides informa-

tion on networking hardware and software to remote SNMP management consoles.

- **COM Internet Services Proxy.** Installed via the Windows Components Wizard, this component permits Distributed Components Object Model (DCOM) elements to travel via HTTP.
- **Network Monitor Tools.** Installed via the Windows Components Wizard, this component enables the local packet analyzer described in the last section of this chapter.
- **Internet Authentication Service (IAS).** Installed via the Windows Components Wizard, this component supports the RADIUS protocol for dialup connection authentication.
- **QoS Admission Control.** Installed via the Windows Components Wizard, this component lets you specify the quality parameters for each network segment.
- **Simple TCP/IP Services.** Installed via the Windows Components Wizard, this component provides character generator, time, echo, and quote of the day services.
- **Site Server Internet Locator Service (ILS) Services.** Installed via the Windows Components Wizard, this component provides current user information.

Other network services, described elsewhere, include DNS, DHCP, WINS, SFM, and Print Services for UNIX.

Study Break

Install Network Services

Practice what you have learned by installing a network service.

For example, if you have installed GSNW, install SAP Agent as well. If you are running TCP/IP, install simple TCP/IP services. Verify that the services are operational in the Computer Management MMC's Services snap-in.

MCSE 13.4   **Working with Remote Access Services**

Thus far we have described Windows 2000 Server networking components and services in terms of their LAN applications. For many organizations, the ability to access these resources remotely is of equal importance. This is made possible through the installation and configuration of Routing and

Remote Access Services (RRAS), which provides the functionality of Dial-Up Networking, multiprotocol routing, and Virtual Private Network (VPN) connections. This material was first touched upon in Chapter 6, and will be covered in more detail in Chapter 17, "Administering Remote Access Services."

Installing Remote Access

RRAS is installed under Windows 2000 Server by default, but not activated. Prior to activating it, you must install and configure the network protocols that will be used with RRAS and verify that all communications components, such as modems and network adapters, are working properly (e.g., using Device Manager). You may then select the Routing and Remote Access item from the Administrative Tools program group to open the Routing and Remote Access MMC, as shown in Figure 13.36.

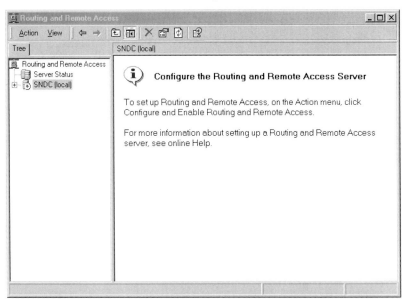

Figure 13.36 *Opening the Routing and Remote Access MMC.*

Next, select the Configure and Enable Routing and Remote Access command from the Action menu to launch the Routing and Remote Access Server Setup Wizard, as shown in Figure 13.37.

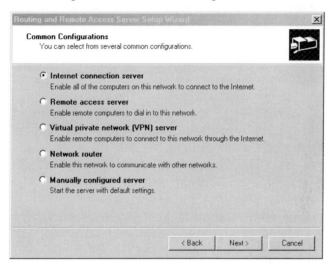

Figure 13.37 *Selecting a RRAS server configuration.*

The wizard will prompt you to choose among the following common configurations:

- **Internet connection server.** This option enables Internet Connection Sharing (ICS) through a modem, network adapter, or some other communications device, making your server a gateway between the Internet and workstations on the local network.
- **Remote access server.** Permits remote computers to connect with your server, and by extension the LAN, over a dialup device.
- **Virtual Private Network (VPN) server.** Permits remote computers to securely connect with your server and network via their own Internet Service Providers (ISPs).
- **Network router.** This option permits you to establish the Windows 2000 Server as a router between separate networks, for which you have separate network adapters installed.
- **Manually configured server.** This option enables a few initial settings for RRAS, then lets you configure the rest. This is useful when the other options will not meet your needs.

Select the Remote access server radio button to continue. In subsequent windows, you will be prompted for the following:

- **Remote Client Protocols.** Confirm that all of the necessary LAN protocols are in place, or choose to install additional protocols.
- **Guest Authentication.** If AppleTalk was among your network protocol choices, you will be informed that remote access can either be granted to anyone via the Guest account or restricted to authenticated users. If you enable unauthenticated access, any dialup client—not just Macintosh clients—can gain server access without name or password.
- **Network selection.** If your server resides on more than one network segment, you will be directed to choose the network adapter attached to the network to which dialup users will be granted access.
- **IP Address Assignment.** Assuming TCP/IP was among your network protocol choices, you will be prompted to determine how dialup clients will receive their own valid IP addresses, either via DHCP or from a range of addresses that you specify.
- **Managing Multiple Remote Access Servers.** If there is more than one remote access server on your network, you can enable the IAS/ RADIUS option to provide a centralized authentication database to serve them.

Configuring Remote Access

After you complete the wizard, RRAS will start, thereafter becoming accessible through the Routing and Remote Access MMC, as shown in Figure 13.38.

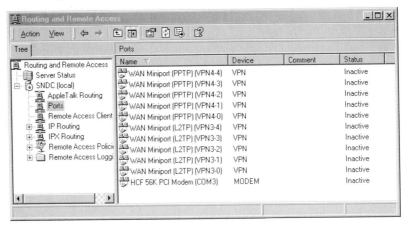

Figure 13.38 *Configuring Remote Access Server.*

You may use the Routing and Remote Access MMC to configure RRAS protocol by protocol and port by port, as well as to adjust policies and view log activity.

CONFIGURING INBOUND CONNECTIONS

Once your remote access server is established, client computers can connect to it in a variety of ways. In so doing, they will call into play devices and ports. For the purposes of RRAS, devices are hardware and software that create physical and logical point-to-point connections between the client and server. For example, analog modems or Integrated Services Digital Network (ISDN) adapters would be considered devices. Ports are the channels that devices provide to support single point-to-point connections. An analog modem has one port, for example. An ISDN adapter has several, such as a port for each "B" channel.

The Routing and Remote Access Server Setup Wizard provides an initial configuration for several ports for you, as can be seen in Figure 13.38. To view the details of these configurations, right-click the Ports branch from the local server listing in the MMC and choose the Properties command from the resulting pop-up menu to open the Ports Properties dialog box, as shown in Figure 13.39.

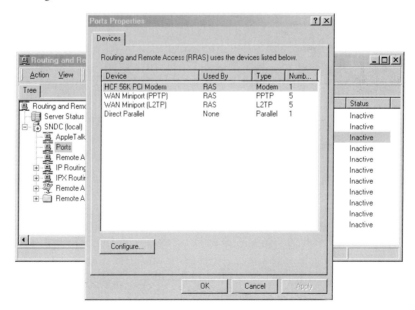

Figure 13.39 *Viewing port configurations.*

To enable or disable the use of a specific device, select it in the list and click the Configure button to open the Configure Device dialog box, as shown in Figure 13.40.

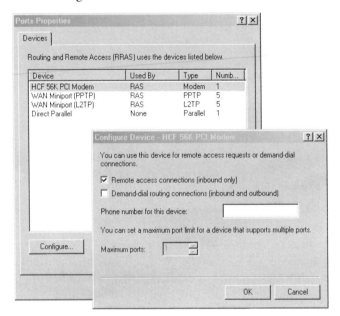

Figure 13.40   *Enabling access through a device.*

By default, a modem is configured to accept incoming calls only. If you wish to use the device for dial-out connections also, perhaps to connect to an ISP, you can enable the Demand dial routing connections checkbox and supply a phone number.

RRAS also enables several VPN ports by default. These can be of the following two types:

- **Point-to-Point Tunneling Protocol (PPTP).** PPTP allows a Dial-Up Networking client to establish secure communication sessions with a RAS server via the insecure Internet. Using the Extensible Authentication Protocol (EAP), PPTP supports encryption for both communications and authentication, making remote access as secure as access on a local network segment. In operation, a remote client connects to the Internet using an ISP dialup account. Once IP connectivity has been established, a PPTP "tunnel" is created through which IP, IPX, and NetBEUI protocols can travel while encapsulated in Point-to-Point (PPP) packets.

- **Layer Two Tunneling Protocol (L2TP).** L2TP is similar in function to PPTP in that it creates an encrypted tunnel through the Internet.

Unlike PPTP, however, it does not encrypt its sessions directly, relying instead on such technologies for tunnel encryption and authentication. In addition, L2TP supports such packet-oriented protocols as X.25, Frame Relay, UDP, and Asynchronous Transfer Mode (ATM), while PPTP is limited to IP.

By default, RRAS enables five ports for each VPN protocol. The PPTP and L2TP WAN Miniports can be configured in the same manner as modem ports, except that you are given the option of increasing the number of ports.

You may also configure ports for direct cable and infrared connections.

CREATING REMOTE ACCESS POLICY

Under Windows NT 3.5 and 4.0, providing RAS access to users was a simple matter of enabling dial-in permissions for their accounts and, if desired, configuring a callback number. Under Windows 2000, security has been enhanced to make user access not only dependent on the permissions assigned to their user accounts, but also on the settings of the server's remote access policy. These policies let you base the decision of whether or not to allow access on such criteria as time of day, connection type, group membership, and so on. When a user dials in, his connection attempt must meet the criteria defined by at least one remote access policy. If not, access is denied regardless of the permission granted the user account.

Windows 2000 Server can use the following three models in implementing dialup access permissions.

ACCESS BY USER • This model, the same under Windows NT Server 4.0, controls user access by enabling or disabling access under the Dial-in tab in the user account dialog box, as shown in Figure 13.41.

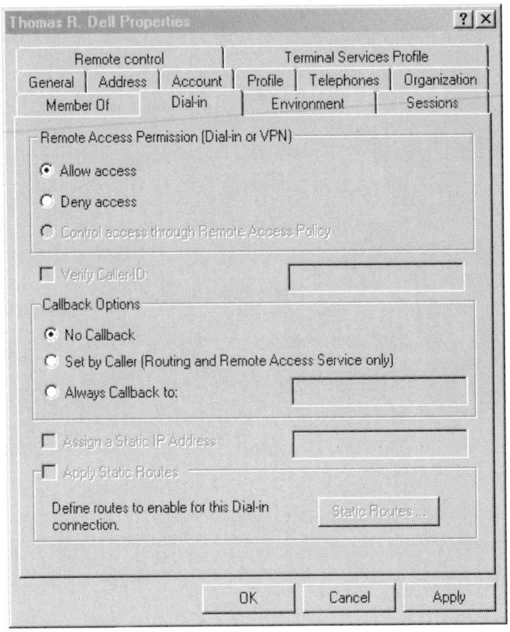

Figure 13.41 *Enabling remote access by user.*

Three scenarios are possible under this model. If you explicitly permit access by enabling the Allow access radio button, access will be permitted if the connection attempt matches conditions specified by the user account's dial-in properties and remote access profile. If you explicitly disallow access by enabling the Deny access button, access will not be permitted. If you explicitly permit access by enabling the Allow access radio button, but the connection attempt does not match conditions specified by the user account's dial-in properties and profile, access will not be permitted!

This option is available when the remote access server is based on a standalone server, a server that is a member of a Windows NT 4.0 domain, or a server that is a member of a Windows 2000 native-mode or mixed mode domain.

ACCESS BY POLICY UNDER NATIVE MODE • Under this model, access is dependent upon the remote access policy set for all users. If the policy's remote access permission is set to grant access and a connection attempt matches policy conditions as well as the settings of the user account's dial-in properties and profile, access will be permitted. If the policy's remote access permission is set to deny access, the connection will be denied even if the connection attempt matches the policy's conditions. If a connection attempt fails to match the conditions of any access policies or settings, access will not be permitted.

This option is available when the remote access server is based on a standalone server or a server that is a member of a Windows 2000 native-mode domain.

ACCESS BY POLICY UNDER MIXED MODE • Under this model, if a connection attempt matches remote access policy conditions and the settings of the user account's dial-in properties and profile, access is permitted. If a connection attempt matches the conditions of the remote access policy but differs from the profile settings, access will not be permitted. (To enable this restriction, enable the Restrict dial-in to this number only option and use a number not used by RRAS.) If the connection attempt does not match the conditions of any remote access policies, access is not permitted.

You may create remote access policies by selecting the Remote Access Policies branch in the Routing and Remote Access MMC and choosing the New Remote Access Policy command from the Action menu. First, you will be prompted to name the policy. Next, you will be prompted by choose the policies criteria by clicking the Add button in the Add Remote Access Policy dialog box, as shown in Figure 13.42.

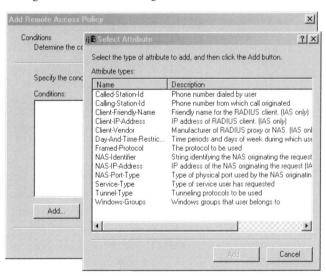

Figure 13.42 *Adding policy conditions.*

In the Select Attribute dialog box, you may select conditions that must be met before access will be granted, such as the incoming call must originate with a certain caller ID or use the specified tunneling protocol. Next, you will be prompted to specify whether access should be granted or denied based on the selected conditions. Finally, you are given the option to create a remote access profile.

CONFIGURING REMOTE ACCESS PROFILES

Remote access profile settings are applied to connections that have been authorized by user account permissions and remote access policy conditions, as shown in Figure 13.43.

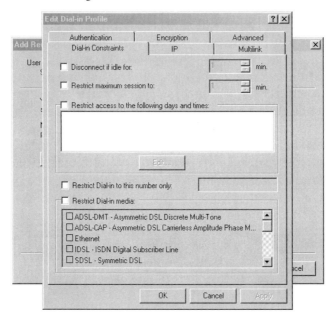

Figure 13.43 *Setting dialin contraints.*

Restrictions can be configured under the following tabs in the Edit Dial-In Profile dialog box:

- **Dial-In Constraints.** Contains such settings as disconnect on idle, restrict session length, restrict access to certain days and times, permit certain dial-in numbers only, or permit only certain dial-in media.
- **IP.** Defines IP address assignment behaviors and applies packet filters.
- **Multilink.** Multilinking increases data transmission rates by combining multiple physical links (e.g., multiple modems and telephone lines) into a logical connection that increases bandwidth. You can allow or deny the use of multilinking under this tab, as well as establish Bandwidth Allocation Protocol (BAP) settings.

- **Authentication.** Lets you choose from several authentication methods, including nonencrypted and nonauthenticated access.
- **Encryption.** Contains permissible encryption settings: No Encryption, Basic, Strong, or any combination thereof.
- **Advanced.** Lets you establish many RADIUS attributes used in communications with the IAS server.

Monitoring Remote Access

You can monitor your RRAS server port by port. Simply right-click a port in the Routing and Remote Access MMC and select the Status command from the pop-up menu to view current condition, connection duration, network addresses and names, bytes in, bytes out, and protocol error statistics.

Troubleshooting Remote Access

If RRAS access fails, first check the Event Viewer snap-in for any useful messages in the System Log. You might also consult the Routing and Remote Access MMC Port Status dialog box to see if it has recorded any error statistics. This can tell you if it is a server-related or connection-related failure.

Some common RRAS problems and solutions are as follows:

- The connection fails during authentication. This situation is often caused by incompatible encryption methods. Try switching both server and client to the clear text authentication option. If it works, then it was probably incompatible encryption methods that caused the problem.
- Multilink does not work with call back. Multilink can be used to establish a session between client and server over multiple phone lines. If the call back option is enabled, however, RAS will only call a user back using one phone line. The exception is with ISDN, where both channels can still be used on call back.

Study Break

Activate RRAS

Practice what you have learned by activating RRAS on the Windows 2000 Server.

First, install any network protocols that will be needed to support client communications. Next, confirm that all communications hardware and software is working correctly using Device Manager. Next, launch the Routing and Remote Access MMC and activate RRAS. Finally, go to a client workstation and confirm RRAS operations by dialing into the server.

MCSE 13.5   Working with Virtual Private Networks

As mentioned in the previous section of this chapter, VPNs make possible secure private communications via the very public and insecure Internet.

Installing VPNs

Installing VPN access to your RRAS server was described in the previous section of this chapter. Installing VPN access between your server and another RRAS server, presumably located at one of your organization's distant locations, requires that you employ the Network Connection Wizard. This can be launched via the Make New Connection item in the Networking and Dial-Up Connections program group.

Configure an outgoing VPN connection by performing the following steps:

1. Select the Connect to a private network through the Internet radio button in the Network Connection Wizard to establish dialup settings for secure connections between your server and another dialup server.
2. Specify the existing dialup connection that should be used, if any. Choose the Automatically dial this initial connection radio button and choose from the options in the drop menu, such as a previously configured private network or Internet connection. Alternately, create an entirely new connection by selecting the Do not dial the initial connection radio button.
3. Supply the host name or IP address of the host to which you are connecting, such as a Windows 2000 Server computer.

4. Apply the connection to all user profiles or yours exclusively.
5. Name the connection.

Configuring VPNs

When completed, the wizard will create a connection icon in the Network and Dial-Up Connections program group under the name you defined. Right-click the item and choose the Properties command from the pop-up menu to configure the connection's various options, as shown in Figure 13.44.

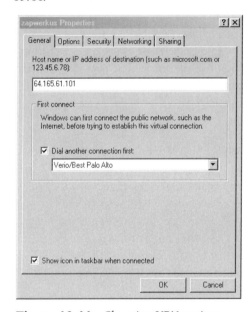

Figure 13.44 *Choosing VPN settings.*

Numerous settings can be configured under the following tabs in the connection properties dialog box:

- **General.** Specifies the remote host and dialup connection.
- **Options.** Specifies dialing options, such as prompting for name and password, and redial options.
- **Security.** Establishes the use of authentication and data encryption. Enable the Advanced radio button and click the Settings button to a make available a more extensive list of security protocol options. You can specify that data encryption be required for all connections, be disabled for all connections, or be made optional depending on the dialup server's capabilities. Similarly, you can choose among various options for how your server will encrypt authentication information,

which may vary between servers. Password Authentication Protocol (PAP) is the least secure. Challenge Handshake Authentication Protocol (CHAP) is the most secure. Enable the Extensible Authentication Protocol (EAP) radio button to override traditional PAP or CHAP settings in favor of some other public key or certificate authentication method, such as Message Digest 5 (MD5)-CHAP and Smart Card or other Certificate. The latter implements Transport Level Security (TLS).

- **Networking.** Lets you choose between PPTP or L2TP line protocols, and choose the LAN protocols supported by the network to which you are calling.
- **Sharing.** Permits you to enable connection sharing and on-demand dialing. If you enable on-demand dialing, you may establish criteria via the Settings button for which applications and services will be allowed to initiate it.

Troubleshooting VPNs

Common problems that affect VPN access include incompatible authentication and/or encryption methods, and a failure to by the user to pass the authentication process because of remote access policy or profile restrictions. If you are having trouble with a client-server VPN connection, make sure that both computers are capable of using the same authentication method, encryption technologies, and are running the same line protocols (e.g., PPTP, L2TP) and network protocols (e.g., IPX, NetBEUI).

VPNs will be covered in more detail in Chapter 17.

Study Break

Create a VPN

Practice what you have learned by creating a VPN connection between a workstation and the Windows 2000 Server.

On the server side, activate RRAS using the Routing and Remote Access MMC. Make sure incoming VPN ports are available and active. On the client side, configure a dialup connection to the server using the Network Connection Wizard. Make sure that your logon is acceptable to the server's remote access policy, user account properties, and profile settings. Make sure both client and server are using the same authentication and encryption techniques and running the same LAN protocols. Finally, test your configuration by establishing a VPN connection.

MCSE 13.6 **Working with Terminal Services**

Terminal Services permits users to run applications from the Windows 2000 Server rather than their own workstations. Candidates for this type of access include the following:

- Workstations running 32-bit Windows operating systems, such as Windows 9x/Me, Windows NT 3.51 or 4.0, or Windows 2000 Professional.
- Workstations running 16-bit Windows for Workgroups 3.11 (with Microsoft TCP/IP-32).
- Handheld and terminal computers running Windows CE.

Built upon TCP/IP and Remote Desktop Protocol (RDP), Terminal Services can be installed to run in one of two modes:

- **Remote Administration Mode.** This mode permits Administrators to connect to, monitor, configure, and troubleshoot the server using its own Windows 2000 Graphical User Interface (GUI) from any networked location. No special licensing is required, but only two administrators can be logged on simultaneously.
- **Application Server Mode.** This mode permits users to run Windows-based applications from the server, a real boon to clients that would not otherwise have the local computing power to run the applications on their own.

In operation, RDP passes the client's keystrokes and mouse navigation to the server for processing, then returns the server's audio and screen display. Based on the International Telecommunications Union (ITU) T.120 protocol, RDP is capable of varying its compression algorithms to meet the needs of different connection speeds and to alter its encryption levels from 40 bits to 128 bits.

Installing Terminal Services

Terminal Services is installed via the Windows Components Wizard. After enabling the checkbox next to its listing, you will be prompted to choose between remote administration and application server mode, as shown in Figure 13.45.

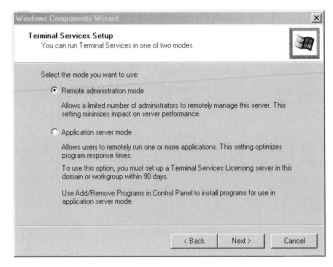

Figure 13.45   *Choosing Terminal Services modes.*

You can run your server in either mode, but not both. Fortunately, you can switch between modes after installation.

If you choose to install Terminal Services in application server mode, you will also need to install the Terminal Services Licensing component. When running the Windows Components Wizard, you will be prompted to choose between Windows 2000 or Terminal Server 4.0 permissions. The former is more secure, while the later is compatible with the Windows NT Server 4.0 implementation of Terminal Services.

Next, you might be presented with a list of previously installed applications that might not run, or run properly, under Terminal Services. They will need to be reinstalled using versions optimized for Terminal Services. Finally, you will be asked which role the server should take in doling out licenses: license server to the entire enterprise or just to the domain/workgroup.

Configuring Terminal Services

A successful installation of Terminal Services will populate the Administrative Tools program group with Terminal Services Configuration, Terminal Services Client Creator, Terminal Services Manager, and Terminal Services Licensing items.

Use the Terminal Services Configuration tool to reconfigure the choices you made in installing Terminal Services, such as the operational mode, as shown in Figure 13.46.

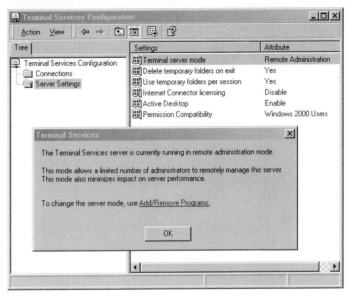

Figure 13.46 *Configuring Terminal Services.*

In addition, you can delete enable settings for temporary folders and Active Desktop, among others. Switch to the Connections branch to modify such connection properties as logon account, encryption level, and network adapter.

REMOTELY ADMINISTERING SERVERS

When running Terminal Services, you can perform practically any administrative task that you would otherwise perform while physically sitting at the machine, even rebooting! The performance drain is mercifully low in remote administration mode, so users will be not be affected by your distant tinkering. You can even copy and paste data between local and remote clipboards.

CONFIGURING APPLICATION SHARING

While remote administration mode is light on the server processor, applications server mode is not so unobtrusive. Terminal Services requires 128 MBs of base RAM and a Pentium or higher processor, plus at least another 3 to 9 MBs of RAM for each user.

CONFIGURING APPLICATIONS

In most cases, you will need to perform some extra steps after installing Terminal Services to get the service up and running for application sharing. First, you will need to install or reinstall the applications that will be shared from the server, using the Add/Remove Programs control panel application. Next, you probably need to run a few compatibility scripts. Be sure to do this prior to letting any users open a session.

Monitoring Terminal Services

Administrators can monitor Terminal Services using the Terminal Services Manager application. This tool lists all users logged on and the processes they are running from the server. It also permits Administrators to close user sessions or kill processes, if necessary.

Troubleshooting Terminal Services

Administrators can also use Terminal Services Manager to jump into a session when a user is having trouble with an application. Administrators can see what the user is doing and intervene with their own keystrokes and mouse movements. As well as send on-screen messages to the users.

Should you need to shut down a computer that is acting as an applications server, it is best to do so via the command line rather than the Start menu by using the TSSHUTDN command. This informs users that the server will be shutting down (in 60 seconds by default) so that they can close out of their work gracefully. Add the /REBOOT switch to the command if you wish to simply restart the server.

Study Break

Enable Terminal Services

Practice what you have learned by installing Terminal Services in remote administration mode.

Run the Windows Components Wizard to install Terminal Services. Next, log into the server from a remote workstation and experiment by performing various administration tasks.

| MCSE 13.7 | **Working with Network Adapters** |

Windows 2000 supports a range of network types and associated adapters.

Installing Network Adapters

When you install Windows 2000 Server, any installed network adapters are detected and configured automatically. Thereafter you can add additional adapters to service other network segments using Plug-and-Play and the Add/Remove hardware Wizard.

Configuring Network Adapters

Network adapter hardware is configured in the same manner as any other hardware device. To view a network adapter's settings, click the Local Area Connection icon in the Network and Dial-Up Connections folder. In the Local Area Connection Status dialog box, click the Properties button to open the Local Area Connection Properties dialog box. Next, select an adapter from the Connect using pop-down menu and click the Configure button to open the properties dialog box shown in Figure 13.47.

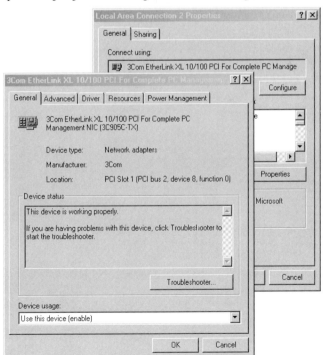

Figure 13.47 *Configuring network adapter settings.*

As with other hardware devices, you can verify operating status, review or adjust resource allocations, and update drivers.

One way in which network adapters differ from other hardware devices is in their use of bindings. Bindings, as the name implies, determine which network protocols will run on any given network adapters. In the case of services such as File and Printer Sharing for Microsoft Networks, they also determine the order in which protocols will be chosen when more than one is running on a network. For example, if you are running both NetBEUI and TCP/IP on the same network, you might wish to give the use of NetBEUI priority over TCP/IP in terms of file sharing because of its inherent speed.

To configure a network adapter's bindings, select the appropriate Local Area Connection item in the Network and Dial-Up Connections folder, then choose the Advanced Settings command from the Advanced menu bar item to open the dialog box shown in Figure 13.48.

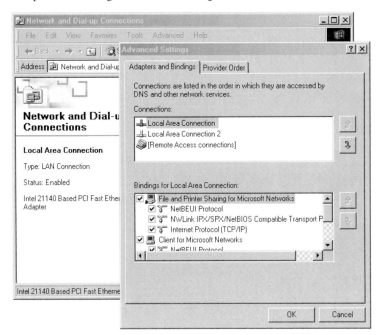

Figure 13.48 *Configuring network adapter bindings.*

Select the protocol to which you want to give priority and click the arrows to move it up or down. To remove an unnecessary protocol from the network adapter, deselect the appropriate checkbox.

Troubleshooting Network Adapters

If a computer cannot access the network at all, try the following:

- Make sure that the network cabling is secure.
- Make sure that the network adapter's "link status" light is on. If not, the cable connection is not powered (10BaseT, Token Ring).
- Make sure that the network is properly terminated (10Base2).
- Make sure the adapter is not affected by an IRQ conflict.
- Make sure network services are running properly.
- Make sure that the protocols are bound to the adapter.

Study Break

Adjust Network Bindings

Practice what you have learned by adjusting a network adapter binding.

Select an adapter via the Network and Dial-Up Connections folder. In the Advanced Settings dialog box, use the arrow buttons to move a protocol binding up or down in the list. If you know that a protocol is unnecessary for use on the adapter, disable it.

■ Summary

In this chapter, we described the issues surrounding Windows 2000 Server network connectivity, including protocols and services.

Working with Shared Access

Windows 2000 Server provides file and printer sharing access on a traditional Microsoft network through its native File and printer sharing for Microsoft Networks. In addition, Windows 2000 Server can be configured to provide support for Windows clients on a Novell NetWare network through its GSNW service. Windows 2000 Server can also be configured to support Mac OS-based file and printer sharing through its SFM components. Finally, Windows 2000 Server supports UNIX-based clients—and Internet-capable clients on most other operating systems—through IIS.

Working with Network Protocols

By default, Windows 2000 Server is configured to use TCP/IP, the network protocol of the Internet. It can be optionally configured to run NWLink IPX/ SPX/NetBIOS Compatible Transport protocol, a protocol used in NetWare environments; NetBEUI, a protocol useful on small Windows LANs; Apple-Talk, the network language of the Apple Macintosh; and DLC, a protocol used by mainframes and printers.

Working with Network Services

In addition to its core File and Printer Sharing for Microsoft Networks service, Windows 2000 Server can be configured with numerous optional network services, including DNS, DHCP, WINS, SFM, Print Services for UNIX, QoS Packet Scheduler, SAP Agent, Connection Manager Components, Network Monitor Tools, SNMP, COM Internet Services Proxy, IAS, Simple TCP/ IP Services, and ILS Services. These are installed either through the Windows Components Wizard or via the Local Area Connection dialog box.

Working with Remote Access Services

RRAS provides direct dial-in and VPN access to remote users and servers. It can be configured as an Internet connection server, becoming a gateway between the Internet and workstations on the local network; a remote access server, permitting remote computers to connect over a dialup device; or a VPN server, permitting remote computers to securely connect by tunneling through the Internet. RRAS can also be configured as a network router for such protocols as IP, IPX, and AppleTalk. In order to connect to the server via RRAS, a client must have permissions to do so enabled in a user account, meet the conditions of remote access policy, and have a valid and acceptable access profile.

Working with Virtual Private Networks

VPNs make possible secure private communications via the public and presumed insecure Internet by encapsulating LAN protocols, such as IP, IPX, and NetBEUI, inside encrypted protocols, such as PPTP and L2TP—a process called tunneling. VPNs are created on the Windows 2000 Server through RRAS.

Working with Terminal Services

Terminal Services allows users to run applications from the Windows 2000 Server rather than their own workstations, thus taking advantage of the server's superior processing power. Terminal Services can be installed to run in one of two modes. Under Remote Administration Mode, it permits Administrators to connect to, monitor, configure, and troubleshoot the server using its own Windows 2000 GUI from any networked location. Under Application Server Mode, it permits users to run Windows-based applications from the server, which is useful to clients that would not otherwise have the desktop power to run the applications.

Working with Network Adapters

Windows 2000 Server can be installed with one or multiple network adapters attached to various network segments. They are configured in the same manner as other hardware devices, with the exception of bindings. Bindings determine which network protocols will be run on a given network adapter, and the order in which they will be selected by such network services as File and Printer Sharing for Microsoft Networks.

▲ CHAPTER REVIEW QUESTIONS

Here are a few questions relating to the material covered in the *Configuring and Troubleshooting Windows 2000 Network Connections* section of Microsoft's *Installing, Configuring, and Administering Windows 2000 Server* exam (70-215).

1. *You can only employ File and Printer Sharing for Microsoft Networks if your server is running TCP/IP.*
    A. True
    B. False

2. *Which of the following network services provide file sharing under Windows 2000 Server? Select all that apply:*
    A. SFM
    B. IIS
    C. Terminal services
    D. GSNW

3. *You must install network protocols before installing the network services they are meant to support.*

   A. True

   B. False

4. *Which of the following are Windows 2000 network protocols? Select all that apply:*

   A. IPX/SPX

   B. PPTP

   C. AppleTalk

   D. DLC

5. *Which of the following are network services installed via the Local Area Connection dialog box? Select all that apply:*

   A. IIS

   B. Terminal Services

   C. SFM

   D. SAP Agent

6. *Windows 2000's HTTP server, FTP server, and Printing for UNIX are all installed as part of IIS.*

   A. True

   B. False

7. *RRAS is not installed with Windows 2000 Server by default.*

   A. True

   B. False

8. *RRAS will sometimes deny a connection even if the user account has permissions to log on.*

   A. True

   B. False

9. *When activated on a server equipped with a modem, RRAS creates three ports by default: one for the modem, and one each for PPTP and L2TP VPN connections.*

   A. True

   B. False

10. *You can control the time of day users are permitted to dial in to the server through remote access policies.*

 A. True

 B. False

11. *Windows NT Server 4.0 remote access policies can be seamlessly integrated into Windows 2000 Server's RRAS.*

 A. True

 B. False

12. *Remote access profiles are analyzed at the end of the dialup access authentication process.*

 A. True

 B. False

13. *Which of the following can be established through remote access profiles? Select all that apply:*

 A. The level of encryption used

 B. The IP address of the caller

 C. The use of multilinking

 D. The days on which access is permitted

14. *RRAS can be used to enable your server to accept or initiate VPN connections.*

 A. True

 B. False

15. *Which of the following are modes in which Terminal Services can be configured? Select all that apply:*

 A. Access by server

 B. Applications server

 C. Remote access server

 D. Remote administration

16. *Remote server administration is supported through Terminal Services for as many Administrators as you have licenses for.*

 A. True

 B. False

17. *Which of the following are computers that can take advantage of Terminal Services application sharing? Select all that apply:*

    A. Windows for Workgroups 3.11

    B. Windows 95

    C. Mac OS

    D. Windows CE

18. *You will probably need to install more RAM in your server as you increase the number of applications server users.*

    A. True

    B. False

19. *You should install all applications for which users will need access prior to installing the applications server.*

    A. True

    B. False

20. *Specially written Terminal Services-enabled applications are required for application sharing.*

    A. True

    B. False

21. *Windows 2000 Server setup should detect installed network adapters during installation.*

    A. True

    B. False

22. *Bindings can only be enabled on the primary network adapter.*

    A. True

    B. False

Securing Windows 2000 Server

▲Chapter Syllabus

MCSE 14.1 Encrypting Hard Disk Data

MCSE 14.2 Working with Windows 2000 Policies

MCSE 14.3 Working with Auditing

MCSE 14.4 Working with Local Accounts

MCSE 14.5 Working with Account Policy

MCSE 14.6 Using the Security Configuration Toolset

In this chapter, we look at material covered in the *Implementing, Monitoring, and Troubleshooting Windows 2000 Security* section of Microsoft's *Installing, Configuring, and Administering Microsoft Windows 2000 Server* exam (70-215).

This chapter builds on material first introduced in Chapter 7, "Securing Windows 2000 Professional." It is important that you know how to enable file encryption, implement local, system and account policy, and work with local accounts and auditing. You should also understand the capabilities of the Security Configuration Toolset.

MCSE 14.1   Encrypting Hard Disk Data

Windows 2000's Encrypting File System (EFS), which can be used on NTFS-formatted drives only, adds an extra layer of security to files in danger of being stolen, such as those on laptop computers or anonymous access FTP sites.

Encrypted files are only easily accessible to the people who created them, so EFS does not lend itself to file sharing. Other users can delete encrypted files, however, so EFS cannot be used instead of NTFS permissions. Finally, EFS does not work with NTFS compression and can make accessing encrypted files somewhat slower. Beyond these things, EFS is easy to enable and its operation is largely transparent to users, making it a useful addition to your file server's overall security.

When a user encrypts a file under EFS, a File Encryption Key (FEK) is randomly generated. After encrypting the file, the FEK is itself encrypted using the user's public key. At least two FEKs are created; one with the user's public key and one with a Recovery Agent's public key.

Some important things to know about EFS include the following:

- EFS requires certificate-based services to support its use of public key cryptography.
- EFS uses the CryptoAPI (CAPI) architecture, and can store keys on secure devices and Smart Cards.
- Where a Certificate Authority (CA) is available, EFS automatically has its user keys certified as needed. Where a CA is unavailable, EFS signs them itself. EFS also renews keys automatically.
- EFS uses Data Encryption Standard-X (DESX) encryption techniques.
- EFS originally shipped with either 56-bit or 128-bit encryption for use domestically and 40-bit encryption for use internationally. With the release of Service Pack 2, Microsoft upgraded EFS to 128-bit encryption. If your server is running under the earlier 56-bit encryption and you install Service Pack 2, you cannot revert back to 56-bit encryption even if you uninstall the Service Pack. Other services affected by the change include Kerberos, RAS, RPC, SSL/TLS, Terminal Services RDP, and IPSec.

Encrypting and Decrypting Data

To encrypt a file on a Windows 2000 Server volume, perform the following steps:

1. Right-click the file to open the Properties dialog box.
2. Switch to the General tab and click the Advanced button to open the Advanced Attributes dialog box, as shown in Figure 14.1.

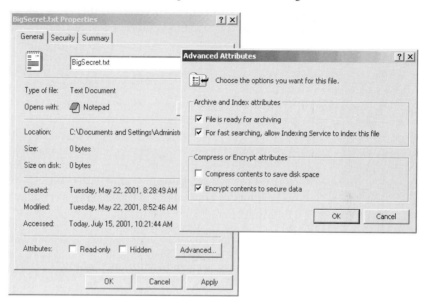

Figure 14.1   *Encrypting a file.*

3. Select the Encrypt Contents to Secure Data check box.
4. Click OK. You are given the further choice of additionally encrypting the folder that contains the file. Be aware, however, that Windows 2000 does not really encrypt a folder, it encrypts files that are added to the folder.
5. Click OK. EFS randomly generates a key to encrypt and decrypt the file. After being used to encrypt the file, the EFS key itself is encrypted using your public key.

To decrypt a file, you require a private key with which to decrypt your public key and gain access to the EFS key. The private key is stored on your workstation, becoming available after your identity is validated by logon authentication.

Only the person who encrypted a file has access to it. To make the file available to others, the person who encrypted the file must decrypt it by reversing the process previously described, deselecting the Encrypt Contents to Secure Data checkbox (see Figure 14.1).

EFS is only supported under Windows 2000's NTFS version 5. When moving or copying an encrypted file to a non-NTFS 5 volume, encryption is lost.

If you move or restore an encrypted file to another computer, encryption is lost unless you use the Windows Backup program. You cannot open the file unless your private key is on the target computer.

ENCRYPTING FROM THE COMMAND LINE

The CIPHER utility can be used to encrypt and decrypt files from the command line. Its options are as follow:

- **/e.** Encrypt file.
- **/d.** Decrypt file.
- **/s: dir.** Perform operation on all subdirectories.
- **/a.** Perform operation on all files of the specified name.
- **/i.** Continue operation regardless of errors.
- **/f.** Force encryption (even on encrypted files).
- **/q.** Minimize reporting.
- **/h.** Perform operation on hidden files.

Working With Private Keys

By exporting your security certificate, you make it possible to carry your private key with you from computer to computer. You can export your certificate to a floppy disk or network share or set up a roaming user profile to make the key accessible when you are working from another system.

To export your private key, you need to add the Certificates snap-in to the Group Policy Editor MMC. This was described in Chapter 7, "Securing Windows 2000 Professional." Thereafter, perform the follow steps:

1. Expand the Certificates node in the MMC and navigate to the Personal/Certificates branch.
2. Select your certificate, then choose the Export command from the Action menu's All Tasks submenu to launch the Export Certificate Wizard.
3. Enable the Yes, export the private key radio button when prompted, option in the Certificate Export Wizard.
4. Choose the default .pfx file format.
5. Deselect the Enable strong protection checkbox if you will be using the certificate on a non-Windows 2000 system or a Windows NT 4.0 system without at least Service Pack 4.

6. Enter a password.
7. Provide a file name and location to save the certificate.

When complete, the wizard creates a small .pfx file that you can copy to a floppy disk or secure network share for use on other computers. When at another computer, simply reverse this process by choosing the Certificate snap-in's Import command.

RECOVERY AGENTS

Should a user's private key be destroyed, Microsoft supplies a fail-safe in the form of Recovery Agents, special users with the power to decrypt files without having the creator's private or EFS keys.

Administrators can create Recover Agents from the Encrypted Data Recover Agents folder under the Local Computer Policy node in the Group Policy MMC. Choose the Add command from the Action menu to open the Add Recovery Agent Wizard. You are prompted to locate a certificate by either browsing the Active Directory or selecting a .cer file on the local computer.

To gain access to a local certificate, you must first save a copy of it as a .cer file. This is done by following the export procedure as previously explained, except that you must choose the "No, do not export private key radio button" and save the certificate under an X.509 .cer file format instead of the .pfx format.

By default, Windows 2000 makes at least the Administrator a Recovery Agent. In addition to determining whether encrypted data can be recovered, Recover Agents also determine whether EFS can be used at all. If you delete all accounts as Recovery Agents, including Administrator, EFS is disabled for the entire system.

Study Break

Create a Recovery Agent

Practice what you have learned by creating a Recovery Agent.

First, navigate to the Encrypted Data Recover Agents folder under the Local Computer Policy node in the Group Policy MMC. Choose the Add command from the Action menu to open the Add Recovery Agent Wizard. Locate a certificate by either browsing the Active Directory or selecting a .cer file on the local computer.

MCSE 14.2   Working with Windows 2000 Policies

You can employ the following Windows 2000 Server policies in managing the ways in which your users use their computers:

- **Local Policy.** Local policies are group policies stored locally on a Windows 2000 member server or Windows 2000 Professional workstation. Applied to each computer and/or user, these policies control configuration settings, auditing policy, user rights, and security. Local policies are most effective when implemented on computers in a nonnetworked environment. On the network, they can be overwritten by the policies of sites, domains, and Organization Unit (OU) objects.
- **System Policy.** System policies modify the Registry to control user and computer settings on Windows NT 4.0 and Windows 9x computers, and standalone Windows 2000 machines. The System Policy Editor utility is used to create Windows 9x policies under the name "config.pol," and Windows NT 4.0 polices under the name "ntconfig.pol." For the most part, these have been superceded by group policies in the Windows 2000 environment.
- **Group Policy.** Like local and system policies, group policies control user operating environments. Unlike local policies, however, these policies are applied to Active Directory objects and can be applied across domains, sites, and OUs. This is described in Chapter 24, "Managing Active Directory Change and Configuration."

Configuring Windows 2000 Policies

Although similar, the process of configuring the various Windows 2000 policies differs in the settings addressed and the tools used.

CONFIGURING LOCAL POLICY

Local security policy can be implemented through the Local Security Settings MMC found in the Administrative Tools program group, as shown in Figure 14.2.

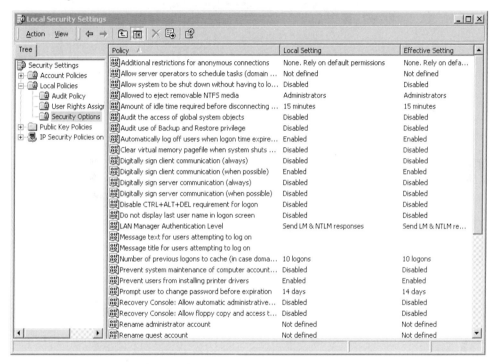

Figure 14.2 *The Local Security Settings MMC.*

Under the Local Policies node, you may establish the criteria for audit policies, user rights, and security options.

To modify a local policy setting, double-click a policy document in the list to open a dialog box in which you may disable/enable the setting, or choose among appropriate options, as shown in Figure 14.3.

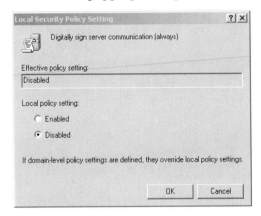

Figure 14.3 *Modifying a policy setting.*

CONFIGURING SYSTEM POLICY

Under Windows 2000, the System Policy Editor tool can be launched from the Run dialog box from its location in the WINNT folder. It can be used to set system variables and Registry configurations on Windows NT 4.0 and Windows 9x computers throughout the network, and standalone Windows 2000 machines.

To begin configure a system policy, select the Policy Template command from the Options menu bar item and choose a policy file in the Policy Template Options dialog box, as shown in Figure 14.4.

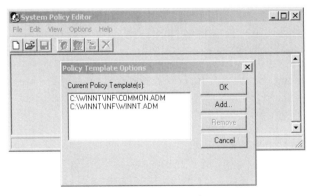

Figure 14.4 *Loading a system policy.*

When using Policy File mode, System Policy Editor acts like a master Registry editor.

When you create a new policy file by choosing the New Policy command under the File menu, two icons appear in Policies dialog box by default, as shown in Figure 14.5. The Default Computer list lets you configure all computer-specific properties within the Registry's HKEY_LOCAL_MACHINE subtree. The Default User list lets you specify settings for all clients who do not already use a specific computer entry in the policy file (as shown in Figure 14.5). This affects the Registry's HKEY_CURRENT_USER subtree. Users of roaming profiles have this information stored in their NTUSER.DAT files.

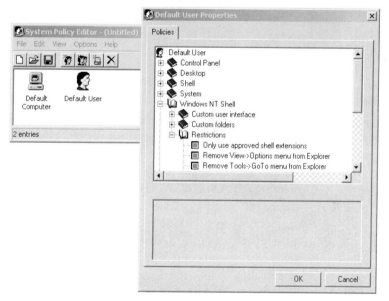

Figure 14.5 *Default User Properties dialog box.*

During the logon process, the computer first looks to the policy file to find settings that affect the computer or user. If there are any, these settings merge with or overwrite the settings in the local Registry. These policy settings can be applied to users and groups, therefore they can be applied to individuals or to entire domains.

In Registry Policy mode, System Policy Editor acts like a local Registry editor. It is not as powerful as the Registry Editor application in this role, but it can be used to configure both local and remote computers and it has a simpler interface.

If you enable customized shared folders, (e.g., Start menu folder, Desktop folder, Programs folder, and Startup folder), one useful trick is to create a "Shares" folder that contains shortcuts to commonly accessed, public shares. Put this folder in the Start menu folder to save users time over browsing through the My Network Places. (This assumes, of course, that you have chosen not to map these shares as network drives.)

Managing Windows 2000 Policies

Whether they are local policies or system policies, it is wise to apply policies only where strictly needed. This requires that you know and understand the settings that can be managed through policies.

MANAGING LOCAL POLICY

When managing local policy under using the Local Security Settings MMC, the following are among the policy settings of particular interest:

- **Digitally sign client/server communications.** By default, Windows 2000 Server uses digital signatures for communications with clients or other servers "when possible." For increased security, you might wish to change these settings to "always."
- **Disable CTRL-ALT-DELETE requirement for logon.** If disabled (the default), this setting ensures that only Windows 2000 is accepting your logon information, rather than some Trojan Horse program whose purpose is to steal that data. If security is no concern, this feature might be considered an annoyance on a workstation. Because of the volume of important data they host, this setting should almost always be enabled on a server.
- **Do not display last user name in logon screen.** If enabled, an unauthorized person who sits down at the server does not see your logon user name if they attempt to log on, making it harder for them to gain access.
- **LAN Manager Authentication Level.** If you have legacy LAN Manager clients on your networks, you might wish to alter the way in which they authenticate logons for the best possible security.
- **Message Text/Title for Users Attempts to Logon.** This setting lets you post a message for all users logging on, such as "Welcome to Company X" or "authorized access only."
- **Prompt user to change password before expiration.** Here you can alter the amount of time that may pass before users are required to

change passwords. The default is 14 days, but in relatively secure environments, you might increase the interval.

- **Recovery Console.** Allow floppy copy and access to all drives and all folders. If enabled, this policy could compromise security by permitting someone to navigate through a hard drive's directory structure and copy files from the Recovery Console command prompt. Recovery Console is still subject to Administrator log-on authentication (unless you also disable that policy), so you might consider this change in policy useful for making last ditch efforts at file recovery.
- **Rename Administrator account.** To increase security, you can use this setting to rename the Administrator logon user name, preferably to something as complex as the password. You may also rename the Guest account, which might improve its security slightly.
- **Digitally encrypt or sign secure channel data.** For increased security, you might wish to change these settings from "when possible" to "always."
- **Unsigned driver installation behavior.** By default, this policy is not defined. You can define a policy of Silently succeed, in which case all unsigned drivers are installed without prompting, Warn but allow installation, or Do not allow installation.

MANAGING SYSTEM POLICY

When managing system policy using System Policy Editor, some of the things an administrator might want to do include the following:

- Configure programs, such as virus scans or disk checkers, to run automatically at startup. The path to this setting is Default Computer/System/Run.
- Make sure all Windows clients create administrative shares (e.g., hidden shares) on startup, permitting their central management. The path to this setting is Default Computer/Windows NT Network/Sharing.
- Enable customized shared folders, such as the Start menu folder, Desktop folder, Programs folder, and Startup folder. By pointing to a network share, you can force multiple computers to use the same set of custom folders. The path to this setting is Default Computer/Windows NT Shell/Custom Shared Folders.
- Present a Logon Banner. This is useful for reminding users of a security policy or informing them of impending server maintenance when they log on. The path to this setting is Default Computer/Windows NT System/Logon.

- Remove the last user name from the User Authentication dialog box. This prevents users from knowing who logged on last and, presumably, from guessing that person's password. The path to this setting is Default Computer/Windows NT System/Logon.
- Lock down display resolution. The path to this setting is Default User/Display/Restrict Display.
- Prevent mapping of, or disconnecting from, network drives. The path to this setting is Default User/Windows NT Shell/Restrictions.
- Set a timeout for dialog boxes that appear on screen when the user is not around. The path to this setting is Default Computer/Windows NT User Profile.

Troubleshooting Windows 2000 Policies

Careful planning and a good understanding of the implications of setting policy usually saves you from a lot of troubleshooting. When troubleshooting is needed, it depends on the types and numbers of policies you have implemented.

TROUBLESHOOTING LOCAL POLICY

If your workstation is a member of a domain, the policies you establish locally are not necessarily the last word on the matter. Local policy settings are always overruled by domain-wide policy settings when conflicts occur. Should you find that a policy you set locally is having no effect, double check the Local Security Settings MMC to make sure that the Local Setting listed matches the Effective Setting (e.g., the domain-wide setting).

TROUBLESHOOTING SYSTEM POLICY

When problems occur involving system policies, make sure the policies are being read properly. The order in which predefined system policies are processed is as follows:

1. When the user logs on to the network successfully, the user profile is read from the authenticating domain controller's NETLOGON share.
2. If a predefined users policy exists on the domain controller, it is merged with the local HKEY_CURRENT_USER Registry subtree.
3. If a predefined machine policy exists on the domain controller, it is merged with the local HKEY_LOCAL_MACHINE Registry subtree.

If no predefined system policies exist, the processing order is as follows:

1. When the user logs on to the network successfully, the user profile is read from the authenticating domain controller's NETLOGON share point.

   Since no predefined user policy exists on the domain controller, the default user policy is processed.

2. The group priority list is then examined to see if the user is a member of any global groups for which there is a policy. If so, processing proceeds along the group priority order (from bottom to top of the group priority list).

3. Each policy processed is merged with the HKEY_CURRENT_USER Registry subtree. If the user is not a member of an applicable global group, the default user policy applies. Since a predefined machine policy does not exist on the domain controller, a default machine policy is merged with the HKEY_LOCAL_MACHINE Registry subtree.

When troubleshooting system and group policies, some areas that merit attention include the following:

- Verify that the user authentication was successful.
- Verify that the user belongs to the domain.
- Verify that no one else has modified the policy.
- Verify that enough time has elapsed for any group policies you have created to be replicated to all domain controllers (known as the convergence time).

Study Break

Establish Local Security Policy

Practice what you have learned by configuring your server's local security policy.

Using the Local Security Settings MMC, configure settings that increase the local security of your server, such as changing the name of the Administrator account or requiring digital signatures. Log on to the server to make sure that your policy settings have been properly adopted. Log on onto the server from a workstation and make sure that the policies you have enabled do not unduly restrict user access.

MCSE 14.3   Working with Auditing

Through Windows 2000 Server's powerful auditing capabilities, any attempt to access a directory or file, whether it was successful, can be tracked and recorded in the Security Log that can be examined in Event Viewer.

Configuring Auditing

Use the Audit Policy node of the Local Security Settings MMC to implement auditing. To configure an audit policy, double-click a policy document in the list to open a dialog box to which you can enable tracking for successes, failures, or both, as shown in Figure 14.6.

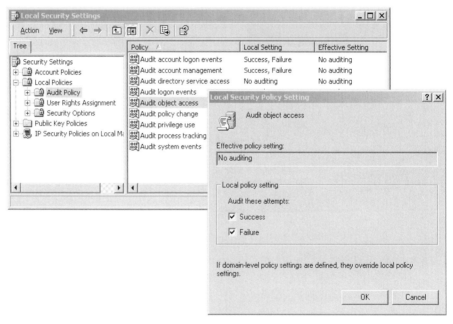

Figure 14.6 *Configuring audit policy.*

Managing Auditing

Auditing policy lets you determine which of your server's resources are monitored. For example, to monitor access to a particular volume, you would first enable the Successes checkbox for the Audit Object Access policy, open the Access Control Settings dialog box from the volume's properties dialog box. Under the Auditing tab, click the Add button to select the groups whose access you wish to watch. After clicking the OK button, enable checkboxes monitor the successes and failures of the group's activities by permission level, as shown in Figure 14.7.

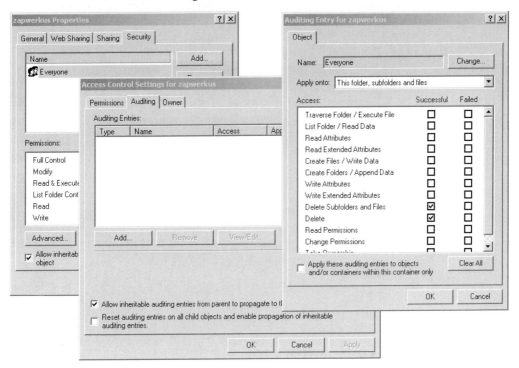

Figure 14.7 *Choosing accounts for auditing.*

Administrators and any users or groups assigned the Manage auditing and security log user right can set directory and file auditing options. They may also view the status of successes and failures in the Security Log, as shown in Figure 14.8.

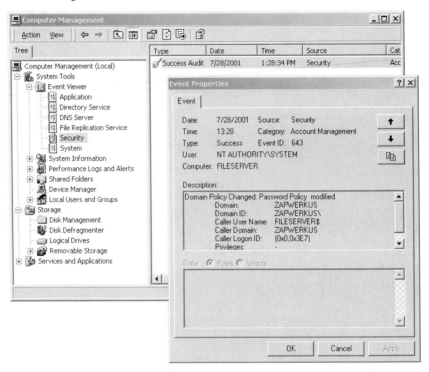

Figure 14.8 *Viewing an auditing event.*

If you are auditing a share volume, you also need to decide if you are extending your auditing to subfolders and existing files. Next, you must decide what events to audit. Among the questions these choices can answer are the following:

- **Read.** Who is trying to read a file?
- **Write.** Who is attempting to modify a file?
- **Execute.** Who is trying to execute a program?
- **Delete.** Who is trying to delete a file?
- **Change Permissions.** Who tried to change access to a directory or file?
- **Take Ownership.** Who attempted to take ownership of a directory or file?

Whether you audit for successes or failures depends on what you are looking for. If someone keeps deleting an important file, for example, you should enable Success auditing to see who it is the next time it happens. If you know your permissions are secure but you suspect someone of malicious intent, you should enable Failure auditing to see who might be probing your security. If you fear that network security has been compromised and there are unauthorized users accessing your resources, enable logon and logoff auditing. Audit for both successes and failures. This points you to the location of failed logon attempts and actual security breaches.

Troubleshooting Auditing

Be aware that auditing slows down your server's performance and should be used sparingly. Also be aware that auditing events can fill up the Security Log quickly, so you might need to either reduce the number of auditing events or increase the size of the Security Log.

MCSE 14.4   Working with Local Accounts

The use of user and group accounts allow an administrator to control the ability of users to perform actions and access resources by assigning rights and permissions. On a domain controller, users and groups are managed through Active Directory, as described in the third section of this book. On standalone servers, however, users and groups are managed through the Computer Management MMC, as described in Chapter 7.

Configuring Local Accounts

On standalone servers and workstations, users and groups can be created and managed using the Computer Management MMC's System Tools node.

To configure a new user account, select the Users folder in the Tree pane, right-click the right windowpane, and choose the New User command from the context menu. This opens the New User dialog box, as shown in Figure 14.9.

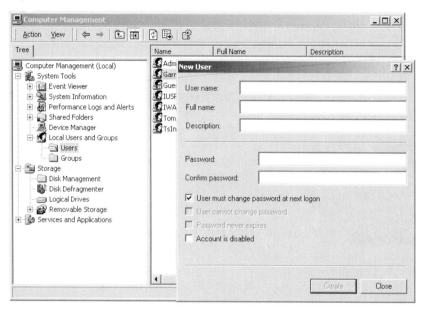

Figure 14.9 *Creating a new user account.*

In the New User dialog box, fill in the fields for user name and password. The user name is not case sensitive and can be as long as 20 characters. It cannot consist solely of periods or spaces and must be unique from any other user or group name in the computer or domain. In addition, it cannot include the following characters:

? " / : \ ; [,] + | = * < - >

The password is case sensitive and can be as long as 127 characters. The best passwords are at least 8 characters long and include both upper and lower case characters mixed randomly with numerals. Longer passwords are better still. Windows NT and 9.x only support passwords of 14 characters, however, the Windows 2000 Server default. You may enable the Users Must Change Password at Next Logon checkbox to force users to create their own passwords when they first log on with the user name you provide. When enabled, this checkbox disables the "User cannot change password" and "Password never expires" checkboxes.

To create a new group account, select the Groups folder in the Tree pane of the Computer Management MMC, right-click the right windowpane, and choose the New Group command from the context menu. This opens the New Group dialog box, as shown in Figure 14.10.

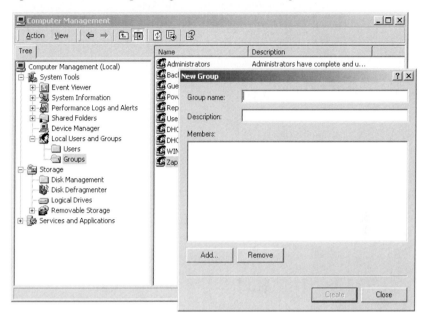

Figure 14.10   *Creating a new group account.*

Name and describe the group, then click the Add button to include members. You may add user accounts, global group accounts, or both. Once created, local groups cannot be renamed or disabled, but they can be deleted (without deleting their member accounts).

Managing Local Accounts

To manage existing user accounts, select the Users folder in the Tree pane of the Computer Management MMC, double-click a user in the right pane to open the User Properties dialog box, as shown in Figure 14.11.

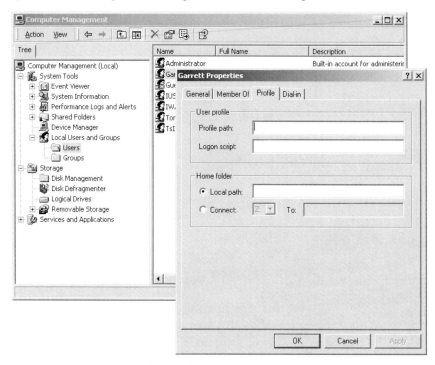

Figure 14.11 *Configuring local account properties.*

You may reconfigure all of the account parameters you established when creating the user account, with the exception of user name and password, under the General tab. If an administrator has enabled the Account Lockout option through Account Policy, you also see an active Account locked out check box.

Add or remove group memberships under the Member of tab.

Switch to Profile tab to configure the following environmental variables:

- **User Profile Path.** This field is used to specify the location on a server of a user profile file. Among other things, this file contains information about the user's Start menu, Desktop, and recently used documents. Specifying this path permits users to have their preferences follow them from workstation to workstation.

The most common user profile path is:

```
\\<server_name>\Profileshare\%username%
```

- **Logon Script Name.** This field is used to specify a .CMD or .BAT file containing scripted instructions, such as to map network drives or display a welcome message.
- **Home Folder.** These fields are used to specify the default location where users store their work. This folder can be local or on a network share. If you create a user's home folder on an NTFS partition, the user is granted Full Control permissions and all other users are denied access by default.

Switch to the Dial-in tab to enable access through RRAS.

In addition to these account settings, specific user rights can be managed through the User Rights Assignment node of the Local Security Settings MMC. User rights do not have to be explicitly assigned under Windows 2000. In general, you do not want to change default user rights. A mistake here can render the workstation inoperable. There are sometimes exceptions to the rule, however. For example, the default membership of the Log on locally user right includes the Guest group. For better security, you might wish to remove this group's access.

Troubleshooting Local Accounts

Among the issues that can be addressed through troubleshooting account settings are the following:

- If a user is unable to access a resource, verify that the proper group memberships have been assigned.
- Should a user report repeated failures in logging on, check to see if an administrator has enabled the Account Lockout option through Account Policy. If so, you will see that the Account locked out check box is active in the user's account properties. It is triggered (enabled) when the user reaches the preset limit of unsuccessful logon attempts. If the Lockout duration is set for a long time, then you must manually disable the check box before the user can access the account again.
- If users report problems with their environmental settings, verify that the path to their profile folders is still accurate.
- If users report they have problems logging on, verify that the settings in the login script are still valid (e.g., NET USE, and so on).

- If users cannot access their home folders, verify that the share on which they are stored is still accessible and that the path is still valid.

  If users report problems with their levels of system access, verify that they belong to the groups appropriate to the user rights they need. Also, be sure to verify that user rights you grant locally correspond to those of the domain at large, where applicable.

Study Break

Secure User Accounts

Practice what you have learned by creating users and groups.

Create several user accounts using the Computer Management MMC. Create a group and assign your new user to it. Next, modify various account settings and note the effects as you log on using the various accounts.

MCSE 14.5 Working with Account Policy

As user accounts determine whether someone is eligible to log on, account policies determine the circumstances under which they are permitted to log on. These policies are implemented through the Password Policies and Account Lockout Policy subfolders of the Account Policies folder under the Local Computer Policy node of the Group Policy Editor MMC, or through the Local Security Settings MMC.

Configuring Account Policy

To configure an account policy, double-click a document in the Policy list to open a dialog box in which you can enable a rule or enforce a parameter, as shown in Figure 14.12.

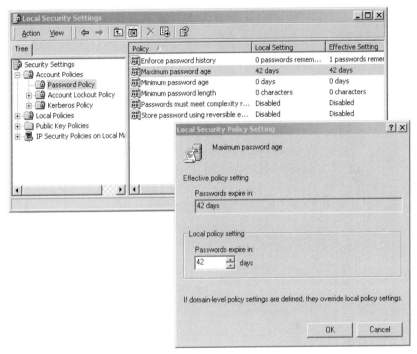

Figure 14.12 *Configuring account policy.*

The Password Policy folder contains group policy objects that let you require more secure passwords for all users. The Account Lockout Policy folder lets you disable access to an account when password authentication has been repeatedly tried and failed.

Managing Account Policy

Among the ways in which password policies should be managed are these:

- **Maximum password age.** Passwords have a habit of falling into the hands of unauthorized persons. One of the best ways to maintain password integrity is to keep them changing. This policy can be used to force users to pick new passwords after the specified interval.
- **Minimum password age.** Some users may attempt to bypass the purpose of the previous feature by setting a new password as required,

then promptly switching back to a favorite password. If you accept the default setting of allowing changes immediately here, users can switch back to their favorite passwords whenever they want. Alternately, you can set an interval of between one and 999 days before they can change the new password to a previous one.

- **Minimum password length.** The longer the password, the more difficult it is to crack. With this field, you can require passwords of up to 14 characters in length. In general, passwords longer than four characters are considered reasonably secure, with eight characters being a common minimum.
- **Password uniqueness.** This setting can be used in conjunction with the Minimum Password Age field to keep users from reusing passwords. It directs Windows 2000 to remember each user's last passwords and refuse to permit their reuse.

Account Lockout policies direct Windows 2000 to lock out an account that has been subject to a certain number of bad log on attempts in a given amount of time, as shown in Figure 14.13.

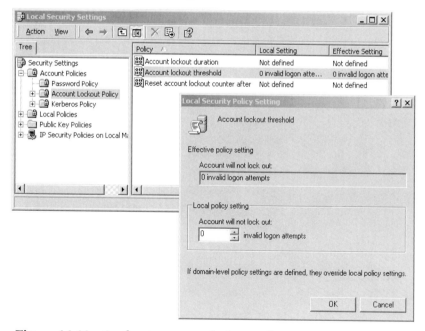

Figure 14.13 *Configuring account lockout policy.*

Such occurrences are the usual sign of someone attempting to gain unauthorized access. One problem here is that once a hacker knows the number and interval by trial and error, the hacker desists before triggering this action. The hacker then tries again later (a process known as nibbling). Be sure, then, to reset the counter only after a reasonably long time. You can also establish how long the account is disabled. Make this interval long enough for you to become aware of the attempted breach and investigate.

On a domain controller, you can also enable the use of Kerberos 5 for server and client computer authentication via Kerberos Policy settings, which issues tickets that permit access to network resources. Kerberos can only be used between Windows 2000 computers.

Troubleshooting Account Policy

If it appears that your account policy settings are not being applied, make sure that the local settings are not working against the effective settings. Group policies can be applied at the local, site, domain, or OU. All other levels have the strength to override what you set locally.

If your settings are in agreement, it might be that the policies have not yet had a chance to propagate. If necessary, you can force a refresh by executing the following command from the Run dialog box:

```
Secedit /refreshpolicy MACHINE_POLICY
```

Study Break

Set Account Policy

Practice what you have learned by enabling account policy.

Using the Local Security Settings MMC, enable more strict settings for user account access. For example, set an expiration date for user passwords, and a limit to the number of failed logon attempts that can occur before accounts are locked out. Verify your settings by making the necessary number of failed logon attempts from a remote workstation.

MCSE 14.6 Using the Security Configuration Toolset

The Security Configuration Toolset is a group of utilities that let you centrally manage multiple computers' security settings. It includes the following components:

- Security Configuration and Analysis MMC snap-in.
- Security Settings Extension to Group Policy.
- Security Templates Snap-in.
- SECEDIT.EXE.

Configuring Security

Because of the inherent security risks they impose, Windows 2000 does not go out of its way to make its security tools obvious. You must therefore create your own MMC to host the Security Configuration and Analysis snap-in through the following procedure:

1. Type "mmc" at the command line to open an empty console in author mode.
2. Select the Add/Remove Snap-ins command from the Console menu to open the Add/Remove Snap-in dialog box.
3. Click the Add button to include Security Configuration and Analysis snap-in and Security Template Snap-in under the Console Root node.

You can import templates into the Security Configuration and Analysis snap-in that can be used to configure local security by applying their settings to the group policy object (GPO) for the local workstation. Security templates are created using the Security Templates snap-in, so add it to the MMC as well.

The Group Policy Editor contains an extension that permits the configuration of local as well as domain and OU-wide security policies.

SECEDIT provides most of the same functionality of the Security Configuration and Analysis snap-in, but is run from the command line.

Managing and Troubleshooting Security

The Security Configuration and Analysis snap-in can be used to analyze system settings and provide recommendations for changing them. It lets you perform the following tasks:

- Create a settings database.
- Import and export security templates.

- Analyze and review security.
- Configure security settings.

After configuring the MMC to include the Security Templates snap-in, expand the C:\WINNT\Security\Templates folder under the Security Templates node to see all of the defined templates and their explanations. Double-click a template document, such as the Windows 2000 Server default template "DC security," to view and modify its settings for Account Policies, Local Policies, Event Log, Restricted Groups, System Services, Registry, and File System.

To analyze your system's settings, perform the following steps:

1. Select the Security Configuration and Analysis node and choose the Import template command from the Action menu to open a file selection dialog box. After the template is imported, a new database will be created.
2. Select the Security Configuration and Analysis node and choose the Analyze Computer Now command from the Action menu. This opens the Perform Analysis dialog box, in which is displayed the path and name of the error log. When you click the OK button, the utility checks the local security configuration against the template, displaying its progress in the Analyzing System Security dialog box.
3. The settings in both the security template and system configuration are displayed for each policy. Any discrepancies appear with a red alert symbol, while consistent settings appear with green check marks in the center. Settings not appearing with one of these symbols are not specified in the template.

To synchronize the two policies, select the Configure Computer Now command from the Action menu to open the Configure System dialog box. After you click OK, the Configuring Computer Security dialog box shows you its progress. When it is complete, verify that the values under the Database Settings now match the values under the Computer Setting column.

Study Break

Analyze Security Configurations

Practice what you have learned by applying and analyzing a security configuration.

Create a new MMC console that contains the Security Configuration and Analysis and Security Templates snap-ins. Next, import a template and create a security database using the "DC security" template document. Next, make some changes to the security configuration. Finally, analyze the system and compare the results to see how your changes compare with the template. Save the MMC.

■ Summary

In this chapter, we described the process of securing your Windows 2000 Server through the use of file encryption, local, system, and account policy, auditing, and the Security Configuration Toolset.

Encrypting Hard Disk Data

Windows 2000's EFS adds an extra layer of security to files in danger of being stolen, such as those on laptop computers or anonymous access FTP sites. Encrypted files are only easily accessible to the people who created them. When a user encrypts a file under EFS, a FEK is randomly generated. After encrypting the file, the FEK is itself encrypted using the user's public key. At least two FEKs are created; one with the user's public key and one with a Recovery Agent's public key. Recover Agents can be used to recover data when the user's key is lost or destroyed.

Working with Windows 2000 Policies

Local policies are group policies stored locally on a Windows 2000 member server or Windows 2000 Professional workstation. Applied to each computer and/or user, these policies control configuration settings, auditing policy, user rights, and security. System policies modify the Registry to control user and computer settings on Windows NT 4.0 and Windows 9x computers, and standalone Windows 2000 machines. For the most part, these have been superceded by group policies in the Windows 2000 environment. Like local and system policies, group policies control user operating environments. Unlike local policies, however, these policies are applied to Active Directory objects and can be applied across domains, sites, and OUs.

Working with Auditing

Through Windows 2000 Server's auditing capabilities, any attempt to access a directory or file, whether it was successful, can be tracked and recorded in the Security Log that can be examined in Event Viewer. Auditing is enabled using the Local Security Settings MMC. It can be configured resource by resource.

Working with Local Accounts

The use of user and group accounts allow an administrator to control the ability of users to perform actions and access resources by assigning rights and permissions. On a domain controller, users and groups are managed through Active Directory. On standalone servers, however, users and groups are managed through the Computer Management MMC. In addition to these account settings, specific user rights can be managed through the User Rights Assignment node of the Local Security Settings MMC, although user rights do not have to be explicitly assigned under Windows 2000.

Working with Account Policy

The Security Configuration Toolset is a group of utilities that let you centrally manage multiple computers' security settings. It includes the Security Configuration and Analysis MMC snap-in, Security Settings Extension to Group Policy, Security Templates Snap-in, and SECEDIT.EXE. The Security Configuration and Analysis snap-in can be used to analyze system settings and provide recommendations for changing them.

Chapter Review Questions

Here are a few questions relating to the material covered in the *Implementing, Monitoring, and Troubleshooting Windows 2000 Security* section of Microsoft's *Installing, Configuring, and Administering Windows 2000 Server* exam (70-215).

1. *EFS makes drive access unacceptably slow when used in conjunction with NTFS compression.*
    A. True
    B. False

2. *Other users can neither read nor delete a file that you have encrypted.*
    A. True
    B. False

3. *Group policy settings overrule local policy settings when conflicts occur.*
   A. True
   B. False

4. *If the Disable CTRL-ALT-DELETE for logon local security setting is disabled, Windows 2000 will only accept actual user-input logon information.*
   A. True
   B. False

5. *You can choose to rename the Administrator account through local security policy.*
   A. True
   B. False

6. *System policies cannot be used to edit Registry settings.*
   A. True
   B. False

7. *System policies are functionally the same as Active Directory-based group policies.*
   A. True
   B. False

8. *Which of the following questions cannot be answered through file access auditing? Select only one.*
   A. Who is trying to read a file?
   B. Who is trying to modify a file?
   C. Who is trying to change file permissions?
   D. Who is trying to audit a file?

9. *Auditing does not have an appreciable effect on server performance.*
   A. True
   B. False

10. *It is unwise to "time out" passwords, because users will likely forget new passwords and incur greater support time.*
    A. True
    B. False

11. *The default password length for Windows 2000 is eight characters.*
     A. True
     B. False

12. *Account policies determine the circumstances under which users are permitted to log on with a user account.*
     A. True
     B. False

13. *Account policy and lockout policy should not be used together.*
     A. True
     B. False

14. *The Security Configuration Toolset can be found in the Administrative Tools program group.*
     A. True
     B. False

15. *SECEDIT is basically just a command line version of the Security Configuration and Analysis MMC snap-in.*
     A. True
     B. False

Windows 2000 Networking

◆ In This Part

◆ **CHAPTER 15**
Administering DNS

◆ **CHAPTER 16**
Administering DHCP

◆ **CHAPTER 17**
Administering Remote
Access

◆ **CHAPTER 18**
Administering Network
Protocols

◆ **CHAPTER 19**
Administering WINS

◆ **CHAPTER 20**
Administering IP Routing

◆ **CHAPTER 21**
Administering Certificate
Services

In this section, we cover material from MCSE exam 70-216, *Implementing and Administering a Microsoft Windows 2000 Network Infrastructure* exam. This gives you the knowledge necessary to install, configure, and manage networked Windows 2000 Server computers and support their Windows 2000-based clients. This part's topics include the following:

- **Administering DNS:** Installing Domain Name Services (DNS) Server, including configuring zones, records, and clients, and managing, monitoring, and troubleshooting DNS.

- **Administering DHCP:** Installing Dynamic Host Configuration Protocol (DHCP) Server, including configuring scopes and DNS/Active Directory integration, and managing, monitoring, and troubleshooting DHCP.

- **Administering Remote Access:** Configuring inbound connections, policy, profiles, Virtual Private Networks (VPNs), multilink, and routing, and managing, monitoring, and troubleshooting remote access.

- **Administering Network Protocols:** Installing and configuring Transmission Control Protocol/Internet Protocol (TCP/IP), Internet Protocol Security (IPSec), and NWLink Internetwork Packet Exchange/Sequenced Packet Exchange (IPX/SPX)/NetBIOS Compatible Transport protocol, and managing, monitoring, and troubleshooting network protocols, security, and traffic.

- **Administering WINS:** Installing Windows Internet Naming Service (WINS) Server, configuring replication and name resolution, and managing, monitoring, and troubleshooting WINS.

- **Administering IP Routing:** Configuring, managing, and troubleshooting routing tables, border routing, internal routing, and demand-dial routing. Installing, configuring, and troubleshooting Network Address Translation (NAT).

- **Administering Certificate Services:** Installing, configuring, and troubleshooting Certificate Authority, issuing and revoking certificates, and removing recovery keys.

Most of this material is common to both Windows 2000 Professional and Windows 2000 Server, and has been touched upon previously in this book. In this section, the topics are covered in greater depth.

Any discussion of networking topics inevitably involves references to the Open Systems Interconnection (OSI) model. The OSI model is comprised of seven layers, each of which provides an abstract way of representing the specific components that enable communications to take place on a network.

These layers break down as follows:

- **Application Layer.** At Layer 7, the languages and syntax that programs use to communicate with each other are defined. Most of the commands needed to open, read, write, transfer and close files over the network are exchanged at this level.

- **Presentation Layer.** The encoding of data so that it can be exchanged between different computer systems is managed at Layer 6. For example, security encryption and decryption occurs at this level.

- **Session Layer.** It is the job of Layer 5 to maintain an orderly process of communications. Among the things that are determined here are whether communications are one-way (half duplex) or two-way (full duplex) and how that dialog is managed so that it can be recovered in the event of a connection failure.

- **Transport Layer.** The responsibility for maintaining the integrity of a transmission overall rests with Layer 4. If a 1 MB file is sent from a server, it is the job of Layer 4 to ensure an identical 1 MB file is received by a workstation.
- **Network Layer.** At Layer 3, the route over which the sending and receiving computers communicate is established. Where a network is segmented, these routes can become quite complicated as data hops across routers.
- **Data Link Layer.** The division of data bits into frames for node-to-node transmission takes place at Layer 2. A process of error checking and retransmission is used to ensure that all the necessary data is ultimately transferred.
- **Physical Layer.** Layer 1 is responsible for the electrical and mechanical signaling that moves data bits from one computer to another. Network cabling resides at this level.

It is important that you remember this model. A mnemonic phrase that can help you remember these layers, from bottom to top, is "*People Don't Need Those Stupid Protocols Anyway.*"

Having said this, we must now point out that TCP/IP — Windows 2000's core protocol — does not truly implement the Presentation and Session layers, as shown in the following illustration:

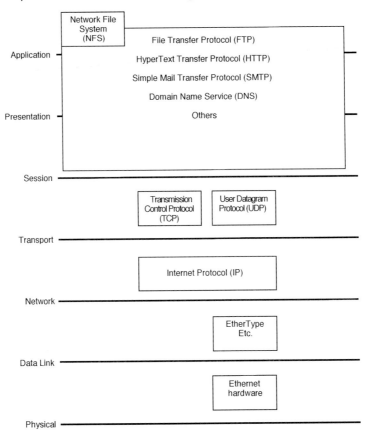

Administering Domain Name Services

▲ **Chapter Syllabus**

MCSE 15.1 **Working with DNS**

In this chapter, we examine the installation topics covered in the *Installing, Configuring, Managing, Monitoring, and Troubleshooting DNS in a Windows 2000 Network Infrastructure* section of Microsoft's *Implementing and Administering a Microsoft Windows 2000 Network Infrastructure* exam (70-216).

The following material gives you the background necessary to understand DNS, and as well as ensure that you can install DNS Server and configure zones, records, and clients. You also learn to manage, monitor, and troubleshoot DNS.

MCSE 15.1 Working with DNS

Like so many of the other services we have addressed in this book, DNS adheres to the client/server model. DNS clients are referred to as resolvers, while its servers are commonly called name servers. Applications that make use of DNS resolvers include Web browsers, FTP utilities, and telnet clients. A DNS resolver is built-in to Windows 2000, and others are included in the applications themselves.

When hunting for an IP address-to-domain name mapping, resolvers query a group of worldwide databases collectively referred to as the domain name space.

First introduced in the 1980s, DNS was designed to allow for the autonomous local administration of domain names by distributing the responsibility for address resolution across multiple sites and many computers. The distributed nature of DNS prevents the responsibility for mapping all the world's hostnames from residing with one overburdened central authority. More importantly, it makes it unnecessary for Internet-based computers to maintain a local "hosts" file containing the address mappings for other computers. Such files would be enormous, as would the amount of network traffic generated to keep them in sync.

The use of DNS is a significant departure from the NetBIOS naming scheme used by all Microsoft networks prior to Windows 2000. First deployed IBM in 1983 and worked into the Session layer of such protocols as NetBEUI (NetBIOS Enhanced User Interface), NetBIOS is a broadcast-based methodology. As shown in Figure 15.1, NetBIOS name resolution begins when one computer broadcasts the name of the desired destination computer throughout the network ("1"). Computers that do not have the requested name (e.g., "server") ignore the message. The computer has the specified name responds by sending back its unique Media Access Layer (MAC) address ("2"). The MAC addresses of both computers can then be used to initiate a point-to-point communications session between them.

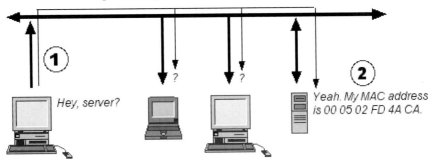

Figure 15.1 *Broadcast-based name resolution.*

This methodology works well enough on small, nonsegmented LANs. On larger LANs, however, it creates a prohibitive volume of broadcast traffic as the number of computers looking for each other increases. In addition, there is no built-in mechanism for routing between multiple network segments, a requirement of any internetwork (of which the Internet is the ultimate example). Perhaps most limiting factor of all, however, is the fact that NetBIOS uses a "flat" name space that requires each computer to have a unique host name. Where two computers have the same name, traffic gets misrouted. Imagine that such a scheme were employed on the Internet. There could be but one "www" in the whole world!

The domain name space is hierarchical, descending from the root domain, usually represented with an empty space (" ") or a dot ("."). Extending from the root domain are primary or top-level domains, the familiar .com, .net, .edu, and so on. The intended uses for these domains are listed in Table 15.1.

Table 15.1 *Common Top-Level Domains*

Domain Name	Description
.com	Commercial, profit-driven organizations (e.g., microsoft.com).
.edu	Educational institutions, mostly universities (e.g., stanford.edu).
.gov	U.S. governmental institutions (e.g., whitehouse.gov).
.int	International organizations (e.g., nato.int).
.net	ISPs and Internet founders (e.g., nsf.net).
.org	Not-for-profit organizations (e.g., redcross.org).
.mil	Military (e.g., navy.mil).

Beneath these are the second-level domains or subdomains, such as "microsoft" or the author's own company network "scionnet."

The last part of any domain address (read from right to left) is the host name, as illustrated in Figure 15.2.

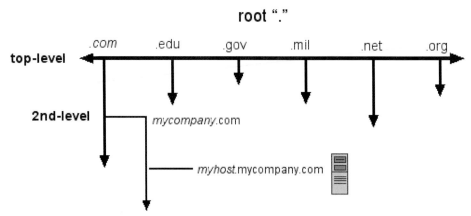

Figure 15.2   *Computers in the DNS hierarchy.*

Because DNS is hierarchical, both Microsoft and Scionnet can have hosts with the name "www" on the same network (the Internet) without concern that they interfere with each other. True, there cannot be two identical domain names at the same level (e.g., there is only one "microsoft.com"), but duplication at the subdomain and host level is permitted.

Requests for name resolutions move through the DNS hierarchy by following a series of pointers. Resolvers first query the root domain, which contains powerful name servers owned by specially designated governmental, educational, and ISP sites. Root domain name servers in turn point to top-level domain name servers (e.g., .com, .edu, net, .org, etc.), which also reside primarily with governments, universities, big companies, ISPs, and the like. Top-level domain name servers then point to name services in their owners' various subdomains (e.g., "scionnet.com"). It is at this level that the Windows 2000 Server DNS server is useful.

Domain name queries originate from resolvers and are sent to name servers. The name servers respond directly to the clients when queries relate to subdomains for which they are authoritative (have address records for). When queried about domains for which they are not authoritative, name servers switch roles and act as resolvers themselves.

In Figure 15.3, you can see that the author's company name server is authoritative for any host in the "scionnet" subdomain. When the author's laptop resolver ("1") asks the company's name server ("2") for the IP address that matches a host name, such as "www.scionnet.com," the name server knows to respond with the correct IP address.

When the same resolver asks for the IP address that matches a remote address, "www.zapwerk.de," things get more complicated. The local name server is not authoritative for "zapwerk.de," so it must forward a query to a root domain name server ("3"). That root domain name server does not know either. It refers the query to a name server in the top-level ".de" domain ("4"), which in turn passes the query to the authoritative name server for "zapwerk" ("5"). The authoritative name server for "zapwerk" then resolves the IP address, passing the data back to the querying laptop.

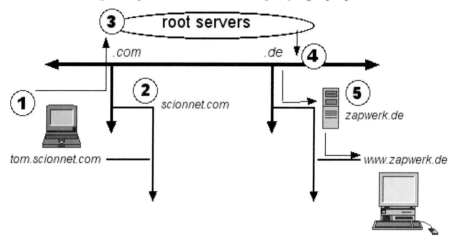

Figure 15.3 *Following the recursion process.*

The process just outlined is called *recursion*. Under this model, the local name server queried the root domain name server and followed successive pointers until it found a host that knew the answer to the laptop's recursive query. In so doing, it used a technique called *iteration*, whereby the queried name server returns either the requested information or the name of another name server that might have the requested information. Recursive queries must be answered either positively (with the IP address) or negatively (with "host not found."). Iterative queries permit the server to refer the question.

When the Windows 2000 Server DNS server receives a query for information that is not in its database, it calls out to a parent server — often that of an ISP — to begin the recursion process. If it receives a query for information that it has looked up recently, however, it recalls the requested information from a cache of recent data. Since the whole query process is not duplicated, caching provides for a faster response.

The DNS Server can maintain hostname-to-IP address mappings for all hosts in a given Zone of Authority (ZOA), which is that part of the domain name space for which a specific name server is authoritative. A network might have one name server responsible for everything in the domain, or it might have multiple name servers with each responsible for different subdomains, or zones, within that domain.

Most domains on the Internet are supervised by at least two name servers, a primary and a secondary, so that if one goes offline the other can maintain DNS. You can set up the Windows 2000 Server in either capacity.

Windows-based network applications address the TCP/IP protocol stack using either the NetBIOS or Windows Sockets (WinSock) Session-layer interface. The NetBIOS interface requires the name of destination computer in order to communicate. The WinSock interface requires an IP address (or a host name that can be resolved to an IP address). To unify this fundamental difference in approaches, Windows 2000 implements NBT (NetBIOS over TCP/IP). Programs written specifically for TCP/IP networks use the WinSock interface to open a communications session using IP addresses. Programs written to use the NetBIOS interface are supported at the Application layer, where NBT resolves a NetBIOS name with an IP address.

To make your network part of the Internet-based domain name space, you must first obtain a unique second-level domain from a registrar. Earlier in Internet history, you could only obtain a domain name from Network Solutions Inc., which had a monopoly. Today, however, there are several registrars and a growing number of primary domains under which you can list your second-level domain.

One requirement when registering a second-level domain is that you must provide primary and secondary name servers that are authoritative, either in conjunction with your ISP or from your own hardware. The primary name server is also a root server for your second-level domain, and must be installed before you can install Active Directory.

Once you have a valid domain name, you can use your Windows 2000 DNS Server to map IP addresses to local host names. Domain names are processed left to right, so in the following domain name:

```
www.scionnet.com
```

"com" refers to the root-level domain, "scionnet" is an example of a company's local domain, and "www" is the host. This is an example of a Fully Qualified Domain Name (FQDN), because it specifies the exact path to the host.

FQDNs are composed of labels and dots. Under Windows 2000, each label can be as large as 63 bytes, with each FQDN totaling no more than 255 bytes. This can be somewhat confusing, as names are traditionally measured in number of characters rather than bytes. That works fine when working with ASCII characters. Under ASCII, any character is equal to eight bits or one byte. Windows 2000 supports Unicode Character Set Transformation Format (UTF)-8 characters, however, which permits character sizes that vary.

In general, characters permissible in a FQDN include the following:

- A-Z (uppercase and lowercase)
- 0-9
- Dashes (-)

Not permitted are underscores (_). This is a big departure from previous Microsoft networking schemes in which the underscore is commonly used in NetBIOS names. When migrating from a Windows NT 4.0 network to a Windows 2000 network, for example, you will find that NetBIOS names containing underscores are translated to dashes. Thus, a computer with a name like "tom_pc" becomes "tom-pc."

Some registrars support labels larger than 200 bytes. It is wise to avoid their use, however, since many WinSock applications are programmed to accept only the 63-byte label. In addition, Windows 2000's support for expanded UTF-8 character sets means that it can actually support labels containing most characters known to human language. Since such support is not universally available across the Internet or in most WinSock applications, however, it's usefulness is limited to homogeneous intranets.

There is no service-level labeling requirement pertaining to FQDNs. For example, if a host is a Web server it does automatically assume the name "www." Such labels are for human identification only, and are irrelevant to the protocol. A Web server with the name "charliethetuna.scionnet.com" is as valid as one named "www.scionnet.com" when it comes to providing services. Windows 2000 does require that name servers support SRV records for use in service recognition, however, as described further on in this chapter.

Installing DNS Server

The steps to installing DNS Server, as covered in Chapter 9, "Administering Windows 2000 Server Resource Access," are as follow:

1. Click the Install Add-on Components link in the installation CD-ROM Autorun screen. This opens the Windows Components window.
2. Choose the Networking Services item in the scrolling list and click the Details button to open the Networking Services window.
3. Enable the Domain Name System (DNS) checkbox, then click the OK button.

4. Click the Next button in the Windows Components window to perform the installation.

It is important that the server on which you install the service have a static IP address.

Configuring DNS Server

Once installed, the server can be configured through the Services and Applications snap-in of the Computer Management MMC, or the more specific DNS snap-in found in the Administrative Tools program group and shown in Figure 15.4.

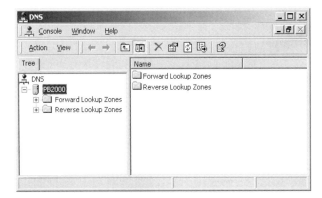

Figure 15.4   *Launching the DNS MMC snap-in.*

The DNS MMC snap-in provides an interface to the zone database, a set of files that contain all of the important information for the domains administered. By default, it is stored in the following location:

```
\WINNT\system32\dns
```

The Windows 2000 DNS server can be deployed in the following roles:

- **Primary name server.** A primary DNS server is responsible for maintaining the master database for a given zone. There can only be one primary DNS server, and addressing changes are made to its database only. The primary DNS server keeps track of the address mappings for Internet-based root domain servers, and caches recent name resolution requests to speed up future requests for the same host.
- **Secondary name server.** Secondary DNS servers provide redundancy by hosting a read-only copy of the master zone database, permitting them to respond to queries when the primary DNS server is unavail-

able because of a server failure or heavy workload. Multiple secondary servers can be deployed on a network to provide fault tolerance and load-balancing functions. Their local databases are regularly updated with that of the primary DNS server through zone transfers.

- **Caching-only server.** Caching-only DNS servers can be deployed to speed up resource access by caching recent external queries, but they do not maintain a copy of the zone database.
- **DNS forwarder.** The DNS forwarder server resolves queries handed to it by another DNS server (forwarding server), rather than from a client directly.
- **Dynamic update server.** New to Windows 2000, the Dynamic DNS (DDNS) server works closely with DHCP to update its database with the proper mappings whenever DHCP assigns an address.

CONFIGURING ROOT NAME SERVERS

In the same way that the Internet's root name servers are authoritative for top-level domains, root name servers deployed in your organization are authoritative for your secondary-level domain, identifying the top of the local hierarchy. In smaller organizations, they might be authoritative for all subdomains as well. Alternately, they might employ delegations, which direct DNS clients to seek out other DNS servers that are authoritative for lower-level subdomains.

To configure the root name server, select the Configure the Server command from the Action menu in the Services and Applications snap-in of the Computer Management MMC to open the Configure DNS Server Wizard. As described in Chapter 9, you are prompted to identify this as the first DNS server on the network, or a secondary that must know the IP address of a pre-existing primary server. If you continue with this wizard, your next task are to configure zones.

CONFIGURING ZONES

Standard zones differ somewhat from the Active Directory integrated zones unique to Windows 2000. We stress the former here, leaving the later for Chapter 23, "Administering DNS and Active Directory." You need to configure the following two types of zones:

- **Forward Lookup Zones.** During a forward lookup query, a client asks the DNS server for the IP address associated with a particular host name. The server either resolves this query from its own database, or passes the request on up the line to the next DNS server. If you enable the creation of the forward lookup zonc, the DNS server creates a database for local address resolution.

- **Reverse Lookup Zones.** In some cases, a user or service might know the IP address of a given host rather than its FQDN. To locate the resource, a reverse lookup is used. A FQDN is processed from right to left, with the left-most designation being that of the host. An IP address, however, is processed from left to right with the right-most octet being the host address. To be used with DNS, then, an IP address such as "64.165.61.70" must become "70.61.165.64." These reserve mappings are maintained in special zones that use the network portion of the address and the in-addr.arpa designator, as in the following example:

```
61.165.64.in-addr.arpa
```

You can configure a new zone through the DNS MMC snap-in by choosing the New Zone command from the Action menu to open the New Zone Wizard. Your first choice is to designate the DNS server as Active Directory integrated, primary, or secondary, as shown in Figure 15.5.

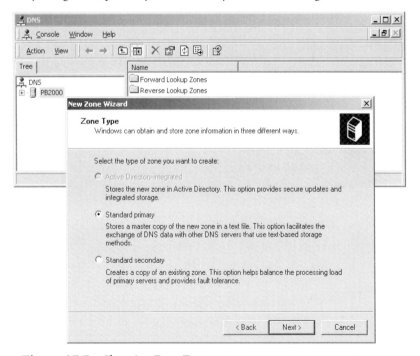

Figure 15.5 *Choosing Zone Type.*

When creating a standard zone, select the Standard primary radio button.

Next, you are prompted to create either a forward lookup zone or reverse lookup zone. Choose to create the forward lookup zone first. You are then prompted to name the zone, in the following format:

```
zone.mycompany.com
```

What naming convention should you use? There are no hard and fast rules, although zones based on resource types, departmental divisions, and geographical locations are common.

Zones may contain multiple domains and subdomians, so long as those domains are contiguous. For example, consider some of the zones in use by international software developer zapwerk Inc., as illustrated in Figure 15.6.

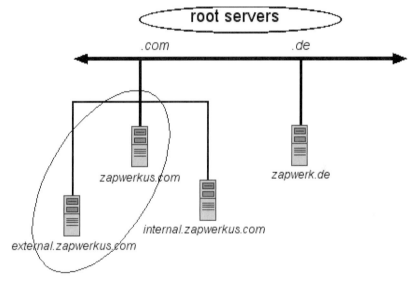

Figure 15.6 *Contiguous and noncontiguous zones.*

The company's U.S. office falls under the "zapwerkus.com" domain, while its German headquarters uses the domain "zapwerk.de." At the U.S. offices, two zones are maintained. One contains the nonpublic resources of the "internal.zapwerkus.com" subdomain while the other contains the more public resources of both the "zapwerkus.com" domain and "external.zap-werkus.com" subdomain. The "zapwerk.de" domain cannot be made part of either zone, however, as it is noncontiguous.

When queries come in for resources in "zapwerkus.com" or "inter-nal.zapwerkus.com," they are immediately resolved. The primary DNS server has records for both "zapwerkus.com" and "internal.zapwerkus.com" because they share the same zone. When requests come in for resources in "external.zapwerkus.com," however, a delegation is used to refer the queries to the DNS server that has a zone file for that subdomain.

Zones can be particularly useful when you wish to distribute the responsibility for the DNS database among multiple administrators in multiple locations. For example, the "scionnet.com" domain might contain "west.scionnet.com" and "east.scionnet.com" zones. One would be administered from offices in San Francisco while the other is administered from offices in New York.

After naming the zone, you are prompted to accept the default file name for the new database file (such as "west.scionnet.com.dns"). Optionally, you can choose to designate an existing file that you have previously copied to the \WINNT\system32\dns folder on the DNS server from some other server. Press the Next button to finish the wizard.

Strictly speaking, you do not have to create a reverse lookup zone. Practically speaking, you must in order to avoid DNS time-outs when using several types of software. Trying to resolve an IP address with a host name is too slow when using a forward lookup zone. It is somewhat like using a phone book. It works fine when you know the name of the person you want to call. Just use alphabetical order to find the name and the number is there. It is not so easy when you know the number but not the name, however. Since the phone book is not ordered by phone numbers, who knows how many pages you have to page through to find a match?

This is essentially the method employed a by DNS inverse lookup. To provide a faster and more workable system, the "in-addr.arpa" domain was created to index host names by network ID.

As with the forward lookup zone, the New Zone Wizard asks whether the zone should be created under Active Directory or for a standard primary or secondary DNS server. You are also asked to specify the network ID portion of the zone's IP address range, as shown in Figure 15.7.

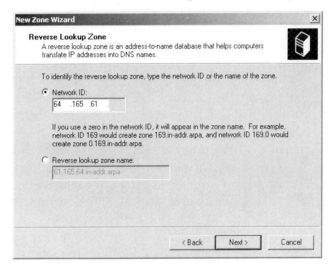

Figure 15.7 *Identifying the network ID.*

The wizard automatically fills in the Reverse lookup zone name field based on the Network ID you supply.

CREATING DNS RESOURCE RECORDS

Once you have created the zone database, you are ready to populate it with resource records. DNS record types are as follow:

- **SOA (Start of Authority).** This record identifies the DNS server that is authoritative for the data within a domain. This is the first record in any domain.
- **NS (Name Server).** This record identifies the DNS servers that can provide authoritative answers to queries for resources within a domain. These include the primary server as well as any secondary servers. NS records also redirect client requests from DNS servers that are not authoritative to those that are. For example, you do not get an answer from the ".com" DNS server when you look for "www.scionnet.com." However, that DNS server has an NS record to redirect the client to the authoritative "scionnet.com" server.
- **A (Address).** The most common, this record contains the IP address-to-host name mapping for a given computer.
- **CNAME (Canonical Name).** This is an alias record that can be created for any host with an address record. If you are running multiple

services on your Windows 2000 computer, you might want to create multiple canonical names to resolve access requests. For example, a host with an address record for "dc1.scionnet.com" might have canonical name records for "www.scionnet.com," "ftp.scionnet.com," and "smtp.scionnet.com."

- **MX (Mail Exchanger).** This record is used to identify mail servers (which must also have a valid address record). DNS assigns a different priority to each mail exchanger host, depending on how desirable it is for that host to receive email. The most desirable host is always the one serving the recipient's email account. When unavailable, email can be sent to a relay host that holds it until the destination host is available. In addition to the host name, this record contains a server priority number. The lower the number the higher the priority. What you actually use for a number is irrelevant, although it is wise to leave some numbers between them in case you choose to slip in a new MX host later. For instance, if you use the priority numbers "10" and "20" your company could easily deploy another MX host at priority "15." If you use "1" and "2" instead, this would not be possible.

- **SRV (Service).** This record identifies the available services running on a given host. These records are particularly important to Windows 2000 domains, as they inform Windows 2000 clients of which hosts are domain controllers that can authenticate their log-on requests.

- **HINFO (Host Information).** These records provide information about the DNS server machine, such as its OS and CPU. This data is handy for some network protocols, such as FTP, which employ special procedures when communicating between computers of the same OS and CPU types.

- **PTR (Pointer).** This record is used for reverse lookups. Reverse lookups are necessary for some security verifications, particularly for email hosts.

After you complete the wizard, the new forward and reverse lookup zones are available in the DNS MMC snap-in. SOA and NS records are created automatically. To create a host record in a forward lookup zone, choose the New Host command from the Action menu to open the New Host dialog box, as shown in Figure 15.8.

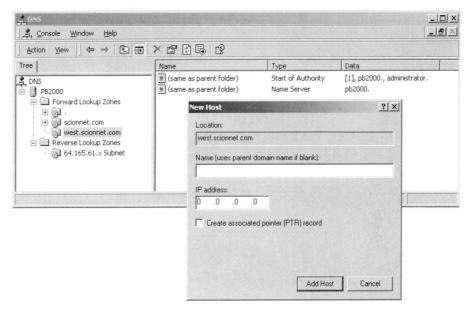

Figure 15.8   *Adding a new host record.*

Enter the host name and IP address, then click the Add Host button to add the new record to the database.

Similar commands exist under the Action menu for CNAME and MX records. Other record types (such as HINFO and SRV) are created using the Other New Records command. When working with reverse lookup zones, specific commands are available to create CNAME and PTR records.

CONFIGURING FOR DYNAMIC UPDATES • New to the Windows 2000 DNS Server is its ability to perform dynamic updates. This ability overcomes the DNS limitation of using static databases that must be updated manually by an administrator. Thanks to the Dynamic DNS update protocol, Windows 2000 clients use the DHCP client service to inform the primary DNS server of their current host names and IP addresses (e.g., A and PTR records).

The primary server can be of either the Active Directory integrated or standard types. To enable dynamic updates, right-click on a zone and choose the Properties command to open the properties dialog box, as shown in Figure 15.9.

Figure 15.9 *Enabling dynamic updates.*

Select Yes in the Allow dynamic updates drop-down menu.

CONFIGURING DELEGATED ZONES

As previously mentioned, zones provide a good way to distribute responsibility for database administration. This is done through zone delegation, a process wherein a DNS server passes on requests to another DNS server for actual resolution. For example, if the "scionnet.com" domain is divided into "west.scionnet.com" and "east.scionnet.com" zones, a delegation could be used to redirect requests coming into the root domain server to subdomain servers located in San Francisco and New York. This is also a handy way to provide load-balancing. You can delegate zones to either primary or secondary servers.

To create a delegation, select a zone, then choose the New Delegation command from the Action menu to launch the New Delegation Wizard. First, you need to supply the zone name, as shown in Figure 15.10.

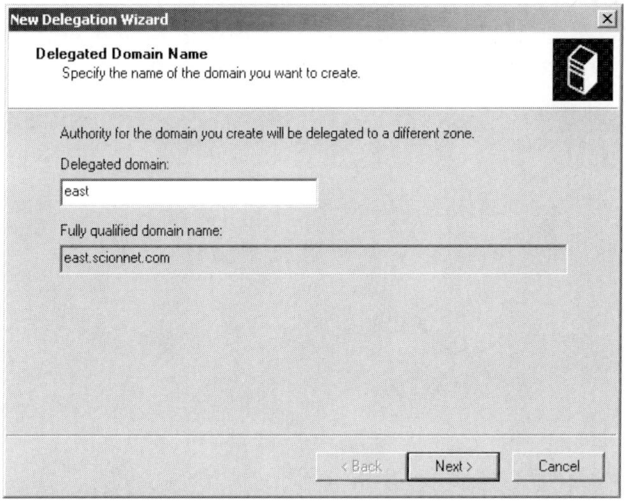

Figure 15.10   *Delegating a zone.*

The wizard automatically creates the appropriate FQDN.

Next, you are prompted to enter the host name and IP address of the DNS server that takes responsibility for the zone. This creates a new NS resource record for the DNS server.

Active Directory integrated zones can be made invulnerable to updates from unauthorized hosts through the use of secure dynamic updates, as described in Chapter 23.

CONFIGURING CACHING-ONLY SERVERS

All DNS servers cache the queries they resolve to speed up future requests. (This information is stored only in RAM, and so is lost after a reboot.) Caching-only servers do not maintain zone files or a zone database, they simply maintain a cache of successful DNS queries. They are useful in network performance tuning, for they can be used to provide faster responses to queries from remote network segments (such as those isolated over WAN links) without generating zone transfer traffic. They can also augment security when deployed as DNS forwarders.

To configure a caching-only server, install the DNS Server as you normally would, but do not add any zones. All DNS servers create a "cache.dns" file to contain the IP addresses of Internet root servers. Under Windows

2000, you can view this cache, also called the root hints file, under the Root Hints tab of the of the DNS server properties dialog box. The caching-only server adds to this file as it issues iterative queries in response to client requests.

CONFIGURING DNS CLIENTS

As previously described, the DNS client is a resolver that queries the DNS name space. It actually looks in several places to achieve host name resolution, in the following order:

1. localhost
2. DNS
3. NetBIOS Remote Name Cache
4. WINS
5. broadcast
6. LMHOSTS file

As described previously in this book, the HOSTS file is a static database of host name-to-IP address mappings located in the \WINNT\system32\drivers\etc folder. Under Windows 2000, the resolver caches the contents of the HOSTS file on startup.

Whenever the resolver receives a query for an entry that contains a period or is longer than 15 bytes, it will initiate the host name resolution sequence. Otherwise, the resolver initiates a NetBIOS name resolution process. When initiating the host name resolution sequence, the resolver first determines whether the destination is the local host. If not, it checks its local DNS cache, which also contains the contents of the HOSTS file. Failing that, it checks with the preferred DNS server. When the DNS server cannot resolve the request, the resolver uses the host name label of the FQDN to initiate the NetBIOS name resolution process.

DNS clients can be configured either manually or via DHCP, as described in Chapter 6, "Networking Windows 2000 Professional."

TESTING DNS SERVER

To test the validity of your configuration, you can enable the use of the following tests under the Monitoring tab of the DNS Server's properties dialog box:

- **A simple query against this DNS server.** This option sends a (non-recursive) query to the local server to resolve a name in a zone for which it is authoritative.

· **A recursive query to other DNS servers.** This option sends a query for NS record information in the root of the Internet domain name space. It requires that the cache.dns file be accurate and up-to-date.

Managing DNS

As previously described, your network is expected to provide some fault tolerance for DNS by having both primary and secondary name servers. These name servers keep their databases in sync through the process of zone transfer. Zone transfers are initiated by the secondary server at boot-up, after a predefined refresh interval has elapsed, or whenever the primary notifies the secondary that an update has occurred.

Parameters that pertain to zone transfers are contained in the primary server's SOA record, as shown in Figure 15.11.

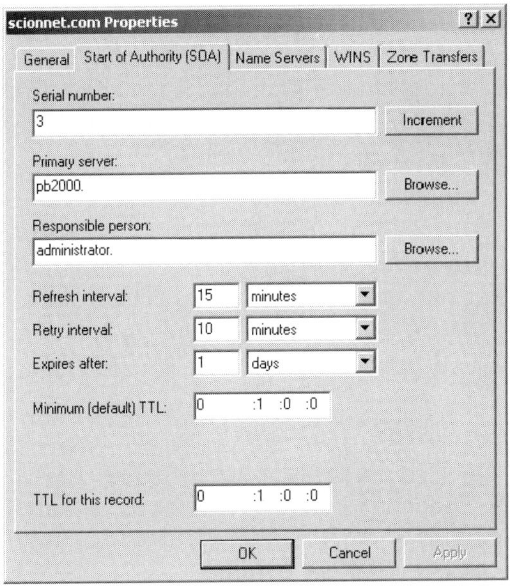

Figure 15.11 *Viewing the SOA record.*

When you create a zone, it has a serial number of "1." Each time a change is made to the database, this number is increased by an increment of one. This serial number is passed on to the secondary during zone transfers. Zone transfers are initiated if the time designated in the Refresh interval field has elapsed and if the secondary server detects that the serial number in the primary server's SOA record is larger than it own. If so, the secondary server begins one of the following zone transfer types:

- **Entire Zone Transfer (AXFR).** As the name implies, a secondary server that uses this type of request receives the entire zone database, even if there is but one change in the records. Windows NT 4.0 DNS servers were restricted to this type.
- **Incremental Zone Transfer (IXFR).** To save time and bandwidth, Windows 2000 DNS servers can use this query type, ensuring that only those records that have actually changed are transferred to the secondary server.

The primary DNS server ignores an IXFR request and perform an entire zone transfer if it does not understand the request, the secondary server's database is too old, or the sum of changes is greater than the entire zone.

For the purposes of zone transfer, the name server providing the database information is the master and the name server receiving the update is the secondary or slave server. The term "primary" is not used, because a primary server can act as a secondary to zones for which it is not authoritative.

Should the primary be unavailable when the refresh interval comes around, the secondary waits for the length of time specified in the Retry Interval field before sending another request. The secondary continues trying to contact the primary until it is successful.

Windows 2000 DNS Server can respond to AXFR or IXFR request types, making it compatible with Windows NT 4.0 and nonWindows DNS servers that do not support IXFR. Windows 2000 DNS servers also support the use of fast transfers, in which multiple records are included in a single message. UNIX-based BIND DNS servers prior to version 4.9.4 do not support this feature, however, so if your are working with such servers as secondaries you need to enable the BIND Secondaries checkbox under the Advanced tab of the DNS Server's properties dialog box.

Unique to Windows NT 4.0/2000 DNS servers are the ability to use WINS servers in performing forward and reverse lookups. If you enable the settings under the WINS tab in a zone's properties dialog box, the DNS server queries a WINS server with the host name label of the FQDN. This feature requires the use of WINS and WINS-R resource records that are not recognized by nonMicrosoft DNS servers, however. To address this, you may disable the transfer of WINS and WINS-R resource records.

Table 15.2 provides a comparison of the features supported by Windows and BIND-based DNS servers.

Table 15.2 *Common DNS Server Features*

DNS Server	Features
Windows 2000	UTF-8, dynamic updates, secure dynamic updates, SRV, WINS, and WINS-R resource records, IXFR transfers, fast transfers.
Windows NT 4.0	SRV (with SP4), WINS, and WINS-R resource records, fast transfers.
BIND 8.2	Dynamic updates, SRV resource records, IXFR transfers, fast transfers.
BIND 8.1.2	Dynamic updates, SRV resource records, fast transfers.
BIND 4.9.7	SRV resource records, fast transfers.

Monitoring and Troubleshooting DNS

Among the tools useful in troubleshooting your DNS server are NSLOOKUP, System Monitor, Event Viewer, and DNS logging.

USING NSLOOKUP

One of the easiest ways to verify the functioning of your newly configured DNS server is to use the NSLOOKUP command from the command prompt. This simple tool queries the zone database directly. For example, if you typed the following:

```
nslookup www.scionnet.com
```

You would get a response similar to the following:

```
Server: ns1.scionnet.com
```

```
Address: 64.165.61.65
```

```
Name: www.scionnet.com
```

```
Address 64.165.61.95
```

USING SYSTEM MONITOR

As described previously in this book, the System Monitor application lets you establish a wide range of statistical measurements for most of the computer's hardware and software components. The DNS Server is no exception. System Monitor's primary DNS-related counters are shown in Table 15.3.

Table 15.3 *DNS-Related Counters in System Monitor*

Counter	Description
AXFR Request Received	Number of full zone transfer requests received by the master server.
AXFR Request Sent	Number of full zone transfer requests sent by the secondary server.
AXFR Response Received	Number of full zone transfer responses received by the secondary server.
AXFR Success Received	Number of successful full zone transfers received by the secondary server.
AXFR Success Sent	Number of successful full zone transfers sent by the master server.
Caching Memory	Amount of memory used for caching.
Database Node Memory	Amount of database node memory used by the server.
Dynamic Update NoOperation	Number of empty dynamic update requests received by the server.
Dynamic Update NoOperation/sec.	Rate at which empty dynamic update requests are being received by the server.
Dynamic Update Queued	Number of dynamic update requests queued at the server.
Dynamic Update Received	Number of dynamic update requests received by the server.
Dynamic Update Received/sec .	Rate at which dynamic update requests are being received by the server.
Dynamic Update Rejected	Number of dynamic update requests rejected by the server.
Dynamic Update TimeOuts	Number of dynamic update timeouts at the server.
Dynamic Update Written to Database	Number of dynamic updates written to the database by the server.
Dynamic Update Written to Database/ sec.	Rate at which dynamic update are being written to the database by the server.
IXFR Request Received	Number of incremental zone transfer requests received by the master server.

Table 15.3 *DNS-Related Counters in System Monitor (continued)*

IXFR Request Sent	Number of incremental zone transfer requests sent by the secondary server.
IXFR Response Received	Number of incremental zone transfer responses received by the secondary server.
IXFR Success Received	Number of successful incremental zone transfers received by the secondary server.
IXFR Success Sent	Number of successful incremental zone transfers sent by the master server.
IXFR TCP Success Received	Number of successful TCP incremental zone transfers received by the secondary server.
IXFR UDP Success Received	Number of successful UDP incremental zone transfers received by the secondary server.
Nbstat Memory	Amount of nbstat memory used by the server.
Notify Received	Number of notifies received by the secondary server.
Notify Sent	Number of notifies received by the master server.
Record Flow Memory	Amount of record flow memory used by the server.
Recursive Queries	Number of recursive queries received by the server.
Recursive Queries/sec.	Rate at which recursive queries are being received by the server.
Recursive Query Failure	Number of recursive query failures.
Recursive Query Failure/sec.	Rate at which recursive queries are failing.
Recursive Send TimeOuts	Number of recursive query sending timeouts.
Recursive TimeOut/sec.	Rate of recursive query sending timeouts.
Secure Update Failure	Number of secure update failures of the server.
Secure Update Received	Number of secure update requests received by the server.
Secure Update Received/sec.	Rate at which secure update requests are received by the server.
TCP Message Memory	Amount of memory used for TCP messages.
TCP Query Received	Number of TCP queries received by the server.
TCP Query Received/sec.	Rate at which TCP queries are received by the server.
TCP Response Sent	Number of TCP responses sent by the server.
TCP Response Sent/sec.	Rate at which TCP responses are sent by the server.
Total Query Received	Number of queries received by the server.

Table 15.3 *DNS-Related Counters in System Monitor (continued)*

Total Query Received/ sec.	Rate at which queries are received by the server.
Total Response Sent	Number of responses sent by the server.
Total Response Sent/ sec.	Rate at which responses are sent by the server.
UDP Message Memory	Amount of memory used for UDP messages.
UDP Query Received	Number of UDP queries received by the server.
UDP Query Received/ sec.	Rate at which UDP queries are received by the server.
UDP Response Sent	Number of UDP responses sent by the server.
UDP Response Sent/ sec.	Rate at which UDP responses are sent by the server.
WINS Lookup Received	Number of WINS lookup requests received by the server.
WINS Lookup Received/sec.	Rate at which WINS lookup requests are received by the server.
WINS Response Sent	Number of WINS lookup responses sent by the server.
WINS Response Sent/ sec.	Rate at which WINS lookup responses are sent by the server.
WINS Reverse Lookup Received	Number of WINS reverse lookup requests received by the server.
WINS Reverse Lookup Received/sec.	Rate at which WINS reverse lookup requests are received by the server.
WINS Reverse Response Sent	Number of WINS reverse lookup responses sent by the server.
WINS Reverse Response Sent/sec.	Rate at which WINS reverse lookup responses are sent by the server.
Zone Transfer Failure	Number of zone transfers from the master server that failed.
Zone Transfer Request Received	Number of zone transfer requests received by the master server.
Zone Transfer SOA Request Sent	Number of SOA resource record requests sent by the secondary server.
Zone Transfer Success	Number of zone transfers from the master server that succeeded.

USING EVENT VIEWER

Also useful in monitoring and troubleshooting the DNS server is Event Viewer, which maintains a DNS Server log, as shown in Figure 15.12.

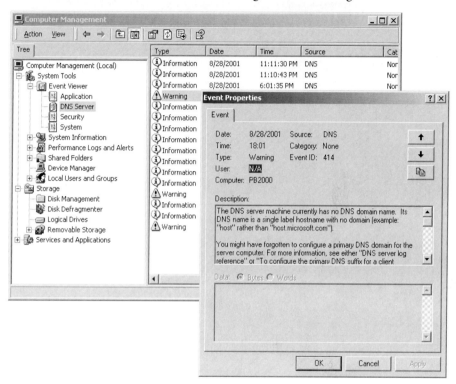

Figure 15.12 *Viewing the DNS Server log.*

Among the events tracked are when zone transfers occurred, when changes occurred in the zone, and when there were problems.

DNS LOGGING

Should you require more detailed information, you can enable the use of a trace log under the Logging tab of the DNS Server's properties dialog, as shown in Figure 15.13.

Enable checkboxes for the categories you wish to log. The results are stored in a text file located in the \WINNT\system32\dns folder. This type of logging is processor intensive, so use it only when necessary.

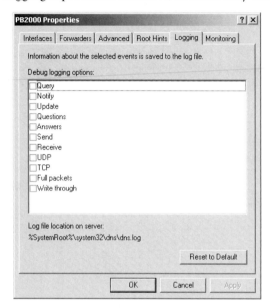

Figure 15.13 *Enabling a Trace Log.*

Study Break

Install and Configure DNS Server

Practice what you have learned by installing and configuring the Windows 2000 Server DNS Server, perhaps in a secondary or caching-only server role.

If possible, create a new zone for which the DNS Server is authoritative, and its associated forward and reverse lookup zones. Verify its proper functioning using the built-in monitoring function and NSLOOKUP. Also verify the proper functioning of zone transfers.

■ Summary

In this chapter, we examined various DNS topics including the configuration of the DNS server, zones, records, and clients.

Working With DNS

DNS adheres to the client/server model. DNS clients are referred to as resolvers, while its servers are commonly called name servers. Applications that make use of DNS resolvers include Web browsers, FTP utilities, and telnet clients. When hunting for an IP address-to-domain name mapping, resolvers query a group of worldwide databases collectively referred to as the domain name space. The domain name space is hierarchical, with primary (.com, and so on.) and second-level (microsoft, and so on.) domains descending from a root domain.

Requests for name resolutions move through the DNS hierarchy by following a series of pointers. Resolvers first query the root domain, which has servers that in turn point to top-level domain name servers. Top-level domain name servers then point to name services in their owners' various subdomains. Name servers respond directly to the clients when queries relate to subdomains for which they are authoritative. When queried about domains for which they are not authoritative, name servers switch roles and act as resolvers themselves through the process of recursion. Queries use a technique called iteration, whereby the queried name server returns either the requested information or the name of another name server that might have the requested information.

The Windows 2000 DNS Server can maintain hostname-to-IP address mappings for all hosts in a given ZOA. A network might have one name server responsible for everything in the domain, or it might have multiple name servers, each responsible for different zones within that domain. The Windows 2000 DNS server can be deployed as a primary name server, responsible for maintaining the master database for a given zone; secondary name server, providing redundancy by hosting a read-only copy of the master zone database; caching-only server, to speed up resource access by caching recent external queries; DNS forwarder, to resolve queries handed to it by another DNS server, or DDNS, working with DHCP to update its database with the proper mappings whenever DHCP assigns an IP address.

Setting up the DNS Server involves the creation of forward lookup zones, for host name-to-IP address resolution, and reverse lookup zones, for IP address-to-host name resolution. You also need to create resource records. The SOA record identifies the DNS server that is authoritative for a domain. The NS record identifies the DNS servers that can provide authoritative answers to queries for resources within a domain. The A record contains the IP address-to-host name mapping for a given computer. The CNAME record is an alias that can be created for any host with an address record. The MX record is used to identify mail servers. The SRV record identifies the available services running on a given host. The HINFO record provides information about the DNS server machine, such as its OS and CPU. The PTR record is used for reverse lookups. The DNS Sever can also be configured as caching-only, without resource records, and with delegations, which pass the work of name resolution to other DNS servers.

Tools useful in monitoring and troubleshooting the DNS Server include NSLOOKUP, Event Viewer, System Monitor, and the DNS trace log.

▲ CHAPTER REVIEW QUESTIONS

Here are a few questions relating to the material covered in the *Installing, Configuring, Managing, Monitoring, and Troubleshooting DNS in a Windows 2000 Network Infrastructure* section of Microsoft's *Implementing and Administering a Microsoft Windows 2000 Network Infrastructure* exam (70-216).

1. *Which of the following statements are true with regards to DNS? Select all that apply:*

   A. It uses broadcast-based name resolution methodology

   B. It uses a hierarchical name space

   C. It maintains IP address-to-host name mappings in centralized databases

   D. It is heavily integrated into Windows 2000 networking

2. *Among the requirements of registering a second-level domain is an agreement to provide a primary and secondary DNS server.*

   A. True

   B. False

3. *DNS Server is automatically installed along with the Windows 2000 Server operating system.*

   A. True

   B. False

4. *The DNS snap-in to the MMC provides an interface to the root name server's zone database.*

   A. True

   B. False

5. Which of the following DNS server roles support deployment as the root name server? Select all that apply:

   A. Primary

   B. Secondary

   C. Caching-only

   D. DNS Forwarder

6. Which of the following may be configured using the New Zone Wizard? Select all that apply:

   A. Standard primary server

   B. Standard secondary server

   C. Active Directory integrated server

   D. DDNS

7. You should create a reverse lookup zone, even though it is not strictly necessary.

   A. True

   B. False

8. Caching-only DNS servers store recent queries in a RAM-based cache that is deleted during reboot.

   A. True

   B. False

9. To configure a caching-only DNS server, you can simply install the DNS Server without adding zones.

   A. True

   B. False

10. The DNS client will perform the NetBIOS name resolution process before contacting a DNS server for name resolution.

    A. True

    B. False

11. Windows 2000 DNS clients automatically cache the contents of the HOSTS file.

    A. True

    B. False

12. *Dynamic updates are only available on Active Directory integrated DNS servers.*
    A. True
    B. False

13. *Dynamic updates permit the updating of DNS records by the client.*
    A. True
    B. False

14. *When testing the DNS Server, you can choose to perform queries against the local name server or against the root name space.*
    A. True
    B. False

15. *When testing the DNS Server, you should not perform a recursive DNS query unless the cache.dns file is up-to-date.*
    A. True
    B. False

16. *Delegations can be used to improve DNS Server fault tolerance by selectively passing queries to another server in times of high-traffic.*
    A. True
    B. False

17. *Delegations can be used to improve overall DNS performance by distributing queries for various zones among various DNS servers.*
    A. True
    B. False

18. *Which of the following are pertinent to zone transfers? Select all that apply:*
    A. AXFR
    B. EXFR
    C. IXFR
    D. DXFR

19. *Which of the following might not be supported by a UNIX-based BIND server? Select all that apply:*
    A. SRV resource records
    B. WINS-R resource records
    C. IXFR transfers
    D. Fast transfers

20. *The NSLOOKUP utility can be used to query the zone database directly.*

    A. True

    B. False

21. *Because it is processor intensive, you should not enable the DNS trace log unless it is really necessary for troubleshooting.*

    A. True

    B. False

Administering Dynamic Host Configuration Protocol

▲ Chapter Syllabus

MCSE 16.1 Working with DHCP

In this chapter, we look at material covered in the *Installing, Configuring, Managing, Monitoring, and Troubleshooting DHCP in a Windows 2000 Network Infrastructure* section of Microsoft's *Implementing and Administering a Microsoft Windows 2000 Network Infrastructure* exam (70-216).

The following material teaches you to install and configure the DHCP Server, set up scopes, and integrate it with DNS and Active Directory. You also learn to manage, monitor, and troubleshoot DHCP. DHCP Server was first described in Chapter 9, "Administering Windows 2000 Server Resource Access."

| MCSE 16.1 | **Working with DHCP** |

As previously described, use of the Windows 2000 Server DHCP Server reduces the amount of work an administrator must perform in configuring workstation IP addresses by automatically loaning out, or *leasing*, IP addresses as needed.

The client-server lease process takes place in the following four phases:

- **DHCPDISCOVER.** The process begins when the DHCP client broadcasts a DHCPDISCOVER message on the local segment. The message is addressed to the IP address 255.255.255.255 and hardware address FFFFFFFFFFFF. While all nodes hear the broadcast, only a DHCP server responds to the DHCPDISCOVER message. In the message, the client provides its MAC address, host name, parameter request list (containing supported DHCP options), network interface hardware type (such as 10 Mbps Ethernet), and a message ID (used in all subsequent client-server communications pertaining to the request.)

- **DHCPOFFER.** DHCP servers maintain pools of available addresses. Upon receiving a DHCPDISCOVER message, they respond to the client with a DHCPOFFER message that is addressed to the client's MAC address. Besides the DHCP server's IP address, the DHCPOFFER message contains an offered IP address, subnet mask, and optional information such as default gateway, DNS server, and WINS server addresses. The DHCPOFFER offer message also contains a lease interval, which determines how long the client may use the offered IP address, and first and second lease renewal intervals, which determines when the lease may be renewed.

- **DHCPREQUEST.** The DHCP client responds to the first DHCPOFFER message it receives with a DHCPREQUEST message. This message is sent as a broadcast even though the DHCP client now knows the IP address of the DHCP server. By doing so, the client informs all other DHCP servers that it has rejected their DHCPOFFER messages and does not require an IP address from their pools. The DHCPREQUEST message confirms the information received in the DHCPOFFER message, containing the server's IP address and the client's hardware address, requested IP address, and host name.

- **DHCPACK.** The DHCP server ends the process by responding with a DHCPACK (acknowledgment) message. Like the DHCPREQUEST message, this is a broadcast addressed to the client's MAC address.

The client's IP address is not officially assigned until this message is sent. The message contains much of the same information that was contained in the DHCPOFFER and DHCPREQUEST messages.

At this point, the client has leased an IP address that can be used in subsequent network communications. By default, the duration of the lease is eight days. By setting a lease limit, the DHCP server ensures that assigned IP addresses are actually in use. After the lease duration has elapsed, an IP address is returned to the pool unless the lease is renewed.

Along with the lease duration, the DHCPOFFER message contains the following information pertaining to when a client is required to renew the lease:

- **Renewal Time Interval (T1).** This value is 50 percent of the lease duration, or four days by default. When this interval is reached, the client attempts to renew its lease by broadcasting a DHCPREQUEST message that contains its current IP address. If the DHCP server that issued the IP address is available and responds, the lease is renewed. If the DHCP server is unavailable, the client is still allowed to keep the IP address, but the clock is ticking.
- **Rebinding Time Value (T2).** This value is 87.5 percent of the lease duration, or 168 hours by default. If the client was unable to renew its lease when the T1 value was reached, it tries again at this point by sending another DHCPREQUEST message. If the DHCP server that issued the IP address is available and responds, the lease is renewed. If the DHCP server that issued the IP address is unavailable, the client enters a *rebinding state* during which it reinitiates the DHCPDIS-COVER process in an attempt to renew the lease from any DHCP server. If the client fails to renew its lease, it then tries to obtain a new address from any available DHCP server.

DHCP clients also send out DHCPREQUEST messages for lease renewal at boot-up, just to make sure that they are still connected to the same network. If the message is not properly acknowledged, the client attempts to obtain a new, valid IP address.

To provide DHCP services on your network, you must install the DHCP Server service and have available a range of unassigned IP addresses with which to configure it.

Installing DHCP Server

The steps to installing DHCP Server, as covered in Chapter 9, are as follows:

1. Click the Install Add-on Components link in the installation CD-ROM Autorun screen. This opens the Windows Components window.
2. Choose the Networking Services item in the scrolling list and click the Details button to open the Networking Services window.
3. Enable the Dynamic Host Configuration Protocol (DHCP) checkbox, then click the OK button.
4. Click the Next button in the Windows Components window to perform the installation.

It is important that the server on which you install the service have a static IP address.

Configuring DHCP Server

The primary task you must perform when configuring the DHCP Server is to create a *scope*, the pool of addresses that the server manages.

WORKING WITH DHCP SCOPES

Once you have installed the DHCP Server, you must provide it with a range of unassigned and unused IP addresses to form a scope. Although only one scope can be created for a given subnet, the DHCP Server can manage multiple scopes on multiple subnets. The DHCP Server need not necessarily be on the same subnet as the scopes it manages, for its services can be extended to clients on remote segments by certain types of routers and DHCP Relay Agents.

It is possible to create a scope using a limited range of addresses within a subnet, thus leaving other addresses, such as those for servers, to be statically assigned. It is recommended that you make all IP addresses on a subnet part of a scope, however. You may then remove the IP addresses that you wish to assign statically from DHCP control through the use of an exclusions list.

CREATING SCOPES • Once installed, the server can be configured through the Services and Applications snap-in of the Computer Management MMC, or the more specific the DHCP MMC snap-in found in the Administrative Tools program group and shown in Figure 16.1.

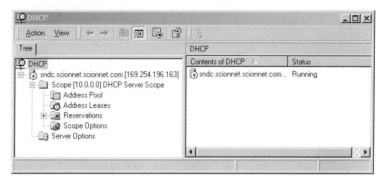

Figure 16.1 *Launching the DHCP MMC snap-in.*

To create a new scope, select the server in the Tree pane and choose the New Scope command from the Action menu to open the New Scope Wizard, as shown in Figure 16.2.

Figure 16.2 *Launching the New Scope Wizard.*

The wizard prompts you to supply the following information in subsequent windows:

- **Scope Name.** Provide a name and description for the scope.
- **IP Address Range.** Provide the first IP address, last IP address, and subnet mask.

- **Add Exclusions.** Provide a range of IP addresses, or individual IP addresses, that should not be managed by the DHCP Server.
- **Lease Duration.** Set a length for time for leases, in days, hours, and minutes. The default is eight days. If your network is populated by mobile computers and dialup clients that access and leave the network often, you may want to reduce the lease duration to ensure the maximum number of unused addresses are always available. Four hours is a common setting. If your network is relatively static, you might want to increase the lease duration to reduce the amount of DHCP-related traffic.
- **Configure DHCP Options.** While the DHCP server requires such information as IP address range and subnet mask, details such as the default gateway, DNS server address, and WINS server address are optional. The wizard gives you the option of configuring this information.
- **Activate Scope.** In the last step, the wizard lets you activate the scope immediately or later.

Once it is installed and activated, you can further configure the DHCP Server via the items under the Scope folder in the MMC Tree pane (see Figure 16.1). For example, select the Scope Options folder and right click the DNS Servers item to open the Scope Options dialog box, as shown in Figure 16.3.

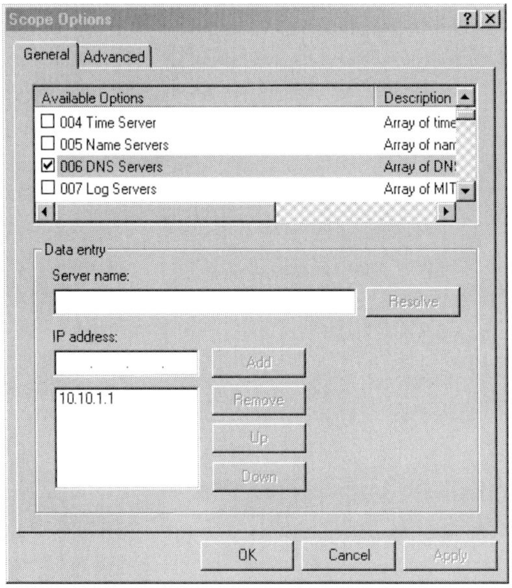

Figure 16.3 *DNS scope options.*

Although there are many entries for optional information that can be supplied to DHCP clients, the Windows client supports only the following:

- **003 Router.** The default gateway's IP address.
- **006 DNS.** The primary DNS server's IP address.
- **015 Domain Name.** The network's domain name.
- **044 WINS/NBNS Servers.** The WINS server's IP address.
- **046 WINS/NBT Node Type.** The NetBIOS node type.
- **047 NetBIOS Scope ID.** The NetBIOS scope ID.

Use the Scope Options dialog box when you wish to configure different options for multiple scopes, such as the default gateway. Where settings are shared, such as for the DNS server, use the Server Options dialog box instead, as these options apply to all scopes.

Although options can be applied in several ways, they are cumulative. When DHCP options conflict, the settings take precedence over each other in the following order:

1. **Locally configured options.** These are settings that have been manually configured at the client.
2. **Vendor/user class options.** Custom vendor-specific options may be added to the DHCP Server for specific hardware and software applications. Microsoft's vendor specific options include disabling NBT, releasing the lease at shutdown, using a router metric base (used to calculate the fastest network routes), and autodiscovering the proxy. User class options let the client communicate a class membership to the DHCP Server, which then returns class-specific settings. You can configure your own user class options on the DHCP Server. For example, you might create a "mobile" class that assigns laptop users a specific gateway.
3. **Client options.** These are settings configured for the client.
4. **Scope options.** These are scope-specific settings.
5. **Server options.** These are global settings.

CONFIGURING BOOTP SUPPORT • Bootstrap Protocol (BOOTP) is an earlier UNIX technique for obtaining dynamic IP addresses. DHCP is based upon this earlier, more limited, protocol. Because of this, DHCP servers can process requests from BOOTP clients as well. To enable this option, select the scope and right-click to open the properties dialog box.

Switch to the Advanced tab, and select either the BOOTP or Both radio button, as shown in Figure 16.4.

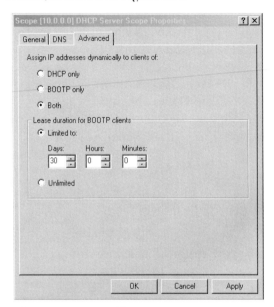

Figure 16.4 *Enabling BOOTP options.*

When supporting BOOTP clients, you might also wish to enable the Show the BOOTP table folder option under the General tab in the DHCP Server's properties dialog box. This displays the table in which are set BOOTP client configuration entries, which vary somewhat from those of DHCP clients.

CONFIGURING RESERVATIONS • In most circumstances, you will find it most convenient to give the DHCP Server a range of addresses and let it assign IP addresses as it sees fit. You can, however, use the DHCP Server to assign static IP addresses of a sort through the use of *reservations*. A reserved client always receives the same IP address, which is handy for servers and other computers mapped to specific host names.

To configure a reserved client, select the New Reservation command from the Action menu to open the New Reservation dialog box, as shown in Figure 16.5.

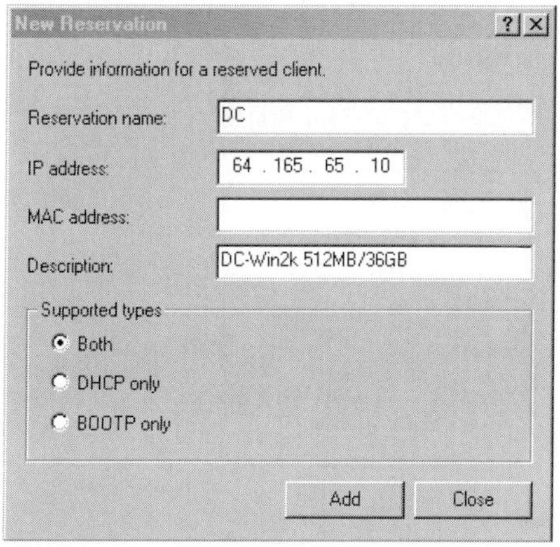

Figure 16.5 *Configuring a reserved client.*

In the New Reservation dialog box, enter an IP address that is part of any existing scope. Also add the host name, MAC address (without dashes), and a description. Once added, the reserved address is removed from the pool of available addresses, just as if it were in the exclusion list.

CONFIGURING DNS INTEGRATION

Under Windows 2000, DHCP can be integrated with the Dynamic DNS (DDNS) server through the settings established under the DNS tab of the server properties dialog box, as shown in Figure 16.6.

If you enable the first radio button under the Automatically update DHCP client information in DNS check box, the DHCP Server updates the DDNS server with a client's A and PTR record at the client's request.

If you enable the second radio button, the DHCP Server can update the DDNS server without the client's request.

Disable the checkbox if you want the DHCP Server to let the client to update its own information with the DDNS server (an option configured at the client).

If you enable the Enable updates for DNS clients that do not support dynamic update checkbox, the DHCP Server will serve as a proxy between incompatible clients (such as those under Windows NT 4.0) and DDNS.

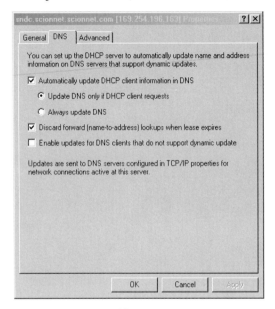

Figure 16.6   *Enabling DDNS integration options.*

AUTHORIZING DHCP SERVER IN ACTIVE DIRECTORY

The DHCP Server is designed to be integrated with Windows 2000 domain security, and must therefore be *authorized* with Active Directory. This helps ensure that no one creates address conflicts on your network by deploying their own DHCP Server somewhere. Unless authorized with Active Directory, any such Windows 2000-based "rogue" servers are automatically detected and forced to shut down their DHCP service.

When you deploy a new DHCP Server in an Active Directory environment, the following occurs:

1. Before initialization, the Windows 2000 DHCP Server broadcasts a DHCPINFORM message on the local segment that contains vendor-specific information designed to let the server to query network information from any existing Windows 2000 DHCP Servers.
2. Any receiving servers respond with a DHCPACK message containing information about the enterprise root name and location.
3. The new DHCP server receives DHCPACK messages from all available servers. If the messages contain information for the enterprise root, the

new DHCP server queries Active Directory to see if its IP address is in the authorized list. If not, the server does not initialize its DHCP service. The DHCP Server only initialize its services if it is authorized with Active Directory, it is the only Windows 2000 DHCP Server on the segment, or other servers are Windows 2000 workgroup servers or older systems (such as Windows NT 4.0 DHCP Server).

To authorize your server, select it in the DHCP MMC pane and right click to choose the Authorize option in the pop-up menu.

Managing DHCP

Beyond the initial configuration, issues that require further management of the DHCP Server include scopes and DHCP relays.

MANAGING SCOPES

One issue you might be confronted with in managing the DHCP Server is the need for additional scopes on a single subnet. This limitation can be overcome through the use of a *superscope*. A superscope is a feature of the Windows 2000 that permits you to deploy multiple scopes on a single subnet as "child" scopes to a parent scope. This permits you to administer DHCP clients on a *multinet*, a network configuration that includes multiple logical networks on the same physical network segment.

Superscopes are most useful when the number of DHCP clients has nearly exceeded the network's available IP addresses. With a superscope, you can continue to use the original "child" scope while adding an additional scope for expansion within the same network name space.

To configure a superscope, right-click the server in the DHCP MMC window and select the New Superscope command from the pop-up menu.

MANAGING DHCP RELAY AGENTS

In general, broadcast messages such as those used by DHCP are limited to the local segment. Broadcasts are not passed on by routers. If you have multiple segments on your network, then, you must either install multiple DHCP servers or use a mechanism that allow your DHCP traffic to traverse routers. Such mechanisms exist in the form of *BOOTP relays* and *DHCP Relay Agents*.

BOOTP relays are implemented on many routers, allowing them to pass BOOTP and DHCP broadcast messages. Where routers with this capability are unavailable, Windows 2000 Server can be configured to act as a DHCP Relay Agent. The DHCP Relay Agent acts as a sort of proxy by intercepting DHCP messages and forwarding them to known DHCP servers on remote segments.

DHCP Relay Agents are configured through the RRAS MMC.

Monitoring and Troubleshooting DHCP

In addition to the Event Viewer, tools useful in monitoring and trouble-shooting DHCP include IPCONFIG, System Monitor, and DHCP logging.

USING IPCONFIG

If the computer is configured to receive its addressing information from DHCP but fails to gain access to the network, you may employ the IPCONFIG utility in your troubleshooting. To determine which network settings a DHCP server has leased to a desktop, type the following command at the Command Line prompt:

```
IPCONFIG /all
```

Here you can verify the accuracy of TCP/IP information, including host name, physical address, IP address, subnet mask, and DHCP use, as shown in Figure 16.7.

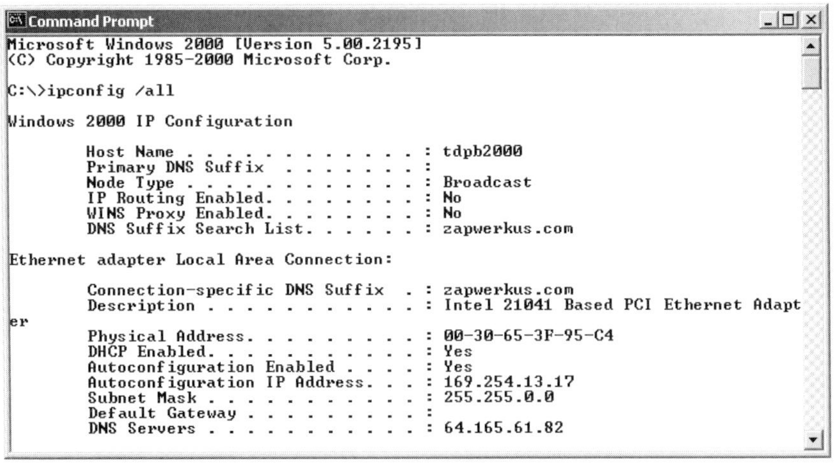

```
Command Prompt                                                        _ □ ×
Microsoft Windows 2000 [Version 5.00.2195]
(C) Copyright 1985-2000 Microsoft Corp.

C:\>ipconfig /all

Windows 2000 IP Configuration

        Host Name . . . . . . . . . . . . : tdpb2000
        Primary DNS Suffix  . . . . . . . :
        Node Type . . . . . . . . . . . . : Broadcast
        IP Routing Enabled. . . . . . . . : No
        WINS Proxy Enabled. . . . . . . . : No
        DNS Suffix Search List. . . . . . : zapwerkus.com

Ethernet adapter Local Area Connection:

        Connection-specific DNS Suffix  . : zapwerkus.com
        Description . . . . . . . . . . . : Intel 21041 Based PCI Ethernet Adapt
er
        Physical Address. . . . . . . . . : 00-30-65-3F-95-C4
        DHCP Enabled. . . . . . . . . . . : Yes
        Autoconfiguration Enabled . . . . : Yes
        Autoconfiguration IP Address. . . : 169.254.13.17
        Subnet Mask . . . . . . . . . . . : 255.255.0.0
        Default Gateway . . . . . . . . . :
        DNS Servers . . . . . . . . . . . : 64.165.61.82
```

Figure 16.7 *Viewing the IP configuration.*

If there is a problem connecting to the DHCP server, you will probably see that the client computer has an invalid address, such as the broadcast address 255.255.255.255. In this case, you should release the client's IP address and try to lease a new one. To do this, type the following sequence of commands at a command prompt:

```
IPCONFIG /release
```

```
IPCONFIG /renew
```

If the DHCP server is available, the client should be granted a new lease for an IP address.

USING SYSTEM MONITOR

As with the DNS Server, System Monitor tracks a large number of statistical measurements for the DHCP Server, such as the number of messages sent and received and how taxing the operations are to the processor. Among System Monitor's more useful DHCP-related counters are those shown in Table 16.1.

Table 16.1 *DHCP-Related Counters in System Monitor*

Counter	Description
Packets Received/ sec.	The number of messages received by the DHCP Server. Create a baseline to determine the average number. If you see a large increase, investigate the cause.
Packets Expired/sec.	The number of messages held in the queue for so long that they eventually expired. If the number is large, determine why the DHCP server is responding to DHCP messages too slowly.
Nacks/sec.	The number of negative acknowledgements received by the server. If the number is large, it could mean that many laptops are moving on and off the network, or that a scope is deactivated.
Declines/sec.	The number of messages sent by clients to turn down an offered IP address. Clients also send this message when they detect a duplicate IP address. If the number is high, enable the DHCP Server's conflict detection feature (under the Advanced tab in the server properties dialog box) to track down the presence of duplicate IP addresses.

USING DHCP LOGGING

You can enable the use of a log under the General tab of the DHCP Server's properties dialog. You can determine where the log is stored in the hard drive under the Advanced tab. By default, the results are stored in a text file located in the \WINNT\system32\dhcp folder.

Study Break

Install and Configure DHCP Server

Practice what you have learned by installing and configuring the DHCP Server.

First, run the New Scope Wizard to create a new scope. Use the options to configure settings for WINS and DNS servers. Use the exclusions list to set aside the addresses of computers requiring static addresses, such as servers. Activate the scope, and authorize the scope with Active Directory if necessary. Finally, move to a client computer and use the IPCONFIG utility to verify that the workstation is receiving its address from the DHCP Server.

■ Summary

In this chapter, we looked at the ways in which the DHCP Server manages and assigns IP addresses.

Working with DHCP

The DHCP Server IP address leasing process takes place in four phases. The process begins when the DHCP client broadcasts a DHCPDISCOVER message on the local segment. Upon receiving a DHCPDISCOVER message, a DHCP server responds to the client with a DHCPOFFER message that is addressed to the client's MAC address, offering an IP address. The DHCP client responds to the first DHCPOFFER message it receives with a DHCPREQUEST message to confirm the information received in the DHCPOFFER message. The DHCP server ends the process by responding with a DHCPACK (acknowledgement) message.

At this point, the client has leased an IP address that can be used in subsequent network communications. By setting a lease duration, the DHCP server ensures that assigned IP addresses are actually in use. After the lease duration has elapsed, an IP address is returned to the pool unless the lease is renewed. When the Renewal Time Interval is reached at 50 percent of the lease duration, the client attempts to renew its lease. It does so again at 87.5 percent of the lease duration, the Rebinding Time Value. If the DHCP server that issued the IP address is available and responds, the lease is renewed. If the DHCP server that issued the IP address is unavailable, the client reinitiates the DHCPDISCOVER process in an attempt to renew the lease from any DHCP server. If the client fails to renew its lease, it then tries to obtain a new address from any available DHCP server.

Once you have installed the DHCP Server, you must provide it with a range of unassigned and unused IP addresses to form a scope. Although only one scope can be created for a given subnet, the DHCP Server can manage multiple scopes on multiple subnets. The DHCP Server need not necessarily be on the same subnet as the scopes it manages, for its services can be extended to clients on remote segments by certain types of routers and DHCP Relay Agents. A superscope is a feature of the Windows 2000 that permits you to deploy multiple scopes on a single subnet as "child" scopes to a parent scope. This permits you to administer DHCP clients on a multinet, a network configuration that includes multiple logical networks on the same physical network segment.

▲ CHAPTER REVIEW QUESTIONS

Here are a few questions relating to material covered in the *Installing, Configuring, Managing, Monitoring, and Troubleshooting DHCP in a Windows 2000 Network Infrastructure* section of Microsoft's *Implementing and Administering a Microsoft Windows 2000 Network Infrastructure* exam (70-216).

1. *Which of the following are messages sent between client and server during the lease process? Select all that apply:*
    A. DHCPDISCOVER
    B. DHCPINFORM
    C. DHCPOFFER
    D. DHCPACK

2. *Before installing a DHCP server, you should first obtain a range of contiguous IP addresses that it will manage.*
    A. True
    B. False

3. *The DHCP Server must be installed prior to the installation of Directory Services.*
    A. True
    B. False

4. *Microsoft recommends that you configure scopes with limited IP address ranges that do not include IP addresses that are statically assigned.*

    A. True

    B. False

5. *If your network is relatively static, you might wish to extend the lease duration to reduce the amount of DHCP traffic on the network.*

    A. True

    B. False

6. *Only Windows 2000 DHCP clients can be used with the DDNS.*

    A. True

    B. False

7. *The DHCP Server will only configure a client's A and PTR records with the DDNS server at the client's request.*

    A. True

    B. False

8. *Under which of the following circumstances does a Windows 2000 DHCP Server activate its services? Select all that apply:*

    A. If it is authorized by Active Directory.

    B. If it is the only DHCP Server on the network segment.

    C. If other DHCP servers are hosted by Windows 2000 workgroup servers.

    D. If other DHCP servers are hosted by Windows NT 4.0 servers.

9. *Active Directory authorization ensures that any rogue DHCP servers on the network will be shut down.*

    A. True

    B. False

10. *Any indication that DHCP is working properly on the client end is the presence of the IP address 255.255.255.255 when viewed from IPCONFIG.*

    A. True

    B. False

11. *A large number of negative acknowledgments, as viewed by the System Monitor Nacks/sec. Counter, is a sign of a relative static network.*

    A. True

    B. False

Administering Remote Access

▲ **Chapter Syllabus**

MCSE 17.1 Working with Remote Access

MCSE 17.2 Configuring Remote Access Security

This chapter covers material in the *Installing, Configuring, Managing, Monitoring, and Troubleshooting Remote Access in a Windows 2000 Network Infrastructure* section of Microsoft's *Implementing and Administering a Microsoft Windows 2000 Network Infrastructure* exam (70-216).

Off-site access to Windows 2000 networking components and services is made possible through the installation and configuration of the Routing and Remote Access Service (RRAS). In this chapter, you examine such issues as configuring and managing RRAS connections, options, and security. This material was partially addressed in Chapter 6, "Networking Windows 2000 Professional," and Chapter 13, "Networking Windows 2000 Server."

RRAS supercedes Windows NT's Remote Access Service (RAS), first introduced in Windows NT 3.51 Service Pack 2. RRAS integrates several services, such as the Multiprotocol Router (MPR) and Remote Access Server, into a single service.

Features new to RRAS include the following:

- RRAS MMC snap-in and Net Shell (NETSH) command line tool.
- Support for Network Address Translation (NAT).
- Support for Layer Two Tunneling Protocol (L2TP) and Internet Protocol Security (IPSec).
- Support for Internet Group Management Protocol (IGMP) and multicast boundaries.
- Expanded support for Remote Authentication Dial-in User Service (RADIUS).

MCSE 17.1 Working with Remote Access

You can deploy RRAS to extend your network to far away locations through *Dial-Up Networking*, which is used to create temporary connections between a RRAS server and remote users over telecommunications media (analog telephone, ISDN, X.25). You can also extend access through *Virtual Private Networking (VPN)*, used to create secure connections between a RRAS server and remote users through an IP network intermediary, such as the Internet.

Incoming connections to your LAN can be made using the following line protocols:

- **Point-to-Point Protocol (PPP).** PPP acts as a bridge for TCP/IP, IPX, NetBEUI, and other protocols. It accepts static or DHCP IP address assignments, and supports encrypted authentication.
- **Point-to-Point Tunneling Protocol (PPTP).** An extension to PPP, PPTP allows a Dial-Up Networking client to establish secure communication sessions with a RRAS server via the Internet. PPTP supports encryption for both communications and authentication and the creation of multi-protocol VPNs. Through PPTP, the Internet can be used as a transport for IPX and NetBEUI by encapsulating their packets.
- **Layer Two Tunneling Protocol (L2TP).** Similar in function to PPTP, L2TP creates an encrypted tunnel through the Internet. Unlike PPTP, however, it does not encrypt its sessions directly, relying instead such technologies as IPSec. It also differs in that while PPTP only supports IP directly, L2TP supports such additional packet-oriented protocols as X.25, Frame Relay, User Datagram Protocol (UDP), and Asynchronous Transfer Mode (ATM).

Dial-Up Networking clients can also use *Serial Line Internet Protocol (SLIP)* to make dialup connections to legacy SLIP servers, but RRAS does not support incoming SLIP connections.

After a remote client uses PPP, PPTP, or L2TP to establish a connection to a RRAS server, the user is authenticated and granted access to either the server or the server plus the local network. The former scenario, referred to as *point-to-point remote access*, involves no routing. The latter scenario, referred to as *point-to-LAN remote access*, requires that the server also act as a multi-protocol router and NetBIOS gateway.

Remote clients capable of accessing RRAS include the following:

- Windows 2000
- Windows NT 3.5, 4.0
- Windows 9x, Me
- Windows for Workgroups
- MS-DOS
- LAN Manager

Many third-party PPP clients, such as Apple's AppleTalk Remote Access (ARA) and various UNIX programs.

The physical connection to RRAS can be made using the following technologies:

- **Public Switched Telephone Network (PSTN).** This is the technology used by your local telecommunications provider to bring analog telephone service to your home or office. RRAS requires a modem to use PSTN.
- **Integrated Digital Services Network (ISDN).** This is a technology used by some local telecommunications providers to bring digital telephone service to homes and offices. RRAS requires an ISDN adapter to use it.
- **Digital Links.** Modems work by converting digital signals to analog signals and back again. You can sometimes eliminate part of this process and some line noise by employing a digital switch on a T carrier or ISDN connection. The client requires a V.90 modem and the server requires a V.90 digital switch to use it.
- **X.25.** This is a packet-switching technology used by many local telecommunications providers to bring analog data service to offices. RRAS requires a Packet Assembler Dissembler (PAD) to use it.
- **Asynchronous Digital Subscriber Line (ADSL).** This technology provides digital transmission speeds over PTSN lines. Its use requires either an ADSL router, which connects to the server via Ethernet, or a dialup adapter, which connects the server via ATM.

- **Null Modem.** This method connects two computers directly rather than via the network. RRAS needs a null modem cable to use it. Similarly, Infrared ports can also be used.

Configuring Routing and Remote Access

Among the issues you will confront in setting up remote access are configuring inbound connections, policies, profiles, VPNs, routing, and DHCP integration.

RRAS is installed under Windows 2000 Server by default, but not activated. Prior to activating it, you must install and configure the network protocols that will be used with RRAS and verify that all communications components, such as modems and network adapters, are working properly. You may then select the Routing and Remote Access item from the Administrative Tools program group to open the Routing and Remote Access MMC, as shown in Figure 17.1.

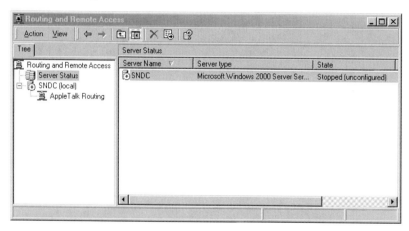

Figure 17.1   *Activating Routing and Remote Access.*

Next, select the Configure and Enable Routing and Remote Access command from the Action menu to launch the Routing and Remote Access Server Setup Wizard. The wizard prompts you to choose among the following common configurations:

- **Internet connection server.** This option enables Internet Connection Sharing (ICS) through a modem, network adapter, or some other communications device, making your server a gateway between the Internet and workstations on the local network.

- **Remote access server.** This option permits remote computers to connect with your server, and by extension the LAN, over a dialup device.
- **VPN server.** This option permits remote computers to securely connect with your server and network via their own Internet Service Providers (ISPs).
- **Network router.** This option permits you to establish the Windows 2000 Server as a router between separate networks, for which you have separate network adapters installed.
- **Manually configured server.** This option enables a few initial settings for RRAS, then lets you configure the rest. This is useful when the other options do not meet your needs.

Select the appropriate option to continue, such as the Remote access server radio button. In subsequent windows, you are prompted for the following:

- **Remote Client Protocols.** Confirm that all of the necessary LAN protocols are in place (AppleTalk, IPX, NetBEUI, TCP/IP) or choose to install additional protocols.
- **Guest Authentication.** If AppleTalk was among your network protocol choices, you are informed that remote access can either be granted to anyone via the Guest account, or restricted to authenticated users only. If you enable unauthenticated access, any dialup client—not just Macintosh clients—can gain server access without name or password.
- **Network selection.** If your server resides on more than one network segment, you are directed to choose the network adapter attached to the network to which dialup users are granted access.
- **IP Address Assignment.** Assuming TCP/IP was among your network protocol choices, you are prompted to determine how dialup clients will receive their own valid IP addresses, either via DHCP or from a range of IP addresses that you specify.
- **Managing Multiple Remote Access Servers.** If there is more than one remote access server on your network, you can enable the IAS/RADIUS option to provide a centralized authentication database to serve them.

After you complete the wizard, RAS starts up, thereafter becoming accessible through the Routing and Remote Access MMC, as shown in Figure

17.2. You may use the Routing and Remote Access MMC to configure RAS by protocol and port, as well as adjust policies and view log activity.

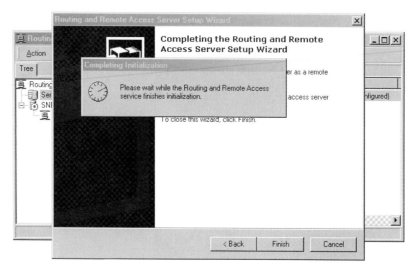

Figure 17.2 *Starting Up RAS.*

CONFIGURING INBOUND CONNECTIONS

Once your remote access server is established, client computers can connect through various devices and ports. For the purposes of remote access, *devices* are hardware and software that create physical and logical point-to-point connections between the client and server (such as analog modems or ISDN adapters). *Ports* are the channels that devices provide to support single point-to-point connections.

The Routing and Remote Access Server Setup Wizard provides an initial configuration for several ports. To view the details of these configurations, right-click the Ports branch from the local server in the RRAS MMC and choose the Properties command to open the Ports Properties dialog box, as shown in Figure 17.3.

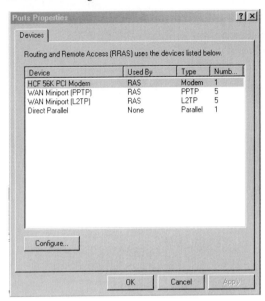

Figure 17.3 *Viewing port configurations.*

To enable or disable the use of a specific device, select it in the list and click the Configure button to open the Configure Device dialog box, as shown in Figure 17.4.

Figure 17.4 *Enabling access through a device.*

By default, a modem is configured to accept incoming calls only. If you wish to use the device for dial-out connections also, enable the Demand dial routing connections checkbox and supply a telephone number.

CREATING REMOTE ACCESS POLICY

Under Windows 2000, RAS security makes user access dependent on the permissions assigned to user accounts plus the settings of the server's remote access policy. These policies let you base the decision of whether to allow access on such criteria as time of day, connection type, and group membership. When a user dials in, his connection attempt must meet the criteria defined by at least one remote access policy. If not, access is denied regardless of the permission granted the user account.

The following models can be used in implementing dialup access permissions:

- **Access By User.** This model, which is the same under Windows NT Server 4.0, controls user access by enabling or disabling access under the dial-in tab in the user account dialog box. If you explicitly permit access, a connection is established if the connection attempt matches conditions specified by both the user account's dial-in properties and remote access profile. This option is available when RAS is based on a standalone server, a server that is a member of a Windows NT 4.0 domain, or a server that is a member of a Windows 2000 native-mode or mixed mode domain.
- **Access by Policy Under Native Mode.** Under this model, access is dependent upon a remote access policy that is set for all users. If the policy's remote access permission is set to grant access and the connection attempt is approved by remote access policy criteria as well as the user account's dial-in properties and remote access profile, the connection is established. If the policy's remote access permission is set to deny access, the connection is not permitted even if the connection attempt matches the policy's other conditions. Likewise, if a connection attempt fails to match the conditions of remote access policy, user account properties, or the remote access profile, access is not permitted. This option is available when RAS is based on a standalone server or a server that is a member of a Windows 2000 native-mode domain.
- **Access by Policy Under Mixed Mode.** Under this model, if a connection attempt matches remote access policy conditions as well as user account dial-in properties and the remote access profile, access is permitted. If a connection attempt matches the conditions of the remote access policy but differs from the remote access profile settings, access is not permitted. (To enable this restriction, enable the Restrict dial-in to this number only option and use a telephone number not actu-

ally used by RRAS.) If the connection attempt does not match the conditions of any remote access policies, access is not permitted.

You may create remote access policies by selecting the Remote Access Policies branch in the Routing and Remote Access MMC and choosing the New Remote Access Policy command from the Action menu. The conditions that can be specified in remote access policy are listed in Table 17.1.

Table 17.1 *Remote Access Policy Conditions*

Condition	Description
Called-Station-ID	Telephone number of the remote access server. Can be used if the telephone line and hardware support caller ID.
Calling-Station-ID	Telephone number of the remote client. Can be used if the telephone line and client-server hardware support caller ID.
Client-Friendly Name	Used when the server acts as a RADIUS client.
Client-IP-Address	Used when the server acts as a RADIUS client.
Client-Vendor	Used when the server acts as a RADIUS client.
Day-And-Time-Restriction	Days and times (relative to the RAS server) when access is permissible.
Framed-Protocol	Used when the server acts as a RADIUS client.
NAS-Identifier	Used when the server acts as a RADIUS client.
NAS-IP-Address	Used when the server acts as a RADIUS client.
NAS-Port-Type	Dial-up media used, such as analog (asynch), ISDN, or VPN (virtual).
Service-Type	Used when the server acts as a RADIUS client.
Tunnel-Type	Protocols to be used (PPTP or L2TP).
Windows-Groups	Domain groups of which the remote user is a member. (No local groups.)

CONFIGURING REMOTE ACCESS PROFILES

Remote access profile settings are applied to connections that have been previously authorized by user account permissions and remote access policy conditions. Among the restrictions that can be configured are the following:

- **Dial-In Constraints.** Contains such settings as Disconnect if idle for "X" minutes, Restrict maximum session to "X" minutes, restrict access to certain days and times, permit access to a certain dial-in number only, or permit only certain dial-in media (Ethernet, ADSL, and so on).

- **IP.** Defines IP address assignment behaviors and contains such settings as whether the client can choose an IP address, which packets are filtered, how long a connect can be idle before it is disconnected, and how long a user can stay connected.
- **Multilink.** *Multilinking* increases data transmission rates by combining multiple physical links (e.g., multiple modems and telephone lines) into a logical connection that increases bandwidth. You can allow or deny the use of multilinking, as well as establish Bandwidth Allocation Protocol (BAP)/Bandwidth Allocation Control Protocol (BACP) settings that reduce multilink connections when the session fails below a minimum capacity.
- **Authentication.** Lets you choose from several authentication methods, including nonencrypted and nonauthenticated access.
- **Encryption.** Lets you choose No Encryption, Basic encryption (PPTP with 40-bit key Microsoft Point-to-Point Encryption (MPPE)/L2TP over IP Sec with 56-bit Data Encryption Standard (DES)), Strong encryption (PPTP with 56-bit key MPPE/L2TP over IP Sec with 56-bit DES) for authentication, or Strongest encryption (PPTP with 128-bit key MPPE/L2TP over IP Sec with 128-bit DES) for authentication.
- **Advanced.** Lets you establish many RADIUS attributes used in communications with the Internet Authentication Service (IAS) server.

CONFIGURING VIRTUAL PRIVATE NETWORKS

To configure a VPN, your network should have a permanent, full-time Internet connection. During installation, RAS enables the following incoming VPN ports by default:

- **PPTP.** Using the Extensible Authentication Protocol (EAP), PPTP supports encryption for both communications and authentication, making remote access as secure as access on a local network segment. In operation, a remote client connects to the Internet using an ISP dialup account. Once IP connectivity has been established, a PPTP "tunnel" is created through which IP, IPX, and NetBEUI protocols can travel while encapsulated in PPP packets.
- **L2TP.** Unlike PPTP, L2TP does not encrypt its sessions directly, relying instead on such technologies as IPSec for tunnel encryption and authentication.

The PPTP and L2TP WAN Miniports can be configured in the same manner as modem ports, except that you are given the option of increasing the number of ports. You may not simply delete one of these miniports if you do not require its use. Instead, decrease the number of available ports or disable its remote access permission.

Installing VPN access between your server and another RAS server, such as a server located at one of your organization's distant locations, is made simple through the Network Connection Wizard. The wizard can be launched via the Make New Connection item in the Networking and Dial-Up Connections program group. Configure an outgoing VPN connection by performing the following steps:

1. Select the Connect to a Private network through the Internet radio button in the Network Connection Wizard to establish dialup settings for secure connections between your server and another dialup server.
2. Specify the existing dialup connection that should be used, if any. Choose the Automatically dial this initial connection radio button and choose from the options in the drop menu, such as a previously configured private network or Internet connection. Alternately, create an entirely new connection by selecting the Do not dial the initial connection radio button.
3. Supply the host name or IP address of the host to which you are connecting, such as a Windows 2000 Server computer.
4. Apply the connection to all user profiles or yours exclusively.
5. Name the connection.

When completed, the wizard creates a connection icon in the Network and Dial-Up Connections program group under the name you defined. Right-click the item and choose the Properties command from the pop-up menu to configure the following options:

- **General.** The remote host and dialup connection settings.
- **Options.** Dialing options, such as prompting for name and password, and redial options.
- **Security.** The use of authentication and data encryption. Enable the Advanced radio button and click the Settings button to make available a more extensive list of security protocol options. You can specify that data encryption be required for all connections, be disabled for all connections, or be made optional depending on the dialup server's capabilities. Similarly, you can choose among various options for how your server encrypts authentication information, which may vary between servers.
- **Networking.** Lets you choose between PPTP or L2TP line protocols, and to choose the LAN protocols supported by the network to which you are calling.

- **Sharing.** Permits you to enable connection sharing and on-demand dialing. If you enable on-demand dialing, you may establish criteria via the Settings button for which applications and services are allowed to initiate it.

CONFIGURING MULTILINK CONNECTIONS

Multilinking supports the combination of multiple physical pathways to increase remote access bandwidth (but not multiple RAS servers). It can be configured under the PPP tab of the remote access server's properties dialog box, as shown in Figure 17.5.

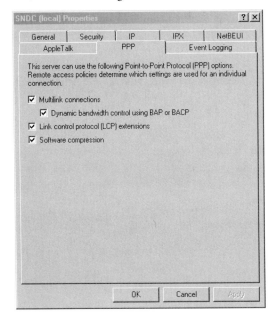

Figure 17.5 *Configuring multilink options.*

Enabling the Dynamic bandwidth control using BAP or BACP checkbox augments the connection by providing a mechanism for adapting to changing conditions. For example, the BAP can add links when throughput requirements increase, or deallocate them when they are not in use.

CONFIGURING ROUTING

RAS's routing features can be configured under the following tabs in the remote access server properties dialog box (see Figure 17.5):

- **IPX.** By default, RAS enables both server and network access via IPX for remote access clients, assigning a network number automatically and using the same network number for all clients. Alternately, you may establish a specific network range for remote clients.

- **AppleTalk.** Enabled by default, a single checkbox extends remote access to ARA clients.
- **NetBEUI.** By default, RRAS enables both server and network access via NetBEUI for remote access clients. Beyond this, NetBEUI cannot be routed.
- **IP.** By default, both IP routing and remote access using DHCP address assignments are enabled. Alternately, you can specify a range of static addresses to be assigned to remote access clients. The intricacies of IP routing are described in Chapter 20, "IP Routing."

CONFIGURING DHCP INTEGRATION • Because of its central administration and better control over such issues as duplicate IP addressing, Microsoft recommends that you employ DHCP for remote access clients' IP address assignment. When this integration is enabled, RAS leases a pool of 10 IP addresses from the DHCP Server at start-up, which it in turn distributes to remote access clients as needed. When this pool is used up, it leases another 10 IP addresses, and so on. These IP addresses are only released when the RRAS service is stopped.

Because the IP address lease is between RAS and the DHCP Server rather than the client and DHCP Server directly, the client does not obtain any scope options that might be specified by DHCP. Instead, it adopts such information as default gateway, DNS server address, and WINS server address from RAS. In most cases, this should suffice for connectivity to take place. If, however, you must extend DHCP scope information to remote access clients, you can do so my installing a DHCP Relay Agent on RAS' internal interface using the following procedure:

1. Double-click the IP Routing item in the RRAS MMC's Tree pane.
2. Right-click the General item in the IP Routing pane, then select the New Routing Protocol command in the pop-up menu.
3. Select DHCP Relay Agent in the New Routing Protocol window and click the OK button.
4. Right-click the newly added DHCP Relay Agent item in the IP Routing pane and choose the Properties command in the pop-up menu.
5. In the DHCP Relay Agent Properties dialog box, add the IP address of at least one DHCP Server.

You cannot install the DHCP Relay Agent if the server is also running the DHCP service or NAT.

If no DHCP Server is available when RAS starts up, the server assigns IP addresses through its Automatic Private IP Addresses (APIPA) feature in the following range:

```
169.254.0.1-169.254.255.254
```

This capability ensures that remote connectivity can still take place when DHCP services are unavailable, but it is not recommended for use in any but the smallest networks because of conflicts that can occur with routers and nonAPIPA addressed computers.

Managing and Monitoring Remote Access

In addition to the Routing and Remote Access MMC, tools that can help you manage and monitor remote access include Net Shell (NETSH), Network Monitor, event logs, authentication and account logs, PPP logs, Simple Network Management Protocol (SNMP), and various third party utilities.

USING NET SHELL

NETSH is a command line utility that can be used to configure and script remote access, DHCP Relay Agent, NAT, and routing on local and remote servers. Located in the \WINNT\system32 folder, this utility can be run in either real-time "online mode" or scripted "offline mode." In offline mode, you can specify a number of batch commands that are not executed until you use the command "commit" (or discard them with the command "flush").

One of NETSH's handiest functions backs up the RRAS server settings to a test file using a command in the following format:

```
NETSH dump file.txt
```

To restore the settings, use a command in the following format:

```
NETSH exec file.txt
```

NETSH tells you which settings were restored successfully and unsuccessfully.

USING NETWORK MONITOR

As with LAN traffic, Network Monitor can be useful in capturing traffic moving between the RAS server and remote client for analysis. Specifically, you can capture PPP traffic relating to the establishment of the connection, and determine if compression and/or encryption is being used.

USING EVENT LOGS

RAS's event logging levels can be configured under the Event Logging tab in the remote access server properties dialog box (see Figure 17.5):

- Log errors only
- Log errors and warnings
- Log the maximum amount of information
- Disable event logging

Among the details that can be gathered in the event log include authentication messages, allocated IP addresses and DHCP data, and connection speeds.

USING AUTHENTICATION AND ACCOUNT LOGS

In addition to the authentication messages recorded in the event log, RAS maintains authentication and account data in the \WINNT\System32\LogFiles folder. This data can be invaluable when troubleshooting connection failures brought on by remote access policies, for they document which settings caused the connection to be accepted or denied.

These files are stored in the IAS 1.0 comma-delimited format by default, but an Open Database Component (ODBC)-compliant format may also be selected for importing into third-party tools.

RAS's authentication logging options can be configured via the Remote Access Logging option in the Tree pane of the RRAS MMC. You can choose to log accounting requests, authentication requests, and periodic status as well as specify a logging interval.

USING PPP LOGS

RAS's PPP logging can be configured under the Event Logging tab in the remote access server properties dialog box (see Figure 17.5). Information on the connection establishment process, protocols, and programming calls are stored in the "ppp.log" file in the \WINNT\tracing folder.

USING SNMP AND THIRD PARTY UTILITIES

Windows 2000 provides support for Management Information Database (MIB) II, making it compatible with numerous third-party SNMP consoles.

RRAS also has robust Application Programmer's Interface (API) sets, making it open to modification and management by third-party tools.

Troubleshooting Remote Access

If RRAS access fails, verify the following:

- RRAS is configured and running properly, and RAS is enabled.
- Dial-up ports are set to receive incoming connections.
- User account properties, remote access policies, and remote access profiles all permit access.
- Remote access policies do not conflict with RAS settings (for authentication, multilink, and so on).
- There are free dialup ports available on RAS.

Among the common issues that can prevent users from connecting with Dial-Up Networking are telecommunications problems, dial-in protocol incompatibilities, authentication method incompatibilities, and security setting misconfigurations.

Logging at either the server or client end can be particularly useful in troubleshooting Dial-Up Networking connections. For example, with a modem log (see Figure 17.6), you can determine if a desktop's communications hardware is communicating with the operating system correctly before troubleshooting higher-level applications and view the communication process to see at which point it is failing.

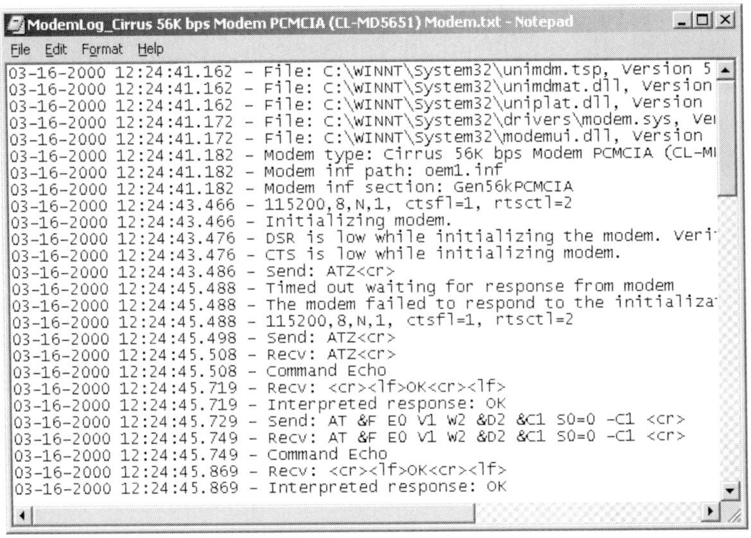

Figure 17.6 *Viewing a modem log.*

Problems with telecommunications technologies are generally beyond what you can troubleshoot without enlisting the aid of the telco. Nevertheless, this is where you should start when users are unable to dial-out for a connection to the RAS server. Before contacting the telco, verify that users' equipment is functional (e.g., is turned on, is correctly attached to the desktop and plugged into the data jack, has dial-tone, and so on) and that it is properly configured (e.g., has the right modem settings, Service Profile Identifiers (SPIDs), X.3 settings, and so on). In cases in which users are unable dial in to your servers, this is commonly the problem.

Poor-quality telecommunications links are also a primary cause of slow and dropped connections. To spot these types of problems, you can direct users to the Dial-Up Networking Monitor, which provides various connection options and status statistics. If users report excessive errors, poor lines or faulty connection components are indicated.

When users are unable to negotiate a connection with your dial-in server, first make sure that their service profiles are using a dialup protocol that your server supports. This can be identified in the Dial-Up Networking phone book entry. If you are providing access through PPP, for example, but a user has selected SLIP in the properties dialog box, that user will be unable to negotiate a connection. In addition, make sure users who have the correct dialup protocols selected also have the correct settings configured for those protocols.

PPP can be configured to use either automatic DHCP or static addressing. Desktops that fail to acquire a unique IP address through these means will not be able to access network resources. In addition, such settings as the Use IP Header Compression checkbox (which reduces the protocol overhead sent over the modem) might not be supported on the server-end. In short, make sure that all dialup protocol settings—including details such as compression—match on both client and server.

One of the most common errors experienced by Dial-Up Networking users attempting to connect to an intranet occurs when the connection fails during authentication. Although the most common reason for this is incorrect password usage, this situation can also be caused by incompatible encryption methods. If this happens, try switching both server and client to the clear text authentication option. If communications then take place, you know that the encryption was the problem. Both client and server must be using the same security settings here, or communications will fail.

A general list of possible dialup connection problems and solutions for Dial-Up Networking clients on all Windows operating systems, as suggested by Microsoft, is provided in Table 17.2.

Table 17.2 *Common Dial-Up Problems and Solutions*

Problem	Solution
The modem does not work because it is incompatible.	Check the list of compatible modems in the Microsoft Windows Hardware Compatibility List at the Microsoft Web site. If the modem in question is not listed, consider replacing it.
The client is unable to connect to a remote server because the modem cable is incompatible.	Be sure that a proper hardware handshaking cable is in use. Do not use the 9-to-25-pin converters that are included with most mouse hardware, for example, because some of them do not carry modem signals. To be safe, you should use a converter made especially for this purpose.
The client is unable to connect to a remote server because the telephone cabling is faulty.	The telephone line does not accommodate the modem speed. Try selecting a lower bps rate.
The client is unable to connect to a remote server. Error message says that the server is not responding.	One cause could be that, at higher bps rates, the modem is incompatible with the modem of the server. Another cause could be an excess of static on the phone line, which prevents a modem from connecting at a higher bps rate. Yet another possibility is that there is switching equipment between the client and server that prevents the two modems from negotiating at a higher bps rate. Try lowering the modem's bps rate.
Connections with the remote server are repeatedly dropped.	It could be that call waiting is disrupting the connection. Disable call waiting (often using the *70 command) and try calling again.
A hardware error is generated when trying to connect.	If the modem is not functioning properly, you can enable modem logging to test the connection. If the modem communicates through a terminal program, but not through Dial-Up Networking, the cable that attaches the modem to the computer is probably incompatible. Try installing a compatible cable.
A hardware error message is generated when trying to connect because of conflicting serial ports.	Adjust the serial port settings. COM1 and COM3 share Interrupt Request (IRQ) 4. COM2 and COM4 share IRQ 3. As a result, you can use neither COM1 and COM3 nor COM2 and COM4 simultaneously for serial communications. For example, you cannot use Dial-Up Networking on COM1 and a terminal program simultaneously on COM3.

Table 17.2 *Common Dial-Up Problems and Solutions (continued)*

A "No Answer" message is generated when trying to connect by ISDN.	It could be that the telephone number is not configured correctly. Each B channel on an ISDN line can have its own telephone number, or both B channels can share a single telephone number. The telco can tell you how many numbers the ISDN line has. If you are located in the U.S. or Canada, it could also be that the Service Profile Identifier (SPID) is configured incorrectly. The SPID normally consists of the telephone number with additional digits added to the beginning, the end, or both. The SPID helps the switch understand what type of equipment is attached to the line and routes calls to the appropriate devices on the line (as many as eight). If an ISDN channel requires a SPID, but it is not entered correctly, then the device cannot place or accept calls. Reconfigure the ISDN device and try again.
Connections made via X.25 fail because the dialup PAD is configured with the wrong X.3 parameters or serial settings.	If you cannot connect to the remote server directly through an X.25 smart card or an external PAD, modify the dialup PAD X.3 parameters or serial settings.
Connections made via X.25 fail because new "Pad.inf" file entries are incorrect.	Check other "Pad.inf" entries for direct connections and external PADs, and view the comments that go with them. You may need a line analyzer or a terminal program to see the response for the PAD.
Connections made via X.25 are dropping.	If a connection has been established, but network drives are disconnecting, sessions are dropping, or sessions are suffering network errors, the cause might be congestion on the leased line for the remote access server. For example, if four clients connect at 9,600 bps (through dialup PADs), they require a 38,400-bps leased line on the server end (four times 9,600 bps). If the leased line does not have adequate bandwidth, it can cause timeouts and degrade performance for connected clients. Consider upgrading the telecommunications link.
Connections made via PPP to TCP/IP utilities are failing.	If you cannot connect to a server using PPP, or the remote computer terminates your connection, the server may not support Link Control Protocol (LCP) extensions. Try disabling the Enable LCP Extensions option. Similarly, it could also be that IP header compression is keeping TCP/IP utilities from running. If you successfully connect to a remote server using PPP, but TCP/IP utilities do not work, try to reconnect after disabling IP header compression.
Connections from a laptop to an ISP do not permit applications to run normally.	Mobile users operating a laptop in a corporate environment might need to disable the Microsoft WinSock Proxy Client when they use the same computer to dial to an ISP or other network.

Study Break

Install and Configure RAS

> Practice what you have learned by installing and configuring RAS using the Routing and Remote Access Server MMC. First, install RAS, and decide if you wish to permit user access to the entire LAN or the server only. Then, decide which protocols will be supported for remote access. Configure communications ports based on your decisions. Next, configure user accounts, remote access policies, and remote access profiles to permit remote connections. Finally, test your configurations by connecting from a remote computer and accessing server resources.

MCSE 17.2   Configuring Remote Access Security

RRAS employs such security features as authentication and data encryption, both at the client end and through remote access policy.

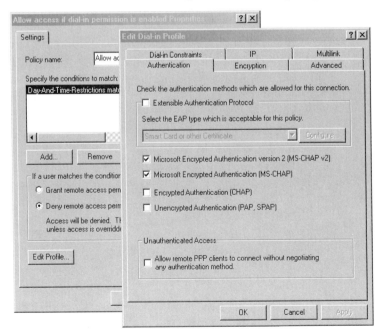

Figure 17.7 *Remote access profile security settings.*

Creating Remote Access Security Policy

To configure a remote access profile, select a remote access security policy and right-click to open the Properties dialog box. Next, click the Edit Profile button to open the Edit Dial-In Profile window, as shown in Figure 17.7.

CONFIGURING AUTHENTICATION PROTOCOLS

Before a remote access connection can take place, both the client and the server must agree on a protocol that will be used to exchange authentication values. They must also agree to use either Windows authentication or RADIUS.

Under RADIUS authentication, RRAS acts as a client a RADIUS server, such as a Windows 2000 Server running the Internet Authentication Service (IAS). User credentials can be verified with the RADIUS server's internal database, a Windows 2000 domain controller, or some other server running an ODBC-compliant interface.

When using either Windows or RADIUS authentication providers, you may choose from the following Authentication protocols:

- **Password Authentication Protocol (PAP).** The least secure option, PAP passes authentication information in clear text. This makes it insecure in any environment where a "packet sniffer" can be deployed on the network to capture the user name and password. PAP should only be used when troubleshooting or to provide compatibility with clients that cannot support more secure methods.
- **Shiva Password Authentication Protocol (SPAP).** Designed for use with Shiva remote access servers, SPAP is a reversible encryption mechanism. While more secure than PAP, it is less secure than other methods and has little practical use except when connecting to Shiva remote access servers.
- **Challenge Handshake Authentication Protocol (CHAP).** This method uses a Message Digest 5 (MD5) one-way encryption scheme in hashing the response to a challenge issued by the remote access server. This option is more secure than PAP, but less secure than other options. Its main application is to non-Windows clients incapable of using MS-CHAP.
- **Microsoft CHAP (MS-CHAP).** Supported by all versions of Windows, MS-CHAP has the capabilities of CHAP and some extra features. For the most part, it has been superceded by MS-CHAP2.
- **MS-CHAP2.** The latest version of MS-CHAP generates separate cryptographic keys for data that is both transmitted and received.

These keys are based on the user's password and an arbitrarily generated challenge variable, so they differ with each connection. MS-CHAP2 also requires mutual client-server authentication. This option is available for Windows 2000 and Windows Me clients as well as Windows NT 4.0 with Service Pack 4 or later and Windows 98 with Service Pack 1 or later. It can be applied to Windows 95 through the Dial-Up Networking 1.3 Performance and Security Upgrade for PPTP connections (but not PPP connections).

- **Extensible Authentication Protocol (EAP).** This option permits you to add various authentication methods as client-server plug-ins that will authenticate a PPP connection. The methods that can be used, referred to as *EAP types*, range from smart cards to fingerprints and retina scans. Only Windows 2000 supports it.

- **EAP-MD5.** This option combines EAP with CHAP.

- **EAP-TLS.** This option combines EAP with the Transport Layer Security (TLS) protocol. This methods supports client and two-way (certificate-based) encryption, negotiation by encryption algorithm, secure exchange of keys, and message authentication codes. Offering the highest EAP security, this option is only available on RRAS servers based on Windows 2000 Servers under the domain model.

- **EAP-RADIUS.** This option passes EAP messages on to the RADIUS server for handling.

The authentication protocol you employ will depend on the kind of security threat your network faces. One possibility, called the *replay attack*, involves an outside party collecting packets on your network which are then resent in an attempt to recreate an authenticated connection. Another threat is *client impersonation*, wherein an intruder takes over an authenticated connection. Yet another threat is *server impersonation*, wherein a rogue server passes itself off as a legitimate server in order to capture user credentials.

You also have the option of employing no authentication. This might be acceptable in some circumstances, such as when you wish to enable unauthenticated guest access. In most cases, however, you should employ more appropriate authentication considering the client types and security risks involved.

Server-specific authentication providers can be configured under the Security tab of the remote access server's properties dialog box, as shown in Figure 17.8.

To enable authentication protocols, click the Authentication Methods button.

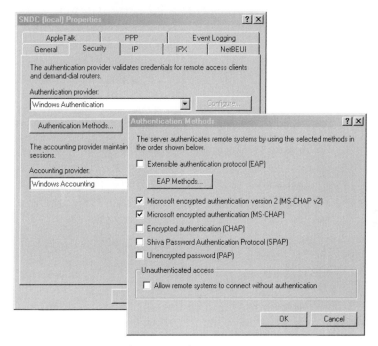

Figure 17.8   *Configuring authentication options.*

CONFIGURING ENCRYPTION PROTOCOLS

Encryption between the client and RRAS can only be used with IPSec, MS-CHAP, MS-CHAP2, or EAP-TLS. If you require encryption beyond the RRAS server, you should employ IPSec with or without L2TP.

Encryption can be set at the client end through Dial-Up Networking, or at the RRAS server end through a remote access profile. In the remote access profile, you can choose among the following options:

- **No Encryption**.
- **Basic Encryption.** Used with PPTP with 40-bit key Microsoft Point-to-Point Encryption (MPPE) or L2TP over IPSec with 56-bit Data Encryption Standard (DES).
- **Strong Encryption.** Used with PPTP with 56-bit key MPPE or L2TP over IPSec with 56-bit DES.
- **Strongest Encryption.** Used with PPTP with 128-bit key MPPE or L2TP over IPSec with 128-bit DES. It requires Service Pack 2.

Available in all Microsoft 32-bit remote access clients, MPPE uses the Rivest-Shamir-Adleman (RSA) RC4 stream cipher with 40-bit, 56-bit, or 128-bit keys that are generated during authentication.

Study Break

Enable Remote Security

Practice what you have learned by configuring security for client-server remote access connections.

First, determine the types of client that will be accessing the RAS server. Next, choose an authentication provider and authentication protocol based on your security needs. Decide whether data encryption should be employed, and if so, decide which method should be used. Configure both the RAS server and a remote client, based on your choices. Finally, verify that authentication and communication are possible between the remote client and server.

■ Summary

In this chapter, you examined the installation, configuration, and administration of remote access and the RRAS server. Before a remote access connection can take place, both the client and the server must agree on a protocol to be used to exchange authentication values. They must also agree to use either Windows authentication or RADIUS.

Working With Remote Access

You can extend your network resources to users in distant locations using Dial-Up Networking, which is used to create temporary connections between a RRAS server and remote users over telecommunications media. You can also extend access through VPNs, which are used to create secure connections between a RRAS server and remote users through an IP network intermediary, such as the Internet. After a remote client uses a line protocol to establish a connection to a RRAS server, the user is authenticated and granted access to either the server, through point-to-point remote access, or the server plus the local network, through point-to-LAN remote access.

RRAS is installed under Windows 2000 Server by default, but not activated. You may activate it using the RRAS MMC. Remote access to RRAS services is dependent upon user account dial-in permissions, remote access policy, and remote access profiles. VPNs can also be created that employ encryption for both communications and authentication, making remote access as secure as access on a local network segment.

Configuring Remote Access Security

RRAS employs such security features as authentication and data encryption, both at the client end and through remote access policy. Encryption can be set at the client end through Dial-UP Networking, or at the RRAS server end through a remote access profile. In the remote access profile, you can choose among none, basic, strong, and strongest encryption methods.

▲ CHAPTER REVIEW QUESTIONS

Here are a few questions relating to the material covered in the *Installing, Configuring, Managing, Monitoring, and Troubleshooting Remote Access in a Windows 2000 Network Infrastructure* section of Microsoft's *Implementing and Administering a Microsoft Windows 2000 Network Infrastructure* exam (70-216).

1. *Which of the following technologies are used in providing remote access under Windows 2000? Select all that apply:*
   A. RAS
   B. MPR
   C. RRAS
   D. VPN

2. *Under Windows 2000 Server, remote access is made possible by configuring Dial-Up Networking on both the client and server.*
   A. True
   B. False

3. *Which of the following line protocols can be used in connecting to the Windows 2000 Server remotely? Select all that apply.*
   A. SLIP
   B. PPP
   C. PPTP
   D. L2TP

4. *In order to gain access to a network through RRAS, remote access users may either have permissions enabled in their user accounts or meet criteria defined by remote access policy.*

    A. True

    B. False

5. *Which of the following are remote access policy conditions? Select all that apply:*

    A. Telephone number of the remote access server

    B. Telephone number of the remote client

    C. Telephone number restricted to "X"

    D. Domain groups of which the user is a member

6. *Which of the following are remote access profile restrictions? Select all that apply:*

    A. Permit only certain dial-in media

    B. Restrict access to certain domain groups

    C. Define permitted IP address assignment methods

    D. Establish RADIUS client attributes

7. *Multilinking increases overall connection bandwidth by permitting remote access clients to connect simultaneously over multiple pathways and through multiple RRAS servers.*

    A. True

    B. False

8. *In a VPN, a protocol such as IP is used to create a tunnel in which PPTP packets are encapsulated.*

    A. True

    B. False

9. *For greater security, you should delete any VPN miniports that are not in use.*

    A. True

    B. False

10. *Multilink connection settings can be enabled under which tab in the RAS server properties dialog box? Select only one:*

    A. General

    B. IP

    C. PPP

    D. Security

11. *BAP/BACP provide dynamic bandwidth control for multilink connections.*
    A. True
    B. False

12. *When DHCP integration is enabled, the RAS server can lease no more than 10 IP addresses.*
    A. True
    B. False

13. *If you wish to provide DHCP scope options to remote access clients that differ from those used by the RAS server, you must install the DHCP Relay Agent.*
    A. True
    B. False

14. *The NETSH utility can be used to back up RRAS server settings.*
    A. True
    B. False

15. *Which of the following logs are available to monitor RRAS? Select all that apply:*
    A. PPP logs
    B. VPN logs
    C. Authentication and Account logs
    D. Event logs

16. *Authentication and encryption are security techniques dependent on each other.*
    A. True
    B. False

17. *Which of the following are authentication providers that can be enabled under Windows 2000 remote access? Select all that apply:*
    A. Windows authentication
    B. PAP
    C. MS-CHAP
    D. RADIUS authentication

18. *Which of the following authentication protocols supports the use of smart cards? Select only one:*

    A. SPAP

    B. EAP

    C. MS-CHAP

    D. MS-CHAP2

19. *Which of the following authentication methods can be used with encryption between the remote access client and RRAS server? Select all that apply:*

    A. PAP

    B. MS-CHAP

    C. MS-CHAP2

    D. EAP-TLS

20. *The strongest encryption requires Service Pack 2.*

    A. True

    B. False

21. *Such settings as authentication methods and encryption types can only be enabled through remote access policy on the RAS server, not on the client.*

    A. True

    B. False

22. *It is possible to permit remote access without requiring authentication.*

    A. True

    B. False

Administering
Network Protocols

▲Chapter Syllabus

MCSE 18.1 Working with Network Protocols

MCSE 18.2 Working with Network Protocol Security

MCSE 18.3 Working with Network Traffic

MCSE 18.4 Working with IPSec

This chapter covers material in the *Installing, Configuring, Managing, Monitoring, and Troubleshooting Network Protocols in a Windows 2000 Network Infrastructure* section of Microsoft's *Implementing and Administering a Microsoft Windows 2000 Network Infrastructure* exam (70-216).

In this chapter, you delve more deeply into the workings of Windows 2000's core networking protocol, TCP/IP. You learn more about its structure and review such concepts as installation, configuration, and troubleshooting. You also learn more about securing TCP/IP connections using such methods as packet filtering and such technologies as Internet Security (IPSec). In addition, you take a brief look at other network protocols, such as NWLink IPX/SPX/NetBIOS Compatible Transport. Finally, you learn how to monitor and manage the traffic that they produce.

Much of this material was described initially in Chapter 6, "Networking Windows 2000 Professional," and Chapter 13, "Networking Windows 2000 Server."

MCSE 18.1 Working with Network Protocols

Network *protocols* are the rules and procedures that govern communications between networked computers. They can be compared to human languages in that, as with humans, two computers must know the same language if communications is to take place between them. More precisely, they can be compared to human etiquette such as parliamentary procedure. Unless computers adhere to rules, such as which of them may talk when, communication becomes garbled.

Among the choices of network protocol under Windows 2000 are the following:

- **Transmission Control Protocol/Internet Protocol (TCP/IP).** The Transmission Control Protocol/Internet Protocol (TCP/IP) is the language of the Internet, and Microsoft's 32-bit native implementation of it is the default protocol for Windows 2000 Server. This routable, cross-platform protocol has become a global industry-standard. To connect a Windows 2000 Server to the Internet, one must use TCP/IP. In addition, TCP/IP is the preferred protocol for routing across Wide Area Networks (WANs), of which the Internet is the ultimate example.
- **NWLink IPX/SPX/NetBIOS Compatible Transport.** Microsoft's NetWare Link (NWLink) Internetwork Packet Exchange (IPX)/ Sequenced Packet Exchange (SPX) Compatible Transport protocol was designed to make Windows 2000-based servers compatible with Novell NetWare networks.
- **NetBIOS Enhanced User Interface (NetBEUI).** Designed by IBM in 1985, NetBEUI was the default network protocol for earlier Microsoft products such as Windows for Workgroups 3.1 and LAN Manager. Windows 2000 is capable of using it, and can therefore communicate with computers running these earlier systems. NetBEUI is Windows 2000's fastest protocol. However, it is useful only on nonextended, and therefore generally small, LANs because it cannot be *routed* (except on Token Ring networks). Routers are used to pass network communications between different networks or network segments. (One can *bridge* NetBEUI network segments if necessary, however.

Bridges connect multiple network segments while treating them all as one logical network. This is really only useful in increasing the size of a LAN). NetBEUI supports as many as 200 computers on a LAN. NetBEUI has some advantages over more robust protocols. It is self-configuring, self-tuning, and incurs little RAM overhead. On the downside, it generates a large number of network broadcasts that degrade network performance on large LANs.

- **Data Link Control (DLC).** The DLC protocol was designed to enable communications between IBM mainframe systems and AS400 servers. Microsoft's Systems Network Architecture (SNA) server uses DLC as its underlying protocol to connect to IBM servers. DLC is often used with Hewlett-Packard LaserJet printers that are equipped with JetDirect NICs. These printing devices can also support TCP/IP, however, so that protocol is often used instead.

- **AppleTalk.** The native networking protocol of the Apple Macintosh, AppleTalk is installed in Windows 2000 Server as part of Services for Macintosh (SFM). It gives Mac OS users connectivity to Windows 2000 servers similar to that of Apple's AppleShare IP line of servers. It also permits Mac OS users to access Windows 2000-based print services. Like NetBEUI, AppleTalk is a self-configuring protocol that requires practically no maintenance. Unlike NetBEUI, it can be routed and supports large numbers of computers per network segment. It is therefore scalable to an enterprise environment.

In preparing for Microsoft's exam objectives, a good understanding of TCP/IP is most important.

Working with TCP/IP

Although TCP/IP is commonly referred to as a protocol, it is more accurately a *protocol suite*. Within the TCP/IP suite are numerous distinct protocols designed for various purposes, such as File Transfer Protocol (FTP), Telnet, Simple Mail Transfer Protocol (SMTP), Simple Network Management Protocol (SNMP), and the ever-popular HyperText Transfer Protocol (HTTP).

TCP/IP PROTOCOLS

TCP/IP is an *open standard*, with no one company owning the rights to it or developing it. Regardless of the implementation — whether provided by Microsoft, Novell, IBM, Sun, Apple or some other vendor — TCP/IP adheres to standards reviewed and published by the Internet Engineering Task Force (IETF) in the form of *Request for Proposals (RFCs)*. TCP/IP also adheres to accepted networking models, such as the International Standards Organization's (ISO's) seven-layer Open Systems Interconnection (OSI) model and U.S. government's four-layer Department of Defense (DOD) model. These models and the relative positions of the protocols in the TCP/IP suite are illustrated in Figure 18.1.

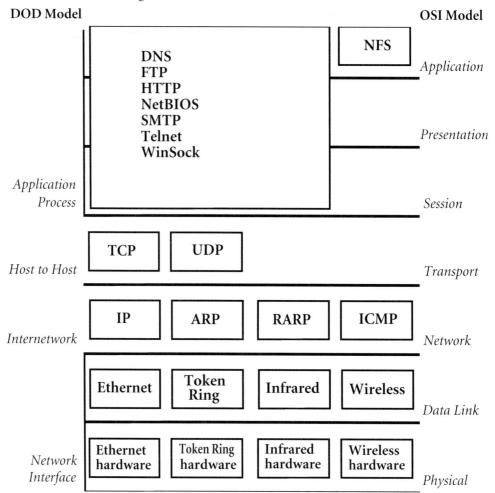

Figure 18.1 *TCP/IP in the DOD and OSI models.*

To understand the history of TCP/IP is to understand the history of the Internet itself. Among the landmarks have been the following:

- The U.S. Department of Defense establishes the Advanced Research Projects Agency (ARPA). In 1969, the *ARPAnet* is launched, connecting university and military sites.

- In 1983, military traffic is split off from ARPAnet to form MILNET. ARPAnet is populated by a growing number of universities and becomes the *NSFnet* under the National Science Foundation (NSF).
- In the late 1980s, commercial enterprises begin moving to what has since been called *the Internet.*
- When Windows 95 was new (1995), there were about 5 million hosts on the Internet. When Windows 98 came around (1998), there were about 30 million. In the time of Windows 2000 (2000), there are about 72 million. Continued exponential growth is anticipated.

Throughout the evolution of the Internet, TCP/IP has grown and flourished despite the fact that it is certainly not the world's best protocol. Other, more modern protocols are faster, easier to administer, and have less operational overhead. TCP/IP does have certain undeniable advantages, however. For one thing, the protocol is based on a "connectionless" packet-switching technology in which no dedicated pathway is maintained between the sending computer and the receiving computer. Eventually, all packets sent from one computer should arrive at the destination computer, but they make take many different routes to get there. This makes TCP/IP very reliable. TCP/IP is also scalable, permitting growth from small LAN segments into planet-spanning internetworks through the deployment of subnets and routers.

Among the protocols in the TCP/IP suite are the following:

- **ARP.** It is the job of the Address Resolution Protocol (ARP) to resolve IP address (software) with Media Access Control (MAC) addresses (hardware). To do this, ARP sends out broadcasts to obtain MAC addressing information, which it stores in a cache. You can view the ARP cache by typing "arp -a" at the command prompt, as shown in Figure 18.2.

Figure 18.2   *Viewing the ARP cache.*

- **RARP.** As the name implies, the Reverse Address Resolution Protocol (RARP) does the same thing in reverse. It resolves MAC addresses with IP addresses.

- **ICMP/IGMP.** The Internet Control Message Protocol (ICMP) lets hosts and routers report status and errors. The PING utility uses this protocol, sending *echo request* packets and recording *echo responses*. The Internet Group Management Protocol (IGMP) is used to send a message to a group of hosts using one destination address through a process called *multicasting*.

- **IP.** Internet Protocol (IP) is responsible for routing and delivering packets from the originating computer to the destination computer. It is a *connectionless protocol*, the workings of which are analogous to mailing a letter. The letter has a sender and recipient address, but beyond that, how it gets from one place to another is up to the postal service.

- **TCP.** It is the job of Transmission Control Protocol (TCP) to handle the establishment of point-to-point communications, acknowledgements, packet ordering, and flow control. To continue with the previous analog, TCP is the postal service. Unlike IP, TCP is a *connection-oriented protocol* that depends on establishing a connection before transferring data. To carry the same analog further, TCP is like a delivery service that will not give the recipient your letter until he signs for it.

  In operation, TCP first creates a point-to-point communications session between hosts. It then breaks down the data it will send into *segments*, which it numbers and puts in sequence for delivery. At the receiving end, TCP responds with *acknowledgments* so that the sending computer knows which segments have arrived. If segments arrive out of sequence, the receiving computer can reorder them based on their numbering. If segments fail to arrive, the sending computer is informed and told to resend them.

- **UDP.** The User Datagram Protocol (UDP) is used in a way similar to TCP. It is a connectionless protocol, however, and so it is not as reliable as TCP and can only offer *best-effort delivery*. It is, therefore, used only when a small amount of data is to be sent quickly, or when such controls as sequencing and acknowledgements are provided at the Application layer.

In addition to the IP address, TCP/IP protocols use *sockets* to route traffic between various services on a host. The socket is a combination of IP address and port number. For example, port "80" is the default for Web services.

IP ADDRESSING

The key to becoming comfortable with IP addressing is accepting its binary (base two) nature and putting aside the inclination to think in terms of base 10. Consider an IP address such as the following:

64.165.61.95

This number is represented to humans in dotted decimal notation. Each number that is separated by dots is an *octet*, because it represents eight binary digits. In binary notation, the same number would look like the following:

01000000.010100101.00111101.01011111

To figure out how we arrived at this conclusion, consider the first octet:

1000000

The trick here is to realize that each numeral is a placeholder for a decimal value, as shown in Figure 18.3.

0	0	0	0	0	0	0	0.	0	0	0	0	0	0	0	0.	0	0	0	0	0	0	0	0.	0	0	0	0	0	0	0	0
128	64	32	16	8	4	2	1.	128	64	32	16	8	4	2	1.	128	64	32	16	8	4	2	1.	128	64	32	16	8	4	2	1
		0				.				0				.				0				.				0					

Figure 18.3 *Binary digits in an IP address.*

As you move from right to left, doubling each time, add the appropriate decimal value for each number represented by a "1." In the case of the first octet, we move seven places to the left before a value is "turned on," which corresponds to "64".

Now consider the last octet. The values in the first five places are turned on, so "1+2+4+8+16" or "31." Then we skip a place. Then the seventh value for "64" is turned on again. The result: 31+64=95.

All IP addresses are composed of two parts. One part is the *host ID*, which designates an individual host on a network. The other part is the *network ID*, which designates the network among all the other networks in the world. If the octets used to identify network and host were consistent, we could end the description here. It does not work that way, however. The octets that represent host and network vary. To tell which is which we need to employ the *subnet mask*.

Like the IP address, the subnet mask is a 32-bit number divided into octets. Its purpose is to "mask" the octets that represent the network ID by "turning on" the appropriate bits. For example, the following subnet mask:

```
255.0.0.0
```

… would be seen as the following in binary:

```
11111111.00000000.00000000.00000000
```

In this case, the subnet mask is representing the network ID as the first octet, leaving the last three octets to represent the host ID. Naturally, the smaller the network ID, the more numbers available for hosts. To represent these divisions, IP addresses are divided into the following address classes:

- **Class A.** As illustrated in Figure 18.4, this class of network spans a range in the first octet from 1 to 127. An example of a class A IP address is "120.8.2.67." The subnet mask is "255.0.0.0." Because the network ID is small, there are not many class A networks. These are held by big organizations and Internet founders such as IBM and General Electric. Because the host ID is large, however, each network can be home to about 16 million hosts. Note that this class includes the *loopback address* used to represent the localhost, "127.0.0.1."

Network		Node			
0 1 1 1 1 0 0 0 .	0 0 0 0 1 0 0 0 .	0 0 0 0 0 0 1 0 .	0 1 0 0 0 0 1 1
128 64 32 16 8 4 2 1 .	128 64 32 16 8 4 2 1 .	128 64 32 16 8 4 2 1 .	128 64 32 16 8 4 2 1
120 .	8 .	2 .	67

Figure 18.4 *Class A addresses.*

- **Class B.** As illustrated in Figure 18.5, this class of network spans a range in the first and second octets from 128.0 to 191.255. An example of a class B IP address is "184.8.2.67." The subnet mask is "255.255.0.0." Thanks to its larger network ID space, there are more than 16,000 class B networks. There are fewer hosts on each, however: 65,536.

Network		Node			
1 0 1 1 1 0 0 0 .	0 0 0 0 1 0 0 0 .	0 0 0 0 0 0 1 0 .	0 1 0 0 0 0 1 1
128 64 32 16 8 4 2 1 .	128 64 32 16 8 4 2 1 .	128 64 32 16 8 4 2 1 .	128 64 32 16 8 4 2 1
184 .	8 .	2 .	67

Figure 18.5 *Class B addresses.*

Class C. As illustrated in Figure 18.6, this class of network spans a range in the first, second, and third octets from 192.0.0 to 223.255.255. An example of a class C IP address is "216.8.2.67." The subnet mask is "255.255.255.0." Because the network ID is large, there are many class C networks — more than 2 million. Each has a small number of hosts, however: 254.

Network			Node
1 1 0 1 1 0 0 0 .	0 0 0 0 1 0 0 0 .	0 0 0 0 0 0 1 0 .	0 1 0 0 0 0 1 1
128 64 32 16 8 4 2 1 .	128 64 32 16 8 4 2 1 .	128 64 32 16 8 4 2 1 .	128 64 32 16 8 4 2 1
216 .	8 .	2 .	67

Figure 18.6 *Class C addresses.*

- **Class D.** This is a special nonnetwork class of "224" that is used in multicasting.
- **Class E.** This is a special nonnetwork class of "240" that is used for testing purposes.

Note that in the previous illustrations, not all of the numbers in the leftmost octet are used when identifying the network ID. That is because a certain portion of the octet is reserved to identify the address class, leaving the rest to identify the network. For the sake of simplicity, however, it is safe to consider the entire octet as part of the network ID.

In addition to the loopback, class D, and class E addresses, there are a few other ranges not assigned for Internet use: 10.x.x.x, 172.16.x.x, and 192.168.x.x. These are private addresses reserved for use on internal networks. If your network is not connected to the Internet and you wish to use TCP/IP without the expense of leasing an IP address range from an ISP, these are the numbers to use. You cannot route traffic from these public addresses to the Internet without the use of at least one public IP address and Windows 2000's built-in Network Address Translation (NAT) support, however.

SUBNETTING • At this point, we have divided the 32-bit IP address space into smaller and smaller Network IDs using default subnet masks. But what if you wish to divide the network still more? This can be done by employing a router and making use of *custom subnet masks.*

To create a custom subnet mask, you must steal a few bits from the host ID to give to the network ID. For example, imagine that you have a class C network with the address range "216.8.2.0" to "216.8.2.255." By default, the subnet mask would look like the following in binary:

11111111.11111111.11111111.00000000

You want to divide this network into four subnets. To do so, you take six bits from the subnet mask to end up with the following:

```
11111111.11111111.11111111.11000000
```

In decimal notation, this translates into the following:

```
255.255.255.192
```

You end up with four subnets in the ranges 1-62, 65-126,19-190 and 193-254, as illustrated in Figure 18.7.

Subnet Mask			Node
1 1 1 1 1 1 1 1.	1 1 1 1 1 1 1 1.	1 1 1 1 1 1 1 1.	1 1 0 0 0 0 0 0
128 64 32 16 8 4 2 1.	128 64 32 16 8 4 2 1.	128 64 32 16 8 4 2 1.	128 64 32 16 8 4 2 1
255 .	255 .	255 .	192

Subnet 1			Node
1 1 0 1 1 0 0 0.	0 0 0 0 1 0 0 0.	0 0 0 0 0 0 1 0.	0 0 0 0 0 0 0 0
128 64 32 16 8 4 2 1.	128 64 32 16 8 4 2 1.	128 64 32 16 8 4 2 1.	128 64 32 16 8 4 2 1
216 .	8 .	2 .	0

Subnet 2			Node
1 1 0 1 1 0 0 0.	0 0 0 0 1 0 0 0.	0 0 0 0 0 0 1 0.	0 1 0 0 0 0 0 0
128 64 32 16 8 4 2 1.	128 64 32 16 8 4 2 1.	128 64 32 16 8 4 2 1.	128 64 32 16 8 4 2 1
216 .	8 .	2 .	64

Subnet 3			Node
1 1 0 1 1 0 0 0.	0 0 0 0 1 0 0 0.	0 0 0 0 0 0 1 0.	1 0 0 0 0 0 0 0
128 64 32 16 8 4 2 1.	128 64 32 16 8 4 2 1.	128 64 32 16 8 4 2 1.	128 64 32 16 8 4 2 1
216 .	8 .	2 .	128

Subnet 4			Node
1 1 0 1 1 0 0 0.	0 0 0 0 1 0 0 0.	0 0 0 0 0 0 1 0.	1 1 0 0 0 0 0 0
128 64 32 16 8 4 2 1.	128 64 32 16 8 4 2 1.	128 64 32 16 8 4 2 1.	128 64 32 16 8 4 2 1
216 .	8 .	2 .	192

Figure 18.7 *The top-most subnet mask divides a class C network into subnets.*

You discard the first and last addresses in each range. The first number signifies the network itself and the last is used for broadcasts. You then assign each range to a different interface on a router, such as the Windows 2000

Server with four network adapters and running RRAS. Possible subnetting configurations are summarized in Table 18.1.

Table 18.1 *Custom Subnet Masks*

Subnet mask	Subnets	Host IP address ranges
255.255.255.0	1	1-254
255.255.255.128	2	1-126, 129-254
255.255.255.192	4	1-62, 65-126, 19-190, 193-254
255.255.255.224	8	1-30, 33-62, 65-94, 97-126, 129-158, 161-190, 193-222, 225-254
255.255.255.240	16	1-14, 17-30, 33-46, 49-62, 65-78, 81-94, 97-110, 113-126, 129-142, 145-158, 161-174, 177-190, 193-206, 209-222, 225-238, 241-254
255.255.255.248	32	1-6, and so on

SUPERNETTING • Supernetting is the same process as subnetting in reverse. Here we take bits from the Network ID and allocate them to the Host ID. For example, you might combine two contiguous class C networks to support 512 hosts instead of 254 by changing the subnet mask to "255.255.255.254."

CLASSLESS ADDRESSING • Yet another method of creating subnets and supernets involves the use of Classless InterDomain Routing (CIDR). These networks are called "/X" networks, where the "X" indicates the number of bits assigned to the Network ID (before subnetting). Under this system, the subnet mask becomes part of the routing table, providing greater flexibility.

Consider the class C network. The last octet of 8 bits is available for the Host ID, leaving three octets or 24-bits for the Network ID. Under CIDR, this is a "/24" network that would be addressed in the format "216.8.2.67/24." Possible CIDR configurations are summarized in Table 18.2.

Table 18.2 *CIDR Network Types*

Subnet mask	CIDR	Number of possible hosts
255.255.255.0	/24	254
255.255.255.128	/25	126
255.255.255.192	/26	62
255.255.255.224	/27	30
255.255.255.240	/28	14
255.255.255.248	/29	6

These topics are addressed again in Chapter 20, "Administering IP Routing."

INSTALLING TCP/IP

TCP/IP is installed on Windows 2000 machines by default. If not present already, you can install TCP/IP or another network protocol in the following steps:

1. Click the Local Area Connection icon in the Network and Dial-Up Connections folder.
2. In the Local Area Connection Status dialog box, click the Properties button to open the Local Area Connection Properties dialog box.
3. Click the Install button to open the Select Network Component dialog box, and choose Protocol from the list.
4. Click the Add button to open the Select Network Protocol dialog box.
5. Select the appropriate protocol and click the OK button. You will then be prompted to restart the server.

You must be logged in as Administartor.

CONFIGURING TCP/IP

To configure TCP/IP LAN settings under Windows 2000, perform the following steps:

1. Double-click the Local Area Connection application to open the Local Area Connection Status dialog box.
2. Click the Properties button to open the Local Area Properties dialog box and select the TCP/IP protocol in the scrolling list.
3. Click the Properties button to open the Internet Protocol (TCP/IP) Properties dialog box.
4. Configure the settings under the General properties tab. Either accept DHCP (automatic) IP addressing or enable the Use the following IP address radio button to type in a static TCP/IP address configuration. In the latter case, type in the appropriate numbers for IP address, Subnet mask, Default gateway (if a router is present), and at least the Preferred DNS server.
5. Click the Advanced button to open the Advanced TCP/IP Settings dialog box, as shown in Figure 18.8.
6. Under the IP Settings tab, choose the Add or Edit buttons to modify settings for multiple IP addresses. You might need to use multiple addresses if the computer resides on both a public network and an

internal network that uses private addressing, or where multiple logical IP networks reside on the same network segment. Choose the Add button to define multiple gateways. Should the top-most router go offline, Windows 2000's *dead gateway detection* feature switches to the next gateway in the list and update the TCP routing table accordingly. Only one default gateway is used at a time. The interface metric helps Windows 2000 determine which route to use when there are multiple routes to a destination by selecting the lowest *hop count*. Each router adds a hop, so the local gateway is "1," an ISP's router might be "2," and so on.

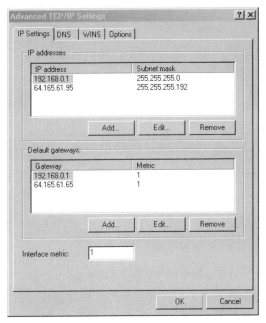

Figure 18.8 *Configuring Advanced TCP/IP properties.*

7. Under the DNS tab, enter the IP addresses for multiple DNS servers in the DNS server addresses field, in order of preference. Should the top-most server fail to answer a query, DNS automatically switches to the next server in the list. Also enter the domain(s) for your network in the Append these DNS suffixes field. The primary suffix is identified under the Identification tab of the System Control Panel application. Additional suffixes can be added for each Network and Dial-Up Connections connection. You direct TCP/IP to resolve unqualified names by appending the primary and connection-specific suffixes for DNS queries, and/or a series of suffixes, using the appropriate checkboxes. Finally, you may enable the Register this connection's addresses in DNS and Use this

connection's DNS suffix in DNS registration if there are DDNS servers on your network.

8. Under the WINS tab, configure the IP addresses of any servers that are running WINS for your network in the WINS addresses field. As with DNS, Windows 2000 goes down the list after failing to connect to the first server. By default, the Enable LMHOSTS Lookup checkbox is selected. This permits the use of a text list of IP address-to-NetBIOS name mappings for computers outside the local subnet, which is stored in the \WINNT\System32\Drivers\Etc folder. If the Enable NetBIOS over TCP/IP radio button is not selected, programs that require Net-BIOS will not run over TCP/IP and you might be unable to connect to older operating systems such as Windows 95 or Windows NT.

9. To configure Internet Protocol Security (IPSec), double-click the IP security item under the Options tab.

CONFIGURING TCP/IP PACKET FILTERS

TCP/IP filtering allows you to specify which types of nontransit network traffic your server is allowed to process. Enable this feature by double-clicking the TCP/IP filtering item under the Options tab in the Advanced TCP/IP Settings dialog box to open the TCP/IP Filtering dialog box, as shown in Figure 18.9.

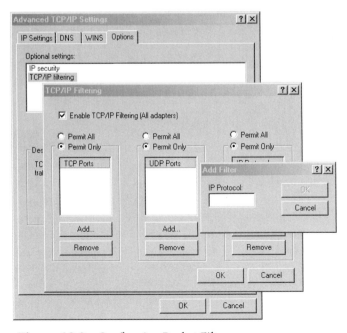

Figure 18.9 *Configuring Packet Filters.*

When you enable TCP/IP filtering, it initially blocks all traffic. The computer does not receive traffic again until you explicitly configure the appropriate protocols and ports. Ports can be configured for TCP, UPD, and IP. For example, you might filter TCP port 80 to permit Web access.

Working with NWLink

NWLink IPX/SPX/NetBIOS Compatible Transport makes Windows 2000-based servers compatible with Novell NetWare networks. Although used almost exclusively for this purpose, it is a complete network protocol in its own right and can easily be used instead of NetBEUI or TCP/IP as a Microsoft LAN's base protocol.

A Windows 2000-based computer can connect to client/server applications on a NetWare server using NWLink. In order to connect to file and print services on a NetWare server, however, Windows 2000 Server must be running both NWLink and Gateway Services for NetWare (GSNW). (Windows 2000 Professional workstations must be running NWLink and Client Services for NetWare (CSNW).)

GSNW running on a Windows 2000-based server also extends access to NetWare resources to Microsoft clients (e.g., Windows 9x/Me, Windows for Workgroups) that use the Server Message Block (SMB) protocol. These NetWare resources appear as Windows networking resources to such clients.

To configure NWLink IPX/SPX/NetBIOS Compatible Transport, perform the following steps:

1. Double-click the Local Area Connection application to open the Local Area Connection Status dialog box.
2. Click the Properties button to open the Local Area Properties dialog box and select the NWLink IPX/SPX/NetBIOS Compatible Transport protocol in the scrolling list.
3. Click the Properties button to open the properties dialog box, as shown in Figure 18.10.
4. Under the General tab, type a number in the Internal Network Number field if you intend to run file and print services, IPX routing, or any service that depends on a Service Advertising Protocol (SAP) agent. This is somewhat like a TCP/IP subnet address. NetWare uses it to determine which servers are on the local network and which are on remote networks. In most cases, the default of "00000000" will work.
5. The second field under the General tab is for Frame Type. Protocols divide data that is destined to move across the network into *packets*. These are passed to the NIC, which encapsulates them in *frames*. The

types of frames used on your network depends on both its physical media and the networking software deployed on it (see Figure 18.10).

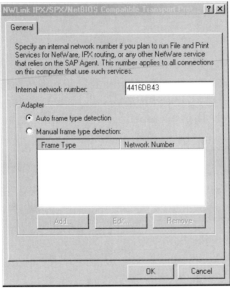

Figure 18.10 *Configuring NWLink properties.*

The possibilities are listed in Table 18.3.

Table 18.3 *NWLink Frame Types*

Topology	Frame Type
Ethernet	Ethernet II, 802.3, 802.2, and Sub-Network Access Protocol (SNAP)
Token Ring	802.5 and SNAP
Fiber Distributed Data Interface (FDDI)	802.2 and 802.3

Configure NWLink IPX/SPX/NetBIOS Compatible Transport protocol to use the same frame types that other servers are using. For example, modern servers running NetWare 3.12 or 4.x, Windows NT Server 3.5x or 4.0, or Windows 2000 Server, commonly use the Ethernet 802.2 frame type. Older servers running NetWare 2.x or 3.11, or Windows NT Server 3.1, commonly use the Ethernet 802.3 frame type. Windows 2000 can also be configured for multiple frame types.

You can determine which network numbers and frame types are in use on your network by typing "IPXROUTE CONFIG" at the command line, as shown in Figure 18.11.

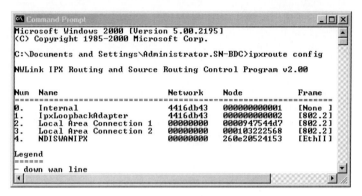

Figure 18.11 *Viewing IPX configurations.*

When NWLink IPX/SPX/NetBIOS Compatible Transport protocol is installed, the NWLINK NetBIOS component is installed alongside it. When enabled, Windows 2000 sends its file and printer sharing information via NetBIOS over IPX. When disabled, these messages are sent over IPX directly through a process called *direct hosting*.

Configuring Network Bindings

Multiple network protocols can be bound to network services. For example, you might bind TCP/IP, NWLink, and NetBEUI to the Microsoft Network Client. When the client attempts to connect to a server, it looks to the order in which the protocols are bound to select them. If the server cannot connect using the selected protocol, the client will try the next in the list, and so on.

To set the binding order, open the Network and Dial-Up Connections folder and select the Advanced Settings command from the Advanced menu. In the Advanced Settings dialog box, switch to the Adapters and Bindings tab and use the arrows and checkboxes to enable/disable and reorder network bindings, as shown in Figure 18.12.

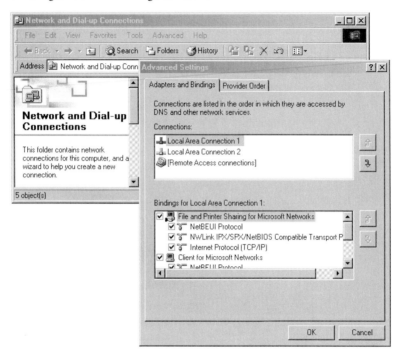

Figure 18.12 *Changing bindings order.*

Troubleshooting Network Protocols

Among the tools helpful in troubleshooting TCP/IP, and network protocols in general, are the following.

PING

Use the Packet Internet Gopher (PING), shown in Figure 18.13, to verify the correct configuration of TCP/IP and to test connectivity to other hosts on the local subnet and beyond.

This was described extensively in Chapter 6.

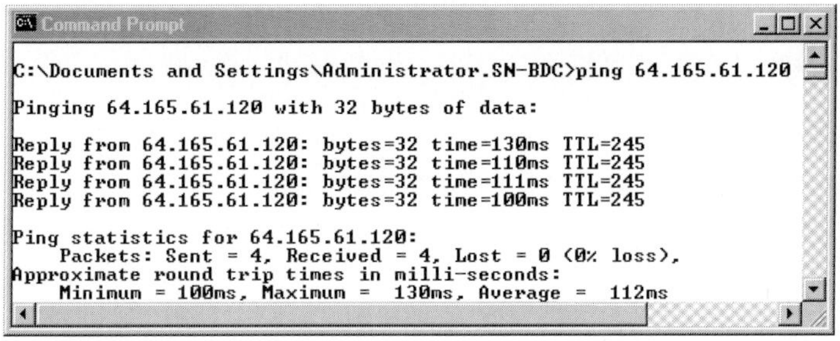

```
Command Prompt                                              _ | □ | x |

C:\Documents and Settings\Administrator.SN-BDC>ping 64.165.61.120

Pinging 64.165.61.120 with 32 bytes of data:

Reply from 64.165.61.120: bytes=32 time=130ms TTL=245
Reply from 64.165.61.120: bytes=32 time=110ms TTL=245
Reply from 64.165.61.120: bytes=32 time=111ms TTL=245
Reply from 64.165.61.120: bytes=32 time=100ms TTL=245

Ping statistics for 64.165.61.120:
    Packets: Sent = 4, Received = 4, Lost = 0 (0% loss),
Approximate round trip times in milli-seconds:
    Minimum = 100ms, Maximum = 130ms, Average = 112ms
```

Figure 18.13   *Using PING.*

TRACERT

Use Trace Route (TRACERT), shown in Figure 18.14, to follow the path between two hosts. This utility sends out ICMP echo packets with varied Time-To-Live (TTL) values to a destination host address. The TTL acts as a hop count, because each router encountered along the way increments it by at least one. When the TTL for a given packet reaches zero, the router sends back a "time exceeded" message to the sending host. This permits TRACERT to determine the routing path taken.

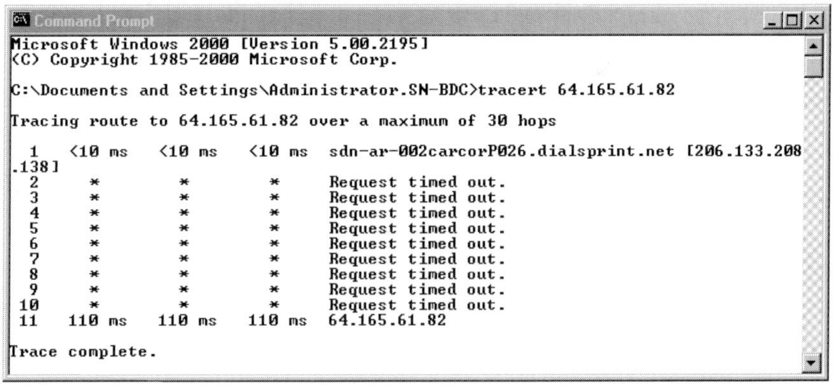

```
Command Prompt                                              _ | □ | x |
Microsoft Windows 2000 [Version 5.00.2195]
(C) Copyright 1985-2000 Microsoft Corp.

C:\Documents and Settings\Administrator.SN-BDC>tracert 64.165.61.82

Tracing route to 64.165.61.82 over a maximum of 30 hops

  1    <10 ms    <10 ms    <10 ms   sdn-ar-002carcorP026.dialsprint.net [206.133.208
.138]
  2      *         *         *      Request timed out.
  3      *         *         *      Request timed out.
  4      *         *         *      Request timed out.
  5      *         *         *      Request timed out.
  6      *         *         *      Request timed out.
  7      *         *         *      Request timed out.
  8      *         *         *      Request timed out.
  9      *         *         *      Request timed out.
 10      *         *         *      Request timed out.
 11    110 ms    110 ms    110 ms   64.165.61.82

Trace complete.
```

Figure 18.14   *Using TRACERT.*

PINGPATH

Use PATHPING, as shown in Figure 18.15, to combine the abilities of PING and TRACERT.

This is useful in evaluating the network's Quality of Service (QoS) by displaying packet loss statistics.

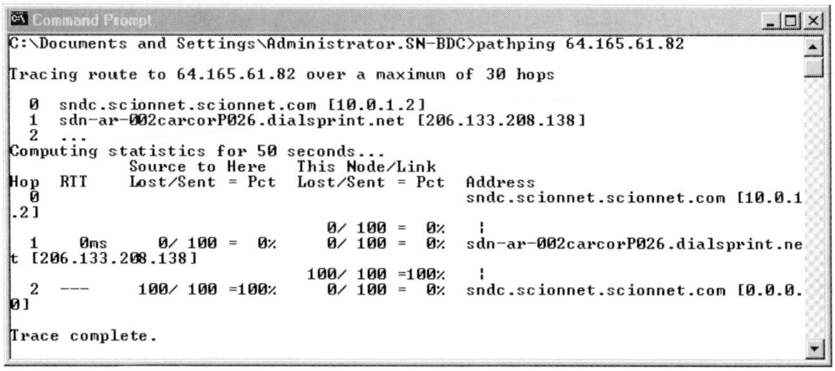

```
CA Command Prompt                                                    _|□|×|
C:\Documents and Settings\Administrator.SN-BDC>pathping 64.165.61.82

Tracing route to 64.165.61.82 over a maximum of 30 hops

  0  sndc.scionnet.scionnet.com [10.0.1.2]
  1  sdn-ar-002carcorP026.dialsprint.net [206.133.208.138]
  2  ...
Computing statistics for 50 seconds...
              Source to Here   This Node/Link
Hop  RTT    Lost/Sent = Pct  Lost/Sent = Pct  Address
  0                                            sndc.scionnet.scionnet.com [10.0.1
.2]
                              0/ 100 =  0%    !
  1   0ms     0/ 100 =  0%    0/ 100 =  0%    sdn-ar-002carcorP026.dialsprint.ne
t [206.133.208.138]
                            100/ 100 =100%    !
  2   ---   100/ 100 =100%    0/ 100 =  0%    sndc.scionnet.scionnet.com [0.0.0.
0]

Trace complete.
```

Figure 18.15   *Using PATHPING.*

IPCONFIG

Use IPCONFIG, as shown in Figure 18.16, to view TCP/IP configuration values (/all), manually renew and release DHCP leases (/renew, /release), and reset domain name registrations (/registerdns).

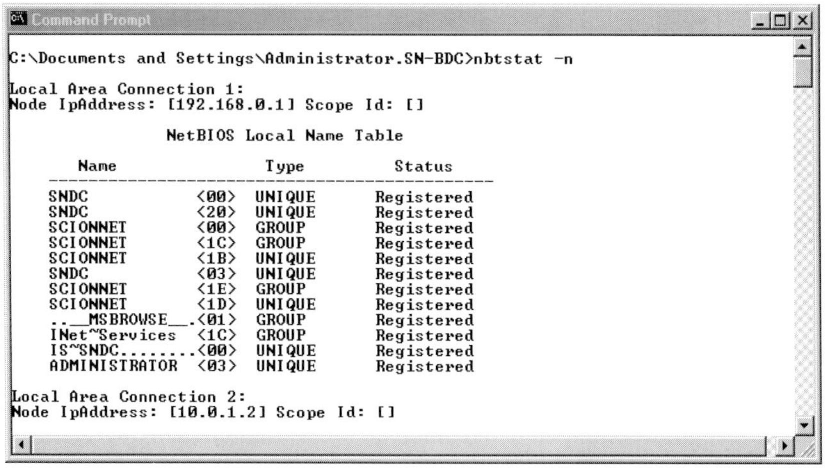

```
CA Command Prompt                                                    _|□|×|
C:\Documents and Settings\Administrator.SN-BDC>nbtstat -n

Local Area Connection 1:
Node IpAddress: [192.168.0.1] Scope Id: []

              NetBIOS Local Name Table

       Name             Type         Status
    ---------------------------------------------
     SNDC        <00>  UNIQUE      Registered
     SNDC        <20>  UNIQUE      Registered
     SCIONNET    <00>  GROUP       Registered
     SCIONNET    <1C>  GROUP       Registered
     SCIONNET    <1B>  UNIQUE      Registered
     SNDC        <03>  UNIQUE      Registered
     SCIONNET    <1E>  GROUP       Registered
     SCIONNET    <1D>  UNIQUE      Registered
     .._MSBROWSE_.<01>  GROUP      Registered
     INet~Services <1C>  GROUP     Registered
     IS~SNDC........<00>  UNIQUE   Registered
     ADMINISTRATOR <03>  UNIQUE    Registered

Local Area Connection 2:
Node IpAddress: [10.0.1.2] Scope Id: []
```

Figure 18.16   *Using IPCONFIG.*

NETSTAT

Use the Network Statistics (NETSTAT) utility, as shown in Figure 18.17, to display connections and listening ports (-a), display Ethernet statistics (-e), display addresses and ports in numerical order (-n), display protocol statistics (-p protocol), and display the routing table (-r).

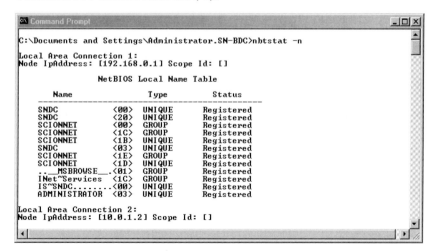

Figure 18.17 *Using NETSTAT*

NBTSTAT

Use the NetBIOS Statistics utility (NBTSTAT), as shown in Figure 18.18, to display locally registered program and service names (-n), display the NetBIOS Remote Name Cache (-c), purge and reload the name cache from the LMHSOST file (-R), release and renew names registered with WINS (-RR), display a remote computer's name table and MAC address, and display current NetBIOS session statistics (-s).

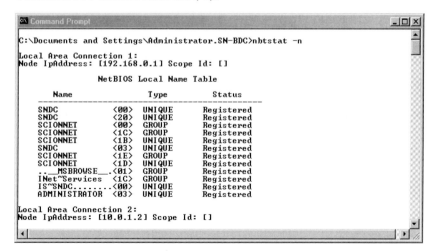

Figure 18.18 *Using NBTSTAT.*

The use of these utilities was described extensively in Chapter 6 and Chapter 13.

Another useful tool in troubleshooting is Network Monitor, described further on in this chapter.

Study Break

Configure TCP/IP Filters

Practice what you have learned by configuring filters for TCP/IP.

First, enable TCP/IP filtering in the TCP/IP Advanced Properties dialog box. Next, explicitly configure appropriate protocols and ports. Ports can be configured for TCP, UPD, and IP. For example, you might filter TCP port 80 to permit Web access. Finally, test various services to ensure the filters have not blocked desired connectivity.

MCSE 18.2   Working with Network Protocol Security

Windows 2000 provides three MMC tools that let you configure security overall settings: The Security Configuration and Analysis snap-in, Security Templates snap-in, and Group Policy snap-in. Among the settings in a Windows 2000 security configuration are security policies (account policies and local policies), access controls (services, files, Registry), event logs, restricted group memberships, IPSec policies, and public key policies. Because of the inherent security risks they impose, Windows 2000 does not go out of its way to make its security tools obvious.

To create an MMC based on the Security Configuration and Analysis snap-in, perform the following steps:

1. Type "mmc" at the command line to open an empty console in author mode.
2. Select the Add/Remove Snap-ins command from the Console menu to open the Add/Remove Snap-in dialog box.
3. Click the Add button to include Security Configuration and Analysis snap-in under the Console Root node.

Upon returning to the MMC, note that an empty Security Configuration branch has been added.

Configuring Network Protocol Security

Windows 2000 includes the following controls that are important to network security:

- **Security Templates.** Lets you establish security-related Registry values, file and Registry access controls, and system service security. They can be configured using the Security Templates MMC snap-in.
- **Kerberos.** This security protocol supports mutual authentication for clients and servers. It is the primary security protocol for Windows 2000 domains.
- **PKI.** Windows 2000 support for Public Key Infrastructure (PKI) augments Kerberos with a public key system based on the X.509 standard.
- **Smart Card.** Windows 2000 supports the use of smart card-aware readers and applications.
- **IPSec.** Supports network-level authentication, data integrity, and encryption. Its configuration is described further on in this chapter.

In addition, you can use firewalls and proxy servers to regulate protocol traffic for the purposes of network security. *Firewalls* examine packets and filter traffic, and therefore network services, based on specified policies. A *proxy server* computer acts on behalf of several client computers that are requesting content from the Internet or elsewhere on an intranet. The proxy server is the secure gateway to the Internet for several client computers.

Troubleshooting Network Protocol Security

The NETSTAT utility is used to list which TCP/IP ports are used during communications sessions. With it you can quickly determine if certain ports are not being accepted across the link, perhaps because they are being blocked at a firewall.

Study Break

Create Security Templates MMC

> Practice what you have learned by creating an MMC based on the Security Templates snap-in.
>
> Type "mmc" at the command line to open an empty console in author mode. Select the Add/ Remove Snap-ins command from the Console menu to open the Add/Remove Snap-in dialog box. Click the Add button to include Security Templates snap-in under the Console Root node.

MCSE 18.3   Working with Network Traffic

In order to optimize network connectivity, you must first monitor the network to determine what type of traffic is being generated on it. This tells you how each of the Windows 2000 services that are generating the traffic is affecting the network. You can optimize network traffic either by providing network services to improve response times (but which increase traffic), or through providing greater network bandwidth by reducing network services (which decreases traffic). As these are mutually exclusive goals, you need to strike a balance between the two.

Each time you add or remove a network service, there is a corresponding affect on network utilization. Analyzing these effects is the goal of *capacity planning*. Services that have an impact on network performance include the following:

- **Computer Browser**. Used by client computers to find network resources in a graphical hierarchy and without using pathnames and command line syntax.
- **DHCP**. Used to dynamically assign IP addresses and DNS server information to clients.
- **Directory Replicator**. Used to duplicate directories across multiple computers.
- **DNS**. Use to map IP addresses to host names.
- **NetLogon**. Used to validate and synchronize domain user accounts.
- **Server**. Used to provide clients with access to shared resources.
- **WINS**. Used to map IP addresses to NetBIOS names.
- **Workstation**. Used to provide access to shared resources from clients.
- **WWW browser**. Used to view data published on intranets or the WWW.

Each network service should be *classified* by its characteristics. To do this, identify the kind of traffic the service generates, how often the traffic is generated, and the impact this traffic has on the rest of the network.

Services can be classified using a packet analyzer such as Windows 2000 Server's Network Monitor. First, isolate the server on a single network segment to exclude extraneous traffic. Next, launch the service that you wish to classify. Finally, identify all the frames that are associated with the service.

Frames are packages of data or control traffic exchanged between networked computers. Each frame can be broken down into fields. Some fields contain protocol, addressing, and frame type information. Some fields contain data. Some fields contain verification information, such as checksums. Frames can be one of the following types:

- **Broadcast**. Used to send messages to all computers on the network. All computers will process this type of frame when they see its reserved destination address.
- **Directed**. Used to send data from one computer to another computer on the network. The most common type, this frame contains the unique MAC address of both the sending and destination computer. Any computer other than the destination machine knows to ignore the frame based on the addressing information.
- **Multicast**. Used to send data to a select group of computers on the network. These frames rely on a *multicast set* of addresses rather than a single MAC address or an all-inclusive broadcast address.

The type of traffic that is generated is determined both by the service that generated it and its protocol type. These details can be determined with the aid of Network Monitor. Windows 2000 Server includes a scaled-down version of the protocol analyzer. The full version is available as part of the Microsoft Systems Management Server (SMS). One of the main differences is that the full-version supports *promiscuous mode*, making it able to monitor all traffic on the network, while the Windows 2000 Server version can only record traffic that has been sent to its network interface.

Managing and Monitoring Network Traffic

To use Network Monitor, launch it from the Administrative Tools program group, select the network adapter connected to the network that you wish to monitor, then choose the Start command under the Capture menu.

The utility begins displaying network statistics in four windowpanes, as shown in Figure 18.19.

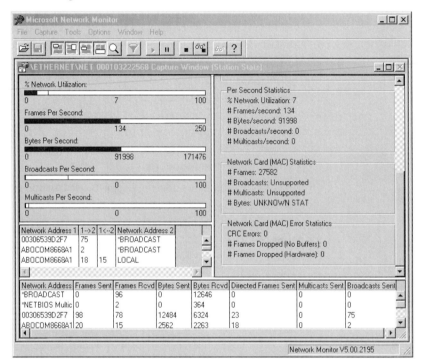

Figure 18.19   *Network Monitor window.*

Network Monitor displays the following statistics:

- **Graph pane.** Displays the current network activity in five bars: Percent Network Utilization, Frames Per Second, Bytes Per Second, Broadcasts Per Second, and Multicasts Per Second.
- **Session Statistics pane.** Shows the exchange of information between nodes on the network, including the amount of data exchanged and its direction of travel, per session. Network Monitor tracks up to 128 sessions.
- **Total Statistics pane.** Displays information about overall network activity. These statistics are listed in five categories: Network Statistics (number of Frames, Broadcasts, Multicasts, Bytes, and Frames Dropped, Network Status), Captured Statistics (number of Frames, Frames in Buffer, Bytes, Bytes in Buffer, Packets Dropped, and percent of Allotted Buffer Space in Use), Per Second Statistics (number of Frames, Bytes/second, Broadcasts/second, Multicasts/second, and percent Network Utilization), Network Card (MAC) Statistics (num-

ber of Frames, Broadcasts, Multicasts, and Bytes), and Network Card (MAC) Error Statistics (number of Cyclical Redundancy Check (CRC) Errors, Dropped Frames Due to Inadequate Buffer Space, and Dropped Packets Due to Hardware Failure).

- **Station Statistics pane.** Displays information about each workstation's activity on the network. These can be sorted by Network Address, Frames Sent, Frames, Bytes Sent, Bytes Received, Directed Frames Sent, Multicasts Sent, and Broadcasts Sent.

Network Monitor lets you capture network traffic as seen from the local system. In addition, the Network Monitor Agent can be deployed on another computer to capture data on it and send it to the computer running Network Monitor. The version of Network Monitor that comes with the SMS can capture frames sent to or from any computer on the network. (Windows 2000 Server's Network Monitor is limited in capabilities for security reasons. Presumably, the ability to read data moving between remote computers is not something all administrators need or should have.)

In order to isolate certain types of traffic, you can set *filters*. This is done by selecting the Filter command under the Capture menu to open the Capture Filter dialog box, as shown in Figure 18.20.

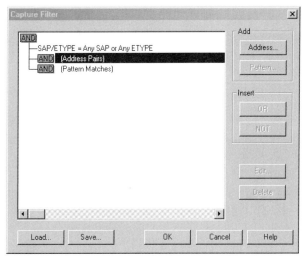

Figure 18.20 *Capture Filter dialog box.*

You can set filters to isolate protocol traffic or addresses. For example, press the Address button to open a dialog box in which you may restrict traffic to only that which passes between two computers (see Figure 18.21).

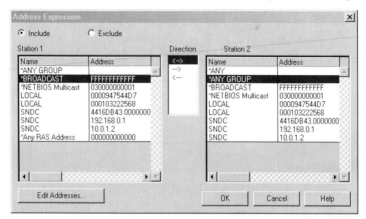

Figure 18.21 *Address Expression dialog box.*

To stop capturing data, choose the Stop command from the Capture menu. Captured data can be saved to the disk drive or displayed for analysis.

To display data, choose the Display Capture Data command from the Capture menu to open the Capture Summary window, as shown in Figure 18.22.

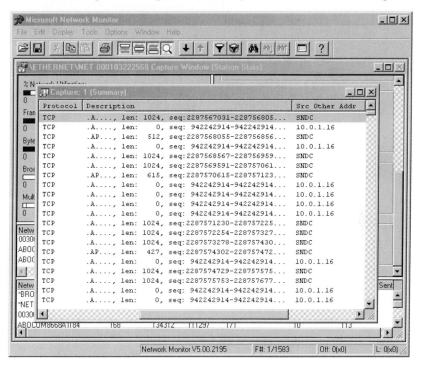

Figure 18.22 *Capture Summary window.*

You may analyze the contents of a frame by double-clicking on it in the Capture Summary window to open additional panes, as shown in Figure 18.23.

The Detail pane (in the middle) provides protocol information for the selected frame. The Hexadecimal pane (on the bottom) shows that actual data carried by the frame.

The data you capture will allow you to analyze network performance in a variety of areas.

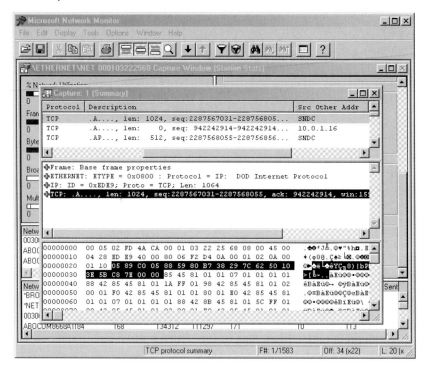

Figure 18.23 *Frame details in Capture Summary window.*

CAPTURING CLIENT-SERVER TRAFFIC

Client-server traffic is generated when a workstation first logs on to the network and thereafter when the workstation exchanges data with a server.

LOCATING A LOGON SERVER • Logon servers can be called upon in one of two ways on a Windows 2000 network. First, a client can send a broadcast request to the NetLogon service of domain controllers. Second, a client can send a query to a WINS server asking for all registered domain controllers in the domain. The client can then send a directed request to one of these.

VALIDATING A LOGON • A client accepts the first server response that comes back, regardless if the request was sent via broadcast or directed traffic. In looking at validation, consider the amount of traffic that was generated in establishing the session. In addition, look at how the session was terminated. Also, pay attention to how much traffic is generated by Window 2000 Professional computers vs. Windows 9x/Me computers.

OPENING A FILE SESSION • In order to transfer data between client and server, a session must be established. To do this under TCP/IP, for example, a client must first resolve the server's NetBIOS name with an IP address. Next, the IP address must be resolved with a MAC address. A TCP session is then established, followed by a NetBIOS session. At that point, the two computers can begin using SMB protocols to send data.

BROWSER TRAFFIC • Browser traffic is generated by servers when they publish lists of available network resources and by clients when they request those lists. Servers register their names with a master browser upon startup. The master browser then makes this list available to master browsers in other domains and to backup browsers. A client computer requests a list of backup browsers from a master browser. Upon receiving this list, the client requests a list of servers from a backup browser. A server's list of available resources is then requested from the selected server.

CAPTURING SERVER-SERVER TRAFFIC

In order to maintain the transparent nature of a Windows 2000 network, a great deal of server-to-server traffic must be generated as well. Much of this traffic is generated at regular intervals.

- Master browsers contact master browsers in other domains on the same subnet every 12 minutes.
- Domain master browsers contact a WINS server for a domain list every 12 minutes.
- Master browsers contact the Domain master browser for an updated browse list every 12 minutes.
- Backup browsers contact master browsers for an updated browse list every 15 minutes.

BROWSER ELECTIONS • *Browser election* is an automatic process for selecting a new master browser should the usual master browser go off line. This process can be triggered if a backup browser or client is unable to contact the master browser. As you might expect, this generates additional network traffic.

TRUSTS • Trust relationships generate a good deal of traffic when a trust is first created. A lot of traffic is also generated when an administrator from a trusting domain assigns permissions to an account from a trusted domain. Finally, pass-through authentication generates considerable traffic.

CAPTURING NETWORK ERRORS

CRC errors are an indicator of problems These can be caused by faulty termi-
nations, reflections, or other wiring problems.

In addition, pay close attention to your network's utilization statistics.
Generally, your Ethernet network should not exceed 35 percent sustained
utilization. If it does, it might be time to segment the network through the
use of routers or switches, or to upgrade the network's topology (such as
from 10 Mbps Ethernet to 100 Mbps Ethernet).

Study Break

Perform Traffic Analysis

Practice what you have learned by using Network Monitor to create a baseline of network activity.

Monitor network traffic to determine utilization trends and spot trouble areas. Some things to look
out for here include dropped frames and high, sustained networked utilization. Also look for nodes
that "ghost," disappearing and then reappearing. These are most often signs of bad network
cabling.

MCSE 18.4 Working with IPSec

Internet Protocol Security (IPSec) is a protocol suite that provides
cryptography-based security for data communications over IP version 4 and
IP version 6. Operating at the Network layer, IPSec extends protection to IP
as well as higher-level protocols, such as TCP, UDP, and ICMP. Because IPSec
operates at such a low-level in the networking model, it works with applications that might or might not know that it exists (unlike such protocols as
Secure Socket Layer (SSL) which requires applications to be written specifically for its use).

Before attempting to configure IPSec, it is important to understand the
underlying concepts on which it is based.

Working with Cryptography

Cryptography is the field dedicated to keeping communications secret. Imagine you are sending a message to someone and you do not want anyone other
than the receiver to view its contents. If the message is sent without employing any security techniques, there is the possibility that it will be intercepted

and read. In cryptographic terms, the message is in *plaintext* or *cleartext*. Alternately, if you encode the contents of the message in such a way that it is protected from view by outsiders (*encryption*), the message is said to be in *ciphertext*. The process of transforming ciphertext back into plaintext is *decryption.*

An encryption/decryption method is called a *cipher.* Most cryptographic methods rely on algorithms that employ a key to control encryption and decryption. There are two classes of key-based algorithms: *Symmetric* (or *secret-key*) and *asymmetric* (or *public-key*). Symmetric algorithms either use the same key for encryption and decryption, or the decryption key is easily obtained from the encryption key. Asymmetric algorithms use a different key for encryption and decryption.

Symmetric algorithms can be divided into *stream ciphers* and *block ciphers*. Stream ciphers encrypt one bit of plaintext at a time, while block ciphers encrypt a number of bits (typically 64) as a single unit.

A commonly used symmetric algorithm is Data Encryption Standard (DES), which was originally published by the U.S. government in the 1970s. DES is the encryption algorithm most commonly used with IPSec. A stronger variant, *Triple DES*, is also available under Windows 2000. As the name implies, it strengthens security by processing each block three times.

In asymmetric ciphers, the encryption key can be public, allowing anyone to encrypt with it. Only the proper recipient (who knows the decryption key) can decrypt the message, however. Rivest-Shamir-Adelman (RSA) and Diffie-Hellman are commonly used public-key algorithms for key exchange. Diffie-Hellman provides a way for two parties to create a shared secret key that is known to them only despite the fact that they are communicating over insecure channels.

Symmetric algorithms are generally faster than asymmetric ones. They are often used together, with a public-key algorithm used to encrypt a randomly generated encryption key, and the random key used to encrypt a message using a symmetric algorithm.

Public-key algorithms are often used to generate *digital signatures*. A digital signature is a block of data created using a secret key and for which there is a public key that can verify that the signature was truly generated using the corresponding private key. It should be impossible to create a signature that can be verified without knowing the secret key. Digital signatures are used to verify that a message truly comes from the alleged sender (with only the sender knowing the secret key corresponding to the public key).

Digital signatures can also certify that a public key belongs to a particular person or entity. This is done by signing the combination of the key and the information about its owner by a trusted key. The trusted key is provided by respected Certificate Authorities (CAs) that are part of a Public Key Infrastructure (PKI).

A digital signature is generally created by computing a message digest from a given document and concatenating it with information about the signer and a timestamp. The resulting string is then encrypted using the private key of the signer, resulting in an encrypted block of bits, or signature. The signature can then be distributed with information about the public key that was used to sign it. To verify it, the recipient decrypts the signature using the public key. If the signature decrypts properly and the information matches that of the message, the signature is considered valid.

Digital signatures are created using a *hash function*, a mathematical calculation that produces a fixed-length string which cannot be deciphered to produce the original.

Digital signatures are described further in Chapter 21, "Administering Certificate Services."

UNDERSTANDING IPSEC

IPSec provides "end-to-end" security, wherein only the sender and receiver need to be IPSec aware. Intervening devices such as routers, bridges, and switches do not know, or need to know, that IPSec exists.

IPSec supports two modes. In *tunnel mode*, IPSec provides protection for VPNs in conjunction with L2TP. This is also referred to as *gateway to gateway*. In *transport mode*, IPSec protects TCP/IP data communications between clients, clients and servers, and remote access connections. This is also referred to as *client to client*.

In tunnel mode, the sending and receiving computers can use any LAN protocol supported by the IPSec tunnel (such as TCP/IP, NetBEUI, IPX/SPX, or AppleTalk). In transport mode, both the sending and receiving computers must use TCP/IP.

IPSec's primary components include the following:

- **AH.** The Authentication Header (AH) is slipped between the original IP header and the TCP or UDP header in a datagram under transport mode. Its purpose is to ensure authentication and data integrity rather than encrypt data. In so doing, it signs the entire packet using Hash-based Message Authentication Code (HMAC) algorithms. Considered a medium security method, the AH ensures that the packet is invalidated if the destination address, source address, or data is changed.

- **ESP.** The Encapsulating Security Payload (ESP) header is slipped between the original IP header and the TCP header in a datagram under transport mode. Like the AH, it provides authentication and data integrity. In addition, however, it provides confidentiality by encrypting packet data.

Unlike AH, ESP does not sign the entire packet (except in tunneling mode), making the IP header potentially insecure. To avoid this, you may use AH and ESP together by creating a Windows 2000 custom security method (as described further on).

IPSec Security Negotiation • The process of *security negotiation* ensures that both a sending and a receiving computer are using the same authentication and encryption methods. A successful negotiation results in the creation of a Security Association (SA), a secure IPSec link, between remote nodes or networks. The negotiation process works as follows:

1. The sending computer transmits an offer list to the receiving computer that contains potential security levels.
2. The receiving computer notifies the sending computer that it either accepts or rejects the offer list.
3. If both the sending and receiving computers have active IPSec-compatible security policies, a *hard SA* is established. If the sending computer has active security policies that permit unsecured communications with non-IPSec hosts, a *soft SA* is established.

Each IPSec connection requires at least two SAs: One for outgoing messages and one for incoming messages. An SA can be applied to either AH or ESP, but not both. (If you employ both AH and ESP, four SAs are created.) Each SA is uniquely identified in the Security Parameters Index (SPI), which is itself derived from the destination host IP address and a randomly generated number.

IPSec Key Exchange • Automated key exchanges involve a combination of Internet Security Association and Key Management Protocol (ISAKMP) and Oakley protocol. Collectively, this combination is referred to as Internet Key Exchange (IKE), and is responsible for exchanging keys, SA negotiation, and peer authentication. The Oakley protocol protects the identities of the negotiating parties.

The first phase of key exchange involves establishing the ISAKMP SA in the following steps:

1. The sending and receiving computer select a common encryption algorithm. This can be DES or Triple DES.
2. The sending and receiving computer select a common hash algorithm. This can be MD5 or SHA1.

3. The sending and receiving computer select a common authentication method. This can be Kerberos version 5, which is based on a shared secret key (in which two or more people have it). It can be based on Public Key Certificates. Finally, it can be based on *Preshared Keys* (in which a secret key was agreed upon prior to its use).

4. The sending and receiving computer select a Diffie-Hellman group that permits the Oakley protocol to manage the key exchange.

The second phase involves negotiating SAs for the security protocols (AH and ESP). Each SA must establish a common encryption algorithm, hash algorithm, and authentication method.

Configuring IPSec

Under Windows 2000, IPSec is administered through security policy. It is integrated into Active Directory and Group Policy, and can be applied to individual computers as well as forests, trees, domains, and Organizational Units (OUs).

To create an MMC based on IPSec, perform the following steps:

1. Type "mmc" at the command line to open an empty console in author mode.

2. Select the Add/Remove Snap-ins command from the Console menu to open the Add/Remove Snap-in dialog box.

3. Click the Add button to include Computer Management snap-in under the Console Root node. You will be prompted to choose among managing the local or a remote computer. Select the Local Computer default and click the Finish button.

4. Select Group Policy in the Add Standalone Snap-in window. You are prompted to choose a group policy object to manage. Accept the Local Computer default and click the Finish button.

5. Select Certificates in the Add Standalone Snap-in window. You are prompted to choose among managing certificates for your user account, a service account, or a computer account. Select the Computer account radio button and click the Next button. You are again prompted to choose between managing the local and a remote computer. Select the Local Computer default and click the Finish button.

6. Close the various dialog boxes to return to the MMC, as shown in Figure 18.24.

This MMC can be used to manage a local computer, such as a file server. Alternately, by selecting the appropriate policy when adding the Group Policy snap-in, you could manage policy for a domain or OU.

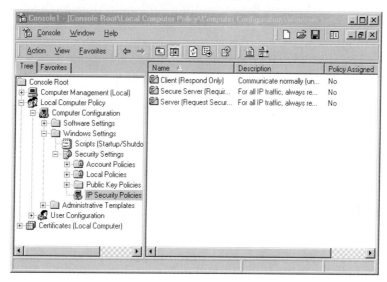

Figure 18.24   *IPSec-related MMC snap-ins.*

The following built-in IPSec policies are available:

- **Client (Respond Only).** Implements IPSec when requested by another computer. For example, a client computer connecting to a server computer that demands IPSec be used. The client itself does not require IPSec for incoming connections.
- **Server (Request Security).** Attempts to implement IPSec for all connections, but does not require it. For example, a server computer might request and implement IPSec when connecting to IPSec-aware Windows 2000 clients, but permit unsecured soft SA connections to non-IPSec-aware Windows 9x clients.
- **Secure Server (Require Security).** Implements IPSec for all connections. For example, a server computer requires that IPSec connections be used, or the connection is dropped. Common examples include high-security servers and the gateways at either end of a L2TP/IPSec tunnel.

In addition, you can create custom IPSec policies by selecting the IP Security Policies item in the Tree pane and choosing the Create IP Security Policy command from the Action menu. This launches the IP Security Policy Wizard.

The IP Security Policy Wizard asks you for the following information:

- **Name and Description.** Identify the policy.
- **Requests for Secure Communication.** Determine how requests for IPSec connections will be handled. The default is to respond to them.
- **Default Response Rule Authentication Method.** Determine how authentication will be performed. The default is through Kerberos 5. Alternately, you can choose to employ certificates or a pre-shared key.

CUSTOMIZING POLICIES AND RULES

To edit an existing policy, double-click its listing in the MMC to open the properties dialog box shown in Figure 18.25.

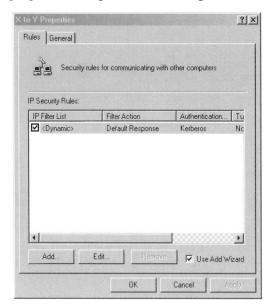

Figure 18.25 *Configuring policy properties.*

Under the Rules tab, you may add or edit IPSec rules that include an IP filter list and IP Filter actions. To perform wizard-based configuration, make sure the Use Add Wizard checkbox is selected and click the Add button.

The Security Rule Wizard prompts the following information:

- **Tunnel Endpoint.** For VPNs, enter the IP address for the destination gateway. Alternately, choose not to specify a tunnel if you are not applying the rule to a VPN.
- **Network Type.** Choose to apply the rule to LAN, remote access, or all network connections.
- **Authentication Method.** Choose the authentication method that will be applied. The default is Kerberos 5. Alternately, you can choose to employ certificates or a preshared key, but not multiple methods.

- **IP Filter List.** Choose to filter certain types of traffic, such as all IP traffic or all ICMP traffic. Click the Add button to open the IP Filter List window, in which you can add additional filters by protocol, port, and address. You must select at least one filter.
- **Filter Action.** Decide how the policy will respond to the filter. The default choices are to permit unsecured packets to pass through, accept unsecured communications but request that clients establish trust and security methods, or accept unsecured communications but require that clients establish trust and security methods. Additional actions can be added by clicking the Add button. You must select at least one filter.

Alternately, you can Edit existing settings by selecting a rule in the Properties window and clicking the Edit button. You would do this, for example, to augment the rule with additional authentication methods.

Each new policy includes a Default Response rule. You cannot remove this rule, however, you can deactivate it by deselecting its checkbox.

CONFIGURING TRANSPORT MODE

In transport mode, IPSec can accept multiple connection types.

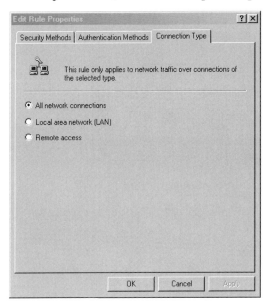

Figure 18.26 *Editing the Connection Type.*

These can be defined by double-clicking a rule and selecting the Connection Type tab in the Edit Rule Properties dialog box, as shown in Figure 18.26.

You may choose to apply the rule to LAN, remote access, or all network connections.

CONFIGURING TUNNEL MODE

In tunnel mode, IPSec requires two separate rules to define tunnel endpoints. These can be defined by double-clicking a rule and selecting the Tunnel Setting tab in the Edit Rule Properties dialog box, as shown in Figure 18.27.

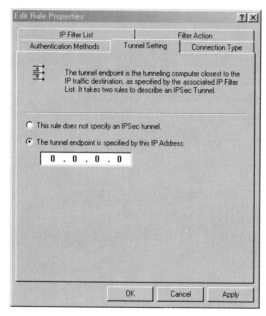

Figure 18.27 *Editing the Tunnel Setting.*

Enter an IP address in each rule, one for each gateway.

Managing IPSec

To test your IPSec policies in the MMC, right-click the IP Security Policies item in the Tree pane and select Check Policy Integrity command from the All Tasks menu in the pop-up menu. If all is well, a dialog box confirms that any changes made have been propogated by Group Policy to the computer accounts in the Group Policy Object.

To revert to default IPSec policies, right-click the IP Security Policies item in the Tree pane and select Restore Default Policies command from the All Tasks menu in the pop-up menu.

To import or export IPSec policies, right-click the IP Security Policies item in the Tree pane and select either the Import Policies or Export Policies from the All Tasks menu in the pop-up menu.

Monitoring IPSec

You may view active SAs for both the local and remote computers using the IPSec Monitor tool. You may launch this tool, as shown in Figure 18.28, from the Run dialog box with the following command:

```
ipsecmon
```

The display is updated every 15 seconds by default, but you can change this interval via the Options button.

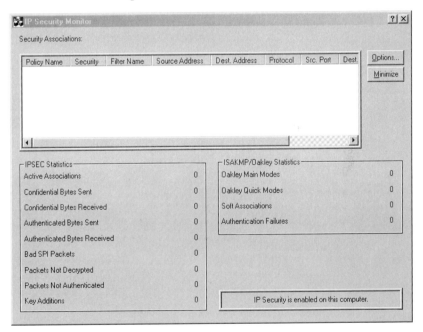

Figure 18.28   *IPSec Monitor.*

Troubleshooting IPSec

Event Viewer's System and Security Logs can be helpful in troubleshooting IPSec. The Security Log can be used in troubleshooting the policy agent. For example, an Event message 279 informs you that an IPSec Policy is in effect and that it is being updated after a change. An Event message 284 reports that the policy agent could not access Active Directory. In the Security log, messages relating to ISAKMP/Oakley are recorded, such as successful logons.

Study Break

Create Custom IPSec Policy

Practice what you have learned by creating a custom IPSec policy.

First, select the IP Security Policies item in the Tree pane of the IPSec MMC and choose the Create IP Security Policy command from the Action menu to launch the IP Security Policy Wizard. When prompted, supply the name and description, determine how requests for IPSec connections are handled, and determine how authentication is performed. When finished, use the Check Policy Integrity command to check your work.

■ Summary

In this chapter, you examined the configuration of such network protocols as TCP/IP, with a special emphasis on security.

Working with Network Protocols

Network protocols are the rules and procedures that govern communications between networked computers. They can be compared to human languages in that, as with humans, two computers must know the same language if communications is to take place between them. Windows 2000 supports such protocols as TCP/IP, NetBEUI, NWLink IPX/SPX/NetBIOS Compatible Transport, DLC, and AppleTalk, with TCP/IP being its default protocol.

Although TCP/IP is commonly referred to as a protocol, it is more accurately a *protocol suite*. Within the TCP/IP suite are numerous distinct protocols designed for various purposes, such as File Transfer Protocol (FTP), Telnet, Simple Mail Transfer Protocol (SMTP), Simple Network Management Protocol (SNMP), and the ever-popular HyperText Transfer Protocol (HTTP). NWLink IPX/SPX/NetBIOS Compatible Transport makes Windows 2000-based servers compatible with Novell NetWare networks. Although used almost exclusively for this purpose, it is a complete network protocol in its own right and can easily be used instead of NetBEUI or TCP/IP as a Microsoft LAN's base protocol.

Multiple network protocols can be bound to network services. For example, you might bind TCP/IP, NWLink, and NetBEUI to the Microsoft Network Client. When the client attempts to connect to a server, it looks to the order in which the protocols are bound to select them.

Tools useful in monitoring and troubleshooting network protocols include Network Monitor, PING, TRACERT, PATHPING, IPCONFIG, NET-STAT, and NBTSTAT.

Working with Network Protocol Security

Windows 2000 security includes Security Templates, which let you establish security-related Registry values, file and Registry access controls, and system service security; Kerberos, which supports mutual authentication for clients and servers; PKI, which augments Kerberos with a public key system based on the X.509 standard; Smart Card, which supports the use of smart card-aware readers and applications; and IPSec, which supports network-level authentication, data integrity, and encryption. In addition, you can use firewalls and proxy servers to regulate protocol traffic for the purposes of network security.

Working with Network Traffic

In order to optimize network connectivity, you must first monitor the network to determine how each of the Windows 2000 services that are generating the traffic is affecting the network. You can optimize network traffic either by providing network services to improve response times, or through providing greater network bandwidth by reducing network services. As these are mutually exclusive goals, you need to strike a balance between the two. The type of traffic that is generated is determined both by the service that generated it and its protocol type. These types of details can be determined with the aid of Network Monitor.

Working with IPSec

IPSec is a protocol suite that provides cryptography-based security for data communications over IP version 4 and IP version 6. Operating at the Network layer, IPSec extends protection to IP as well as higher-level protocols, such as TCP, UDP, and ICMP. Because IPSec operates at such a low-level in the networking model, it works with applications that might or might not know that it exists. IPSec provides "end-to-end" security, wherein only the sender and receiver need to be IPSec aware. Intervening devices such as routers, bridges, and switches do not know, or need to know, that IPSec exists.

In tunnel mode, IPSec provides protection for VPNs in conjunction with L2TP. This is also referred to as gateway to gateway. In transport mode, IPSec protects TCP/IP data communications between clients, clients and servers, and remote access connections. This is also referred to as client to client. In tunnel mode, the sending and receiving computers can use any LAN protocol supported by the IPSec tunnel (such as TCP/IP, NetBEUI, IPX/SPX, or AppleTalk). In transport mode, both the sending and receiving computers must use TCP/IP.

IPSec's primary components include the Authentication Header (AH), used to ensure authentication and data integrity rather than encrypt data, and Encapsulating Security Payload (ESP) header, which provides authentication and data integrity as well as by encrypting packet data.

▲ CHAPTER REVIEW QUESTIONS

Here are a few questions relating to the material covered in the *Installing, Configuring, Managing, Monitoring, and Troubleshooting Network Protocols in a Windows 2000 Network Infrastructure* section of Microsoft's *Implementing and Administering a Microsoft Windows 2000 Network Infrastructure* exam (70-216).

1. *Which of the following network protocols can be routed? Select all that apply:*
   A. TCP/IP
   B. NetBEUI
   C. NWLink IPX/SPX/NetBIOS Compatible Transport
   D. AppleTalk

2. *Which of the following IP addresses in numerical notation corresponds to "11000001.10101000.11100000.00001001" in binary notation? Select only one:*
   A. 192.168.10.12
   B. 192.168.128.23
   C. 193.168.224.9
   D. 212.10.1.4

3. *To create a custom subnet, you must take some bits from the network ID to give to the host ID.*

   A. True

   B. False

4. *Before attempting to use NWLink IPX/SPX/NetBIOS Compatible Transport, you must configure an internal network number.*

   A. True

   B. False

5. *NWLink IPX/SPX/NetBIOS Compatible Transport can only used one frame type at a time.*

   A. True

   B. False

6. *Network services can only use one network protocol at a time.*

   A. True

   B. False

7. *Where are network bindings configured? Select only one:*

   A. In the Network and Dial-Up Connections folder

   B. In the Computer Management MMC

   C. In the Local Area Network Properties dialog box

   D. Via the command line

8. *Which of the following may be configured using TCP/IP filtering? Select all that apply:*

   A. TCP

   B. UDP

   C. IP

   D. ICMP

9. *To properly filter TCP/IP traffic you must know the ports that are used by the service you wish to block.*

   A. True

   B. False

10. *Which of the following are components of Windows 2000 protocol security? Select all that apply:*

    A. Kerberos

    B. PKI

    C. Subnetting

    D. IPSec

11. *You might be able to determine if a service is being blocked by a firewall using NETSTAT.*

    A. True

    B. False

12. *The Windows 2000 Server version of Network Monitor supports promiscuous mode.*

    A. True

    B. False

13. *Ethernet redesign may be necessary when network utilization consistently meets are exceeds which level? Select only one:*

    A. 3 percent

    B. 35 percent

    C. 50 percent

    D. 87.5 percent

14. *Cryptoanalysis is the field dedicated to keeping communications secret.*

    A. True

    B. False

15. *Before enabling the use of IPSec, you must configure such devices as routers, bridges, and switches to be aware of it.*

    A. True

    B. False

16. *IPSec is enabled and configured through security policy.*

    A. True

    B. False

17. *IPSec only supports TCP/IP in transport mode.*

    A. True

    B. False

18. *IPSec in transport mode can support which of the following connections? Select all that apply:*

    A. All network connections

    B. Remote access connections

    C. LAN connections

    D. VPN connections

19. *IPSec in tunnel mode can support which of the following protocols? Select all that apply:*

    A. L2TP

    B. PPTP

    C. IPX

    D. AppleTalk

20. *Which IPSec policy would you use to request security but permit insecure communications when linking with non-Windows 2000 computers? Select only one:*

    A. Client

    B. Server

    C. Secure Server

    D. Custom

21. *When adding or editing IPSec rules, you should first delete the Default Response rule.*

    A. True

    B. False

22. *Which of the following authentication methods can be applied to IPSec rules? Select all that apply:*

    A. Kerberos

    B. NTLM

    C. Certificates

    D. Pre-shared key

23. *For security reasons, you cannot export IPSec policies.*

    A. True

    B. False

24. *You can use the NETSTAT utility to view active SAs.*

A. True

B. False

Administering Windows Internet Naming Service

▲ **Chapter Syllabus**

MCSE 19.1 Configuring NetBIOS Name Resolution

MCSE 19.2 Working with WINS

MCSE 19.3 Configuring WINS Replication

In this chapter, we look at material covered in the *Installing, Configuring, Managing, Monitoring, and Troubleshooting WINS in a Windows 2000 Network Infrastructure* section of Microsoft's *Implementing and Administering a Microsoft Windows 2000 Network Infrastructure* exam (70-216).

After reading the material in this chapter, you will understand the workings of NetBIOS, Net-BEUI, and NetBIOS over TCP/IP (NBT). You also learn about the NetBIOS name resolution process, as performed with and without the use of the Windows Internet Naming Service (WINS). Finally, you learn to install, configure, manage, monitor, and troubleshoot WINS and such features as the dynamic database, burst mode, tombstoning, replication, and persistent connections.

| MCSE 19.1 | **Configuring NetBIOS Name Resolution** |

Microsoft Networking prior to Windows 2000 was NetBIOS-based, using NetBEUI as the protocol of choice. With the rise in the popularity of the Internet, and subsequently the install base of TCP/IP, Microsoft abandoned NetBEUI as its standard protocol. The transition has not been seamless, however, for there are many applications that were written specifically for NetBIOS, and NetBIOS does things differently from TCP/IP (e.g., WinSock) applications.

To begin with, NetBIOS is broadcast-based. Applications written for NetBIOS access its network protocols via a Session layer interface. When two applications wish to communicate, the sending computer broadcasts the name of the destination computer over the network and waits for the receiving computer to respond with its MAC address.

This methodology has some inherent limitations. First, each computer must have a unique name in the flat NetBIOS name space, a requirement that is more difficult to implement than it might sound when users are able to define their own workstations' names. Second, a lot of broadcast traffic is generated, limiting the number of nodes that can effectively chatter away on one segment to about 200. Third, routers do not pass broadcast traffic, so NetBEUI cannot be used to create internetworks.

As described earlier in this book, TCP/IP uses the more indirect hierarchical DNS for name resolution, relying on IP addresses and port numbers to direct traffic on one segment or many. The trick for Microsoft has been to provide a way for applications written for NetBIOS to work with TCP/IP. The answer is the NetBIOS over TCP/IP (NBT) Session layer interface. Its job, simply put, is to resolve NetBIOS computer names with IP addresses, permitting NetBIOS-aware applications to use TCP/IP as a transport without being rewritten.

Working with NetBIOS Names

NetBIOS are 16 bytes in size, with the first 15 bytes used for characters and the last byte reserved for identifying a service. In general, characters permissible in a NetBIOS name include the following:

- A-Z (uppercase)
- 0-9
- # $! - _ @ % ( ) [ ]

Note that underscores (_) are permitted. These are not permitted in FQDNs, however. When migrating from a Windows NT 4.0 network to a

Windows 2000 network, you will find that NetBIOS names containing underscores are translated to dashes. Thus, a computer with a name like "tom_pc" becomes "tom-pc." With this in mind, you should only create Net-BIOS names that would also be legal FQDNs.

A computer running NBT has multiple NetBIOS names, each with a different service identifier, as listed in Figure 19.1.

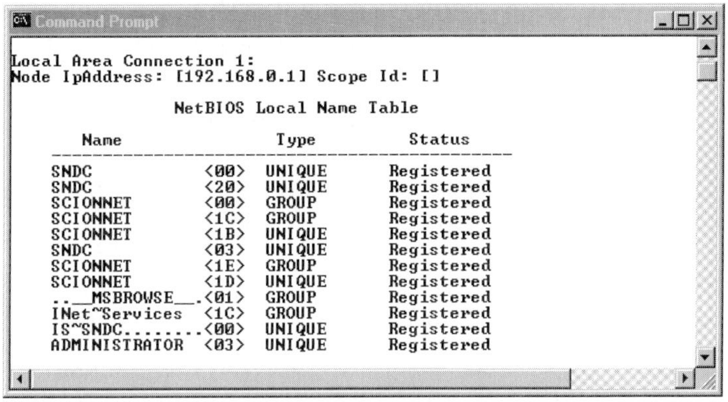

Figure 19.1 *Viewing NetBIOS names in NBTSTAT.*

Some common service identifiers are listed in Table 19.1.

Table 19.1 *NetBIOS Service Identifiers*

NetBIOS Name	Service
computer <00>	Workstation service (Microsoft Networking Client).
domain <00>	Server service, when LAN Manager Announcements are enabled.
MSBROWSE <01>	Master browser, announcing the domain on the local subnet.
domain <1b>	Domain master browser, on a PDC or PDC emulator.
domain <1c>	Internet group name, a dynamically generated list of as many as 25 domain controllers that can be used for Windows NT 4.0 pass-through authentication.
domain <1d>	Segment master browser.
domain <1e>	Domain-wide browser service announcements in a Windows 2000 domain.
computer <03>	Messenger service, on a WINS client.
computer <1f>	Network Dynamic Data Exchange (NetDDE) service.
computer <20>	Server service, on a Windows 2000 WINS client.
computer <Be>	Network Monitor service, unique name.
computer <Bf>	Network Monitor service, group name.

NetBIOS Name Resolution

The primary methods of NetBIOS name-to-IP address resolution involve broadcasts, name servers, or the LMHOSTS file.

BROADCASTS

NBT can resolve a NetBIOS name to an IP address on a local segment only. When the IP address is returned, a second Address Resolution Protocol (ARP) broadcast is sent to resolve the IP address with the MAC address. A communications session can then be established.

LMHOSTS

Like the "HOSTS" file used in DNS, the "LMHOSTS" file contains the NetBIOS names and IP addresses of the network's computers in a static text document. You can create an LMHOSTS file in a text editor such as Word Pad, as shown in Figure 19.2.

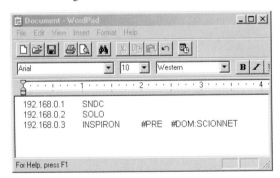

Figure 19.2 *Creating an LMHOSTS file.*

The LMHOSTS file does not have an extension. Its tags are listed in Table 19.2.

Table 19.2 *LMHOSTS File Tags*

File Tag	Description
#BEGIN_ALTERNATE	Used in grouping multiple #INCLUDE statements.
#END_ALTERNATE	Denotes the end of an #INCLUDE statements grouping.
#DOM:*domain*	Used with the #PRE statement to define a NetBIOS name mapping for a domain controller.

Table 19.2 *LMHOSTS File Tags (continued)*

#INCLUDE *file name*	Specifies the name of an LMHOSTS file shared on another computer using UNC naming. When the remote server is beyond the local subnet, you must include a mapping for it above the #BEGIN_ALTERNATE statement. Must be used with the #PRE statement.
#MH	Used on multihomed systems to search for the same NetBIOS name on up to 25 interfaces (with up to 25 IP addresses).
#PRE	Preloads the entry into the NetBIOS remote name cache.

The file is read from top to bottom, with parsing stopping after the first successful resolution (unless the #MH tag is present). The tags need to be in uppercase, but the NetBIOS names do not. Entries containing #PRE tags should come at the end.

The LMHOSTS file is saved in the WINNT\System32\Drivers\Etc folder.

NETBIOS NAME SERVERS

The NetBIOS Name Server (NBNS) is a database application dedicated to resolving NetBIOS names with IP addresses. The most commonly used NBNS is the Windows Internet Naming Server (WINS).

When an application running on a WINS client calls on the NetBIOS Session layer interface, Windows first examines the name in the query to make sure that it is not longer than 15 characters or contains any dots. If it does, the query is handed off to DNS. Otherwise, name resolution generally occurs in the following order:

1. Windows checks to see if the name is in the NetBIOS remote name cache.
2. If the name is not found, Windows contacts the WINS server defined in the client's TCP/IP properties.
3. If the name is not resolved by the WINS server, a broadcast is issued.
4. If the broadcast fails, Windows looks to the LMHOSTS file (if TCP/IP properties are configured for it to do so).
5. If the LMHOSTS lookup fails, Windows looks to the HOSTS file.
6. If all else fails, Windows queries DNS.

The actual name resolution sequence differs somewhat depending on how the client is configured. *Node types* are used to define how NetBIOS clients process queries. The choices are as follow:

- **B-node.** A Broadcast-node (B-node) uses broadcasts rather than WINS for NetBIOS name resolution. This includes any computer whose WINS server properties are not configured. The B-node's query sequence is NetBIOS remote name cache, broadcast, LMHOSTS, HOSTS, and then DNS. An *enhanced B-node* client parses entries preloaded from the LMHOSTS file (using #PRE tags) before sending a broadcast.
- **P-node.** A Peer-node (P-node) client does not issue broadcasts. This can greatly reduce network traffic, but it also makes the client highly dependent upon the availability of the WINS server. The P-node's query sequence is NetBIOS remote name cache, WINS, LMHOSTS, HOSTS, and DNS.
- **M-node.** The Mixed-node (M-node) client uses both broadcast and WINS name resolution methods, with preference given to broadcasts. The M-node's query sequence is NetBIOS remote name cache, broadcast, WINS, LMHOSTS, HOSTS, and DNS.
- **H-node.** The Hybrid-node (H-node) client uses both broadcast and WINS name resolution methods, with preference given to WINS. The H-node's query sequence is NetBIOS remote name cache, WINS, broadcast, LMHOSTS, HOSTS, and DNS.

Nodes types can be automatically assigned using the DHCP Server, or manually set through the Registry.

Study Break

Set Node Types

Practice what you have learned by changing the node type for a workstation.

First, determine which node type is most appropriate for your network environment. For example, M-node might be best applied to a network with remote locations, ensuring that name resolution traffic will be restricted to the local segment in most cases.

The node type can be set by changing the following Registry key:

`HKLM\System\CurrentControlSet\Services\NetBT\Parameters`

Possible REG_DWORD values for the Node Type entry are: B-node, 0x1; P-node, 0x2; M-node, 0x4; and H-node, 0x8.

MCSE 19.2   **Working with WINS**

Like the previously described DNS and DHCP, WINS adheres to the client-server architecture. WINS servers can be installed on a standalone Windows 2000 Server or a domain controller, in either primary or secondary roles. A single primary/secondary combination can easily accommodate 10,000 WINS clients.

WINS supports clients running under Windows 2000, NT, 9x/Me, Windows for Workgroups 3.11, MS-DOS/LAN Manager 2.2c, and MS-DOS/Microsoft Network Client 3.0 (with the real mode TCP/IP driver). WINS client configuration was described in Chapter 6, "Networking Windows 2000 Professional."

WINS services can also be extended to non-WINS NetBIOS services through WINS Proxy Agents, which intercept NetBIOS name resolution requests from non-Windows B-node computers.

In action, WINS clients and servers communicate through the following processes.

Name Registration

The name registration process proceeds as follows:

1. Upon launch, the WINS client attempts to register its NetBIOS names with the Primary WINS server.
2. The primary WINS server checks the database to see if the NetBIOS names already exist in its database. If not, it sends the client a Positive Name Registration Response.
3. If the NetBIOS computer name is in the database, the WINS server sends a Wait for Acknowledgement (WACK) message. It then sends as many as three separate challenges, at 500 ms intervals, to the IP address of the client. If it receives no response, the WINS server sends the client a Positive Name Registration Response. If the WINS server receives a response from the queried IP address, the client receives a Negative Name Registration Response.

When a client attempts to register its own NetBIOS name when it already exists in the database, it performs the name renewal process.

If the client is unable to contact the primary WINS server when it boots up, it tries twice more at 500 ms. intervals. It then attempts to contact each secondary WINS server, going down the list. There can be as many as 12. If none of the secondary WINS servers respond, it tries the primary WINS server again, and so on.

Name Renewal

Along with the Positive Name Registration Response, the WINS server sends the client a Renewal Interval. In order to keep its name active in the database, the client must renew its registration at regular intervals. To do so, the client sends a Name Refresh Request to the primary WINS server at 50 percent of the Renewal Interval. In most cases, the client then receives a new Renewal Interval of the same length of time.

If the client cannot contact the primary WINS server, it keeps trying at 10-minute intervals for an hour before trying a secondary WINS server. Failing that, it returns to the primary WINS server.

Name Release

During a normal shutdown, the WINS client sends the primary WINS server a NetBIOS Name Release message. If the client's IP address matches the one in the WINS server's database, the record is marked inactive. Otherwise, the message is ignored.

An inactive record will enter an *extinction period*, during which time the WINS server does not issue a challenge if another client attempts to register it. After the extinction period has elapsed, the record is marked *extinct* and is *tombstoned* for another period of time, the *extinction timeout*. Thereafter, it is removed, or *scavenged*, from the database.

Name Resolution

To resolve a NetBIOS name with an IP address, WINS clients perform the following steps:

1. The client checks the NetBIOS remote name cache.
2. If the information is not in the NetBIOS remote name, the client sends a Name Query Request to the primary WINS server.
3. The WINS server responds with either a positive or negative Name Query Response.
4. If a Negative Name Query Response is received, the WINS client broadcasts as many as three Name Query Request messages on the local segment, at 750 ms. Intervals.
5. If the broadcasts fail, the WINS client may attempt name resolution through other methods, as previously described.

Windows 2000 adds several improvements to WINS, including the following:

- **Dynamic database.** The WINS database is distributed and works in conjunction with DHCP to register and query dynamic NetBIOS names.
- **Burst mode.** WINS has an increased capability to handle a burst of NetBIOS registration requests, such as when computers are started at the beginning of the workday or after a power outage. When in burst mode, the WINS server responds to requests immediately and does not take the time to check NetBIOS names against its database, send challenges to avoid duplicate names, or commit any entries to its database.
- **Manual Tombstoning.** This permits a record's removal across all WINS servers, ensuring that a record that was not deleted on one server never gets propagated back to the rest of the system.
- **Persistent connections.** Using this feature, WINS servers can keep their connections between replicating partners open, saving time and overhead that would be generated by constantly opening and closing connections.

Installing WINS

The steps to installing WINS Server, as covered in Chapter 9, "Administering Windows 2000 Server Resource Access," are as follow:

1. Click the Install Add-on Components link in the installation CD-ROM Autorun screen. This opens the Windows Components window.
2. Choose the Networking Services item in the scrolling list and click the Details button to open the Networking Services window.
3. Enable the Windows Internet Name Service (WINS) checkbox, then click the OK button.
4. Click the Next button in the Windows Components window to perform the installation.

You do not need to restart the server.

Configuring WINS

The WINS server can be configured through the Services and Applications snap-in of the Computer Management MMC, as shown in Figure 19.3, or through its own MMC found in the Administrative Tools program group.

Using the WINS snap-in, you can display records by name (NetBIOS) or owner (IP address), verify name records, and delete owners.

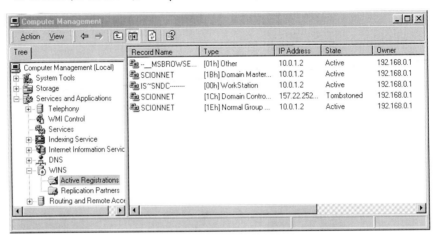

Figure 19.3 *Configuring the WINS server.*

You can also establish static mappings for computers that are not WINS clients by selecting the New Static Mapping command from the Action menu to open the New Static Mapping dialog box, as shown in Figure 19.4.

Figure 19.4 *Creating a static mapping.*

In addition to Computer name, NetBIOS scope, and IP address, you can choose among the following Type settings:

- **Unique.** Used when the computer has a single IP address. NetBIOS names are created for workstation (redirector), server, and messenger services.
- **Group.** Used when the computer is member of a workgroup. Name resolution is performed via broadcasts.
- **Domain Name.** Used to create mappings to Windows NT domain controllers (creating a 1Ch entry).
- **Internet Group.** Used to create mappings for Administrative Groups of shared resources (creating a 20h entry).
- **Multihomed.** Used when the computer has multiple IP addresses.

You can configure the WINS Server overall by right-clicking its name in the MMC and choosing the Properties command from the pop-up window to open the Properties dialog box, as shown in Figure 19.5.

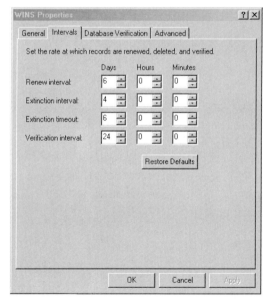

Figure 19.5 *Configuring WINS Server properties.*

Various features can be configured under the following tabs:

- **General.** Enable/disable and define the statistics update interval (10 minutes by default). Also enable/disable database backup at shutdown and define the backup file's pathname.

- **Intervals.** Specify a Renew interval (6 days by default), Extinction interval (4 days by default), Extinction timeout (6 days by default), and Verification interval (24 days by default).
- **Database Verification.** Enable/disable database verification and define the interval (24 hours by default). If enabled, define beginning time, maximum records to verify, and verify against owner servers or randomly generated partners.
- **Advanced.** Enable/disable detailed logging, enable/disable burst mode and set the level of client requests, define database pathname, and enable/disable LAN Manager compatibility.

Managing WINS

The WINS database is largely self-tuning. Based on the same Extensible Storage Engine used by Active Directory and Microsoft Exchange, the database has no specific limit on the number of entries that it may contain. What can be done to manage WINS mostly involves managing its server databases.

PERFORMING COMPACTION

As entries are removed from the database, the amount of space they once consumed is not reclaimed until the database undergoes compaction. WINS performs its own *online compaction* routines during idle times. This is not completely efficient, however, so you might wish to perform manual compaction occasionally. To do this, first stop the WINS service from the command line with the command: *net stop WINS*. Next, change to the \WINNT\system32\wins directory and type the command: *jetpack wins.mdb winstemp.mdb*. You should then see the message "jetpack completed successfully." Type the command: *net start WINS*.

CONSISTENCY CHECKING

As previously described, WINS servers update their database records by communicating with push and pull partners at regular intervals. In addition, you can force the process by right-clicking the server in the WINS MMC and selecting the Verify Database Consistency command from the pop-up menu. You can also verify the consistency of version IDs by right-clicking the server in the WINS MMC and selecting the Verify Version ID Consistency command from the pop-up menu.

BACKUP AND RESTORATION

As previously described, you can configure the WINS Server to automatically back up its database under the General tab of the server's Properties dialog box. When enabled, this feature backs up the database every three hours. Alternately, you may perform this task manually by right-clicking the server in the WINS MMC and selecting the Back Up Database command from the pop-up menu.

To restore a WINS database, first stop the service. Next, right-click the server in the WINS MMC and select the Restore Database command from the pop-up menu.

Monitoring and Troubleshooting WINS

As described previously in this book, the System Monitor application lets you establish statistical measurements for the computer's hardware and software components. System Monitor's primary WINS-related counters are shown in Table 19.3.

Table 19.3 *WINS-Related Counters in System Monitor*

Counter	Description
Queries/sec	Rate at which queries are being received by the server.
Releases/sec	Rate at which NetBIOS Name Release Requests are being received by the server.
Successful Queries/sec	Rate at which queries are being resolved successfully by the server.
Successful Releases/sec.	Rate at which NetBIOS Name Release Requests are being processed successfully by the server.
Total Number of Conflicts/sec	Rate at which NetBIOS name conflicts are being detected by the server.
Total Number of Registrations/ sec.	Rate at which NetBIOS Name Registration Requests are being processed by the server.
Total Number of Renewals/sec.	Rate at which NetBIOS Name Renewel Requests are being processed by the server.
Unique Conflicts/sec	Rate at which unique name conflicts are being detected by the server.
Unique Registrations/sec	Rate at which unique NetBIOS names are being registered by the server.
Unique Renewals/sec	Rate at which unique NetBIOS names are being renewed by the server.

When WINS problems manifest themselves, some areas to examine in troubleshooting include the following:

- **Database.** If the server crashes or shuts down improperly, the database can become corrupted. Such problems can often be identified in the Event Log.
- **Service Startup.** If low resources cause the service to "hang" at startup, there will likely be a message in the Event Log.
- **Network.** Problems with the network interface, or an overburdened network segment, can lead to WINS problems. Check to see if WINS clients and servers are experiencing timeouts. If so, inspect network components and run Network Monitor to analyze the level of network utilization.

Study Break

Install and Configure WINS

Practice what you have learned by installing and configuring the Windows 2000 Server WINS Server, perhaps in a secondary role.

After setting up the WINS server, use the Verify Database Consistency command to update its records. Next, use the Back Up Database command to create an archive of the WINS database.

MCSE 19.3 Configuring WINS Replication

In order to provide the highest possible level of fault tolerance on your network, you should employ multiple WINS servers, such as a primary and at least one secondary. In that way, if a WINS client is unable to contact the primary WINS server, it will have a number of secondary WINS servers with which to register instead. To maintain address consistency, WINS servers share their database information through the process of *replication*.

For the purposes of synchronization, WINS servers are configured as replication partners of the following two types:

- **Pull partners.** This server receives database information after a replication interval has elapsed. This decision is made based on a database version ID. If the pull partner's database version ID has a higher value than the last database that was pulled, it requests an update.
- **Push partners.** This server sends database information to a push partner based on the number of changes that have been made to the

database. After the specified number of changes, the server sends the push partner a pull notification. The push partner may then request an update. Under Windows 2000, WINS push partners can maintain persistent connections, allowing them to update changes as they occur.

Microsoft recommends that you configure your WINS servers as both push and pull partners to ensure the maximum possible database security. An exception might be when WINS servers are separated by relatively slow WAN links. In this case, configuring the servers at either end of the WAN link as pull partners ensure the least possible impact on throughput.

WINS servers are capable of creating their own partnerships automatically. With *Automatic Partner Discovery* enabled, WINS servers use a multicast address of 224.0.1.24 to locate each other.

To configure WINS replication, right-click the Replication Partners item in the MMC's Tree pane and select the Properties command to open the Properties dialog box, as shown in Figure 19.6. Switch to the Push Replication tab to define how many changes are to be made to the database before the server notifies its push partner that it is time for an update.

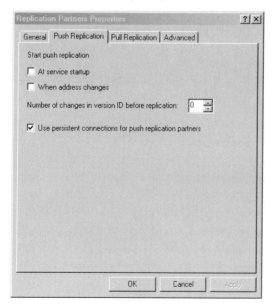

Figure 19.6 *Configuring push replication.*

Alternately, you can elect to start the push replication process at startup, or whenever an address change is recorded. By default, the use of persistent connections is enabled.

Next, switch to the Pull Replication tab to define the Replication interval, start times, and number of retries, as shown in Figure 19.7. By default, pull replication starts at service startup and persistent connections are used.

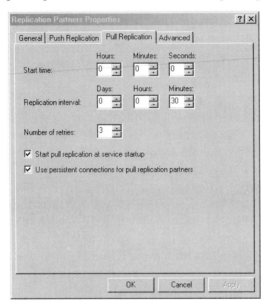

Figure 19.7 *Configuring pull replication.*

Next, switch to the Advanced tab to identify the replication partners by IP address, or enable the Automatic partner discovery features.

Study Break

Configure Replication Partners

Practice what you have learned configuring replication partners manually.

Configure at least two WINS servers to act as both push and pull partners in the server Properties dialog box. Also enable the use of persistent connections.

■ Summary

In this chapter, we looked at issues surrounding the installation and management of WINS, including NetBIOS, primary and secondary WINS servers, and replication partners.

Configuring NetBIOS Name Resolution

NetBIOS is broadcast-based. Applications written for NetBIOS access its network protocols via a Session layer interface. When two applications wish to communicate, the sending computer broadcasts the name of the destination computer over the network and waits for the receiving computer to respond with its MAC address. TCP/IP uses the more indirect hierarchical DNS for name resolution, relying on IP addresses and port numbers to direct traffic on one segment or many. Microsoft provides a way for applications written for NetBIOS to work with TCP/IP through the NBT Session layer interface. Its job is to resolve NetBIOS computer names with IP addresses, permitting NetBIOS-aware applications to use TCP/IP as a transport without being re-written. The primary methods of NetBIOS name-to-IP address resolution involve broadcasts, name servers, or the LMHOSTS file. The actual name resolution sequence differs somewhat depending on how the client is configured. Node types are used to define how NetBIOS clients process queries.

Working with WINS

WINS adheres to the client-server architecture. WINS servers can be installed on a standalone Windows 2000 Server or a domain controller, in either primary or secondary roles. The WINS name resolution process involves name registration. Name renewal, name release, and name resolution phases. The WINS server can be configured through the Services and Applications snap-in of the Computer Management MMC or through its own MMC found in the Administrative Tools program group. Among WINS management tasks are compaction, consistency checking, and backup. WINS services can be monitored using the System Monitor utility.

Configuring WINS Replication

In order to maintain address consistency, WINS servers share their database information through replication. For the purposes of synchronization, WINS servers are configured as replication partners of two types. Pull partners receive database information based on a database version ID when a certain interval has elapsed. Push partners send database information based on the number of changes that have been made to thc database. WINS servers are capable of creating their own partnerships automatically, or they can be identified manually.

▲ CHAPTER REVIEW QUESTIONS

Here are a few questions relating to the material covered in the *Installing, Configuring, Managing, Monitoring, and Troubleshooting WINS in a Windows 2000 Network Infrastructure* section of Microsoft's *Implementing and Administering a Microsoft Windows 2000 Network Infrastructure* exam (70-216).

1. *NetBIOS and TCP/IP name resolution works similarly.*
     A. True
     B. False

2. *It a good idea to use underscores (_) in place of spaces in NetBIOS names.*
     A. True
     B. False

3. *Which of the following are involved in the WINS name registration process? Select all that apply:*
     A. Positive Name Registration Response
     B. Wait for Acknowledgment
     C. Negative Name Registration Response
     D. Renewal Interval

4. *Only Windows-based computers can have records in the WINS Server database.*
     A. True
     B. False

5. *WINS Server database compaction must be performed manually.*
     A. True
     B. False

6. *WINS Server database back ups can be performed automatically.*
     A. True
     B. False

7. *A WINS Server sends updates to a push partner after a specified interval has elapsed.*

    A. True

    B. False

8. *WINS Servers can locate each other using multicasting for the purposes of creating push and pull partnerships.*

    A. True

    B. False

Administering IP Routing

▲Chapter Syllabus

MCSE 20.1 Working with IP Routing

MCSE 20.2 Working with NAT

In this chapter, we cover the *Installing, Configuring, Managing, Monitoring, and Troubleshooting IP Routing in a Windows 2000 Network Infrastructure* section of Microsoft's *Implementing and Administering a Microsoft Windows 2000 Network Infrastructure* exam (70-216).

From this material, you learn to enable IP routing using Windows 2000's Routing and Remote Access Service (RRAS), as well as manage routing tables, border routing, internal routing, and demand-dial routing. You also learn to use private IP addressing through Network Address Translation (NAT) and Internet Connection Sharing (ICS).

MCSE 20.1 **Working with IP Routing**

At its simplest, *Routing* involves forwarding packets from a computer on one network to a computer on another network. Several devices and services can accomplish this function, including gateways and proxy servers, but this work is most commonly accomplished by *routers*. Routers can be hardware devices, such as those produced by Cisco, Bay Networks, Shiva, and others, or software-based, such as Windows 2000 Server's built-in RRAS.

Routers decide whether to leave packets on the segment from which they originated or forward them to another segment based on IP address. When it is determined that a packet is destined for a host beyond its originating network, the router figures out the best way to get it there based on its understanding of available routes. *Static routes* are manually established by an administrator. This is the most cumbersome way to set up routes, as each must be explicitly configured, but the one that incurs the least performance overhead thereafter. *Dynamic routes* are learned and updated by routers automatically. These are the easiest to set up and administer, but their use results in greater performance overhead as routers need to spend time and use network bandwidth in communicating with each other.

Routers are identified to clients in the TCP/IP Properties dialog box, as shown in Figure 20.1.

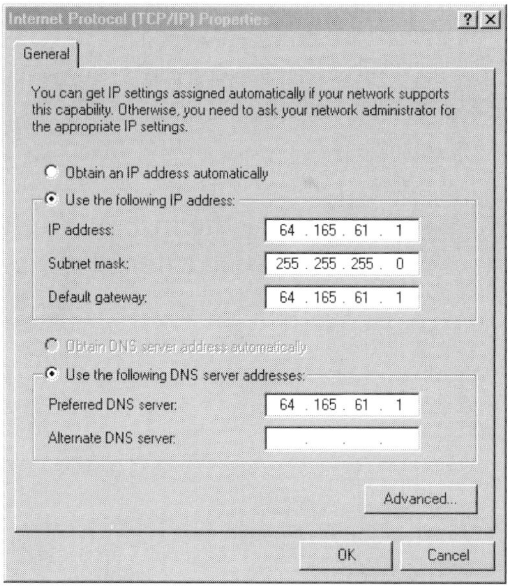

Figure 20.1 *Configuring the default router.*

Although the TCP/IP Properties dialog box refers to a default *gateway*, this is somewhat of a misnomer. Gateways usually operate further up in the OSI model, permitting conversion between two protocols (e.g., Gateway Services for NetWare). Gateways can also convert one IP packet into another IP packet, however, so the reference is not completely inaccurate. Whatever you call it, the IP address that you type into the Default gateway field should be the device responsible for forwarding packets beyond the local segment to another subnet or the Internet.

Microsoft's implementation of TCP/IP only supports a single route table, so all traffic is forwarded through a *single* default gateway whenever its destination is nonlocal. You can configure multiple gateways (using the Advanced button) in the event the default gateway is unavailable, which the workstation then tries sequentially using Windows 2000's *Dead Gateway Detection* feature. No more than one gateway will ever be used at one time, however.

A *routing interface* is any route into the router that has an IP address. A typical implementation would be a Windows 2000 Server with two network adapters, each with a different IP address, as shown in Figure 20.2.

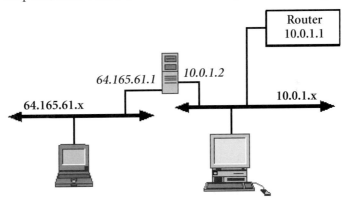

Figure 20.2 *Simple Windows 2000 Router Configuration.*

Routers consult *routing tables* to determine where a packet arriving from one interface should go. If the sender and destination addresses reside on the same network, the router leaves the packet alone. If the sender and destination addresses reside on different networks, the router determines the path that the packet must take to the remote host and forwards it on its way through another interface. If there are multiple routes possible, the router chooses the most efficient route.

Microsoft TCP/IP clients also have a routing table, albeit a smaller one. It contains information for the installed network adapters and the loopback address (127.0.0.1). You can view this routing table by typing "route print" at the command line to view a list like the one shown in Figure 20.3.

```
Command Prompt                                                        _ |□| X
Microsoft Windows 2000 [Version 5.00.2195]
(C) Copyright 1985-2000 Microsoft Corp.

C:\Documents and Settings\Administrator.SN-BDC>route print
===========================================================================
Interface List
0x1 ........................... MS TCP Loopback interface
0x2 ...00 00 94 75 44 d7 ...... Intel DC21140 PCI Fast Ethernet Adapter (Microso
ft's Packet Scheduler)
0x3 ...00 01 03 22 25 68 ...... 3Com EtherLink PCI (Microsoft's Packet Scheduler
)
===========================================================================
===========================================================================
Active Routes:
Network Destination        Netmask          Gateway       Interface  Metric
          0.0.0.0          0.0.0.0         10.0.1.1        10.0.1.2       1
         10.0.1.0    255.255.255.0         10.0.1.2        10.0.1.2       1
         10.0.1.2  255.255.255.255        127.0.0.1       127.0.0.1       1
   10.255.255.255  255.255.255.255         10.0.1.2        10.0.1.2       1
        127.0.0.0        255.0.0.0        127.0.0.1       127.0.0.1       1
      192.168.0.0    255.255.255.0      192.168.0.1     192.168.0.1       1
      192.168.0.1  255.255.255.255        127.0.0.1       127.0.0.1       1
    192.168.0.255  255.255.255.255      192.168.0.1     192.168.0.1       1
        224.0.0.0        224.0.0.0         10.0.1.2        10.0.1.2       1
        224.0.0.0        224.0.0.0      192.168.0.1     192.168.0.1       1
  255.255.255.255  255.255.255.255      192.168.0.1     192.168.0.1       1
Default Gateway:          10.0.1.1
===========================================================================
Persistent Routes:
  None
```

Figure 20.3 *Windows 2000 TCP/IP client routing table.*

Host routing permits the computer to make decisions about which of its attached interfaces it should route a packet to. *Router routing* is more capable. Routers can send packets to networks not directly attached their local interfaces by forwarding packets to other routers and hosts that do reside on the destination network.

Windows 2000 computers have a single routing table, regardless of the number of interfaces or protocols installed. Multiroute routers can be configured with a routing table on each interface.

Routing tables contain at least the following information:

- **Destination Address.** The network ID and subnet mask for each route.
- **Interface.** The network interface over which packets are forwarded to reach the destination address.
- **Metric.** The preference number, or *hop count*, for various network routes, with the lowest numbers being the most desirable. To save time, Windows 2000 only stores the shortest route when multiple routes are learned.
- **Lifetime.** The time during which a route is considered valid. Static routes have infinite lifetimes, but dynamic routes are subject to refresh intervals.

Configuring IP Routing

Windows 2000 routing is configured using the Routing and Remote Access MMC, just as RAS was, as shown in Figure 20.4.

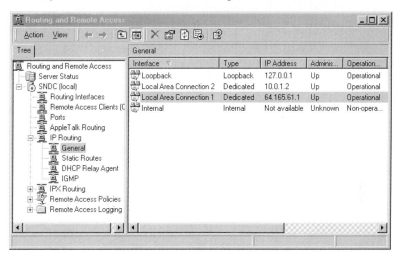

Figure 20.4   *IP routing in the RRAS MMC.*

Having already configured RRAS once, you need not run the Routing and Remote Access Server wizard again.

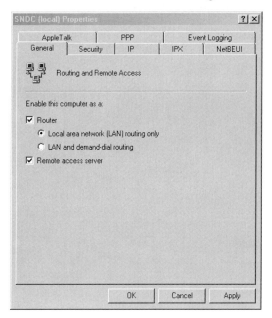

Figure 20.5   *Enabling RRAS routing.*

Instead, you may select the RRAS server in the Tree pane and right-click to choose the Properties command from the pop-up menu. Switch to the General tab in the Properties dialog box and enable the Router checkbox, as shown in Figure 20.5.

You may also enable checkboxes for LAN routing only, or LAN plus demand-dial routing (described further on). Close the dialog box, at which time Windows 2000's routing services restart.

UPDATING ROUTING TABLES

The enabling of routing makes changes to the Registry, permitting packet forwarding between network interfaces. If there are multiple routers on your network, you need to update the routing table to include the possible routes, either through static or dynamic configuration.

CONFIGURING STATIC ROUTES • To enable a static route, expand the IP Routing item in the RRAS MMC, right-click the Static Routes item, and select the New Static Route command from the pop-up menu. In the Static Route dialog box, enter the appropriate network information for each interface, as shown in Figure 20.6.

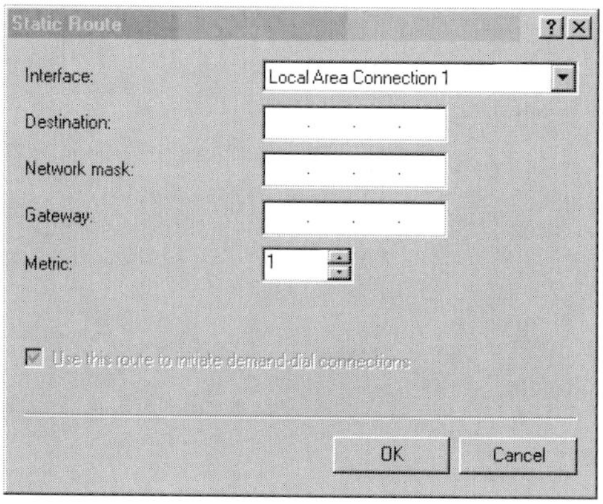

Figure 20.6 *Configuring a Static Route.*

To check your work, right-click the Static Routes item and select the Show IP Routing Table command to view the routing table, as shown in Figure 20.7.

Static routes can also be configured using the "route add" command or NETSH command line utility.

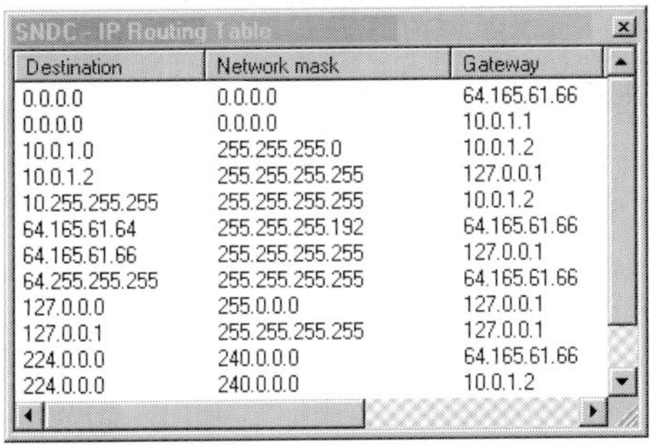

SNDC - IP Routing Table

Destination	Network mask	Gateway
0.0.0.0	0.0.0.0	64.165.61.66
0.0.0.0	0.0.0.0	10.0.1.1
10.0.1.0	255.255.255.0	10.0.1.2
10.0.1.2	255.255.255.255	127.0.0.1
10.255.255.255	255.255.255.255	10.0.1.2
64.165.61.64	255.255.255.192	64.165.61.66
64.165.61.66	255.255.255.255	127.0.0.1
64.255.255.255	255.255.255.255	64.165.61.66
127.0.0.0	255.0.0.0	127.0.0.1
127.0.0.1	255.255.255.255	127.0.0.1
224.0.0.0	240.0.0.0	64.165.61.66
224.0.0.0	240.0.0.0	10.0.1.2

Figure 20.7 *Viewing the Routing Table.*

CONFIGURING DYNAMIC ROUTING • Routing tables can also be updated automatically using dynamic routing protocols.

When all dynamic routing tables on an internetwork agree, they are said to be in *convergence*. When a change occurs, such as one router going offline, all routers on the network must reconfigure themselves to understand the new topology. The time it takes for all routers to agree again is termed the *convergence time*. In dynamic routing, you wish to achieve the shortest possible convergence time while generating the least amount of network traffic.

Routing protocols are based on either a *distance vector* or *link state* algorithm. Distance vector routing protocols listen for the information periodically supplied by other routers about their routing tables, as well as send out similar data of their own. Such communications are neither synchronized nor acknowledged. Distance vector routing is easy to configure and administer. However, it requires a lot of bandwidth, has a high convergence time, creates unwieldy routing tables on large internetworks, and is limited to no more than 15 routers per route.

Link state routing protocols build routing tables based on multicast Link State Advertisements (LSAs), which are both synchronized and acknowledged, including a network ID for all routers. Link state routing is more complex, but requires less bandwidth, has lower convergence times, and creates small routing tables. It is also scalable to large internetworks.

You can configure Windows 2000 routing tables to be updated automatically using one of the following routing protocols:

- **Router Information Protocol (RIP).** RIP uses a distance vector algorithm. Windows 2000 supports both RIP version 1 and RIP version 2.

- **Open Shortest Path First (OSPF).** OSPF is a link state routing protocol, designed primarily for use in large internetwork environments
  (supporting as many as 255 routers).

To install a routing protocol, right-click the General item under the IP
Routing branch in the RRAS MMC and select the New Routing Protocol
command. In the New Routing Protocol window, select either RIP or OSPF.

The routing protocols you choose are added to the IP Routing branch
of the RRAS MMC. Next, right-click a routing protocol and select the New
Interface command from the pop-up menu. You are prompted to choose the
interface to which the routing protocol should be bound. Thereafter, the
routing protocol Properties dialog box opens, in which you can modify settings as necessary.

DEMAND-DIAL ROUTING

Demand-dial routing is employed on impermanent connections, such as
those made to the Internet over a nondedicated link such as dialup modem.
On-demand connections are opened when there is data to transfer or a
demand for a remote service. They are closed when the connection is idle.
The advantage of such a connection is that you do not pay for idle time, only
for the time during which the connection is actually needed.

To configure demand-dial routing, right-click the server in the RRAS
MMC Tree pane to choose the Properties command from the pop-up menu.
Switch to the General tab in the Properties dialog box and enable the LAN
and demand-dial radio button (see Figure 20.5).

After you click the Apply button, the router is restarted.

Next, right-click the Ports item and open the Ports Properties dialog
box to choose from available ports.

Double-click a port to open its configuration dialog box, as shown in Figure 20.8.

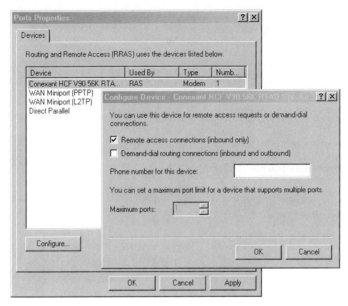

Figure 20.8 *Configuring ports for demand-dial routing.*

Enable the Demand-dial routing connections checkbox.

Next, right-click the Routing Interfaces branch in the RRAS MMC Tree pane and select the New Demand-Dial Interface command to open the Demand Dial Interface Wizard. The Wizard prompts you for the following information:

- **Interface Name.** Name the connection, or accept the default of "Remote Router."
- **Phone Number.** Enter the telephone number of the remote router.
- **Protocols and Security.** Make sure that the LAN protocols that you wish to route are selected. In addition, select the Add a user account so that a remote router can dial in checkbox if you want the remote router to be able to dial-in, creating a *two-way initiated connection*. If you leave this checkbox unselected, only a *one-way initiated connection* is permitted, with the local router calling the telephone number you previously specified. You can also select options for plaintext authentication and scripted logons.
- **Dial In Credentials.** For two-way initiated connections, enter user account information.

- **Dial Out Credentials.** For one-way and two-way initiated connections, enter user account information that is valid for the remote network.

When the wizard is completed, a new demand-dial interface is added to the RRAS MMC.

Although it contradicts the idea of "dial-on-demand," you can make a demand-dial connection permanent by opening the demand-dial interface Properties dialog box and enabling the Persistent connection radio button under the Options tab. This must be enabled on both the local and remote router.

Managing and Monitoring IP Routing

How IP routing is managed depends upon the routing protocols employed.

MANAGING AND MONITORING RIP

Among important RIP management issues is how the protocol handles convergence. Under RIP version 2, the following configurations are possible:

- **Split Horizon.** This feature prevents routers from advertising network information in the direction from which the path was learned. This ensures that the only data sent in routing announcements is for networks beyond neighboring routers and in the other direction. Split horizon helps to eliminate *routing loops*, wherein out-of-date routing tables cause packets to be routed back to the originating network rather than the destination network.
- **Split Horizon with Poison Reverse.** This feature permits routers to advertise all networks, but networks learned in a given direction are identified as having a hop count of 16, an "unreachable" network.
- **Triggered Updates.** This features permits a router to advertise changes in route metrics immediately, rather than after the typical period of time has elapsed. This helps reduce convergence time.

You can also configure your router to use *silent RIP*. In this case, the router updates its own routing table with information gleaned from neighbor routers, without sharing its own routing data. This is done to reduce network traffic where possible.

Finally, you can explicitly identify the routers that your router should listen to under the Security tab of the RIP Properties dialog box, as shown in Figure 20.9.

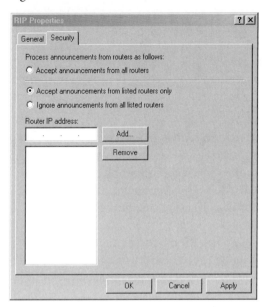

Figure 20.9   *Configuring RIP Security.*

MANAGING AND MONITORING OSPF

To manage OSPF routing, you first need to understand its terminology.

A group of routed networks with shared protocols and administration is referred to as an Autonomous System (AS). OSPF-routed networks are further divided into *areas*. Each area is defined by *boundaries*, which determine how far LSAs can travel. All routers within a boundary contain an identical routing table called the Link State Database (LSDB), which maps the topology of its area. Rather than hop counts, routes are identified with *costs*, which help determine the most efficient path between a packet's sender and destination. The paths with the least cost become part of the Shortest Path First (SPF) Tree.

All OSPF-routed networks require at least one area. Where there is more than one area, an additional *backbone* area is created. Usually networks are divided into areas when they exceed 40 routers. Routers are identified with unique IDs that use the same 32-bit notation as, but are not related to, IP addressing. For example, a backbone would be identified as "0.0.0.0" and attached routers could be identified as "0.0.0.1," "0.0.0.2," and so on.

OSPF networks can be configured for the following network types:

Broadcast. Used on networks that can support hardware broadcasts (although multicasting is actually used). These include Ethernet, Token Ring, and FDDI topologies.

Point-to-Point. Used on networks connected by just two routers. These include WAN and T-carrier links.

Nonbroadcast Multiple Access (NBMA). Used on networks that can contain multiple routers but which do not support hardware broadcasts. Here OSPF uses *unicasting*, where packets are directed to known IP addresses that you specify. These topologies include ATM, Frame Relay, and X.25.

MANAGING AND MONITORING BORDER ROUTING • Routers that sit on the border between one or more areas are referred to as Area Border Routers (ABRs). These routers are responsible for exchanging routing information between areas. To reduce the amount of data exchanged, ABRs send summary routing information rather than individual routes.

Similarly, Asynchronous System Border Routers (ASBRs) are responsible for exchanging information between ASs.

You can use a tool such as Network Monitor to determine how much network traffic an OSPF network is generating.

Where greater efficiency is desired, you can employ the use of external route filters, which exclude external route information that is not required by an ASBR.

These filters can be configured under the Exteranl Routing tab in the OSPF Properties dialog box, as shown in Figure 20.10.

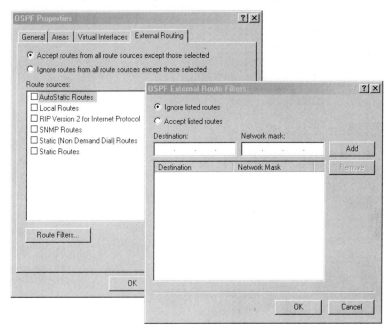

Figure 20.10   *Configuring OSPF external routing.*

You can filter external routes individually or by route source (e.g., RIP, SNMP, static).

MANAGING AND MONITORING INTERNAL ROUTING • An Internal Router (IR) routes traffic within its area only. To keep external routes from being imported into an area, thus reducing the amount of unnecessary routing information, you can create a *stub area*. This area defines a default route to limit the size of the topology database. The default route and a route summary must be advertised to the stub area by at least one ABR.

To enable the use of a stub area, open the OSPF Properties dialog box from the RRAS MMC and make sure the router is configured as an IR under the General tab (e.g., the Enable Autonomous system boundary router option is not enabled).

Next, switch to the Areas tab and click the Add button to open the OSPF Area Configuration dialog box, as shown in Figure 20.11.

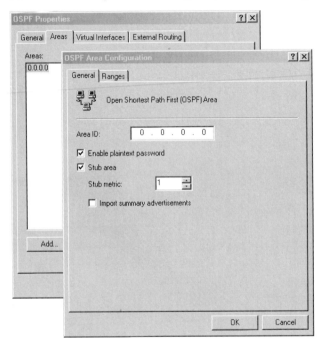

Figure 20.11 *Enabling a stub area.*

Enter an Area ID an enable the Stub area checkbox.

Troubleshooting IP Routing

Among the tools useful in monitoring and troubleshooting routing issues are PING, TRACERT, PATHPING, Network Monitor, and the "route print" command. These tools were described extensively in Chapter 6, "Networking Windows 2000 Professional," and Chapter 13, "Networking Windows 2000 Server." In troubleshooting, you should use these tools to verify each component in the routing process: TCP/IP host configurations, routing tables, and router configurations. If dynamic routing protocols are in use, additional factors come into play.

TROUBLESHOOTING RIP

Among the issues that relate to troubleshooting RIP are the following:

- RIP supports not more than 15 routers, so any hop count beyond 15 results in the error message "destination unreachable." If you have more than 15 routers, consider a switch to OSPF.
- On networks that contain both RIP version 1 and RIP version 2 routers, the RIP version 2 routers should be configured to send announcements using broadcasts rather than multicasts.
- Where authentication is used, make sure that routers are configured with the correct authentication credentials (RIP version 2).
- Where IP packet filtering is used, make sure that input and output filters are not configured to block necessary router traffic (such as UDP port 520).

TROUBLESHOOTING OSPF

Among the issues that relate to troubleshooting OSPF are the following:

- Each router must be properly configured in its assigned role if all routing tables are to be complete. Verify that authentication, the Hello interval, the Dead interval, area ID, and stub setting are the same on all adjacent routers.
- No adjacent routers should have the same router ID.
- One router in each area should be assigned as a Designated Router (DR).
- All ABRs should be connected to the backbone.
- On NBNA networks, multicast addresses must be properly assigned.

Study Break

Deploy a Router

Practice what you have learned by deploying a Windows 2000 Server-based software router.

First, install two or more network interfaces, such as two network adapters. Next, enable routing in the RRAS MMC. Configure each interface with different network information. In this case, the use of routing protocols is unnecessary. In a multiple router environment, however, you may also install and configure dynamic routing protocols. Finally, use the "route print" command to verify routing tables and the TRACERT utility to verify routing paths.

MCSE 20.2 — Working with NAT

Internet Connection Sharing (ICS) and Network Address Translation (NAT) allow you to turn a Windows 2000 Computer into a gateway between the Internet and other workstations on a small local network, such in a Small Office/Home Office (SOHO) environment. By enabling this feature, you can cut the costs that would be incurred by setting up multiple dialup lines and ISP accounts, as well as reduce the complexity of administering them. This is particularly useful when you have a fast dialup connection, such as through Digital Subscriber Lines (DSL), ISDN, or broadband cable. All that is required on your computer is dialup access to the Internet, such as through a modem, and a separate network adapter for access to your LAN. ICS/NAT then provides dynamically assigned private IP addresses for other computers on the network and makes it possible for them to access the Internet as if they were connected directly.

The previous section described routed networks, in which packets maintain the source and destination address regardless of the number of hops that must be traversed between sender and recipient. ICS/NAT connections are *translated*, with packets being altered to adopt the source address of the computer serving as the ICS/NAT gateway. In this way, internal IP addresses are "hidden" to the outside, with all traffic appearing to come from one computer.

Although functionally similar, ICS and NAT differ in implementation and features. Essentially, ICS is a simplified version NAT configured through Network and Dial-Up Connections, as described in Chapter 6, "Networking Windows 2000 Professional." NAT is configured as a routing protocol addition to RRAS.

Installing Internet Connection Sharing

To enable ICS, open an Internet connection's Properties dialog box in the Network and Dial-Up Connections program group and switch to the Sharing tab. Select the Enable Internet Connection Sharing for this connection checkbox, as shown in Figure 20.12.

Unless you have a dedicated Internet link, you also want to select the Enable on-demand dialing checkbox.

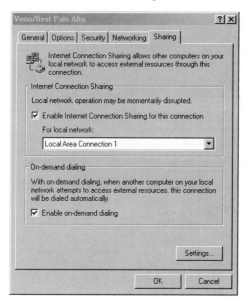

Figure 20.12 *Enabling Internet Connection Sharing.*

If your internal computers will only seek service from the outside (such as Web browsing), your configuration work is done. If, however, you wish to offer services to the outside, such as email, FTP, or Web sites, you need to configure static mappings for inbound connections by clicking the Settings button and switching to the Services tab to open the dialog box shown in Figure 20.13.

Click the Add or Edit buttons to open the Internet Connection Sharing Service dialog box, in which you may identify the name or IP address of the computer that should receive incoming traffic for a given service and port number.

Similarly, you can configure static mappings for outbound connections under the Applications tab, if required by multiuser applications connecting on specific ports.

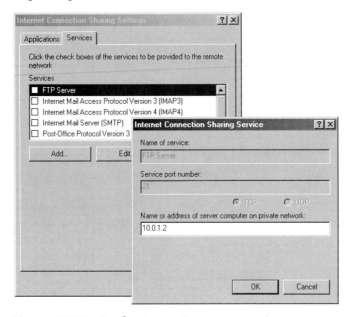

Figure 20.13 *Configuring static service mappings.*

Although ICS should meet the needs of most SOHO environments, it has the following limitations:

- ICS cannot support many DHCP options, such as identifying the default DNS and WINS servers.
- ICS supports only a single IP address.
- ICS requires dynamic port mappings.
- ICS cannot reserve an IP address for incoming server access, such as for a Web site.
- ICS cannot be used on a network that is running such network services as DHCP, routers, domain controllers, and so on.
- ICS can only be run on one computer and one network segment.
- ICS does not permit the simultaneous use of both static and dynamic addressing for clients.
- ICS cannot be used with WINS proxies.
- ICS has no monitoring utilities (other than Event Viewer's System log).
- If any one of these limitations is relevant to your environment, you should look instead to the more robust NAT.

Configuring NAT

To install NAT, right-click the General item under the IP Routing branch in the RRAS MMC and select the New Routing Protocol command. In the New Routing Protocol window, select NAT. It is added to the IP Routing branch of the RRAS MMC. Next, right-click NAT and select the Properties command to open the Network Address Translation Properties dialog box, as shown in Figure 20.14.

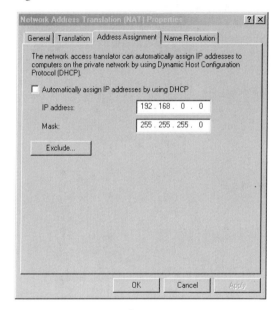

Figure 20.14 *Configuring NAT properties.*

NAT properties can be configured under the following tabs:

- **General.** Provides options for various logging levels.
- **Translation.** Provides options for setting the refresh intervals for dynamic and static mappings between privately addressed worksta- tions and the publicly addressed NAT computer. The default is 24 hours.
- **Address Assignment.** Provides options for allocating internal IP addresses through DHCP, and for excluding some IP addresses. If you do not have a DHCP Server already running on your network, you must enable the Automatically assign IP addresses by using DHCP checkbox for NAT to work.
- **Name Resolution.** Provides options for whether NAT resolves DNS names for connecting clients.

Configuring NAT Interfaces

In addition to specifying NAT global properties, you must also configure at least two interfaces to use NAT, such as a network adapter and dialup connection. To do this, right-click the NAT item in the RRAS MMC and select the New Interface command. Next, choose a connection in the New Interface dialog box to open the NAT Properties dialog box shown in Figure 20.15.

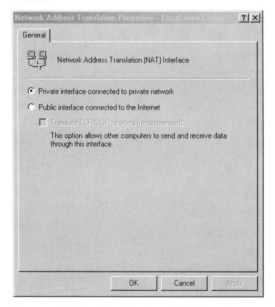

Figure 20.15 *Configuring a NAT interface.*

For the internal network interface, select the Private interface connected to private network radio button. For the external network interface (e.g. Internet), select the Public interface connected to the Internet radio button. Enabling the latter choice makes an Address Pool tab available. If you have more than one public address, you can identify additional addresses here. A Special Ports tab also appears, under which you may statically assign port service mappings for incoming connections.

Troubleshooting NAT

Common NAT problems and their solutions include the following:

- **The modem connection fails.** Troubleshoot the modem as described in Chapter 2, "Administering Windows 2000 Professional."

- **The network connection fails.** If you have multiple network adapters installed, make sure that you are sharing the one that is accessing the Internet connection (such as to a cable modem or DSL router).
- **TCP/IP fails.** Make sure that TCP/IP is properly installed on all client computers, and that they are configured to receive their addressing information automatically through DHCP. Make sure clients are receiving the proper IP addressing by using the "ipconfig /all" command at the command prompt.
- **NAT service fails.** Make sure there is no conflict with another service, as can often be detected in the Event Viewer's System log.

Study Break

Enable NAT

Practice what you have learned by installing and configuring NAT services.

First, install NAT as a routing protocol in the RRAS MMC. Next, configure NAT properties on the appropriate network interfaces for such options as translation timing intervals and address assignment. Finally, verify that connectivity can be achieved between the local and public (e.g., Internet) networks from a client computer.

■ Summary

In this chapter, we examined the installation, configuration, and administration of IP routing and NAT.

Working with IP Routing

Routing involves forwarding packets from a computer on one network to a computer on another network. Several devices and services can accomplish this function, including Windows 2000 Server's built-in RRAS. Routers decide whether to leave packets on the segment from which they originated or forward them to another segment based on IP address. When it is determined that a packet is destined for a host beyond its originating network, the router figures out the best way to get it there based on its understanding of available routes. Static routes are manually established by an administrator. Dynamic routes are learned and updated by routers automatically.

Routers consult routing tables to determine where a packet arriving from one interface should go. If the sender and destination addresses reside on different networks, the router determines the path that the packet must take to the remote host and forwards it on its way through another interface. Microsoft's implementation of TCP/IP only supports a single route table, so all traffic forwarded through a single default gateway whenever its destination is nonlocal. Routers can send packets to networks not directly attached their local interfaces by forwarding packets to other routers and hosts that do reside on the destination network.

Windows 2000 routing is configured using the Routing and Remote Access MMC. You can configure Windows 2000 routing tables to be configured manually, or to be updated automatically using a routing protocol. The RIP routing protocol uses a distance vector algorithm. Windows 2000 supports both RIP version 1 and RIP version 2. OSPF is a link state routing protocol, designed primarily for use on large internetworks. RIP is easier to implement, while OSPF is more scalable.

Working with NAT

ICS and NAT allow you to turn a Windows 2000 Computer into a gateway between the Internet and other workstations on a small local network, such in a SOHO environment. By enabling this feature, you can cut the costs that would be incurred by setting up multiple dialup lines and ISP accounts, as well as reduce the complexity of administering them. All that is required on your computer is dialup access to the Internet, such as through a modem, and a separate network adapter for access to your LAN. ICS/NAT then provides dynamically assigned private IP addresses for other computers on the network and makes it possible for them to access the Internet as if they were connected directly.

ICS/NAT connections are translated, with packets being altered to adopt the source address of the computer serving as the ICS/NAT gateway. In this way, internal IP addresses are "hidden" to the outside, with all traffic appearing to come from one computer.

Although functionally similar, ICS and NAT differ in implementation and features.

▲ CHAPTER REVIEW QUESTIONS

Here are questions relating to the material covered in the *Installing, Configuring, Managing, Monitoring, and Troubleshooting IP Routing in a Windows 2000 Network Infrastructure* section of Microsoft's *Implementing and Administering a Microsoft Windows 2000 Network Infrastructure* exam (70-216).

1. *Which of the following are routing protocols that can be configured through RRAS? Select all that apply:*

   A. RIP version 2

   B. OSPF

   C. LSA

   D. NAT

2. *Configuring routers with static routes is the most cumbersome method.*

   A. True

   B. False

3. *Which of the following utilities or commands can be used to configure static routes?*

   A. Route add command

   B. NETSH

   C. RRAS MMC

   D. IPCONFIG

4. *It is dangerous to enable two-way initiated demand-dial connections, as it opens an insecure path into your network by any router that knows the correct telephone number.*

   A. True

   B. False

5. *Demand-dial connections are always impermanent.*

   A. True

   B. False

6. *OSPF routing is easier to configure than RIP routing.*

   A. True

   B. False

7. *Which of the following are examples of OSPF border routers? Select all that apply:*

   A. AS

   B. ABR

   C. ASBR

   D. IR

8. *Border routers sit between one or more areas.*

   A. True

   B. False

9. *Internal routers forward traffic within a single area only.*

   A. True

   B. False

10. *Internal routers are always aware of external routes.*

    A. True

    B. False

11. *OSPF networks can accommodate as many as 15 routers per route.*

    A. True

    B. False

12. *NBMA networks use multicasting to overcome the inability to support hardware address broadcasts.*

    A. True

    B. False

13. *ICS can only be installed under Windows 2000 Server.*

    A. True

    B. False

14. *You would not want to install ICS on a domain controller.*

    A. True

    B. False

15. *NAT can only be installed under Windows 2000 Server.*

    A. True

    B. False

16. *NAT cannot be used with DHCP.*
    A. True
    B. False

17. *You can configure NAT to provide DNS name resolution for connecting clients.*
    A. True
    B. False

18. *NAT's default dynamic address mapping interval is one day.*
    A. True
    B. False

19. *You must configure at least one NAT interface.*
    C. True
    D. False

20. *NAT cannot be used with more than one public address.*
    A. True
    B. False

Administering Certificate Authorities

▲ **Chapter Syllabus**

MCSE 21.1 **Working with Certificate Authorities**

In this chapter, we cover the *Installing, Configuring, Managing, Monitoring, and Troubleshooting Certificate Services in a Windows 2000 Network Infrastructure* section of Microsoft's *Implementing and Administering a Microsoft Windows 2000 Network Infrastructure* exam (70-216).

This material teaches you to deploy certificates on your organization's network for use in securing client-server communications, including installing Windows 2000 Certificate Services, issuing and revoking certificates, and working with Encrypted File System (EFS) recovery keys. Windows 2000 Certificate Services is based on the Public Key Infrastructure (PKI) described in Chapter 18, "Administering Network Protocols."

MCSE 21.1 **Working with Certificate Authorities**

Many Microsoft products use industry-standard X.509 version 3 *digital certificates* to verify the identity of individuals and organizations, as well as to ensure the integrity of downloadable files. Certificates contain their owner's public key, owner's name or alias, an expiration date, a serial number, the name of the issuing entity, and the digital signature of the issuing entity. Certificates can optionally contain such information as postal address, email address, country, postal code, user age, user gender, and so on. You can use certificates to verify the identity of email senders, Web clients, and Web servers, encrypt client-server communication channels and email communication, and verify the source and integrity of signed, downloaded executable code.

Certificates are authenticated, issued, and managed by third-party Certification Authorities (CAs). These authorities are responsible for providing such technology as security protocols and standards, secure messaging, and cryptography. CAs must provide an infrastructure that includes secure facilities, backup systems, and customer support. Finally, CAs provide a trust model with a legally binding framework for managing subscriber actions and resolving disagreements.

There are numerous commercial CAs that issue and renew certificates, authenticate the identities of individuals and organizations, and verify the registrations of individuals and organizations. In addition to handling legal and liability issues that relate to security, commercial CAs publish and maintain a Certificate Revocation List (CRL) containing all certificates that have been revoked. Some commercial CAs are listed in Table 21.1.

Table 21.1 *Certification Authorities*

Organization	URL
BankGate	http://www.bankgate.com
Digital Signature Trust	http://www.digsigtrust.com
GlobalSign NV-SA	http://www.globalsign.com
GTE CyberTrust	http://www.cybertrust.gte.com
Thawte Consulting	http://www.thawte.com
Verisign	http://www.verisign.com

You can obtain various types of certificates from CAs, including personal certificates used by individuals to digitally sign communications, client and server authentication certificates for managing secure transactions, and software publisher certificates that allow developers and organizations to digitally sign the software that they create.

CAs must operate within the framework of their Certification Practices Statements (CPSs), which are posted on the CA's various Web sites. When choosing a CA, you should verify that it is a trusted organization with a good reputation, that it is familiar with the interests of your organization, and that it provides services and products that integrate well with your existing security models.

Your organization might choose to act as a CA on its own by providing a certificate server, such as Windows 2000's Certificate Services, to issue, renew, and revoke certificates. The certificates you issue can be used in conjunction with servers that support Secure Sockets Layer (SSL), Transport Layer Security (TLS), and Private Communications Technology (PCT) to build a secure Internet or intranet communications system. This option is particularly appealing to large organizations with more complex security needs, as it lowers costs while providing greater control over certificate management.

Certificates can be used to support user authentication and secure communications with various clients, such as Web browsers. Servers can present clients with server authentication certificates from trusted authorities that verify their identities. The same is true of clients, such as Internet Explorer, which can present their own trusted certificates to servers. The exchange of certificates between clients and servers is done using a secure transmission protocol, such as SSL.

Using SSL, secure, encrypted connections can be created between the server and client using the public key encryption system. This type of security should be used whenever private data, such as credit card information, is passed over the Internet.

SSL has two protocol layers. The first layer, the *SSL Handshake Protocol*, is used at the beginning of the client-server communications process to establish the encryption algorithm. The second layer, the *SSL Record Protocol*, is used to handle the encapsulation of data communicated over TCP and other higher-level protocols. This capability allows SSL to operate independent of applications, services, and data types.

In a typical Web server-to-browser connection, SSL works as follows:

The Web browser requests a URL to a secured resource on the server, initiating the communications process.

The server sends a certificate to the Web browser. This contains the Web site's unique digital identification. It might also request a certificate from the Web browser.

The Web browser sends a certificate to the server, if requested.

The Web browser attempts to verify the server's certificate with a public key. If the certificate is verified, the Web browser requests an encryption specification, called the *session key*, from the server. This is encrypted using the Web browser's private key.

The Web server attempts to verify the Web browser's certificate with a public key, if requested.

The Web server receives the session key, which it decrypts using the Web browser's public key. It then modifies its encryption specification to match that requested by the Web browser.

The Web server and Web browser begin normal communication over the encrypted connection.

If any of these steps is executed incorrectly, SSL communications fails. It is mandatory for both the client and server to be able to supply the correct encryption, certificates, and other information.

SSL 2.0 supports server authentication only. SSL 3.0, TLS 1.0, and PCT 1.0 support both client and server authentication.

Traffic encryption using secure channels adds a significant overhead to client-server connections, and should therefore generally be used only for small volumes of information, such as user authentication or credit card information.

The highest possible level of security is afforded by the use of Server Gated Cryptography (SGC). This encryption method enables a 128-bit server with an SGC certificate, such as IIS 3.0 or newer, to communicate securely with Internet Explorer 4.0 or newer using 128-bit SSL encryption. If your organization requires such a high-level of security, perhaps to support financial transactions, you could make use of it with a 128-bit SSL Windows 2000-based Internet server and Internet Explorer.

The underlying security services for certificate management, secure channels, code signing, and Authenticode are provided by the *CryptoAPI* 2.0. With it, developers integrate Cryptographic Service Provider (CSP) modules into their applications that interface with CryptoAPI to perform such functions as key generation and exchange, data encryption/decryption, hashing, and digital signature creation/verification.

Installing Certificate Authority

Use the Add/Remove Programs wizard to install Windows 2000's Certificate Services. After selecting the Certificate Services item and clicking the Next button, as shown in Figure 21.1, you are warned that the computer cannot be renamed or removed to another domain after installation.

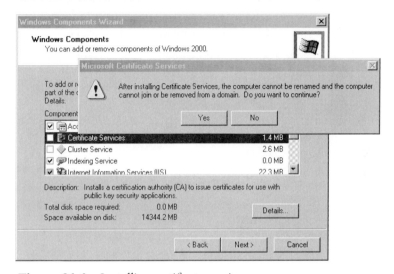

Figure 21.1 *Installing certificate services.*

Next, you are prompted to determine which type of CA you want to install, as shown in Figure 21.2.

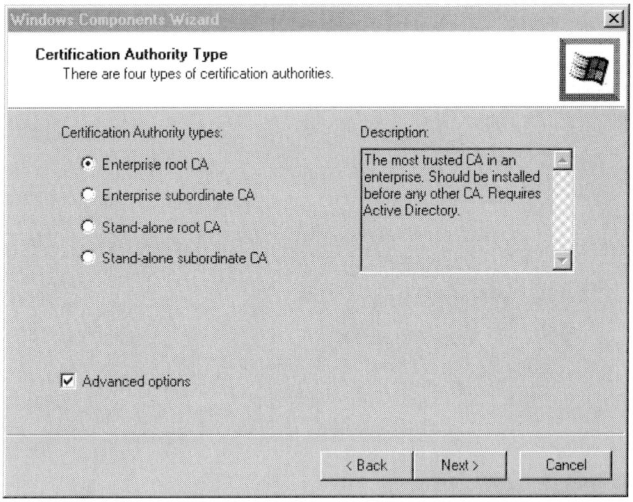

Figure 21.2 *Selecting a CA type.*

Windows 2000 certificate services are deployed hierarchically. Under Active Directory, there is one Enterprise root CA under which are arranged Enterprise subordinate CAs. Stand-alone root and subordinate CAs can be deployed with or without Active Directory, but are only visible to other Active Directory domain clients if made part of an Active Directory tree.

If you enable the Advanced options checkbox, you have an opportunity to choose the CSP and related hash algorithm to be used in generating a key pair in the next window, as shown in Figure 21.3.

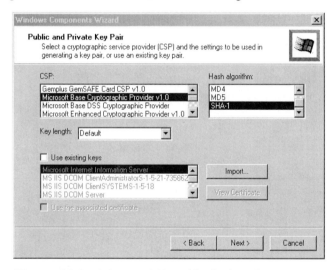

Figure 21.3 *Selecting CSP and hash algorithm.*

Next, you are prompted to enter information identifying your organization, as shown in Figure 21.4.

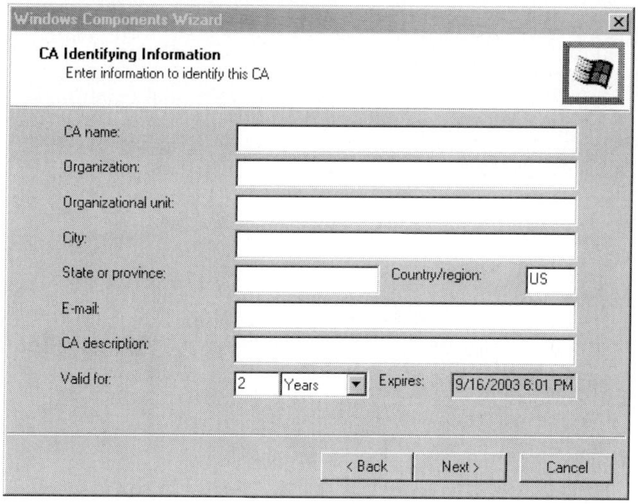

Figure 21.4 *Providing CA identification data.*

Next, you may designate where the certificate database and log should be stored, as shown in Figure 21.5.

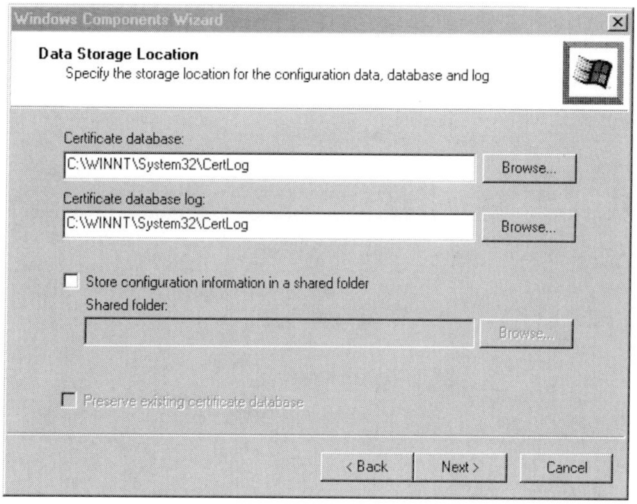

Figure 21.5 *Selecting certificate data storage location.*

You do not have to reboot the computer after installation.

Configuring Certificate Authority

Once installed, Certificate Services can be configured via the Certification Authority MMC, as shown in Figure 21.6.

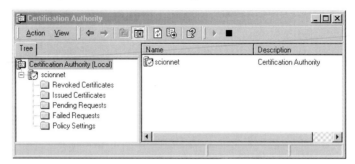

Figure 21.6 *Using the Certification Authority MMC.*

ISSUING CERTIFICATES

Certificates can be issued through a Web browser, such as Internet Explorer, using a URL in the following format: http://server_name/certsrv

Once logged on, simply follow the steps in sequential pages to create a Web Browser Certificate or email Protection Certificate. You are prompted to enter identification information, and then issued a certificate such as the one shown in Figure 21.7.

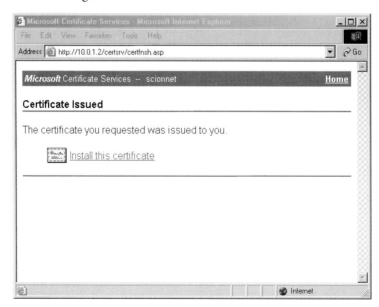

Figure 21.7 *Issuing a Web browser certificate.*

REVOKING CERTIFICATES

To revoke a certificate, select the Issued Certificates folder in the Certification Authority MMC Tree pane. Next, right-click the certificate to be revoked in the right pane and choose the Revoke Certificate command from the All Tasks menu to open the Certificate Revocation dialog box, as shown in Figure 21.8.

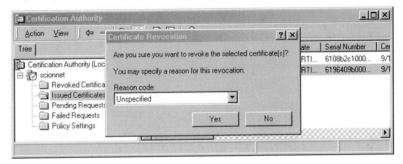

Figure 21.8 *Revoking a certificate.*

You are prompted to provide a reason for the revocation. Click the Yes button to complete the process.

REMOVING EFS RECOVERY KEYS

Another form of certificate security involves EFS keys, as described in Chapter 7, "Securing Windows 2000 Professional." Since these private keys are portable and can be destroyed, Microsoft supplies a fail-safe in the form of *Recovery Agents*, special users with the power to decrypt files without having the creator's private or EFS keys.

Administrators can create Recover Agents using the Group Policy MMC. Likewise, administrators can remove recovery keys for greater security using the Local Security Policy MMC, as shown in Figure 21.9.

Select the Encrypted Data Recovery Agents folder under the Public Key Policies folder in the Tree pane to view available recovery keys in the right pane. Right-click each recovery key and select the Export command from the All Tasks menu to move the recovery keys to removable media (using the Certificate Export Wizard).

Next, right-click each recovery key and select the Delete command from the pop-up menu.

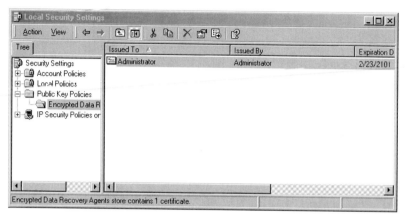

Figure 21.9 *Removing EFS recovery keys.*

Administrators can still designate backup Recovery Agents for use when the default agents have been removed.

Troubleshooting Certificate Authority

Among problems that can affect certificates are the following:

- **Bad request formats.** Results in an unusable certificate when a request is incorrectly processed because of the format. To resolve this, recreate the certificate with the proper format.
- **Bad certificate mapping.** Occurs when a certificate is mapped to the wrong user or computer account. Resolve this by remapping the certificate or revoking it.
- **Corrupted certificates.** Manifests itself in invalid password messages, and can be resolved by recreating the certificate.

Study Break

Install Certificate Services

Practice what you have learned by installing Windows 2000 Certificate Services.

Once the server is installed, use Internet Explorer to obtain a Web Browser Certificate. Verify that the certificate is visible in the Certification Authority MMC. Finally, revoke the certificate.

■ Summary

In this chapter, we examined the installation, configuration, and administration of certificate services.

Working with Certificate Services

Your organization may choose to act as a CA by using Windows 2000's Certificate Services to issue, renew, and revoke certificates. The certificates you issue can be used in conjunction with servers that support SSL, TLS, and PCT to build a secure Internet or intranet communications system. Certificates can be used to support user authentication and secure communications with various clients, such as Web browsers. Servers can present clients with server authentication certificates from trusted authorities that verify their identities. The same is true of clients, such as Internet Explorer, which can present their own trusted certificates to servers. The exchange of certificates between clients and servers is done using a secure transmission protocol, such as SSL.

Windows 2000 Certificate Services are deployed hierarchically. Under Active Directory, there is one Enterprise root CA under which are arranged Enterprise subordinate CAs. Stand-alone root and subordinate CAs can be deployed with or without Active Directory.

Certificates can be issued through a Web browser, such as Internet Explorer, using a URL in the following format.

▲ CHAPTER REVIEW QUESTIONS

Here are a few questions relating to the material covered in the *Installing, Configuring, Managing, Monitoring, and Troubleshooting Certificate Services in a Windows 2000 Network Infrastructure* section of Microsoft's *Implementing and Administering a Microsoft Windows 2000 Network Infrastructure* exam (70-216).

1. *Once Windows 2000 Certificate Services are installed, you cannot rename the host computer or remove it from the domain.*

    A. True

    B. False

2. *Only Enterprise CAs can be installed in Active Directory domains.*
    A. True
    B. False

3. *Certificates can only be issued via the Certification Authority MMC.*
    A. True
    B. False

4. *You must specify a reason when revoking a certificate.*
    A. True
    B. False

5. *You should copy recovery keys to removable media before deleting them from the Local Security Policy MMC.*
    A. True
    B. False

6. *Once recovery keys are removed, there is no other way to recover encrypted data if the original keys are lost.*
    A. True
    B. False

Active Directory

◆ **In This Part**

◆ **CHAPTER 22**
Installing Active Directory

◆ **CHAPTER 23**
Administering Active
Directory and DNS

◆ **CHAPTER 24**
Managing Change
Configuration

◆ **CHAPTER 25**
Optimizing Active Directory

◆ **CHAPTER 26**
Securing Active Directory

In this section, we cover material from MCSE exam 70-217, *Implementing and Administering a Microsoft Windows 2000 Directory Services Infrastructure* exam. This gives you the knowledge necessary to install, configure, and manage networked Windows 2000-based computers under Active Directory. This part's topics include the following:

• **Installing Active Directory:** Installing and configuring Active Directory components, such as forests, trees, domains, sites, operations master roles, and Organizational Units.

• **Administering DNS for Active Directory:** Installing, configuring, managing, and monitoring DNS for Active Directory.

• **Managing Change and Configuration:** Administering Group Policy, including user environments, software, network configurations, and Remote Installation Services (RIS).

- **Optimizing Active Directory Components:** Managing Active Directory objects, optimizing performance and replication, and performing backup and restoration.
- **Securing Active Directory:** Applying security policy and configurations, using audit policy, and monitoring security events.

Most of this material is common to both Windows 2000 Professional and Windows 2000 Server, and has been touched upon previously in this book. In this section, the topics are covered in greater depth.

Installing Active Directory

▲ **Chapter Syllabus**

MCSE 22.1 Installing Active
Directory

In this chapter, we examine the installation topics covered in the *Installing and Configuring Active Directory* section of Microsoft's *Implementing and Administering a Microsoft Windows 2000 Directory Services Infrastructure* exam (70-217).

Active Directory has been mentioned throughout this book, a fact that should stress its integral importance to Windows 2000. While directory services are nothing new to Windows, there is a great deal of difference between how they are implemented under Windows NT vs. Windows 2000. Windows NT's services involved a variety of interrelated but separate applications, while Active Directory's components are integrated. Windows NT's directory services were flat, while Active Directory's are hierarchical. Windows NT permitted pass-through authentication of logons through explicitly configured one-way trusts, while Active Directory supports Kerberos-authenticated two-way trusts.

MCSE 22.1 Installing Active Directory

Windows NT's Security Account Manager (SAM) database was limited by RAM, effectively restricting the size of domains to 40,000 accounts. Active Directory stores such object information on the hard disk, removing such size limitations. The list of superior features goes on, but Active Directory should suffice to say that it is far more scalable than what came before. Active Directory is not just an upgrade, it is a whole new system.

Terms important to Active Directory include the following:

- **Active Directory Services Interface (ADSI).** A set of COM interfaces that Windows applications use to interface with Active Directory. ADSI permits developers to create migration tools for other systems, such as Novell Directory Services (NDS), NT Directory Services (NTDS), and Lightweight Directory Access Protocol (LDAP).
- **Child Domain.** A domain that is directly beneath a parent domain in the Active Directory hierarchy, and which therefore shares the same namespace.
- **Delegation.** The process of assigning administrative control over part of the namespace to a user or group.
- **Directory.** A database that contains information about objects. Such information is made available to users and applications by *directory services*. This data is stored in the "NTDS.NIT" file, which is kept on a Windows 2000 domain controller or other NTFS-formatted volume. It includes both *private* and *public* data (subject to replication).
- **Distinguished Name (DN).** A unique name used to identify an object and its location in a tree. An attribute of an object is a Relative Distinguished Name (RDN).
- **Domain.** A grouping of computers that share a directory database, security policies, and trust relationship with other domains. Domains are in turn grouped into trees, which can be further grouped into forests. Under Windows NT, domains were peers. Under Windows 2000, domains are hierarchical, as illustrated in Figure 22.1.
- **Forest.** A grouping of trees that share a schema, Global Catalog, and configuration. They do not share a contiguous namespace.
- **Global Catalog (GC).** A source of information about objects in the directory that permit users to locate resources without knowing upon which server they reside.
- **Globally Unique Identifier (GUID).** Assigned to objects when created, a 128-bit number that is unique on the network.

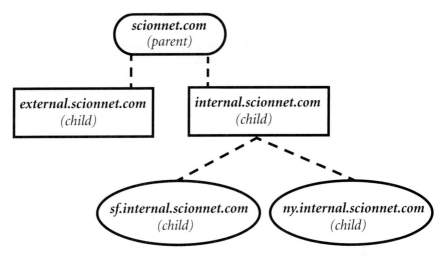

Figure 22.1 *Domain hierarchies.*

- **Group Policy.** Rules that control user environments, security, and software deployments. A Group Policy Object (GPO) is a set of Group Policy settings that can be applied to sites, domains, or Organizational Units.
- **Kerberos.** The authentication protocol used in trust relationships.
- **Lightweight Directory Access Protocol (LDAP).** A general industry standard with which Active Directory is compatible.
- **Native Mode.** A condition that can be implemented by an administrator when all domain controllers are running under Windows 2000.
- **Object.** An element with a particular set of attributes, such as a file, server, printer, or account.
- **Organizational Unit (OU).** A container used to group objects, such as users, groups, printers, servers, in a hierarchy that mirrors an organization's working structure.
- **Parent Object.** An object that contains another object.
- **Replication.** A process that distributes and synchronizes directory data between domain controllers. This can involve *inter-site* and *intra-site* replication. Windows 2000 uses *multi-master replication*, which makes all domain controllers equally capable of distributing and accepting information changes. Data that is replicated includes *domain data*, information about domain objects such as share points and printers; *configuration data*, information relating to directory structure such a domain names and catalog locations; and *schema data*, which includes object class types and attributes.

- **Schema.** Rules that dictate object classes, attributes, limitations, and naming conventions used in the directory.
- **Security Services Provider Interface (SSPI).** A set of security interfaces that Windows applications use to interface with Active Directory, performing such functions as authentication.
- **Site.** IP subnets connected by fast network links. Sites optimize network traffic by restricting such things as logons to local areas rather than permitting authentication over slow connections, such as WAN links. Similarly, sites optimize replication traffic.
- **Tree.** A grouping of domains that share a contiguous namespace and transitive trust relationship.
- **Trust.** A mechanism that defines resource sharing relationships between domains. Under Active Directory, all domains in a tree or forest maintain two-way transitive trusts with other, meaning that access to resources is implicitly granted through intermediary domains. In short, domain A trusts domain B and domain C trusts domain B, therefore domain C trusts domain A.
- **User Principal Name (UPN).** A combination of user name and domain name in the format: username@domain
- **X.500.** A general industry standard with which Active Directory is compatible.

Before installing Active Directory, you should determine both your network's current and future needs. Among the details you should have on hand are the number and names of current domains, domain-specific services that are in use (e.g., Directory Replication, etc.), and the way in which management tasks are currently performed. Overall, you need to define the resources your network needs and consider where to deploy them.

Microsoft does not define extraordinary hardware requirements for a Windows 2000 Server that hosts Active Directory, however, a computer with a greater than minimum configuration is recommended (see Chapter 8, "Installing Windows 2000 Server"). You must have a DNS server installed on your network, whether Microsoft's or some other. You also need at least 250 MB of hard disk space to store the Active Directory database and log files. An NTFS partition is not strictly required for this, but it is strongly recommended. Another part of Active Directory, the Shared System Volume (SYSVOL), requires an NTFS version 5 partition.

The easiest way to install Active Directory is through the Windows 2000 Configure Your Server Wizard, from which you can launch the Active Directory Installation Wizard. As shown in Figure 22.2, your first choice is to define the Windows 2000 Server as a domain controller for a new domain, or a new domain controller in an existing domain.

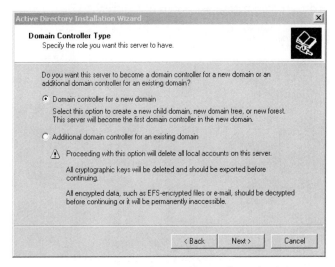

Figure 22.2 *Selecting domain controller roles.*

Working with Forests, Trees, and Domains

As previously described, *forests* contain groups of trees, *trees* contain groups of domains, and *domains* contain resources. After selecting the Domain controller for a new domain radio button, you are prompted to create either a domain tree or child domain, as shown in Figure 22.3.

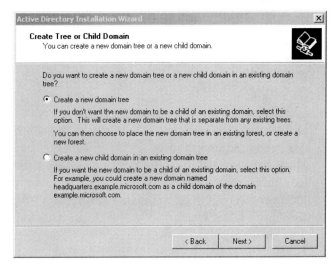

Figure 22.3 *Selecting domain trees.*

After selecting the Create a new domain tree radio button, you are prompted to create either a forest of domain trees or add the new domain tree to an existing forest, as shown in Figure 22.4.

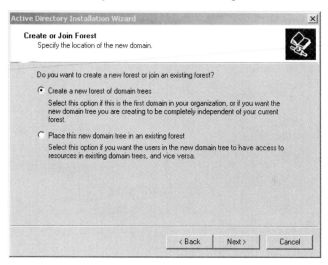

Figure 22.4 *Selecting forests.*

In creating a new forest, you are creating a DNS root domain from which other domains in the hierarchy descend. In subsequent wizard screens, you are prompted for the following:

- **New Domain Name.** The new forest's FQDN (such as "scionnet.com").
- **NetBIOS Domain Name.** The new forest's name as seen by pre-Windows 2000 Microsoft networking clients. It is recommended that you accept the Windows 2000 default name, which is the left-most name in the domain name (e.g., "scionnet").
- **Database and Log Locations.** The directory paths for storage location of the Active Directory database and logs. The default location is \WINNT\NTDS, but it is recommended that you store the database and logs on separate hard disks where possible for better performance and easier recovery.
- **Shared System Volume.** The directory path for the domain controller's public data, which is replicated to other domain controllers. The location specified must be on an NTFS version 5 partition.
- **Configure DNS.** You are given the choice to configure the Windows 2000 DNS Server, a task described in Chapter 15, "Administering DNS."

- **Permissions.** Choose to employ default permissions that are compatible with Windows 2000-based servers only (e.g., Native Mode), or both Windows 2000 and earlier servers (e.g., mixed mode).
- **Directory Services Restore Mode Administrative Password.** Define the password that are required to restart the Active Directory server in restore mode.

Upon completion of the wizard, your actions are summarized in a final screen, as shown in Figure 22.5.

Figure 22.5 *Finishing the Active Directory Installation Wizard.*

Additional verification can be performed at the DNS server, where you should find that 15 new records have been added, if the server supports Dynamic DNS (DDNS). If your DNS server does not support DDNS, a file is manually generated in the \WINNT\System32\config folder called "NETLOGON.DNS." In it are the entries that must be added to your network's DNS server manually.

Further verify that the SYSVOL folder has been created, and that it contains a SYSVOL share as well as Policy and Script folders.

Finally, verify that the Active Directory Users and Computers MMC has been added to the Administrative Tools program group, and that your domain controller is present in the Domain Controller's folder (in the MMC's Tree pane).

AUTOMATING DOMAIN CONTROLLER INSTALLATION

Running the Active Directory Installation Wizard automatically creates a domain controller. You can reassign your server to the role of member server, or promote a member server to domain controller, by entering the command "dcpromo" in the Run dialog box.

New domain controllers are automatically assigned to the correct sites if they are configured properly ahead of time.

Working with Sites, Subnets, Site Links, and Connection Objects

Sites are defined as subnets and domain controllers that are *well-connected*. For example, in an organization with two Ethernet networks in two locations connected by a 56K dialup connection, a logical configuration would be two separate sites with the dialup connection forming a boundary, as illustrated in Figure 22.6.

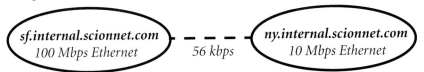

Figure 22.6   *Example of logical site configuration.*

CREATING SITES

Sites are created and managed through the Active Directory Sites and Services MMC snap-in, as shown in Figure 22.7.

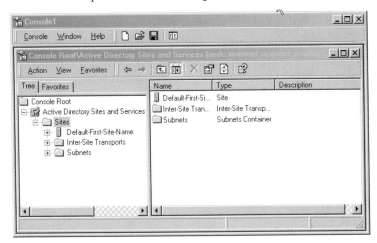

Figure 22.7   *Using the Active Directory Sites and Services MMC snap-in.*

The first domain controller you set up appears here as "Default-First-Site-Name," and should be given a more meaningful name.

To create a new site, select the New Site command from the Action menu to open the New Object-Site dialog box, as shown in Figure 22.8.

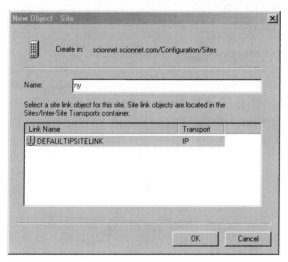

Figure 22.8   *Creating a new site.*

Give the site a logical name and assign at least one site link. *Site links* define the paths between sites over which replication occurs. Initially, the site is placed in the "DEFAULTIPSITELINK" container, which can be modified after additional sites have been created.

After pressing the OK button, a dialog box summarizes the following tasks that must also be completed:

- Ensure site links are configured where necessary.
- Add subnets to the Subnets container.
- Install one or more domain controllers.
- Identify a licensing computer.

CREATING SUBNETS

To create subnets, right-click the Subnets folder in the Tree pane and choose the New Subnet item from the Action menu to open the New Object-Subnet dialog box, as shown in Figure 22.9.

Select the site to which the subnet is assigned, then type in the appropriate beginning IP address and subnet mask.

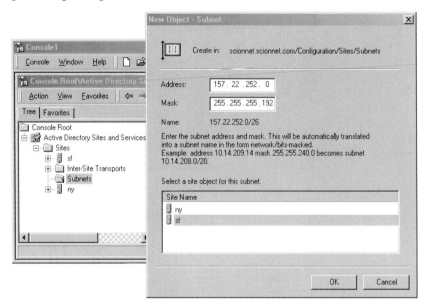

Figure 22.9 *Creating a subnet.*

CREATING SITE LINKS

When sites and subnets are linked, they are able to use Knowledge Consistency Checker (KCC) services, which run on all domain controllers, to evaluate the relative costs of links in determining how and when data is replicated.

To create a site link, select the Inter-Site Transports item in the Tree pane under the Sites folder, as shown in Figure 22.10.

Two replication protocols are available, IP and SMTP. When IP is used, replication is *synchronous*, requiring that one transaction be completed and acknowledged before another is begun. When SMTP is used, replication is *asynchronous*, permitting multiple transactions to take place simultaneously. This can be helpful on particularly slow WAN links.

Right-click a transport and select the New Site Link command to open the New Object-Site Link dialog box. Provide a logical name for the site links, and use the Remove button to exclude sites that should not be linked.

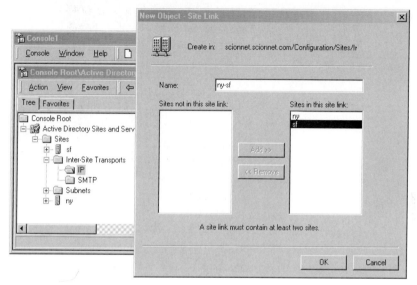

Figure 22.10 *Creating site links.*

CREATING CONNECTION OBJECTS

Connection objects enable inbound links to domain controllers. Connection objects are created and managed by KCC automatically, so in most cases, the replication topology does not require administrator intervention. You can manually create connection objects, but such objects are not managed by KCC. This has implications for fault tolerance, as only a KCC-managed replication topology can be automatically rebuilt if one of its servers fails. Nevertheless, you might wish to manually create connection objects to adjust their replication schedules or to take a more hands-on role in creating a replication topology.

To create a connection object, expand a site in the MMC's Tree pane and right-click the NTDS Settings item to select the New Active Directory Connection command. You will be prompted to select the appropriate domain controller, and then to name the new connection object.

The new connection object appears in the MMC, where you can double-click it to open its properties dialog box, as shown in Figure 22.11.

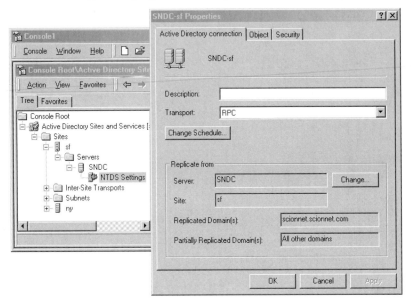

Figure 22.11 *Configuring a connection object.*

Among the attributes you can define for the connection object are the following:

- **Transport.** Choose IP, SMTP, or Remote Procedure Call (RPC). IP and RPC transports are essentially the same, except that RPC is used at the level of domain controllers (intra-site) while IP is used at the level of sites (inter-site). The IP method compresses replication data, making it more efficient on slow links. SMTP, because of its asynchronous nature, is the most appropriate for slow links and problematic network connections.
- **Schedule.** Determine when replication is allowed to take place.
- **Replication from.** Identify the server and site from which replication will come, as well as the domain information to be replicated.

Configuring Server Objects

Domain controller server objects are installed into a site automatically by the Active Directory Installation Wizard, as previously described.

A new server object appears beneath a site in the MMC, where you can double-click it to open its properties dialog box, as shown in Figure 22.12.

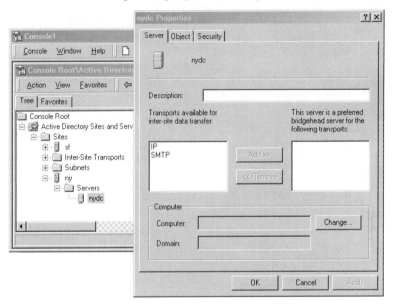

Figure 22.12 *Configuring a Server Object.*

Among the items you can configure are a description, available transports, and the actual computer and domain.

WORKING WITH SITE MEMBERSHIP

On occasion, it might be necessary to change the membership of objects such as servers. To move a server object from one site to another, select it in the MMC and right-click to choose the Move command from the pop-up menu. This opens the Move Server dialog box, in which you can select the site to which the server should be moved.

Similarly, you can remove a server object from a site by selecting the Delete command.

WORKING WITH GLOBAL CATALOGS

Global Catalog servers host a copy of the local Active Directory and a partial replica of the objects from all other domains. As they are required for successful logons, their placement is important to network performance. In general, it is recommended that GC servers be deployed in each site. This increases the amount of replication traffic on your network, however, so this might not be practical in some cases.

To create a GC server, expand a domain controller in the MMC's Tree pane and right-click the NTDS Settings item to open the NTDS Settings Properties dialog box, as shown in Figure 22.13.

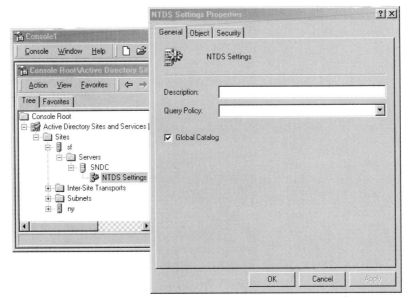

Figure 22.13 *Configuring a Global Catalog Server.*

Enable the Global Catalog checkbox.

The first domain controller you install is automatically configured as a GC server.

Transferring Operations Master Roles

In general, Active Directory employs built-in multi-master replication techniques in which all domain controller's databases are synchronized with each other and perform equal roles. In those instances where multimaster replication does not permit domain-wide changes to be made, single-master replication is employed. Under this model, a domain controller is configured as an *operations master* that maintains certain Active Directory data while other domain controllers serve only as backups.

FOREST-WIDE OPERATION MASTER ROLES

Forest-wide operations master roles include the following:

- **Schema Master Role.** This domain controller makes all modifications to the forest schema.
- **Domain-Naming Master Role.** This domain controller keeps track of domain additions and deletions.

There can be only one schema master and domain-naming master in a forest.

DOMAIN-WIDE OPERATIONS MASTER ROLES

Doamin-wide operations master roles include the following:

- **Relative ID Master Role.** This domain controller generates security Ids (SIDs) for each object in the domain. The SID consists of a domain SID, which is the same for all objects, and relative ID (RID), which is unique to each object. It is from this domain controller that objects can be moved across domains.
- **PDC Emulator Role.** This domain controller acts as a Primary Domain Controller (PDC) on mixed mode networks that contain Windows NT computers.
- **Infrastructure Master Role.** This domain controller makes changes in the global catalog relating to group memberships.

There can be only one RID master, PDC emulator, or infrastructure master in a domain.

On small networks containing only one domain controller, that domain controller performs all operations master roles. Having just one domain controller is bad design, however. At least two domain controllers should be deployed as replication partners so that should one fail, network operations can continue uninterrupted from the other.

On networks with multiple domain controllers, you might wish to move operations master roles around for load balancing or while performing maintenance on the host domain controllers. Initially, these roles are all assigned to the first domain controller you install. The schema master and domain-naming master should be assigned to the same domain controller, but other operations master roles can be spread among domain controllers.

To identify the domain controllers currently performing domain-wide operations master roles, launch the Active Directory Users and Computers MMC and right-click the Active Directory Users and Computers item to select the Operations Masters command from the pop-up menu.

This opens the Operations Master dialog box, in which you can see which servers have been assigned to which roles, as shown in Figure 22.14.

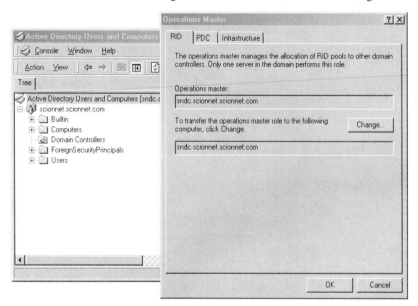

Figure 22.14   *Viewing operations master roles.*

To transfer a domain-wide operations master role, select the Connect to domain command from the Action menu. Once connected, open the Operations Master dialog box again and use the Change button under various tabs to reassign operations master roles.

The process of seizing operations master roles is described in Chapter 25, "Active Directory Backup and Restoration."

Verifying and Troubleshooting Installation

If Active Directory has been properly installed, the Windows 2000 Configure Your Server Wizard tells you so when you restart the server, as shown in Figure 22.15.

In addition, the following tools are added to the Administrative Tools program group:

- Active Directory Users and Computers
- Active Directory Domains and Trusts
- Active Directory Sites and Services

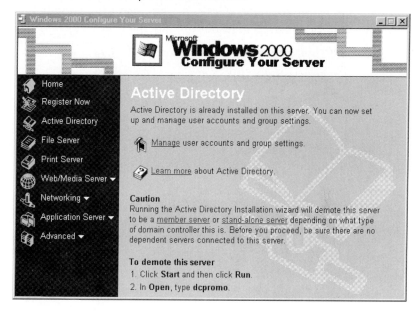

Figure 22.15 *Sign that Active Directory is properly installed.*

Finally, the new domain should appear in My Network Places, as shown in Figure 22.16.

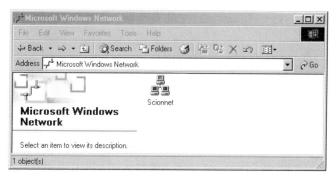

Figure 22.16 *Newly created domain.*

You can verify that your domain controller has been properly installed if it is visible when you click the Domain Controllers folder in the Active Directory Users and Computers MMC.

Finally, you can verify that DNS is working properly (if you installed the Windows 2000 DNS Server) by selecting the server in the DNS MMC and right-clicking to open the Properties dialog box, as shown in Figure 22.17.

Switch to the Monitoring tab, select the checkbox for simple queries, and click the Test Now button. The test results appear in the bottom pane.

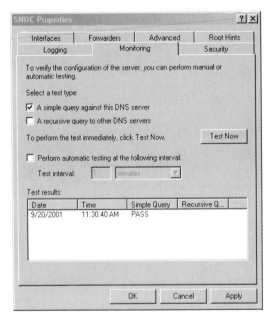

Figure 22.17 *Verifying the DNS server.*

If the test fails, troubleshoot the DNS Server as described in Chapter 15.

Creating Organizational Units

Organizational Units (OUs) are Active Directory containers designed to reflect your organization's hierarchical structure. For example, you might create OUs that are function-based, such as by department, location-based, such as by geographical address, or a combination of both. Functionally, OUs contain relevant objects, such as computers and user accounts, and can be used to apply Group Policies and resource restrictions.

To create an OU, select a domain in the Tree pane of the Active Directory Users and Computers MMC and right-click to choose the Organizational Unit command from the New menu in the pop-up menu. In the New Object-Organizational Unit dialog box, you are prompted to name the OU.

To configure an OU, right-click its folder in the MMC to open the Properties dialog box, as shown in Figure 22.18. Under the General tab, type in address information associated with the OU. Under the Managed By tab, select an individual who administers the OU. Address information is taken from the user's account information. Select links to group policies under the Group Policy tab. These properties can be changed at any time.

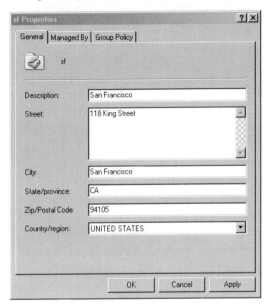

Figure 22.18 *Configuring OU Properties.*

Once OUs have been created, you can create objects within them by right-clicking an OU's folder in the MMC's Tree pane and choosing from the options in the New menu. Objects created in one OU can be moved to other OUs.

OUs can be created, deleted, and moved between domains using the MMC.

Study Break

Install Active Directory

Practice what you have learned by installing Active Directory.

Perform the steps in the Active Directory Installation Wizard to install Active Directory on your first domain controller. Verify the installation. Create an initial forest, tree, and domain. Give thought to naming, so that your Active Directory will be logical and scalable. Create sites, subnets, site links, and connection objects as necessary. If multiple domain controllers are available, consider transferring the roles of domain-wide operations masters. Finally, create at least one OU.

■ Summary

In this chapter, we considered various issues surrounding the installation and configuration of Active Directory.

Installing Active Directory

Active Directory is of integral importance to Windows 2000. While directory services are not new to Windows, there are differences in how they are implemented under Windows NT and Windows 2000. Windows NT's directory services were flat, while Active Directory's are hierarchical. Domains are groupings of computers that share a directory database, security policies, and trust relationship with other domains. Domains are in turn grouped into trees, which can be further grouped into forests. A child domain is directly beneath a parent domain in the Active Directory hierarchy, and therefore shares the same namespace.

The Active Directory is a database that contains information about objects. Objects are elements with a particular set of attributes, such as a file, server, printer, or account. Such information is made available to users and applications by directory services. This data is stored in the NTDS.NIT file, which includes both private and public data, the latter of which is subject to replication. Replication is a process that distributes and synchronizes directory data between domain controllers. This can involve inter-site and intra-site replication. Windows 2000 uses multi-master replication, which makes all domain controllers capable of distributing and accepting information changes. Data that is replicated includes domain data, information about domain objects such as share points and printers; configuration data, information relating to directory structure such a domain names and catalog locations; and schema data that includes object class types and attributes.

Other terms important to Active Directory include the Global Catalog, a source of information about objects in the directory that permit users to locate resources without knowing upon which server they reside; Group Policy, the rules that control user environments, security, and software deployments; and Organizational Unit, a container used to group objects according to an organization's working hierarchies.

Active Directory can be configured using the Active Directory Users and Computers, Active Directory Domains and Trusts, and Active Directory Sites and Services MMC snap-ins.

▲ CHAPTER REVIEW QUESTIONS

Here are questions relating to material covered in the *Installing and Configuring Active Directory* section of Microsoft's *Implementing and Administering a Microsoft Windows 2000 Directory Services Infrastructure* exam (70-217).

1. *Forests, trees, and domains exist as peers under Active Directory.*

    A. True

    B. False

2. *Domain controllers can be demoted to the role of member server with the command "dcpromo."*

    A. True

    B. False

3. *Sites contain groupings of resources that are well connected, while site links are not so well connected paths over which replication traffic travels.*

    A. True

    B. False

4. *Connection objects can be either manually or KCC-managed.*

    A. True

    B. False

5. *Server objects cannot be moved between sites.*

    A. True

    B. False

6. *Global Catalog servers do not increase replication traffic on a network.*

    A. True

    B. False

7. *Which of the following are domain-wide operations master roles? Select all that apply:*

    A. RID Master Role

    B. PDC Emulator Role

    C. Domain-Naming Master Role

    D. Infrastructure Master Role

8. *There can be multiple RID Operations Masters deployed domain-wide.*

    A. True

    B. False

9. *One easy way to verify Active Directory installation is to look for the newly created domain in My Network Places.*

   A. True

   B. False

10. *OUs can be configured by functional area or geographical location.*

   A. True

   B. False

Administering Active Directory and DNS

▲**Chapter Syllabus**

MCSE 23.1 **Administering DNS for Active Directory**

In this chapter, we examine the installation topics covered in the *Installing, Configuring, Managing, Monitoring, and Troubleshooting DNS for Active Directory* section of Microsoft's *Implementing and Administering a Microsoft Windows 2000 Directory Services Infrastructure* exam (70-217).

In this chapter, you build upon the knowledge gained from previous chapters to cover several Active Directory/DNS integration issues, such as installation, configuration, and management. This augments material that was originally covered in Chapter 9, "Administering Windows 2000 Server Resource Access," and Chapter 15, "Administrating Domain Name Services."

MCSE 23.1   Administering DNS for Active Directory

Under Active Directory, DNS replaces NetBIOS as the Windows domain naming and resource location service. Many of the issues surrounding DNS have already been described in this book, but in this section, a few issues that pertain to Active Directory/DNS integration in particular are covered.

Installing DNS for Active Directory

There are several methods for installing the DNS Server under Windows 2000 Server, as described in previous chapters. It can be installed when you originally install the Windows 2000 Server. You can also install the DNS Server when installing Active Directory, or when promoting a server to a domain controller. Finally, you can install the DNS Server using the Add/Remove Programs Control Panel application.

    If there are already DNS servers installed on your network, you do not necessarily have to install the Microsoft version. Active Directory can work in conjunction with other DNS applications. The Windows 2000 DNS Server is recommended, however, because it ensures the availability of advanced services such as dynamic updates and fast transfers.

Configuring DNS for Active Directory

Once installed, the DNS Server can be configured through the Services and Applications snap-in of the Computer Management MMC, or the more specific DNS snap-in found in the Administrative Tools program group. As described in previous chapters, DNS Server can be configured as standard primary, standard secondary, or Active Directory-integrated server.

INTEGRATING ACTIVE DIRECTORY AND DNS ZONES

If you choose to install zones for an Active Directory-integrated DNS Server (using the New Zone Wizard), the master copy of the zone database is created and stored in Active Directory.

    Active Directory-integrated zones differ from standard zones in several ways. For example, standard zones are synchronized using a single-master update model, with the primary server hosting the master database and secondary servers updating their resource records from the primary. Active Directory-integrated zones are more fault tolerant because they employ the multi-master update model in which the master database is replicated across all domain controllers. Active Directory-integrated zones are updated according to the same replication schedule applied to other Active Directory data.

If you previously installed the DNS Server as a standard primary server, as described in earlier chapters, you can switch to an Active Directory-integrated DNS Server using the DNS MMC. Select the zone in the Tree pane and right-click to open the Properties dialog box. Under the General tab, click the Change button to open the Change Zone Type dialog box, as shown in Figure 23.1.

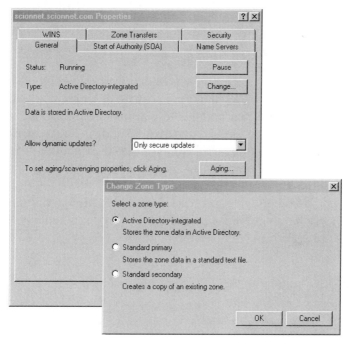

Figure 23.1   *Enabling Active Directory/DNS integration.*

CONFIGURING ZONES FOR DYNAMIC AND SECURE UPDATES

The Windows 2000 DNS implementation is a Dynamic DNS (DDNS) server that works closely with DHCP to update its database with the proper mappings whenever DHCP assigns an IP address.

To enable the use of dynamic updates, use the pop-up menu next to the Allow dynamic updates field under the General tab in the zone Properties dialog box (see Figure 23.1) to choose the Yes or Only secure updates options. If you choose the latter, only those users, groups, or computers that are granted rights under the Security tab will be allowed to create zone records.

CREATING DNS RECORDS

Where DNS records cannot be added dynamically, you can create them manually by choosing the New Host command from the Action menu to open the New Host dialog box. Enter the host name and IP address, then click the Add Host button to add the new record to the database.

Similar commands exist under the Action menu for CNAME and MX records. Other record types (such as HINFO and SRV) are created using the Other New Records command. When working with reverse lookup zones, specific commands are available to create CNAME and PTR records. SOA and NS records are created automatically.

Managing and Monitoring DNS

Windows 2000's aging and scavenging features are useful when you deploy DDNS. When DDNS adds records to the database, it marks them with a time/date stamp that pertains to when they were created and/or refreshed. When a computer leaves the network suddenly, such as because of a crash, invalid records can be left behind. By setting aging options, you ensure that stale records are properly removed and cannot interfere with the host name resolution process.

To enable scavenging, click the Aging button in the zone Properties dialog box to open the Aging/Scavenging Properties dialog box, as shown in Figure 23.2.

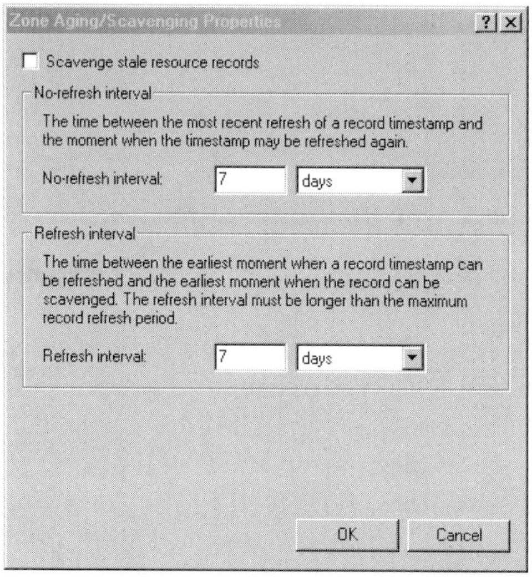

Figure 23.2 *Enabling resource record scavenging.*

Select the Scavenge stale resource records checkbox. For zones originally created as Active Directory-integrated, this feature is already enabled. If you have changed a zone from standard to Active Directory-integrated, however, you need to manually enable this feature.

For more information on managing and monitoring the DNS Server, review Chapter 15.

Troubleshooting DNS

For information on troubleshooting the DNS Server, review Chapter 15.

Study Break

Enable Active Directory Integration

Practice what you have learned by configuring the Windows 2000 DNS Server with Active Directory-integrated zones.

If you previously created zones for a standard primary DNS server implementation, change this configuration to one that is Active Directory-integrated. Also enable dynamic updates, and make sure the aging/scavenging features are enabled for all zones.

■ Summary

In this chapter, we looked at issues relating to Active Directory/DNS integration.

Administering DNS for Active Directory

Under Active Directory, DNS replaces NetBIOS as the Windows domain naming and resource location service. Active Directory-integrated zones differ from standard zones. Standard zones are synchronized using a single-master update model. Active Directory-integrated zones are more fault tolerant because they employ the multi-master update model. Active Directory-integrated zones are updated according to the same replication schedule applied to other Active Directory data. Active Directory also benefits from the abilities of the Windows 2000 DDNS server that works closely with DHCP to update its database with the proper mappings whenever DHCP assigns an IP address.

▲ CHAPTER REVIEW QUESTIONS

Here are a few questions relating to the material covered in the *Installing, Configuring, Managing, Monitoring, and Troubleshooting DNS for Active Directory* section of Microsoft's *Implementing and Administering a Microsoft Windows 2000 Directory Services Infrastructure* exam (70-217).

1. *Which of the following are possible ways to install DNS Server and Active Directory integration? Select all that apply:*

   A. Using the Add/Remove Programs Wizard

   B. When promoting a domain controller

   C. When installing Active Directory

   D. When installing Windows 2000 Server

2. *You must be careful when initially installing the DNS Server because once installed as a standard primary or secondary server, it cannot be migrated to Active Directory integration.*

   A. True

   B. False

3. *Dynamic updates can only be implemented in conjunction with users, groups, or computer accounts.*

   A. True

   B. False

4. *DNS resource records can be created either dynamically or manually, but not both.*

   A. True

   B. False

5. *Scavenging must be manually enabled for a standard primary DNS Server.*

   A. True

   B. False

Managing Change Configuration

▲ Chapter Syllabus

MCSE 24.1 Working with Group Policy

MCSE 24.2 Managing Change Configuration

In this chapter, we examine the installation topics covered in the *Configuring, Managing, Monitoring, Optimizing, and Troubleshooting Change and Configuration Management* section of Microsoft's *Implementing and Administering a Microsoft Windows 2000 Directory Services Infrastructure* exam (70-217).

In this chapter, you learn about the numerous remote workstation configuration capabilities made possible through the use of group policy and the creation and management of Group Policy Objects (GPOs). Similarly, you learn how you can save money and time by deploying programs and even the Windows 2000 Professional operating system through the use of group policy and other Active Directory features.

MCSE 24.1 Working with Group Policy

GPOs are groupings of common configuration settings that can be applied to individual or multiple user and computer accounts. Although Windows NT provided similar functionality through its System Policy Editor application, GPOs are only available under Windows 2000 and Active Directory.

Creating Group Policy Objects

As described in Chapter 5, "Configuring Windows 2000 Professional," you can set group policy using the Group Policy MMC snap-in. Typing "mmc" in the Run dialog box opens an empty MMC to which this snap-in can be added. When you select the Group Policy item in the Add Standalone Snap-in dialog box, you are presented with the Select Group Policy Object Wizard, as shown in Figure 24.1.

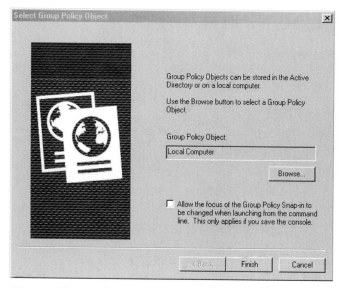

Figure 24.1 *Selecting a GPO in the MMC.*

By default, the Local Computer GPO is selected. Click the Browse button to open the Browse for a Group Policy Object window, as shown in Figure 24.2.

You can create GPOs at the domain, OU, or site level by switching to the desired tab, right-clicking, and selecting the New command from the pop-up menu.

You may then rename the new GPO, and select it to be returned to the Select Group Policy Object Wizard.

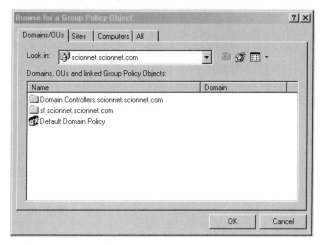

Figure 24.2   *Selecting or creating a GPO.*

Dismiss the various windows to end up with an MMC that includes your newly created GPO, as shown in Figure 24.3.

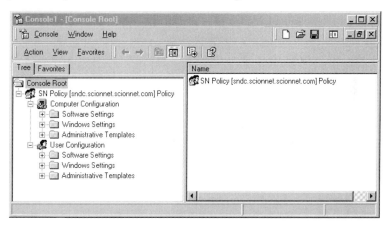

Figure 24.3   *New GPO in the MMC.*

MODIFYING GPOS

In the Tree pane are configuration categories that can be modified for both a computer and its users: Software Settings, Windows Settings, and Administrative Templates.

For example, expand the Windows Settings branch and its Security Settings item to see a list of possible policies in the right pane, as shown in Figure 24.4.

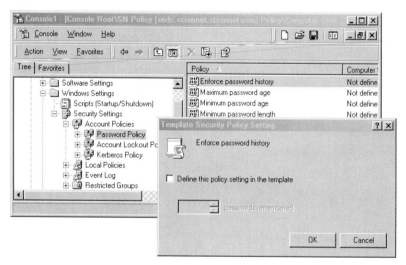

Figure 24.4 *Enabling a group policy.*

Double-click a policy and choose the Enabled radio button to define and apply it. Most policies are disabled by default.

LINKING GPOS

GPOs exist within the container in which they were created. To apply a GPO's policies to groups that exist in other containers, you may link them to sites, domains, or OUs.

To link a GPO to a site, domain, or OU container, right-click the object in the Active Directory Users and Computers MMC to open the Properties dialog box. Next, switch to the Group Policy tab, where currently assigned GPOs are listed, as shown in Figure 24.5.

Use the Add button to open the Add a Group Policy Object link window, from which you can select additional GPOs. Alternately, click the New button to create a new GPO.

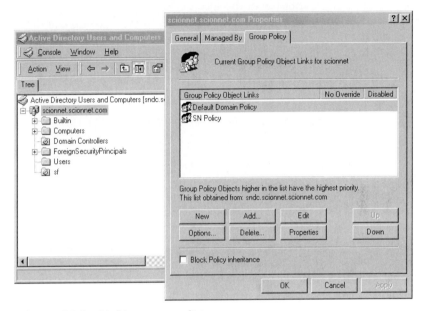

Figure 24.5   *Linking group policies.*

Delegating Administrative Control

By delegating administrative control over group policy, you can share the workload while ensuring that only individuals you deem capable have input into this powerful feature.

To delegate administrative control over a GPO, right-click a site in the Active Directory Sites and Services MMC to open the site Properties dialog box. Next, switch to the Group Policy tab and click the New button to create a new GPO. Rename the GPO, then select it and click the Properties button to open its Properties dialog box. Finally, switch to the Security tab, as shown in Figure 24.6.

Use the Remove button to delete default groups and the Add button to extend control to new users and groups.

Permissions can be extended in the following categories:

- **Full Control.** Users or groups have all permissions associated with the object.
- **Read.** Users or groups can open and read the object, but not modify or apply it.

- **Write.** Users or groups can modify the object, but not read or apply it.
- **Create All Child Objects.** Users or groups can create objects that are children of the specified object.
- **Delete All Child Objects.** Users or groups can delete objects that are children of the specified object.
- **Apply Group Policy.** Users or groups can apply objects that are linked to the container. This permission also includes the Read permission.

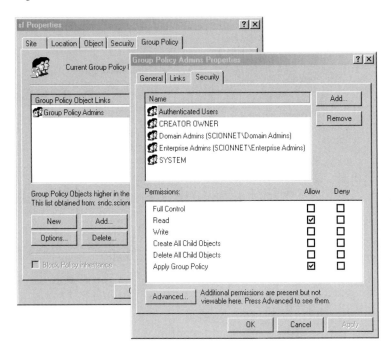

Figure 24.6 *Configuring GPO security.*

CONFIGURING GROUP POLICY OPTIONS

To configure overall options for a group policy, select it in the Group Policy MMC and right-click to open the Properties dialog box, as shown in Figure 24.7.

You can choose to link to other GPOs under the Links tab, and assign administrative control under the Security tab. Under the General tab, you can select checkboxes to disable either Computer Configuration settings or User Configuration settings.

If no modifications have been made to policies in either category, disabling them speeds up the computer's parsing process.

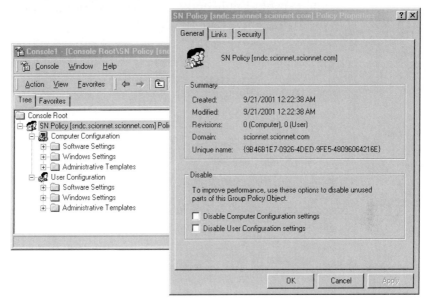

Figure 24.7   *Configuring group policy properties.*

FILTERING SECURITY SETTINGS

Using security groups in conjunction with group policies, you can get quite particular in applying a GPO to only certain users or computers even while they belong to a larger domain or OU group.

To apply a security filter to a GPO, first create a security group that contains the users that you wish to provide access. Next open the GPO Properties dialog box and switch to the Security tab, where you can use the Add button to include the security group. Remove the Authenticated Users group to make limit general access. Finally, give the security group the Read and Apply Group Policy permissions.

MODIFYING PRIORITIES

An important group policy issue is *inheritance*, through which GPO settings are applied from group policies higher in the processing hierarchy. The GPO processing order is as follows:

- Local Computer GPO
- Site GPOs
- Domain GPOs
- OU GPOs (including nested GPOs)

Microsoft uses the acronym LSDOU to refer to this process. At the same time, multiple GPOs for objects are applied from the bottom up.

You can block inheritance by right-clicking the object in the Active Directory Users and Computers MMC to open the Properties dialog box, switching to the Group Policy tab, and enabling the Block Policy Inheritance check box (see Figure 24.5). This directs the object to ignore all other policies.

Similarly, you can enable a No Override setting as a policy option that functions like the Block Policy Inheritance setting, but for a specific GPO only. This option prevents all settings in a GPO from being overwritten by any other GPO during processing.

Managing and Troubleshooting User Environments

Although you cannot add to the settings under the Software Settings and Windows Settings branches, you can add to the settings under the Administrative Templates branch by creating and importing your own custom templates. Specifically, you can modify Registry settings within the HKEY_LOCAL_MACHINE and HKEY_CURRENT_USER hives. Your custom templates should be saved to the \WINNT\INF folder with an ".ADM" extension. You can then import them into a GPO by selecting the Administrative Templates branch in the Group Policy MMC and right-clicking to choose the Add/Remove Templates command. If your template file has settings for both computers and users, you need to import it into both the GPO's Computer Configuration and User Configuration branches. The file is then copied to the SYSVOL folder so that it can be replicated to all domain controllers.

Your template will be parsed and verified during the import process. If errors are detected, recheck the syntax in your ADM file.

For more details, review Chapter 5. For more information on creating administrative templates, obtain Microsoft's *Group Policy White Paper* from *www.microsoft.com*.

Study Break

Create a GPO

Practice what you have learned by creating a GPO. First, create a MMC based on the Group Policy snap-in. Next, create a GPO at the domain, OU, or site level. Finally, delegate administrative control to trusted users.

Managing Change Configuration

Microsoft's *IntelliMirror* provides several technologies designed to reduce computer's Total Cost of Ownership (TCO) by allowing an administrator to perform tasks remotely and automatically that previously required their physical presence. Among IntelliMirror's components are the *Windows Installer service*, which supports automated software installation; *Software Installation and Maintenance,* which uses GPOs in administering software; and *Folder Redirection*, which automatically backs up data in such folders as My Documents to a secure, central location.

Administering Software

Administering software through group policy involves first deploying it and then maintaining it.

INSTALLING SOFTWARE

There are two primary steps in deploying software using the Windows Installer service. First, a Microsoft Windows Installer (.MSI) package must be created. Second, the installer package must be either published or assigned using a GPO. The Windows Installer service can deploy software to Windows 9x/Me, NT 4.0, and 2000 computers.

The software you wish to deploy can come in one of two forms. A *native package* comes prepackaged in .MSI files. Where there is no native package, a third-party utility can be used to repackage the software. This process was described in Chapter 5.

There are many benefits to using group policy to distribute software. When GPOs are placed in OUs, filtering can be used to apply their settings to any user, group, or computer. GPOs give you options for how software will be distributed, such as in a mandatory or optional installation, and permit you to restrict users from having full administrative control over their workstations.

DEPLOYING SOFTWARE TO COMPUTERS • To deploy a software package to a group of computers, expand the Software Settings folder under the Computer Configuration branch of the Group Policy MMC, right-click the Software Installation item, and choose the Package command from the New menu, as shown in Figure 24.8.

First, you are prompted to select the .MSI file that is to be distributed. Next, you are asked to choose a deployment method. In most cases, you can accept the default Assigned radio button.

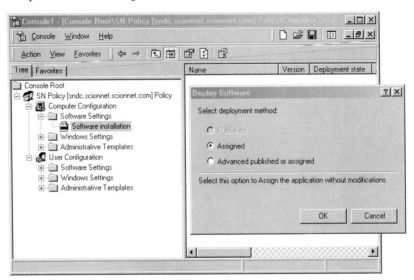

Figure 24.8 *Deploying software to computers.*

An *assigned* package is installed the next time the computer is rebooted, regardless of the logon. Such an installation is self-repairing, in that each time the computer reboots the package is checked. If any files have gone missing since installation, they are replaced.

DEPLOYING SOFTWARE TO USERS • To deploy a software package to a group of users, expand the Software Settings folder under the User Configuration branch of the Group Policy MMC, right-click the Software Installation item, and choose the Package command from the New menu.

You are prompted to select the .MSI file that is to be distributed. You are then asked to choose between the Assigned and Published deployment methods. A *published* package is available for user installation, but is not advertised. Users are unaware of it until they launch the Add/Remove Programs Wizard.

Similarly, when a package is assigned to users, it is not actually installed, although its icon appears in the Start menu. It cannot be installed unless a user chooses its icon or it is called upon by a file type through *document invocation* (e.g., a .DOC file invokes Microsoft Word, and so on). This ensures that the application is available, but not installed unless users really need it. Here, too, the software is self-repairing.

CONFIGURING SOFTWARE

Select the Advanced published or assigned radio button if you need to modify the package or its installation options. You are then presented with the Properties dialog box, as shown in Figure 28.9.

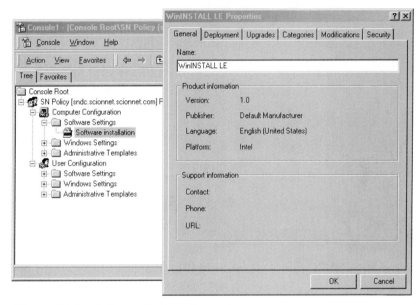

Figure 24.9 *Software Package Properties.*

You may choose from options under the following tabs:

- **General.** Rename the application.
- **Deployment.** Choose to enable/disable document invocation, uninstall the application when it is no longer under the scope of management, show/hide the application in the Add/Remove Programs Wizard, and select Basic or Maximum user interface options. Click the Advanced button enable settings that ignore language options and remove previously installed, but not Active Directory-managed, copies of the application.
- **Upgrades.** Define packages that will be upgraded from the current GPO.
- **Categories.** Define the categories in which the application appears in the Add/Remove Programs Wizard.
- **Modifications.** Identify and order the transformation package (.MST) files that will be used to modify the software installation package.
- **Security.** Set user and group permissions.

Managing Software

Once software has been deployed through group policy, it can be easily upgraded, redeployed, or removed.

UPGRADING SOFTWARE

You can deploy a *mandatory upgrade* that updates an application the next time a user accesses it. Alternately, you can deploy an *optional upgrade*, which appears in the Add/Remove Programs Wizard but is not installed unless the user explicitly chooses to do so. Either way, the new version of the application is identified under the Upgrades tab in the installation package Properties window (see Figure 28.9). To make an upgrade mandatory, select the Required upgrade for existing packages checkbox.

REDEPLOYING SOFTWARE

Should you need to redeploy an application, perhaps because a service pack was applied or a previously unused feature is implemented, you can do so by right-clicking the package in the GPO and choosing the Redeploy command from the All Tasks menu.

REMOVING SOFTWARE

Should you need to remove an application, you can do so by right-clicking the package in the GPO and choosing the Remove command from the All Tasks menu. You are then prompted to choose between removal methods. If you choose the Immediately uninstall the software from users and computers option, a forced removal occurs. If you select the Allow users to continue to use the software, but prevent new installations radio button, an optional removal is specified.

Troubleshooting Software

Among the problems that can occur when deploying software through group policy are the following:

- **Software package does not install.** Make sure that group policy has been properly configured. For example, make sure the specified user has both Read and Apply Group Policy permissions assigned. Also make sure that the network path to the share containing the .MSI file is available and that the computer can log on to it.

- **Software package does not install completely.** Verify the software repackaging process and recreate the .MSI file, if necessary. Make sure you create your software packages on a "clean" machine so that all necessary files are identified and included in the snapshot.
- **Software package has not been installed.** If you want to ensure that an application is installed, assign it rather than publish it.

The installation of a new application, whether or not it is successful, is recorded in the Event Viewer's Application log.

Managing Network Configurations

To configure group policy related to networking configurations, expand the Administrative Templates branch and its Network item to see a list of possible policies in the right pane, as shown in Figure 24.10.

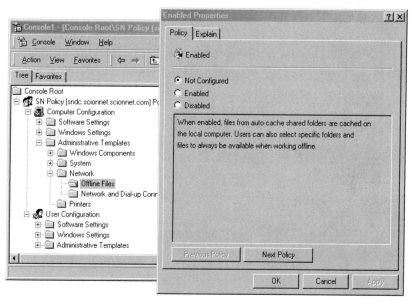

Figure 24.10 *Enabling a Network group policy.*

Double-click a policy and choose the Enabled radio button to apply it, or choose among the options presented.

Among the group policies related to networking are the following:

- **Offline Files.** Although the use of offline files is configured through shared folder properties, they way in which it is used can be configured through the use of group policy, such as synchronization and logging options.

- **Network and Dial-Up Connections.** Although the use of a network or RAS connection is configured elsewhere, you can define how such connections behave here, such as by prohibiting connection sharing.

Other network-related group policies can be applied for printers, logon scripts, Internet Explorer, and NetMeeting.

Supporting Remote Installation Services

Remote Installation Services (RIS) is an optional component of Windows 2000 Server that lets you install Windows 2000 Professional remotely on multiple computers of the same or differing configurations. Under RIS, you create a disk image of a properly configured Windows 2000 Professional workstation using any disk duplication tool, preferably the companion Remote Installation Preparation Wizard. This image is then distributed to additional workstations from the RIS server. The Remote Installation Preparation Wizard strips hardware-specific settings and the security identifier (SID) from the master image, making its duplicates useable by any workstation.

In action, the RIS installation process works as follows:

1. A target client computer starts up from its Preboot eXEcution (PXE)-based BIOS or the boot ROM on its network adapter—if so enabled—or from a Remote Boot Disk that can be prepared on the RIS server using the Remote Boot Floppy Generator tool.
2. The client computer uses the Boot Protocol (BootP) to locate a Dynamic Host Configuration Protocol (DHCP) server and obtain an IP address. The DHCP server provides the client with an IP address, and Boot Information Negotiation Layer (BINL) extensions redirect the client to the RIS server.
3. The RIS server downloads the Client Installation Wizard (CIW) to the computer, which opens with a log-in screen.
4. When the user logs in, RIS uses the Domain Name System (DNS) to locate the Active Directory server.
5. Active Directory determines which options the CIW may display to the user, as well as which images the user is allowed to choose from. Active Directory then downloads the initial installation files to the client using the Trivial File Transfer Protocol (TFTP).
6. The user chooses the appropriate image, launching the setup.

Careful planning is required, since the client computer's boot mechanism, RIS, DHCP, DNS, and Active Directory must all work in harmony. RIS requires an Active Directory domain controller with the DNS Server integrated with the domain.

RIS limitations include the following:

- RIS can only be used to duplicate the Windows 2000 Professional operating system.
- Only a single partition, such as the C: drive, can be duplicated.
- The Remote Boot Disk only contains drivers for 25 Peripheral Connection Interface (PCI)-based network adapters. Laptops with PC Card adapters, for example, are therefore out of luck.

INSTALLING RIS

To set up RIS, you must first designate a Windows 2000 Server that will be the RIS server. It must meet the following requirements:

- The server must be a member of a domain.
- The shared volume on which images are stored must be formatted as NTFS.
- The shared volume must have between 800MB and 1GB of free space for an initial image.
- The shared volume cannot contain the Windows 2000 Server system files.
- The server must be authorized as a DHCP server with Active Directory.

To begin, install RIS via the Add/Remove Programs Wizard and reboot the server.

USING RISETUP

With RIS installed, type "risetup.exe" in the Run dialog box to open the RIS Setup Wizard as shown in Figure 24.11.

Follow the wizard's instructions to prepare the share drive and install the initial image.

If you have multiple images, there will be a great deal of file duplication that would consume server disk space. To lessen this impact, Microsoft creates a Single-Instance-Store (SIS) volume in which duplicate files are not saved.

Figure 24.11 *Running the RIS Setup Wizard.*

USING RIPREP

Next, you must add new images as needed using the Remote Installation Preparation Wizard (RIPrep.exe). To use the Remote Installation Preparation Wizard, first install Windows 2000 Professional on a master computer remotely from the RIS server. Next, install the appropriate applications (as determined by your organization's policies). Finally, run the Remote Installation Preparation Wizard on the master computer to create a disk image that is uploaded to the RIS server.

You can only duplicate a single partition. However, identical machine configurations are not required so long as they share the same Hardware Abstraction Layer (HAL). When differences occur between the master and target computers, Plug and Play support is employed.

CONFIGURING SECURITY • Restrict user access to various images as necessary by applying group policy through the Active Directory Users and Computers MMC snap-in. This ensures that users only apply the appropriate images to their workstations. If you only authorize a given user to download one image, the user can only be shown that image, which can then be installed automatically.

CONFIGURING OPTIONS

To define the configuration choices that are presented to users, select the Remote Installation Services item in the Windows Settings folder in the User Configuration branch in the Group Policy MMC. Double-click the Choice Options icon in the right pane to open the Choice Options Properties dialog box, as shown in Figure 24.12.

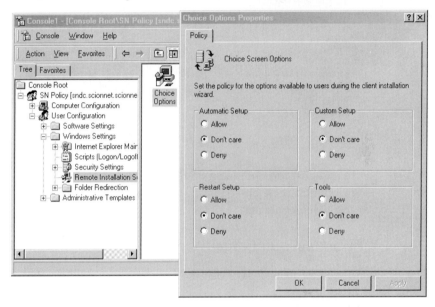

Figure 24.12 *Configuring Choice Options.*

Users may be presented with some combination of the following four options after the Client Installation Wizard launches:

- **Automatic Setup.** The default, this option only requires that the user select the appropriate image. The image is then installed using all of its preconfigured settings.
- **Custom Setup.** This option lets the user name the computer and select the Active Directory location in which its computer account will be created. Most of the installation's parameters can be specified manually using this option.
- **Restart a Previous Setup Attempt**. In the event of a connection failure, this option picks up where the previous setup left off without prompting the user for previously entered information.
- **Maintenance and Troubleshooting**. This option permits a third-party tool to be run prior to the installation.

Once users choose an option here, they are prompted to select the appropriate image, beginning the setup process.

Study Break

Deploy a Software Package

Practice what you have learned by deploying a software package.

First, either create a new .MSI package, or select a third-party application from the Windows 2000 Server installation CD-ROM. Try installing the package to both computers and users, using both assigned and published options. Remove the package after verifying successful deployment.

■ Summary

In this chapter, we looked at numerous ways of remotely managing changes throughout networked computers using group policy, with a special emphasis on deploying and managing software.

Working With Group Policy

GPOs are groupings of common configuration settings that can be applied to individual or multiple user and computer accounts. You can create GPOs at the domain, OU, or site level. To apply a GPO's policies to groups that exist in other containers, you may link them to sites, domains, or OUs. By delegating administrative control over group policy, you can share the workload while ensuring that only individuals you deem capable have input into this powerful feature. Using security groups in conjunction with group policies, you can get very particular in applying a GPO to only certain users or computers even while they belong to a larger domain or OU group. An important group policy issue is *inheritance*, through which GPO settings are applied from group policies higher in the processing hierarchy. Microsoft uses the acronym LSDOU to refer to this process.

Managing Change and Configuration

Microsoft's IntelliMirror provides several technologies designed to reduce computer's TCO by allowing an administrator to perform tasks remotely and automatically. Among IntelliMirror's components are the Windows Installer service, which supports automated software installation; Software Installation and Maintenance, which uses GPOs in administering software; and Folder Redirection, which automatically backs up data in such folders as My Documents to a secure, central location. Administering software through group policy involves first deploying it and then maintaining it. Installation can be mandatory or optional.

RIS is an optional component of Windows 2000 Server that lets you install Windows 2000 Professional remotely on multiple computers of the same or differing configurations. Under RIS, you create a disk image of a properly configured Windows 2000 Professional workstation. This image is then distributed to additional workstations from the RIS server.

▲ CHAPTER REVIEW QUESTIONS

Here are a few questions relating to the material covered in the *Configuring, Managing, Monitoring, Optimizing, and Troubleshooting Change and Configuration Management* section of Microsoft's *Implementing and Administering a Microsoft Windows 2000 Directory Services Infrastructure* exam (70-217).

1. *GPOs are available for use on computers running Windows NT 4.0 and Windows 2000.*
   A. True
   B. False

2. *GPOs can be created at which of the following levels? Select all that apply:*
   A. Forest
   B. Tree
   C. Domain
   D. Site

3. *By linking to a GPO, you move it from the container in which it was created.*
   A. True
   B. False

4. *Which of the following permissions must be assigned in addition the Apply Group Policy permission when delegating GPO administrative control? Select all that apply:*
   A. Full Control
   B. Read
   C. Write
   D. Create All Child Objects

5. *If you do not need settings from the Computer Configuration or User Configuration branches of a policy, you should disable it to speed up parsing.*

   A. True

   B. False

6. *If you wish to apply security filtering to GPOs, you should remove access by the Authenticated Users groups and enable access by a security group of your own creation.*

   A. True

   B. False

7. *Which of the following GPOs has the highest priority in inheritance? Select only one:*

   A. OU

   B. site

   C. local computer

   D. domain

8. *You can manage user environments through templates saved under which of the following file extensions? Select only one:*

   A. .MST

   B. .MSI

   C. .ADM

   D. .INF

9. *The Windows Installer service is available for Windows 2000 computers only.*

   A. True

   B. False

10. *Network policies can be used to enable or disable such capabilities as the use of offline files and RAS.*

    A. True

    B. False

11. *Which of the following are prerequisites of installing the RIS server? Select all that apply:*

    A. Server must be a domain member.

    B. RIS shared volume must be NTFS formatted.

    C. Server must be running the DNS Server and be authorized by Active Directory.

    D. Server must have at least 800 MB of free disk space.

12. *The RIPrep.exe utility is run on a Windows 2000 Professional workstation.*

    A. True

    B. False

13. *By applying security restrictions, you can ensure that users only apply the RIS disk image that is appropriate for their workstations.*

    A. True

    B. False

Optimizing Active Directory

▲ **Chapter Syllabus**

| MCSE 25.1 | Managing Objects |

| MCSE 25.2 | Optimizing Performance and Replication |

| MCSE 25.3 | Backup and Restoration |

In this chapter, we examine the installation topics covered in the *Managing, Monitoring, and Optimizing the Components of Active Directory* section of Microsoft's *Implementing and Administering a Microsoft Windows 2000 Directory Services Infrastructure* exam (70-217).

In this chapter, we expand on Active Directory management topics, such as moving, publishing, and locating objects. We describe the process of monitoring and troubleshooting Active Directory to optimize its performance. Finally, we review backup and restoration procedures.

MCSE 25.1 Managing Objects

As previously described, the Active Directory database is made up of *objects*, which include computers, users, groups, shared folders, printers and some network services. Managing Active Directory involves creating, moving, publishing, and controlling accessibility to these objects.

Moving Objects

When changes occur in your network's environment, you can expect to make corresponding changes to Active Directory. Many of these changes involve moving objects. For example, when a user leaves one department in your organization to take up residence in another, the user's move might be reflected at the OU and/or domain level and involve the movement of computer, user account, and printer objects. In general, events that occasion the movement of objects include modifications to the organization's hierarchy, the addition or subtraction of domains, the migration of users between locations, the deployment of new hardware, and the adjustment of network components for performance or maintenance reasons.

MOVING OBJECTS WITHIN A DOMAIN

You can move objects from one OU to another within a domain by selecting them in the Active Directory Users and Groups MMC and choosing the Move command from the Action menu, as shown in Figure 25.1.

When moving objects within a domain, the original permissions that were established for them are kept. When moving objects from one OU to another within a domain, the permissions set for the destination OU are applied. In short, original object permissions are preserved while inherited permissions are lost, being replaced by those of the destination OU.

MOVING OBJECTS BETWEEN DOMAINS

Moving objects between domains requires the use of the MOVETREE and NETDOM utilities, available in the \Support\Tools folder on the Windows 2000 Server installation CD-ROM. Special utilities are required because a move between domains requires a change to the object's SID.

Windows 2000 in native mode preserves the object's security settings through its SIDHistory feature, however.

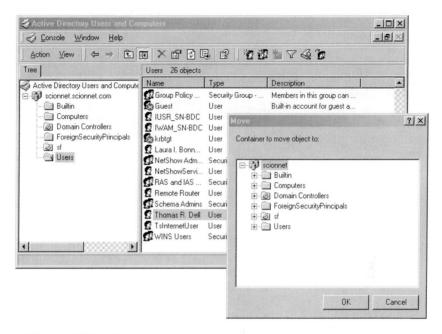

Figure 25.1 *Moving a user account object.*

USING MOVETREE • The MOVETREE command can be executed from the command line, at which time the utility will provide you with a lengthy explanation of its parameters, as shown in Figure 25.2.

Important considerations for MOVETREE include the following:

- Objects can only be moved between domains in the same forest.
- Neither local groups nor domain-level global groups that contain user accounts can be moved.
- Locked objects cannot be moved.
- System objects cannot be moved.
- Objects in special containers (such as Built-in or ForeignSecurityP-rinicpals) cannot be moved.
- Domain controller objects, or children of domain controller objects, cannot be moved.
- Members of global groups cannot be moved.
- Group policies associated with objects are not preserved. New group policies must be applied after the move.

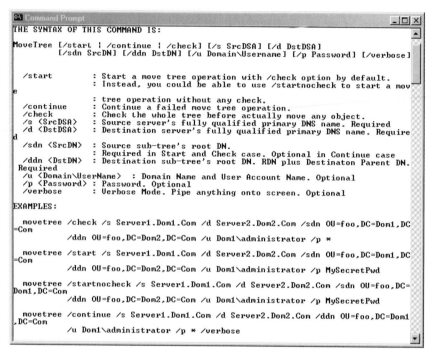

Figure 25.2 *Viewing MOVETREE command line parameters.*

USING NETDOM • The NETDOM utility can be used to move member servers and workstations between domains. It can be executed from the command line, at which time the utility will provide you its list of parameters, as shown in Figure 25.3.

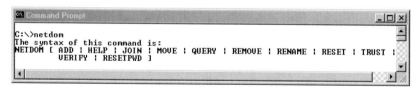

Figure 25.3 *Viewing NETDOM command line parameters.*

Publishing Resources

One of the conveniences provided by Active Directory is its searchable database, which gives users a central location in which to find such resources as users, groups, computers, shared folders, shared printers, and network services. Any resource that can be searched for is considered *published*. When published, users need not concern themselves about the actual, physical location of resources.

In many cases, objects are published as they are created. The exceptions are as follow:

- **Shared folders.** These resources can be published manually using the Active Directory Users and Computers MMC.
- **Shared printers.** Windows 2000's Add Printer Wizard publishes printers by default. They can also be shared from the Active Directory Users and Computers MMC. Non-Windows 2000 printers, such as those shared from Windows NT computers, must be published in this manner.
- **Network Services.** Binding information, which allows clients to automatically connect to services, and Configuration information, which advertises data on an application to all clients, can be configured using the Active Directory Sites and Services MMC.

Locating Objects

The Find dialog box can be used to locate objects in the Active Directory database. To use it, open the Directory folder in the My Network Places program group, right-click a domain, and select the Find command from the pop-up menu, as shown in Figure 25.4.

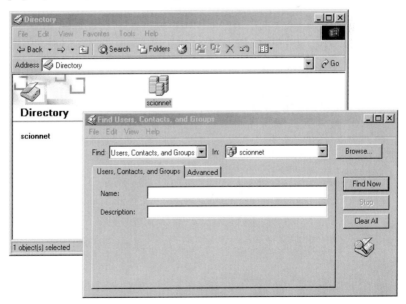

Figure 25.4 *Locating objects in the Find dialog box.*

General search categories include Users, Contacts, Groups, Computers, Printers, Shared Folders, and OUs. A Custom Search option can also be selected, through which you can define criteria by Computer, Contact, Container, Domain, Foreign Security Principal, Group, OU, Certificate Template, Printer, Remote Storage Service, RPC Service, Trusted Domain, User, or Shared Folder. For example, you might search for a user by email address, or a computer by operating system. The amount of searchable data is extensive.

You can also execute an Advanced search by entering an LDAP query.

Managing Objects Manually

You can create and modify objects manually using the Active Directory Users and Computers MMC. For example, to create a new object, simply open the New menu from the Action menu, as shown in Figure 25.5.

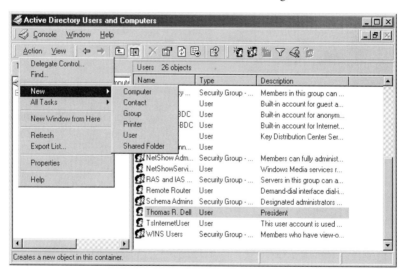

Figure 25.5 *Creating a new object.*

This opens a New Object wizard, in which you can configure the object's properties.

Managing Objects Through Scripting

You can also automate object creation through scripting. If you are familiar with Windows Scripting Host, VBScript, or JScript, it is a relatively straightforward process to create a batch file that will create objects and input the data requested by Setup Wizards.

Controlling Object Access

Users are permitted access to various Active Directory objects by virtue of the permissions granted them by Access Control Lists (ACLs). These work in much the same way as the standard NTFS permissions described in Chapter 2, "Administering Windows 2000 Professional Resources."

Active Directory permissions include the following:

- **Full Control.** Users or groups have all permissions associated with the object.
- **Read.** Users or groups can open and read the object, but not modify or apply it.
- **Write.** Users or groups can modify the object, but not read or apply it.
- **Create All Child Objects.** Users or groups can create objects that are children of the specified object.
- **Delete All Child Objects.** Users or groups can delete objects that are children of the specified object.

You can also apply special permissions as you would under NTFS.

Delegating Administrative Control

In the previous chapter, the process of delegating control over group policy was described. Similarly, you can delegate control for Active Directory objects at the OU or container level.

To delegate administrative control over an object, such as an OU, right-click its listing in the Active Directory Users and Computers MMC to open the Delegation of Control Wizard, as shown in Figure 25.6.

You are prompted to identify the users and/or groups to which you will delegate authority.

You are also prompted to identify the tasks that you wish your assistants to perform, such as resetting passwords or modifying group memberships. (You can also select a Custom Task option.)

You are further prompted to identify the scope of the work as applying to objects in the selected folder only, or to additional objects.

Finally, you are prompted to assign permissions.

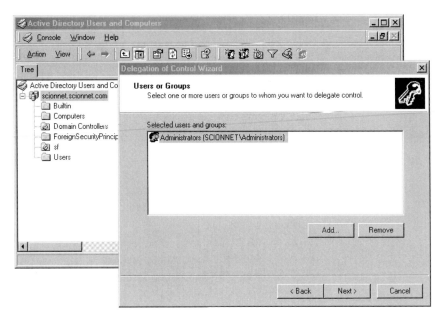

Figure 25.6 *Running the Delegation of Control Wizard.*

Study Break

Create an Object

Practice what you have learned by manually creating an object.

First, launch the Active Directory Users and Computers MMC and create a new object, such as for a user account. Enter the data requested by the New Object Setup Wizard. Finally, verify that the object has been published in the Active Directory database by running the Find command.

MCSE 25.2 ‖ Optimizing Performance and Replication

Active Directory is designed to be relatively self-sufficient. Nevertheless, there are a few monitors to be watched and tasks to be performed in making sure the service runs at its best.

Monitoring and Optimizing Performance

As with the other services described in this book, the primary tools useful in evaluating the performance of Active Directory are Performance Monitor and Event Viewer.

USING EVENT VIEWER

In addition Event Viewer's Application, System, and Security logs, domain controllers maintain additional logging services for domain controllers, as shown in Figure 25.7.

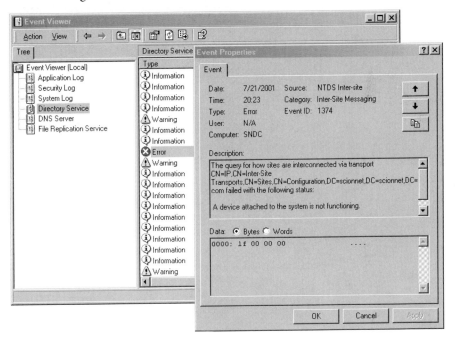

Figure 25.7 *Domain controller event logs.*

The Directory Service log records problems related to Active Directory in general. The DNS Server log reports problems associated with DNS, which is an integral part of Active Directory. Finally, the File Replication Service log provides a history of domain controller to domain controller database transfers.

Using Performance Monitor

In addition to the Performance Monitor counters previously described in this book, the System Monitor snap-in contains several that relate to Active Directory directly, such as the NTDS object shown in Figure 25.8.

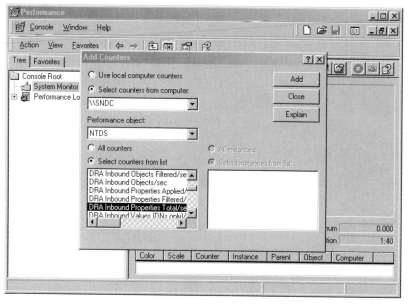

Figure 25.8 *Adding NTDS performance counters.*

Of particular usefulness are the services of DRA Inbound and DRA Outbound counters. Also useful are client session counters labeled DS, LDAP, NTLM, and XDS. Important counters related to Active Directory are listed in Table 25.1.

Table 18.1 *Useful Active Directory Counters*

Counter	Description
DRA Inbound Bytes Compressed (Between Sites, After Compression)/Sec	Compressed size of compressed replication data received per second.
DRA Inbound Bytes Compressed (Between Sites, Before Compression)/Sec	Original size of compressed replication data received per second.
DRA Inbound Bytes Not Compressed (Within Site)/Sec	Amount of data received through inbound replication that was not compressed at the source, per second.

Table 18.1 *Useful Active Directory Counters (continued)*

DRA Inbound Bytes Total/Sec	Amount of data received through replication, per second. (Sum of uncompressed bytes and compressed bytes.)
DRA Inbound Full Sync Objects Remaining	Objects remaining until full synchronization completed.
DRA Inbound Objects/Sec	Objects received from replication partners through inbound replication, per second.
DRA Inbound Objects Applied/Sec	Rate at which replication updates are received from replication partners and applied by the local directory service.
DRA Inbound Objects Filtered/Sec	Objects received from inbound replication partners that contained no updates to be applied, per second.
DRA Inbound Object Updates Remaining in Packet	Object updates received in the current directory replication update packet that have not yet been applied.
DRA Inbound Properties Applied/Sec	Properties that are applied through inbound replication through reconciliation logic.
DRA Inbound Properties Filtered/Sec	Property changes that are already known when received during replication.
DRA Inbound Properties Total/Sec	Total object properties received from inbound replication partners, per second.
DRA Inbound Values (DNs Only)/Sec	Object property values received from inbound replication partners that are DNs, per second.
DRA Inbound Values Total/Sec	Total object property values received from inbound replication partners, per second.
DRA Outbound Bytes Compressed (Between Sites, After Compression)/Sec	Compressed size of outbound compressed replication data from DSAs in other sites.
DRA Outbound Bytes Compressed (Between Sites, Before Compression)/Sec	Original size of outbound compressed replication data from DSAs in other sites.
DRA Outbound Bytes Not Compressed (Within Site)/Sec	Amount of data replicated but not compressed from DSAs in the same site.
DRA Outbound Bytes Total/Sec	Total bytes replicated per second. (Sum of uncompressed bytes and compressed bytes.)
DRA Outbound Objects/Sec	Objects replicated per second.
DRA Outbound Objects Filtered/Sec	Objects acknowledged by outbound replication, requiring no updates.
DRA Outbound Properties/Sec	Properties replicated per second.

Table 18.1 *Useful Active Directory Counters (continued)*

DRA Outbound Values (DNs Only)/Sec	Object property values containing DNs and sent to outbound replication partners.
DRA Outbound Values Total/Sec	Object property values sent to outbound replication partners, per second.
DRA Pending Replication Synchronizations	Directory synchronizations queued for the server but not yet processed.
DRA Sync Requests Made	Synchronization requests made to replication partners.
DS Directory Reads/Sec	Directory reads per second.
DS Directory Writes/Sec	Directory writes per second.
DS Security Descriptor Suboperations/Sec	Security Descriptor Propagation suboperations per second.
DS Security Descriptor Propagations Events	Security Descriptor Propagation events queued but not yet processed.
DS Threads in Use	Current threads in use by the directory services.
Kerberos Authentications/Sec	Number of times that clients use a ticket to the domain controller to authenticate the domain controller, per second.
LDAP Bind Time	Time required for last successful LDAP binding (in milliseconds).
LDAP Client Sessions	Connected LDAP client sessions.
LDAP Searches/Sec	Search operations performed by LDAP clients, per second.
LDAP Successful Binds/Sec	Successful LDAP binds, per second.
NTLM Authentications	NT LAN Manager (NTLM) authentications, per second.
XDS Client Sessions	Extended Directory Service (XDS) client sessions. (Connections from Windows NT services and the Windows NT Administrator program.)

Troubleshooting Performance

One of the most important components to examine when troubleshooting Active Directory is DNS. Always verify that the DNS servers are available and running properly, as was described in Chapter 15, "Administering Domain Name Services."

Microsoft makes the following advanced Active Directory administration tools available in the \Support\Tools folder on the Windows 2000 Server installation CD-ROM:

- **ACLDIAG.** Diagnoses problems with Active Directory object permission sets.
- **DSACLS.** Lets you view and change security permissions on Active Directory objects.
- **DSASTAT.** Detects differences in domain controller naming contexts.
- **LDP.** Lets you perform LDAP operations.
- **NLTEST.** Forces trust synchronization. Can also force domain controller shutdown.
- **REPADMIN.** Diagnoses Replication problems.
- **REPLMON.** Monitors replication and can force synchronization between domain controllers.
- **SDCHECK.** Lets you view the ACLs for Active Directory objects.

Monitoring, Optimizing, and Troubleshooting Replication

As with general Active Directory traffic, you can monitor replication in particular using the Performance Monitor tool. Among the counters to watch are those that measure inbound and outbound replication traffic (see Table 25.1).

Event Viewer dedicates a special log to Active Directory, the Directory Services log. Among messages useful in monitoring and troubleshooting are the following:

- **ID 700/701.** The directory is being defragmented (every 12 hours).
- **ID 1009/1013.** KCC is updating the replication topology.
- **ID 1265.** Replication to a replication partner failed.
- **ID 1404.** Server is performing in the inter-site topology generator role.

Microsoft also makes available the Replication Monitor (REPLMON) and Replication Administration (REPADMIN) tools. Among the tasks that can be performed using the Replication Monitor MMC are checking the replication topology as well as showing domain controllers, replication topologies, GPOs' status, current performance data, GC servers, bridgehead servers, trust relationships, and object meta-data attributes. You can also use the tool to search for replication errors among domain controllers, and to manually force replication between replication partners.

Study Break

Review Event Viewer

Practice what you have learned by reviewing the messages displayed in Event Viewer.

Pay particular attention to the Directory Service log, DNS Server log, and File Replication Service log.

MCSE 25.3   Backup and Restoration

The importance of regularly backing up your domain controllers cannot be over-emphasized. The importance of backing up Active Directory is even greater, for if its objects become unavailable, users lose access to vital network resources such as shared folders and printers, if they are able to log on at all!

In this section, we examine Active Directory-specific requirements for backup and recovery. General backup and recovery issues, as well as the use of the Backup Wizard, were described in Chapter 4, "Optimizing Windows 2000 Professional," and Chapter 11, "Optimizing Window 2000 Server."

Backing Up Active Directory

To back up Active Directory components using the Backup Wizard, select the Only back up the System State radio button in the What to Back Up screen, as shown in Figure 25.9.

For more information on other wizard settings, review Chapter 4 and Chapter 11.

Restoring Active Directory

Before attempting to restore Active Directory data, make sure that you have access to all of the locations to which files must be restored and that the Remote Storage Manager service is running (if you are restoring from a media pool). Then determine whether or not you need to perform an authoritative restore.

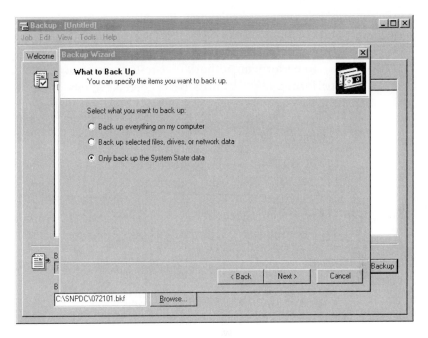

Figure 25.9 *Choosing to back up system data.*

NONAUTHORITATIVE RESTORATIONS

When Active Directory data changes on a domain controller, it receives an update sequence number that is higher than that of the data on other domain controllers. This informs other domain controllers that replication is needed to bring their databases up to date.

When you perform a *nonauthoritative* restore, the system data recovered maintains the same update sequence number it had when backed up. Since its older update sequence number is likely to be lower than that of surrounding domain controllers, the restored domain controller uses replication to update its data after restoration.

For information on restoring a system data backup, review Chapter 4 and Chapter 11.

AUTHORITATIVE RESTORATIONS

In some circumstances, it might not be wise to permit a nonauthoritative restore. If, for example, a virus or malicious hacker has damaged the Active Directory data that has been replicated throughout the network, there would be little purpose in restoring clean data only to have it overwritten by corrupt data through replication. In this instance, you might wish to perform an *authoritative restore*, giving the older recovered data a higher update sequence number than the current corrupted data and effectively taking your network back in time.

To perform an authoritative restoration, first follow the steps necessary to perform a non-authoritative restore. Next, reboot the server and perform the following steps after pressing the F8 key during bootup:

1. Choose the Directory Services Restore Mode command in the Windows 2000 Advanced Startup Options menu.
2. Log on to the server as Administrator.
3. Click OK in the Safe Mode dialog box.
4. Open the Command Prompt and enter the command "ntdsutil."
5. Type "authoritative restore" at the NTDSUTIL prompt.
6. Select the RESTORE DATABASE option to authoritatively restore the entire database.
7. Type "quit" to exit Authoritative Restore Mode and "quit" again to exit NTDSUTIL.
8. Reboot the server in Normal Mode.

Recovering from System Failures

The two main methods for recovering Active Directory from a system failure is backup restoration, as just described, and replication, assuming that the other domain controllers on the network have uncorrupted data. For information on recovering from system failures, see Chapter 4 and Chapter 11.

The process of recovering from system failures is complicated somewhat when the affected domain controller is serving in an operations master role.

SEIZING OPERATIONS MASTER ROLES

Should a domain controller that is in an operations master role go offline due to a system failure that cannot be repaired within a reasonable amount of time, it might be necessary to perform a forceful transfer of the operations master role, or *seize* the role.

This is not a task that should be performed lightly. For example, when you seize the roles of RID, schema, or domain-naming operations master, the servers that formerly performed the role should not be brought online again unless you have reformatted the hard drive and reinstalled the operating system.

Operations master roles can be seized using the NTDSUTIL tool.

Important considerations pertaining to each role include the following:

- **Domain-Naming Operations Master.** This domain controller controls the addition and removal of domains in a forest. Its loss has no immediate impact on network operations. It will not be missed until an administer attempts to add or remove domains. If you seize it, it cannot be restored to the domain controller that originally hosted it.
- **Infrastructure Operations Master.** This domain controller controls group renaming and tracks membership changes. There is no immediate impact on network operations when it goes offline. It will not be missed until an administer attempts to move or rename user and group accounts. If you decide to move this operations master, make sure that the domain controller seizing it is, or has a good connection to, the GC server.
- **PDC Emulator Operations Master.** This domain controller controls password changes and serves as PDC for Windows NT-based BDCs. Its loss will be immediately noticed by non-Windows 2000 computers, and so it should seized immediately. Fortunately, its role can be reassigned to the original domain controller when it is brought back online.
- **RID Operations Master.** This domain controller controls SID assignments. Its loss will only be noticed when administrators attempt to add or delete Active Directory objects.
- **Schema Operations Master.** This domain controller controls updates and modifications to schema data. Its short-term loss is not critical. If you seize it, however, it cannot be restored to the domain controller that originally hosted it.

Study Break

Back Up Active Directory

Practice what you have learned by backing up Active Directory.

To back up Active Directory components, select the Only back up the System State radio button in the Backup Wizard's What to Back Up screen. It is also wise to perform a nonauthoritative restoration thereafter to ensure that you know what to expect in an emergency.

■ Summary

In this chapter, we looked at additional Active Directory management topics, including monitoring and troubleshooting Active Directory to optimize its performance, and backing up and restoring system data

Managing Objects

When changes occur in your network's environment, you can expect to make corresponding changes to Active Directory. The Active Directory database is made up of objects that include computers, users, groups, shared folders, printers and some network services. Managing Active Directory involves creating, moving, publishing, and controlling accessibility to these objects. Tools useful in performing such tasks include the Active Directory Users and Computers MMC, MOVETREE, and NETDOM.

Optimizing Performance and Replication

Active Directory is designed to be relatively self-sufficient. Nevertheless, there are a few monitors to be watched and tasks to be performed in making sure the service runs at its best, including Event Viewer and Performance Monitor. Others include ACLDIAG, DSACLS, DSASTAT, LDP, NLTEST, REPADMIN, REPLMON, and SDCHECK.

Backup and Restoration

The importance of regularly backing up your domain controllers using the Backup Wizard cannot be over-emphasized. The importance of backing up Active Directory is even greater, for if its objects become unavailable, users will lose access to vital network resources such as shared folders and printers. In addition, should a domain controller that is in an operations master role go offline due to a system failure that cannot be repaired within a reasonable amount of time, it might be necessary to seize the role.

▲ CHAPTER REVIEW QUESTIONS

Here are a few questions relating to the material covered in the *Managing, Monitoring, and Optimizing the Components of Active Directory* section of Microsoft's *Implementing and Administering a Microsoft Windows 2000 Directory Services Infrastructure* exam (70-217).

1. *Which of the following would be considered Active Directory objects? Select all that apply:*
   A. Replication partner
   B. User account
   C. Nonshared printer
   D. Folder

2. *Objects can only be moved within a domain.*
   A. True
   B. False

3. *All objects must be published manually.*
   A. True
   B. False

4. *It is possible to locate objects by such attributes as email address or operating system using the Find dialog box.*
   A. True
   B. False

5. *Which of the following are scripting methods supported by Windows 2000 for use in automating object creation? Select all that apply:*
   A. Java
   B. JScript
   C. VBScript
   D. Windows Scripting Host

6. *Active Directory objects rely on NTFS ACLs.*
   A. True
   B. False

7. *In delegating administrative control over an object, you are limited to delegating only the tasks presented by the Delegation of Control Wizard.*
   A. True
   B. False

8. *Which of the following Event Viewer logs relate most directly to Active Directory?*

    A. Security log

    B. DNS Server log

    C. File Replication Service log

    D. System log

9. *Backing up Active Directory is especially important because it can affect the ability of users to access network resources.*

    A. True

    B. False

10. *During a nonauthoritative restoration, the update sequence number is reset.*

    A. True

    B. False

11. *In the event of a system failure, Active Directory data can only be recovered from backups.*

    A. True

    B. False

12. *Which of the following operations master roles may be restored on a domain controller from which they were previously seized? Select all that apply.*

    A. Domain-naming

    B. PDC Emulator

    C. Infrastructure

    D. Schema

Securing Active Directory

▲ **Chapter Syllabus**

| MCSE 26.1 | Working with Security Policy |

In this chapter, we examine the installation topics covered in the *Configuring, Managing, Monitoring, and Troubleshooting Security in a Directory Services Infrastructure* section of Microsoft's *Implementing and Administering a Microsoft Windows 2000 Directory Services Infrastructure* exam (70-217).

In this chapter, you expand on your knowledge of local security to extend it to networked computers through Active Directory. This material was first addressed in Chapter 7, "Securing Windows 2000 Professional," and Chapter 14, "Securing Windows 2000 Server."

MCSE 26.1   Working with Security Policy

In previous chapters, the process of establishing local security policy was described, including audit policy and user policy. While powerful, these policies are restricted to the local computer only. To extend such policies network-wide, you must import them into a Group Policy Object (GPO).

Using Group Policy

Security policies can be applied at the local, site, domain, or OU level through the use of group policies established with the Active Directory Group Policy MMC. The following are components of group policy:

- **Group Policy Object (GPO).** Containing a group policy's configuration settings, GPOs can be applied to sites, domains, and OUs.
- **Group Policy Container (GPC).** This object contains GPOs and properties.
- **Group Policy Templates (GPT).** Stored in the SYSVOL folder, these documents store frequently changing group policy information.

Areas in which security can be adjusted through group policy are as follows:

- **Account Policy.** Security settings include Password Policy, Account Lockout Policy, and Kerberos Policy.
- **Local Policy.** Security settings, which affect the local computer only, include Audit Policy, User Rights Assignment, and Security Options.
- **Event Log.** Specifies event log settings for user permissions and file size.
- **Restricted Groups.** Specifies settings for built-in user groups (Power Users, Backup Operators, Domain Admins, and so on).
- **System Services.** Specifies startup types and user permissions.
- **Registry.** Specifies user rights for Registry keys.
- **File System.** Security settings for files and folders.
- **Public Key Policies.** Security settings for certificate authorities and EFS recovery agents.
- **IP Security Policies.** Security settings for IPSec.

Such security policies can be used to enforce uniform security throughout an organization. When set at the root level of the domain, these policies become active on all domain controllers and member servers on the network. Only one account policy can be defined.

To apply security settings through Active Directory, perform the following steps:

1. Launch the Active Directory Users and Computers MMC.
2. Select the Advanced Features command from the View menu.
3. Right-click the domain or OU in which you will create a GPO, and choose the Properties command to open the Properties dialog box.
4. Switch to the Group Policy tab and click the New button to create a GPO. Rename the GPO. Close the Properties dialog box.
5. Right-click the domain or OU in which the GPO was created, and choose the Properties command to open the Properties dialog box.
6. Switch to the Group Policy tab, select the newly created GPO, and click the Edit button to open the Group Policy MMC.
7. In the Group Policy MMC, navigate to the User Rights Assignment item under in the Local Policies subfolder of the Security Settings subfolder under the Windows Settings subfolder under the Computer Configuration branch, as shown in Figure 26.1.

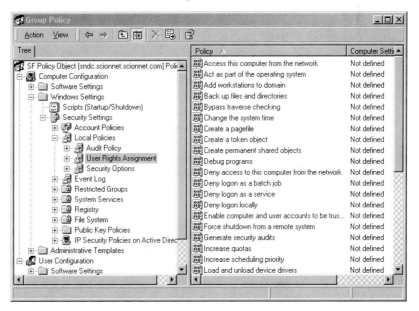

Figure 26.1 *Configuring user rights assignments.*

8. Double-click a policy to open the Security Policy Setting dialog box, in which you can define its use, as shown in Figure 26.2.
9. Enable the Define these policy settings checkbox.
10. Click the Add button to open the Select Users or Groups dialog box, in which you can identify the accounts to which the policy will be applied.
11. Close all windows when finished.

Figure 26.2 *Enabling policy settings.*

Creating and Analyzing Security Configurations

As described in Chapter 7, the Security and Configuration Analysis MMC lets you compare the security settings of Windows 2000 computers with those recommended by Microsoft. Where differences are found, you may choose to alter the security settings. Ordinarily, you might perform this task on each computer individually. A timesaving alternative, however, is to use the Security Templates MMC to apply modified security templates to a GPO.

Working with Audit Policy

As described in Chapter 7, the audit policy defines the types of user actions that will be monitored and recorded to log files, such as logons and logoffs or Active Directory object modifications. Audited events are recorded in the Event Viewer's Security log.

Auditing is disabled by default, and can only be enabled by Administrators and on NFTS partitions. To apply audit policy, you must first establish the audit settings and then enable auditing on the target computers. This can be done via the Audit Policy item under the Computer Configuration branch in the Active Directory Users and Computers MMC.

By default, security policies are not put into effect for eight hours. You can override this behavior by restarting the computers or by using the following command at the command prompt:

```
secedit /refreshpolicy machine_policy
```

Monitoring Security Events

Among the questions you seek to answer in auditing network resource access are the following:

- **Logon.** Who is attempting to log on to the resource?
- **Access.** Who is attempting read or modify data stored on the resource?
- **Administer.** Who is has user rights to administer resources, and are they using these right responsibly?

Whether you audit for successes or failures will depend on what you are looking for. If someone keeps deleting an important file, for example, you should enable Success auditing to see who it is the next time it happens. If you know your permissions are secure but you suspect someone of malicious intent, you should enable Failure auditing to see who might be probing your security.

Audited events appear the in Event Viewer Security log, which only Administrators can view.

Study Break

Implement OU Security Policy

Practice what you have learned by implementing a simple security policy at the OU level.

Create a special GPO for this purpose. In addition, implement audit policy to see how your security settings are being used.

■ Summary

In this chapter, we reviewed the process of applying security policies with an emphasis on Active Directory implementations.

Working with Security Policy

To extend security policies network-wide, you must import them into a GPO. Security policies can be applied at the local, site, domain, or OU level through the use of group policies established with the Active Directory Group Policy MMC. The Security and Configuration Analysis MMC lets you compare the security settings of Windows 2000 computers with those recommended by Microsoft. You may perform this task on multiple computers by using the Security Templates MMC to apply modified security templates to a GPO. Audit policy defines the types of user actions that will be monitored and recorded to log files, such as logons and logoffs or Active Directory object modifications. Audited events are recorded in the Event Viewer's Security log.

▲ CHAPTER REVIEW QUESTIONS

Here are a few questions relating to the material covered in the *Configuring, Managing, Monitoring, and Troubleshooting Security in a Directory Services Infrastructure* section of Microsoft's *Implementing and Administering a Microsoft Windows 2000 Directory Services Infrastructure* exam (70-217).

1. *Which of the following are levels at which security policies can be applied through Active Directory? Select all that apply:*

   A. local computer

   B. forest

   C. domain

   D. OU

2. *The Security and Configuration Analysis MMC is used to analyze audit logs.*

   A. True

   B. False

3. *Changes made to object auditing are not applied for several hours.*

   A. True

   B. False

4. *One danger of audit policy is that its results can be seen by all in the Event Viewer Security log.*

   A. True

   B. False

APPENDIX: CHAPTER REVIEW ANSWERS

▲ Chapter 1: Installing Windows 2000 Professional

1. A, B, C, D. You can also run the Setup program with the /checkupgrade-only switch.

2. B, C. You can launch the initial phase of the installation from four boot floppy disks, but thereafter the setup files must be present from the CD-ROM or network share.

3. B. However, it is easy to convert a FAT drive to NTFS.

4. B, C. Windows 95/98 can both be updated directly. Windows NT 3.5 can be upgraded if you first upgrade to Windows NT 3.51 or NT 4.0. Windows Me is too new to have been included in the Windows 2000 upgrade path.

5. B. Setup (WINNT32.EXE) can also be launched from the command line.

6. B. Computer names must be unique from any other computer, domain, or workgroup name on the network.

7. D. Setup makes the computer a member of its own workgroup. A computer can only join a domain if it has a predefined computer account.

8. D. Unattended Answer Files (UAFs) are used to script installations. RIPrep and Sysprep are used in disk duplication. Update.EXE is used to install Services Packs.

9. A, B, C. The Hardware Abstraction Layer (HAL) must be similar between the master and clone computers. It has nothing to do with network services, however.

10. B, C, D. RIS is designed to facilitate installation from a Windows 2000 Server-based distribution volume.

11. A, D. The System Preparation tool (Sysprep) has no distribution method of its own, nor can it be used with RIS. It is designed for use with third-party tools.

12. A, C, D. The SYSDIFF.EXE utility can be used in scripted installations.

13. A, C. Setup Manager creates an Unattended Answer File (UAF) and a distribution folder from which to install Windows 2000.

14. A. "/uaf" and "/sysman" are invalid. "/udf" is used in scripted installations that include an Unattended Database File (UDF), but is not required.

15. B. You can perform a clean installation and dual-boot between the older and newer operating systems.

16. B. Update packs might be available from each application's vendor. Some applications might remain incompatible and require replacement.

17. B. While this is preferable, you can also install update packs during the installation process.

18. B. Update.exe is used to install Service Packs, "/hcl" is invalid, "winver" ius used to determine the installed version of Windows 2000.

19. A, B, C, D. These are known to be incompatible.

20. B. Service Packs can be included in the installation process through slip-streaming.

21. A, B, C. Service Packs are not installed automatically, but you can schedule when UPDATE.EXE is run.

22. B. You can always choose a workgroup, then attempt to join a domain another time.

23. B, C. "unattend.txt" is the default UAF. "winsetup.log" is invalid.

▲ Chapter 2: Administering Windows 2000 Professional Resources

1. A. The only difference between moving and copying files between partitions is that the original files are then deleted on the original partition.

2. B, C. Although most other system files can.

3. B. It is enabled using the COMPACT.EXE utility.

4. A, C, D. Change Permissions is a special permission granted to users with Full Control permissions.

5. B. Traverse Folder is a special permission. Read & Execute and Modify are common to both files and folders.

6. B. Inheritance is the default.

7. B. Windows 2000 applies to whichever is most restrictive.

8. A. Although IIS must be installed to enable access over HTTP.

9. A, C, D. The Creator/Owner group is applied to printer access.

10. B. You need only disable sharing in the Properties dialog box.

11. A, B, D. The Deny status overrides access through the affected permission.

12. B. NTFS permissions are separate from share permissions.

13. C. Client for NetWare Services (CSNW) does not apply. HTTP is generally used for Web access, not FTP. Peer Web Services were available under Windows NT Workstation 4.0, but are now rolled into IIS 5.0.

14. B. If you enable Directory Browsing, users see the contents of the folder from Internet Explorer.

15. A. Windows 2000 Professional can therefore often install printer drivers automatically.

16. B. You must know the printer's URL, such as its domain name or IP address.

17. B. You can disable this behavior through Properties or by disabling the Print Spooler service.

18. A, C, D. Modify is an NTFS permission.

19. A. If they affect the printer's access to the spooler folder.

20. B. Internet printers must support TCP/IP.

21. B. Internet printers are configured as network printers.

22. A. Although LPT1 is the default.

23. B. Local printers become network printers through sharing.

24. A, B, C, D. Although Windows 2000 is designed to upgrade to, and work with, NTFS 5.0.

25. B. You must use the CONVERT.EXE utility.

26. B. This involves reformatting and erasing all data on that hard disk.

27. A, D. FAT is best on drives of less than 2 GBs. FAT does not provide security, nor built-in compression. FAT can dual-boot with Windows 95.

28. B. The MMC's Storage snap-in handles multiple file systems.

▲ Chapter 3: Managing Windows 2000 Professional Devices

1. A. It has been approved by the Windows Hardware Quality Labs.

2. B, C. CD-ROMs are not formatted using the UNIX File System (UFS) or New Technology File System (NTFS).

3. B. You may access device properties through the Device Manager snap-in to the MMC.

4. B. You cannot format CD-ROMs without additional third-party software.

5. A, B, C, D. Volume sets are called spanned volumes on dynamic disks.

6. B. Dynamic volumes are new, and only supported under Windows 2000.

7. A, B, C, D. In addition, you cannot extend system or boot volumes.

8. B. Removable media has it own snap-in under the Storage branch of the MMC.

9. A, B, C, D. Firewire and IEEE 1394 are the same.

10. B. Multiple display support permits Windows 2000 to share display space with as many as nine monitors.

11. B, C. The Test button and Boot Loader option were used under Windows NT 4.0.

12. A. Even so, adapters that support primary monitors might not support secondary monitors.

13. B. The POST should appear on the primary display.

14. A. This might be an issue with laptops.

15. B, D. Accelerated Graphics Port (AGP) pertains to displays. Compatible BIOS is required to enable power management support.

16. B. ACPI is the newer of the two standards, a superset of the APM standard.

17. B. Windows 2000 is fully compliant with ACPI. Power Schemes are used to group various power management settings for user convenience.

18. B. Card services refer to Windows 2000 support for any PCMCIA-based devices.

19. B. You should run the Add/Remove Hardware Wizard first to inform Windows 2000 that the device will be removed.

20. A, B, C, D. All are examples, as are microphones, speakers, video cameras, and card readers.

21. B. Most I/O devices can be configured via the Device Manager snap-in to the MMC.

22. A. This permits you to troubleshoot all I/O devices at a glance.

23. A. The Control Panel can be used to configure both incoming and outgoing data settings.

24. A. Under the Hardware tab.

25. B. There is no I/O Hardware Control Panel application. There is a Phone and Modem Options Control Panel application.

26. A. If the modem and software are TAPI-compliant.

27. A. This includes IR and RF devices.

28. B. Direct line of sight between devices is essential.

29. B. All or true. Devices should also maintain line of sight.

30. A, D. Both USB and Firewire are based on wired interfaces.

31. D. Each device can be as much as five meters from the hub.

32. B. USB buses seldom require configuration.

33. A. Right-click to bring up the Properties dialog box and select the Driver tab.

34. B. The Add/Remove Hardware Wizard and Upgrade Device Driver Wizard are very similar.

35. B. Multiprocessing relies on preemptive multitasking.

36. A. Although other versions of Windows 2000 support more.

37. A. Physical topologies supported include Ethernet, Token Ring, FDDI, and ATM.

38. B. The Network Control Panel, present under Windows NT 4.0, was dropped from Windows 2000 professional.

▲ Chapter 4: Optimizing Windows 2000 Professional Devices

1. B. Thanks to digital signatures, you can easily check for corrupted system files using the System File Checker tool.

2. A, C, D. You can block the installation of an unsigned driver, but you cannot disable it once installed using as a configuration option.

3. B. As an option, you may specify that tasks only be run at idle times, after a given number of minutes.

4. A, B, C. Tasks cannot be scheduled at shutdown, but they can be scheduled at startup and logon.

5. A, B, C, D. Also Name, Type, and Access.

6. B. You must configure offline access through a shared folder's Properties dialog box.

7. A, B, D. Performance optimization is not meant to apply to power management.

8. B. Paged memory is Virtual Memory created from hard disk space. Disk access is slower than RAM access.

9. B. This is a sign that high levels of paging are occurring.

10. B. It is likely to be a bottleneck when this counter, or the Percent Processor Time counter, exceeds 75 percent.

11. A. Two processors may be employed.

12. B. PhysicalDisk counters are, LogicalDisk counters are not.

13. A. This is a PhysicalDisk counter.

14. B. Even unused protocols contribute to a certain amount of bandwidth overhead.

15. B. Start at the Physical layer and work up to the Application layer.

16. D. 0 through 15 are assigned to user applications, usually eight by default.

17. B. You can both alter priorities and end processes with Task Manager.

18. A. An example might be the video card on a laptop's docking station, which would be unavailable when the laptop is at a different location.

19. A. Identical profiles serve no purpose, and it slows the startup process because you have to select a profile to load.

20. B, C, D. The File Signature Verification tool might identify problems, but will not help you recover from them.

21. B. Unless you are a member of the Administrators or Backup Operators groups.

22. B. Normal jobs take the longest to create, but Incremental backups take the longest to restore.

23. B. Although this still has a bearing on what you may do once logged on.

24. B. You may choose to boot up with networking support in Safe Mode.

25. B. Only Administrators may run Recovery Console, and even they may only copy file to the hard drive.

26. A. If the Registry was first backed up using the Backup utility.

▲ Chapter 5: Configuring Windows 2000 Professional Environments

1. B. User Profiles are created in the Documents & Settings folder at the root level of the system drive.

2. A, C, D. Only administrators can create roaming user profiles, which are server-based.

3. B. Computers are numerically based and cannot interpret human language conventions without number to character mappings.

4. A, C. RTL refers to a programmer's API, ISO refers to a standards-forming organization rather than a standard itself.

5. A, B, C, D. Even the non-Roman Chinese language is included.

6. B. RTL is not a user-configurable interface option. It is an API. You should ensure that software you buy or deploy makes use of this feature.

7. A. Windows 2000 can be purchased in 24 localized versions, and one "MultiLanguage" version that contains all 24 languages.

8. B. Language groups are added through the Regional Options Control panel application.

9. A, B, C, D. All are part of the Western Europe and United States language group.

10. A. New Locales become available with new languages.

11. B. Once configured through the Regional Options Control Panel application, you can easily toggle between input methods from the Taskbar.

12. B. Installer packages can often be scripted to run silently, without user interaction.

13. B, C, D. Installer packages can be scripted so that they do not overwrite system or other existing files, which could cause problems for software already present on the system.

14. B. Local computer group policy applies to all users.

15. B. You make it less accessible. Users may still browse the computer to find a utility you wish to hide, for example, or access features from the Command Line.

16. A. You can enable Fax receiving through the Fax Service Management Console.

17. A. The Initialization/Termination log is accessible through the Fax Service Management Console.

18. A, B, C. The On-Screen Keyboard is aimed at serving the mobility impaired.

19. A. As well as commands and dialog box messages.

▲ Chapter 6: Networking Windows 2000 Professional

1. A. "0" refers to the network and "255" to the broadcast address.

2. A, C, D. Other options take into account situations where secure communications cannot be achieved.

3. B. Although it can only support outgoing connections.

4. B, D. While PPP supports authentication encryption, it does not support data encryption. EAP is used in authentication encryption and might or might not be implemented in a VPN.

5. A. L2TP supports such protocols as x.25, Frame Relay, and ATM, while PPTP is limited to IP.

6. A. Through dialup, serial, or VPN clients.

7. B. It is limited to 10. Windows 2000 Server is relatively unlimited.

8. B. The Internet Connection Wizard allows you to locate and sign-up with a local ISP through the Microsoft Internet Referral Service.

9. A. Although almost all ISPs support PPP over the more limited SLIP.

10. B. ICS cannot be used on networks with preestablished addressing or services such as DHCP and DNS.

11. B. Its use is optional.

12. B. It can work with NetBEUI, TCP/IP, or IPX/SPX-compatible protocols.

13. A, B, C, D. All except C let you browse the network. UNC command work best when you know the names of the resources for which you are seeking.

▲ Chapter 7: Securing Windows 2000 Professional

1. A. If one is enabled, the other cannot be enabled.

2. A. Recovery Agents are Windows 2000's only fail-safe.

3. B. Local policy settings are the weakest in the Windows 2000 security model.

4. A, C, D. Logon authentication is vital to Windows 2000 security.

5. B. Since only user accounts can be used to log on, only user accounts require passwords.

6. B. Audited events are recorded in the Security Log, accessible through the Event Viewer application.

7. A, B, C, D. You can also determine who is trying to take ownership of the file.

8. A, D. The other options are disabled when the User must change password at next logon is enabled.

9. B. Which can cause logon problems for some users.

10. B. Account policies determine the circumstances under which users are permitted to log on.

11. A. Also make sure users do not just reuse their previous passwords.

12. B. By definition, a user is a step above a guest because users may log on locally.

13. A. The other settings are recommended, but not required. They can also be added later.

14. A. In general, you need to assign permissions explicitly, but user rights are assigned implicitly.

15. B. Ownership can only be taken, never granted. Taking ownership is discretionary.

16. B. NTFS permissions are embodied in the ACL attribute and are stored with a directory or file. User rights are stored with user account information in the Registry.

17. B. The workstation's security database only comes into play when working locally.

18. A. Security settings include group membership information and user rights.

19. B. Kerberos protocol is Windows 2000's default authentication and security protocol.

20. A. Users changes will then not be saved.

21. B. You must create an MMC based on the Security Configuration and Analysis snap-in by typing "mmc" at the command line to open an empty console and adding the snap-in.

22. A. Settings with icon are not specified in the template.

▲ Chapter 8: Installing Windows 2000 Server

1. A. Windows NT Server 3.5 must be upgraded to version 3.51 or 4.0 before it can be upgraded. Windows NT Enterprise Server 4.0 can only be upgraded to Windows 2000 Advanced Server or Windows 2000 Datacenter Server.

2. B. Because clients are likely to log on to multiple servers in an enterprise environment, it makes more sense to go with per seat licensing. That way, you do not need to keep track of the number of clients accessing your server at a given time.

3. A, B, C. RIS can only be used to install Windows 2000 Professional.

4. A, B, C, D. All can be specified in an UAF, although such parameters as user name and computer name can also be specified in an UDF.

5. B. Windows 9x is a 32-bit operating system, so you should use WINNT32.EXE.

6. C, D. SysPrep and RIS both work through disk duplication.

7. C, D. Disk duplication methods cannot be used for upgrades.

8. A. Thereafter, you can upgrade other servers in whatever order you wish.

9. B. Member servers are not made part of Active Directory unless promoted to domain controllers.

10. B. Although this was an issue under Windows NT.

11. A. This is a good idea, although it requires extra disk space.

12. A. These can be created from the installation CD-ROM.

13. A. The netsetup.log file documents the domain or workgroup logon process.

▲ Chapter 9: Administering Windows 2000 Server Resource Access

1. B. Such services as DNS server, DHCP server, and WINS server must be installed explicitly.

2. A, C, D. DFS is limited to Windows clients.

3. B. A printer is software that controls a print device.

4. B, C. There is also a Manage Documents permission.

5. A. Only NTFS supports local file and folder security.

6. A. With Service Pack 3 or later.

7. B. DFS information resides in the standalone server's Registry alone.

8. A. In addition, DFS information is synchronized on multiple servers through Active Directory.

9. D. Only those operating systems that can participate in Active Directory are supported.

10. B. Standard permissions are composed of various special permissions.

11. A. You can assign file permissions separately.

12. A. The are applied to folders and subfolders.

13. B. Windows 2000 applies the most restrictive.

14. B. Web folders use their own Read and Write permissions, but are still secondary to NTFS permissions.

15. A. You can apply Windows authentication instead, however.

16. B. IIS is limited to the bandwidth level you set.

17. A. A failure in any step results in failure for the connection.

▲ Chapter 10: Managing Windows 2000 Server Devices

1. B. You may install other device drivers, but you should check with their manufacturers to ensure that they are compatible with Windows 2000 Server.

2. C, D. Plug-and-Play devices are installed automatically, and non-Plug-and-Play devices are installed via the Add/Remove Hardware Wizard.

3. B. If a driver a driver has a critical update that has not yet undergone testing by the WHQL, you might wish to bypass its approved status.

4. A, B, D. There is no Administrator Only option, although only administrators can reduce driver signing security, such as from Warn to Ignore.

5. A. They can then be reinstalled as needed.

6. A. The device remains installed, it drivers are simply prevented from starting up.

7. A. Although both Device Manager and System Information tool identify a faulty configuration, only Device Manager permits you to make adjustments.

8. B. It can be accessed through the device driver properties dialog box found in Device Manager.

▲ Chapter 11: Optimizing Windows 2000 Server

1. B. You may use the System Monitor utility, accessible through the Performance MMC snap-in.

2. B, C, D. Baselining a server under no load is of little practical use, since all measurements should be optimal.

3. A. This allows low-priority threads to run, which would not otherwise have enough memory space.

4. A, C, D. There is no "medium." There is "normal."

5. B, D. The command is End process rather than kill process. There is no pause process.

6. A. More RAM promotes larger disk caches and less paging.

7. A, B, C. The use of compression always leads to some performance degradation.

8. A. This is a primary goal of server optimization.

9. A, B, C, D. All give you access to the server's disk drives, and therefore, user data.

10. B. Both can be backed up using the Backup program.

11. A. As well as user data.

12. A. You must also run the "ntdsutil" program.

13. B. Not necessarily. If you know a problem does not reside in the networking components, you can boot into safe mode with networking support enabled.

14. B. Login authentication is preserved under safe mode.

15. B. Recovery Console can access all partitions.

16. A, C, D. You are not permitted to copy files from the disk drive, such as to floppy disks.

▲ Chapter 12: Administering Windows 2000 Server Storage

1. B. Only Windows 2000 recognizes dynamic disks, whatever the format.

2. B. Only striping with parity, RAID 5, is fault tolerant.

3. B. Compression cannot be used with encryption at all.

4. B. Compression can only be used on NTFS volumes.

5. B, D. Disk quotas can be applied differently to multiple volumes on one physical disk.

6. B. Disk quotas apply uncompressed file sizes only.

7. B. It must be specified in the BOOT.INI file.

8. A. They may be listed as "offline" or "missing."

▲ Chapter 13: Networking Windows 2000 Server

1. B. TCP/IP is the server's default, however File and printer sharing for Microsoft Networks also works with NetBEUI and NWLink IPX/SPX/Net-BIOS Compatible Transport protocol.

2. A, B, D. Terminal services cannot be used to exchange files.

3. B. Most supporting network protocols are installed along with their network services, such as SFM and GSNW.

4. A, C, D. PPTP is a line protocol that supports network protocols in remote access implementations.

5. D. This service is used in conjunction with NWLink IPX/SPX/NetBIOS Compatible Transport protocol.

6. B. Printing for UNIX is installed separately.

7. B. It is installed by default, but not activated.

8. A. Access is also dependent on remote access policy.

9. B. RRAS enables five connections each for VPN access.

10. A. As well as other variables such as permissible group memberships and authentication parameters.

11. B. Windows NT Server 4.0 did not use remote access policies, concerning itself with only user account permissions.

12. A. User account permissions and remote access policy are examined first.

13. A, B, C, D. You can also specify settings for authentication type and RADIUS attributes.

14. B. You need to configure outgoing connections through the Network and Dial-up Connections folder.

15. B, D. In the first case, clients are permitted to run applications from the server. In the second case, Administrators are permitted to control the server.

16. B. It supports two simultaneous Administrator log-ons.

17. A, B, D. Only Windows operating systems are supported, albeit even those running on handheld devices.

18. A. The base allocation is 128 MBs, and Microsoft recommends that you install as much as 9 MBs additionally, per user.

19. B. Applications must often be reinstalled after the installation of Terminal Services.

20. B. But you will often need to install some compatibility scripts to optimize application sharing for many programs.

21. A. If it does not, troubleshoot the hardware and drivers using Device Manager.

22. B. Bindings can be enabled on all network adapters.

▲ Chapter 14: Securing Windows 2000 Server

1. B. EFS cannot be used with NTFS compression at all.

2. B. Other users can delete your encrypted files, if the have the NTFS permissions to do so.

3. A. Local policies settings are overwritten by site, domain, and OU level policies.

4. A. Without it, you leave the server open to Trojan horse program whose purpose is to steal that data.

5. A. Which increases security as the new name is likely to be unknown to outsiders.

6. B. System policies are used primarily to edit Registry settings.

7. A. System polices are most effective on Windows NT 4.0 and Windows 9x computers, and standalone Windows 2000 machines.

8. D. Only Administrators can audit access.

9. B. It can, depending on the hardware involved and the amount of activity.

10. B. Old passwords are pose an unnecessary security risk.

11. B. Windows NT and 9.x only support passwords of 14 characters, so that is the Windows 2000 Server default.

12. A. User accounts determine whether or not they have the right to logon.

13. B. They should be used together to ensure that hacker's are not permitted an unlimited number of logon attempts.

14. B. You must explicitly configure its components as snap-ins to the MMC.

15. A. It gives the administrator greater flexibility in how security maintenance is performed.

▲ Chapter 15: Administering Domain Name Services

1. B, D. NetBIOS used a broadcast-based methodology, while DNS is based on address tables. These tables are not managed centralized, by distributed among numerous primary domain and subdomain servers.

2. A. These can be supplied by your ISP, or yourself using the Windows 2000 DNS Server.

3. B. You need to install it explicitly.

4. A. This database is a set of files that contain all important information for the domains administered.

5. A. By definition, the primary name server is also the root name server.

6. A, D, C. DDNS server functionality is configured elsewhere.

7. A. Some applications seek name resolution using the IP address rather than the host name.

8. A. All DNS servers store query data in this manner.

9. A. The server stores its iterative queries.

10. B. It first verifies that the address sought does not belong to the local host, then query DNS, and only then attempts NetBIOS name resolution.

11. A. This is a change from the Windows NT 4.0 DNS client's behavior.

12. B. Standard servers can also be used.

13. A. Specifically, the client can update it's a and PTR records.

14. A. These tests can be specified in the DNS Server's properties dialog box.

15. A. If not, results are inconclusive.

16. B.The process is not selective. It is all or nothing.

17. A. This is especially helpful when some zones are located on remote network links, such as over WAN links.

18. A, C. AXFR pertains to entire zone transfers and IXFR pertains to incremental zone transfers.

19. B, C. WINS and WINS-R resource records are not commonly supported. IXFR is only supported in version 8.2.

20. A. It is executed from the command line.

21. A. Be sure to disable it when the problem is found.

▲ Chapter 16: Administering Dynamic Host Configuration Protocol

1. A, C, D. The DHCPINFORM message is not used, rather the DHCPREQUEST message is used.

2. A. You should also make sure that none of these IP addresses is being managed by another DHCP server and that you know of any static IP address assignments.

3. B. This is not true of the DNS Server, although it is true of the DNS server.

4. B. It is recommended that you make all IP addresses part of the scope, then use the exclusions list and reservations to handle static IP address assignment.

5. A. Likewise, if there are numerous mobile computers moving on and off the network, you might want to decrease the lease duration to reclaim IP addresses that might not otherwise be needed.

6. B. Older and incompatible clients can use the DHCP Server to works as proxy with the DDNS.

7. B. This is one option. Alternately, the DHCO Server can update the record regardless of the client request, or leave the client to do so itself.

8. A, B, C, D. In the last case, IP addressing conflicts are possible.

9. B. Only if they are Windows 2000 DHCP Servers and Active Directory is being used to begin with.

10. B. This is a sign that the client has not yet received an IP address.

11. B. It indicates that clients are moving on and off the network a lot, which might be a sign of connectivity problems.

▲ Chapter 17: Administering Remote Access

1. A, B, C, D. RAS and MPR are both configurable through RRAS.

2. B. RAS must be configured on the server.

3. B, C, D. Dial-Up Networking clients can use SLIP, but RRAS does not support it.

4. B. The user's connection attempt must meet the criteria defined by remote access policy, regardless of the permissions granted by the user account.

5. A, B, D. This restriction is enabled through the remote access profile setting.

6. A, C, D. Domain group restrictions are defined in remote access policy.

7. B. Multilinking increases overall connection bandwidth by permitting remote access clients to connect over multiple pathways, but through only one RRAS server at a time.

8. B. PPTP is used to create a tunnel in which IP, IPX, or NetBEUI packets can travel while encapsulated in PPP packets.

9. B. This cannot be done. You must instead decrease the number of available ports or disable its remote access permission.

10. C. You can enable multilink connection use as well as the use of BAP, software compression, and LCP extensions.

11. A. For example, it can add or tear down links to meet changing throughput requirements.

12. B. It leases IP addresses 10 at a time.

13. A. Which cannot be done if the DHCP Server is running on the same machine.

14. A. Using the command "NETSH dump file.txt."

15. A, C, D. VPN information is recorded in the PPP log.

16. B. While commonly used in combination, they are configured separately.

17. A, D. PAP and MS-CHAP are examples of authentication protocols, not authentication providers.

18. B. EAP accepts various authentication methods as EAP types.

19. B, C, D. IPSec is also an option.

20. A. Service Pack 2 introduced 128-bit encryption.

21. B. Both the server and client must agree on authentication and encryption settings.

22. A. But there are few circumstances in which this is appropriate.

▲ Chapter 18: Administering Network Protocols

1. A, C, D. NetBEUI cannot be routed, only bridged.

2. C. A quick way to figure these out is by using the Windows Calculator in scientific mode (set under the View menu).

3. B. This is done to create a supernet.

4. B. This becomes important if you are running certain SAP applications or routing. In most cases, the default number will do.

5. B. NWLink IPX/SPX/NetBIOS Compatible Transport can use multiple frame types.

6. B. Network services can use the network protocols to which they have been bound.

7. A. Under the Advanced menu.

8. A, B, C. As soon you enable it, you filter out all traffic using these protocols.

9. B. Port numbers are essential.

10. A, B, D. Subnetting is not intrinsically a security operation.

11. B. You should be able to determine which protocols are being filtered.

12. B. This is only available in the SMS.

13. B. At this point, it is time to consider segmenting or a topology upgrade.

14. B. "Cryptography" is the field dedicated to keeping communications secret. Cryptoanalysis is a field dedicated to breaking cryptographic codes.

15. B. IPSec provides end-to-end security, meaning that only the sender and receiver need to be aware of it.

16. A. Using the Group Policy snap-in to the MMC, and others.

17. A. Between clients or clients and servers.

18. A. B, C. Transport mode is not applied to VPNs.

19. A, C, D. IPSec does not support PPTP.

20. B. One for each tunnel end point.

21. B. It can only be disabled.

22. A, C, D. Kerberos has replaced NTLM authentication in Windows 2000.

23. B. Use the Export Policies command in the MMC.

24. B. Use the IPSec Monitor (IPSECMON) utility.

▲ Chapter 19: Administering Windows Internet Naming Service

1. B. NetBIOS name resolution is broadcast-based, while TCP/IP relies on DNS.

2. B. To be compatible with DNS, Windows 2000 will changes underscores to hyphens (-).

3. A, B, C, D. All can be part of the process, although a server only sends a Renewal Interval along with a Positive Name Registration Response.

4. B. Other computers can be added as well through static address mappings.

5. B. It is performed automatically through online compaction, but can be performed manually for greatest efficiency.

6. A. Every three hours to in the path you specify.

7. B. Push partners perform updates after a specified number of changes have occurred in the database.

8. A. They use the multicast address 224.0.1.24.

▲ Chapter 20: Administering IP Routing

1. A, B, D. Link State Advertisements (LSAs) are a component of OSPF routing rather than a routing protocol.

2. A. But it is also the method that incurs the lowest bandwidth and processor requirements.

3. A, B, C. IPCONFIG is not useful in configuring static routes.

4. B. Such connections are subject to authentication.

5. B. Although a contradiction in terms, persistent demand-dial connections can be enabled.

6. B. OSPF is more complicated, but also more scalable.

7. B, C. Autonomous Systems (ASs) and Internal Routers (IR) are not related to border routers.

8. A. Or between one or more ASs.

9. A. Although they communicate with border routers.

10. B. This information can be filtered out with a stub area.

11. B. This is a limitation of RIP. OSPF can accommodate as many as 255 routers.

12. B. Unicasting is used.

13. B. It is also available under Windows 2000 Professional and Windows 98 (Second Edition)/Me.

14. A. It is incompatible with such network services, so NAT should be used instead.

15. A. As part of RRAS.

16. B. NAT must be used with DHCP, in conjunction with either a DHCP Server or its own built-in DHCP allocation.

17. A. Which has nothing to do with NetBIOS name resolution.

18. A. Defined as 24 hours.

19. B. Two. One for the private network and one for the public network.

20. B. This is a limitation of ICS.

▲ Chapter 21: Administering Certificate Authorities

1. A. You are warned of this during installation.

2. B. Either Enterprise or standalone CAs can be deployed in Active Directory managed domains, but standalone CAs must made part of Active Directory Trees.

3. B. Certificates can be issued via a Web interface.

4. A. Even if the reason is "unspecified."

5. A. Assuming you wish to still be able to recover encrypted data.

6. B. Administrators can still designate backup Recovery Agents.

▲ Chapter 22: Installing Active Directory

1. B. Active Directory is hierarchical.

2. A. This launches the Active Directory Installation Wizard.

3. A. Slow links generally serve as good site boundaries.

4. A. Or, in some configurations, both.

5. B. You can also remove and delete server objects from sites.

6. B. Nevertheless, it is recommended that one be deployed for each site.

7. A, B, D. The Domain-Naming Master and Schema Master are deployed forest-wide.

8. B. There can be only one operations master of whichever type deployed in a domain.

9. A. Another is to view the Windows 2000 Install Your Server Wizard.

10. A. Or both, as parent OUs can contain child OUs.

▲ Chapter 23: Administering Active Directory and DNS

1. A, B, C, D. You can also integrate none-Microsoft DNS servers.

2. B. A standard DNS server can be migrated to Active Directory integration through the DNS MMC.

3. B. This is required only where secure dynamic updates are implemented.

4. B. Even when dynamic updates are used, resource records can still be created manually.

5. A. It is automatically enabled for Active Directory-integrated DNS Servers.

▲ Chapter 24: Managing Change Configuration

1. B. Although Windows NT 4.0 had similar capabilities through its System Policy Editor application, GPOs are only available under Windows 2000 and Active Directory.

2. C, D. As well as the OU level.

3. B. You make its policies applicable to groups that exist in other containers.

4. B. Although naturally, Full Control would also suffice.

5. A. There is no value in parsing default, unspecified settings.

6. A. Providing such general access would defeat the point of security filtering.

7. C. The order is local computer, site, domain, and OU.

8. C. They should be saved to the WINNT\INF folder.

9. B. The Windows Installer service is available for Windows 9x, Me, NT 4.0, and 2000 computers.

10. B. These features are enabled through their own properties dialog boxes, but group policies can be applied to such behaviors as synchronization schedules and connection sharing.

11. A, B, D. The server must be an authorized DHCP server.

12. A. It is used to create the operating system disk image.

13. A. The user can only access one disk image, which can then be installed automatically.

▲ Chapter 25: Optimizing Active Directory

1. A, B. Under Active Directory, all domain controllers are replication partners, and domain controllers are objects. Neither a non-shared printer nor a nonshared folder need be Active Directory objects, because they are not published.

2. B. Although moving objects between domains requires different tools than those required to move objects within a domain.

3. B. Most objects are published automatically.

4. A. When using the Custom Search option.

5. B, C, D. Java is a programming language that would not be applied to creating simple batch files.

6. B. They have their own ACLs that function in much the same manner.

7. B. There is also a Custom Task option.

8. B, C. While applicable, these logs are more general. There is also a Directory Services log.

9. A. Was well as their ability to log on, assuming there is but one domain controller on the network.

10. B. The update sequence number is maintained in the backup.

11. B. Active Directory data can also be restored through replication.

12. B, C. Domain-naming, schema, and RID operations masters should not be brought back online after those roles were seized by another domain controller.

▲ Chapter 26: Securing Active Directory

1. A, C, D. As well as the site level.

2. B. It is used to compare current security with that recommend by Microsoft.

3. A. At least eight hours unless you restart or refresh the computer.

4. B. This access is restricted to Administrators.

INDEX

A

A record, 725
Accessibility services, 289–295
ACE, 388
ACL, 388, 497, 621
ACPI, 41
Active Directory,
    administering software, 933–942
    and DNS, 920–923
    and Kerberos, 899
    and LDAP, 899
    and RIS, 938
    and X.500, 900
    authorizing DHCP, 754
    backup, 960
    connection objects, 907
    delegation, 898, 929, 953
    directory, 898
    distinguished name, 898
    domain, 898, 901
        child, 898
    forest, 898, 901
    global catalog, 898, 909
    globally unique identifier, 898
    group policy, 899, 926–932
        objects, 926
        securing, 968
    installing, 898–915
    native mode, 899
    object, 899
        access, 953
        locating, 951
        managing, 952

        moving, 948
        parent, 899
    operations master, 910
        Domain-Naming, 911
        Infrastructure, 911
        PDC Emulator, 911
        Relative ID, 911
        Schema, 911
        seizing, 962
    organizational unit, 899
        creating, 914
    performance, 954–960
    printing, 474
    publishing, 950
    replication, 899, 959
        asynchronous, 906
        inter-site, 899
        multi-master, 899
        synchronous, 906
    restore, 562, 960
        authoritative, 962
        nonauthoritative, 961
    schema, 900
    security, 970
    Security Services Provider
        Interface, 900
    server objects, 908
    services interface, 898
    site, 900
        creating, 904
        link, 906
        membership, 909
    subnet,
        creating, 905

Active Directory, subnet, (cont'd)
    SYSVOL, 903
    tree, 900, 901
    trust, 900
    User Principal Name, 900
ADSI, 898
ADSL, 763
AFP, 625, 626
AGP, 148
APCI, 150
API, 45, 147
APIPA, 774
APM, 41, 150
AppleShare, 625
AppleTalk, 92, 634, 791
    configuring, 643
    routing, 626
Application,
    performance, 224–227
ARA, 763
ARC, 597
ARP, 793, 840
ARPA, 792
AS, 867
ASBR, 868
ASCII, 269, 719
ATM, 171, 545, 657, 762
Auditing, 380–384, 690–693
AXFR, 732

B

Backup, 231–244, 556–561
    copy, 236, 558
    daily, 236, 558
    differential, 236, 557

incremental, 236, 557
    normal, 236, 557
    remote storage, 558
    restoring, 243, 561–563
        system data, 562
    strategies, 242
Bandwidth, 544
Baselining, 213, 540
BDC, 433
BIND, 461, 732
BINL, 22
BOOT.INI, 597
BootP, 22, 459, 751, 755
Bottlenecks, 214

C

CA, 678, 822, 884
CAL, 14
CAPI, 678
CAT, 523
CDFS, 10, 71, 113
CD-ROM drives, 113–122
Certificate Authorities, 884–892
CHAP, 664, 781
Characterization file, 90
CIDR, 799
CIPHER, 360, 680
CIW, 22
CNAME, 725
Codec, 158
COMPACT.EXE, 59
CRL, 884
Cryptography, 820
CSNW, 82, 803
CSP, 886

D

DAT, 141, 234
DCOM, 651
DDNS, 721, 753, 903
Dead gateway detection, 859
Debugging, 565–569
DECnet, 91
DES, 770, 821
DESX, 678
DFS,
    administering, 498–503
    domain-based, 501
    managing, 502
    standalone, 498
    troubleshooting, 502
DHCP, 22, 305, 450, 746–758
    BootP support, 751
    configuring, 455–459, 748–755
    DNS integration, 753
    installing, 747
    leases, 746
    logging, 757
    managing, 755
    monitoring, 756
    operations, 746–747
    rebinding state, 747
    Relay Agent, 459, 755, 773
    reservations, 752
    scopes, 456, 748
        creating, 748
        managing, 755
        multinet, 755
        superscope, 755
    troubleshooting, 756
Dial-Up Networking, 324–338
Diffie-Hellman, 821
Disk Defragmenter, 220

Display devices, 145–148
DLC, 91, 634, 791
    configuring, 643
DLL, 90, 468
DLT, 141, 234
DMA, 518
DNS, 305, 306, 450, 459, 714–738
    caching-only, 729
    clients, 730
    configuring, 459–466, 720–731
    dynamic updates, 727
    installing, 719
    iteration, 717
    logging, 737
    managing, 731
    monitoring 733
    name resolution, 646
    operations, 714–719
    recursion, 717
    resource records, 725
    root domains, 460, 715
    server,
        Active Directory-integrated, 463
        caching-only, 461, 721
        dynamic, 461, 721
        forwarder, 461, 721
        primary, 461, 720
        root, 721
        secondary, 461, 720
    troubleshooting, 733
    zones,
        configuring, 721–729
        delegated, 728
        forward lookup, 721
        reverse lookup, 722
DOD model, 792
Dolby Digital, 113

Domain, 19, 898
DOS,
  8.3 naming convention, 56
DoubleSpace, 14
DRAM, 541
Driver signing, 182–186
  managing, 182
  troubleshooting, 183
DriveSpace, 14, 61
DSL, 872
DVD, 112
DVD drives, 113–122

E

EAP, 656, 664, 782
EBCDIC, 269
EFS, 352, 678, 883
  recovery keys, 891
El Torito, 113
EMF, 91
ERD, 139, 556, 562, 589
Ethernet, 642, 804

F

FAT, 10, 61, 71, 101, 415, 481, 586
FAT32, 10, 11, 56, 71, 101, 415, 586
Fax, 287–289
FDDI, 172, 804
FDISK, 9, 125
FEK, 678
Files,
  accessing, 56–70, 489–498
  compressing, 57–61
  copying, 56, 70
  decrypting, 354
  encrypting, 352
  moving, 56, 70
  naming, 56
  permissions, 61–70, 482–484
  securing, 481–493
Firewall, 811
Firewire, 112, 141
Folders,
  accessing, 56–70, 489–498
  caching, 72
  compressing, 57–61
  naming, 56
  permissions, 61–70, 74–78, 484–487
  securing, 481–493
  shared, 71–89
FQDN, 305, 460, 718
Frame Relay, 657
FTP, 83, 493, 604, 614–618, 791
  authentication, 615
  bandwidth, 614
  directory listings, 617
  ports, 616
  virtual directories, 618
  virtual servers, 618

G

GC, 898
GPC, 968
GPO, 968
GPT, 968
Group,
  accounts, 370
  default, 365
  global, 366
  local, 365
  special, 367

GSNW, 82, 604, 803
    configuring, 612
    installing, 606
GUID, 898

H
HAL, 24
Hard disk,
    basic disks, 125, 577–580
        mirror set, 579
        partitioning, 577
        stripe set, 578
        stripe sets with parity, 579
        volume sets, 578
    caching, 551
    cluster sizes, 11
    compressing, 591–593
    configuring, 125–130, 576–587
    controllers, 550
    diskperf commands, 543
    dynamic disks, 129, 580–586
        configuring, 580, 583
        mirrored volumes, 584
        RAID 5, 585
        simple volume, 583
        spanned volume, 584
        striped volumes, 584
    encrypting, 352–360, 678–681
        Recovery Agents, 678, 681
    formatting, 7
    fragmentation, 551
    monitoring, 122–124, 587
    partition, 7, 125, 414
        active, 8
        boot partition, 9
        extended, 8

primary, 8, 127
    system, 9
performance, 218–221, 543–544,
        550–554
quotas, 593–597
recovering, 597–599
sector sparing, 13, 560
specifications, 550
troubleshooting, 590
volume,
        configuring, 133–138, 576–587
        duplexing, 137
        mirrored, 136
        monitoring, 130–133, 587
        spanned, 134
        striped, 136
        troubleshooting, 138–141, 590
Hardware,
    configuring, 518–522
    disabling, 527
    disk drives, 113–144
    drivers,
        signing, 522–524
        updating, 524–526
    installing, 111–112
    profiles, 227–231
    removing, 526
    troubleshooting, 528–531
Hardware Compatibility List, 5
HCL, 112, 410, 413, 518
HINFO, 726
Hosts file, 459
HTTP, 83, 493, 506, 604, 619–625, 791
    authentication, 621
    bandwidth, 619
    Keep-Alives, 504, 625
    ports, 622

I

IAS, 651, 770
ICMP, 312, 644, 794
ICS, 336–338, 653, 764, 857, 872
    installing, 872
IDE, 550
IEEE, 141, 642
IETF, 791
IGMP, 762, 794
IIS, 83, 493, 506, 604, 886
    configuring, 614
    installing, 608
IKE, 823
ILS, 651
IME, 272
INF, 31, 32, 523
Input/Output devices, 155–167, 522
Installer packages, 275–281
InstallShield, 276
Internet Explorer, 506
InterNIC, 459
IP, 794
IPCONFIG, 311, 756, 808
IPSec, 308, 639, 762, 820–830
IPXROUTE, 805
IR, 164
IrDA, 165
IRQ, 518, 521
ISAKMP, 823
ISDN, 655, 763, 872
ISO, 270
IXFR, 732

K

KCC, 906
Kerberos, 824

L

L2TP, 326, 656, 762
Languages, 268–275
LDAP, 898
Linux, 6
LIP, 82, 604
LMHOSTS,
    file tags, 840
LPD, 470
LPR, 92, 470
LSA, 863

M

MAC, 714, 793
Mac OS,
    printing, 471
MAU, 171
MBR, 141, 569
MD5, 664
Member server, 20
Memory,
    performance, 214–216, 541–542
    virtual, 541
MFT, 141
MIB, 775
Microsoft,
    File and Printer Sharing,
        configuring, 610
        installing, 605
MILNET, 793
Modems, 159–164
    configuring, 160
    installing, 159
    managing, 162
MOVETREE, 949
MPEG-2, 113

MPPE, 770
MS-CHAP, 781
MS-DOS, 6
MSI, 933
Multimedia devices, 157
Multiple processing units, 169
Multitasking, 169
MX, 726
My Network Places, 78

N

NAT, 762, 797, 857, 872–877
    configuring, 875–876
    troubleshooting, 876
NBMA, 868
NBNS, 841
NBT, 718, 837
NBTSTAT, 809, 839
NCP, 82, 604
NCSA, 509
NDS, 82, 604, 898
NetBEUI, 633, 714, 790, 838
    configuring, 643
NetBIOS,
    name resolution, 838–842
        B-node, 842
        broadcasts, 840
        H-node, 842
        LMHOSTS, 840
        M-node, 842
        P-node, 842
        Registry key, 842
    name servers, 841
    names, 838
    over TCP/IP, 838
    service identifiers, 839
NETDOM, 950

Netscape Navigator, 506
NETSH, 762, 774
NETSTAT, 318, 646, 808
NetWare, 6, 82, 341–343, 604, 633
    printing, 470
Network,
    bindings, 805
    frames, 803
    packets, 803
    performance, 222–224, 544–545
    protocols, 632–649, 790–810
        best-effort delivery, 794
        configuring, 635
        connectionless, 794
        connection-oriented, 794
        installing, 634
        monitoring, 647–649
        multicasting, 794
        security, 810–812
        troubleshooting, 643–649, 806
    services, 649–662
        configuring, 649
        installing, 649
    traffic, 812–820
Network adapters, 170, 669–671
    configuring, 170, 669
    installing, 170, 669
    troubleshooting, 171, 671
NIC, 544
NOS, 411
NS, 464, 725
NSF, 793
NSFnet, 793
NSLOOKUP, 733
NTDS, 898
NTFS, 10, 12, 56, 62, 71, 101, 415, 481,
    586, 591

NTFS, (cont'd)
    converting, 102, 587
    permissions, 62–68
NWLink, 633, 790, 803–805
    configuring, 641–642

O

ODBC, 509
Offline File Synchronization, 191–197
OnPower Management, 112, 152
OS/2, 10
OSI model, 222, 710–712, 792
OSPF, 864
    border routing, 868
    managing, 867
    stub area, 869
    troubleshooting, 871
OU, 899

P

PAP, 664, 781
PATHPING, 317, 645
PC Card, 152
PCI, 23, 148
PCL, 626
PCMCIA, 152
PCT, 885
PDC, 433, 911
PING, 312–317, 644, 806
PINGPATH, 807
PJL, 92
PKI, 811, 822, 883
Plug and Play, 111, 522
Policies,
    account, 384–388
    group, 282–286
    local security, 361–363

POST, 148
Power schemes, 151
PPP, 325, 656, 762
PPTP, 326, 656, 762
Printing, 90–100, 468–481
    connecting, 92
    devices, 90, 468
    drivers, 90, 468
    Internet, 95
    managing 96
    monitor, 91, 469
    monitoring, 476
    network protocols, 468
    permissions, 98, 475
    printer, 468
    processor, 91, 469
    queue, 90, 468
    router, 91, 469
    server, 468
    sharing, 344–346, 471–481
    spooler, 90, 98, 469
    troubleshooting, 478
Processor,
    killing processes, 549
    managing, 546–549
    performance, 216–218, 542–543
    priorities, 546
Proxy server, 811
PSTN, 763
PTR, 726
PXE, 22

Q

QIC, 141, 234
QoS, 650, 651

R

RADIUS, 762, 782
RAID, 551, 558–560, 579
    mirroring, 559, 597
    striping, 559
    striping with parity, 559, 599
RARP, 793
RAS, 651–662, 762–784
    authentication, 781
    clients, 763
    configuring, 654, 764–774
    DHCP integration, 773
    encryption, 783
    inbound connections, 655, 766
    installing, 652
    logging, 775
    managing, 774
    monitoring, 661, 774
    multilinking, 660, 772
    policies, 657, 768
    profiles, 660, 769
    security, 780–784
    troubleshooting, 661, 776–780
Recovery Agents, 357
Recovery console, 245, 556, 569–570
Registry, 7, 140
Removable media,
    devices, 141, 141–144
Rendering, 91
RF, 164
RFC,
    1034, 461
    1035, 461
    2052, 23
    2136, 23
    974, 461
RID, 911

RIP, 471, 642, 863
    managing, 866
    split horizon, 866
    troubleshooting, 870
RIPrep, 23, 940
RIS, 22–24, 426, 431, 938–942
RISETUP, 23, 939
Routing,
    AppleTalk, 773
    configuring, 772
    IP, 773
    IPX, 772
    NetBEUI, 773
RPC, 470
RRAS, 652, 857
RSA, 821
RTL, 270

S

Safe Mode, 244–245, 531, 555, 563
SAM, 615, 898
SAP, 650
SCSI, 141, 550, 586
Security,
    configuring, 393–400, 702–703
    policies, 682–689
        configuring, 682
        group, 682
        local, 682, 683, 686, 688
        managing, 686
        system, 682, 684, 687, 688
        troubleshooting, 688
Setup Manager Wizard, 35–39, 429–433
Setupcl, 25
SFM, 471, 604, 625–630, 791
    installing, 608

SGC, 509, 886

SID, 22, 267, 911

SIMM, 541

SIS, 23, 939

SLIP, 325, 763

SMB, 604

SMS, 813

SMTP, 791

SNMP, 650, 774, 775, 791

SOA, 464, 725

SOHO, 872

SPAP, 781

SPF, 867

SRV, 726

SSL, 507, 820, 885

SSPI, 900

Stop screen errors, 564

Symmetric Multi-Processing, 6

SYSDIFF, 26, 30–33

Sysprep, 25, 426, 431

System File Checker, 185

System Monitor, 199–212

    DHCP, 757

    DNS, 733

System Preparation tool, 24–26

T

Task Scheduler, 186–191

    configuring, 186

    managing, 188

    troubleshooting, 190

TCP, 794

TCP/IP, 302–323, 632, 790, 791–803

    addressing, 795–800

        Class A, 796

        Class B, 796

        Class C, 797

        Class D, 797

        Class E, 797

        classless, 799

    classes, 304

    configuring, 302–310, 635–641, 800, 800–803

    filtering, 309, 802

    host ID, 795

    network ID, 795

    protocols, 791

    routing, 858–871

        configuring, 861

        convergence, 863

        demand-dial, 864

        dynamic routes, 858, 863

        gateway, 859

        host, 860

        interface, 859

        static routes, 858, 862

        tables, 862

        troubleshooting, 870

    subnet mask, 795

    subnets, 304, 797

    supernets, 799

    troubleshooting, 311–323, 644

Terminal Services, 665–668

    configuring, 666

    installing, 665

    monitoring, 668

TFTP, 23

Thinnet, 171

TLS, 664, 885

Token Ring, 171, 804

TRACERT, 317, 645, 807

U

UAF, 22, 26, 28–30, 426, 427–428, 431
UAM, 627
UDF, 28–30, 113, 427, 428–429
UDP, 640, 657, 762, 794
unattend.doc, 29
UNATTEND.TXT, 33, 34
UNC, 80, 340, 618
Unicode, 269
UNIX, 6, 617
    printing, 470
UPN, 900
USB, 112, 142, 165
User,
    accounts, 260–263, 267–268, 367, 693–698
        security, 364–380, 698–701
    authenticating, 388–393
    profiles, 256–259
        local, 259, 263
        mandatory, 259
        remote, 267
        roaming, 259
    rights, 375–380
UTF, 719
UTP, 171

V

VBBasic, 270
Video adapters, 148–150
    troubleshooting, 149
VPN, 331–336, 653, 662–664, 762
    configuring, 663
    installing, 662, 770
    troubleshooting, 664

W

W3C, 509
WACK, 843
WDM, 112
Web,
    server,
        accessing, 493–498, 503–512
        bandwidth throttling, 504
        host header names, 506, 624
        logging, 509, 511
        pages, 623
WHQL, 112, 182, 522
Win32 Driver Model, 112
Windows 2000 Advanced Server, 411
Windows 2000 Datacenter Server, 411
Windows 2000 Professional,
    clean installs, 7
    desktop settings, 281–287
    installing,
        automated, 14–21
        disk cloning, 21
        disk imaging, 21
        floppy disks, 15, 44
        planning, 3–14
        unattended, 21–39
        upgrading, 39–42
    licensing, 14
    Service Packs, 42
    system requirements, 5
    troubleshooting, 44–47
    update packs, 40
    upgrading, 6
Windows 2000 Server,
    alerts, 539
    clean installs, 412

Windows 2000 Server (cont'd),
installing,
  attended, 417–426
  automated, 430
  licensing, 416
  network services, 451–467
  planning, 410–416
  unattended, 426–433
  upgrading, 411, 433–438
  upgrading BDCs, 437
  upgrading domains, 434
  upgrading PDC, 436
  upgrading Windows NT Server,
    435
logging, 539
monitoring, 536–546
network protocols, 450
Service Packs, 438
system requirements, 412
troubleshooting, 440
Windows 3.1, 7
Windows 95, 6
Windows 98, 6
Windows for Workgroups, 7
Windows Me, 6
Windows NT 3.51, 6
Windows NT 4.0, 6
WinINSTALL, 276
WinINSTALL Lite, 276
WINNT32, 27–28
WINS, 307, 451, 639, 837–854
  backup and restore, 849
  burst mode, 466, 845

clients, 466, 843
compaction, 848
configuring, 466–467, 845–849
consistency checking, 848
dynamic database, 845
installing, 845
managing, 848
monitoring, 849
name registration, 843
name release, 844
name renewal, 844
name resolution, 646, 844
persistent connections, 845
Proxy Agents, 467
replication, 850–852
tombstoning, 466, 845
troubleshooting, 849
WinSock, 718
Wireless devices, 164–165
Wise, 276
Workgroup, 19

X

X.25, 657
X.509, 884

Z

ZOA, 717

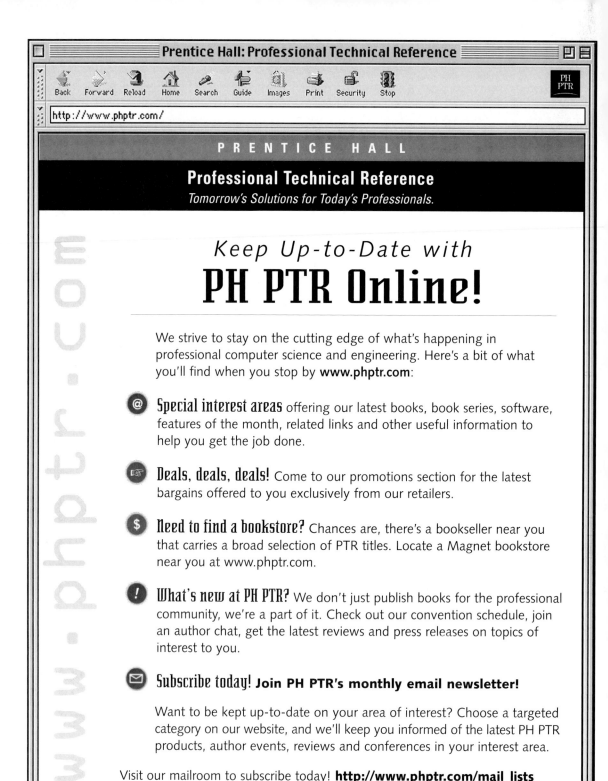